Energy in the developing world

Energy in the developing world

Energy in the developing world

The real energy crisis

EDITED BY

VACLAV SMIL AND WILLIAM E. KNOWLAND

Oxford New York Toronto Melbourne

OXFORD UNIVERSITY PRESS

1980

Oxford University Press, Walton Street, Oxford OX2 6DP

OXFORD LONDON GLASGOW
NEW YORK TORONTO MELBOURNE WELLINGTON
KUALA LUMPUR SINGAPORE HONG KONG TOKYO
DELHI BOMBAY CALCUTTA MADRAS KARACHI
NAIROBI DAR ES SALAAM CAPE TOWN

Published in the United States of America by
Oxford University Press, New York

British Library Cataloguing in Publication Data

Energy in the developing world.
1. Underdeveloped areas – Power resources – Addresses, essays, lectures.
I. Smil, Vaclav II. Knowland, William E.
333.7 HD9502.A2 79–41127
ISBN 0–19–854421–9 Pbk
ISBN 0–19–854425–1

Typeset by Cotswold Typesetting Ltd., Gloucester
Printed in Great Britain at the University Press, Oxford
by Eric Buckley, Printer to the University

Preface

This is a book about the energy crisis facing the developing world, the three-quarters of mankind where the average consumption of energy per capita is at the level achieved in most of the European nations and in North America a century ago. Such low energy usage is accompanied by inadequate diets, poor health care, a low degree of industrialization, and, too often, a general socio-economic malaise.

There are, consequently, few global problems which, in decades to come, could equal the task of substantially increasing the energy availability for some 3 billion people in Asia, Africa, and Latin America. This book tries to bring together a variety of perspectives needed to appreciate the nature and the magnitude of this formidable problem and the options available for its alleviation.

Global and general views in the first two sections, dealing with energy and development and energy resources and uses, are followed by about a dozen national profiles. The energetics of the world's two most populous countries—China and India—and of Brazil, Latin America's largest nation, is dealt with in greater detail in three separate sections. Shorter reviews are presented in the last two parts devoted to Africa and to Asia and Central America.

Separate coverage of each and every developing nation would be impracticable and is also unnecessary. Most of the more than 100 developing countries are small—both territorially and in population—states with hardly any modern energy sector worth describing and with commonly low usage of traditional fuels. On the other hand, we have also decided not to include any information on the hydrocarbon-rich OPEC nations with relatively small populations, such as Saudi Arabia, Iraq, and Libya: although these nations still certainly belong to the developing category (above all in terms of demographic, health, and cultural indicators) their predicament has little in common with the rest of the Third World.

Focusing the book on the largest and most populous countries, the national and regional profiles summarize the energy situation in developing nations with a combined population of some 2.2 billion people, or nearly 75 per cent of the Third World. Future social and economic successes and failures in these countries will have deep global repercussions and we hope that this book will contribute toward understanding the critical factor of the developmental process: the acquisition and the usage of energy.

December 1979 V.S. W.E.K.

Contents

I Energy and development

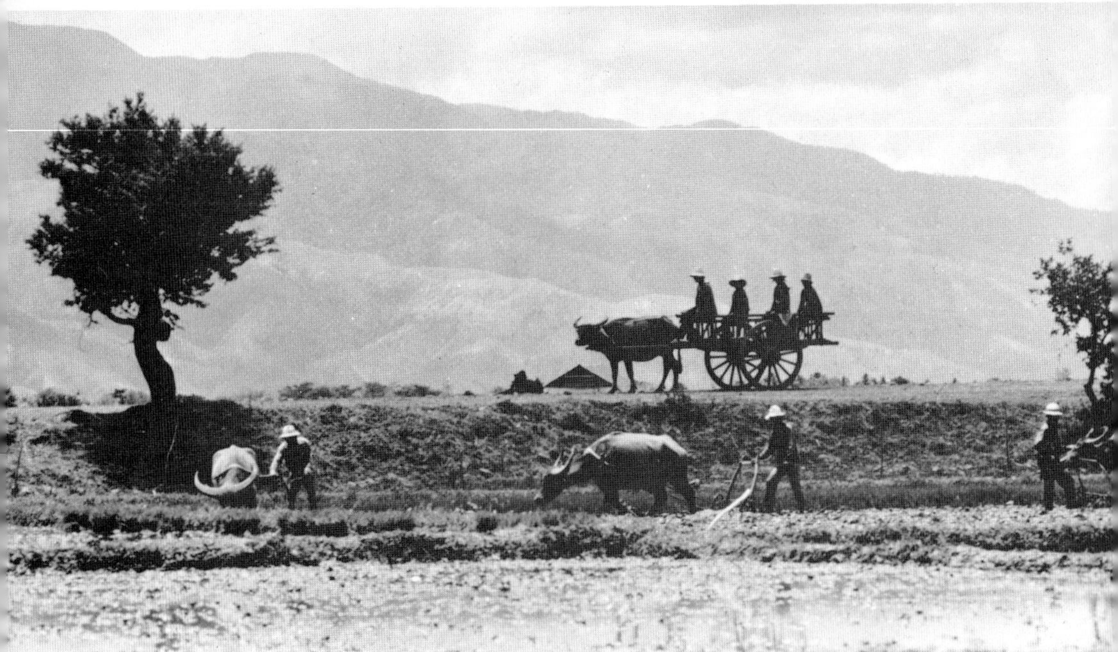

TOP: Modern Wood Stove in Colombia. Unlike in the developed nations, most of the energy consumed throughout the developing world revolves around growing and preparing food.

US Agency for International Development Photo.

BOTTOM: Water Buffaloes in the paddies and on the road in Central Luzon, Philippines. Draft animals supply essential motive power for field tasks and transportation in most of the poor nations.

World Bank Photo by Edwin G. Huffman.

Only about a quarter of the more than 4 billion people on this planet live in countries where the average food consumption is well above the physiological needs, where infant mortality is low (typically below 25 per 1000 live births) and life expectancy is high (around 70 years), where literacy touches on 100 per cent, and most of a nation's inhabitants cluster in growing cities. These are the world's developed nations: a quarter of mankind consuming four-fifths of the global use of fossil fuels and primary electricity and enjoying a quality of life unsurpassed in history.

Statistical averages, or just best estimates because good data are often missing, for the remaining three-quarters of the human population are painfully different. Although in most of these 110 nations there is an urban and land-owning elite of various sizes, the overwhelming majority of their people are illiterate or semi-literate poor villagers, surviving on less than adequate diets, whose infant mortality is an order of magnitude higher than in the developed world—and whose life expectancy is as much as three decades shorter. The difficult present and the less than promising future of this developing world—or, as some prefer, the less developed, underdeveloped, or Third World—is, to a very large extent, the result of energy starvation, a very low consumption of fossil fuels and electricity.

. Our opening paper ('Energy in the developing world') attempts to survey the key realities: the close, yet far from simple, relationship of energy and economic growth; continuing heavy reliance on traditional fuels and on animate power; necessities of new integrative energy policies; and of reducing the dependence on crude oil imports. It also scans the resource alternatives and discusses what is undoubtedly the most important and also the most intractable task for energy development in poor nations—to bring the benefits of modern energetics to rural areas.

The majority of people in developing countries are, of course, living in villages or small towns: more than 90 per cent in many poor African nations, four-fifths in China and in India, some 60 per cent in Turkey. Their energy needs are hardly extravagant and, as A. Makhijani ('Energy in the rural Third World') argues, they could be best satisfied with a small-scale, labour-intensive approach, with ecologically sound technologies which would also preserve human dignity.

Regardless of the nature of technical solutions eventually chosen, the developing world will require a relatively fast expansion of primary energy consumption for decades to come and detailed long-ranged analyses, done as a part of comprehensive study of world energetics undertaken by the Worskhop on Alternative Energy Strategies ('Energy and economic growth prospects for the developing countries'), indicate well the magnitude of the task.

The WAES study focused on the non-communist industrialized nations but could not ignore energy supply and demand in both OPEC and non-OPEC developing countries outside of Communist areas. Its medium-term and long-range forecasts—for the years 1985 and 2000—are based on alternative economic growth and energy-price scenarios and the resulting demands are contrasted with potential supplies to determine probable levels of exports and imports.

The results indicate that by the end of this century OPEC nations will be still the principal crude oil exporters (at a level about equalling the 1975 total), while the non-OPEC countries, as a group, might need to import between 7.6 and 4 million barrels per day, although they might become, again as a group, modest exporters of coal and natural gas.

The remainder of this century would then appear to be a time of lasting balance of payment difficulties and of a slower than previously anticipated growth rates for most developing nations. Should it also be a time of comprehensive energy planning and of increasing exploitation of renewable resources, the necessary foundations might be laid for a more promising century.

Energy and development: selected readings

Brookhaven National Laboratory (1978). *Energy needs, uses and resources in developing countries.* Brookhaven National Laboratory, Upton, NY.

Friedmann, E. (1976). Financing energy in developing countries. *Energy Policy* **2** (1), 37–49.

Hayes, D. (1977). *Energy for development: Third World options.* Worldwatch Institute, Washington, DC.

Howe, J. W., Bever, J., Knowland, W. E., and Tarrant, J. (1978). *Energy for developing countries.* Overseas Development Council, Washington, DC.

Jequier, N. (1976). *Appropriate technology: problems and promises.* OECD, Paris.

Makhijani, A. (1978). *Energy policy for the rural Third World.* International Institute for Environment and Development, London.

El Mallakh, R. (1977). The organization of the Arab Petroleum Exporting Countries: objectives and potential. *Annual Review of Energy* **2**, 399–415.

—— and McGuire, C. (eds.) (1974). *Energy and development.* The International Research Center for Energy and Economic Development, Boulder, Co.

Odum, H. T. (1971). *Environment, power and society.* Wiley-Interscience, New York.

—— and Odum, E. C. (1976). *Energy basis for man and nature.* McGraw-Hill, New York.

Schumacher, E. F. (1973). *Small is beautiful: economics as if people mattered.* Blond and Briggs, London.

Sherbiny, N. A. and Tessler, M. A. (eds.). (1976). *Arab oil: impact on Arab countries and global implications.* Praeger, New York.

Workshop on Alternative Energy Strategics (1977). *Energy: global prospects 1985–2000.* McGraw-Hill, New York.

World Bank (1975). *Rural electrification.* World Bank, Washington, DC.

World Bank (annually). *World Bank atlas.* World Bank, Washington, DC.

1

Energy in the developing world

VACLAV SMIL AND WILLIAM E. KNOWLAND

The energy problems of the industrialized nations, serious though they are, pale in comparison to those facing most of the world's developing countries. In the well-off nations of Europe and in Australia, New Zealand and Japan the energy consumption per capita exceeds 5 tonnes of coal equivalent per year, and in North America it is more than double this.[1] Much of this, of course, is from imported petroleum. And much of the energy consumed in the industrialized countries is either used inefficiently or for purposes that do not significantly enhance peoples' well-being or quality of life.[2] Just as when an obese patient is suddenly prohibited by his physician from eating too many carbohydrate foods, the 'energy crisis' of the rich countries may merely be the initial trauma of converting to a leaner, but adequate—and certainly healthier—energy diet. But for most developing countries, the existing energy situation is more one of debilitatingly inadequate nutrition, virtually a condition of energy starvation.

In most developing countries, measured (that is modern commercial) energy consumption is barely a quarter tonne of coal equivalent per capita annually.[3] The industrial countries are not only starting from much higher consumption levels, but they also have the research capability and wealth to develop aggresively additional and novel energy resources while only the largest and most technologically advanced developing nations are capable of major energy research and development programmes of their own. And the poor developing countries will be unable to compete in international energy markets if future supply shortages (and their resulting price increases) occur. Worst of all, a worsening trend of overconsumption of what is still the developing world's most important energy resource, fuelwood, is leading to an agricultural–ecological crisis of perhaps unprecedented dimensions.[4]

Energy and economic growth

Energy is, naturally, the prime mover of economic growth and development—but the linkages between energy and development are complex and still imperfectly understood. To begin with, it has been elusively difficult to define the concept of *economic development* itself.[5] The basic readily available denominator of economic growth, gross national product (GNP), is generally acknowledged to be imprecise and inadequate for fully measuring productivity or improvements in welfare within a single country—let alone to be compared among different nations with different kinds of economies, different cultural values, and widely varying environmental settings.[6] Moreover, both the strategies and goals of economic development are open to debate, and are continuously evolving.

Similarly, *energy* is not a single, uniform commodity. For comparisons and for statistical accounts different energies—fossil fuels (coals, crude oils, natural gases), electricity (generated in hydro-stations, fossil-fuelled, nuclear, or geothermal power plants), and biomass fuels (fuelwood, crop residues, dung, biogas)—can be converted to common denominators (ergs, joules, calories, Btu's, tonnes of oil or coal equivalent, etc.),[7] but all of these are merely equivalent measures of quantity, and tell nothing about the quality or form that is actually available or is needed for a given purpose.

Again, an analogy to food and nutrition is fitting. Food contains several groups of essential nutrients: proteins, lipids, glycids, vitamins, and minerals; each of these is necessary in varying amounts to sustain life and the amounts for an adequate diet vary according to an individual's age, sex, body weight, activity level, and metabolic rate. Similarly, various economic activities demand varying energy 'diets'. There may be considerable latitude in what mix of energy nutrients can satisfy a particular economic 'hunger'. But speaking simply in terms of, say, tonnes of oil equivalent of demand for energy is talking in the same order of generalization as talking of food needs in kilograms or pounds.

Consequently, it is impossible to judge a country's well-being just on the basis of total energy consumption or to state what level of equivalent energy usage is to correspond to a specific level of economic development. A comprehensive global energy–GNP regression analysis will, of course, indicate a strong positive relationship between aggregate economic performance and total commercial energy consumption, but a closer look will reveal very sizeable variations and disappearance of strong correlation within more homogeneous groupings.[8]

Traditional energies

Another serious difficulty in establishing energy and economic development relationships is that much of the energy used in the developing world is never measured. Traditional fuels in rural areas, such as firewood, crop residues, and animal dung, have always been available to whoever takes the effort to collect and gather them. Unlike fossil fuels or electric power, the bulk of all traditional, or non-commercial, fuels is not sold, so there are neither sales receipts nor production data for them. Similarly, draught animals and human labour still provide most of the motive power and transportation in the developing world. For example, in 1972 India's 85 million draught animals were estimated to provide some 34 million horsepower to agricultural production, compared with less than 3 million horsepower from 130000 tractors.[9] Especially if draught animals and human labour are factored in, it is very difficult to say with any certainty how much energy most people in the developing world presently consume, or how much they use for specific tasks in farming, households, and manufacturing.

Energy accounting and consumption comparisons are further complicated due to a very low conversion efficiency of most non-commercial energy sources. Fuelwood is usually burned in an open fire or in a partially enclosed stove. Draught animals are often inefficiently harnessed or are weakened by poor nutrition or disease. It is therefore difficult to say how much of the statistical growth in energy consumption in developing countries in recent years has been due to actual increase in energy use, or how much it has been a substitution or 'upgrading' from unmeasured non-commercial energy sources to measured commercial sources.

It seems unlikely that reasonably accurate statistics of non-commercial energy use will ever be possible. But traditional energies will continue to play a major role in most developing countries for decades to come. Reasonable estimates are that the non-commercial fuels presently account for about one-third of China's primary energy use, half of all the energy consumed in India, three-quarters of the energy consumption of Bangladesh, and 90 per cent or more in several African countries.[10] On the other hand, the World Bank estimates that only 4 per cent of black Africa's rural population have access to electric power, the most convenient and versatile form among modern energies. The situation is somewhat better in the Asian and Latin American countryside, but at present rates of rural electrification only a quarter of the developing world's villagers is likely to use electricity by the end of the century.[11]

Use of traditional fuels is not limited only to rural areas. In many parts of the developing world, charcoal is the preferred cooking fuel even among the wealthiest families, and large quantities of fuelwood and charcoal are being imported from the countryside to satisfy the cooking and heating needs of rapidly growing urban populations.

There is an old African proverb: It costs as much to heat the pot as to fill it.[12] Never has this been more true. Despite the difficulty of quantifying traditional energy use, it is becoming apparent that its cost can be alarmingly dear. When traditional fuels enter into commerce, as in most cities, and, increasingly in smaller towns and villages, the cost is approaching, or even exceeding the cost of the food it is to cook. In Mali, a full third of a typical urban labourer's income may be needed to purchase cooking fuel for his family.

Although the cooking fires of the developing world have always been limited to the energy sources available from the immediate environment, a major alteration is presently occurring in the traditional system. As some of the benefits of modern medicine, sanitation, and nutrition have bolstered survival rates in most of the developing world, populations that had long been in approximate equilibrium or only very slowly growing have suddenly begun a steady increase. One of the results is that firewood is now being consumed more rapidly than it is being regrown in many areas. A vicious circle results, in which it is necessary for each family to devote more of its time and labour to searching ever farther away from its home for fuelwood. As forests are at first badly damaged and then eliminated entirely, vast areas of topsoil are left exposed to rain and wind.

Erosion of the topsoil, especially in mountainous regions, not only contributes to the silting of waterways and eventual flooding downstream, but also accelerates the loss of the land's productivity. This effect is further exacerbated by the increasing tendency to burn dung where firewood is scarce, dung that formerly served as a vital soil fertilizer. In other words, because of an increasing lack of traditional fuel sources and an inability to afford the purchase of commercial alternatives, the energy situation of the poorest people in the developing countries is actually declining, and they are simultaneously undermining their ability to produce their own food.

Need for new energy policies

To halt this dangerous environmental degradation, to expand their food production, and to support serious economic modernization drives, developing nations need, obviously, both to consume much larger quantities of fossil fuels and electricity and to change fundamentally the way their renewable biomass energies are being depleted.

Until very recently, however, developing countries had no institutions, plans, or policies to deal with these critical and complex questions. Such a situation should not be too surprising. For most nations, industrialized or developing, energy and energy policies have become high-ranking governmental and public concerns only during this decade. Only the quintupling of international crude-oil prices and the concomitant recognition of rapidly approaching limits of cheap and easily accessible hydrocarbon resources brought the recognition of the obvious: energy's key role in economic well-being and human progress.[13]

Nowhere has this been more true than in the developing nations. Except in those dozen or so countries blessed with substantial quantities of readily exploitable crude oil, 'energy policy' has been largely limited to development of electric power systems. And for those nations with large petroleum production or potential, an energy ministry in the government would have been primarily concerned only with questions of foreign participation in oil exploration, granting of concessions, and national control of the oil industry.

Moreover, most developing countries have gained their national independence and begun significant use of modern fuels and electric power only since the Second World War, an era during which energy prices were not only stable but, at times, were actually declining and when the crude-oil price stood at just around US$2.00 per barrel. Not only were large quantities of petroleum readily available, but it was widely perceived that nuclear power technologies being developed and commercialized in the United States, Canada, Western Europe, and Japan would eventually be a source of almost unlimited quantities of low-cost energy. The leaders of most developing countries therefore turned their attention to more pressing issues, such as employment, health care, education, food production, and development of raw materials and export industries.

But the events of the early 1970s have changed that. Beginning in 1970, when the US—by far the largest consumer of petroleum—first became a net crude-oil importer, the importance of those relatively few nations—all developing countries—with large petroleum reserves destined mainly for exports rose immensely, and was dramatically demonstrated during 1973–4 when the 13 members of the Organization of Petroleum Exporting Countries (OPEC) exercised their oligopolistic powers and raised the international trading price of petroleum to more than four times its former level.[14]

In the industrialized countries, the effect of the sharp oil price increases included a sudden acceleration of inflation, higher unemployment, and the severest economic recession since the great Depression of the 1930s. But it became soon obvious that it was those developing countries that are petroleum importers that were the hardest hit. Many oil-importing nations in Asia, Africa, and Latin America were actually dependent on imported petroleum for a larger share of their liquid fuels than were most industrialized countries and because of their relative economic weakness, were immediately confronted with difficult choices.[15] Either they would have to borrow funds to pay for the crude oil they needed to maintain economic growth, thereby greatly increasing their indebtedness to foreign banks or other foreign investors, or they would have to sacrifice economic growth. These difficulties were worsened by the simultaneous decline in the industrialized countries' ability to purchase the raw materials that are generally the primary—if not the sole—source of foreign exchange for most developing nations.

Lowering the dependence on imported oil

There are, naturally, three principal courses to lower the dependence on imported oil: to conserve the fuel for essential uses and to maximize its conversion efficiencies; to develop, if possible, domestic hydrocarbon resources; and to switch gradually to other energies.

The first option, so imperative for the advanced nations, is, obviously, of a limited use in most of the developing world where refined fuels are not wasted on inefficient individual transportation, energy-intensive leisure activities, and wasteful space heating and cooling. There is, naturally, room for improved conversion efficiencies but such steps alone cannot even perceptibly slow down the growing demand.[16]

Possibilities of discovering and developing new crude oil resources are, at least for some developing nations, fairly promising. Currently only a dozen of more than 100 developing nations outside OPEC are producing in excess of 5 million tonnes of crude oil annually but this number will increase, not least because of the sharp rise in oil prices.[17] During the 1950s and 1960s when crude-oil prices were low, and even declining, only the largest and most readily accessible and exploitable fields were worth developing. Not surprisingly, those developing countries without proven petroleum potential had little likelihood of attracting the technical skill and foreign capital necessary for expensive and risky oil exploration. In fact, they had little incentive for doing so.

Since 1973, however, new oil discoveries have occurred in virtually all developing countries that were already producers and nearly a dozen additional developing nations have discovered oil for the first time and are now beginning or preparing commercial production (Benin, Cameroon, Chad, Guatemala, Ivory Coast, Papua New Guinea, Philippines, Tanzania, and Vietnam).[18] Exploration has been intensified in some three dozen additional countries which had received only cursory drilling attention before 1973. Since some geologists estimate that half of all the crude oil yet to be globally discovered will be found in the non-OPEC developing areas, the potential contribution of these countries to the world petroleum supply can no longer be ignored. Indeed, discoveries in Mexico during the past several years have suddenly put that country into the category of major oil producers, with proved reserves almost as great as those of Nigeria or Venezuela.[19] On the other hand, many nations have had a very disappointing history of unproductive search.

Substitution of crude oil and refined oil products by other forms of energy is not an easy task. Crude oil is a very concentrated, high-quality energy source: in comparison with good bituminous coal the identical mass of crude oil typically contains 1.5 times more energy.[20] It can be conveniently stored for long periods of time unlike coal, natural gas, or electricity, and it is easily and inexpensively transported in large or small quantities; and through refining, of course, it can be broken into a variety of specific end-products having a very wide range of final uses. Precisely these relative advantages over most other energy sources have made crude oil the universal fuel of choice for most modern economic needs. They also explain why, as the cheap accessible deposits of crude oil are shrinking, advanced nations are currently engaged in complex and costly research and development to extract liquid oil from solids—oil sands and oil shales—and to liquefy the still abundant coal resources.

Production of synthetic liquid fuels is, however, still far from being commercial even in the USA and Canada, the two nations which have devoted most attention to such technologies. And, moreover, substantial resources of coal and oil sands and shales are concentrated in even fewer developing countries than are conventional hydrocarbon deposits.[21] Smaller coal and oil-shale deposits are much more abundant and they can be, certainly, tapped directly for local rural modernization, but, as the Chinese example shows, they cannot be a foundation of large-scale industrialization programmes.

Consequently, it seems very unlikely that the developing nations, excepting the minority with sizeable hydrocarbon deposits, will ever again have access to abundant supplies of a very inexpensive, conveniently concentrated, and versatile energy source such as crude oil has been. Precisely how much of a factor the availability of inexpensive petroleum was in the unprecedented economic growth of the industrialized countries during the nearly three decades following the Second World War will be a moot point, but there is little doubt that it was a critical contribution, and one not to be repeated for most of mankind. Naturally, this predicament spurs a search for alternatives.

Alternative energies

Perhaps the most significant common characteristic of non-fossil-fuel alternatives in the developing countries is the difficulty with which they can be put to a widespread practical use.

Nuclear power technology can be readily transferred from North America and Western Europe, but the introduction of large-scale fission power to even the richer or more populous developing nations remains economically questionable and fraught with serious technical safety and security problems. Environmental impacts of nuclear generation and the uncertainty surrounding the viability and safety of fast-breeder reactors aside, fission generation, whose development and operation has been subsidized in countless ways by fossil fuels, remains an offspring of advanced economies and not a viable means for an alternative self-supporting energy basis in developing countries.

Wind and solar energy for large-scale power generation are, by any account, quite complex, as yet poorly mastered and hence excessively expensive; tides and ocean thermal differences are being much written about but it is safe to predict that their actual contribution will remain insignificant even for technically competent advanced nations for decades to come.[23] Geothermal power is more promising although the exploratory drilling is expensive and operation of power plants is hardly simple, and in many locations potential appears to be very good, if not for power generation at least for some food producing and household tasks.

Undoubtedly the greatest promise is in using a variety of renewable energies on small scale. During the 1970s the advocacy of this approach spread tremendously and 'small is beautiful' and 'appropriate technology' gained an almost unassailable and revered status.[24] The basic soundness of the small-scale strategy cannot be doubted: it is to produce fuels and electricity in rural areas for farming, households, and manufacturing with relatively simple and inexpensive technology which would allow for large-scale labour participation, rely on local resources for manufacture of components, and would reduce dependence on costly imports of advanced machinery and materials. Appropriate technology would also gradually prepare unskilled labour for more complex future advances, would perceptibly improve standard of living (household lights, better cooking) and should have beneficial environmental implication.

Practical applications, however, face a variety of obstacles. Very few countries or regions have reliable inventories of renewable resources to be harnessed by small-scale applications. It is difficult to set the policies and to plan the programmes without knowing the magnitude of potentially exploitable small-scale hydro-power, phytomass for bioconversion, solar radiation, or wind—as well as without having reliable information on the current utilization of renewables.[25] Some of these resource inventories, moreover, require fairly demanding and time-consuming research to give a useful basis for viable planning.

Although many small-scale technologies are fully proven and operate satisfactorily in a particular setting, their transfer to many tradition-dominated rural societies, even if subsidized, faces a formidable array of technical, economic, cultural, institutional, and social obstacles which may take very long time to recede.

The introduction of new, more efficient, energy conversion methods—small hydro stations, biogas generation, direct solar applications, wind generators—must also be well co-ordinated and integrated with the many other closely related facets of the national or local economy: domestic manufacture capabilities, availability of foreign exchange for necessary imports, flow of investment capital (grants, loans, subsidies), presence of skilled labour, and means of diffusing the needed information to build, operate, and maintain the small-energy projects, all of these must be carefully considered before making a commitment to a new technology if a particular programme is to succeed.

Mainly for these reasons a recent comprehensive evaluation of renewable energies in the rural areas of the developing world had to conclude that 'at least a decade or two must pass before any of what are now regarded as promising "unconventional" energy sources will play an important role in the energy-supply picture' and that 'the "energy crisis" will continue to be, in essence, a fossil-fuel crisis (specifically, an oil crisis)'.[26]

The future

The needs are clear and overwhelming: to provide three-quarters of mankind with enough energy for a decent life. The solutions cannot follow any set prescription: diversity of resource endowment, environmental, demographic, cultural, economic, and political conditions will force each developing nation to pursue a specific path.

During the remaining two decades of this century the less populous OPEC nations—the small Persian-Gulf States, Saudi Arabia, and also Venezuela—will certainly move into the 'developed' category not only in terms of their income per capita and energy consumption but also as far as their health and social indicators are concerned. Iran, Algeria, and Iraq might follow closely, while the two most populous OPEC states, Nigeria and Indonesia, will need much more time, and will encounter more problems, before they will truly develop their economies.

Among the non-OPEC developing nations those with newly discovered major hydrocarbon deposits or with plentiful hydropower potential may look toward the future with some confidence—providing they pursue rational development policies, promote rural modernization, and strive to control their population growth. Malaysia, Zaire, Egypt—and above all Mexico—are among the populous states in this category: their inhabitants, on the average, can hardly become affluent within one or two decades, but their real incomes per capita may at least double and their quality of life might improve markedly. Brazil, if successful in harnessing alternative energies and in developing the Amazon Basin potential, would join them.

For most developing nations, however, the prospects are much less promising. Resource-rich China has embarked on a large-scale programme of economic modernization but her predicament is best illustrated by the fact that even a rapid expansion of energy supply will bring the annual consumption per capita in the 1990s no higher than the mid-1970s levels in Mexico or Iran.[27] If the current expansion plans for Indian energetics in the 1980s are fulfilled, consumption per capita of modern energy would slightly more than double—but that would still leave the population with a far from desirable supply.[28]

Indonesian energy consumption per capita is expected to reach only a third of the projected average for the developing countries by the year 2000[29] and other large populous nations—Bangladesh, Burma, Pakistan, Philippines, Ethiopia—will also not change radically their current poor standing. Many smaller nations in Asia (e.g. Afghanistan, Nepal, Sri Lanka, Laos, Cambodia), tropical Africa (at least two dozen, ranging from Mauritania to Somalia and from Niger to Botswana) and Central America and the Caribbean are in a similar situation: without significant domestic fossil-fuel resources and with low export earnings they will continue to face the interrelated and trying problems of energy scarcity, inadequate food production, serious underemployment, income maldistribution, indebtedness, and environmental degradation.

Ample energy supply is not an automatic guarantee of smooth economic advance, social progress, and political stability; it is, undisputably, their essential precondition. The future state of our increasingly interdependent world will be thus very much influenced by the success or failure of the developing countries to assure sufficient and sustainable flows of energies.

References and notes

1. Production and consumption figures for all the world's nations are published regularly by the Department of Social and Economic Affairs of the UNO in *World energy statistics* (UNO, New York, annually) and aggregate values are converted to millions of tonnes and to kilograms of *coal* equivalent. OECD in its series—*Statistics of energy* (OECD, Paris, annually)—and some other international statistics convert different energies to *oil* equivalents.
2. For details on final energy consumption in the major non-Communist developed nations see Basile, P. S. (ed.) *Energy demand studies: major consuming countries*, The MIT Press, Cambridge, Mass. (1976).
3. Extreme values range from mere 10 kg of coal equivalent per capita annually in Nepal to more than 18 000 kg in Qatar.
4. These developments are discussed in detail by E. Eckholm and K. Openshaw in papers reprinted in the second section of this volume (Energy Resources and Uses).
5. Analyses and discussions of development—ranging from rigorously quantitative to radically philosophical—are best covered in the following periodicals: *World Development*, *Economic Development and Cultural Change*, *The Developing Economies*, *The Journal of Development Studies*, and *The Journal of Developing Areas*.
6. Data and estimates on GNP (gross national product) are regularly published by the UNO in *Yearbook of national statistics* (UNO, New York, annually) and by the World Bank in *World Bank atlas* (World Bank, Washington, DC, annually). For GNP comparisons see Kravis, I. B., *et al.* (1975), *A system of international comparison of gross national product and purchasing power*, Johns Hopkins Press for the World Bank, Baltimore, Md. (1975).
7. Important energy and power conversions are listed in Appendix A of this volume.
8. For a global look at the energy–GNP relationship see Smil, V. and Kuz, T. (1976), Energy and the economy—global and national analysis, *Long Range Planning* **9** (3), 65–74. For a detailed analysis of commercial energy consumption and gross national product in advanced nations see Darmstadter, J., Dunkerley, J., and Alterman, J. *How industrial societies use energy*, Johns Hopkins Press, Baltimore, Md. (1977).
9. Estimates according to the *Asian agricultural survey: 1976* (Asian Development Bank, Manila, 1977); similar comparisons for China can be found in Smil, V. China's energetics: a system analysis, reprinted in section III of this volume.
10. For further details see the papers by Smil, V. and Henderson, P. D. in this volume and also Goldemberg, J. (1978), *Energy strategies for developed and less developed countries*, Center for Environmental Studies, Princeton University, NJ.
11. World Bank, *Rural electrification*, World Bank, Washington, DC (1975).
12. The worry about cooking fuel is common to many areas of the developing world. Peasants in the central Chinese province of Hunan have a saying very similar to the African one: 'It's not what's in the pot, but what is under it, that worries you.'
13. Perhaps the most elegant, yet rigorous and lucid, exposé of energy's role in human affairs remains H. T. Odum's *Environment, power and society*. Wiley Interscience, New York (1971).
14. Posted price of Saudi Arabian light crude oil (34° API gravity), the largest single export stream in the world, rose from $US2.591 per barrel on 1 January 1973 to $3.00 on 1 October 1973, $5.176 on 1 November 1973, and $11.651 on 1 January 1974.
15. For example, small Central-American countries were importing over 90 per cent of their consumption in the early 1970s, Philippines over 95 per cent, South Korea 54 per cent, and Brazil 45 per cent. An informative summary of the effect of OPEC oil price rise is in *Implications of recent organization of Petroleum Exporting Countries (OPEC) oil price increases* (USGPO, Washington,DC, 1974).
16. Primary energy demand for non-Communist developing nations as a group rose from 139 to 752 million tonnes of coal equivalent between 1950 and 1974, an average exponential growth of 7 per cent annually (that is doubling each 10 years). China's demand during the same period grew, on the average, by 10.5 per cent annually.
17. These nations are China, Mexico, Argentina, Oman, Egypt, Trinidad, Brunei, Syria, Angola, Brazil, Colombia, and India.

18. The new developments in global search for hydrocarbons are perhaps best chronicled in *The Oil and Gas Journal* and in its *International petroleum encyclopedia* (Petroleum Publishing Co., Tulsa, annually).
19. Estimated proved reserves as of 1 January 1978 were 14 billion (10^9) barrels in Mexico, 18.7 billion barrels in Nigeria, and 18.2 billion barrels in Venezuela.
20. For energy equivalents of common fuels see Appendix B of this volume.
21. Recoverable solid fuel reserves in excess of 1 billion tonnes are only in a handful of developing nations: China, India, Turkey, Swaziland, Brazil, Rhodesia, and Indonesia.
22. Current nuclear capacities and future plans for fission generation in developing nations are reviewed in Lane, J. A., Covarrubias, A. J., Csik, B. J., Fattah, A., and Woite, G. *Nuclear power in developing countries*, International Atomic Energy Agency, Vienna (1977).
23. For one of the most informative reviews of alternative-energy potentials see: Congressional Research Service, *Project Interdependence: U.S. and world energy outlook through 1990*, USGPO, Washington, DC (1977).
24. The essential work has been, of course, Schumacher, E. F. *Small is beautiful: economics as if people mattered*, Harper, New York (1973), followed by a profusion of theoretical and applied writing.
25. For example, there is not even any reliable inventory of the primary productivity and standing biomass in tropical rain forests, the planet's largest depository of renewable energy.
26. US National Academy of Sciences, *Energy for rural development*, pp. 4–5, US National Academy of Sciences, Washington, DC (1976).
27. For details see the third section of this volume.
28. A good review of India's future energy requirements is in Pachauri, R. K. *Energy and economic development in India*, pp. 47–68, Praeger, New York (1977).
29. According to the estimates of A. Arismunandar, (see section VII of this volume).

2

Energy in the rural Third World

ARJUN MAKHIJANI*

Development is about meeting today's needs and assuring a brighter future for our children. Yet often these two aspects of development are seen as mutually antagonistic. If we consume what we have today, the argument goes, we cannot meet our needs tomorrow, let alone build a brighter future for all.

This paper challenges such dismal pessimism. As a premise for development policy to meet the urgent needs of the poor it is both unacceptable and unnecessary. There exist many approaches which make meeting poor peoples' needs today consonant with investing in the future. Indeed, the two are often synonymous. So long as they exist the policy maker, who has enough for today, must seek and adopt these approaches. But to do so he must first become a champion of the poor.

In the Third World an overwhelming majority of the poor, and of all people, live in rural areas. Most development resources, though, have been applied to the cities. A first imperative for development policy in poor countries is thus to focus on rural communities and small towns, where productive jobs to meet human needs can nearly always be created with far less capital than in cities. Such an emphasis on rural development can produce a prosperous countryside which may in turn help to slow and perhaps even reverse the migration of the rural poor to the cities.

As shown later, village organization combined with investments in carefully selected small-scale technologies can provide all the basic life essentials such as domestic water, adequate food, fuel, sanitation, and health care to the poor through their own efforts. Labour-intensive programmes such as composting and building minor irrigation works can provide enormous numbers of needed jobs. Development 'take off' with the production not only of enough basic essentials for all but of surplus wealth is easily possible. In short, the root causes of poverty lie in the neglect of the countryside and that is where remedies must begin.[1,2]

While there are some stirrings in the international community and in some countries towards such an approach, the inertia of the past still carries the day. The large scale, centralized approach with its heavy emphasis on capital intensive industrialization still takes up most of the available investment capital. This approach has not served the poor well. For them we need to create one permanent, productive job for a few hundred or even a few tens of dollars.* Capital-intensive projects use up

*The use of US dollars as a currency measure throughout this paper does not, of course, imply foreign exchange transactions.

From *Energy Policy for the Rural Third World* by A. Makhijani (International Institute for Environment and Development, London, 1976), pp. 1–13. Reprinted by permission of the IIED and of the author who wishes to state that in view of his more recent experience many of the opinions expressed here have been altered and a revised version of the paper can be found in *Economic and Political Weekly*, Vol. XII, Nos. 33–4.

thousands of dollars per workplace. A second imperative is thus to search for and adopt village-scale and family-scale technologies, sophisticated in their conception, simple in their application. This paper reviews ideas of this kind, with special emphasis on the provision of energy as an essential basis for development.

There are even more fundamental reasons for adopting development strategies that focus on the rural poor. The direction and purpose of development policy has been to achieve, in the long run, what the industrial revolution achieved for the now rich countries. This is one of the reasons why poor countries are variously called 'developing' or 'less developed' or 'underdeveloped' in relation to the 'developed countries'. Implicit in this is the assumption that there is some immutable linear spectrum of development and that the poor countries should aspire to achieve the conditions now found in the industrialized world. This view entirely ignores the idea that there are many possible paths of development.

It ignores also the fact that most people in the industrialized countries are trapped in meaningless, dull jobs over which they have little or no control; that they must befoul their air and water by endless consumption on pain of losing their jobs; that most are locked into a transportation system where a good portion of their work time goes to purchasing and maintaining a car so that they can get to and from work; that beyond a certain point increases in the the gross national product have an inverse correlation with well-being and freedom as witnessed by increasing expenditures on drugs (over and under the counter), by rising crime and increasing police forces and armaments, by the alienation of people in urban areas, and by the way people have come to derive their spiritual satisfaction from the things rather than the people around them.

Ignoring these realities, the poor countries have been directing their efforts primarily towards an imitative industrialization—towards the city at the expense of the countryside. This path is at once undesirable, unaffordable, and ecologically unsound. It has caused the population influx to the cities because of the failure to create enough productive jobs in the countryside. It has created small pockets of vast wealth in the cities to which the rural poor are attracted in the hope of sharing some of it by being beggars or servants or factory work slaves.

Moreover, these facts are routinely ignored or sidestepped in the discussion and formulation of development policies. For example, engineering colleges in poor countries routinely have automobile engineering as a large part of their curricula. Bullock carts, which are the vital transport of the poor and which have a large potential for simple technical development, are almost entirely ignored. Even the technologies that are introduced into the countryside are usually imitations of Western technology. They are put there without much thought as to alternatives that would more easily and more cheaply meet the needs of the poor.

In their rush to imitate the West, the planners and politicians of poor countries consistently opt for what is known as 'high technology' or 'advanced technology', terms usually undefined but implicitly taken to mean 'capital-intensive technology'. Many of these technologies are ecologically unsound and debasing to human dignity. A humanist development policy cannot be based on such technologies. It must be based on technologies which people can understand and control, which produce meaningful jobs, which are compatible with long-term ecological constraints, which are accessible to the poorest, and which are coupled with an educational system that enables their use for individual as well as common benefits. The solutions to the problems of development call for the use of resources in a manner that is radically different from the way they are, or have been, used in the industrialized countries. This paper is about such solutions.

Human needs

Each human need has two aspects—the physical and the spiritual. We need calories and protein to survive, and we need to relish our food and even to embellish it. We need houses for shelter and warmth and we need homes for emotional and intellectual strength and integrity. We need jobs to produce and equitably distribute the physical needs and we need satisfaction and dignity in our work so that the pursuit of happiness can be a 24-hour affair rather than a 2-weeks-a-year vacation-escape from mindless and repetitive service of monstrous technologies and bureaucracies. Moreover, we need to accomplish these things in a way that is compatible with ecological realities and particularly with the long-term integrity and productivity of the rural environment.

Physical needs are easily listed:

(1) food of adequate quality and quantity;
(2) clean domestic water;
(3) shelter including ventilation and protection from extremes of weather;
(4) clothing;
(5) sanitation; and
(6) light.

Energy is also needed to meet these needs but is not a need in itself, except in the form of food and sunlight. For example, energy is needed for cooking but is only one of many requirements included in the category 'food'. Thus, when this paper speaks of 'energy needs' it is merely as shorthand for 'energy needed to produce and equitably distribute the wherewithal to meet human needs'. In this sense, the quantity of energy needed can vary widely from time to time, with climate, with different forms of social organization, and so on. The physical needs are fairly invariant.

These physical needs are related to the needs for meaningful and productive jobs, personal mobility, physical and mental health, and education which in turn are related to each other. With respect to education, it should be borne in mind that it is not only the poor or illiterate that need it, but also the literate who must understand the point of view of the poor, the reasons for the existence of poverty and the many-sided effects that result from actions to ameliorate poverty. It is vital for the policy maker to be keenly aware of local skills and materials, traditional modes of transfer of information and knowledge, and so on. For example, the poor often use resources such as water with great care: the literate have much to learn from them. Human development requires an educational system in which segments of society grow together, not a unilateral dictation to the poor by the elite. (It is noteworthy that in discussions about poverty and poor people, the elite often use the terms 'illiteracy' and 'ignorance' interchangeably, whereas they are manifestly distinct concepts.)

Energy needs

The principal energy needs that correspond to the human needs are:

(1) agricultural fuels (irrigation, draught power, fertilizers, manufacture of implements, crop processing, food transport, food storage);
(2) energy for cooking;
(3) energy for providing clean domestic water supply which, in some places, includes energy for boiling drinking water;
(4) house heating and warm water for bathing in cold climates;
(5) hot water and soap for washing clothes;
(6) energy for lighting (household and community);
(7) energy for personal transport;
(8) energy for processing and fabricating materials needed for house construction, pots and pans, clothes, tools, bicycles, etc.;
(9) energy for transport of goods; and
(10) energy needed to run local health services, schools, government and other community uses.

The people of the Third World fulfil these energy needs, to the extent that they can, primarily and in many cases almost exclusively, by the use of solar energy. This use of solar energy is dominated by photosynthetic conversion. The energy captured through agriculture in crops and crop residues provides food for people and fodder for draught animals. In some areas dung and crop residues are used for cooking and heating.[3,4,5] In the past two decades these traditional energy sources have been supplemented by the use of coal, oil, and electricity in agriculture, transport, industry, and homes. However, these 'commercial' energy supplements are used almost exclusively by the wealthiest 20 per cent of the people in poor countries.

It is manifest that the needs of a great number of people in the poor countries* are not being met. This is partly due to a lack of sufficient investments and effort aimed at creating productive jobs for the poor, and equally important, the poor return, in terms of production and jobs, of the investments that are made.

The situation in energy use is the same. Energy use in the Third World is much greater than is usually supposed. When food, fodder and wood are included, annual energy use is seen to be 20 to 80 billion† joules per capita instead of 1 to 15 billion joules per capita when only commercial energy (coal, oil, gas, electricity, etc.) is counted (Table 2.1).

One of the most striking features of energy use in the Third World, shown in Table 2.1, is that *the amount of useful work which the poor obtain from the energy they use is small.* This is attributable to their poverty, for obtaining more useful work entails investments which they often cannot afford on an individual basis, and often because they are cut off from technological developments that may benefit them owing to a lack of organization and effective extension work. Thus the energy needs of the poor are not met only partly because of the inadequate level of energy use—the neglect by government policies of rural development, which is responsible for the low efficiency of energy use, is equally important. It will be shown in this paper that the best way to meet some of the pressing energy needs in a short time involves increasing the efficiency of energy use rather than increasing energy supply.

Energy use in rural areas of the Third World is also characterized by distressingly hard and unproductive labour by human beings and their animals, and by the expenditure of ecological capital as in the excessive burning of wood. Again the poverty of the people and the neglect of rural development are responsible. The energy needs to increase the productivity of labour are related principally to making agriculture more productive while creating a large number of jobs. Making agriculture more productive not only requires fertilizers, irrigation, etc., but also water conservation and the arrest of soil erosion.

Agricultural energy needs

Agriculture is essentially the organized trapping of solar energy in crops and crop residues. *In general, the energy content of the crops plus the crop residues exceeds the energy inputs to farming including energy for irrigation, manufacture of chemical fertilizers and the energy to make and power farm machines.*‡ In fact, when inputs to agriculture, including *useful* energy, are increased properly the energy output per unit of land increases—that is, the plants capture solar energy more efficiently. This means that subsistence agriculture which

*I exclude the People's Republic of China from the categorization 'poor countries', but not from the categorization 'Third World'. In many ways China is, among nations, a class by itself.

†*Editors' note:* Billion is used here and elsewhere as a thousand million.

‡The energy for threshing grain is included, but further processing, transport, storage, and cooking are excluded.

Table 2.1. A rough sketch of energy use in a few areas of the Third World

	Non-commercial energy: wood, food, crop residues, grazing land (principal sources except north Mexico)										*Commercial energy*		*Total energy*	
	Rural domestic energy use per capita (billion joules/yr)		*Agricultural energy use, farm work, irrigation, chemical fertilizers (billion joules/yr) per capita*		*(per hectare)*		*Energy use in transportation crop processing and other activities per capita (billion joules/yr)*		*Sub-total energy use per capita (billion joules/yr)*		*Oil, coal, hydro, etc., per capita (billion joules/yr)*		*Total energy use per capita (billion joules/yr)*	
	Useful energy	*Energy input*	*Useful energy*	*Energy input*	*Useful energy*	*Energy input*	*Useful energy*	*Energy input*	*Useful energy*	*Energy input*	*Useful energy*	*Energy input*	*Useful energy*	*Energy input*
India (East) Gangetic Plain)	0.2	4	0.5	7.7	1.6	25.6	0.1	3.4	0.8	15.1	0.5	2.5	1.3	17.2
China (Hunan)	1	20	1.4	8.3	6.5	41.5	0.1	3.2	2.5	31.5	1.6	8	4.1	39.5
Tanzania	1.1	22	0.06	2.3	0.1	3.8	0.02	0.7	1.2	25.0	0.2	1	1.4	26
Nigeria	0.75	15	0.16	2.4	0.4	7.3	0.03	0.9	0.9	18.3	0.14	0.7	1.14	19.2
Mexico (North)	1.6	17	13.5	41	14.9	45.5	0.1	3.6	15.2	61.6	3.0	15	18.2	75.6

Sources: Refs. 6 and 7.

Notes: (1) These numbers are rough estimates, particularly with regard to the breakdown of animal labour into field and non-field activities. (2) Of the areas shown agriculture is productive only in northern Mexico and China (Hunan). (3) Efficiency of draught animals and wood use assumed to be 5 per cent; efficiency of oil, coal, hydro, etc., assumed to be 20 per cent.

barely supplies enough food and fodder for the poor can be transformed into *one that provides surplus energy (in the form of excess food and crop residues) to other parts of the economy* even while it provides enough food and fodder for the villagers and their draught animals.

As an example, when the energy inputs and outputs of two of the prototypical villages of Table 2.1 are compared[8] (one in Bihar, India and the other in northern Mexico), the net energy output of food and crop residues is found to increase much faster than the energy inputs needed for irrigation, fertilizers, and double cropping. The north Indian village, Mangaon, relies almost exclusively on human and animal labour with little use of either chemical fertilizers, manure or irrigation. In Arango, northern Mexico, heavy use is made of irrigation, chemical fertilizers and double cropping. Most of the useful mechanical energy in Arango is provided by machines, though there are some draught animals. The animal energy input in Mangaon is about 28 billion joules per hectare and the output 40 billion joules per hectare. Only 0.07 per cent of the incident solar energy is captured. The corresponding figures for Arango are 50 billion joules per hectare, 120 billion joules per hectare, and 0.2 per cent. In each case about 30 per cent of the energy output is food, the rest crop residues. The most important feature of the increase in energy inputs is that the annual *useful* energy input is increased from 2 billion joules per hectare to 15 billion joules per hectare. However, the needed increase in energy inputs would be smaller if organic fertilizers were used to as large an extent as feasible. Broadly speaking, the principal energy needs of agriculture are related to increases in:

(1) the number of jobs;
(2) the output per worker; and
(3) the output per unit of land.

While expansion of cultivated land can be, and is being undertaken, it is expensive. The heavily populated river valleys and plains regions throughout the Third World (with some notable exceptions such as the Zaire river in tropical Africa and the Amazon region) do not have much additional land available. Indeed *a vast portion of the poverty and suffering in the poor countries is concentrated in a single region—the Indo-Gangetic Plain*, which includes Pakistan, Bangladesh, and the Indian States of Uttar Pradesh, Bihar, and West Bengal. In this region there is little additional land available. I will concentrate on the three factors listed above, because of their importance to all poor countries and particularly to the densely populated regions.

To accomplish large increases in employment and productivity, fertilizers and irrigation are usually essential. Either of these, or both in combination, can help achieve simultaneous increases in all three factors. This is reinforced by the fact that the warm climates prevalent in the area permit harvesting several crops a year, but the erratic rainfall is largely limited to a single monsoon season.

Widespread irrigation using underground water resources generally requires mechanical energy from sources other than human labour and draught animals, particularly if the land is to be productively cultivated in the dry season. During the rainy season, human and animal labour can and do provide supplemental irrigation where the water is not too far below the surface.

The *useful* energy requirements for pumping underground water can vary from 0.5 billion to 5 billion joules per hectare per crop. This may be more for very deep tubewells. The corresponding fuel requirements for the machines operating the pumps at 20 per cent efficiency would be 2.5 to 25 billion joules per hectare per crop.

Certain labour-intensive water conserving methods of irrigation for cultivating vegetables may not require power from machines. One of the promising ones involves the use of earthen pots buried in the soil up to the neck and filled with water. The seeds are planted around the pots and water seeps through the porous walls of the pots to the roots. The pots can be refilled manually. This system used only 2 cm of water to grow a crop of melons with an 88-day growing season.[9]

Fertilizers from organic sources require little or no fuel input, but chemical nitrogen requires about 75 billion joules per tonne of nitrogen content. The need for chemical fertilizers depends on the number and variety of crops, practice with regard to manure use, and soil characteristics. With two or three crops a year, 200 kg/hectare or more of nitrogen may be required. This requirement can probably be substantially reduced—perhaps to small quantities—by planting legumes and recovering the fixed nitrogen by composting or by gasifying (by anaerobic digestion) crop residues, dung, and human excrement.

Immediate initiation of composting schemes, followed later by community biogas plants, can provide enormous quantities of badly needed fertilizers in poor countries (composting is already widely practised in China). Additional nitrogen fertilizer of the order of 10 to 15 million tonnes per year could be had if only half the available nitrogen in human and animal excrement is used.* This has the potential of increasing to 20 to 25 million tonnes as diets improve (i.e. protein intake increases), recovery of wastes is increased and biogas plants are used to conserve nitrogen. In addition roughly 5 million tonnes each of phosphorus (P_2O_5) and potassium (K_2O) would be available in the compost. These figures exceed present use of chemical fertilizers significantly. In 1971 chemical fertilizer use in poor countries was: nitrogen 5.7 million tonnes; phosphorus (P_2O_5) 2.7 million tonnes; potassium (K_2O_5) 1.5 million tonnes. A comprehensive composting programme could increase *annual* food production by over 100 million tonnes or more than four times the current deficit in terms of need. *This increase can be accomplished by the use of labour alone: the composting programme can create* 50 *to* 100 *million productive jobs*. In many areas, such a programme has to be tied to reduction of dung used for cooking.

Total fuel requirements for irrigation and fertilizers can vary from 5 to 30 billion joules per hectare per crop depending on the method of irrigation, source of water, the source of fertilizers, etc. A typical range for the Gangetic plain may be 5 to 10 billion joules per hectare per crop because of the easy accessibility of ground water.

The other major requirement for energy in the fields is draught energy. Today, this is provided primarily by human and animal labour and in some places by tractors. A characteristic feature of energy requirement for field operations is that they peak sharply at certain times of the year (ploughing, planting, harvesting, and in some instances crop processing). Thus, many farmers experience acute shortages of human and animal labour during brief periods while many are unemployed for a good part of the year. In certain areas, such as the Deccan plateau of India, there is a severe lack of power to till the fields because the hard soil may require 2 to 3 horsepower to turn the soil effectively. This is more than the ½ to 1 hp available even to a farmer with one or two draught animals and a medium-sized plot (5 to 20 acres of dry land).

In some areas, shortages of draught power and labour may be a factor in preventing the adoption of labour-intensive methods, such as rice transplantation, which increase production. In such areas increasing draught animal power or selective mechanization can help increase output. However, this can cause large losses of jobs for the landless unless other measures are taken *prior to* and during the mechanization period. Mechanization cannot succeed in alleviating the problems of the poor where a small minority controls most of the land and there are large numbers of landless people. The organization of labour co-operatives and

*Calculations are based on references 10 and 11.

unions, and sharing of animals, can considerably ease the labour shortages that small farmers commonly experience. Such organizations should include the guarantees of increases in employment to the landless (labour unions) and should precede efforts at providing machines to solve peak labour problems. In some places such efforts can significantly postpone the need for selective mechanization while increasing both output and employment.[12] In any case, where mechanization endangers jobs, particularly those of the landless, insecure tenants and small farmers, it must be postponed until measures are taken to ensure it will not. As Gandhi said in 1934, machines must not be pitted *against* human beings.

It is worthwhile to digress here and note that sharp peaks in agricultural labour requirements coupled with poor health care are among the principal causes of the high birth-rate in poor countries. First, a poor Indian villager must have six children to be reasonably certain (95 per cent confidence level) that one son will survive to maturity—his only hope of security in his old age.[13] Second, because they are denied capital by governments and because of the lack of organization for development, the poor are forced to rely on children as one of the principal sources of labour. Their labour for tending animals, collecting wood, fetching water, looking after their younger siblings, becomes critical at peak periods in the agricultural season. We cannot hope to reduce birth-rates substantially unless development policy takes these fundamental realities into account.

Thus, there are five principal changes in energy inputs to the land that are usually essential to an increase in food and crop residue output as well as jobs and labour productivity:

(1) labour organization;
(2) sharing draught animals at peak periods;
(3) increasing energy used for irrigation by partly or wholly mechanizing it as dictated by the water resources, soil characteristics, etc.;
(4) increasing the use of fertilizers by returning organic matter and supplementing the organic fertilizers with chemical fertilizers as needed; and
(5) where necessary, increasing the draught power for ploughing and other field operations by improving the quality of draught animals, by increasing their number and by supplementing draught animals with small walking tractors.

The increased energy inputs for human labour and draught animals must come from improved health, and food and crop residues. Organic fertilizers require little energy input except for application to the soil (draught energy). Fuels must be used for chemical fertilizers and either fuels or wind for irrigation.

References

1. Myrdal, Gunnar, *Asian drama*. Part 5. Pantheon Press, New York (1968).
2. Makhijani, Arjun and Poole, Alan. *Energy and agriculture in the Third World*. Chapter 1. Ballinger Publishing Co., Cambridge, Mass. (1975).
3. Makhijani and Poole, op. cit., Chapter 2.
4. Openshaw, Keith. 'The Gambia: a wood consumption survey and timber trend study, 1973–2000'. Unpublished report to the ODA/LRD Gambia Land Resources Development Project, Midlothian, Great Britain (1973).
5. Eckholm, Eric. *Losing ground*. W. W. Norton. New York (1976).
6. Makhijani and Poole, op. cit., Table 2.2
7. *World energy supplies 1960–1970*, statistical papers Series J. No. 15. United Nations, New York (1971).
8. Makhijani and Poole, op. cit., Tables 2.4, 2.5, 2.18, 2.19, and 4.6.
9. *More water for arid lands*. National Academy of Sciences, Washington, DC (1974).
10. Food and Agriculture Organization, *Production yearbook*, *1972*, Vol. 26, Rome (1973).
11. Makhijani and Poole, op. cit., Table 4.5.
12. Myrdal, Jan. *A report from a Chinese village*. Vintage Books, New York (1965).
13. Rich, William. 'Smaller Families through Social and Economic Progress'. Overseas Development Council, Washington, DC (1973).

3

Energy and economic growth prospects for developing countries

WORKSHOP ON ALTERNATIVE ENERGY STRATEGIES*

The Workshop on Alternative Energy Strategies has focused on projected energy supply and demand in the industrialized world. Members of WAES come from 15 countries, most of them in the industrialized world outside of Communist areas (WOCA). We believe that the actions of these countries—or their failure to act—to alleviate possible future shortages of world energy will significantly affect the energy prospects of the developing nations.

In the WAES analyses, it is necessary to make assumptions about the energy supply and demand patterns in what is termed 'Rest of WOCA'—WOCA countries outside Western Europe, North America, and Japan. These countries consist primarily of the developing countries (both OPEC and non-OPEC) but also include Australia, New Zealand, and the Republic of South Africa.

We have relied extensively on others with knowledge of these countries to help analyse their future energy supply and demand prospects. In particular, individuals from the International Bank for Reconstruction and Development (World Bank) have been most helpful in estimating developing country economic growth rates to 1990, deriving relevant income elasticities of energy demand, and providing energy supply estimates to 1980.

The energy supply estimates by fuel type for 1980 to 1985 come from World Bank and WAES sources, and the 1985 to 2000 figures are taken from the WAES global supply estimates for oil, gas, and coal.

The energy supply–demand estimates in this paper are very tentative. Historical data on energy consumption in developing countries are generally incomplete and are clouded by the fact that a significant proportion of total energy consumption comes from non-commercial sources such as firewood, cow dung, and vegetable waste. The survey also attempts to cover over 90 countries and so is exceedingly general in nature.

This report attempts to answer the following questions, which are essential to the WAES global supply–demand analysis: (1) Given certain assumptions regarding economic growth, what is the probable range of commercial energy consumption in the developing countries during 1985 and 2000? (2) What potential domestic energy supplies are available to help these countries

*This report was prepared jointly by William F. Martin (WAES Staff) and Frank J. P. Pinto (Consultant to WAES and the World Bank). The authors gratefully acknowledge the written papers and verbal communications received from Nicholas Carter, John Foster, and William Humphrey of the World Bank and Alan Strout of the MIT Energy Laboratory.

meet their anticipated demands? (3) What would be the probable range of desired imports (or exports) of energy by these countries? Possible answers to these questions represent the boundaries of the study. We recognize that the developing countries will need appropriate mechanisms to help them achieve desired levels of economic growth and that new arrangements may be needed to assist developing countries in meeting the rising costs of energy. Such arrangements must be part of a broad and complex system of existing economic relationships and institutions, an analysis of which is outside the scope of the WAES study.

Introduction

This paper focuses on the energy and economic growth prospects of the OPEC and non-OPEC developing economies in the world outside Communist areas (WOCA).

Primary energy consumption in the developing countries during 1972 constituted approximately 15 per cent of total WOCA energy consumption. As these countries industrialize, their share will rise relatively faster than that of the industrialized world. The WAES global supply–demand integrations suggest that the developing countries could consume as much as 25 per cent of total world energy by the year 2000, as Fig. 3.1 illustrates.

The 93 developing nations in WOCA considered in this analysis are divided into two major groups: (1) the 13 OPEC countries and (2) the non-OPEC developing nations of Asia, Africa, and Latin America. The latter group is further divided into two classifications according to income per capita (the number of countries in each category is in parentheses):

Lower-income countries comprising those developing economies with annual income per capita below $200. The countries in this group fall into two regions: South Asia (7) and lower-income sub-Sahara Africa (20).

Middle-income countries comprising those developing economies with annual income per capita above $200. These countries can be grouped into three regions: East Asia (9); Caribbean, Central and South America (21); middle-income sub-Sahara Africa and West Asia (23). Per capita incomes range from $200 to around $1000 with the mean being about $550.[1]

These classifications are identical to those used by World Bank. A detailed list of the countries in each major group is given in Table 3.1.

An important factor in the analysis of energy consumption in the developing world is the present level and future growth rate

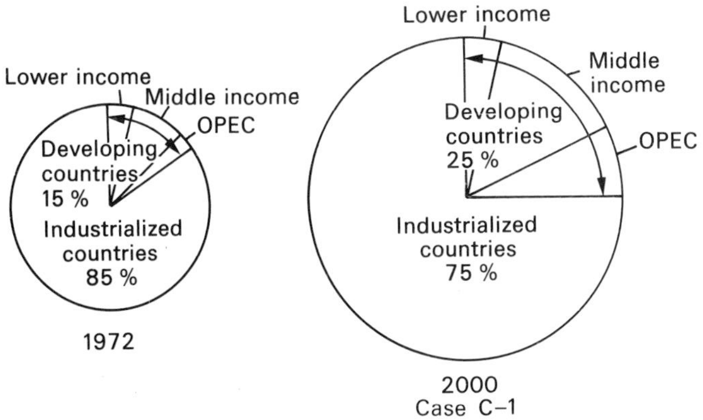

Fig. 3.1. Shares of WOCA energy consumption.

Table 3.1. Classification of developing countries

OPEC countries

Algeria	Iran	Qatar
Ecuador	Iraq	Saudi Arabia
Gabon	Kuwait	United Arab Emirates
Indonesia	Libya	Venezuela
	Nigeria	

Non-OPEC developing countries

Lower-income countries (annual income per capita under $200 (1972 US$))

South Asia	*Lower-income sub-Sahara Africa*	
Afghanistan	Burundi	Niger
Bangladesh	Central African Republic	Rwanda
Burma	Chad	Sierra Leone
India	Dahomey	Somalia
Nepal	Ethiopia	Sudan
Pakistan	Guinea	Tanzania
Sri Lanka	Kenya	Togo
	Madagascar	Uganda
	Malawi	Upper Volta
	Mali	Zaire

Middle-income countries (annual income per capita over $200 (1972 US$))

East Asia	*Middle-income sub-Sahara Africa and West Asia*	*Caribbean, Central and South America*
Fiji	Angola	Argentina
Hong Kong	Bahrein	Barbados
Korea (South)	Cameroon	Bolivia
Malaysia	Congo P.R.	Brazil
Papua New Guinea	Cyprus	Chile
Philippines	Egypt	Colombia
Singapore	Ghana	Costa Rica
Taiwan	Israel	Dominican Republic
Thailand	Ivory Coast	El Salvador
	Jordan	Guatemala
	Lebanon	Guyana
	Liberia	Haiti
	Mauritania	Honduras
	Morocco	Jamaica
	Mozambique	Mexico
	Oman	Nicaragua
	Rhodesia	Panama
	Senegal	Paraguay
	Syria	Peru
	Tunisia	Trinidad and Tobago
	Turkey	Uruguay
	Yemen AR, DM	
	Zambia	

of population. WOCA had a population of around 2.7 billion in 1975, and it is estimated that this figure will increase to 4.5 billion by the year 2000. The industrialized nations of North America, Europe, Japan, and Oceania constituted approximately 28 per cent of the total population in 1975 and will probably constitute around 20 per cent by the year 2000.

Table 3.2 presents estimates of the absolute levels and growth rates of population for the developed and developing nations for the years 1970, 1975, 1985, and 2000. Most of these figures have been derived from United Nations population projections. The energy problems facing the developing economies are more severe because of their 2.4–2.7 per cent average population growth between now and 2000, as compared to 0.7–0.9 per cent for the industrialized world.

WAES uses the scenario approach in its studies 1985 and 2000. The scenario variables include economic growth (high or low), real energy price (rising, constant, or falling), government policy (vigorous or restrained), and, for 1985 to 2000, principal replacement fuel (coal or nuclear). For the developing economies, only a constant real energy price to 1985 was examined. Furthermore, government policy response to 1985 is not included as a variable owing to the uncertainty in modelling an aggregate policy response for over 90 countries. The WAES scenario cases considered in the analysis of developing country prospects are more fully specified in Table 3.3.

The first step is the determination of economic growth rates for the developing nations, primarily from the World Bank's SIMLINK model.[2] High and low economic growth rate assumptions for the developed economies, as well as the WAES oil price assumption of $11.50 (per barrel of light Arabian crude, FOB Persian Gulf, in constant 1975 (US$) are special inputs to the model, whose simulations then provide economic growth projections for the major developing regions of WOCA to 1985. Figure 3.2 illustrates the SIMLINK flow from the exogenous input to the output.

The historical (1960 to 1972) relationship between regional economic growth and energy consumption is then examined by considering the income elasticity of demand for energy use. This is defined as the growth rate of energy consumption divided by the growth rate of real income. Since real energy prices rose substantially between 1972 and 1976 and are assumed to either remain constant (WAES Cases C and D in 1985, Cases D-7 and D-8 in 2000) or increase by 50 per cent by the year 2000 (WAES Cases

Table 3.2. Estimated developed and developing country population levels and growth rates, 1970–2000

	Population (in millions, rounded)				*Population growth rate (per cent/year)*		
	1970	*1975*	*1985*	*2000*	*1970–75*	*1975–85*	*1985–2000*
Total population in WAES analysis	2399	2661	3310	4475	2.1	2.2	2.05
Developed economies	702	732	792	872	0.9	0.8	0.7
Developing economies	1697	1929	2518	3603	2.6	2.7	2.4
OPEC	255	292	388	566	2.8	2.9	2.6
Non-OPEC developing countries	1442	1637	2130	3037	2.6	2.7	2.4
Lower-income countries	889	1005	1301	1835	2.5	2.65	2.3
South Asia	740	835	1076	1487	2.4	2.6	2.2
Lower-income Africa	149	170	225	348	2.7	2.9	2.9
Middle-income countries	553	632	829	1202	2.7	2.75	2.5
East Asia	138	158	207	290	2.8	2.7	2.3
Middle-income Africa and West Africa	162	184	240	353	2.6	2.7	2.6
Caribbean, Central and South America	253	290	382	559	2.8	2.8	2.6

Table 3.3. WAES scenario assumptions

	Economic growth	*Energy price**	*Principal replacement fuel*
1976–1985			
C	High	$11.50	
D	Low	$11.50	
1985–2000			
C-1	High	$11.50–$17.25	Coal
C-2	High	$11.50–$17.25	Nuclear
D-7	Low	$11.50	Coal
D-8	Low	$11.50	Nuclear

*Price per barrel light Arabian crude FOB Persian Gulf in 1975 US dollars.

C-1 and C-2), the historical income elasticities were revised downward for the period 1976 to 2000 to reflect the more energy-efficient use of resources in the future.

The primary energy demand growth rates are obtained from the real economic growth rates and the income elasticities of energy demand. The total primary energy consumption of developing countries in 1985 and 2000 can then be determined.

The energy supply estimates by fuel type for 1975 to 1985 come from World Bank[3] and WAES sources. The 1985 to 2000 estimates come primarily from the WAES global supply studies described in chapters 3 to 7 of the second WAES technical report.

Supply–demand integrations then balance available energy supplies with expected energy demands. The resulting figures show the range of energy exports and imports of

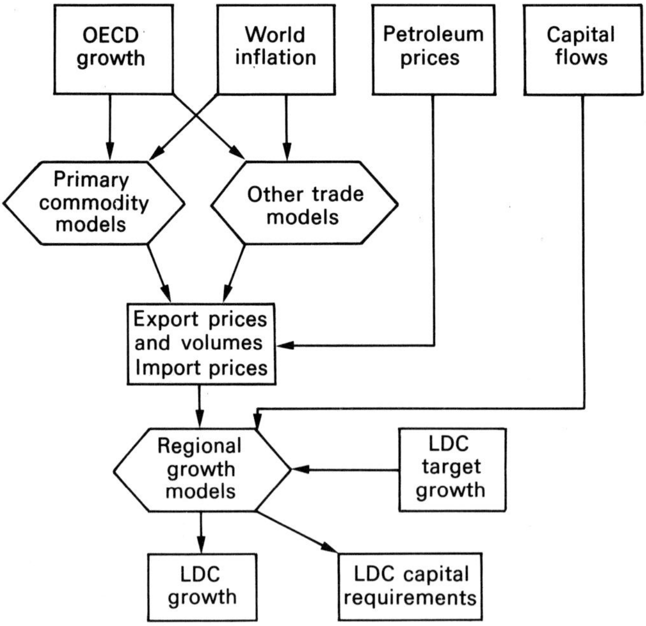

Fig. 3.2. Flow diagram for SIMLINK III.

both OPEC and non-OPEC developing countries.

Demand for energy

The historical and projected economic growth rates for the developing economies for the period 1960 to 2000 are presented in Table 3.4. The 1976 to 1985 growth estimates have been derived primarily from simulation of the World Bank's SIMLINK model using the WAES high (Case C) and low (Case D) economic growth assumptions for the OECD countries as well as the WAES constant oil price assumption of $11.50 per barrel (1975 US$). Because SIMLINK is primarily a medium-term forecasting system, extrapolations were made to determine the 1985 to 2000 developing countries' economic growth rates.

Several of the middle-income countries profited by the commodity boom of 1972–3 and should be able to achieve comparatively rapid growth over the next decade. Latin American and East Asian countries are expected to show the highest economic growth patterns among the non-OPEC developing countries owing to higher capital productivity, an increase in the rate of investment, and export promotion. The lower-income countries will probably grow much slower than the middle-income countries, and they will continue to suffer from the effects of higher oil prices and agricultural shortfalls. The projected growth rates assume, however, that improvements will be achieved in domestic policies with special emphasis on increasing exports.

As a group, the non-OPEC developing countries are expected to maintain a growth rate higher than that of the OECD area. In the long run, middle-income countries are expected to grow 1–2 per cent faster and low-income countries about 0.5 per cent slower than the developed nations.

OPEC countries are expected to achieve high economic growth rates from 1976 to 1985, possibly as high as 7.2 per cent per year in the high growth case and 5.5 per cent per year in the low growth case. Several OPEC countries—mainly those with larger populations such as Algeria, Ecudaor, Indonesia, Iran, Iraq, Nigeria, and Venezuela —are expected to have current-account deficits in their balance of payments by 1985. From 1985 to 2000 OPEC growth will likely decrease since many OPEC countries have undertaken large development projects that may cause foreign exchange shortages and curtailed imports after 1985.

From 1960 to 1972 the nations of the developing world more than doubled their consumption of commercial energy and increased their demand for electric power by more than 250 per cent. In 1972 the developing countries accounted for around 15 per cent of total world energy consumption in WOCA.

Sixteen countries accounted for about three-quarters of all developing world energy

Table 3.4. Real GNP growth rate assumptions, 1972–2000 (average annual percentage growth)

Period	*1960–1972*	*1972–1976*	*1976–1985*		*1985–2000*	
Economic growth WAES case			*High C*	*Low D*	*High C-1, C-2*	*Low D-7, D-8*
Non-OPEC developing countries	5.6	5.1	6.1	4.1	4.6	3.6
Lower-income countries	3.7	2.3	4.4	2.8	3.1	2.5
Middle-income countries	6.2	5.9	6.6	4.5	4.9	3.9
OPEC	7.2	12.5†	7.2	5.5	6.5	4.3
Developed countries* (OECD)	4.9	2.0	4.9	3.1	3.7	2.5

*As derived by WAES analyses of individual countries.
†Preliminary estimate.

demand.[4] They are Argentina, Brazil, Chile, Colombia, Egypt, India, Indonesia, Iran, Korea, Mexico, Pakistan, Philippines, Taiwan, Thailand, Turkey, and Venezuela.

Total commercial energy demand within the developing world (including OPEC) during 1972 was approximately 9.5 MBDOE (excluding international oil bunkers), distributed among the developing regions as shown in Table 3.5.

Table 3.5. Distribution of total commercial energy demand in the developing world, 1972 (per cent)

Lower income countries South Asia	23.0
Lower-income Africa	2.0
Middle-income countries East Asia	13.5
Middle-income Africa and West Asia	11.0
Caribbean, Central and South America	33.0
OPEC	17.5
All developing countries	100.0

Table 3.6 summarizes the actual quantities of commercial energy consumed by the OPEC and non-OPEC developing countries for the period 1960 to 1972 in both tonnes of coal equivalent (TCE) and millions of barrels per day of oil equivalent (MBDOE). The energy and real income growth rates for the period are also included.

We have estimated only commercial fuel consumption. In several developing countries non-commercial energy in the form of firewood, cow dung and vegetable waste constitutes a significant share of total energy consumption. In India, non-commercial energy was estimated at 59 per cent of total energy consumption in 1960 and 48 per cent in 1970; it is expected to retain a significant though decreasing percentage of total energy consumption.[5] Owing to the great difficulty in obtaining accurate data, the non-commercial energy sources have been excluded from this study. A detailed study

Table 3.6. Developing country commercial energy consumption and income elasticity of energy demand, 1960–1972

	Energy consumption				*Energy growth rate, 1960–1972 (per cent year)*	*GNP growth rate, 1960–1972 (per cent/year)*	*Income elasticity of energy demand, 1960–1972*
	(10^6 tonnes of coal equivalent)		*(MBDOE)*				
	1960	*1972*	*1960*	*1972*			
Non-OPEC developing countries	260.40	594.50	3.43	7.81	7.10	5.50	1.29
Lower-income countries	88.50	177.40	1.17	2.33	6.00	3.70	1.62
South Asia	83.40	165.10	1.10	2.17	5.80	3.60	1.61
Lower-income Asia	5.10	12.30	0.07	0.16	7.60	4.00	1.90
Middle-income countries	171.90	417.10	2.26	5.48	7.70	6.20	1.24
East Asia	27.80	97.60	0.37	1.28	11.00	7.70	1.43
Middle-income Africa and West Asia	32.90	79.30	0.43	1.04	7.60	5.80	1.31
Caribbean, Central and South America	111.20	240.20	1.46	3.16	6.60	5.90	1.12
OPEC	48.30	127.90	0.64	1.68	8.40	7.20	1.17
Total developing countries	308.70	722.40	4.07	9.49	7.40	5.80	1.28

Sources: For energy consumption: (1) UN, *World Energy supplies, 1950–74*, Series J, No. 19. (2) *Report of the Fuel Policy Committee*, Government of India (1974), and also J. D. Henderson, *India: the energy sector*, World Bank. (3) A. Lambertini, Energy and petroleum in non-OPEC developing countries, *World Bank Staff Working Paper* No. 229, February 1976. (4) William Humphrey, Estimation of energy growth for non-OPEC LDCs by region and OPEC countries for 1972–85 and 1985–2000, Cambridge, *WAES Associates Report*, 15 January 1976.

For GNP data: *World Bank Atlas*, 1975 (in constant US 1973 dollars).

Table 3.7. Projected developing country income elasticity of energy demand, 1960–2000

Period / *WAES case* / *Oil price*	*1960–1972*	*1976–1985*	*1985–2000*	*1985–2000*
		C, D	*C-1, C-2*	*D-7, D-8*
	$2.00	$11.50	$11.50–17.25	$11.50
Non-OPEC developing countries*	1.29	1.19	1.04	1.10
Lower-income countries	1.62	1.50	1.20	1.30
Middle-income countries	1.24	1.10	1.00	1.05
OPEC	1.17	1.10	1.05	1.10

*The ratios for the non-OPEC developing countries have been weighted using the following year-end weights:

Year / *WAES case*	*1972*	*1985*	*1985*	*2000*	*2000*
		C	*D*	*C-1, C-2*	*D-7, D-8*
Lower-income countries	0.246	0.215	0.219	0.176	0.186
Middle-income countries	0.754	0.785	0.781	0.824	0.814
Total	1.000	1.000	1.000	1.000	1.000

on the developing world's energy prospects would have to consider such fuels explicitly.

Table 3.7 shows our assumptions regarding the historical (1960–72) and projected relationship between energy consumption and real economic growth. This relationship is termed the *income elasticity of demand for energy use*. The price of oil quadrupled between 1972 and 1976. A simple extrapolation of the historical (1960–72) income elasticity would result in an overestimation of energy demand. The much higher current and expected energy prices assumed in the WAES cases to 1985 would tend to reduce the energy intensiveness in economic activity. Specifically, the income elasticity of energy demand would decrease if current energy prices were maintained. For the period 1985 to 2000, the C cases assume a 50 per cent increase in real energy prices, and this would serve to lower the income elasticity of energy demand even further.

From the World Bank study,[6] one can derive interesting relationships between developing-country income growth and energy consumption for the period 1970 to 1980. In the lower-income countries, per capita income elasticity of energy demand is about 40 per cent higher than the corresponding total income elasticity, where per capita income elasticity = (growth rate of energy consumption per capita)/(growth rate of real income per capita) and total income elasticity = (growth rate of energy consumption per capita + population growth rate)/(growth rate of real income per capita + population growth rate).

For the middle-income countries, however, per capita and total income elasticities are found to be noticeably closer. In other words, the process of industrialization that raises income per capita also results in a gradual reduction in the growth rate of energy consumption with respect to growth in real income.[7]

Table 3.8 specifies the percentage decrease assumed in the income elasticity of energy demand for the period 1976 to 1985 as compared to 1960 to 1972 and for 1985 to 2000 as compared to 1976 to 1985. The lower-income countries are dominated by India, whose energy consumption in 1972 was around 75 per cent of the total, while Argentina, Brazil, and Mexico together account for around 42 per cent of the energy consumption of the middle-income countries. The long-run income elasticities for the lower-income countries are consistent with those implied in the 1974 report of the

Table 3.8. Per cent change assumed in the income elasticity of energy demand over the preceding period*

Period	*1976–1985*	*1985–2000*	*1985–2000*
WAES case	*C, D*	*C-1, C-2*	*D-7, D-8*
Oil price	*$11.50*	*$11.50–17.25*	*$11.50*
Non-OPEC developing countries	−8	−13	−8
Lower-income countries	−7	−20	−13
Middle-income countries	−11	−9	−5
OPEC	−6	−5	nil

*Rounded to nearest per cent. Elasticity for 1976–85 period is compared to that of 1960–72.

Indian Fuel Policy Committee, while the income elasticities for the middle-income countries are consistent with estimates provided by the WAES Mexican team.

While the income elasticities of energy demand for non-OPEC developing countries are assumed to decline, the decrease will be more pronounced in the lower-income than in the middle-income countries. Their elasticities, however, will still be higher than the developed country elasticities, which, in the WAES analysis, have been shown to drop below unity.

Obviously, using such a simple relationship between economic growth and energy growth is inadequate in some respects, in that it fails to include factors that may significantly affect energy consumption, such as changes in the industrial structure or increased mechanization in agriculture. Alan Strout, for instance, considers the production of a small group of key energy-intensive materials (such as iron and steel, cement, aluminium), when combined using energy weights, as an indication of the 'energy-intensiveness' of a country's industry.[8] For developing countries achieving rapid industrialization, the production of energy-intensive goods would have to grow even faster than normal, and income elasticities would accordingly be higher.

This raises the important issue of whether or not developing countries will choose to develop energy-intensive industries. Some feel that a significant transfer of industry to the developing countries endowed with energy resources will occur. For example, a significant proportion of the industrialized world's aluminium processing industry might be relocated in Brazil, where abundant hydroelectric reserves would allow for large-scale, relatively inexpensive production. Likewise, many chemical plants might be 'exported' to the OPEC countries where abundant gas reserves permit manufacturing of chemicals such as ammonia at lower cost. It is an assumption of this chapter that while such transfers may occur, there will be no major transfer of energy-intensive industries from the developed to the developing world.

Furthermore, the immense complications of such a transfer—for both the developed and the developing countries—suggest that most developing countries will continue to be net importers of these products. Strout has also shown that most developing countries did not develop significant energy-intensive industries when oil prices were low, and the higher prices assumed by the WAES cases would, if anything, discourage them from major investment in energy-intensive industry. This important issue needs further research and is certainly beyond the scope of this analysis.

A somewhat different approach to the problem is that of Charpentier and Beaujean, who replace the GNP indicator with a long list of non-energy variables describing the level of development of the economy.[9] Their study uses the technique of factor analysis to sum up and reduce a given set of data by

Table 3.9. Primary energy consumption targets for the developing world (MBDOE)*

Year / *WAES case*	*1972*	*1985* / *C*	*1985* / *D*	*2000* / *C-1, C-2*	*2000* / *D-7, D-8*
Non-OPEC developing countries	7.81	18.20	14.90	35.60	26.50
Lower-income countries	2.33	4.90	4.00	8.40	6.50
Middle-income countries	5.48	13.30	10.90	27.20	20.00
OPEC	1.68	4.90	4.20	13.10	8.40
All developing countries	9.49	23.10	19.10	48.70	34.90

*Excludes bunkers.

extracting factors that are linear combinations of non-energy variables. Multiple correlation analysis then gives a series of factors. The first factor, termed *degree of development*, determines the greatest amount of variance between countries. This first factor is highly correlated with steel and electricity consumption per capita, total energy consumption, and the number of newspapers and cars. Their choice of variables was, however, biased in favour of the industrialized nations (e.g., number of newspapers and cars) and hence is not really applicable here. Selecting key variables in the development process of poorer nations would make this approach useful and relevant.

Table 3.9 shows the estimates of developing country consumption of energy for the principal WAES cases based on the analysis in the preceding sections. Non-OPEC developing countries are expected to increase their energy consumption from four to as high as five times their 1972 level by the year 2000. This is based on an average economic growth rate of between 4 and 5 per cent per year during the period. OPEC countries are expected to achieve a five- to eightfold increase in their energy consumption by the year 2000 based on an economic growth rate of between 6 and 7 per cent per year from 1972 to 2000.

Supply of energy

The OPEC and non-OPEC developing countries have the potential to significantly increase their domestic energy supplies by the year 2000. There are a number of reasons for this. First, the higher energy prices will encourage exploration for and production of fuels in many developing countries where such activities have been seen as uneconomic. This is particularly true for oil, natural gas, and coal. Developing countries with adequate reserves of coal and natural gas may choose to develop these resources rather than risk further deterioration in their balance of payments because of higher oil import bills.

It is difficult to generalize for over 90 countries. Therefore in discussing energy supply, we shall distinguish between OPEC and non-OPEC developing economies. Even within these two groups differences are substantial. OPEC countries differ widely in their economic growth potentials, development plans, population, and revenue needs. The non-OPEC developing countries also vary greatly in their energy supply potentials and revenue needs. Some, such as Mexico and Brazil, will most likely attain a high degree of energy self-sufficiency, while others, particularly the low-income countries of Africa and Asia, will continue to depend on energy imports.

Table 3.10 shows the resource base for middle- and lower-income non-OPEC developing countries. The middle-income countries are relatively well-endowed with energy resources, especially oil and natural gas. The lower-income countries do not have abundant supplies of oil and natural gas but do have plentiful coal reserves. These

Table 3.10. Non-OPEC developing countries' medium-term energy resources (10^6 tonnes of oil equivalent)

	Oil	*Natural gas**	*Coal†*	*Hydro-power‡*	*Nuclear power†*	*Total*
Middle-income	3480	1835	5320	190	350	11175
Lower-income	180	480	9250	185	1050	11145
Total	3660	2315	14570	375	1400	22320

*Economically recoverable at current prices and costs.
†The measured or reasonably assured fraction of resources that could be economically exploited in the coming 5 years.
‡All estimated reserves.

Source: Energy and petroleum in non-OPEC developing countries, 1974–1980, *World Bank Staff Working Paper* 229, February 1976.

Table 3.11. Projected production of primary energy in developing countries, 1985–2000 (MBDOE)

Year	*1985*		*2000*			
WAES case	*Case C*	*Case D*	*Case C-1*	*Case C-2*	*Case D-7*	*Case D-8*
Economic growth	*High*	*Low*	*High*	*High*	*Low*	*Low*
*Oil/energy price**	*11.50*	*11.50*	*11.50–17.25*	*11.50–17.25*	*11.50*	*11.50*
Principal replacement fuel			*Coal*	*Nuclear*	*Coal*	*Nuclear*
Oil						
Non-OPEC developing countries	6.70	5.10	11.50	11.50	7.00	7.00
OPEC	40.00	36.00	45.00	45.00	39.00	39.00
Total	46.70	41.10	56.50	56.50	46.00	46.00
Solid fuels						
Non-OPEC developing countries	2.67	2.24	5.26	5.00	4.10	3.60
OPEC	0.42	0.30	1.46	1.30	0.80	0.80
Total	3.09	2.54	6.72	6.30	4.90	4.40
Natural gas						
Non-OPEC developing countries	2.40	2.10	4.56	4.50	3.88	3.40
OPEC	5.47	5.08	13.60	11.60	12.30	10.20
Total	7.87	7.18	18.16	16.10	16.18	13.60
Hydroelectricity						
Non-OPEC developing countries	1.70	1.80	3.80	3.10	2.70	2.10
OPEC	0.10	0.10	0.40	0.40	0.30	0.30
Total	1.80	1.90	4.20	3.50	3.00	2.40
Nuclear electricity						
Non-OPEC developing countries	1.10	0.40	4.00	8.30	2.80	5.90
OPEC	0.10	0.10	0.46	1.00	0.30	0.60
Total	1.20	0.50	4.46	9.30	3.10	6.50
Total primary energy						
Non-OPEC developing countries	14.57	11.64	29.12	32.40	20.50	22.00
OPEC	46.09	41.58	60.92	59.30	52.70	50.90
Total	60.66	52.22	90.04	91.70	73.20	72.90

*In 1975 US dollars per barrel of Arabian light crude oil FOB Persian Gulf or equivalent.

resource statistics indicate that, as a group, the developing countries have sufficient reserves of the major fossil fuels. Table 3.11 is a summary table of the energy production potential of the developing countries by fuel type.

Oil

OPEC countries currently account for about 80 per cent of WOCA oil reserves—about 450 billion barrels. OPEC production in 1975 was about 27 million barrels per day (MBD), most of which was exported to Western Europe, Japan, and North America. OPEC oil production will continue to be of critical importance to the world oil supply, and therefore an assessment of the potential production over the next 25 years is an important part of the WAES oil supply assessment (Chapter 3 in the second technical report).

If OPEC countries produce at a rate sufficient to meet the import requirements of the major consuming countries for as long as possible, limited only by a theoretical reserve-to-production (R/P) ratio of 15 to 1, they could be producing 57 MBD by 1995, assuming that additions to reserves over the next 25 years average 10 billion barrels a year.

However, it is likely that the OPEC countries will decide for economic, conservation, or other reasons to limit their production to a level below the theoretical maximum. WAES therefore chose three alternative assumptions to represent possible ceilings to total OPEC oil production:

(1) 33 million barrels a day;
(2) 40 million barrels a day; and
(3) 45 million barrels a day.

Assumption (1) appears to be most likely if future additions to reserves are low (5 billion barrels) and oil prices remain constant, so it is coupled with the year 2000 Case D scenarios. Assumption (3) is more likely if additions to reserves are high (10 billion barrels) and oil prices rise, so it is coupled with the Case C scenarios.

These levels define the maximum potential production of oil by OPEC. Once OPEC oil production reaches such a limit, it is assumed to remain at that level until the R/P ratio falls to 15 to 1. From then on, maintaining this R/P ratio will result in declining OPEC production. The OPEC production rates given by these assumptions are shown in Table 3.12. Table 3.13 presents an overview of OPEC oil reserves and production in 1975.

Non-OPEC oil production

Proven oil reserves in non-OPEC developing countries are equal to about 40 billion barrels —7 per cent of total WOCA reserves. However, the region is vast and is to a large extent relatively unexplored for oil. Thus, extensive exploration and development encouraged by a desire to reduce dependence on imported oil could lead to a significant increase in production. A high future

Table 3.12. OPEC oil production rates, 1975–2000 (MBD)

	Cases C, C-1			*Cases D, D-8*		
	Limit 33 MBD	*Limit 45 MBD*	*No government limit*	*Limit 35 MBD*	*Limit 40 MBD*	*No government limit*
1975 (actual)	27	27	27	27	27	27
1980	32	32	32	29	29	29
1985	33	39	39	33	36	36
1990	33	45	47	33	40	42
1995	33	45	57	33	40	44
2000	33	45	56	33	39	34

Table 3.13. OPEC oil reserves and oil production, 1975

	Proven reserves (*10⁶ bbl*)	*Production* (*10³ BD*)
Algeria	7370	965
Ecuador	2450	160
Gabon	2200	200
Indonesia	14000	1315
Iran	64500	5395
Iraq	34300	2230
Kuwait	68000	1840
Libya	26100	1490
Nigeria	20200	1785
Qatar	5850	435
Saudi Arabia	148600	6970
United Arab Emirates	36750	1995
Venezuela	17700	2410
Total	448020	27190

discovery rate was set at 4 billion barrels a year. This would permit production to more than triple today's levels—reaching 11.5 MBD by year 2000. A less optimistic discovery rate (around 2 billion barrels a year) would probably allow oil production to be twice as high as current levels by the year 2000.

Much of this production will probably be limited to a few countries. Walter Levy notes that three countries—Mexico, Brazil, and Egypt—could account for as much as 40 per cent of total non-OPEC developing country oil production by 1985.[10] Production in Mexico alone could be 25 per cent of the non-OPEC developing country production by the year 2000. Thus, although production for the non-OPEC developing countries as a whole is likely to increase, there is still the problem of the non-oil-producing developing countries who will continue to face large oil import bills and corresponding balance-of-payments deficits. Table 3.14 shows crude oil reserves and oil production in 1974 for selected non-OPEC developing countries.

Table 3.14. Selected non-OPEC developing countries' crude oil reserves and production, 1974

	Reserves (*10⁶ bbl*)	*Production* (*10³ BD*)
High-income		
Argentina	2459	413
Brazil	779	178
Brunei	2000	191
Chile	210	27
Colombia	627	167
Malaysia	2700	82
Mexico	3087	575
Peru	830	77
Trinidad and Tobago	651	186
Tunisia	533	85
Middle-income		
Angola	1409	172
Bolivia	216	46
Congo	950	46
Egypt	2761	148
Syria	2776	123
Low-income		
Burma	117	22
India	926	183
Pakistan	30	8

Source: Energy and petroleum in non-OPEC developing countries, 1974–1980, *World Bank Staff Working Paper* 229.

Note: These are selected countries, so the sum of these countries does not add up to total non-OPEC developing country production.

OPEC gas production

Proven reserves of natural gas in OPEC are estimated to be 140 billion barrels of oil equivalent (BOE)—about 60 per cent of WOCA reserves. There is at present only a limited demand within OPEC for natural gas, though future consumption is expected to increase substantially. Future natural-gas production will depend primarily on two factors:

(1) domestic requirements for natural gas (including gas for reinjection into oil wells to improve recovery rates); and
(2) expected level of exports to major consuming countries.

It is likely that OPEC countries will increasingly use this plentiful, inexpensive, and convenient fuel and that 3 to 5 MBDOE could be consumed domestically by year 2000. Iran has already announced that it

Table 3.15. Projected coal supply and demand in the developing countries (10^6 tonnes of coal equivalent)

	Cases C, C-1			*Cases D, D-8*		
	Production	*Consumption*	*Export*	*Production*	*Consumption*	*Export*
1985						
OPEC	31	31	—	23	23	—
Non-OPEC	202	182	20	170	160	10
Total developing countries	233	213	20	193	183	10
2000						
OPEC	110	35	75	61	15	46
Non-OPEC	400	306	94	274	243	31
Total developing countries	510	341	169	335	258	77

plans to increase its natural gas component from 18 per cent to as high as 35 per cent of total primary energy consumption by 1987. If other OPEC countries follow this lead, we could expect as much as 40 per cent of total OPEC primary energy consumption by year 2000 to be in the form of natural gas.

The economies of Western Europe, North America, and Japan may increasingly look to OPEC gas reserves as a supplement to their energy needs. Maximum planned and potential natural-gas imports from OPEC in 1985 are estimated at about 3.5 MBDOE. If all planned projects are realized, about 2.5 MBDOE could be delivered as liquefied natural gas (LNG). This would require OPEC production of 3.3 MBDOE for export, allowing for 25 per cent losses in the processing of LNG. Another 0.6 MBDOE could be delivered by pipeline from North Africa and the Middle East, resulting in a total OPEC capacity of 3.9 MBDOE of gas exports. If all import demands of the major consuming countries are to be met in year 2000 by OPEC, then these countries would need to produce as much as 9 MBDOE for export in addition tp their internal demand requirements of up to 5.0 MBDOE.

Proven reserves of natural gas are sufficient to support such a large expansion in international trade. Because of its desirable qualities as a fuel compared with oil and coal, gas may command a premium price.

Uncertainties about the growth of world gas trade lie in (1) the attitudes of the governments of OPEC countries toward export of gas versus domestic use, including use as a chemical feedstock, (2) availability of capital for investment in LNG systems, and (3) possible repercussions of an LNG tanker incident.

Non-OPEC gas production

Despite natural-gas reserves of approximately 20 billion BOE, current natural gas consumption in non-OPEC developing countries is small. The World Bank reports that only about 65 per cent of the gas produced in 1973 was marketed, with the remainder either flared, vented, or reinjected. Reserves have remained largely undeveloped due to lack of markets. With rare exceptions, natural gas has been produced only to meet export demand or for use in maintaining pressure in oil fields. Afghanistan, Bolivia, and Brunei have been small exporters of natural gas.

There are indications that gas consumption is rising. Between 1960 and 1974, its share in total energy consumption rose from 4 to 8 per cent. It seems plausible from a resource perspective that natural gas production and consumption will continue to increase. By the year 2000 the resource base would enable production in non-OPEC developing countries

Table 3.16. Reserves and resources of solid fossil fuels in Africa, East and South Asia, and Latin America (10^6 tonnes)

	Reserves		
	Recoverable	*Total*	*Total resources*
Africa			
South Africa	10584	24224	44339
Rhodesia	~1390	1760	6613
Swaziland	1820	2022	5022
Zaire	720	720	720
Botswana	506	506	506
Mozambique	80	100	400
Tanzania	180	309	370
Nigeria	225	449	449
Zambia	51	74	154
Morocco	15	15	96
Malagasy	39	78	92
Malawi			38
Egypt	~13	25	25
Algeria	~5	9	20
Total	15628	30291	58844
Asia			
India	11580	23160	82977
Japan	1026	8628	8628
Turkey	2025	2893	7282
Indonesia	1060	2123	2533
Pakistan	172	804	1941
Bangladesh	519	780	1491
Korea, Republic of	544	890	1450
China, Republic of	261	479	660
Iran	193	385	385
Burma	7	13	286
Thailand	~118	235	235
Philippines	~38	75	88
Afghanistan			85
Vietnam, Republic of	~6	12	12
Total	17549	40477	108053
Latin America and Greenland			
Mexico	629	5316	12000
Peru	105	211	6964
Colombia	109	150	5330
Chile	58	97	3945
Brazil	1790	3256	3256
Venezuela	11	14	871
Argentina	100	155	555
Honduras			5
Greenland	1	2	2
Total	2803	9201	32928

Source: World Energy Conference, 1974.

to reach 4.5 MBDOE. This level would satisfy domestic consumption needs and also allow for some export.

Solid fuels

Coal deposits can be found in several countries, but the largest known reserves are concentrated in comparatively few areas, notably the United States, the USSR, and China. Most of the coal discovered so far lies in the northern temperate zone where most of the exploration has been concentrated. Few of the developing countries have ever had to search for coal since historically their development processes got underway after oil was generally available. However, there could be significant reserves in many parts of the developing world. Rising oil prices may encourage non-OPEC developing countries to look toward coal to help meet domestic energy needs and, in certain cases, possibly contribute to exports.

OPEC coal production

Only Indonesia and Venezuela, among OPEC nations, have significant coal reserves. Abundant oil and gas reserves in other OPEC countries have discouraged exploration for coal. Therefore, future coal production is expected to be principally confined to Indonesia and Venezuela. As shown in Table 3.15, it is estimated that OPEC coal

Table 3.17. Primary electricity generation in developing countries, 1972–2000

Year	*1972*	*1985*		*2000*			
WAES case		*C*	*D*	*C-1*	*C-2*	*D-7*	*D-8*
Primary electrical generation (MBDOE)							
Oil	0.81	1.13	0.95	2.85	1.66	2.00	1.16
Gas	0.13	0.63	0.53	1.28	0.47	0.57	0.35
Coal	0.29	1.13	0.95	1.45	1.66	1.53	1.16
Hydro	0.97	1.76	1.85	4.24	3.50	3.00	2.40
Nuclear	0.01	1.17	0.53	4.46	9.24	3.10	6.50
Total	2.21	5.82	4.81	14.28	16.53	10.20	11.57
Share of total primary electrical generation (per cent)							
Oil	37	20	20	20	10	20	10
Gas	6	11	11	9	3	6	3
Coal	12	20	20	10	10	15	10
Hydro	44	31	38	30	21	29	21
Nuclear	—	18	11	31	56	30	56
Total	100	100	100	100	100	100	100

Table 3.18. Sector share of final energy demand (excluding processing losses), 1972–2000 (per cent)

	1972	*1985*	*2000*
Transport	34	35	34
Industrial	42	42	41
Domestic and commercial	18	16	17
Non-energy	6	7	8

production could grow to 31 million tonnes by 1985. Production in the year 2000 could be as high as 110 million tonnes.

Non-OPEC coal production

Coal is not widely used in the non-OPEC developing countries. Only two countries, India and Korea, mine significant amounts. In Korea, coal accounts for about half, and in India for about 70 per cent, of total commercial energy consumption.

Total coal production in the non-OPEC developing countries was about 125 million tonnes in 1972. There is increasing incentive for developing countries to expand their coal production, and the resource base could support much higher levels of coal production in many of these countries. By 1985 coal production could reach 230 million tonnes, rising to as much as 510 million tonnes by year 2000, with about half of this production coming from India.

These levels would require developing new coalmines and handling facilities as networks for delivery to consumers. The capital costs for such development are high, but probably not prohibitive in light of increasing oil import bills. Clearly, developing countries, especially lower-income countries with large reserves of coal, have the potential and the motivation to develop this energy source.

Table 3.16, from the World Energy Conference (1974), shows the reserves and total resources of solid fossil fuels in Africa, East and South Asia, and Latin America.

Electricity generation

Electrical capacity nearly tripled in the developing world during the period 1960 to 1973, and this rapid growth is expected to

Table 3.19. Developing country fuel mix assumptions by demand sector (per cent)

	Oil	*Coal*	*Gas*	*Electricity*
1972				
Transport	91	9	—	—
Industry	48	26	15	11
Domestic and commercial	66	9	8	17
1985 C, D				
Transport	97	2	—	1
Industry	42	20	24	14
Domestic and commercial	61	3	13	23
2000 C-1				
Transport	95	2	—	3
Industry	35	17	31	17
Domestic and commercial	55	5	15	25
2000 C-2				
Transport	95	2	—	3
Industry	37	16	28	19
Domestic and commercial	55	3	15	27
2000 D-7				
Transport	95	2	—	3
Industry	31	17	36	16
Domestic and commercial	55	5	15	25
2000 D-8				
Transport	95	2	—	3
Industry	37	18	27	18
Domestic and commercial	55	3	15	27

continue into the future. Over the next 5 years, the World Bank estimates that electrical generation will increase another 50 per cent in the non-OPEC developing countries.[11]

Table 3.17 summarizes electricity growth by fuel type for the WAES scenario cases. Primary electricity use is expected to increase from 2.2 MBDOE in 1972 to 5.8 MBDOE in 1985 in the high growth case (Case C). By the year 2000, total installed electrical capacity in a high nuclear growth future could be as high as 16.5 MBDOE (730 GW(e) installed).[12] The International Atomic Energy Agency estimates that about 11 per cent of total generating capacity in developing countries would be in OPEC countries and 89 per cent in non-OPEC countries.[13]

Most of this increased demand for electricity will be met by expanded hydroelectric and nuclear capacity. Reserves of hydroelectric power are abundant in developing countries, and only 4 per cent of current potential is being utilized.[14] In 1972, hydroelectricity constituted about 44 per cent of the non-OPEC developing countries' electrical generation. The World Bank estimates that this percentage share could increase over the next 5 years, and the WAES assumptions extend this growth to 1985. Hydroelectric capacity is projected to increase over fourfold by year 2000 in one of the WAES cases.

Similarly, nuclear power is expected to grow rapidly. The maximum potential nuclear installed capacity for the developing countries (OPEC and non-OPEC) in the year 2000

Table 3.20. Projected developing country consumption of primary energy, 1985–2000 (MBDOE)

Year	*1985*		*2000*			
WAES case	*C*	*D*	*C-1*	*C-2*	*D-7*	*D-8*
Oil						
Non-OPEC developing countries	10.70	8.94	20.87	19.15	15.20	14.60
OPEC	3.30	2.76	6.33	7.80	3.85	4.50
Total	14.00	11.70	27.20	26.95	19.05	19.10
Solid fuels						
Non-OPEC developing countries	2.40	2.11	4.03	4.19	3.63	3.20
OPEC	0.42	0.30	0.46	0.46	0.20	0.20
Total	2.82	2.41	4.49	4.65	3.83	3.40
Natural gas						
Non-OPEC developing countries	1.92	1.63	3.56	3.50	2.88	2.40
OPEC	1.54	1.15	5.00	3.97	3.42	2.76
Total	3.46	2.78	8.56	7.47	6.30	5.16
Hydroelectricity						
Non-OPEC developing countries	1.70	1.80	3.80	3.10	2.70	2.10
OPEC	0.10	0.10	0.40	0.40	0.30	0.30
Total	1.80	1.90	4.20	3.50	3.00	2.40
Nuclear electricity						
Non-OPEC developing countries	1.10	0.40	4.00	3.30	2.80	5.90
OPEC	0.10	0.10	0.46	1.00	0.30	0.60
Total	1.20	0.50	4.46	9.30	3.10	6.50
*Total primary energy**						
Non-OPEC developing countries	17.82	14.88	36.26	38.24	27.21	28.20
OPEC	5.46	4.41	12.65	13.63	8.07	8.36
Total	23.28	19.29	48.91	51.87	35.28	36.56

*Totals are from supply–demand integration worksheets and may not exactly equal the targets in Table 3.9.

could be as high as 416 GW(e). This high estimate is from the IAEA/OECD survey of December 1975, but there are now indications that installed capacity may be considerably less. Our analysis assumes that in the high economic growth, high nuclear scenario case (C-1) almost all the nuclear potential is utilized. In this case, nuclear power would meet about 56 per cent of the demand for electricity by the year 2000. All other cases (having scenario assumptions of low nuclear growth or low economic growth or both) are scaled downward.

Energy supply–demand integration

The interactions between energy demand and supply are complex. WAES has developed methods of comparing desired demands and potential supplies, termed *supply–demand integrations*. The techniques used in the developing country analysis are simpler than those used in the other national and global integrations. We have assumed certain shares of energy demand for various sectors—transport, industry, domestic and commercial, and non-energy uses. And we have further made the simplifying assumption that energy use in all sectors will grow at about the same rate as total energy demand. These assumptions are shown in Table 3.18. Fuel mix assumptions to the year 2000 for the various sectors are shown in Table 3.19. Oil is expected to constitute almost all of transportation's energy requirements in all cases. The industrial sector's fuel needs are met by substantial amounts of oil and gas, some coal, and in the latter years, some electricity. The relatively large share of gas in the industrial sector is due largely to the probable large-scale use of gas by OPEC countries. The domestic and commercial sectors use substantial amounts of oil and electricity. Non-energy demands for feedstocks and asphalt are made up largely of oil and some gas. Table 3.20 shows the total amount of each fuel consumed for the WAES cases when these fuel mix assumptions are incorporated.

Imports and exports

By comparing the tables on energy production (Table 3.11) and energy consumption (Table

Table 3.21. Projected (imports) and exports of primary energy for all developing countries, 1985–2000 (MBDOE)

Year	*1985*		*2000*			
WAES case	*C*	*D*	*C-1*	*C-2*	*D-7*	*D-8*
Oil						
Non-OPEC developing countries	(4.00)	(3.84)	(9.37)	(7.65)	(8.20)	(7.60)
OPEC	36.70	33.24	38.67	37.20	35.15	34.50
Total	32.70	29.40	29.30	29.55	26.95	26.90
Solid fuels						
Non-OPEC developing countries	0.27	0.13	1.23	0.81	0.47	0.40
OPEC	0	0	1.00	0.84	0.60	0.60
Total	0.27	0.13	2.23	1.65	1.07	1.00
Natural gas						
Non-OPEC developing countries	0.48	0.47	1.00	1.00	1.00	1.00
OPEC	3.93	3.93	8.60	7.63	8.88	7.44
Total	4.41	4.40	9.60	8.63	9.88	8.44
Total primary energy						
Non-OPEC developing countries	(3.25)	(3.24)	(7.14)	(5.84)	(6.73)	(6.20)
OPEC	40.63	37.17	48.27	45.67	44.63	42.54
Total	37.38	33.93	41.13	39.83	37.90	36.34

3.20), desired imports and potential exports by fuel type can be determined for OPEC and non-OPEC developing countries. Table 3.21 shows these balancing calculations.

OPEC exports

OPEC countries will continue to be large fuel exporters. The potential for export does, however, vary among OPEC countries. Saudi Arabia and other Arabian Peninsula countries have the potential to maintain their high export levels. Other OPEC countries, such as Venezuela and Indonesia, have growing domestic needs that will limit their exports. Total OPEC oil exports could range between 33 and 37 MBD in 1985 and between 35 and 38 MBD in 2000. These year 2000 estimates are based on OPEC production ceilings described earlier.

OPEC countries with plentiful gas reserves could export large quantities of gas, but this depends on whether they want to increase exports significantly and on whether the importing countries will construct the expensive and complicated LNG systems needed. As noted earlier in the section on natural gas, consuming countries of Western Europe, North America, and Japan could have import requirements as high as 8.5 MBDOE by year 2000. About 1 MBDOE could be imported from the USSR. The remainder would have to come largely from OPEC countries.

Non-OPEC imports and exports

Non-OPEC developing countries have traditionally been large importers of energy. During the period 1960 to 1972, they imported about 30 per cent of their overall energy needs. Our projections show that in 1985 they will have to import 18–22 per cent and by year 2000, 15–25 per cent of their energy needs, depending on the scenario.

The non-OPEC developing countries differ widely in their dependence on imports. Some developing countries such as Mexico and Brazil may be able to achieve energy self-sufficiency, but most will continue to depend on imports—especially of oil. These countries may require oil imports as high as 4 MBD in 1985 and between 7.6 and 9.4 MBD in the year 2000.

As described earlier, certain countries could produce substantial amounts of coal and gas. Therefore, the non-OPEC developing countries as a group will require no imports of coal or gas, and in fact may be modest exporters. However, this statistic masks the fact that, as in the case of oil, production of coal and gas will most probably be concentrated in a few countries.

Notes and References

1. These distinctions are based on data in the 1974 and 1975 *World Bank atlas*. They relate to the year 1972.
2. The SIMLINK model of trade and growth for the developing world, *World Bank Staff Working Paper* **220**, October 1975. Also in *European Economic Review* **7**, 239–255 (1976). SIMLINK is primarily a medium-term forecasting system in which exports of the non-OPEC developing countries are related to the level of economic activity in the OECD countries through a series of individual commodity models. Growth in the developing countries is linked to investment levels and imports; imports in turn depend on export earnings and inflows of foreign capital. Given assumptions as to OECD growth, the availability of foreign capital to the developing countries, and the international price of petroleum, the model may be run to determine either the import-constrained GDP growth rates to be anticipated in developing countries or the real resource transfer they would need to support a specified GDP growth target.
3. Lambertini, A. Energy and petroleum in non-OPEC developing countries, 1974–80, *World Bank Staff Working Paper* **229**, February 1976.
4. *Modern power prospects in developing countries*. Richard Barber Associates (1976).
5. Report of the Fuel Policy Committee. Government of India (1974).
6. Lambertini. Energy and petroleum, op. cit., ref. 3.
7. Variances in total energy elasticity with respect to GNP at different income levels per capita have been found to disappear when price-adjusted GNPs are used as independent

explanatory variables in place of official exchange-rate GNPs. While attempts are being made to determine the price-adjusted GNPs for several developing nations (see the pioneering study by Kravis, Kenessy, Heston, and Summers, *A system of international comparisons of gross product and purchasing power*, 1975), our study uses readily available official exchange-rate GNPs.

8. Strout, Alan. 'The Future of Nuclear Power in the Developing Countries', unpublished working paper, MIT Energy Laboratory, 1976.
9. Charpentier, J. P. and Beaujean, J. M. Toward a better understanding of energy consumption. II. Factor analysis—a new approach to energy demand? draft paper (1976).
10. OPEC in the medium-term, W. J. Levy Consultants, New York, September 1976.
11. Lambertini, Energy and petroleum, op. cit., ref. 3.
12. 100 GW of installed capacity = 2.4 MBDOE primary energy, assuming 35 per cent efficiency and a 60 per cent load factor.
13. International Atomic Energy Agency, *Market survey for nuclear power in developing countries* (1974).
14. Lambertini, Energy and petroleum, op. cit., ref. 3.

II Energy resources and uses

Fuelwood Market in the old town of Harar, Ethiopia. Fuelwood is still the principal source of thermal energy for most of the developing world.

World Bank Photo by Kay Muldoon.

Geothermal Power Plant in Ahuachapan, El Salvador. A number of developing nations in Latin America, Asia and Africa have considerable geothermal potential that can be harnessed for power generation.

World Bank Photo by Jaime Martin.

To develop their economies, poor nations will have to take advantage of any energy resources which can be harnessed, converted, transported, and used in practical and reasonably efficient ways. Those countries which discover significant deposits of oil and gas will have the least number of problems in their development, as testified by many successful examples (e.g. Libya, Algeria, Nigeria, Mexico).

The nations which possess, or discover, commercial quantities of coal are in a less enviable situation: solid fuels are neither sought as eagerly on the international market nor are they transported as easily as hydrocarbons, and it is thus more difficult to use them, in the absence of strong domestic demand, for exports to finance development. However, their internal use faces no unusual technological problems and, in the overwhelming majority of cases, amounts to arranging the initial financing and, if necessary, transferring the needed technology and know-how from the industrialized nations. Development of large hydro sites falls in the same category.

In essence, developing fossil-fuel and hydro-power resources in a large-scale commercial fashion in the Third World is not profoundly different from their exploitation in the advanced nations. Most of the time the required technology is brought in directly (often as turnkey project deliveries frequently financed by World Bank loans) or it is produced domestically on the basis of foreign experience and selective purchases (a strategy followed in many instances by the People's Republic of China, India, and Brazil). And, naturally, small-scale exploitation of some of these resources—for example rural coal mines and tiny hydro stations in China (see Section III)—may become just a variant of this experience.

However, most poor nations do not have commercial deposits of good quality coals, oils, and gases and even the majority of those who do (e.g. China, Indonesia, Nigeria, Egypt) have energy needs potentially so huge as to be unsupportable over long period of time by fossil fuels alone. A similar situation prevails with respect to large hydro-energy sites. Consequently, virtually all the developing countries, the only exceptions being oil-rich and sparsely populated nations, have a strong need to utilize the alternative sources of energy, above all the renewable ones.

They have been, of course, doing so for millenia: forest fuels (wood, branches, leaves, roots, and bark), crop residues (cereal straws, corn stover, legume, tuber, and vegetables vines, cotton roots, chaff) and, in some regions, dried cattle dung, have traditionally been providing most of the energy in rural areas, as well as in cities of the poor world—and still do so to an amazing extent (see Sections III–V for specific examples).

Demand for forest fuels (for simplicity labelled fuelwood or firewood), burned either directly or as charcoal, has risen with expanding populations and with growing manufacturing activities to such an extent that the physical shortages of firewood in countless villages of the developing world and exorbitant prices charged for it in the cities are directly affecting vastly larger numbers of people than does the multiplication of imported crude oil costs.

E. Eckholm ('The other energy crisis: firewood') traces the genesis, and describes the frightening extent and implications of this true ecological crisis, while Keith Openshaw ('Woodfuel—a time for reassessment') attempts to estimate the current and the future global woodfuel consumption and provides interesting information about final uses and prices of fuelwood and charcoal in several developing nations highly dependent on phytomass energy.

Rapidly shrinking areas of the natural forest and steadily growing demand for fuelwood and for industrial wood will increasingly necessitate the introduction and maintenance of tree plantations which could, potentially, provide a very fast return above all in the tropical regions. N. E. Johnson ('Tropical forest plantations') makes clear that while the rewards may be indeed quite impressive, the risks and concerns associated with soil degradation, fertilization, and diseases will demand extensive research and careful matching of trees with the environment to make the plantations succeed.

Solar energy can be, of course, used in many more ways than just as phytomass. It can be captured directly for heating, cooking, drying, cooling, distillation, and power generation and indirectly as wind, hydro-power, and also as liquid and gaseous fuels via microbiological conversion. The US National Academy of Sciences reviews ('Direct and indirect uses of solar energy') summarize all of these options and evaluate their current status and likely prospects.

Geothermal energy is perhaps the only non-solar alternative which could soon contribute significantly to national energy balances of many developing countries. All circum-Pacific nations, large regions of East Africa and mountainous areas of Asia have numerous potential geothermal sites. The US National Academy of Sciences summary ('Geothermal energy') points out the variety of possible applications and evaluates the tasks and the costs associated with field exploration and with power generation.

Although any further expansion of nuclear generation has become a matter of bitter scientific and political controversy throughout most of the industrialized world, virtually all populous or richer developing nations are eager to acquire this technologically most sophisticated alternative to fossil-fuel power production. As K. Gottstein, of the Max Planck Institute of Physics and Astrophysics in Munich, puts it in his paper ('Nuclear energy for the Third World'), these countries, after they had missed the industrial revolution and ended up in colonial dependency, do not want to let the same thing happen with regard to the atomic age. Gottstein, of course, recognizes the problems associated with nuclear technology transfer to the developing nations but he argues there is no turning back—that the discovery is irreversible and we will have to learn how to make it work safely and peacefully.

Harnessing renewable energies and new alternative sources (geothermal and nuclear) on a large scale and in an efficient, ecologically safe and sustainable way is a technological, economic, and social challenge of no smaller proportions than was the development of fossil-fueled energetics in the Western nations since the industrial revolution. But only a success in this difficult endeavour will usher a solution to energy starvation in the developing world.

Energy resources and uses: selected readings

Arthur D. Little, Inc. (1974). *An overview of alternative energy sources for LDCs*. Arthur D. Little, Inc., Cambridge, Mass.

Armstead, H. C. (ed.) (1973). *Geothermal energy: a review of research and development*. UNESCO, Paris.

Arnold, J. E. M., *Wood, energy and rural communities*, Paper presented at the 8th World Forestry Congress, Jarkarta, October 17 1978.

Brown, N. L. (ed.) (1976). *Renewable energy resources and rural applications in the developing world*. American Association for the Advancement of Science, Washington, DC.

Darrow, K. and Pam, R. (1976). *Appropriate technology sourcebook*. Volunteers in Asia, Stanford, Ca.

Duffie, J. A. and Beckman, W. A. (1974). *Solar energy thermal processes*. John Wiley, New York.

Earl, D. E. (1975). *Forest energy and economic development*. Clarendon Press, Oxford.

Eckholm, E. P. (1976). *Losing ground*. W. W. Norton, New York.

Lane, J. A. *et al.* (1977). *Nuclear power in developing countries*. International Atomic Energy Agency, Vienna.

Lieth, H. and Whittaker, R. H. (eds.) (1975). *Primary productivity of the biosphere*. Springer-Verlag, New York.

Lovins, A. B. (1975). *World energy strategics: facts, issues and options*. Ballinger, Cambridge, Mass.

Makhijani, A. with Poole, A. (1975). *Energy and agriculture in the Third World*. Ballinger, Cambridge, Mass.

Mitsui, A., Miyachi, S., San Pietro, A. and Tamura, S. (eds.) (1977). *Biological solar energy conversion*. Academic Press, New York.

Richard J. Barber Associates, Inc. (1975). *LDC nuclear power prospects, 1975–1990: commercial economic and security implications*. National Technical Information Service, Springfield, Va.

UNESCO (1973). *Proceedings of the International Congress The sun in the service of mankind*. UNESCO, Paris.

US National Academy of Sciences (1976). *Energy for rural development*. US National Academy of Sciences, Washington, DC.

—— (1977). *Methane generation from human, animal and agricultural wastes*. US National Academy of Sciences, Washington, DC.

World Energy Conference (1974). *Survey of energy resources 1974*. World Energy Conference, London.

World Energy Conference (1978). *World energy resources 1985–2020*. IPC Science and Technology Press.

4

Direct and indirect uses of solar energy

UNITED STATES NATIONAL ACADEMY OF SCIENCES

Heating, cooling, distillation, crop drying, and power generation

Current applications of solar energy that seem appropriate for use in rural areas, depending of course on local conditions, include:

heating of water (for domestic and commercial use);
heating of buildings;
cooling of buildings;
drying of agricultural and animal products; and
salt production by evaporation of seawater or inland brines.

From the technological standpoint, many other solar energy applications are possible. These include electricity generation, food refrigeration, cooking, production of pure water from salt water, and chemical manufacture. Their economic status is such, however, that near-term use cannot be expected; either the cost of conventional energy sources for these applications is well below solar costs, or there is very little need for such substitution in the economy of developing countries.

The applications listed are in use in various parts of the world today, but this is not to say that the technology does not need further development. It means simply that some equipment is commercially available, and applications in developing nations during the next 5 years can be expected to involve currently available equipment. Conversely, not every application for which commercial equipment is currently available can be expected to be adopted in rural communities in developing nations within the next 5 years without further significant research and development.

Within the next 5 years, only four of the applications listed can be reasonably expected to be adopted in rural areas of less developed countries (LDCs).

Agricultural uses of solar energy include the drying of various crops, employing both direct exposure to sunlight and the use of heated air passed through or over the material to be dried. These processes are available for immediate application, using locally available materials, labour, and expertise. Further, the reliability of the technology is proven, and recent research has resulted in design improvements. The costs of drying grain, fruit, lumber, and other products by solar-heated air have not yet been reliably appraised. Although they appear to be slightly more costly than conventional heating schemes, they are within economic reach.

Solar energy to produce hot water has long been used successfully for domestic hot-water

From *Energy for Rural Development* (NAS 1976), pp. 21–45, and *Methane Generation from Human Animal and Agricultural Wastes* (NAS 1977), pp. 9–15. Reprinted by permission of the National Academy of Sciences, Washington DC.

supply. Since such systems are often economically competitive with others, the economic advantage of this system compared to those using fossil fuels will increase as the price of fuels rises. Where fuels such as wood or peat are locally available at little or no cost—though such supplies are diminishing—the capital cost of a solar-heated domestic hot-water supply cannot be justified.

Residential heating by solar energy often suffers economically wherever fossil-fuel supplies are cheap and plentiful, a situation that appears to be vanishing rapidly. In the case of residential heating, hot-air systems have been used successfully instead of hot water. These systems are technologically unsophisticated, generally reliable, and can often be implemented with locally available materials, labour, and expertise.

The production of salt by evaporation of seawater or inland brines is an ancient practice sufficiently well known for it not to be treated extensively here. Suffice it to say that it is a current direct use of solar energy that is immediately available for use wherever salt-containing water occurs in conjunction with appropriate climate; the practical and economical use of this method does not depend significantly on technological improvements.

For the most part, these four applications appear to exhaust the available direct uses of solar energy that could be adopted by developing countries within the next 5 years. There is, perhaps, one other application that might be available toward the end of this period—the solar-driven cooling system employing the absorption cycle. About the only technology that will be available during this time, however, will be a redesigned lithium bromide water system. The reliability of the equipment is expected to become adequate within about 5 years, but the cost competitiveness is still open to question; depending upon local conditions, it may not be possible for LDCs in this time period to rely on local materials, industry, labour, and expertise. If the technology is found to be applicable, however, units of this type will probably make sense economically only if used in fairly large buildings where commercial activity provides the capital for defraying the high investment cost.

In the period from 5 to 10 years, one can expect the development of improved cooling systems both of the absorption type and the compression type. In the compression-type system, improvements and economies in the organic Rankine cycle and possibly in the Stirling cycle can be expected. With respect to absorption processes, research should include multistage systems and new working fluids. Some new modifications of absorption cycles will have to be proven, and there may also be success in developing desiccant systems suitable for regeneration by use of solar energy. Research and development in all these areas is needed.

It is possible that near the end of this period small solar-powered electrical generators may become practical. (This subject is more thoroughly discussed in the section on photovoltaics.) Especially for communities remote from electric networks, pumping of water, cooling, and perhaps lighting and communications may be solar operated. In areas of exceptionally high fuel price and abundant solar energy, this technology could be introduced if capital is available.

With respect to the large-scale generation of electrical power, there is little that can be accomplished in terms of in-place power in the next 10 years in the developing countries. This may not be the fault of the rate of technological progress so much as the fact that the very sophisticated industrial infrastructure and the considerable capital requirements may militate against successful implementation within this period. With respect to the technology for solar-driven electrical generating systems, there are numerous approaches in the research and development stage at present: Stirling, organic Rankine, and other cycles, as well as photovoltaic, thermionic, and thermoelectric systems. It is too early to single out one approach that is clearly superior, although some indications favour the 'power-tower' approach. These approaches need further sorting out before a clear direction emerges. During the next 5–10 years, it is not expected that there will be sufficient agreement in the field to permit successful implementation of a single approach on a significant scale, even in the industrialized countries.

In the 0- to 5-year period, viable solar-energy applications in the LDCs can be implemented by the introduction of capital and the exploitation of local materials. Some materials will have to be imported, but the bulk of the material would be available in most countries. Capital availability is unquestionably the major factor in the near-term application of solar energy in the LDCs.

For the 5- to 10-year period, capital again is the limiting factor. But research and development on promising new applications and on improving and reducing the cost of solar systems already in use will also be needed. Support of these programmes by the local governments, by intergovernmental organizations such as the United Nations and UNESCO, and by the international banking community can be effective. In addition to research on these systems in the technologically advanced countries, practical development projects in the LDCs should be of greatest benefit to the introduction of the technology. Monitoring of results by the sponsoring agencies and dissemination of these results through the existing technical and international reporting channels are necessary concomitants of any programme of this kind.

Photovoltaic devices

Direct conversion of the visible part of the solar spectrum—sunlight—to electricity is perhaps the neatest and most aesthetically pleasing of all schemes for the exploitation of solar energy. It is also, unfortunately, among the farthest from feasibility for widespread application in the developing nations.

Direct photovoltaic conversion can be achieved with basically simple devices that involve no moving parts, no additional sources of energy, and little if any maintenance. These photovoltaic devices, which have become known as solar cells, are based on the properties of certain crystalline solids that enable these materials to supply an electric current capable of performing useful work when the material is exposed to sunlight. Although the devices are indeed basically simple—consisting of a wafer of crystalline material to which two metal contacts are fastened—their fabrication requires the sophisticated technological capabilities of the industrialized nations. In fact, it is this very technology that is now developing methods that may (by reducing the cost of the product) make it economically feasible and justifiable for rural areas to make use of solar cells. Thus, with very few exceptions, developing countries can avail themselves of this technology only by acquiring its products through international trade. This will continue to be the case until more of the Third-World nations develop the necessary techological and industrial infrastructure, and the industrial fabrication processes are sufficiently developed through large-scale production, to make transfer of the fabrication technologies themselves economically justified.

Solar cells were first used commercially in 1955. Their development since then has been primarily a by-product of space research. The very properties that make them attractive for use in developing countries—simplicity, low weight, efficiency, reliability, lack of moving parts—have made them indispensable in supplying power needs of spacecraft. Unfortunately, mass-production techniques (geared to high-volume demand and economic competition) have not yet been implemented in the manufacture of these devices. It is not surprising, therefore, that solar cells have remained so costly. The current concern over the availability and price of fossil fuels and the massive infusion of R and D funds into energy research may provide added stimulus to the recent trends toward cost-cutting, mass-production techniques for solar cells.

Photovoltaic systems with 10 per cent solar-conversion efficiency and with peak power capacities from 1 watt to tens of kilowatts are available from manufacturers in Japan, the United States, England, France, and the Federal Republic of Germany (West Germany). Packaged systems for use in remote applications, such as navigational buoys and lighthouses, environmental monitoring stations, microwave relay stations, and forest ranger communications, are available as commercial products in the range of a few watts to a kilowatt; larger systems are available on a custom basis. Costs of a complete system are dominated by the photovoltaic array; prices of \$20–\$30 per peak watt, corresponding to \$100000–\$150000 per average kilowatt installed capacity, are now being quoted, though these costs are expected to decrease by as much as a factor of four within the next few years. These systems all incorporate silicon solar cells produced by modifications of the technology used to produce spacecraft solar cells and include batteries, voltage and current regulation, and other components such as d.c./a.c. inverters as options.

During the coming 5 years, over \$100 million will be spent by industry and government in the United States, Japan, West Germany, France, and England on the development of lower-cost terrestrial photovoltaic power systems. During this period the emphasis will be on the research and development of new processes for mass production of integrated solar modules and, by 1980, of integrated solar-cell arrays using cells made from mass-produced silicon ribbon. Arrays incorporating wide-aperture concentrators without diurnal tracking requirements will probably also be on the market. As a result of the intense research and development effort currently under way on these terrestrial systems, even greater cost reductions can be expected; solar cell modules with a cost of a few thousand dollars per average kilowatt (down by a factor of about 50), and having conversion efficiencies approaching 15 per cent, could be available by 1980.

If the economic stimulus of fuel shortages and high prices continues, there is a good chance that commercial photovoltaic conversion arrays at costs of a few hundred dollars per average kilowatt will be available by 1985 or sooner. The integration of such arrays into a complete system incorporating energy storage, power conditioning, and transmission and distribution will be required before these are useful on any substantial scale for power generation greater than a few kilowatts per system. In this regard, availability of economically interesting storage systems will be a crucial factor in determining the extent to which such technology is used.

In this price range there would be great interest in the potential use of such technology, perhaps in the establishment of local (village and community-size) 'minigrids' with the eventual growth and interlinking of these into larger and more diverse electrical networks. However, if this technology is to be transformed into something that can meet the special technical, economic, and cultural constraints and needs of various developing countries, a deliberate and specific effort will be required; otherwise, the direct 'transfer' to the remote village level of photovoltaic systems developed for integration into modern utility grids is unlikely.

Wind energy

The exploitation of 'free' wind energy is as attractive in its way as photovoltaics are in theirs. It, too, is not free of problems, though for LDCs the problems may be more manageable. Wind was one of the earliest sources of power used to multiply the productive capacity of muscle. On the seas it has been used to propel ships, and on land it has served a variety of purposes on a village scale. These include:

pumping fresh water for domestic livestock and agricultural needs;

irrigating fields;
powering agricultural tasks, such as grinding corn, wheat, and sugar-cane and threshing, chaff cutting, and winnowing;
cutting wood;
pumping saline water in saltworks; and
generating electricity for a variety of purposes.

This section concentrates on small-scale wind machines producing up to 10–20 hp (7.5–15 kW).

A variety of windmills is currently available, either commercially or in the form of working prototypes that could be readily manufactured as a market developed. These include both vertical- and horizontal-axis rotational machines. Among the vertical machines are the Savonius rotor—particularly well suited to local construction—the Darrieus rotor, and the vertical sailmill. Horizontal-axis machines most common are 2-, 3-, and 4-bladed propellers usually associated with wind-powered electrical generators, the multiblade fanmill commonly used for pumping water, and the horizontal version of the sailmill characteristic of the well-known windmill of the Greek islands. In addition, simple windmills of the paddlewheel type, with either horizontal or vertical rotational axes, are used.

In terms of assessing the availability of this technology within the next 5 years, there are enough commercially built units currently available to permit immediate application, whether it be for pumping water, compressing air, or generating electricity.

The water-pumping units vary significantly in price from $4000 to $8000/hp ($5000 to $10000/kW) for fractional size units, to $1000 to $2000/hp ($1300 to $2600/kW) for units of 5–15 hp (7–20 kW). Few larger-scale pumping units are commercially available today.

Electrical generating units cost from $3000 to $6000/kW for fractional-kW generators or from $1000 to $2000/kW for units in the 5- to 15-kW range. One unit just going into production in the United States is expected to sell for about $500/kW. No larger-scale commercial units are currently being sold.

Most commercially available windmill units sold today are safe, dependable, require little maintenance, and are built with an expected life of 10–20 years (sometimes more), with proper maintenance.

In addition, a number of windmill designs are available that villagers themselves can construct, often utilizing locally available materials.* In small sizes, these units will produce mechanical shaft power at a cost of $1000–$1500/hp ($1300–$2000/kW). In general, however, they will be characterized by slightly higher maintenance and operational requirements—principally labour—than most commercially available units.

In developing areas, classical windmills will often cost much less than the figures quoted above, because a considerable amount can be done with locally available technologies.

Technological and economic improvements could be expected in 5–10 years if research and development can be encouraged. Such a programme should include the following:

(a) materials-engineering studies of existing commercial windmills, designed to improve production techniques and reduce costs;
(b) development of windmill systems for the production of mechanical shaft power and the generation of electricity, utilizing as many indigenous or locally available materials and technologies as possible;
(c) investigation and redesign, where necessary, of equipment to be powered by windmills to carry out the required unit operations—such as pumping, agricultural tasks (milling, threshing, grading), and electrical generation—with a view to their fabrication in local workshops;

*For example: *How to construct a cheap wind machine for pumping water*. Leaflet No. L-5. Brace Research Institute, MacDonald College, McGill University, Ste. Anne de Bellevue 800, Quebec, Canada ($1.00). Also: *Low cost windmill for developing nations* by Hartmut Bossel. Available from VITA (Volunteers in Technical Assistance), 3706 Rhode Island Avenue, Mt. Rainier, Md 20822, USA ($2.00).

(d) development of decentralized power systems that are simple, reliable, and that may be serviced—if not fabricated—in village areas;
(e) application of known technologies to adapt windmill systems to a variety of environmental conditions (such as winds, rainfall, snow, ice, temperature extremes), which may include development of new forms of rotors for small-scale applications (although significantly improved efficiency in this area should not be expected); and
(f) a programme of public education in rural areas to show what windpower can do.

Such a programme could be expected to result in the development and use of equipment capable of delivering 1–15 hp (750 W–11 kW) in a 10-mph (16-kmph) wind, from improvements in existing equipment.

The development of units in the 25- to 50-hp (20- to 40-kW) range would be more costly, but needs attention nonetheless. Considerable spinoff advantage can be expected from development programmes currently under way in industrialized nations.

The research and development programme outline would most efficiently be undertaken by a central organization, supported by multilateral funding and having an international staff. At present, there are several groups engaged in windpower research in the developed countries, all with different purposes and financing. Among them are academic groups, such as those at Oklahoma State University at Stillwater, Oklahoma, and at the Technische Hogeschool Eindhoven in the Netherlands; the non-profit Brace Research Institute at McGill University, Montreal; the commercially supported group, Windworks, in Mukwonago, Wisconsin; and the Swedish Technical Board in Stockholm, a government body. In the developing countries, the institute of Technology Bandung in Indonesia, for example, has done some development and field work on windpower devices.

The panel feels that the work of all these groups could be co-ordinated to the best advantage for windpower applications in developing countries only by the creation of a central research and development organization having this as a specific objective, working through regional energy research and development institutes; this is suggested in the section on the panel's conclusions. This organization would be in a position to develop co-ordinated collaborative design and testing programmes with groups such as the Appropriate Technology Development Unit at the Ghandian Institute of Studies in Rajghat, Varanasi, India; the Solar Energy Laboratories in Karachi, Pakistan; the National Physical Laboratory in Jerusalem, Israel; and the Ministry of Electricity in Cairo, Egypt.

Such an organization would function with the collaboration of the Advisory Council for the Application of Science and Technology to Development (ACAST) of the United Nations, as well as with national, bilateral, and multilateral donor agencies, to facilitate the exchange of information on work in progress and ensure widest dissemination of results achieved.

Hydro-power

The first power source extensively used (other than that available from the muscles of men and animals) was that derived from flowing water, either impinging directly upon paddles attached to a wheel or filling buckets attached to a wheel. These are the waterwheels, the precursors of the water turbine, whose origins can be traced to ancient Egypt, China, and Persia.

Waterwheels took over many laborious and monotonous tasks such as grinding grain for flour and animal feed, raising water for irrigation and water supply, textile manufacture, and metallurgical processing.

As the demands for power increased over the centuries, the simple waterwheel became larger. By the middle of the nineteenth century, the revolutionary development of the water turbine by Fourneyron in France began to displace the waterwheel as a power source; in fact, the steam engine had begun this displacement process a half century earlier.

The water turbine was vastly superior to the waterwheel from almost any practical point of view. It could generate much more power than the largest waterwheel in a much smaller volume or appratus. It could perform adequately at high or low heads that could not be handled by waterwheels. It also could operate at a greater number of revolutions per minute than the waterwheel, principally by virtue of its smaller diameter.

In New England, during the last half of the nineteenth century, there were more than 50 manufacturers of water turbines supplying the needs of small, rural mill owners. It was not unusual, however, for a millwright to design and build his own water turbine; indeed there are a few 'homemade' installations still in existence. By the end of the nineteenth century, the small water turbine in a mill was often belt-connected to an electric generator, principally for lighting purposes.

With the development of large-scale hydro- and thermal-electric central generating stations and the extension of electric power lines to rural areas, the manufacture of small water turbines began to decline rapidly. In recent years, however, no doubt because of the energy crisis, there is renewed international interest in the small-scale hydroelectric unit. Such units are currently available for use in developing nations.

By small-scale, low-head hydroelectric units, we refer to those capable of generating 5–15 kW at heads of 10–20 ft (3–6 m). While the discussion will be primarily in terms of generation of electricity, it must be recognized that the same apparatus can perform useful mechanical tasks directly; it may be connected via belts or gears to grain mills, pumps, wood- and metal-working machinery, and other machines of production.

For use with low water heads, the fixed-propeller type of turbine or the more familiar Francis type is more suitable than the more complicated types such as the Kaplan, which adjust themselves to the electrical load. Small hydroelectric generators are currently available from several manufacturers in the United States and Europe. Also, there appears to be vigorous manufacture and use of such turbines in the People's Republic of China, but this panel has no information regarding their availability for export.

Because of the limited production of such small hydroelectric units, their cost per kilowatt is quite high. Units capable of generating 10 kW cost about $1000/kW. The cost per kilowatt rises for smaller capacity units. These costs do not include the cost of other necessary parts of the system, such as the dam, the piping connecting (penstock) between the dam and the turbine, and the housing. With all costs considered, the cost of electricity at the generator would probably range from 8¢ to 10¢ per kilowatt-hour.

Significant cost reductions could probably be achieved in developing countries through the construction of propeller-type turbines from wood. (The more complicated Francis turbine does not lend itself easily to wood construction.) Reports from China, the Soviet Union, and Rumania indicate that this approach has been used successfully in these countries.

The propeller and the Francis turbines are a mature, time-tested technology; further advances can be expected to be limited to cheaper manufacturing methods and materials and to the incorporation of new technology (solid-state devices) in the electrical controls.

The study of hydropower developments of the past may also be helpful to LDCs. Actual small-scale mills using turbines for many rural needs may still be seen in the United States (New England), China, Switzerland, the Balkans, Norway, and Sweden.

The hydraulic ram is a simple, ingenious pump, operated solely by flowing water, that was developed in Europe at the end of the eighteenth century. Like the waterwheel, it experienced a period of popularity in the industrialized countries and then a decline coincident with the surge in production and distribution of economical electrical energy. There is still one hydraulic ram manufacturer in the United States who does business on an international scale.

The hydraulic ram can be described as a completely automated device that uses the energy in flowing water to pump part of that water to a height above that of the source. It can also be used to compress air for operating machinery. It is a simple device that contains only two moving parts.

Manufactured hydraulic rams are currently available at costs ranging from $159 to about $2700, depending on size.

Hydraulic rams can operate 24 hours a day for many months with no maintenance. No significant improvements are anticipated for the next 5 years.

Additional research and development are suggested for the adaptation of the hydraulic ram to air compression for use in reciprocating engines and turbines.

The trompe, or hydraulic air compressor, is a simpler device than the hydraulic ram. It has no moving parts, but utilizes hydraulic potential energy very effectively in the compression of air. This system, which would operate continuously, day and night, without attendance, could store energy in the form of compressed air that can be used to drive turbines and reciprocating engines that, in turn, can drive production machinery or electric generators.

It is suggested that large-scale studies of this simple, low-cost device be undertaken to verify the scant but impressive performance data available from the literature.

Photosynthesis as an energy source

The one renewable energy source on which mankind has relied since the discovery of fire is photosynthesis. Even though nature performs the initial function in the conversion of solar energy to an energy-rich biomass, the photosynthetic process is subject to technological advances as sophisticated in their own way as those that apply to photovoltaics.

Mankind has long found important and diverse uses for the by-products of the photosynthetic process—food, fibre, fuel, and shelter. In terms of the concerns of this panel, the exploitation of the by-products of the photosynthetic process is, in effect, a long-established technology for energy conversion and storage. The deliberate development of an agronomic energy resource, however, is not. The emphasis in this report is placed, therefore, on energy resources that can be developed by supplementing current agricultural practices in rural areas.

The space available to a village can be divided into arable and non-arable land; we are concerned here primarily, but not exclusively, with the more efficient use of the former. Although the panel concerned itself with culturing of plants as an energy feedstock the terms of reference for this study did not permit considerations of the end use of the plant material produced. That final use clearly will depend upon the needs of the population and the methods available to convert the plant material to more useful energy forms, and will dictate many aspects of the specific research, development, and exploitation schemes pursued. (One conversion technology, however, is discussed in the section on microbial conversion.)

When agriculture is viewed from the point of view of human utilization of sunlight as an energy source, the criteria for choice and timing of crops differ from those conventionally used; factors commonly ignored now become very important. One of the first that should be considered is the energy content of the plant material. This is particularly important where there is a choice among alternative food or fibre crops having differing amounts of residue whose energy content could be exploited.

A second factor that should be considered

is that maximum use of available sunlight requires that farmland be kept covered with green plants throughout as much of the year as possible. This involves, for example, multiple cropping, intercropping, nurse crops (i.e. later-maturing crops planted with early-maturing crops so that the former will have a substantial start when the latter are harvested), and the use of cool-, warm-, wet-, and dry-season plants in those seasons when traditional crops may not be planted. Of course, water supply or some other environmental factor may prevent year-round coverage, but bare ground must be covered with green plants—where there are no green plants, no photosynthesis occurs.

A third concept has recently emerged on a sound experimental basis. Most agricultural schemes convert into plant material less than 1 per cent of the solar energy available during a growing season. However, some plants, because of an efficient photosynthetic system, can convert 2–3 per cent of the incident solar energy. These plants, known as 'C_4' plants, require warm growing seasons and high levels of solar radiation. They are already widely grown in many developing countries, but in appropriate climates where they are not grown, they should be given serious consideration as crops, especially during periods of high isolation. These species have the added feature of being able to use water more efficiently and thus are more tolerant of drought than many common crop species.

Finally, there exists another group of plants known as Crassulacean Acid Metabolism (CAM) plants that, by virtue of a genetically controlled metabolic characteristic, are among the plant world's most efficient water users and therefore do well in semi-arid regions. They are slow-growing plants, but in dry areas, where plants could be harvested on long-term rotation (2–6 years), they could make the land more productive and utilize the available water more efficiently.

The choice of food and fibre plants to be grown is usually governed by tradition, which in turn is usually based on generations of experience with local environmental conditions. However, a careful reassessment of these factors, including such fundamental aspects as water supply, temperature, light intensity, and nutrient supply, should be made if maximum capture and storage of solar energy by plants is to be included among the goals of agriculture. The ideas that have been briefly described are based on current practice and investigations of plants that are available now. These plants would need to be tested in given areas over several growing seasons, but well-known procedures for introducing new plants could be initiated now. In each area, the procedures to maximize energy capture would have to be worked out over a 2- to 5-year period, with a variety of plants and management techniques.

Microbiological conversion of plant materials to liquid fuels

Another process in which biological phenomena are responsible for useful energy production involves the action of micro-organisms on plant material substrates and the gathering of the fuel products that result.

Consideration, for example, of the ancient and honoured art of fermentation of a variety of plant products to produce alcoholic beverages naturally leads to the idea that the alcohol could be oxidized outside, rather than inside, the body—thereby providing a useful source of sensible heat. Indeed, the single major obstacle to utilizing this idea in rural areas of developing countries is the technological difficulty in separating the alcohol—or other combustible liquids produced by fermentation—in sufficiently pure form to be used as a liquid fuel.

Production of ethyl alcohol by fermentation as a chemical process, is quite similar to the microbial production of acetone, butyl alcohol, and isopropyl alcohol—all of which are flammable liquids. The processes all involve the growth of microbial populations under anaerobic conditions—i.e., not in contact with air—utilizing the nutrients found in various plant sources, and converting the carbohydrates (sugars and starches) of those plant sources to product systems such as: (1) ethyl alcohol; (2) acetone, butyl alcohol, hydrogen; (3) butyl alcohol, isopropyl alcohol, hydrogen; and (4) acetone, ethyl alcohol, hydrogen.

In three of the cases shown, a gaseous fuel is also produced as a by-product, although not in very large quantities. A similar anaerobic fermentation process does produce large quantities of methane, another gaseous fuel.

All of the materials listed above have been produced by microbial systems on a commercial scale, particularly during the critical years of materials needs of the 1940s and, to some extent, in the early 1950s. However, with the possible exception of ethyl alcohol, they are now produced industrially, by non-microbial means, from petrochemical sources, and even the major part of the world production of ethyl alcohol is manufactured in this way.

While the chemicals listed can indeed be used as liquid fuels, that use depends on their availability in a sufficiently concentrated form; otherwise the water present will interfere with the combustion process (e.g., within an internal combustion engine) or simply dilute the energy density—the heat available from a given weight—to such an extent as to diminish the economic value of the material. Since the microbial processes produce these chemicals in water solution, mixed with a variety of other suspended and dissolved materials, recovery in a sufficiently concentrated form becomes the critical issue in evaluating the usefulness of the process. Because the technology required to effect the necessary separation is not likely to be available in rural areas, the panel does not feel that microbial processes can be considered for such use at the village level in developing countries within the next 5 years.

For fuel production utilizing microbiological processes to become realistic in rural areas of developing nations, research and development are needed on materials, equipment, and processing. To reduce capital investment and the need for sophisticated technical skills currently required, it will be necessary to explore the availability of local raw materials, to investigate the microbiology and physical chemistry of the fermentation systems, and to examine recovery operations and equipment.

Biogas generation

The biogas system includes the gas production process, the use of the gas produced, and the use of the sludge remaining after fermentation is complete.

The production of methane during the anaerobic digestion of biologically degradable organic matter depends on the amount and kind of material added to the system. The efficiency of production of methane depends, to some extent, on the continuous operation of the system. As much as 8–9 ft^3 of gas (containing 50–70 per cent methane) can be produced per pound of volatile solids added to the digester (0.5–0.6 m^3/kg) when the organic matter is highly biodegradable (e.g. night soil or poultry, pig, or beef-cattle faecal matter). Combustion of 1 ft^3 (about 30 l) of gas will release an amount of energy equivalent to lighting a 25-watt bulb for about 6 hours.

In general, lower gas-production rates result when the wastes are less biodegradable. In developing countries, an important consideration will be the differences in the quantity and quality of waste material produced from various sources; for example, the quality and quantity of animal manure is influenced by the diet and general health of the animals. Table 4.1 lists potential sources of organic matter for methane generation.[1]

The use to which the gas is put depends upon removal of noncombustible components (such as carbon dioxide) and corrosive components (such as hydrogen sulphide).

Table 4.1. Organic matter with potential for methane generation[1]

Crop wastes	Sugar-cane trash, weeds, corn and related crop stubble, straw, spoiled fodder
Wastes of animal origin	Cattle-shed wastes (dung, urine, litter), poultry litter, sheep and goat droppings, slaughterhouse wastes (blood, meat), fishery wastes, leather, wool wastes
Wastes of human origin	Faeces, urine, refuse
By-products and wastes from agriculture-based industries	Oil cakes, bagasse, rice bran, tobacco wastes and seeds, wastes from fruit and vegetable processing, press-mud from sugar factories, tea waste, cotton dust from textile industries
Forest litter	Twigs, bark, branches, leaves
Wastes from aquatic growth	Marine algae, seaweeds, water hyacinths

Among the many potential uses of digester gas are hot-water heating, building heating, room lighting, and home cooking. Gas from a digester can be used in gas-burning appliances if they are modified for its use. Conversion of internal-combustion engines to run on digester gas can be relatively simple; thus the gas could also be used for pumping water for irrigation. Past experience has shown that where methane is generated in significant quantities in rural areas of developing countries, its use is primarily for lighting and cooking.

The gas produced by digestion of organic waste is colourless, flammable, and generally contains approximately 60 per cent methane and 40 per cent carbon dioxide, with small amounts of other gases such as hydrogen, nitrogen, and hydrogen sulphide. It has a calorific value of more than 500 Btu/ft^3 (18 676 kJ/m^3). Methane itself is a non-toxic gas and possesses a slight but not unpleasant smell; however, if the conditions of digestion produce a significant quantity of hydrogen sulphide, the gas will have a distinctly unpleasant odour.

The organic fraction of sludges from an anaerobic digester operating on plant and animal waste may contain up to 30–40 per cent of lignin and undigested cellulose and lipid materials, on a dry-weight basis, depending on the type of raw material used. The remainder consists of substances originally present in the raw material but protected from bacterial decomposition by lignin and cutin, newly synthesized bacterial cellular substances, and relatively small amounts of volatile fatty acids. The amount of bacterial cell mass is small (less than 10–20 per cent of the substrate is converted to cells). Therefore there is less risk of creating odour and insect-breeding problems when anaerobically digested sludges are stored or spread on land than there is when untreated or partially treated organic waste materials are similarly handled or are indiscriminately disposed of or stored.

One of the direct benefits of the anaerobic process mentioned earlier is that the nutrient elements in the plant residues and animal wastes used as raw materials are conserved for the production of subsequent crops. Among these nutrients is nitrogen, practically all of which is conserved. Since it is often present in the sludge in the form of ammonia, proper storage of sludge and application to the land is needed to minimize the loss of this volatile chemical. All other chemical elements (except carbon, oxygen, hydrogen, and some sulphur) contained in plant residues and animal wastes are conserved in anaerobically digested sludge.

The end result of applying anaerobically digested sludge to soils has the same effect as that obtained from applying any other kind of organic matter. The humus materials formed improve physical properties of soil: for example, aeration, moisture-holding capacity, and water-infiltration capacity are improved and cation-exchange capacity is increased. Furthermore, the sludge serves as a source of energy and nutrients for the development of microbial populations that, directly and indirectly, improve the solubility, and thus the availability to higher plants, of essential chemical nutrients contained in soil minerals.

Experience has shown that anaerobically digested sludge from municipal waste-water treatment plants receiving large loads of industrial waste have not caused conditions toxic to plants even in heavy applications to agricultural lands in industrialized countries.[2] Thus the possibility is remote that heavy metals or pesticides contained in digested plant and animal waste would cause any problem with digester sludge applied to soils in developing countries. Using the sludge as fertilizer may result in enhanced levels of concentration of some elements in plant tissues, but from the standpoint of animal and human nutrition this is more likely to be a benefit than a detriment. For the most part, the elements likely to be increased in plant tissues are essential animal nutrients.

The main requisites for successful operation of a methane-generation system are acceptance by potential users, ability to use the gas when produced, sufficient demand for the gas, availability of sufficient raw material to meet the production requirement, and adequate maintenance and operational control.

Many scientists and engineers with experience in the anaerobic-digestion process are cautiously optimistic about the prospects of extracting energy from organic wastes. The fundamentals of the process are well known and there is a significant quantity of unused organics in rural areas. These organics will produce large quantities of methane gas. The present technology can be utilized and adapted to local conditions where necessary, but this must be done with competent guidance.

In sum, then, before the anaerobic digester concept is adopted in any country or applied to specific wastes, the panel recommends that the following conditions obtain:

the equipment must be demonstrated to be functional at the scale of the proposed operation;

the installation should be accompanied by clear instructions—including written instructions where practical—for operation;

the equipment and its capacity must be suitable for the quantities and types of material to be handled and compatible with other components; and

users and/or operators must be capable of properly maintaining and operating the equipment.

Adequate methane production requires proper digester conditions. Maximum gas generation per unit of input material in the shortest time depends on obtaining and maintaining optimal conditions for bacterial activity and anaerobic fermentation. The critical factors are outlined in Table 4.2.

Digester design, and output expectations, must be tailored to the resources, climatic conditions, and building materials found in each locale; thus a technical assistance programme may be required in each region of the country in which methane generation is feasible. To minimize capital outlay for equipment, digesters should be of a size suitable for local demand and, whenever possible, should be constructed of local materials available close to the site of operation. Fabrication from corrosion-resistant materials such as wood, ferrocement, concrete, brick, or stone, rather than metal, may also reduce costs by extending equipment life.

Some technical assistance may also be required to determine start-up conditions for each region of the country.

In addition, once the digesters are functioning, there may be need for occasional technical assistance. Digester operation can be relatively simple, however, once a knowledge of construction materials, available organic matter, energy requirements, and user technical expertise have been acquired.

The criteria for determining the design parameters for a methane-generating system

Table 4.2. Critical factors affecting methane production

Initiating digester operation	Anaerobic conditions Appropriate substrates Appropriate bacterial type Appropriate environmental conditions in the digester
Maintaining output of a functioning digester	Protection of digester from sudden environmental changes—maintains adequate population of the anaerobic bacteria
	Steady supply of substrate—continuous operation ensures a higher output than intermittent use; semicontinuous operation is more practical on a small scale
	Removal of inert wastes such as sand and rocks—prevents wear on mechanical parts
	Digester temperature—heating the digester will increase the rate of bacterial activity within the mesophilic (30–40 °C) and thermophilic (50–60 °C) tempertaure ranges, thus increasing methane yield and decreasing the detention time of the substrate in the digester

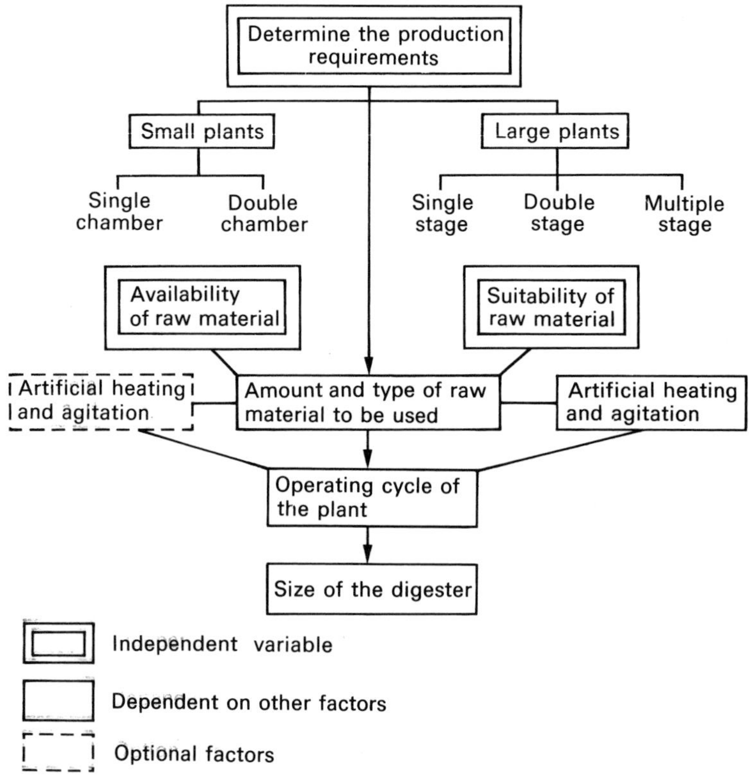

Fig. 4.1. Design parameters for methane-generating systems. (Adapted from Singh Ref. 3.)

are illustrated in Fig. 4.1 and outlined below:

1. *Determine the production requirements of biogas*. The size of a methane unit depends on the quantity of gas needed. The total production requirements can be determined by itemizing the applications for which the methane will be used and summing up the quantities of gas needed for each use.

2. *Inventory the raw waste materials*. This should include animal, agricultural, human, and any other wastes that can be digested for the production of methane.

3. *Determine the time needed to accomplish the optimal digestion of the waste materials* (*'detention time'*). The detention time will be shorter if the digester is heated. In the case of the small digesters (producing less than 500 ft^3 (14 m^3) of gas per day), it may not be advisable to incorporate heating with fuel because of the maintenance required. It may, however, be advisable to consider solar heating of the digester contents.[4]

4. *Determine the size of the digester*. The minimum volume of the digester can be determined by multiplying the detection time by the volume of material that must be added each day to produce the desired volume of gas daily.

5. *Decide whether to compartmentalize and divide the digester volume into two or more stages*. In plants intended to serve an entire village or community, a digester with large capacity is usually needed, and adequate mixing may be difficult to achieve in a large undivided digester.

6. *Determine the size of the gas holder*. The volume of the gas holder depends upon daily production and usage and may be as low as

Table 4.3. Advantages and disadvantages of anaerobic digestion

Advantages	*Disadvantages*
Produces large amount of methane gas. Methane can be stored at ambient temperature.	Possibility of explosion.
Produces free-flowing, thick, liquid sludge.	High capital cost. (However, if operated and maintained properly, the system may pay for itself.)
Sludges are almost odourless, odour not disagreeable.	May develop a volume of waste material much larger than the original material, since water is added to substrate. (This may not be a disadvantage in the rural areas of developing countries where farm fields are located close to the village, thus permitting the liquid sludge to be applied directly to the land, serving both for irrigation and as fertilizer.)
Sludge has good fertilizer value and can be used as a soil conditioner.	Liquid sludge presents a potential water-pollution problem if handled incorrectly.
Reduces organic content of waste materials by 30–50 per cent and produces a stabilized sludge for ultimate disposal.	Maintenance and control are required.
Weed seeds are destroyed and pathogens are either destroyed or greatly reduced in number.	Certain chemicals in the waste, if excessive, have the potential to interfere with digester performance. (However, these chemicals are encountered only in sludges from industrial waste-waters and therefore are not likely to be a problem in a rural village system.)
Rodents and flies are not attracted to the end product of the process. Access of pests and vermin to wastes is limited.	Proper operating conditions must be maintained in the digester for maximum gas production.
Provides a sanitary way for disposal of human and animal wastes.	Most efficient use of methane as a fuel requires removal of impurities such as CO_2 and H_2S, particularly when the gas is to be used in internal-combustion engines.
Helps conserve scarce local energy resources such as wood.	

50 per cent of the total volume of gas produced daily, provided the gas is used frequently. It should be larger if gas is used at irregular intervals.

Safety concerns related to methane generation include health hazards and risks of fire or explosion. Since methane gas is flammable and can be explosive when mixed with air, suitable safety instructions should be provided when the digester is installed.

A minor impurity of the biogas produced by anaerobic fermentation is hydrogen sulphide, a toxic gas that is highly corrosive in water solution. However, hydrogen sulphide can be safely removed from the digester gas by a variety of methods, including bubbling the gas through lime water.

On the other side of the safety coin are advantages inherent in this process: properly operated methane generating units reduce not only the public health hazard of faecal pathogens but the transfer of plant pathogens between successive cops, and provide a valuable, nutrient-rich fertilizer.

Table 4.3 summarizes some of the advantages and disadvantages of the use of anaerobic digestion as a method of processing biodegradable organic waste materials.

References

1. Garg, A. C., Idnani, M. A. and Abraham, T. P. *Organic manures*. Bulletin (Agric.) No. 32. Indian Council of Agricultural Research, New Delhi (1971).
2. Hinesly, T. D., Jones, R. L., Ryler, J. J., and Ziegler, E. L. Soybean yield responses and assimilation of Zn and Cd from sewage sludge-amended soil. *Journal of the Water Pollution Control Federation* **48**, 2137–52 (1976).
3. Singh, Ram Bux. *Bio-gas plant: generating methane from organic wastes*, p. 36. Gobar Gas Research Station, Ajitmal, Etawah (U.P.), India (1971).
4. National Academy of Sciences. Commission on International Relations. *Energy for rural development: renewable resources and alternative technologies for developing countries*. Report of an *ad hoc* panel of the Advisory Committee on Technology Innovation. Board on Science and Technology for International Development. US National Academy of Sciences, Washington, DC (1976).

5

The other energy crisis: firewood

ERIK P. ECKHOLM

Dwindling reserves of petroleum and artful tampering with its distribution are the stuff of which headlines are made. Yet for more than a third of the world's people, the real energy crisis is a daily scramble to find the wood they need to cook dinner. Their search for wood, once a simple chore and now, as forests recede, a day's labour in some places, has been strangely neglected by diplomats, economists, and the media. But the firewood crisis will be making news—one way or another—for the rest of the century.

While chemists devise ever more sophisticated uses for wood, including cellophane and rayon, at least half of all the timber cut in the world still serves in its original role for humans—as fuel for cooking and, in colder mountain regions, home heating. Nine-tenths of the people in most poor countries today depend on firewood as their chief source of fuel. And all too often the growth in human population is outpacing the growth of new trees—not surprising when the average user burns as much as a tonne of firewood a year.[1] The results are soaring wood prices, a growing drain on incomes and physical energies in order to satisfy basic fuel needs, a costly diversion of animal manures from food production uses to cooking, and an ecologically disastrous spread of treeless landscapes.

The firewood crisis is probably most acute today in the countries of the densely populated Indian subcontinent and in the semi-arid stretches of central Africa fringing the Sahara Desert, though it plagues many other regions as well. In Latin America, for example, the scarcity of wood and charcoal is a problem throughout most of the Andean region, Central America, and the Caribbean.

As firewood prices rise, so does the economic burden on the urban poor. One typical morning on the outskirts of Kathmandu, Nepal's capital city, I watched a steady flow of people—men and women, children and the very old—trudge into the city with heavy, neatly chopped and stacked loads of wood on their backs. I asked my taxi driver how much their loads, for which they had walked several hours into the surrounding hills, would sell for. 'Oh wood, a very expensive item!' he exclaimed without hesitation. Wood prices are a primary topic of conversation in Kathmandu these days. 'That load costs 20 rupees now. Two years ago it sold for 6 or 7 rupees.' This 300 per cent rise in the price of fuelwood has in part been prompted by the escalating cost of imported kerosene, the principal alternative energy source for the poor. But firewood prices have risen much *faster* than kerosene prices, a rise that reflects the growing difficulty with which wood is being procured. It now costs as much to run a Kathmandu household on wood as on kerosene.

The costs of firewood and charcoal are

From *Losing Ground* by E. Eckholm (W. W. Norton & Co., New York, 1976), pp. 101–13. Reprinted by permission of the author and Worldwatch Institute.

climbing throughout most of Asia, Africa, and Latin America. Those who can, pay the price, and thus must forgo consumption of other essential goods. Wood is simply accepted as one of the major expenses of living. In Niamey, Niger, deep in the drought-plagued Sahel in West Africa, the average manual labourer's family now spends nearly one-fourth of its income on firewood. In Ouagadougou, Upper Volta, the portion is 20 to 30 per cent.[2] Those who can't pay so much may send their children, or hike out into the surrounding countryside themselves, to forage—if enough trees are within a reasonable walking distance. Otherwise, they may scrounge about the town for twigs, garbage, or anything burnable. In many regions, firewood scarcity places a special burden on women, who are generally saddled with the tasks of hiking or rummaging for fuel.

In some Pakistani towns now, people strip bark off the trees that line the streets; thus, meeting today's undeniable needs impoverishes the future. When I visited the chief conservator of forests in Pakistan's North West Frontier Province at his headquarters in the town of Peshawar, he spoke in a somewhat resigned tone of stopping his car the previous day to prevent a woman from pulling bark off a tree. 'I told her that peeling the bark off a tree is just like peeling the skin off a man,' he said. Of course the woman stopped, intimidated by what may be the most personal encounter with a senior civil servant she will have in her lifetime, but she doubtless resumed her practice shortly, for what else, as the chief conservator himself asked, was she to do?

It is not in the cities but in rural villages that most people in the affected countries live, and where most firewood is burned. The rural, landless poor in parts of India and Pakistan are now feeling a new squeeze on their meagre incomes. Until now they have generally been able to gather free wood from the trees scattered through farmlands, but as wood prices in the towns rise, landlords naturally see an advantage in carting available timber into the nearest town to sell rather than allowing the nearby labourers to glean it for nothing. This commercialization of firewood raises the hope that entrepeneurs will see an advantage in planting trees to develop a sustainable, labour-intensive business, but so far a depletion of woodlands has been the more common result. And the rural poor, with little or no cash to spare, are in deep trouble in either case.

With the farmland trees and the scrubby woodlands of unfarmed areas being depleted by these pressures, both the needy and the ever-present entrepreneurs are forced to poach for fuelwood in the legally protected, ecologically and economically essential national forest reserves. The gravity of the poaching problem in India has been reflected in the formation of special mobile guard-squads and mobile courts to try captured offenders, but law-enforcement measures have little effect in such an untenable situation. Acute firewood scarcity has undermined administrative control even in China, where trees on commune plantations are sometimes surreptitiously uprooted for fuel almost as soon as they are planted.[3]

Trees are becoming scarce in the most unlikely places. In some of the most remote villages in the world, deep in the once heavily forested Himalayan foothills of Nepal, journeying out to gather firewood and fodder is now an *entire day's* task. Just one generation ago the same expedition required no more than an hour or two.[4]

Because those directly suffering its consequences are mostly illiterate, and because wood shortages lack the photogenic visibility of famine, the firewood crisis has not provoked much world attention. And, in a way, there is little point in calling this a world problem, for fuelwood scarcity, unlike oil scarcity, is always localized in its apparent dimensions. Ecnomics seldom permit fuelwood to be carried or trucked more than a few hundred miles from where it grows, let alone the many thousands of miles traversed by the modern barrel of oil. To say that firewood is scarce in Mali or Nepal is of no immediate consequence to the boy scout building a campfire in Pennsylvania, whereas his parents have already learned that decisions in Saudi Arabia can keep the family car in the garage.

Unfortunately, however, the consequences of firewood scarcity are seldom limited to the economic burden placed on the poor of a particular locality, harsh as that is in itself. The accelerating degradation of woodlands throughout Africa, Asia, and Latin America, caused in part by fuel gathering, lies at the heart of the profound challenges to environmental stability and land productivity reviewed in this book—accelerated soil erosion, increasingly severe flooding, creeping deserts, and declining soil fertility.

The Dust Bowl years in the Great Plains of the thirties taught Americans the perils of devegetating a region prone to droughts. The images provided by John Steinbeck in *The Grapes of Wrath* of the human dislocation wrought by that interaction of people, land, and climate could easily describe present-day events in large semi-arid stretches of Africa along the northern and southern edges of the Sahara, and around the huge Rajasthan Desert in north-west India. Overgrazing by oversized herds of cattle, goats, and sheep is the chief culprit, but gathering of fuelwood is also an important contributor to the destruction of trees in these regions. Firewood is a scarce and expensive item throughout the sub-Saharan fringe of Africa, all the way from Senegal to Ethiopia, but citizens in towns like Niamey are paying a much higher price than they realize for their cooking fuel. The caravans that bring in this precious resource are contributing to the creation of desert-like conditions in a wide band below the desert's edge. Virtually all trees within 70 kilometres of Ouagadougou have been consumed as fuel by the city's inhabitants, and the circle of land 'strip-mined' for firewood—without reclamation—is continually expanding.

In the Indian subcontinent, the most pernicious result of firewood scarcity is probably not the destruction of tree cover itself, but the alternative to which a good share of the people in India, Pakistan, and Bangladesh have been forced. A visitor to almost any village in the subcontinent is greeted by omnipresent pyramids of hand-moulded dung patties drying in the sun. In many areas these dung cakes have been the only source of fuel for generations, but now, by necessity, their use is spreading further. Between 300 and 400 million tonnes of wet dung—which shrink to 60 to 80 million tonnes when dried—are annually burned for fuel in India alone, robbing farmland of badly needed nutrients and organic matter. The plant nutrients wasted annually in this fashion in India equal more than a third of the country's chemical fertilizer use. Looking only at this direct economic cost, it is easy to see why the country's National Commission on Agriculture recently declared that 'the use of cow dung as a source of non-commercial fuel is virtually a crime'. Dung is also burned for fuel in parts of the Sahelian zone in Africa, Ethiopia, Iraq, and in the nearly treeless Andean valleys and slopes of Bolivia and Peru, where the dung of llamas has been the chief fuel in some areas since the days of the Incas.[5]

Even more important than the loss of agricultural nutrients is the damage done to soil structure and quality through the failure to return manures to the fields. Organic materials—humus and soil organisms which live in it—play an essential role in preserving the soil structure and fertility needed for productive farming. Organic matter helps hold the soil in place when rain falls and wind blows, and reduces the wasteful, polluting runoff of chemical nutrients where they are applied. Humus helps the soil absorb and store water, thus mitigating somewhat the impact on crops of drought periods. These considerations apply especially to the soils in tropical regions where most dung is now burned, because tropical topsoils are usually thin and, once exposed to the burning sun and torrential monsoon rains, are exceptionally prone to erosion and to loss of their structure and fertility.

Peasants in the uplands of South Korea have adopted a different, but also destructive way to cope with the timber shortage. A United Nations forestry team visiting the country in the late 1960s found not only that live tree branches, shrubs, seedlings, and grasses were cut for fuel; worse, many hillsides were raked clean of all leaves, litter, and burnable materials. Raking in this fashion to meet needs for home fuel and farm compost, robs the soil of both a protective cover and organic matter, and the practice was cited by the UN experts as 'one of the principal causes of soil erosion in Korea'. Firewood scarcity similarly impairs productivity in eastern Nigeria, where the Tiv people have been forced to uproot crop residues after the harvest for use as fuel. Traditionally, the dead stalks and leaves have been left to enrich the soil and hold down erosion.[6]

The increasing time required to gather firewood in many mountain villages of Nepal is leading to what the kingdom's agricultural officials fear most of all. For once procuring wood takes too long to be worth the trouble some farmers start to use cow dung, which was formerly applied with great care to the fields, as cooking fuel. As this departure from tradition spreads, the fertility of the hills, already declining due to soil erosion. will fall sharply. In the more inaccessible spots, there is no economic possibility whatsoever of replacing the manure with chemical fertilizers.

And so the circle starts to close in Nepal, a circle long completed in parts of India. As wood scarcity forces farmers to burn more dung for fuel, and to apply less to their fields, falling food output will necessitate the clearing of ever larger, ever steeper tracts of forest—intensifying the erosion and landslide hazards in the hills, and the siltation and flooding problems downstream in India and Bangladesh.

Firewood scarcity, then, is intimately linked in two ways to the food problem facing many countries. Deforestation and the diversion of manures to use as fuel are sabotaging the land's ability to produce food. Meanwhile, as an Indian official put it, 'Even if we somehow grow enough food for our people in the year 2000, how in the world will they cook it?'

B. B. Vohra, a senior Indian agricultural official who has pushed his government ahead on numerous ecological causes, shook his head as we talked in his New Delhi office. 'I'm afraid that we are approaching the point of no return with our resource base. If we can't soon build some dramatic momentum in our reforestation and soil conservation programmes, we'll find ourselves in a downward spiral with an irresistible momentum of its own.' Without a rapid reversal of prevailing trends, in fact, India will find itself with a billion people to support and a countryside that is little more than a moonscape. But the politicians, in India and other poor countries, will take notice when they realize that, if people can't find any firewood, they will surely find something else to burn.

The firewood crisis is in some ways more, and in others less, intractable than the energy crisis of the industrialized world. Resource scarcity can usually be attacked from either end, through the contraction of demand or the expansion of supply. The world contraction in demand for oil in 1974 and early 1975, for example, helped to ease temporarily the conditions of shortage.

But the firewood needs of the developing countries cannot be massively reduced in this fashion. The energy system of the truly poor contains no easily trimmable fat such as that represented by 4000 to 5000 pound private automobiles. Furthermore, a global recession does little to dampen the demand for firewood as it temporarily does in the case of oil. The regrettable truth is that the amount of wood burned in a particular country is almost completely determined by the number of people who need to use it. In the absence of suitable alternative energy sources, future firewood needs in these countries will be determined largely by population growth. Firewood scarcity will undoubtedly influence the urgency with which governments address the population problem in the years ahead.

Even if the demographers are surpised by quick progress on the population front over the next few decades, the demand for basic resources like firewood will still push many countries to their limits. Fortunately trees, unlike oil, are a renewable resource when properly managed. The logical immediate response to the firewood shortage, one that will have many incidental ecological benefits, is to plant more trees in plantations, on farms, along roads, in shelter belts, and on unused land throughout the rural areas of the poor countries. For many regions, fast-growing tree varieties are available that can be culled for firewood inside of a decade.

The concept is simple, but its implementation is not. Governments in nearly all the wood-short countries have had tree-planting programmes for some time—for several decades in some cases. National forestry departments in particular have often been aware of the need to boost the supply of wood products and the need to preserve forests for an habitable environment. But several problems have generally plagued tree-planting programmes.

One is the sheer magnitude of the need for wood and the scale of the growth in demand. Population growth, which surprised many with its acceleration in the post-war era, has swallowed the moderate tree-planting efforts of many countries, rendering their impact almost negligible. Wood-producing programmes will have to be undertaken on a far greater scale than most governments presently conceive if a significant dent is to be made in the problem.

The problem of scale is closely linked to a second major obstacle to meeting this crisis: the perennial question of political priorities and decision-making time-frames. With elections to win, wars to fight, dams to build, and hungry people to feed, it is hard for any politician to concentrate funds and attention on a problem so multi-dimensional and seemingly long-term in nature. Some ecologists in the poor countries have been warning their governments for decades about the dangers of deforestation and fuel shortages, but tree-planting programmes don't win elections. This phenomenon is, of course, quite familiar to all countries, not just the poorest. In the United States, resource specialists pointed out the coming energy crisis throughout the 1960s, but it took a smash in the face in 1973 to wake up the government, and, years later the country still can hardly be said to have tackled the energy challenge head-on.

Despite these inherent political problems, India's foresters made a major breakthrough a few years back as the government drew up its 5-year development plan for the mid-to-late seventies. Plans were laid for the large-scale establishment of fast-growing tree plantations, and for planting trees on farms and village properties throughout the country.[7] A programme is going ahead now, but there have been some unexpected events since the projects were first contemplated 2 or 3 years ago: the quintupling of the world price of petroleum, the tripling in price and world shortages of grains and fertilizers, and the subsequent wholesale diversion of development funds to maintenance and emergencies in order to merely muddle through 1974 without a major famine and a total economic breakdown. India's development efforts have been set back several years by recent events, and forestry programmes have not been immune to this trend.

Even with the right kind of political will and the necessary allocation of funds, implementing a large-scale reforestation campaign is a complex and difficult process. Planting millions of trees and successfully nurturing them to maturity is not a technical, clearly defined task like building a dam or a chemical-fertilizer plant. Tree-planting projects almost always become deeply enmeshed in the political, cultural, and administrative tangles of a rural locality; they touch upon, and are influenced by, the daily living habits of many people, and they frequently end in failure.

Most of the regions with too few trees also have too many cattle, sheep, and goats. Where rangelands are badly overgrazed, the leaves of a young sapling tempt the appetites of foraging animals. Even if he keeps careful control of his own livestock, a herdsman may reason that if his animals don't eat the leaves, someone else's will. Marauding livestock are prime destroyers of tree-planting projects throughout the less developed world. Even if a village is internally disciplined enough to defend new trees from its own residents, passing nomads or other wanderers may destroy them. To be successful, then, reforestation efforts often require a formidable administrative effort to protect the plants for years—not to mention the monitoring of timber-harvesting and replanting activities once the trees reach maturity.

Village politics can undermine a programme as well. An incident from Ethiopia a few years back presents an extreme case, but its lessons are plain. A rural reforestation programme was initiated as a public works scheme to help control erosion and supply local wood needs. The planting jobs were given to the local poor, mostly landless labourers who badly needed the low wages they could earn in the planting programme. Seedlings were distributed, planting commenced, and all seemed to be going well—until the overseers journeyed out to check the progress. They found that in many areas the seedlings had been planted upside down! The labourers, of course, well knew the difference between roots and branches; they also knew that given the feudal land-tenure system in which they were living, most of the benefits of the planting would flow one way or another into the hands of their lords. They were not anxious to work efficiently for substandard wages on a project that brought them few identifiable personal returns.[8]

In country after country, the same lesson has been learned: tree-planting programmes are most successful when a majority of the local community is deeply involved in planning and implementation, and clearly perceives its self-interest in success. Central or state governments can provide stimulus, technical advice, and financial assistance, but unless community members clearly understand why lands to which they have traditionally had free access for grazing and wood gathering are being demarcated into a plantation, they are apt to view the project with suspicion or even hostility. With wider community participation, on the other hand, the control of grazing patterns can be built into the programme from the beginning, and a motivated community will protect its own project and provide labour at little or no cost.

An approach like this—working through village councils, with locally mobilized labour doing the planting and protection work—is now being tried in India. There are pitfalls; Indian villages are notoriously faction-ridden, and the ideal of the whole community working together for its own long-term benefit may be somewhat utopian. But if it can get underway on a large scale, the national programme in India may succeed. Once given a chance, fast-growing trees bring visible benefits quickly, and they just could catch on. The Chinese have long used the decentralized, community labour-mobilizing approach to reforestation, apparently with considerable success.

A new programme of global public education on the many benefits of reforestation, planned by the United Nations Environmental Program, will hopefully direct more attention to the tremendous global need for tree planting. Whatever the success of reforestation projects, however, the wider substitution of other energy sources for wood can also contribute greatly to a solution of the firewood problem. A shift from wood-burning stoves to those running on natural gas, coal, or electricity has indeed been the dominant global trend in the last century and a half. As recently as 1850, wood met 91 per cent of the fuel needs of the United States, but today in the economically advanced countries, scarcely any but the intentionally rustic, and scattered poor in the mountains, chop wood by necessity any more. In the poor countries, too, the proportion of wood users is falling gradually, expecially in the cities, which are usually partly electrified, and where residents with any income at all may cook their food with bottled gas or kerosene. Someone extrapolating trends of the first seven decades of this century might well have expected the continued spread of kerosene and natural gas use at a fairly brisk pace in the cities and into rural areas, eventually rendering firewood nearly obsolete.

Events of the last 2 years, of course, have abruptly altered energy-use trends and prospects everywhere. The most widely overlooked impact of the fivefold increase in oil prices, an impact drowned out by the economic distress caused for oil-importing countries, is the fact that what had been the most feasible substitute for firewood, kerosene, has now been pulled even farther out of reach of the world's poor than it already was. The hopes of foresters and ecologists for a rapid reduction of pressures on receding woodlands through a stepped-up shift to kerosene withered overnight in December 1973 when OPEC announced its new oil prices. In fact, the dwindling of world petroleum reserves and the depletion of woodlands reinforce each other; climbing firewood prices encourage more people to use petroleum-based products for fuel, while soaring oil prices make this shift less feasible, adding to the pressure on forests.

The interconnections of firewood scarcity, ecological stress, and the broader global energy picture set the stage for some interesting, if somewhat academic, questions about a sensible disposition of world resources. In one sense it is true that the poor countries, and the world as a whole, have been positively influenced by the OPEC countries, which, through price hikes and supply restrictions, are forcing conservation of a valuable and rapidly disappearing resource, and are not letting the poor countries get dangerously hooked on an undependable energy supply. In a world in which energy, ecology, and food were sensibly managed, however, the oil distribution picture would look far different. The long-term interest in preserving the productive capacity of the earth and in maximizing welfare for the greatest number of people might argue for lower prices and a rapid *increase*, not a halt, in the adoption of kerosene and natural gas in the homes of the poor over the next two decades. This, in turn, would be viable for a reasonable period of time only if the waste and comparatively frivolous uses of energy in the industrial countries, which are depleting petroleum reserves so quickly, were cut sharply. It is not so far-fetched as it might first seem to say that today's driving habits in Los Angeles, and today's price and production-level decisions in the Persian Gulf, can influence how many tons of food are lost to floods in India, and how many acres of land the Sahara engulfs, in 1980.

Fossil fuels are not the only alternative energy source under consideration, and, over the coming decades, many of those using firewood, like everyone else, will have to turn in other directions. Energy sources that are renewable, decentralized, and low in cost must be developed. Nothing, for example, would be better than a dirt-cheap device for cooking dinner in the evening with solar energy collected earlier in the day. But actually developing such a stove and introducing it to hundreds of millions of the world's most tradition-bound and penniless families is another story. While some solar cookers are already available, the cost of a family unit, at about $35 to $50, is prohibitive for many, since, in the absence of suitable credit arrangements, the entire amount must be available at once. Mass production could pull down the price, but the problem of inexpensively storing heat for cloudy days and evenings has not been solved.[9] The day may come in some countries when changes in cooking and eating habits to allow maximum use of solar cookers will be forced upon populations by the absence of alternatives.

Indian scientists have pioneered for

decades with an ideal-sounding device that breaks down manures and other organic wastes into methane gas for cooking and a rich compost for the farm. Over 8000 of these biogas plants, as they are called, are now being used in India. Without a substantial reduction in cost, however, they will only slowly infiltrate the hundreds of thousands of rural villages, where the fuel problem is growing. Additionally, as the plants are adopted, those too poor to own cattle could be left worse off than ever, denied traditional access to dung, but unable to afford biogas.[10] Still, relatively simple and decentralized devices like solar cookers and biogas plants will likely provide the fuel sources of the future in the poor countries.

In terms of energy, Nepal is luckier than many countries in one respect. The steep slopes and surging rivers that cause so many environmental problems also make Nepal one of the few remaining countries with a large untapped hydroelectric potential. The latent power is huge, equalling the hydroelectric capacity of Canada, the United States, and Mexico combined. Exploitation of this resource will be expensive and slow, but will relieve some of the pressures being placed on forests by the larger towns of Nepal and northern India. On the other hand, cheap electricity will only partly reduce firewood demands, since the electrification of isolated villages in the rugged Himalayas may never be economically feasible.

The firewood crisis, like many other resource problems, is forcing governments and analysts back to the basics of human beings' relationship with the land—back to concerns lost sight of in an age of macro-economic models and technological optimism. Awareness is spreading that the simple energy needs of the world's poorest third are unlikely ever to be met by nuclear power plants, any more than their minimum food needs will be met by huge synthetic-protein factories.

Firewood scarcity and its attendant ecological hazards have brought the attitude of people toward trees into sharp focus. In his essay 'Buddhist economics', E. F. Schumacher praises the practical as well as esoteric wisdom in the Buddha's teaching that his followers should plant and nurse a tree every few years.[11] Unfortunately, this ethical heritage has been largely lost, even in the predominantly Buddhist societies of south-east Asia. In fact, most societies today lack a spirit of environmental co-operation—not a spirit of conservation for its own sake, but one needed to guarantee human survival amid ecological systems heading toward collapse.

This will have to change, and fast. The inexorable growth in the demand for firewood calls for tree-planting efforts on a scale more massive than most bureaucrats have ever even contemplated, much less planned for. The suicidal deforestation of Africa, Asia, and Latin America must somehow be slowed and reversed. Deteriorating ecological systems have a logic of their own; the damage often builds quietly and unseen for many years, until one day the system falls asunder with lethal vengeance. Ask anyone who lived in Oklahoma in 1934, or Chad in 1975.

References and notes

1. Openshaw, K. Wood fuels the developing world. *New Scientist* **61**, No. 883 (31 January 1974). See also Food and Agriculture Organization *Wood: world trends and prospects*, Basic Study No. 16, FAO, Rome (1967) for a better overview of world fuelwood trends.
2. Delwaulle, J. C. Désertification de l'Afrique au sud de la Sahara. *Bois et forêts des Tropiques* No. 149 (Mai–Juin 1973), 14; and DuBois, V. D. *The drought in West Africa.* American Universities Field Staff, West African Series, Vol. XV, No. 1 (1974).
3. India's enforcement efforts are discussed in Government of India, Ministry of Agriculture (1973) *Interim Report of the National Commission on Agriculture on Social Forestry*, p. 37. New Delhi (1973). Tree-protection problems in China are noted in Richardson, S. D. *Forestry in Communist China*, pp. 14, 66. Johns Hopkins University Press, Baltimore, Md. (1966).

4. See, for example, Bishop, Lila, M. and Bishop, Barry C. Karnali, Roadless world of western Nepal, *National Geographic* **140** (5), 671 (1971).
5. Government of India, Ministry of Agriculture, op. cit., ref. 3 (1973); Adeyoju, S. K. and Enabor, E. N. *A Survey of drought affected areas of northern Nigeria*, p. 48. University of Ibadan, Department of Forestry (1973); US Department of the Interior, Bureau of Reclamation, *Land and water resources of the Blue Nile Basin Ethiopia Appendix VI Agriculture and economics*. Washington DC (1964); Brown, L. H. *Conservation for survival: Ethiopia's choice*, pp. 63, 64. Haile Selassie I University (1973); FAO/UNDP *Forestry research, administration, and training, Arbil, Iraq*, Technical Report 1, A forestry improvement programme. FAO/UNDP, IRQ-18 Rome Food and Agriculture Organization (1973); Republica del Peru, Oficina Nacional de Evaluacion de Recursos Naturales, and Organizacion de los Estados Americanos (1974). *Lineamentos de politica de conservacion de los recursos del Peru*, p. 18. Lima (1974); and Mason, J. A. *The ancient civilizations of Peru*. Penguin, Harmondsworth (1957).
6. FAO/UNDP *Agricultural survey and demonstration in selected watersheds, Republic of Korea, Vol. 1, General report*, FAO/SF 47/KOR 7 (1969) and Vermeer, D. E. Population pressure and crop rotational changes among the Tiv of Nigeria. *Annals of the Association of American Geographers* **60**, 311 (1970).
7. Government of India, Ministry of Agriculture op. cit. (1973).
8. Thomas, J. W. Employment creating public works programs: observations on political and social dimensions. In *Employment in developing nations* (ed. Edgar O. Edwards). Columbia University Press, New York (1974).
9. See Potentials for solar energy in the Sahel. Interview with A. Moumoumi. *Interaction* (Washington DC), Vol. III, No. 10 (July 1975); National Academy of Sciences, Office of the Foreign Secretary, *Solar energy in developing countries: perspectives and prospects*. Washington DC (1972); Daniels, F. *Direct use of the sun's energy*. Ballantine, New York (1974) (Reprint of 1964 edition.); Hayes, D. Solar power in the Middle East. *Science*, **188**, 1261.
10. Prasad, C. R., Krishna Prasad, K., and Reddy, A. K. N., Biogas plants: prospects, problems and tasks. *Economic and Political Weekly* (New Delhi), Vol. IX, Nos. 32–4 (special issue August 1974); and Makhijani, A. with Poole, A. *Energy and agriculture in the Third World*. Ballinger, Cambridge, Mass. (1975).
11. Schumacher, E. F., Buddhist economics. In *Small is beautiful: economics as if people mattered*. Harper and Row, New York (1973).

Additional sources

Beating a drought, organically. *Organic gardening and farming*, January 1975.

Dhua, S. P. Need for organo-mineral fertilizer in tropical agriculture. *Ecologist* **5**, No. 5 (1975).

Eckholm, Erik P. *The other energy crisis: firewood*. Worldwatch Paper No. 1. Washington, D.C.

—— The firewood crisis. *Natural history* **84**, No. 8 (October 1975).

FAO, *Fuelwood plantations in India*. Occasional Paper No. 5. Rome (1958).

—— *Organic materials as fertilizers*. Report of the FAO/SIDA Expert Consultation, Rome, 2–6 December 1974. Soils Bulletin 27. Rome (1975).

Garg, A. C., Idnani, M. A., and Abraham, T. P. *Organic manures*. Technical Bulletin No. 32. Indian Council of Agricultural Research, New Delhi (1971).

Horvath, Ronald J. Addis Ababa's eucalyptus forest. *Journal of Ethiopian Studies*, Vol. VI, No. 1 (January 1968).

Lamoureux, C. H. Observations on conservation in Indonesia. In Kuswata Kartawinata and Rubini Atmawidjaja (eds.). *Papers from a Symposium on Coordinated Study of Lowland Forests of Indonesia*. Darmaga, Bogor, 2–5 July 1973. Sponsored by SEAMEO Regional Center for Tropical Biology and Bogor Agricultural University. Bogor, Indonesia (1974).

Sagrhiya, K. P. The energy crisis and forestry. *Indian Forests* **100** (1974).

Swaminathan, M. S. Organic manures and integrated approaches to plant nutrition. Presented to Consultative Group in International Agricultural Research, Technical Advisory Committee, Eighth Meeting. Washington, DC, 24 July–2 August 1974.

Thulin, S. Wood requirements in the savanna region of Nigeria. Savanna Forestry Research Station, Nigeria, Tech. Rep. 1 (1970).

World of forestry. *Unasylva*, **26**, No. 105 (Summer, 1974).

6

Woodfuel — a time for reassessment

KEITH OPENSHAW

Fuelwood and charcoal have always been important sources of heat and energy, both for domestic and industrial purposes. Even today in many countries wood is the principal fuel, especially in the subsistence sectors of the population. It probably accounts for over 80 per cent of total wood consumption in less developed countries. Indeed, for the world as a whole, woodfuel consumption may be nearly 65 per cent of wood raw material requirements. Nevertheless, its relative importance has been declining over the years both in the forest products field and the energy sector. However, the energy crisis has highlighted the fact that the world cannot rely indefinitely on fossil fuels. Once again we may have to fall back on such renewable resources as a prime source of energy. It seems appropriate that an analysis of present consumption and use of woodfuel and an assessment of its potential and supply be made.

Present consumption

The latest FAO yearbook of forest products[1] estimates that the production of woodfuel in 1976 was 1184 million m^3 of roundwood, with consumption rising at about 1 per cent per year (Table 6.1).

However, it is known that production figures published by the FAO may be considerably underestimated because no accurate records are kept by many of the reporting countries of self-collected or self-produced products such as fuelwood, charcoal, building poles, roughly sawn wood, and handsawn timber. Even the statistics for machine-sawn timber are unreliable owing to illegal felling practices in many countries.

Table 6.1. World production of roundwood for selected years (million m^3)

	1961	*1965*	*1969*	*1972*	*1976*
Woodfuel*	1030	1082	1107	1145	1184
Industrial wood	1019	1131	1232	1288	1340
Total	2049	2213	2339	2433	2524

*Fuelwood and charcoal.

A number of consumption surveys have been undertaken in African and Asian countries, with the help of the FAO and other development agencies, to give a more accurate picture of present consumption and to assist with development planning in the forest and forest industries sector. These surveys endeavour to overcome the shortcomings of official statistics by taking a sample survey of household and non-household consumers and recording the actual use of the various wood products over a fixed time period. From these records a country estimate can be made by product,

First published in *Natural Resources Forum*, Vol. 3, No. 1 (October 1978), a journal of the United Nations in the fields of energy, minerals and water resources. Reprinted by permission of the author and *Natural Resources Forum.*

end-use, and perhaps income group. Data compilation of fuelwood and charcoal presents a difficulty because these products are non-durable items in daily use whose consumption may have seasonal variations depending on climatic changes and food availability. In surveys undertaken to date only one was continued for a year, others being carried out over a shorter period, although one is being extended. Nevertheless, efforts were made to obtain data during seasonal fluctuations so a reasonable degree

Table 6.2. Estimate of world wood consumption in 1976 (million m^3 roundwood equivalent)

	Official figures		*Estimated total*		*Amount in developing countries*	
	Quantity	*Per cent*	*Quantity*	*Per cent*	*Quantity*	*Per cent*
Woodfuel	1184	47	3050	63	2460†	82
(fuelwood)					(1890)	(63)
(charcoal)*					(570)*	(19)
Poles	204	8	300	6	194	7
Sawnwood	723	29	1045	22	310	10
Panel products	178	7	178	4	6	} 1
Wood pulp products	235	9	235	5	35	
Total	2524	100	4808	100	3005	100

*The consumption of wood for charcoal may be twice this figure because the bulk is produced by traditional earth kiln which uses about 12 m^3 to produce 1 tonne and not 6 m^3 as assumed.
†Some of this wood is in the form of branch wood and twigs which strictly speaking is not counted in inventory work. The underestimate in charcoal could compensate for this overestimate.

Source: FAO Yearbook of forest products, 1976, revised by the author as a result of consumption surveys in various countries.

Note: The developing countries are those in economic Class II of the UN classification, which excludes China. The 1976 population of these countries was about 2008 million out of a world total of 4161 million.

Table 6.3. Number of housholds using woodfuel by income class in Thailand (1970)

	Rural (85 per cent of popn)		*Urban (15 per cent of popn)*		*Total*	
Cash income per household per month (US dollars)	*Per cent using*	*Per cent popn in each group*	*Per cent using*	*Per cent popn in each group*	*Per cent using*	*Per cent popn in each group*
Less than 12.50	100	38	97	4	100	33
12.50–24.99	99	30	92	8	98	27
25.00–49.99	98	24	90	23	95	24
50.00–99.99	96	6	87	33	88	10
More than 100	95	2	72	32	73	6
Country	98		87		97	
Average size of household	5.7		6.0		5.8	

Source: Thailand: present and future forest policy goals. A timber trend study 1970–2000. FAO, Rome, 1971.

Table 6.4. Consumption per capita of woodfuel in rural and urban areas of selected countries (m^3 roundwood equivalent)

Country and year of survey	*Population (million)*	*Household*			*Non-household*			*Total*			*Percentage using woodfuel*
		FW	*CH*	*WF*	*FW*	*CH*	*WF*	*FW*	*CH*	*WF*	
Rural											
Gambia (1972)	0.4	1.20	0.12	1.32	0.10	0.13	0.23	1.30	0.25	1.55	100
Sudan (1962)	11.3	1.01	0.26	1.27		negligible		1.01	0.26	1.27	99
Tanzania (1970)	11.6	2.16	0.02	2.18	0.15	—	0.15	2.31	0.02	2.33	99
Thailand (1972)	30.7	0.77	0.51	1.28	0.05	—	0.05	0.82	0.51	1.33	98
Weighted average	54.0	1.12	0.35	1.47	0.06	0.00	0.06	1.18	0.35	0.53	
Urban											
Nigeria (1972)	1.5	0.97	0.09	1.06	0.31	0.01	0.32	1.28	0.10	1.38	95
Gambia	0.1	0.66	0.78	1.44	0.18	0.09	0.27	0.84	0.87	1.71	96
Sudan	1.0	0.38	1.06	1.44	0.14	0.15	0.29	0.52	1.21	1.73	80
Tanzania	0.7	0.86	0.59	1.45	0.15	0.06	0.21	1.01	0.65	1.66	82
Thailand	5.3	0.11	0.90	1.01	0.29	0.24	0.53	0.40	1.14	1.54	87
Weighted average	8.6	0.36	0.75	1.11	0.26	0.17	0.43	0.62	0.92	1.54	
Country											
Gambia	0.5	1.06	0.29	1.35	0.13	0.11	0.24	1.19	0.40	1.59	99
Sudan	12.3	0.96	0.32	1.28	0.01	0.02	0.03	0.97	0.34	1.31	97
Tanzania	12.3	2.07	0.06	2.13	0.15	0.01	0.16	2.22	0.07	2.29	98
Thailand	36.0	0.68	0.56	1.24	0.08	0.04	0.12	0.76	0.60	1.36	97
Weighted average	62.6	1.02	0.40	1.42	0.09	0.02	0.11	1.11	1.42	0.53	

Key: FW = fuelwood; CH = charcoal; WF = woodfuel (FW + CH).
Only an urban survey was undertaken in northern Nigeria, but this has been included in the country weighted average. The Nigerian survey did not record actual consumption of charcoal, but from the information contained an estimation of charcoal consumption has been made. The report indicated small quantities of cornstalks, coal, paraffin, and electricity were additional sources of energy.

The weighted average has been calculated by dividing the consumption by the total population.

Note: (a) For charcoal a standard conversion factor 6 m^3 of roundwood per tonne of charcoal has been applied, except for charcoal made from mangrove where a factor of 4.2 m^3 per tonne is used. This is about average for metal and brick kilns. However, the Sudan report states 'it takes 12 m^3 of roundwood to produce 1 tonne', and the Nigerian report gives a figure of 24 m^3 per tonne—both by traditional earth kiln method. A carefully controlled experiment in Zambia (7) using the earth kiln and traditional 'miombo' (open woodland) species gave an average figure of 11.85 m^3 wood per tonne. Apparently efficiency is increased by 50 per cent when manufactured kilns are used. (b) More wood raw material is used when charcoal is burned than if the wood has been burned directly as fuel, but of course charcoal is a much more convenient fuel to transport and use. 1 tonne charcoal: calorific value 790000 kcal, 6 m^3 fuelwood: calorific value 1 550000 kcal. (c) In Africa, metal charcoal stoves are traditional whereas in Asia clay or bone china stoves are universal. The thermal efficiency of the clay stoves is superior to the metal by about 50 per cent.

Source: The Gambia: A wood consumption survey and timber trend study, 1973–2000. Gambia Land Resources Project, London, 1973. Other countries—FAO Wood consumption surveys.[2–7]

of reliability could be established for the results. If anything, the estimates are on the conservative side.

These surveys have shown that official statistics may be underestimating the consumption of woodfuel by as much as twenty times, poles by up to ten times, and sawnwood about three times. If these underestimates are representative of all the less developed countries, then a more likely consumption estimate of wood products may be as seen in Table 6.2.

Total world consumption of wood products may therefore be nearly twice the official consumption figures, the largest difference being accounted for by woodfuel, which the surveys show to be three times greater than reported consumption (woodfuel accounted for 63 per cent of consumption by volume). However, to put the consumption figures in perspective, woodfuel accounts for only about 10 to 15 per cent of total value, mainly because of its limited cash trade. Nevertheless, in terms of consumer satisfaction its importance is great.

Present consumption

Consumption patterns in developing countries

In rural areas of developing countries especially in the subsistence sector, fuelwood is the dominant fuel. However, in regions of poor wood availability dung, grass, cornstalks, and bamboo often supplement or substitute for wood. In the rural cash-crop economy, charcoal competes with fuelwood; if distribution channels are adequate, paraffin and liquid petroleum gas make minor inroads, although the latter fuels require a relatively large investment for cooking equipment.

In towns, charcoal is usually the principal fuel, but if wood is available as sawmill waste, packing case material, splits, or in the round, it will be purchased or collected. More convenient fuels such as paraffin and bottled gas are making inroads into the 'medium' and 'high' income families but tradition can have an important effect on use. Many 'high' income families still prefer their main meal to be cooked on a charcoal stove. Table 6.3 illustrates the gradual shift from woodfuel to more convenient fuels in the rural areas and a more rapid switch in the towns. However, because of the small number of people in the high income groups, the overall percentage of woodfuel users is still large; this fact is as pronounced in other sample countries (Table 6.4).

Results from a similar study in northern Nigeria[3] indicate that in urban areas, where fuelwood is purchased, low income groups also consume less than middle income groups and similarly, high income groups consume less than their middle income counterparts because of a switch to other fuels.

Consumption per capita varies from 1.3 m^3 to 2.3 m^3 with the weighted average of the sample equal to 1.5 m^3 (the larger consumption in Tanzania being due to the fact that much of the country is above 1000 metres where extra fuel is required for heating purposes). Generally, more fuel is used in the towns than in the countryside. Apart from the industries and services using woodfuel in the towns a large proportion of town dwellers use charcoal instead of fuelwood: this is more extravagant in terms of wood raw material (Table 6.5).

Between 15 and 25 per cent of woodfuel consumption appears to be used for non-household purposes. Fuelwood is important for drying agricultural crops, such as cassava, tea, and tobacco, baking bread, for curing fish, and producing bricks and tiles. Charcoal is used by the cement and metal industries and is used in restaurants and canteens and by blacksmiths. The importance of woodfuel has declined over the years as industry turns to more convenient fuels, but this decline may be reversed because of the large increases in the price of oil and gas. This reversal has already occurred in segments of the Ugandan tea industry and on Thailand's railways.

Household use of fuelwood can be

Table 6.5. Breakdown of consumption between household and non-household use. Unit—percentage of total consumption

Country	*Household*	*Cottage industry*	*Industrial and service sectors*	*Cottage industries*	*Industrial and service sectors*
				in some or all countries	
Northern Nigeria	75	25		Baking	Baking
Gambia	85	7	8	Brewing	Cassava drying
rural	(85)	(9)	(6)	Blacksmith	Tea drying
urban	(83)	(–)	(17)	Fish curing	Fish curing
Sudan	98		2	Heating animal food	Tobacco curing
					Brick manufacture
Tanzania	93		7	Hot food traders	Ceramic manufacture
					Cement manufacture
Thailand	84	7	9	Palm oil production	Metal manufacture
rural	(89)	(7)	(4)		Blacksmiths
urban	(74)	(8)	(18)	Sweet making	Railways
					Sawmills
					Restaurants
					Canteens

Source: As noted in Table 6.4.

conveniently divided into four categories: cooking, heating, protection, and ironing. The latter two are relatively unimportant. Cooking usually accounts for over 50 per cent of total use, although in cool climates heating may be as important.

Table 6.6 shows the incidence of householders using fuelwood for various purposes in Thailand. All households use woodfuel for cooking, but only about 50 per cent of the sample use woodfuel for either heating or warming water to wash in. However, there were marked differences between and within rural and urban populations. Neraly 30 per cent of rural population use wood for heating, mainly in relatively cool areas, whereas in the urban sample it was hardly used for this purpose. The end column gives a breakdown of the amount of woodfuel used for the different activities. Similarly Table 6.7 shows the approximate consumption of woodfuel in Gambia for each purpose. Cooking and heating accounting for about 90 per cent of household use (and 75 per cent of total use) in both Gambia and Thailand. Tables 6.5, 6.6, and 6.7 generalize the pattern of use in developing countries.

Table 6.6. Household use of woodfuel in Thailand (percentage)

Use	*Rural*	*Urban*	*Total*	*Consumption*
Cooking	100	100	100	(59)
Washing	27	45	30	(18)
Heating	29	1	26	(15)
Protection	9	1	8	(5)
Ironing	5	7	5	(3)

Source: As noted in Table 6.4.

Woodfuel plays an important role in supplying the energy needs of the developing countries, but this is also true of some industrialized nations, especially in forest-rich areas. Wood is used extensively for domestic heating in Canada, Northern Europe, and the USSR. Also, many of the wood processing industries in these countries use the 'waste' wood to generate heat and power.

World consumption patterns

If the total number of woodfuel consumers

Table 6.7. Household use of woodfuel in Gambia (percentage)

	Rural			*Urban*			*Total*		
Use	*FW*	*CH*	*WF*	*FW*	*CH*	*WF*	*FW*	*CH*	*WF*
Cooking	52	1	53	29	27	56	46	8	54
Heating*	35	1	36	17	13	30	30	4	34
Protection†	3	—	3	0	—	0	2	—	2
Ironing	—	8	8	—	14	14	—	10	10
Total	90	10	100	40	54	100	78	22	100

Source: Consumption surveys as noted in Table 6.4.

Key: As for Table 6.4.

*Heating includes warming water for washing.

†Protection includes lighting fires to ward off wild animals and insects.

is added for the various continents, it may be that between 40 and 50 per cent of the world's population rely solely or to a great extent on wood for their cooking and heating requirements. Thus wood may still be the primary fuel in terms of actual consumers, although in terms of quantity, it is the third most important fuel after oil and coal. The estimated 1973 consumption of fuel, excluding transport requirements (in millions of tonnes of coal equivalent) is oil 3600; coal 1800; wood 1300; liquid petroleum gas 50; others about 50. Wood, therefore, supplies about one-fifth of the world's fuel requirements.

If the supply of woodfuel is exhausted in many areas, and many people decide to switch to more convenient fuels, then the demands placed on other forms of energy, both in the short and medium term, would become intolerable.

Future consumption

Future household consumption in developing countries

Future consumption of woodfuel in developing countries will depend on

(i) population increase and rate of urbanization;

(ii) increase and distribution of wealth;

(iii) the price of woodfuel *vis-à-vis* other fuels;

(iv) the physical availability of wood for the subsistence sector.

In these countries, the consumption per capita of woodfuel decreases with increasing wealth, but there appears to be a much slower switch in rural as opposed to urban areas. So it can be anticipated that increase in rural consumption will keep pace with population increase.

In developing countries, the population is increasing at an annual rate of about 2.5 per cent. This means that because of a drift to towns, the rural population is currently increasing at about 1 per cent per year. It may stabilize in 20 or 30 years' time, after which the net increase will be in urban areas. Therefore, it may be assumed that rural household consumption will increase initially by about 1 per cent per year, reaching a peak in 20 years and then gradually declining, provided, of course, that there is sufficient wood to meet requirements.

The trend in urban household consumption is complicated by a number of variables. First, charcoal is being substituted more and more for fuelwood at all income levels. In wood raw material terms this will lead to an increased consumption, for charcoal requires a larger quantity of wood to produce it than would be needed if the fuel had been burned directly. Second, as the cash income of a household rises, there is an increasing switch to other fuels. However, because of the actual income distribution pattern in many countries —a pattern which indicates that 50 per cent of the population may receive less than one-quarter of the cash income—the switch from charcoal to non-wood fuels will be relatively small. Also, there will be a tendency for the lowest income group to increase consumption as its income rises. Third, the urban population is growing at between 7 and 10 per cent per year. Combining all of the above assumptions may mean that there will be an increase in consumption of between 3 and 5 per cent in urban areas, giving an overall increase for urban and rural areas of between 1.5 and 2 per cent.

However, there may be physical shortages of fuelwood and charcoal, especially in towns, because of the large increases in urban population, resulting in price rises and accelerated substitution. Typically the producer of charcoal or fuelwood systematically clears, legally or otherwise, areas of woodland and forest radiating from urban centres, until the point is reached when it either becomes uneconomic to transport the charcoal or the raw material supplies are exhausted. If there are relatively cheap means of transport, such as by river, or returning 'empty' lorries, then the economic transport distance can be extended considerably. A prime example is in Thailand where charcoal is transported distances of up to 500 km by road and well over that by river.

Even if charcoal is the desired fuel, physical shortages will lead to a switch. This could mean that governments have to spend foreign exchange importing fuels, and rural employment will decline because of a falling production of fuelwood and charcoal. With foresight, governments could overcome this problem by establishing fuelwood plantations and village woodlots in anticipation of future consumption patterns. Such plantations, if properly managed, could not only be profitable, but could guarantee rural employment and save foreign exchange. It is therefore essential that additional wood consumption and resource surveys be undertaken to establish demand and supply patterns so meaningful plans can be drawn up.

Future non-household consumption in developing countries

The large increase in oil prices over recent years has caused many industries and services either to halt the changeover from wood to other fuels or to reverse it. Industry is once again looking at the use of wood as an energy source; forestry departments and governments should welcome this opportunity for supplying needs from local sources. Plantation grown fuelwood on a 6 to 10 year rotation with such species as eucalyptus, wattle or gmelina, and an expected annual yield of 15 m^3 per hectare, could give a real return of about 7 per cent per year on money invested, if the stumpage fee is about \$2.50 per m^3 (1976 US dollars). This stumpage fee may seem high by current prices in developing countries but it is low enough to make the fuel competitive with its rivals provided the plantations are sited near the industry (Table 6.8).

It is shown in Table 6.8 that fuelwood has a comparative advantage over other fuels and it may be economical for developing countries to consider generating electricity using fuelwood or other vegetable material such as bagasse. Boiler efficiency is very crucial in the calculation and a given boiler type may not be suitable for burning a variety of materials. The moisture content of the fuelwood is an important factor. Unless fuelwood is dried before burning, charcoal could be more advantageous. However, if fuelwood is only required for drying, kilning, or baking its advantage appears to be significant.

Charcoal may be used in a number of processes. For example, cement manufacture and metal extraction where fuelwood cannot readily be used. Indeed, for certain grades

Table 6.8 The cost of various fuels delivered to an industry in a developing country (US dollars)

Cost per tonne	*Fuelwood** *(air dry)* $		*Charcoal†* $	*Fuel oil‡* $
Ex-producer/dockside	6		38	79
Transport costs (80 km)	6		6	5
Load/unload	1		1	—
Factory cost	13		45	84
Calorific value	20 per cent m.c.	55 per cent m.c.		
Kilocalories per gramme (kcal g)	4.0	3.4	7.9	11.25
Price per 100000 kcal $US§	3.25	3.82	5.7	7.47
Efficiency in a boiler, per cent	66	55	80	85
Price per 'efficient' 100000 kcal $US	4.92	6.95	7.12	8.79

*Assume 1.4 m^3 = 1 tonne air dry wood, m.c. = moisture content.

†Includes profit margin.

‡UK delivered price 1974.

§Included stumpage, felling, and extraction to roadside.

Delivered prices of woodfuel: (US dollars)

(a) Woodfuel per m^3:
  (1) Tanzania (1976)—bulk purchase $3.50.
  —small quantities $7.00.
  (2) Gambia (1972) —small quantities $13.00.

(b) Charcoal per tonne:
  (1) Tanzania (1976) Dar es Salaam $40.00.
  (2) Thailand (1970) Bangkok—mixed spp $28.00.
  (1970) Bangkok—mangrove $36.00.
  (1) Gambia (1972) Banjul $32.00.
  (2) Ghana (1972) Accra $55.00.

of steel, charcoal is the preferred fuel and reducing agent.

It appears, then, that there could be a growing market for woodfuel in the service and industrial sectors of developing countries, and there are sound economic reasons why its demand could increase, albeit at a modest rate. However, the supply position is not certain unless plantations specifically for woodfuel are developed.

Future consumption in developed countries

It is anticipated that the traditional use of woodfuel in developed countries will slowly decline. Much depends on its relative price and availability. The economics of growing fuelwood plantations in temperate climates is doubtful, but fuelwood and wood waste is and will continue to be used for domestic heating and industrial steam and electrical production.

With the increases in oil prices, since 1973–4, renewed interest has been taken in the production of various combustible materials such as petrol, methanol, and gas from cellulosic material, including wood waste. During the Second World War many vehicles ran on either water gas combined with produced gas, wood alcohol, or motor spirit made from wood. A detailed account can be found in Egon Glesinger's book *The coming age of wood.*[8] The techniques of producing oil, gas, and methanol by such processes as pyrolysis or the Fischer–Tropsch reaction (hydrogenation) are described in several publications such as those of the US Bureau of Mines.[9, 10, 11] Heating cellulose with carbon monoxide, water, and catalysts at a temperature of 350 to 400 °C and a pressure of 4000 psi will yield about 1 tonne of partially refined oil per $3\frac{1}{2}$ to $5\frac{1}{2}$ tonnes of air dry cellulose (5 m^3 to 8 m^3 of wood). The United States is establishing pilot plants to produce oil from waste material and with the continuing high price of oil—$95.00 per tonne ($13.00 per barrel)—such plants could be the forerunners of commercial ventures. Because of favourable climatic conditions and relatively low labour costs, many areas of the developing world could be in a position to enter this market with large scale short rotation forest plantations, especially if the 'refinery' was situated in the middle of the plantation. However, such refineries require substantial capital investment and technical skills.

There is an expanding market in developed countries for charcoal, especially in the activated form. Such charcoal has fairly unique absorption properties and is used for the purification and absorption of gases and liquids in such processes as sugar decolorizing water purification, solvent clarification, herbicidal deactivation, and air and gas purification. Activated charcoal is made by treating charcoal, usually produced from a uniform material such as coconut shells, bones, bagasse, lignite, or a single species of wood, with a suitable solvent or by heating it in a stream of inert gas or steam. This process removes the woodtars which clog the cells. However, activated charcoal is not an easy substance to make or transport. If developing countries wish to enter this potentially large export market it may be more logical, as a first step, to produce charcoal for activation rather than activated charcoal. In most developing countries charcoal is sold in the market-place within the price range $30 to $55 per tonne (Table 6.8 footnote). The c.i.f. price in industrial countries for charcoal is between $120 and $170 per tonne (activated charcoal $240 per tonne). Therefore, there seems to be potential export market both for the traditional uses and for activation.

Developed countries will undoubtedly increase their production of charcoal, but developing nations, with their climatic advantages for raw material production, could enter this market.

Charcoal is produced in a number of ways ranging from a very simple earth kiln to a complex retort costing upwards of $70000. However, the more sophisticated the production method, the more control there is on the quality and quantity of the product. The efficiency is also increased and by-products may be collected. Table 6.9 gives the approximate capital cost and production costs for charcoal made by various methods. It also gives the area of plantations required to feed the different kilns.

An ex-factory price of $38 per tonne appears to be a possibility. This would allow a reasonable profit to the producer and an adequate return to the grower of the raw material. If charcoal can be produced at around this price from plantation grown wood, then the prospects both in the local and export markets seem assured.

Future world consumption

Total demand for woodfuel in its traditional and anticipated uses might increase by about 2 per cent per year. Consumption forecasts for the year 2000 for woodfuel and all timber products are shown in Table 6.10 The projections indicate that potential consumption in the year 2000 may be nearly double the present figures. The supply situation must therefore be examined to see if such demands can be met from existing sources and if not what steps should be taken to meet them.

Future supply

The optimal supply position

Although wood is a renewable raw material, its supply can only be guaranteed if sufficient

Table 6.9. Charcoal production costs in developing countries with various production processes

Kiln type	*Earth*	*Portable steel*	*Beehive brick*	*Steel furnace*	*Steel retort*
Input/year (airdry) m^3	112	500	2030	40600	50600
Output/year tonnes	12	72	312	7250	9000
Conversion ratio m^3/t	9.3	6.9	6.5	5.6	5.6
Plantations required ha	5.6	25	100	2000	2500
Capital cost $	Nil	570	2380	35700	71400
Expected life years	0.1	3	5	30	30
Running costs per year $					
Depreciation, loan repayment and interest	—	430	1095	25600	51170
Purchase of wood, felling and transport to factory	415	1845	8675	198100	245900
Kiln cost—labour, maintenance and repair	310	155	465	7280	12850
Total running costs $	725	2430	10235	230980	309920
Cost per ton $	60.4	33.8	32.8	31.9	34.4
Cost per ton exluding load repayment and interest $	(60.4)	(30.5)	(30.7)	(30.0)	(31.4)

Notes: (1) Constant costs and prices have been assumed. (2) Upper 1972 price ranges for kilns and retorts have been taken. These costs were obtained from *Charcoal and forest management*, by D. E. Earl.[12] (3) A standard stumpage price of $2.50 per m^3 has been charged for all wood, including branches and stems. Branchwood is usually free and much of the wood used in earth kilns will be self-collected branchwood and scrub. Labour has been charged at full cost ($620 per man per year for labour plus $2380 per man per year for management), irrespective of method of production, but earth kiln operators are usually self-employed susbistence farmers. (4) It is assumed that the money to buy the kiln is borrowed. However, replacement kilns are paid for out of depreciation and so the future production costs will be less and are shown on the last line. (5) For the retort the entire cost has been set against the charcoal production; in fact some of the cost should be set against the by-products. (6) If mangrove is used as a raw material for charcoal production, the input requirements will be reduced by about 30 per cent for the same output.

areas of woodlands and forests are conserved and managed. It may be economically wise to liquidate some forest capital to obtain money for development, and it may be expedient to clear woodland for the expanding rural population to have sufficient land for subsistence agriculture and cash crops. However, it is essential that governments plan for self-sufficiency in wood products, especially fuelwood, in the subsistence sector. Also, it seems prudent and appears economically sound for many developing countries to aim for complete self-sufficiency. Not only is there a comparative advantage in growing fuelwood in many tropical countries but such a policy could lead to more rural employment and a saving of foreign exchange with the possibility of exports. However, there are many areas in developing countries where shortages of woodfuel already occur. Dung, grass and cornstalks are burned, not used for manure and compost; young trees are cut, thus halting succession and regeneration. Priority must be given to solving these shortages.

How to meet current demands from the present forest area

The world's natural forests occupy nearly 28 per cent of the land area, but about 40 per cent of them are unproductive because

Table 6.10 Potential consumption of wood products by the year 2000 (million m^3 roundwood equivalent)

Product	*Estimated present consumption* (*1976*)	*Potential consumption 2000* *Per cent*	*Low*	*Per cent*	*High*	*Per cent*	*Assumed growth rate in consumption per cent per year* *Low*	*High*
Woodfuel	3050	63	5060	56	3840	46	2	1
Poles	300	6	360	4	280	3	2	1
Sawnwood	1045	22	2050	23	2350	28	$2\frac{1}{2}$	3
Panels	178	4	600	7	780	9	5	6
Paper	235	5	910	10	1190	14	4	5
Total	4808		8980		8440			
Volume available from the increment	6610			6610				
Popn (millions)	4161			6110				
Per capita consumption m^3	1.18		1.47		1.38			

Notes: (1) Low and high refer to the anticipated rate of increase in the world's wealth. For woodfuel and poles a higher rate of increase leads to a greater substitution, hence the lower consumption of these products at the 'high' rate. (2) The assumed growth rates in the end column are average world figures but of course many factors contribute to these averages. These estimtaes have been made to show the order of magnitude rather than the actual estimates. (3) The potential consumption in the year 2000 is considerably greater than the increment of the growing stock: if the potential demand is to be satisfied some of the forest capital will have to be liquidated unless steps are taken now to increase the growing stock and hence the increment.

of low economic exploitation and lack of industrial infrastructure. Man-made forests are insignificant, covering less than 1 per cent of the land area, but are an important source of wood because of their high productivity. Table 6.11 illustrates the world's forest resources and how they are divided between the broad economic groups.

Estimated total growing stock amounts to some 357 500 million m^3, which is 75 times the estimated present consumption (4810 million m^3). However, in order to preserve the forest capital, only the increment (in banking terms the interest) should be removed. The current annual increment is estimated to be 6610 million m^3. This is only 1.4 times the consumption figure, and with 40 per cent of the growing stock classified as unproductive, it may be that world consumption is presently in balance with growth. But, as mentioned in the previous section, in some areas the forest capital is being liquidated. The warning bells already are sounding.

Meeting future demands

An estimate of the possible consumption of wood products has been made for the year 2000 (Table 6.10).

It is anticipated that the potential demand for wood products may double by the turn of the century to about one-third more than the potential increment. The demand may grow to about 8700 million m^3 roundwood, whereas the increment will be about 6600

Table 6.11. World forest resources

	Forest								
			Composition		*Growing stock per ha*				
	Total area	*of which unproductive*	*Coniferous*	*Non-coniferous*	*Coniferous*	*Non-coniferous*	*Estimated total growing stock*	*Estimated increment*	*World population 1976*
		million hectares			m^3/ha		*million* m^3	*million* m^3	*million*
Developed	1672	380	1092	555	106	74	156600	2510	1176
Developing E.C. II	1901	1006	55	1800	80	103	189400	3845	2008
Developing E.C. III (China, N. Korea, Vietnam, Laos and Khmer)	139	45	58	80	81	85	11500	255	977
Total developing	2040	1051	113	1880	81	102	200900	4100	2985
World	3712	1431	1205	2435	103	96	357500	6610	4161

Source: FAO, *World forest inventory*, 1963. Revised Table in *Unasylva*. Rome, 1971, vol. 25.

Note: Increment estimates made by the author.

million m^3 roundwood. Woodfuel alone could account for between two-thirds and three-quarters of the increment. Therefore, other things being equal, it appears that the forest capital will have to be reduced to supply requirements. At the same time, some of the expanding population will require forest land for cultivation, leading to further reduction of forest capital. Because population and forests are not spread evenly throughout the world, there are bound to be large inroads into the forest capital in certain areas. The only way to counter those inroads is through better forest management and a much larger investment in plantations. Managed natural and plantation forests covering an area of one-tenth of the world's surface (1300 million hectares) could produce an annual increment of 13000 million m^3. This would more than meet anticipated future requirements by the turn of the century. A plantation grown on a 30-year rotation will give at least 10 m^3/ha/year. However, the productive phase of a plantation does not start until 10 years after planting and the bulk of the volume will not be realized until the end of the rotation (30 years). If one hectare of land was planted each year for 30 years, then from the 31st year onwards the plantation will yield 300 m^3 or 10 m^3 per hectare (and from the 11th year the yield will gradually increase from 1 m^3/ha to 10 m^3 in the 31st year). At the present time plantations cover only about 80 million hectares. There will have to be a tenfold increase over the next 25 years, calling for considerable investment, probably of the order of \$1500 million—\$6000 million per year. This may seem a large sum but it is only \$1.50 per head per year, and the returns can be measured not only in monetary gain, but in new employment, consumer satisfaction, and environmental safeguards. Given the means and having the will, the way is open to solve this problem.

Summary and conclusions

Present consumption of fuelwood and charcoal may be nearly three times the recorded production. This is because much woodfuel is freely collected, especially by the subsistence sector of the population. There is an urgent need to increase the accuracy of production and consumption statistics in order that proper forest and forest industry planning can be undertaken. This should go together with inventory and survey work.

Household consumption per capita of woodfuel in developing countries is of the order of 1 tonne of wood per year (1.4 m^3) with an additional 8 per cent used in the manufacturing and service sectors. The total consumption per capita is approximately 1.5 m^3 per year. Cooking accounts for over 50 per cent of household use while heating, the next most important, accounts for 30 per cent. This latter item, of course, varies according to climatic conditions.

Fuelwood is of minor importance in developed countries. It is used primarily in the timber rich regions of the northern temperate zone for household heating. Industry in these areas burns wood-waste for steam and heat generation.

Woodfuel accounts for about 65 per cent of total raw material consumption, and although it is only the third most important fuel in quantity terms after oil and coal, it is still probably the premier fuel in terms of actual number of consumers. Its importance in both the forest and energy sectors should be fully recognized.

As the world's population becomes more prosperous there will be a move away from fuelwood use, first to charcoal and then to other more convenient non-wood fuels. Much depends on the relative price and convenience of the competing fuels. However, this substitution does not occur in the subsistence sector unless local supplies of fuelwood have been exhausted and users are forced to burn dung and other forms of vegetable matter. The needs of this sector of the population should be planned for by the establishment of village woodlots in areas of timber shortages. Self-sufficiency should be the goal and with assistance and training many people in this sector are only too willing to start self-help schemes.

The population increase will more than balance the move away from woodfuel. Woodfuel consumption may increase at a rate of between 1.5 to 2 per cent per year, provided there is sufficient wood available to meet some of the needs now supplied by fossil fuels.

The *World forest inventory* indicates that for the world as a whole, the merchantable annual increment may, at present, just balance removals. Unfortunately, supply and demand do not match everywhere resulting in local shortages or the reduction of stock. Demand is likely to nearly double by the turn of the century. Even with the opening of virgin forests, potential demand will be larger than annual increment so that forest capital will be reduced. Again, more farm land will be required by an expanding population: this land will have to come from the forest reserve, further reducing the growing stock.

However, if many more plantations are established (from part of the existing forest reserve) and management of the natural forest intensified, there could be a significant increase in production, despite a reduction of area. The greatest gains could be achieved in the tropical areas, and this is where most effort should be concentrated. The developed nations must be prepared to give much more aid and assistance to help solve this problem. One lesson that the energy crisis has spelt out is that renewable natural resources are the most precious resources that mankind has. If they are effectively managed, they will be able to supply all our needs. This is true of woodfuel in particular.

References

1. FAO, *1976 Yearbook of forest products.* Rome (1978).
2. *The Gambia: a wood consumption survey and timber trend study, 1973–2000.* Report to ODA (U.K.)/LRD. London, Gambia Land Resources Development Project (1973).
3. FAO, *Nigeria: The Market for Firewood, Poles and Sawnwood in the Major Towns and Cities in the Savanna Region.* Technical Report No. 6, SF/NIR 16, Rome (1972).
4. FAO, *Sudan: Present Wood Consumption and Future Requirements.* T.A. No. 1820. Rome (1964).
5. FAO, *Tanzania: Present Consumption and Future Requirements of Wood in Tanzania.* Technical Report No. 3, SF/TAN 15 and Project Working Document, Rome (1971).
6. FAO, *Thailand: Present and Future Forest Policy Goals. A Timber Trend Study, 1970–2000* T.A. 3156 and Project Working Document, Rome (1972).
7. *Zambia: Charcoal Study in the Chati and Kafue Areas.* Private communication.
8. Glesinger, Egon. *The Coming Age of Wood.* Secker and Warburg (1950).
9. *Converting Organic Wastes to Oil,* Report No. 7560. United States Bureau of Mines, Washington (1971).
10. *Conversion of Municipal and Industrial Refuse into Useful Materials by Pyrolysis.* Report No. 7428. United States Bureau of Mines, Washington (1970).
11. *Energy Potential from Organic Wastes.* Information Circular 8549. United States Bureau of Mines, Washington (1972).
12. Earl, D., *Charcoal and forest management.* Oxford University Press (1973).

7

Tropical forest plantations

NORMAN E. JOHNSON

Why is there such intensive interest developing for plantation management in the tropics? Included in the many reasons are projected increases in the world population, projected increases in world wood products demand, and the apparent growth potential of the moist tropical climate.

By the year 2000 (Fig. 7.1), the number of people in developed regions will increase by 300 million—but in the developing regions by 2.2 billion. Since many of these undeveloped countries lie in the tropics certain tropical forests are in strategic locations. On the other hand, the demand for wood in developed countries in the year 2000 is expected to be nearly three times that of the developing regions (Fig. 7.2). Yet, some tropical regions are in a position as favourable, or more favourable, to provide wood to Japan, Europe, and the Americas as is Russia, where exists the world's largest untapped temperate forest. Many of the oil-rich nations lack the capability to grow wood. As the standard of living rises in these countries so will their consumption of paper and solid-wood products. The demand for paper products will show a greater increase than will solid wood, indicating that the price for smaller, long-fibred trees will increase compared to trees that produce clear lumber and plywood (Fig. 7.3).

Logging costs rise as the harvesting of indigenous forests recedes further and further from the coast, but these increases may be offset by plantation production close to tidewater. This is to be expected even though felling, bucking, and loading costs per unit of wood are usually higher for small trees. In the south-eastern United States, for example, the average log being sawed in the 'chip-n-saw' sawmills is around 20 cm in diameter and plywood logs only slightly larger.

Growth of the tropical forest

We have all heard of the supposed productivity of the tropical rain forests. What is the truth of the matter?

On the West Coast of North America early loggers commonly found Douglas-fir forests with over 2000 m^3 per hectare; yet, in East Kalimantan, Indonesia, we log less than 60 m^3 from the average hectare. Even clear cutting and full utilization of all trees 15 cm in diameter and above would only double this value. The length of the cutting cycle in Indonesia and Malaysia is 35 years. Assuming the volume cut will be replaced in that time, the annual growth rate of the partially cut forest is about 1 to 3 m^3 per hectare. Lowe (1973) cites the growth of Nigerian rain forests as 2 m^3/ha/year. Momoh and Gibson (1975) state that in the Guinea savannah yields of 1 m^3 /ha/year are common. On the island of Mindanao in the

First published in *Journal of Forestry*, Vol. 74, No. 4 (April 1976), pp. 206–11. Reprinted by permission of the author and the Society of American Foresters.

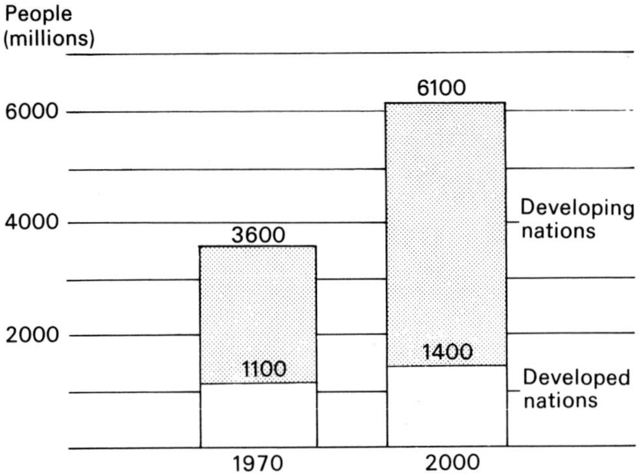

Fig. 7.1. United Nations estimate of world population levels in developed and developing nations for 1970 and 2000.

Philippines, Tagudar (1974) reports selectively logged dipterocarp forest will produce 2.9 to 4.3 m^3/ha/year. His company practises some residual stand silviculture, but he does not say in his report what benefits they produce. Lowe (1973) is sceptical that residual stand silviculture produces increased growth. And Catinot (1970) in reviewing the literature on enrichment planting concluded: 'Enrichment planting . . . now has fewer and fewer supporters in the tropics . . . on the whole it has not given satisfactory results.'

There is also the character of the forest itself to be considered. On an average hectare of tropical rain forest there may be up to a hundred species. Although modern manufacturing technology does allow better utilization of mixed tropical species than

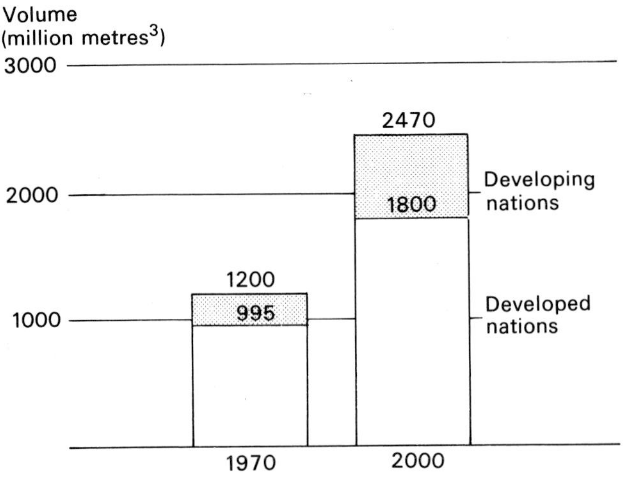

Fig. 7.2. World demand for industrial wood in developed and developing nations for 1970 and 2000.

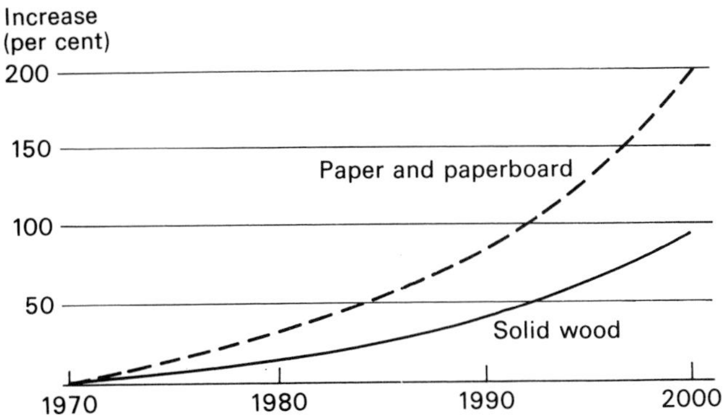

Fig. 7.3. World trends in demand for solid wood and paper and paperboard 1970–2000.

previously, the variable wood quality presents a number of problems that may be eliminated in plantations.

Plantation growth in the tropics

An abundant literature on the yields of various trees grown under tropical conditions raises some suspicion that perhaps only the best yields are reported. All too often plantation failures go unmentioned. However, those growth rates reported are impressive. King and Steinbrenner (1970) compared the height growth of *Pinus caribaea* with loblolly pine and Douglas-fir (Fig. 8.4). At age 12, for example, *Pinus caribaea* may be 85 feet (29 metres) tall while Douglas-fir is still around 30 feet (10 metres), and loblolly pine around 50 feet (17 metres). The yield of *Pinus caribaea* at this age may be 300 m³/ha while Douglas-fir at the same age is still unmerchantable and loblolly pine on the best sites will show less than 200 m³/ha. Tagudar (1974) reports that *Albizia falcataria* plantations in the Philippines can easily produce 44 to 50 m³/ha/year over 8 years and *Eucalyptus deglupta* up to 25 m³/ha/year over 12 years. Hulster (1972) lists plantation growth rate in Indonesia from a low of 6 m³/ha/year for teak up to 30 m³/ha/year for *Gmelina arborea*. This latter species in Surinam and Brazil is growing at between 30 and 40 m³/ha/year.

Growth rates of fast-growing tropical tree species are compared with those for indigenous forests in Fig. 7.5. It is this comparison that intrigues the timber industry. Why are the differences so great? Are plantation species more efficient than those evolved on a given site over millions of years? When an analysis is made of biomass productivity it appears there is nothing mysterious about this difference at all.

According to Sanchez (1973) the total biomass of the indigenous tropical forest lies between 200 and 400 ton/ha of dry matter distributed as follows:

	Low	*High*
Stems and branches	150	300
Roots	36	72
Leaves	10	20
Litter	4	8
	200	400

In tropical plantations pine can average 20 m³/ha/year for 15 years for a total of 300 m³; *Albizia* and other fast-growing broadleaved trees often will produce 40 m³/ha/year for 8 years or a total of 320 m³. There are even reports of up to 60 m³ over 8 years or 480 m³. Assuming that this wood is half water (specific gravity of 0.50 at 0 per cent M.C.) we would have between 150 and 240 tonnes of dry usable wood per hectare. If we add 10 per cent for limbs and small tops we would get between 165 and 264 tonnes of stems and branches, figures that fall within the range of stem and branch

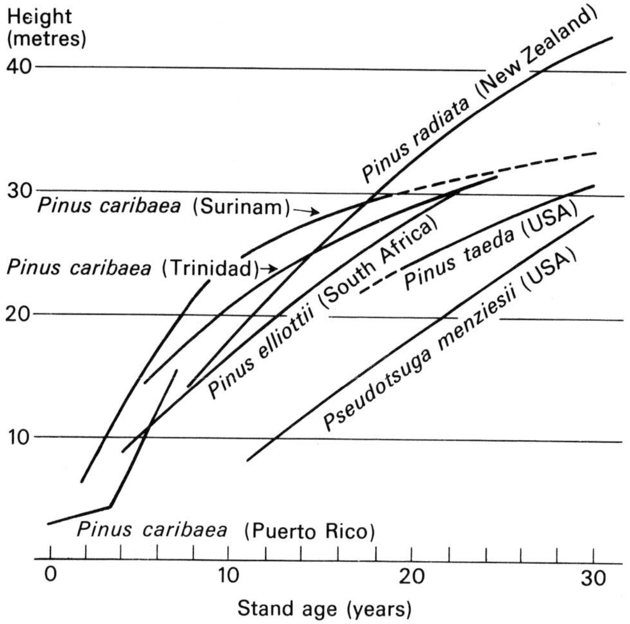

Fig. 7.4. Trends in height growth over time for five conifers growing in widely separated locations.

biomass of the virgin jungle.

Interestingly, Sanchez (1973) says that 90 per cent of the total jungle regrowth occurs within 8 years. If true, this is especially interesting from both a biological and economic point of view. Growth of the fastest-growing plantation trees usually culminates between the ages 8 and 10 years. Therefore, what we're doing is transferring the growth of the natural forest, consisting of a multiplicity of trees, vines and weeds, on to a tree species of our choice. Likewise, as a natural forest matures, the shift is from a high proportion of vines, weeds, and fast-growing pioneer species to those species of trees that dominate the older jungle. In East Kalimantan these are predominantly dipterocarps.

The importance of short time periods in economic calculations is well known, but worth reviewing. We can examine a simplified example of the financial consequences of a $250 per hectare establishment cost over short and long rotations at interest rates of 7, 10 and 13 per cent (Fig. 7.6). The cost of establishing Douglas-fir on an intensively managed southern pine plantation in the United States or a tropical plantation in Borneo, the Philippines, Brazil, or Africa is approximately $250/ha. For purposes of comparison, the example uses a single establishment cost and a constant wood yield of 21 m^3/ha/year. This rate is high for US forests, about average for non-coniferous plantations, and high for pines in tropical areas.

The first example might be a fast-growing broad-leaved tropical species established at $250 per hectare and growing 21 m^3/ha/year. The cost of the wood, at 10 per cent interest, 10 years after establishment will be $3.09/$m^3$. Increasing the rotation to 20 years will increase the cost to $4.00, 30 years will increase it to $6.92, and 40 years to $13.47. With a higher interest rate the differences will be greater. Comparing 10-year and 40-year rotations at 13 per cent, wood costs will be $4.04 and $39.52 respectively per m^3.

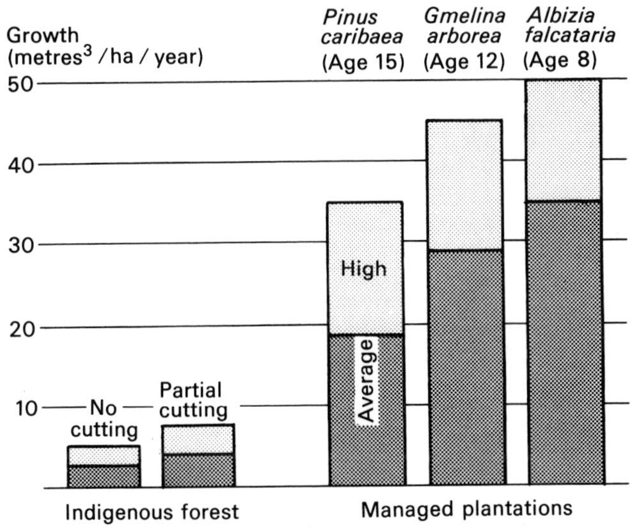

Fig. 7.5. Growth rates compared for undisturbed and partially cut indigenous tropical forests and selected species growing in plantations.

Realistically, the economic considerations are much more complex than this and often confusingly intertwined with social and political issues. In this analysis no consideration is given to carrying costs, tax benefits, or costs of successive generations. But the fact remains that if the costs of establishment, the rate of growth, and the value of the wood are constant, a forestry investment of the shortest duration will offer the highest rate of return.

From the point of view of growth, things look good. What then are the major concerns? There are many and they include problems of transportation, markets, politics, and labour. Two others I would like to examine are forest soils, and insects and diseases.

Soils and productivity

Tropical soils vary so much in texture and nutrient status that broad generalizations are difficult, but a few seem to be relevant. Because of the pattern and intensity of tropical rainfall, many of the available soil nutrients are leached out; the soils have a low level of incorporated organic matter; they tend to have a poor structure, and as a result are not resilient under cultivation; and erosion by surface water presents a constant danger (Ruthenberg 1971). Because of these characteristics, plus the ever-present weed problem, a high proportion of tropical agriculture is so-called 'shifting agriculture'.

Foresters beginning to practise plantation forestry in the tropics may avoid certain mistakes by examining agricultural experience. For example, temperate-region land-clearing practices can have a devastating effect on crop yields. In Brazil, an experiment compared the yields of several crops and cropping techniques on land that had been cleared and burned using typical hand techniques, with land cleared with a medium-sized tractor (Annual report 1973, AID). Soils on tractor-cleared sites were 1/20 as permeable and contained less organic matter; nutrient levels, especially of phosphorus, were also less. All crop yields were lower and returned only 20 per cent of those from ground cleared by traditional hand methods. Although fertilizers increased yields at both sites, they did not right the damage.

A visit to a large-scale tree plantation on the Amazon showed the same results. The

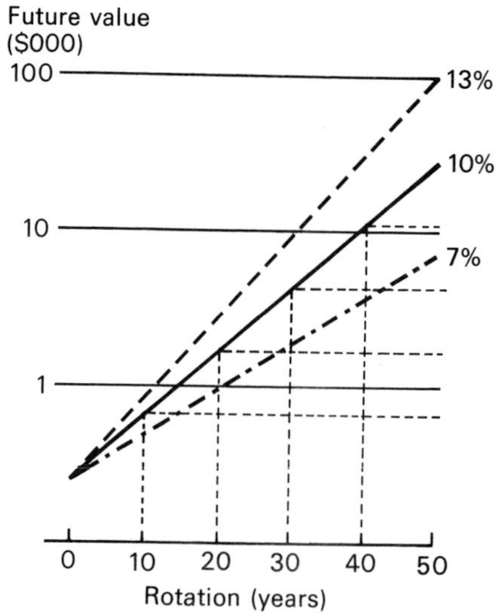

10% interest	
Rotation (years)	Cost ($/metre³)
40	13.47
30	6.92
20	4.00
10	3.04

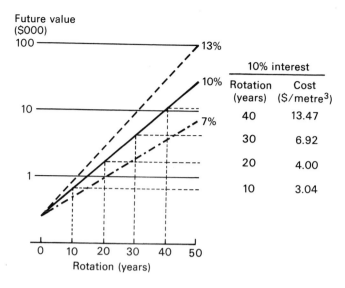

Fig. 7.6. Future cost of wood assuming an initial plantation establishment cost of $250 per hectare, an average mean annual increment of 21 cubic metres and three rates of interest (7 per cent, 10 per cent, and 13 per cent).

tree *Gmelina arborea* growing on soils cleared with tractors grew at only a fraction of the rate of trees growing on undisturbed soils. In East Kalimantan this same species at age 16 months on compacted soil may average 2 metres in height and on undisturbed soil 10 metres.

Yields of agricultural crops on unfertilized tropical soils tend to fall off rapidly. A rule of thumb is that the second crop will yield only one-half that of the first and the third crop even less. So we ask, will the same thing happen with trees? According to Ruthenberg (1971), provided the fallow periods are long enough (from 3 to 30 years), a slash-and-burn system is not harmful to the soil. 'In fact,' he says, 'the yields after a fallow period under secondary forest are in some cases higher than those after the first clearing.' Perhaps so, but we still don't know whether periodic tree cropping will remove more nutrients from the soil than can be restored between harvests. Replacement of nitrogen has been suggested through planting nitrogen-fixing trees or cover crops. The removal of stem wood every rotation will take nutrients with it, but the leaves and roots will be left behind, as will accumulated litter.

According to Sanchez (1973), the top layer of tropical soils contains 260 per cent as much N, 75 per cent as much K, and about the same amount of exchangeable Ca and Mg as the plant biomass. At any one time, however, most of the available P is contained within the biomass itself so tree removals are, therefore, likely to create shortages of P ahead of other nutrients. Since 68 to 85 per cent of the root system of a tropical forest occupies the soils' uppermost 25 to 30 cm, it is extremely critical not to lose soil in the cropping process (Sanchez 1973). In rubber plantations, nutrient additions may well be required after the first crop (Watson 1973). Reduced growth in subsequent rotations, in my view, remains a high priority research item, but should not hold up the establishment of tropical plantations on some portion of the millions of hectares of land being harvested now, or abandoned following careless agriculture. Certainly, experience with rubber and oil palm indicates that with proper care several generations of trees can be grown on the same site without loss of productivity.

Insect and disease problems of tropical plantations

Perhaps the most often-stated hazard to plantations of exotic species is attack by diseases and insects. Common belief has it that so-called monocultures are more susceptible to these attacks than are mixed forests. Generally this is probably true, but there appear to be enough exceptions to make the risks worth taking. Certainly, experience with *Pinus radiata* in New Zealand has been favourable although in parts of Australia diseases have discouraged planting this species. Elsewhere, various species of pines from the south-eastern United States, Mexico, and Central America have been grown successfully in Africa, South America, and Asia. *Gmelina arborea* in Brazil seems to be relatively free from insect pests.

Space prohibits a thorough review of plantation pest problems. For example, 106 forest insects are listed as attacking *Eucalyptus saligna* in Australia alone (Podger 1975). I will mention several specific cases illustrating problems that have developed in exotic plantations.

The foliage disease *Dothistroma pini* causes no appreciable damage to *Pinus radiata* in California, but it is a serious pest of this and other pines elsewhere. Reis and Hodges (1975) report that it has completely eliminated *P. radiata* and possibly *P. pinaster* from consideration as suitable plantation trees in Brazil. Because of this disease, *Pinus radiata* has also been abandoned in East and Central Africa (Ram Reddy and Singh 1975). In New Zealand, effective chemical control has been developed.

Various root diseases are pests of plantations the world over. Diseases well known in the temperate regions such as *Armillariella mellea*, *Phytophthora cinnamomi*, and *Fomes annosus* are problems in tropical plantations as well. *P. cinnamomi* is currently damaging 10000 hectares of *Eucalyptus* forest in Western Australia and another 400000 hectares in Victoria and Tasmania (Gilmour *et al.* 1975). The root disease *Cylindrocladium clavatum* recently was found to be an important pathogen of pines in Brazil.

Canker diseases are another major problem in *Eucalyptus* plantations, with *Diapothe cubensis* causing considerable losses to young plantations in Brazil and Surinam (Hodges and Reis 1975). *Eucalyptus* trials that I have seen on the Amazon have severe stem cankers and cankers are showing up in our 2-year-old *E. deglupta* in East Kalimantan.

A mycoplasma disease carried by the bug *Cryptopeltis tenuis* has nearly wiped out the *Paulownia tomentosa* plantations of Korea (La and Yi 1975) and a similar disease is attacking *Zizyphus jujuba* in the same area. Since *Paulownia* is native to China and Korea, even endemic species are not always safe.

In any plantation one is likely to find insect pests of consequence. For example, in $1\frac{1}{2}$-year-old *Gmelina* plantations in East Kalimantan, a small hemipteran is causing premature leaf fall while termites are eating away at the roots and stems. Plantations of the native tree *Anthocephalus chinensis* are defoliated repeatedly by larvae of a moth and by crickets. Nearby, moth larvae bore into the stems of *Eucalyptus deglupta* and others into the tips of *Swietenia macrophylla*. An as-yet-unidentified insect cuts off the roots of newly planted seedlings and the overall damage is substantial, although not yet quantified.

Termites of the genera *Coptotermes* and *Termes* are a problem in living trees in Malaysia, Indonesia, Australia, New Guinea, British Honduras, and Africa. Pong (1974) reports that in the Pahau Forest Reserve in Peninsular Malaysia termites killed all of the trees in *Araucaria* research plots and a survey showed that nearly all exotic trees species were attacked. Greaves *et al.* (1967) found that *Coptotermes acinaciformis* and *C. frenchi* were responsible for 92 per cent of the mortality occurring in plantations of *Eucalyptus pilularis* in New South Wales. Wilson (1965) found that 80 per cent of *Pinus caribaea* in some British Honduras plantations were attacked by *Coptotermes niger*. In many parts of Africa, species of

Eucalyptus cannot be established without treatment with the insecticide aldrin (Momoh and Gibson 1975).

Insecticide treatment to control leaf-cutting ants (*Atta* species) is routine in some South American plantations (Smith 1975) and a great number of defoliating insects cause problems in plantations throughout the world. Reis and Hodges (1975) report that *Dirphia araucariae* is a new defoliator of pine plantations in Brazil causing moderate to severe damage of *Pinus elliottii* in Sao Paulo. The defoliator *Glena bisulea* causes widespread defoliation of plantations in Columbia (Inderena 1975) and at least two species of butterfly plague *Albizia* plantations in the Philippines (Gatmaiton 1974). Natawiria (1972/73) indicates that because of insect pests primarily, *Albizia falcataria* is being replaced by other tree species in certain plantations in Indonesia.

According to Brunck (1975) the most serious reforestation problems in certain North African countries are attacks on *Eucalyptus* by the beetle *Phoracantha semipunctata* and on pine by the moth *Thaumetopoea pityocampa.* The shootborer *Hypsipyla robusta* is a constant pest of *Swietenia macrophylla* throughout Asia (Chaiglom 1975) and the sucking insects, too, are not to be unaccounted for in the tropics. Ram Reddy and Singh (1975) report that the woolly aphids of the genera *Adelges* and *Pineus* have caused widespread and serious epidemics on pines planted in various countries of the world.

In spite of all the data relating to threats to exotic plantations from pests, it is still not possible to identify the risks with certainty. There are many successful tropical plantations. Some introduced tree species have been surprisingly free from pests. This seems to be true where the tree species finds soil and climate to its liking; but a species on a non-suitable site will soon have pest problems no matter where it may be.

Any arguments against managed plantations in the tropics seem hollow when one considers the real problem and that is the rate that the tropical rain forest is disappearing primarily due to poor land management. One example should suffice. Oemi (1975) points out that in Indonesia there are currently 44 million hectares of once forested land now covered with grass and brush, primarily as a result of shifting agriculture. This is more than the remaining amount of land classed as productive forest and at the present rate of planting in that country it would take over 400 years to correct the situation. This omits the nearly half million hectares being turned to brush and grass each year. Plantations of both native and introduced species will be needed on a portion of the area to maintain future wood supplies in the tropics. But, we will have to learn to match the tree with the environment and to be constantly on the watch for problems that may develop. And just think of what could be accomplished with a genetics programme in the tropics where some species go from seedling to bearing fruit in 2 to 4 years.

References

AID (1973). Agronomic-economic research on tropical soils. *Annual report.* NC State Univ. Soils Science Dept.

Brunck, F. (1975). Principal problems connected with animal or vegetable pests in natural forest stands and man made forests of French speaking tropical countries and North Africa. Second FAO World Technical Consultation on Forest Diseases and Insects. New Delhi, 7–12 April, FAO/IUFRO/DI/75/1-0 (b).

Catinot, R. (1970). Results of enrichment planting in the tropics. FAO committee on forest development in the tropics. Rome, October 1969, FAO: FDT-69/4.

Chaiglom, D. (1975). Dangerous insect pests of forest plantations in Thailand. Second FAO World Technical Consultation on Forest Diseases and Insects. FAO/IUFRO/DI/75/1-1.

Gaitmaitan, F. M. (1974). The yellow butterflies of *Albizia falcataria. Proceedings of the Forest Research Symposium on Industrial Forest Plantations.* Philippine Forest Research Society, Manila, 26 June.

Gilmour, J. W., Alma, P. J., Marks, G. C., and Neumann, F. G. (1975). The status of diseases and insects in New Zealand and Australia.

Second FAO World Technical Consultation on Diseases and Insects. New Delhi. 7–12 April 1975. FAO/IUFRO/DI/75/2-0.

Greaves, T., Armstrong, O. F., McInnes, R. J., and Dowse, J. F. (1967). Timber losses caused by termites, decay and fire in two coastal forests in New South Wales, Tech. Paper No. 7 CSIRO.

Hodges, C. S. and Reis, M. S. (1975). A canker disease of *Eucalyptus* in Brazil caused by *Diaporthe cubensis* Brunder. Second World Technical Consultation on Forest Diseases and Insects. New Delhi. 7–12 April. FAO/IUFRO/DI/75/16-19.

Hulster, I. A. (1972). Tropical silviculture. Department Management Hutan Fakultas Kehutanan. Institut Pertanian Bogor.

Inderena, J. B. M. (1975). El defoliador de las coniferas *Glena bisuela* Rindge. Second FAO World Technical Consultation on Forest Diseases and Insects. New Delhi. 7–12 April. FAO/IUFRO/DI/75/2-5.

King, J. E. and Steinbrenner, E. C. (1970). Observations on forest soils and *Pinus caribaea hondurensis* plantation in the Surinam project. Weyerhaeuser Co. Forestry Research Center, limited distribution.

La, Y. J. and Yi, C. K. (1975). Mycoplasma incited witches broom diseases of Paulownia and Jujube in Korea. Second World Technical Consultation on Forest Diseases and Insects. New Delhi, 7–12 April. FAO/IUFRO/DI/75/16-54.

Lowe, R. G. (1973). *Nigerian experience with natural regeneration in tropical moist forests.* Mimeographed.

Momoh, Z. O. and Gibson, I. A. S. (1975). Status of diseases and insect pests in Africa and Eurasia. Second FAO World Technical Consultation on Forest Diseases and Insects. FAO/IUFRO/DI/75/1-0. New Delhi, April.

Natawiria, D. (1972/3). Hama dan penyakit *Albizia falcataria* (L.) Rimba Indonesia. 17 (1-2):58–69.

Oemi, H. (1975). Pemikiran usaha akselerasi pembangunan hutan buatan di Indonesia. Seminar reforestation and afforestation Gadjah Mada Univ. 23–24 August 1974, pp. 187–200.

Podger, F. D. (1975). Fast growing hardwoods for developing countries—the forest disease and insect pest position. Second FAO World Technical Consultation on Forest Diseases and Insects. New Delhi, 7–12 April 1975. FAO/IUFRO/1/75/16-0/(b).

Pong, T. Y. (1974). *The termite problem in plantation forestry in Peninsula Malaysia.* Forest Research Institute Kepong, mimeo.

Reis, M. S. and Hodges, C. S. (1975). Status of forest diseases and insects in Latin America. Second FAO World Technical Consultation on Forest Diseases and Insects.

Ram Reddy, M. A. and Singh, P. (1975). Diseases and insect pests of fast-growing trees for developing countries—softwoods. Second FAO World Technical Consultation on Diseases and Insects. New Delhi. 7–12 April 1975. FAO/IUFRO/DI/75/5-0.

Ruthenberg, H. (1971). *Farming systems in the tropics.* Clarendon Press, Oxford.

Sanchez, P. A. (1973). Review of soils research in Tropical Latin America. *N. C. Agri. Exp. Stn. Tech. Bull.* **219**.

Smith, R. K. (1975). Status of insects and diseases in the Americas. Second FAO World Technical Consultation on Forest Diseases and Insects. New Delhi, 7–12 April. FAO/IUFRO/DI/75/2-0 (b).

Tagudar, E. T. (1974). Development of industrial plantations inside Paper Industries Corporation of the Philippines. *Proceedings of the Forest Research Symposium of Industrial Forest Plantations. Manila, June 26, 1974.*

Watson, G. A. (1973). Soil and plant nutrient studies in rubber cultivation. FAO/IUFRO/F/73/24.

Wilson, R. M. C. (1965). Infestation of *Pinus caribaea* by the termite *Coptotermes niger* Snyder. Proc. XII International Congress Entomol., London, 1964.

8

Geothermal energy

UNITED STATES NATIONAL ACADEMY OF SCIENCES

Geothermal resources have been known since ancient times when they were widely utilized to support establishments for therapeutic hot bathing. For hundreds of years this was their only use, particularly in Europe, where cities grew up as spas based upon the therapeutic use of hot springs. At the beginning of the twentieth century, a new application of geothermal energy was found at Larderello, in Italy, where geothermal steam was used for the generation of electricity.

Exploitable geothermal resources are most likely to exist in those parts of the world that have experienced geologically recent volcanism (in the past million years), though they may exist in other areas also. Known geothermal areas include the circum-Pacific 'circle of fire', which is a region of active earthquakes and volcanoes. This comprises the western part of South America and the Andes, most of Central America, large parts of the western United States and the Rocky Mountains, the Aleutian Islands, the Kamchatka peninsula, Japan, Taiwan, Indonesia, the Phillipines, New Zealand, and many South Pacific Islands. A large part of East Africa, associated with the Rift Valley System, also has geothermal activity in Ethiopia, Kenya, Uganda, Tanzania, and Zaire. In Asia and Europe hot springs extend from Nepal, India, Afghanistan, Iran, and Turkey to Greece and Italy.

Many other countries and geological provinces possess geothermal resources, although they are devoid of hot springs or other evidence of hot water at depth. For example, it has been estimated that as much as one-third of the Soviet Union is underlain by exploitable geothermal energy.

Geothermal energy is the natural heat contained within the earth. Temperatures in the earth increase with depth. At a depth of 20 km the temperature is close to 750 °C. However, most of this heat is too deeply buried to be exploited. The depth from which heat may be extracted economically is unlikely to exceed 10 km; even in this outer 10 km most natural geothermal heat cannot easily be extracted and put to practical use. Geothermal energy does, however, have economic significance where the hot rock at depth is fractured or has pore spaces that permit water or steam to circulate and carry heat from the rock to the surface if a natural channel exists or if a geothermal well is drilled. It has been proposed that in order to exploit the heat contained in rocks that are not penetrated by fractures or pore spaces, fractures could be induced artificially, using explosives or hydraulic fracturing techniques. These proposals are now under active practical investigation in the United States, but it seems unlikely that this technology will be available for practical use in the near future.

From *Energy for Rural Development* (NAS 1976), pp. 193–200. Reprinted by permission of the National Academy of Sciences, Washington DC.

Past and current uses

The main uses of geothermal energy have been to generate electricity and to heat buildings and greenhouses. Geothermal energy is used for space heating and in greenhouses in Iceland, Hungary, the Soviet Union, and the United States. It is used for air-conditioning buildings, product-processing in a paper-pulp plant in New Zealand, drying diatomite in Iceland, recovering salt from sea water in Japan, and for heating soil for agriculture in Israel. Some chemical products may be associated with geothermal energy utilization, such as the production of dry ice from geothermal carbon dioxide in the United States, the production of borax associated with geothermal steam in Italy, and the production of calcium chloride from geothermal brines in the Imperial Valley, California.

Applications of current technology to exploit geothermal sources are relatively simple or complex, depending on the temperature of the source—hot water sources that are below the normal boiling point, or sources of steam or superheated water.

Applications involving water at a temperature below the boiling point—in general, those using water for heating or bathing—do not involve a complex technology. All that is required is an ability to dig shallow wells, to lift water through small vertical distances, and to construct channels or pipes to conduct water to the point of use. When applied on a small scale where hot springs occur naturally, this type of thermal energy use can be had at virtually zero cost. There are few locations in the world, however, where opportunities for this type of development occur that have not already been exploited.

The development of geothermal resources in other circumstances (where high-temperature water and steam are required or where the resource lies at a considerable depth) presents special problems in technology and finance.

Geothermal resources have attracted considerable interest among energy users in the recent past as a possible substitute for oil in the generation of electricity and heat.

In many places in the world, there is high probability of finding hot water for space heating and process heating. High-temperature geothermal water and steam have been exploited in countries such as Iceland, Italy, Indonesia, Japan, the Philippines, South America, the western United States, and Central America, where volcanic activity has occurred within the geologically recent past. In general, high-temperature geothermal water and steam are suitable for electricity production at delivered costs that are significantly lower than those for electricity produced from fuel oil at current prices. Plant requirements are similar to those of standard thermal power stations, with the difference being that neither boiler nor fuel is required to produce the steam. The capital cost of a geothermal electricity-generating plant, therefore, is lower than that of a fossil-fuelled thermal plant, and there are, of course, no fuel costs. There is, however, an element of financial risk and expense in exploring and drilling for water and steam, since it cannot be guaranteed that they will be found in adequate quantity and quality for electricity generation. This must be considered part of the total cost of production.

Some high-temperature geothermal water contains dissolved mineral salts that, when present in high concentration, make it difficult to discard necessarily substantial quantities of geothermal water without causing unacceptable pollution of surface or ground water. Disposal by channel to the sea has been adopted in the Ahuachapan Field in El Salvador, where alternative reinjection beneath the surface has also been tested. Apart from being an environmental problem, this is also a cost item.

Geothermal exploration makes use of advanced technology; geothermal drilling requires the use of equipment and techniques similar to those in use in the oil and gas industry, though it requires the use of drilling personnel with geothermal experience. It follows, therefore, that there is a minimum scale of activity and investment of risk capital that is required if geothermal exploration is to be carried out with good prospects of success. Exploration that is economically and technically justified normally must be undertaken where there is a requirement for electricity production of several megawatts or several tens of megawatts. When the requirement for electricity is in the kilowatt range—as, for example, in some rural applications—geothermal sources will not be economically viable unless steam-production costs can be shared among several communities.

Exploration

Exploration and prospecting are field activities that must be carried out before drilling if the risk of unproductive drilling is to be minimized. Exploration for geothermal resources in many countries is likely to take place in at least two phases: an initial phase of reconnaissance, and a second phase of more-detailed investigations and possibly exploratory drilling.

Surveys commonly undertaken as part of the reconnaissance phase include: (a) airborne infrared scanning surveys, in situations where little information on the location of hot springs is available; (b) regional studies of the hydrogeochemistry of known hot springs and associated cold-water springs; and (c) studies of the regional geology, particularly of the principal tectonic features and the relation of these to known hydrothermal activity.

A variety of surveys is undertaken during the second phase of investigation. Detailed hydrogeochemical investigations of the prospect area are conducted to locate and evaluate those anomalies in mineral or gas content that may be related to the existence of hot water or steam beneath the surface. Geophysical surveys—most commonly electrical resistivity surveys—are used to determine the sites of the initial 'wild-cat' or exploration wells. Exploration experience indicates that steam-producing areas are commonly associated with indications of low electrical resistivity at a depth of several hundred metres beneath the surface. Other geophysical exploration techniques, such as micro-earthquake or ground-noise surveys, are still in the process of evaluation. Still others, such as seismic reflection surveys and gravity surveys, may be useful where previous experience indicates an association of the geothermal resource with a structural feature exhibiting a contrast in seismic velocity or in density.

The cost of geothermal reconnaisance surveys ranges between several cents and several dollars per square kilometre; the actual cost depends on whether airborne infrared, hydrochemical, and reconnaissance geological surveys are all carried out and whether the survey covers all potentially productive areas. Costs can be minimized in the case of rural projects if financial considerations require that some limit be set to the distance over which any electricity developed may be transmitted. If this distance is, say, 50 km, then the reconnaissance can be limited to an area within a 50-km radius of the communities to be served.

Detailed geophysical and geochemical surveys each may cost up to \$1000–\$2000 per day. Typical expenditures for detailed investigations of a prospect several tens of square kilometres in area may amount to \$100000.

Availability of turbo-generating equipment

Steam turbines in sizes suitable for use in rural geothermal applications are readily available. Single-stage back-pressure turbines are available in power ranges up to 400 kW and small turbines with two or three stages, usable as back-pressure or as condensing machines, are available in power ranges up to 4 or 5 MW.

A geothermal plant using a condensing turbo-generator of 30-MW capacity was commissioned in El Salvador in 1975.

Installed costs, estimated at \$257/kW in 1972, actually were approximately \$500/kW; however, almost one-half of this figure represents the cost of installing the plant for disposal of the geothermal brine produced.

The cost of steam in geothermal electricity generating plants is a function of the ratio of dry wells to productive wells drilled and of the productivity of the wells. If, for example, each well costs \$300000, if four dry wells are drilled for each productive well, if the productive well yields steam equivalent to 5 MW, if the life of the well is 10 years and the interest is 10 per cent, then the cost of steam will be \$0.006/kWh at a load factor of 0.9. Analysis of operating-plant economics indicates that if the life of the generating plant is 25 years and a 10 per cent interest rate is used, then fixed charges, including maintenance, will be \$0.004/kWh and the total generating cost (that is, steam charges plus fixed charges) will be \$0.010/kWh for geothermal-generated electricity when the plant is used for base-load operation (at a load factor of 0.9).

This kind of installation—consisting of a condensing turbo-generator of a few megawatts capacity—would seem to be economically feasible in rural applications only where a number of sizable rural communities cluster around a geothermal field so that electricity generated at a central location near the geothermal field could be distributed to the surrounding communities by relatively short transmission lines. In rural communities the load factor would not usually be 90 per cent; costs in rural applications would, therefore, be higher than \$0.010/kWh, depending on the load factor.

An alternative approach that may be economically feasible where geothermal resources are located in areas with few and relatively small communities, would be to make use of non-condensing turbo-generators. These would minimize capital costs as well as maintenance and operating costs. Communities in such an area might also rely upon some central organization, external to the rural community being served, to provide the steam wells required. This organization could, of course, be financed either from public funds or from private venture capital.

Geothermal wells drilled in such scattered rural areas would be more expensive than wells drilled within a geothermal field. If the cost per well in a rural area is, therefore, taken to be \$300000, the steam produced is equivalent to 2 MW, and other factors are the same as those given above, then the cost of steam will be \$0.015/kWh. If, as a reasonable approximation, we take the installed cost of a rural non-condensing generating plant at 50 per cent of a condensing turbo-generator, then fixed charges will be roughly \$0.002/kWh and the total cost of electricity \$0.017/kWh if the load factor is 0.9. This cost is still significantly lower than the cost of electricity generated using oil-fired thermal or diesel generators that would range from \$0.02/kWh to much higher values in a rural area in a developing country, but two factors must be considered. First, the costs depend on the actual costs of fuel transport and maintenance. The additional costs that may be involved in transporting the fuel from the port to the point of use in a rural area in a developing country may result in very high fuel costs at the point of use. Second, at lower load factors the cost would rise in inverse proportion to the load factor; for example, in rural areas and in small communities where the main use of electricity is for lighting, load factors may be in the range of 0.2–0.5.

Direct applications for heating

Lower-temperature geothermal water resources that are less suitable for electricity production are highly suitable for many applications requiring thermal energy, such as district heating and greenhouse heating. Such resources are found not only in volcanic areas, but also in areas with thick accumulations of permeable sediments, for example, the Gulf of Mexico in the United States, and the Paris Basin and the

Hungarian Basin in Europe, all of which are areas without recent volcanic activity. Geothermal water is already in use in district-heating and greenhouse-heating applications in Iceland, Hungary, Japan, New Zealand, and the Soviet Union, and on a somewhat smaller scale in the United States, France, Czechoslovakia, and Romania.

In rural areas, the use of low-temperature geothermal water as a source of heat in agricultural applications appears to be promising in those developing countries with a cold season that ordinarily prevents crop production and processing. Experiments are taking place in Israel, for example.

The cost of thermal energy from geothermal wells producing water below the boiling point at atmospheric pressure depends upon such factors as seasonal variation in demand and the actual temperatures of the water before and after use, as well as upon the productivity of the wells. Representative costs in Europe fall within the range of $1 to $5/Gcal, which is about one-half to one-eighth the cost of such thermal energy at current (1976) local prices for imported oil. Furthermore, low-temperature geothermal waters are less commonly highly charged with mineral salts and therefore present fewer problems of disposal of waste water. The deposition of carbonate scale in pipes carrying low-temperature geothermal water has occurred in some cases, but control measures have proved effective in dealing with the problem.

In situations where information on the presence of geothermal waters is available as a by-product of the search for oil and gas, the element of financial risk is largely absent from subsequent geothermal development. This will occur where low-temperature geothermal waters occur in deep sedimentary basins that have been investigated for the presence of petroleum.

Current research and development

Geothermal energy can be used in many places in the world where power requirements are small. This is true provided adequate equipment is available for utilizing hot water/steam mixtures directly from one or two hot-water wells of moderate size capable of producing mixtures of steam and hot water. However, conventional steam/water separators and steam turbines of the type available at present may not function efficiently when used in conjunction with geothermal water that deposits mineral scale, because of the mechanical and thermal problems caused by these deposits. During the past 3 years, engineering tests have been made on new equipment that has been proposed as a possible way to overcome these problems.* Tests performed in Mexico on brine from a well at the Cerro Prieto field, using a helical rotary screw expander as a prime mover, demonstrated that this device can operate with such brines and produce power at reasonable efficiencies. These results have been supplemented by further tests, with larger units, using brine from a well in the East Mesa field of the Imperial Valley, California.

Those countries that have not yet begun to evaluate or develop their geothermal-resource potential may be assisted in determining policy if they take the following points into consideration:

(1) base-load electricity produced from high-temperature geothermal resources is likely to be substantially cheaper than electricity produced at solid-fuel-fired or oil-fired thermal generating stations, considering the present world prices of oil and coal;

(2) most countries having geologically recent volcanic activity are likely to possess high-temperature geothermal resources;

*McKay, R. A. and Sprankle, R. S. (1974). Helical rotary screw expander power system. In *Proceedings of the Conference on Research for the Development of Geothermal Energy Resources, Pasadena, California, 23–25 September*, pp. 301–7. California Institute of Technology, Jet Propulsion Laboratory, Pasadena.

(3) exceptionally great thicknesses of sediment and an exceptionally high regional heat flux are not necessary for these geothermal resources to be exploitable economically;
(4) exploration and development of high-temperature geothermal resources involve an element of financial risk;
(5) low-temperature geothermal sources can be developed to satisfy a need for heating in winter, for example, and thus substitute for oil or coal; and
(6) in many locations, where petroleum exploration has taken place, low-temperature geothermal resources can be developed at less financial risk.

9

Nuclear energy for the Third World

KLAUS GOTTSTEIN

Large amounts of capital have been invested in the construction of nuclear power stations by nuclear industries in the industrially developed countries. For this capital expenditure to be amortized a minimum number of reactor units must find a market each year. Because of limited domestic markets, export markets must be found for a certain share of the total number of units produced. However, the only potential importers are the United States and the developing countries. This is because the major West European countries generating nuclear power—the Federal Republic of Germany, the United Kingdom, France, Italy, Sweden, Switzerland, and Belgium, as well as Japan—prefer to purchase products from their own national firms. An open market in this field, therefore, exists only in a small part of Western Europe, as in Spain. The United States economy, to be sure, offers conditions of free competition; but in actual practice it is hardly possible to compete with US industry in her own territory.

There is a rapidly growing demand for nuclear energy from the developing countries. Out of the 514 nuclear power stations in operation, under construction, or contracted for by mid-1975 on a world-wide scale, seven are in South and Central America and twenty-five in Asian countries, excluding Japan and the Soviet Union.* Additional orders have been placed by Iran and Korea, and the German industry has successfully concluded a major export contract with Brazil.

The large order Brazil placed with the German nuclear industry in 1975 has caused much public discussion. The volume itself was significant; the agreement called for construction of eight 1300-megawatt nuclear power stations and the joint mining and processing of uranium ore. In addition, it provided for the construction of installations for uranium enrichment, production of fuel elements, and reprocessing of the spent fuel. Thus, under the terms of the agreement, an entire nuclear fuel cycle is to be located on Brazilian soil, subject to the safeguards system of the International Atomic Energy Agency (IAEA) in Vienna.

Fuel processing yields plutonium, which can be used as an explosive. And uranium enrichment plants for the production of fuel for civilian power stations can in principle be modified, with more or less technical effort, to produce material highly enriched in uranium-235, which is also suitable as an explosive. The purpose of IAEA controls is to discover any such illicit use and to

**Jahrbuch der Atomwitschaft 1976*, Handelsblatt GmbH. Verlag für Wirtschaftsinformation, Düsseldorf-Frankfurt, Seite B 8.

English translation (by Suzanna Libish) first published in *Bulletin of the Atomic Scientists*, Vol. 33, No. 6 (June 1977), pp. 44–8.
Original German version first published in *Physikalische Blätter*, Vol. 32 (November 1976), pp. 481 ff.

prevent it. Incidentally, official spokesmen for the United States, particularly former Secretary of State Henry Kissinger, have expressed satisfaction at the fact that the German–Brazilian agreement provides for safeguard regulations which are particularly comprehensive and far-reaching.

The anxieties still voiced in the United States on this score do not, as it is sometimes assumed, stem from the competitive interests of American industry. American firms were certainly ready to get into business with Brazil and, if anything, blame the Administration for not having given them adequate support in the negotiations. In the main, the criticisms and concern regarding the consequences of the German–Brazilian agreement come from certain groups in Congress, in the press, and from academics, who have used this case for general reflections on the future spread of nuclear energy over the globe and the conditions in which this process will develop.

Governments, of course, are also having second thoughts. The recent confidential London talks of the supplier nations, in which the Soviet Union was also a participant, served to exchange and clarify ideas regarding nuclear export policy.

Nuclear exports and non-proliferation

What is the nature of the problems? On the one hand, various countries want to export or import nuclear technology. On the other, there is the desire not to further the proliferation of nuclear weapons. Regarding this latter point the governments of the United States and of the Soviet Union, and the governments of most other countries as well, are in agreement. The Non-Proliferation Treaty (NPT) which is intended to prevent the spread of nuclear weapons has so far been ratified by about two-thirds of all the states of the world. The views of General Pierre M. Gallois, a former adviser to General de Gaulle, that the world would only be safe when *all* states possessed nuclear weapons, will hardly find any influential supporters today, at any rate not in the industrially developed countries.

Nonetheless, caution is required. There are states whose existence is at stake and whose governments may feel that the possession of atomic weapons might enhance their chances of survival. Other governments might be motivated to 'go nuclear' simply because of a desire for more security and prestige. In this regard one must reckon with the eventuality of emotionally inspired and scarcely calculable decisions, even if some comfort may be derived from the fact that the number of nuclear nations has only been increased by one during the past decade. There must be reasons against joining the nuclear club. However, the possibility of countries possessing untested nuclear weapons cannot be disregarded.

The question then is how can the readiness of countries willing to forgo membership in the nuclear club be reinforced?

The policy advocated and pursued by most of the supplier nations (France being the exception) is based on the NPT and involves:

(a) getting more and more countries to ratify the NPT in the hope that in time this will give rise to a sense of concerted action which will make it increasingly difficult to remain a 'non-party' to the Treaty,
(b) agreements regarding export controls, which obviously require a considerable measure of consensus among the suppliers, and
(c) providing material incentives for observation of the NPT, for example, through agreements on economic and and technological co-operation.

The question of controls is complex. The NPT provides that its signatories—in so far as they are not themselves nuclear-weapons powers—will submit all their nuclear installations to IAEA safeguards, and will only make nuclear facilities available to other countries that are ready to place them under the safeguards administered by the IAEA. (This, by the way, applies also to Brazil, although Brazil has not as yet joined the NPT.)

But can one and should one rely on the IAEA safeguards?

The IAEA is a service agency with limited funds and very limited powers. Its task is only to detect a diversion of nuclear materials after it has happened. In this it depends on the co-operation of those running the installations to be controlled. Its work in this field is based on book-keeping about the amounts of plutonium and uranium-235 in circulation, supported by measurements and statistical analyses. In this, errors of measurement and statistical uncertainties have to be taken into account.

Sceptics predict that confidence in IAEA controls will be shaken the day the first country withdraws from the NPT and asks the IAEA inspectors to leave its territory, and when 'serious diplomatic reasons' preclude any action against the country concerned. It is argued, therefore, that agreement should be reached regarding the sort of sanctions to be taken against a country taking this step, prior to any suspicions being raised.

True enough, a country that is not a signatory of the NPT is not acting in violation of any treaty obligations when it manufactures a bomb. And even NPT members can avail themselves of the legal means stipulated by the Treaty to withdraw from it. The NPT provides that a signatory can withdraw from the Treaty with 3 months advance notice if 'it decides that extraordinary events . . . have jeopardized the supreme interests of its country'.

This is why, in the United States in particular, the view has come to prevail that no risks should be taken and that sensitive installations, such as enrichment and reprocessing plants, should not be exported, as a matter of principle, not even to states party to the NPT. This, of course, would create a third under-privileged class of NPT partners.

According to non-proliferation mentality the world is already divided into two camps: those who have the bomb, and those who are not allowed to acquire it. Among the latter group, a ban on exports would set up another distinction: a distinction between those capable of selling the technology required to make the bomb, and those who want to buy the technology but who would be prohibited from acquiring it because they are not held to be 'trustworthy'.

Naturally, this can and will be regarded as discriminatory. Moreover, India has demonstrated that in the long run it is impossible to prevent the dissemination of the technological know-how needed to make a nuclear explosive device.

The advocates of tight controls on nuclear exports, however, view the possible postponement of such dissemination as presenting such advantages that they are prepared to accept the hurt feelings such discrimination will inevitably produce as well as the political drawbacks.

On the other hand, nobody seems to have any clear idea as to how the time so gained could be profitably used. Naturally it is hoped that it might prove possible to use this time to create better international procedures to prevent proliferation and to provide sanctions against infringements of the NPT. But exactly the opposite might also happen. One cannot, out of hand, reject the argument that time is working against us.

Thus, for instance, the technology for laser enrichment now being developed may in the future make it increasingly simple to gain possession of material suitable for making bombs. In that event, perhaps 10 or 20 years from now, the control problem would be even more difficult than it is at present. If that should turn out to be the case, it would be advisable to share nuclear technology while it can still be shared under controlled conditions.

The counter-argument is that the risk of proliferation is a matter of security and not of morality. A cost-benefit analysis would have to show how much discrimination one could still afford. And if hurt feelings cannot be avoided completely, so the argument runs, they can be kept to a minimum if secrecy prevails regarding the export guidelines agreed upon or still to be settled by the supplier countries.

It is argued that publication carries the risk that the critical reaction of the general public in the supplier countries *vis-à-vis* the recipient countries might cause offence among the recipients. The impression that a cartel was being formed could be created. This would lead to tensions and additional confrontation. One would lose all elements of flexibility in the dialogue with the recipient countries. Admittedly, strict secrecy is not really feasible. But it makes a difference whether information regarding export guidelines is officially or unofficially made public.

Naturally there are those who argue that secrecy in this context is a bad thing. In the supplier countries, it can give rise to the suspicion that it is intended to cover up disagreements among the governments concerned. In the recipient countries, it might provoke suspicions that the conditions of the contract offered are less favourable than admissible under the export guidelines.

The United States and the other supplier countries have reached agreement to keep the export of sensitive installations under careful control. But beyond this consensus, the ideas vary about the kind of policy to be pursued in relation to the recipients.

The United States, it would seem, starts from the assumption that nuclear co-operation offers economic benefits, and that the possibilities inherent in international nuclear collaboration—exerting a positive influence and building up a climate of trust—are conducive to reaching a higher level of security against the illicit use of nuclear materials. Hence, the United States has concluded many bilateral agreements on co-operation in the field of nuclear energy.

However, when the question of authorizing the export of sensitive installations arises, the condition that the recipient had signed the NPT, or equivalent assurances, is not considered sufficient by the United States. Usually additional inquiries will be initiated to make certain that an illicit use of the devices and material to be delivered is ruled out. The Americans have shown particular concern about such questions as where the plutonium extracted by the recipient countries is stored, where it can be subjected to supervision, and how to avoid lowering the security threshold as a consequence of competition between supplier firms.

Another case is that of France, which has decided that all future large-scale power stations in that country will be nuclear, and has expanded its industrial capacity to cover all elements in the fuel cycle. France has not acceded to the NPT. Its foreign policy has always emphasized its independence from the superpowers and the equal rights of smaller nations.

At the same time, however, the French government has officially stated that it would do nothing to encourage nuclear-weapons proliferation. In this sense, therefore, French policy will be no different from that of an NPT party.

Thus, France obligates recipients of French-produced nuclear materials and equipment to accept the IAEA safeguards. On the other hand, the French government has no 'hegemonial claims', and its declared goal is not to interfere with the freedom of decision-making on the part of the recipients. But it is said that France would be ready to reconsider its policy in this field should the French government reach the conclusion that European security required reconsideration.

As French official spokesmen have indicated. France's policy has been to persuade potential buyers of nuclear materials and equipment that it makes better economic sense to let France reprocess the spent fuel from the reactors than to operate the reprocessing facilities themselves. However, in those cases where the clients insist on getting reprocessing installations, France is ready—as was the Federal Republic of Germany in the case of Brazil—to supply them, provided the IAEA safeguards are accepted. The latter is the type of agreement concluded between France and Pakistan on the construction of a reprocessing plant. Negotiations with South Korea, which were proceeding along similar lines, were broken off by Korea when the United States and Canada intervened. Korea will now get a reactor from Canada.

The export of Soviet reactors is always combined with complete fuel service. The fuel comes from the Soviet Union; the spent fuel elements return to the Soviet Union, which does not let enrichment and reprocessing pass out of its hands. It seems that the Soviet Union has put pressure on the Arab countries to join the NPT. Libya became a signatory and then got a Soviet reactor. Cuba has not joined the Treaty but did participate in the NPT review conference, thereby indicating its interest.

The positions of the United States and of the Soviet Union coincide in that they take a negative view with regard to the export of enrichment and reprocessing installations, while Germany, and perhaps France, too, are ready to export these facilities subject to appropriate international supervision.* However, Germany, as a signatory of the NPT, holds itself committed to the stringent implementation of its provisions; while France, as a non-party to the Treaty, intends to apply the control measures of the Treaty only voluntarily and at its own discretion.

By the very nature of things the supplier industries of all the Western countries tend toward the German or French position. They favour the position whereby exports are impeded as little as possible but, at the same time, recognize the necessity of effective safeguards and of not allowing the safeguards to be affected by commercial competition. This latter objective could be realized through international agreements or through obligatory standards set by the IAEA. In all of these matters industry proceeds from the assumption that effective and technically functional safeguards are feasible with respect to all elements of the fuel cycle.

Multinational centres

The requirement of effective control of the future flow of increasing quantities of fresh and spent reactor fuel to more and more places all over the world and the wish for undiminished export possibilities on the part of the nuclear industry could in principle be reconciled in two ways:

(1) By increasing the financial and manpower resources of the IAEA as well as by enhancing its powers. The IAEA could thus become an international institution capable of meeting the rising demands the future will bring with respect to effective control and safeguard activities.
(2) By establishing international or regional fuel centres. These would, at least for certain regions or countries, establish a monopoly with respect to enrichment, reprocessing, and storage. The participation of a number of countries in the operation of these centres would provide more adequate guarantees against diversion than would be the case if such facilities were operated by the government alone.

The idea of regional centres has been advocated very strongly, particularly by the United States. In Europe, and also in the Federal Republic of Germany, the predominant reaction is rather sceptical. It seems hard to imagine that precisely in those critical areas where the danger of diversion may be particularly high, and the establishment of such multinational centres therefore particularly desirable, that the parties concerned would show great readiness to engage in such collaboration.

These difficulties notwithstanding, efforts should certainly be made to advance in both directions. For unless this is done, in periods of economic stagnation, pressures to put through major export deals may well prevail over other considerations, without the control capacities such a situation would require having been developed on an adequate scale.

As a matter of fact, efforts are even now

*As of January 1977, there was some indication that the position of the French government had changed in this respect.

being made to get various smaller countries to join in the venture of operating a multinational fuel centre. For these countries, such a project would have the advantage of being more economical. And international centres of this type, which would come under the IAEA safeguards, would make their services available to any country interested. This might for some countries reduce the incentive for setting up indigenous reprocessing facilities.

If these centres could also offer as one of their services the final disposal of radioactive waste, many countries would probably want to avail themselves of this chance of not having themselves to deal with the problem of radioactive waste management and would extend support to the establishment of these centres. The proposal made on various occasions that the IAEA should also assume responsibility for the physical protection of the nuclear fuel centres, is, admittedly, not compatible with the principle of national sovereignty of the host countries concerned. Nonetheless, the IAEA could set certain security standards.

What prospects for the future arise from these considerations? World wide the number of nuclear power stations will increase to more than 500 in a few years time, and presumably will continue to grow. The Third World will participate in this growth. Many developing countries have made it clear that they demand a share in the benefits of these modern technologies simply on the grounds of equity. As one of their spokesmen recently put it, after they had missed the Industrial Revolution, to be caught up in colonial dependency as a result, they certainly do not intend to allow the same thing to happen as far as the atomic age was concerned.

As to the ways and means by which this modern technology is to be deployed, there exists a variety of conceptions, not all of them very clear. Nuclear energy is perceived as an aid to industrialization; as a source of energy for remote areas lacking any other resources; as a technique for desalting seawater; as a precautionary replacement for oil resources, which may be depleted in a few decades, as in the case of Iran; or, even if not stated explicitly, as a way to keep open the option of nuclear deterrence.

(Reprocessing plants, however, should not be regarded solely as a means for acquiring plutonium for military purposes. They also serve as a way to process radioactive wastes, to render them innocuous, and thus constitute an important element in the fuel cycle. Moreover, technological advances in isotope enrichment will presumably make the use of reprocessing plants, as a source of plutonium for nuclear weapons, seem relatively irrelevant in a few decades.)

The economies of the industrial countries are more or less strongly export-oriented and they cannot debar the nuclear field from exports. They compete with each other in the world's markets; but most are members of a common alliance and within this frame are jointly engaged in finding a peaceful new order in their mutual relations and in their relations with the rest of the world.

The problems arising from international commerce in nuclear technologies are hence but part and parcel of a wider problem. This more universal set of problems—the question of what will be the world order in the twenty-first century; how, on the passage to it, will mankind be able to avoid new world catastrophes—is, however, impressively illustrated by all the unresolved problems arising in connection with the use of nuclear energy.

Man has discovered nuclear energy and this discovery is irreversible. If mankind wants to continue, it will have to learn to live with nuclear energy and to master all the potential dangers characterized by such catchwords as fuel cycle, terrorism, and war. This will require new institutions and a new readiness to co-operate. But other developments of our age present similar demands. Nuclear energy is but one particularly momentous example.

A great sense of responsibility and a

readiness to renounce traditional rights of sovereignty will be required for the creation of institutions effective enough for providing the conditions under which mankind can avoid major catastrophes. But this sense of responsibility and the readiness to surrender certain rights, which must become a corollary to the spread of nuclear power as a peaceful source of energy for all countries in the world, is not something that can be demanded unilaterally only from those who, owing to historical developments, were not in a position themselves technologically to gain access to nuclear energy. To the extent that they still lack experience in this field, they will only be able to gain it on the basis of international co-operation.

Technological superiority does not imply moral superiority. The question posed to the so-called recipient countries, regarding their sense of responsibility and their good faith, can well be addressed to the supplier countries: how responsible and how reliable, from the point of view of the recipients, are, and will be, the supplier nations if we also take a period of a decade or more into consideration? In the field of nuclear energy, as in other fields, the industrially developed countries should make use of their technological lead with wisdom and assist the vast, materially much poorer, majority of mankind with the solution of its problems. This implies drawing attention to potential dangers and to possibilities of avoiding them.

Nuclear energy offers a great chance. In the long range it promises to satisfy human needs for energy and thereby also for food to such an extent that perhaps this may induce the inhabitants of our planet to avail themselves of this potential, to use it on a large scale, and to create the institutions essential for precluding harmful side effects. In that event nuclear energy might provide the momentum for the world to give itself something like a working constitution, a *modus vivendi* which would prevent major wars. That the path to this end is a long and dangerous one is amply indicated by the unresolved problems and the controversial views which we have sought to describe here.

III China

Kao-ching Thermal Power Station near Peking. This power plant is typical of the large relatively modern thermal stations in China: it has six 100 MW units and it burns a good quality bituminous coal from Shansi.

Peasants terracing a hillside in the Loess Region of Shansi. Heavy huma labor, unaided by any mechanization is still a key energy input throughout the Chinese countryside.

Each country is, naturally, unique, but most smaller nations can be loosely grouped on the basis of numerous socio-economic and resource-endowment similarities. China stands truly alone: the planet's most populous nation, nearly a quarter of mankind; a continent, rather than a country in terms of environmental diversity; the world's largest poor developing nation with many attributes of a superpower.

The uniqueness of China is also mirrored in her energetics. In aggregate global terms, the country is now the fourth largest producer of primary energy and its third largest consumer; annual coal output in excess of half a billion tons is surpassed only by the USSR and the USA; crude oil recovery has been expanding at a very fast pace and natural gas potential is undoubtedly quite large. Yet in per capita terms the figures are decidedly those of a poor developing nation: average annual consumption per capita of primary energy is only around 500 kilograms of coal equivalent; installed capacity of China's thermal and hydro power plants amounts to mere 50 watts per head; and a large part of the rural population continues to live almost completely outside the reach of modern fuels and electricity.

China's energy system is thus an intricate mixture of the traditional and the modern, of advanced technologies and inefficient practices and of large and small enterprises. The reliance on appropriate small-scale energy technologies in rural areas is particularly notable: nearly half of China's huge coal output now originates in small local mines, more than 87000 small hydro stations generate one-third of the country's hydro-electricity, and biogas production is spreading fast especially in the warm areas of the south and the south-west. Coal and electricity from small locally built and managed enterprises serve as inputs into small rural industries, above all iron and steel making, and also production of fertilizer and of cement.

Small-scale technologies will undoubtedly retain much of their importance, but the post-Mao leadership—aiming ambitiously to modernize the country and elevate its economy to the world's advanced levels by the end of this century—intends to expand greatly large coal-mining centres, to open up new huge oilfields, and to construct increasingly bigger thermal and hydro power plants.

V. Smil ('China's energetics: a system analysis') surveys all of these various aspects of the current Chinese energy scene—ranging from solar flow, primary plant production, food consumption, and the usage of traditional fuels (firewood and crop residues) to widespread application of small-scale processes (small coal-mines, rural hydrostations, biogas generation), appraisal of fossil-fuel resources and survey of sectoral energy uses. In conclusion he points out the existing inefficiencies of China's industrial energy conversions and evaluates the future needs of the country's massive agricultural modernization effort.

A key task in modernizing China's economy is a substantial increase of power generation. W. Clarke of the US Department of Commerce ('China's electric power industry') offers a systematic look at the weaknesses, technological levels, plans, and likely future performance of the country's power-generating industry. He argues that the Chinese will have to resort to large-scale imports of generating technology to meet the rising demand and that they will have to engage in massive investment, construction, and research programmes to expand their coal output, improve rail transportation, reduce plant-building times, develop high voltage systems, and upgrade the plant equipment if they are to support the planned economy growth rates with adequate flows of electrical energy.

China's new 8-year (1978–85) modernization plan calls for annual growth rates of 4–5 per cent in agriculture and in excess of 10 per cent in industry. The plan mentions specifically the construction of 120 important projects, including 10 iron and steel complexes, 9 non-ferrous metal conglomerates, 8 large mines, 10 oil and gas fields, 30 power stations, 6 new trunk railways, and 5 key ports. This all will require prodigious amounts of energy in relatively short time and, consequently, to watch the country's actual performance will be one of the most intriguing tasks for any student of the international energy scene. If the new leadership is able to assure the political stability and if it further expands the acquisition of advanced foreign technology the odds for success seem considerable.

Energy in China: selected readings

Carin, R. (1969). *Power industry in Communist China.* Union Research Institute, Hong Kong.

Chu-yuan Cheng (1976). *China's petroleum industry.* Praeger, New York.

Clarke, W. W. (1978). China's electric power industry. In Joint Economic Committee: *Chinese economy post-Mao.* US Government Printing Office, Washington, DC.

Ikonnikov, A. B. (1975). *Mineral resources of China.* Geological Society of America, Boulder, Co.

Ling, H. C. (1975). *The Petroleum industry of the People's Republic of China.* Stanford University Press, Ca.

Meyerhoff, A. A. and Williams, J.-O. (1976). Petroleum geology and industry of the People's Republic of China. *CCOP Technical Bulletin* **10**, 103–212.

National Council for US–China Trade (1976). *China's petroleum industry.* National Council for US–China Trade, Washington, DC.

Smil, V. (1976). *China's energy achievements, problems, prospects.* Praeger, New York.

—— (1978). China's energetics: a system analysis. In Joint Economic Committee: *Chinese economy post-Mao*, pp. 323–369. US Government Printing Office, Washington, DC.

—— and Woodard, K. (1977). Perspectives on energy in the People's Republic of China. In J. M. Hollander, M. K. Simmons, and D. O. Wood (eds.), *Annual Review of Energy* **2** 307–42.

US Central Intelligence Agency (1976). *China: The coal industry.* CIA, Washington, DC.

—— (1977). *China: oil production prospects.* CIA, Washington, DC.

—— (1977). Energy balance projections for the People's Republic of China, 1975–1985. In Congressional Research Service: *Project Interdependence: US and world energy outlook through 1990*, pp. 858–77. US Government Printing Office, Washington, DC.

Wang, K. P. (1975). *The People's Republic of China: a new industrial power with a strong mineral base.* US Government Printing Office, Washington, DC.

Williams, B. A. (1975). The Chinese petroleum industry: growth and prospects. In Joint Economic Committee: *China: a reassessment of the economy*, pp. 225–63. US Government Printing Office, Washington, DC.

Williams, J.-O. (1975). China's off-shore oil: application of a framework for evaluating oil and gas potentials under uncertainty. Doctoral thesis, Department of Ocean Engineering, Massachusetts Institute of Technology, Cambridge, Mass.

Woodard, K. (1978). *The international energy policies of the People's Republic of China.* Stanford University Press, Ca.

Yuan-li Wu with Ling, H. C. (1963). *Economic development and the use of energy resources in Communist China.* Praeger, New York.

10

China's energetics: a system analysis

VACLAV SMIL

Introduction

Chinese energetics presents a thoroughly intriguing, highly complex, and, in not a few aspects, continuously puzzling case. In absolute terms, the country's fossil fuel and hydro-power resources rank with—or even above—those of the United States and the Soviet Union. Globally, China has risen to the fourth place in primary energy production (following the United States, the Soviet Union, and Saudi Arabia) and to the third place in consumption (behind the two super-powers) and, in the process, has become not only self-sufficient but also a minor fuel exporter. And yet, at the same time, China's energetics is definitely that of a rather poor, developing country where large segments of rural population still depend on plant fuels and animate power and whose modern energy consumption per capita ranks close to the one-hundredth place in the global array of some 175 countries and territories.

The future seems no less ambiguous. While the probabilities for retaining the energy self-sufficiency and expanding the crude oil and coal exports are very high throughout the 1980s, the potential fuel and electricity requirements for the modernization of the Chinese economy are immense and it seems quite improbable that they could be filled satisfactorily with the sole reliance on domestic technology. And even under circumstances favouring a very fast expansion, the country's energy consumption per capita by the year 2000 would equal the levels attained by most of the Western societies already during the first two or three decades of this century.

Although these developments and prospects have recently attracted a good deal of research attention,[1] their assessment remains a rather difficult and, repeatedly, very frustrating task for any energy analyst familiar with the work and data base available for other major consuming nations. The amount of information completely missing in the Chinese case is staggering and much of what is accessible is unpredictably fragmentary and, too often, of dubious quality. What follows, then, is just the best attempt—under rather restrictive circumstances—to apply the approaches of general system analysis to the energetics of the world's most populous nation.

Rural energy flows

One of the major shortcomings of most national energy studies is, as R. H. Socolow puts it, that 'solar energy doesn't count'.[2] Attention is focused on fossil fuels and solar energy other than as hydroelectricity is not included in the analysis. While always

From *Chinese Economy Post-Mao*, A Compendium of Papers Submitted to the Joint Economic Committee, Congress of the United States, (US Government Printing Office, New York, 1978), pp. 323–69.

regrettable, the omission is not critical for the Western industrialized nations, or for Japan, with their heavy dependence on oil, coal, and natural gas; for developing countries, however, it represents a serious error. Most of the population in these countries is rural, and until fairly recently it has been either completely separated from, or only marginally involved in, the flows of modern commercial fuels and electricity.

China, with four-fifths of its vast population living in the countryside, is the foremost example of a nation where most of the people are still relying on solar energy to produce, via photosynthesis, not only their food and feed for the animals—but also the necessary fuel and raw materials. For a better appreciation of China's solar energetics I have attempted to quantify all the essential sources, conversions, and uses of energy in the country's rural areas during 1 year.[3] They are systematically discussed below and a simplified flow graph is shown in Fig. 10.1.

Insolation and phytomass production

Average annual solar radiation with cloudless sky would range between 160 kcal per cm^2 in the northernmost Heilungkiang to 235 kcal per cm^2 in Hainan and China would receive approximately 20×10^{18} kcal of energy each year.[4] Actual duration of sunshine is strongly reduced by frequent heavy cloudiness accompanying summer cyclonic flows over much of the eastern half of the country and intensity of insolation is appreciably attenuated during late winter and spring months by large quantities of sand and dust swept up from the arid northern regions by continental anticyclonic winds. Solar energy received at the surface is thus only between 100 and 140 kcal per cm^2 per year for most of China, and the annual total does not exceed 11.5×10^{18} kcal.

More than half of this radiation is either reflected or absorbed and reradiated by barren or only sparsely vegetated surfaces: mountain and plateau tundra, stone and sand deserts, and low-productivity shortgrass steppes cover about 56 per cent of China's territory—mostly in Sinkiang, Tibet, Tsinghai, Kansu, and Inner Mongolia—and their combined net primary production is less than 4×10^{15} kcal of plant mass annually. Tibetan plateau meadows and temperate grasslands of the north and the north-west occupy 20 per cent of the total area and produce each year about 4×10^{15} kcal of phytomass. Forests, concentrated above all in Heilungkiang and in the south and the south-west, account for only less than 12 per cent of the land, and their total productivity—just over 4×10^{15} kcal—is actually smaller than that of the grasslands (Table 10.1).

While the above plant productivity figures are merely approximation of the proper order of magnitude, net energy conversion of agricultural crops, which cover nearly 11.5 per cent of China's land, can be established more reliably by accounting for all principal harvested plants and then increasing these totals by appropriate amounts of by-products and unharvested roots. In 1974, China's harvest reached approximately 250 million tonnes (Mt) of dry matter in food and industrial crops and nearly twice that amount in crop residues for a total of 3×10^{15} kcal; roots increase the total by another 20 per cent. Net primary production of all of China's ecosystems is thus around 15×10^{15} kcal, which means that approximately 0.14 per cent of solar energy reaching the surface is being converted annually by autotrophs into new plant mass.[5]

Domestic animals

Domestic animals provide several very important links in a predominantly solar economy: they function well on light energy, feeding mostly on plant tissues unsuitable for human consumption—grasses, crop by-products, and crop processing residues—supplemented with only minor amounts of grain;[6] they deliver the essential power for many farm tasks (fieldwork, irrigation, food processing, transportation); they recycle the valuable nutrients by their often copious

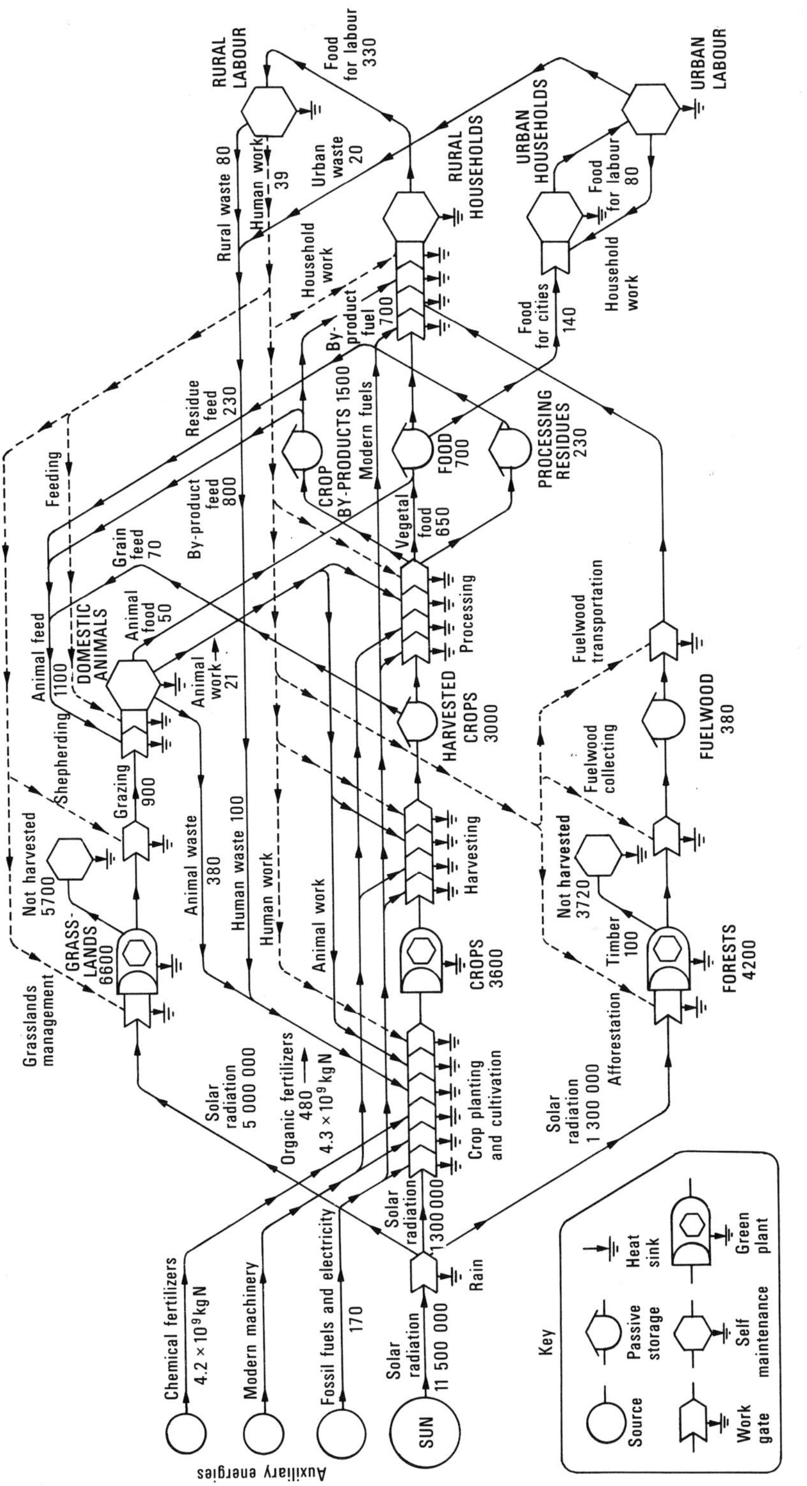

Fig. 10.1. Rural energy flows in China in 1974. All figures, except those for nitrogen fertilizers, are in trillions (10^{12}) kcal.

Table 10.1. Primary productivity of China's major vegetation units

Vegetation unit	Net primary productivity: Area (10^3 km^2)	Average ($g/m^2/year$)	Total production (10^6 tons)	Annual energy fixation: Mean caloric value (kcal/g)	Average (10^3 kcal) m^2/year	Total (10^{15} kcal)
Forest	1100		935			4.18
Boreal forest	660	500	330	4.8	2.4	1.58
Temperate mixed forest	110	1000	110	4.7	4.7	0.52
Raingreen forest	330	1500	495	4.2	6.3	2.08
Grassland	4150		1645			6.58
Shortgrass steppes	2150	300	645	4.0	1.2	2.58
Temperate grassland	2000	500	1000	4.0	2.0	4.00
Tundra	2150	100	215	4.0	0.4	0.86
Desert	1070	70	75	4.5	0.3	0.34
Cultivated land	1090	810	880	4.1	3.3	3.60
Total for China	9560		3750			15.56

and, when mostly stall- or pen-fed, conveniently concentrated manure production; and finally, they are a critical source of protein (in meat, entrails, and milk) and fat (lard, butter, tallow) for the population.

More than four-fifths of the total feed energy for China's domestic animals—over 100 million of large beasts, some 130 million of sheep and goats, about a quarter billion of pigs, and nearly 1.3 billion of chickens, ducks, and geese—is supplied by roughages provided by grazing, collection of field weeds, and a variety of crop by-products (millet, rice, and oat straw and legume and potato vines are fed most widely). Concentrates come predominantly as milling and extraction residues (chaffs, brans, oilseed cakes, sugar refining wastes) and, to a smaller degree, from direct feeding of grains (barley, corn millet, oats), legumes and potatoes (mainly the sweet ones). The total energy equivalent of animal feed amounted to some 2×10^{15} kcal in 1974 and nearly 40 per cent of it was consumed by large domestic animals—cattle, water buffaloes horses, asses, and mules—which are still an indispensable workforce in China's agriculture: an evaluation of animal labour shows that the draught beasts performed the equivalent of some 20×10^{12} kcal of useful work in 1974 (Table 10.2).

No less important is the animals'

Table 10.2. Useful work performed by China's draught animals in 1974

Animals	Average weight (kilograms)	Average draught (kilograms)	Average speed of work (metres per second)	Average horsepower	Hours worked per year	Total numbers in 1974 (10^6)	Useful work performed in 1974 (10^{12} kcal)
Cattle	385	39	0.70	0.36	1000	63.5	9.7
Buffaloes	500	50	0.70	0.46	1200	30.0	7.0
Asses	350	35	0.70	0.32	1100	11.7	1.7
Horses	350	53	1.00	0.70	1100	7.0	2.3
Mules	350	53	0.95	0.66	1100	1.6	0.5
Total						113.8	21.2

Table 10.3. Availability of food energy in China in 1974

	Total food (million tonnes)	*Total energy (10^{12} kcal)*	*Share (per cent)*
Vegetal foods	302.6	650.0	92.9
Cereal products	138.7	492.0	70.3
Tubers	69.4	64.5	9.2
Legumes	14.1	48.5	6.9
Other vegetal foods	80.4	45.0	6.5
Animal foods	27.4	50.0	7.1
Meat, poultry, and fish	19.6	35.5	5.1
Other animal foods	7.8	14.5	2.0
Total	330.0	700.0	100.0

contribution to maintain the fertility, as well as to improve the tilth, of the country's soil. China's domestic animals produce annually about 1.1 billion tonnes (Bt) of manure (approximately 200 Mt of dry solids) and nearly two-thirds of this huge total are carefully gathered, fermented, and returned to the fields.

Human energetics

Conversion of solar radiation by edible plants is, naturally, the main source of food energy for China's large population. Construction of a national food balance sheet indicates that out of the total 1974 harvest of approximately 470 Mt (field weight) of food crops no more than 65 per cent became actually available for human consumption: processing (milling, oil and sugar extraction) and storage wastes, seed and feed account for the difference. Rice, wheat, corn, sweet potatoes, and millets are by far the most important sources of calories providing some four-fifths of plant food energy available in China; legumes, vegetables, and vegetal oil are also indispensable, while the contribution of animal foods to national consumption total was only about 7 per cent in 1974 (Table 10.3).

Depending on the mid-1974 population total used—862 million people according to Leo A. Orleans and 917.25 million people estimated by John S. Aird—the average daily consumption per capita would be no less than 2090 kcal and as much as 2225 kcal.[7] These figures alone are insufficient to evaluate the country's food energy status: for this food consumption must be compared with energy needs which are the function of age, sex, weight, and physical activity.

Precise recent information is not available for any of these variables but reasonable estimates can be made to calculate the likely energy requirements. Age–sex distributions have been computed by John S. Aird, typical Chinese weights can be derived by reducing the Harvard–Iowa age–weight table values by about 10 per cent, and the standard calculations can be done assuming moderately active populations at a given age and weight. These assumptions result in the nationwide energy needs of about 710×10^{12} kcal (Table 10.4), and would indicate a rough balance between the requirements and availability.

However, the standard calculations undoubtedly underestimate the energy needed by the rural labour force. Much of the Chinese agriculture is still traditional and most of its labour tasks—ploughing, hoeing, watering, weeding, mowing, loading—belong to the heavy, rather than moderate, energy expenditure category. So do other activities which are now prominent in many villages: forestry, coal mining, and, above all, off-season repair or building of water-control projects and extension of cultivable lands.

Table 10.4. Calculations of food energy requirements for the Chinese population in 1974

Age group (years)		*Average body weight (kilograms)*	*Energy requirements for moderate activity (kcal/day/capita)*	*Population distribution (millions)*	*Total energy requirements (10^{12} kcal)*
Children	Less than 1		1000	26.45	9.65
	1 to 3	12	1400	79.85	40.80
	4 to 6	19	1800	76.05	49.96
	7 to 9	26	2200	69.17	55.54
Males	10 to 12	34	2600	32.18	30.54
	13 to 15	48	2200	30.14	24.20
	16 to 19	57	2700	39.81	39.23
	20 to 39	60	2800	132.70	135.61
	40 to 49		3600	43.14	40.94
	50 to 59		2500	28.82	26.30
	60 to 69		2100	17.96	13.77
	70 plus		1800	8.95	5.88
Females	10 to 12	34	2300	31.55	26.49
	13 to 15	45	2000	29.68	21.67
	16 to 19	50	2100	39.03	29.92
	20 to 39		2000	127.68	93.20
	40 to 49		1900	42.78	29.67
	50 to 59		1800	30.67	20.15
	60 to 69		1500	19.70	10.79
	70 plus		1300	10.94	5.19
Total				917.25	709.50

These projects require exceptionally heavy exertion in digging, ridging, lifting, and moving heavy loads and the Chinese claim that at least 100 million people have been engaged in these activities every winter and spring since 1971. Eleven provincial totals (adding up to 62 million people participating in the water-control work) released during the winter months of 1974–5 indicate that on the average about 65 per cent of the rural labour force took part in such off-season work.

Considering these facts it would seem reasonable to conclude that at least half of China's economically engaged (16–59 years) rural population (80 per cent of the national total) should be classified as very active. This assumption would raise the total energy requirements of the rural labour force by some 30×10^{12} kcal annually and would imply a slight national food energy deficit of about 5 per cent. Such a deficit would not be a sign of nationwide chronic malnutrition; rather it would indicate the existence of regional disparities—the areas where the people are consuming more than their essential energetic balance requirements and the regions where caloric intake is, at best, sufficient to cover the basic metabolic and work needs but where recurrent food shorages are not compatible with vigorous and healthy life. This interpretation has been lately confirmed by reports coming from China.[8]

As for the accounting of useful work performed by the rural labour force, three different methods yield very similar totals —around 100000 kcal per adult per year.

Economically active rural population of 390 million men and women would then contribute some 39×10^{12} kcal of useful energy in 1974, implying an overall efficiency of about 11 per cent. Finally, recycling of human waste, both rural and urban, returned about 1.6 Mt of nitrogen to the country's fields.

Traditional fuels

For millennia the Chinese civilization has been deriving its kinetic energy from human and animal muscles and its thermal requirements from forests. Extensive use of wood not only as a household and industrial fuel but also for building cities, cremating the dead, and producing black writing ink resulted in dangerous deforestation over vast areas. Prodigious afforestation efforts during the past quarter-century have not always had the expected results: proper forest management has been almost non-existent, survival in terms of number of stems was typically no more than 10 per cent and new plantings were often crippled by reckless pruning; the situation has improved only in the last few years.[9]

Not surprisingly, there is no official record of forest fuel use in China and there are no plantations maintained specifically for firewood. The fuel comes from scavenging of forest-floor debris, lopping of branches and removal of dead trees (and also from illegal cutting and uprooting of the healthy ones) in accessible wooded areas and from pruning of remaining or newly planted roadside trees in deforested regions, where any other kind of vegetal matter—reeds on the stream and canal banks, leaves and grasses—is also collected.[10] Fuelwood consumption in China, as anywhere else in the developing world, cannot be quantified with a high reliability. A Chinese source put it at 35 million m^3 in 1952, Richardson estimated that at least 100 million m^3 were used annually in the early 1960s and the latest FAO figures range between 129 and 142 million m^3 for the years 1970–5. An ecological derivation of forest fuel consumption in China provides an excellent confirmation of the FAO estimates. It is most likely that an equivalent of some 140 million m^3 of wood was removed for fuel from China's forests in 1974.[11]

Grasses are widely collected in deforested regions but by far the most important plant fuel in such areas comes from crop residues. Although all of the principal crop by-products—rice, wheat, and millet straw, corn, and cotton stalks, and potato, legume, and vegetable vines—have a wide variety of competitive uses as animal feed and bedding, for composting, thatching, fencing, and packing as well as raw materials for the manufacture of hats, sandals, ropes, bags, mats, and paper, their consumption as fuel continues to be very important throughout China; a conservative accounting yields the annual usage of 175 Mt, the equivalent of some 700×10^{12} kcal.

Solar economy in transition

In their effort to modernize agricultural production and to raise the rural living standard the Chinese have substantially increased the flow of modern energies in the countryside: 1974 direct fossil fuels and hydroelectricity consumption in agriculture reached perhaps as much as 170×10^{12} kcal[12] and the total rural use of commercial energy, including coal and hydro-power from small enterprises consumed by local industries and households, climbed to nearly 500×10^{12} kcal, nearly four times the amount a decade ago.

Nevertheless, in the same year crop by-products and wood still contributed more than twice as much fuel energy—some 1100×10^{12} kcal. Similarly, the capacity of mechanical pumps and tractors had more than quintupled in a decade to 49 million horsepower,[13] yet the capability of the draught animals (approximately 30 million horsepower) and the rural labour force (the equivalent of another 30 million horsepower) was still about one-fifth larger.[14] And although the importance of organic fertilizers has been relatively shrinking they, too, retain their essential role: in 1974 some 4.2 million tonnes of nitrogen were available in China from domestic production and imports of synthetic fertilizers[15]—but even a conservative estimate yields at least an equal amount of nitrogen recycled from animal and human wastes.

These figures clearly demonstrate that most of China's rural population continues to live as do hundreds of millions of other poor peasants around the world—in solar-dominated ecosystems, largely independent on external energy subsidies. Even for the nation as a whole solar energy recently transformed by green plants still predominates: approximately 4.1×10^{15} kcal of phytomass energy—as food, feed, fuel, and raw material—were used to support China's people and animals in 1974, while the total flow of fossil fuels and primary electricity amounted to less than 2.65×10^{15} kcal.[16] In contrast, the commercial energy consumption in the United States, a nation with almost identical size of the territory though with only less than a fourth of China's population, reached about 18.4×10^{15} kcal in 1974, surpassing about 7.5 times the energy value of plants harvested as food, feed, or raw material.[17]

However, China is today in the midst of a massive rural modernization effort and her countryside is approaching the crucial energy divide: before too long the system will be more dependent for its functioning on auxiliary energies (fossil fuels and electricity) than on organic fuels and wastes and on animate power. It is a unique characteristic of the Chinese energetics that the foundations of this critical transformation have not been laid solely by a hierarchical transfer of advanced technology but, to a large degree, through the application of appropriate small-scale processes.

Modernization with small-scale technologies

Although the Chinese commitment to small energy technologies has not been an unqualified success, the basic soundness of the approach cannot be questioned: for the world's largest developing nation with vast and poor countryside, deep regional disparities, meagre transportation infrastructure and limited investment capacities, a huge labour force, and scattered resources are certainly among its crucial assets and their utilization through appropriate technologies represents undoubtedly a rational strategy at this stage of development. The Chinese have turned into reality, on a scale larger than anywhere else in the world, Ernst F. Schumacher's advice to developing, and also to developed, nations: (1) make things small where possible. (2) reduce the capital-intensity because labour wants to be involved. (3) make the process as simple as you can; and (4) design the process to be non-violent.[18]

The approach—adopted by necessity during Yenan years, discarded during the first 5 year plan in favour of the Stalinist model and employed indiscriminately and injuriously during the 'Great Leap' years—seems to have found its proper niche during the past 10 years and its contribution to China's energetics has become very significant.[19]

Small coal-mines

Since they started to recover from the post-'Great Leap' slump in the early 1960s, small coal-mines, financed and operated by administrative regions, counties, communes, and production brigades, have been steadily gaining in importance and now they produce 45 per cent of China's raw coal, a higher share than at the height of the 1958 native pits campaign (for annual output figures see Appendix B to this Chapter). Most of the new small-mine capacity has been added since 1969 and located in the coal-deficient southern half of the country to reduce the area's traditional dependence on the imported northern coal. Every province and region south of Yangtze, and also Tibet, has a large number of permanent or seasonal small mines which have been instrumental in increasing the area's coal self-sufficiency to more than 70 per cent in 1976.[20] Small- and medium-size coal mines are also very important in some northern provinces: in Shansi, the nation's leading coal producer, these enterprises provide more than 40 per cent of total production, enough to cover all basic local needs and to free the higher quality large-mine output for shipment to coal-deficient provinces.[21]

The total number of small mines is now over 20000, with a typical output of about 1000 tonnes of coal per year, although the largest enterprises in this category produce as much as 100000 tonnes annually.[22] Most of the mines are open pits established in less than a year on suitable outcrops, or single shallow shafts located at deposits too small to be developed by mechanized mining. Human and animal labour dominates the extraction and distribution of the low-quality fuel which is used, without any sorting or preparation, either as household fuel or as the primary heat source—or raw material—in local small industries. The lifespan of many small mines relying solely on traditional technology is often very short, labour productivity is dismal, and safety conditions are appalling. All of these considerations have led the Chinese to embark on a modest programme of modernizing the largest small mines and expanding their capacity to maintain their important role in the national coal production.

Small hydro-power stations

Mass construction of small hydro stations started during the 'Great Leap' years, was abandoned during the early 1960s and has been successfully revived after 1969. Dependence on local resources, maximum thrift, and construction speed have been the main characteristics of the programme. Stations are built predominantly with locally accumulated funds with central investment used only for occasional design, equipment manufacturing or operator training assistance. Massed labour, equipped with traditional tools (chisels, picks, shovels, shoulder-poles and carrying baskets, wheelbarrows, and pull carts) is used in almost all instances, and the dams are either rock-filled or earth-filled structures, requiring only a minimum of cement, steel, and timber. Many counties are now equipped to produce their own small water turbines (ranging from primitive wooden devices to modern Pelton, Francis, and Nagler propellers) and generators, transformers, cement poles, wire and switches, and can also train the needed operators.

More than 87000 stations are now operating throughout China,[23] but naturally the rainy provinces south of the Yangtze account for most of the total—approximately four-fifths—and Kwangtung alone has almost 20 per cent of all small hydro plants. The typical installed capacity of a station is very small indeed: available provincial figures result in the weighted average of about 45 kW per hydro station. Prefecture and county figures, collected for some 10500 stations during 1972–7, indicate better the highly skewed size distribution and significant local variations: most stations are very small (less than 25 kW per station) and higher averages are rather meaningless owing to the inclusion of a few larger medium-sized plants in the totals. Extreme turbogenerator sizes range from miniature devices (0.4–12 kW capacity) produced by the Tientsin Electro-Driving Research Institute to tap spring and creek waters to units in excess of 1000 kW.

The total generating capacity of small- and medium-size hydro plants rose sharply from 500 MW in 1969 to nearly 3000 MW in 1975. As might be expected, the load factor of small stations is considerably lower than the average for large installations: available figures translate into the mean time of 2726.5 hours per kW per year (load factor 31 per cent) in Kwangtung and 2000 hours per kW annually in Chekiang and Honan (load factor of merely 22.8 per cent), with some county averages as low as 1250 hours;[24] nevertheless, the small stations accounted for one-third of total hydro generation—or at least 10 billion kW h—in

1975, contributing considerably to the rudimentary electrification of the Chinese countryside. Besides providing power for local small industries, as well as irrigation and drainage, food and fodder processing and timber sawing, small hydro reservoirs regulate water supplies, help prevent floods, and are used to breed fish and other aquatic products. This multipurpose nature of small hydro projects seems to be the best proof of their utility and the best assurance of their continuous development.

Biogas generation

Biogas (the Chinese use the term 'marsh gas') is a mixture of roughly two-thirds methane, one-third carbon dioxide, and traces of hydrogen sulphide, hydrogen, and nitrogen, which can be produced in sealed, insulated containers, by the controlled anaerobic fermentation of animal and human excrements, vegetation pieces (grasses, leaves, crop residues), household garbage, organic industrial waste (sugar-making and oil-pressing residues), and waste water. Mass production of biogas in China is only of recent origins—yet the Chinese can already claim the world leadership in this relatively simple but immensely useful energy technology.[25] Construction of biogas digesters—typically 5–10 m^3 airtight concrete, brick, or rock containers buried in the ground and consisting of loading, fermentation, and slag compartments (Fig. 10.2)—originated on a large scale in Szechwan Basin in the early 1970s and by 1978 the nationwide total of fermenters of different capacities, ranging from a few m^3 to communal tanks of 100 m^3, reached nearly 6 million.

Digesters are not expensive to build (available figures from Szechwan and Hunan quote 30–40 yuan for a typical 10 m^3 tank with the smallest units costing as little as 10 yuan) but their efficient operation demands careful attention to several environmental factors. Proper liquidity of the load, approximately 25:1 carbon-to-nitrogen ratio of digestible materials, neutral or slightly alkaline (pH 7–8) fermenting fluid, tank temperature between 28–45 °C and regular addition, removal, and mixing of ingredients are all essential for maintaining the sustained high yield of biogas. However, when properly managed, a typical 10-m^3 digester running on pig manure, human

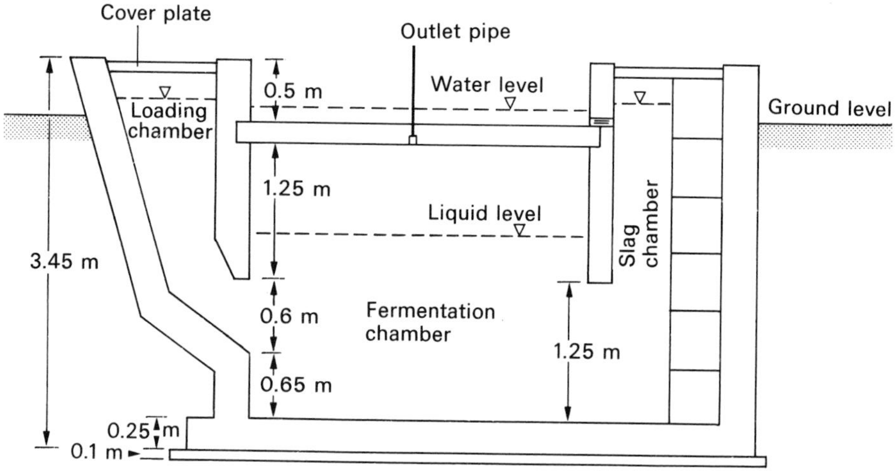

Fig. 10.2. Typical Szechwanese biogas digester. This cross-section, originally published in K'o-hsueh Shih-yen, No. 5 (May 1973) p. 32 is not drawn to scale. The flow of the water through a small hole in the wall separating the gas and slag chambers maintains a relatively stable pressure inside the digester.

waste, and crop residues or grasses will provide all the energy needed for both cooking and lighting during summer and autumn months for a southern Chinese commune family of five.

Biogas is not suitable only for household cooking (the process is faster, easier, and less expensive than with wood or straw) and lighting (a gas lamp brighter than a 100-watt incandescent bulb can be used) but it can also generate electricity and power water pumps and crop processing machinery. Moreover, the benefits go beyond the availability of a clean and versatile fuel: savings of fossil fuels and reduction of fuel expenditures offer a significant economic advantage; conservation of forests and grasses has favourable ecological implications; elimination of many insect pests and diseases markedly improves hygienic conditions of rural areas;[26] burning of biogas largely eliminates the tedious, everyday gathering of firewood or grasses and lightens household labour; finally, methanogenic fermentation yields an excellent organic fertilizer, an essential ingredient of the Chinese farming.

Large-scale fossil fuel production

Although the reliance on local small-scale energy production has been a crucial element in rudimentary rural modernization, it cannot ever be considered a viable basis for advanced industrialization which requires large and steady flows of fossil fuels and electricity.[27] Chinese achievements in providing these requirements have been fairly substantial—both in absolute terms (see annual output figures in Appendix B to this chapter) and in relative international comparisons—but new major advances will be needed to satisfy the greatly expanded demands of agricultural mechanization, industrial and defence modernization as well as to raise the living standard of population.

China's raw coal output is now exceeding 600 Mt a year, the total surpassed only by Soviet and U.S. production. Coal is still the country's principal fuel and large northern and north-eastern mines (Fig. 3) remain its biggest suppliers. Collieries of Ta-t'ung, Fu-hsin, Fu-shun, Ho-kang, Chi-hsi, and P'ing-ting-shan each extract over 10 Mt of raw coal annually, and K'ai-luan, China's oldest and largest commercial mine concentration, surpassed alone 25 Mt in 1975 before it was devastated by the July 1976 earthquake.[28] The best available provincial estimates indicate that the north and the north-east produced no less than 60 per cent of the national output and that the south, with no more than 17 per cent of the production, remains an uncomfortably coal-deficient region.

There are other similarly intractable problems in China's coal industries. Investment in new mines has been clearly inadequate during this decade with most of the output increases coming from existing collieries. For example, before the earthquake five of the seven K'ai-luan's mines were producing twice as much as was their designed capacity and similar indications of intensive exploitation of old mines are available for other coalfields around the country. Mechanization of large mines remains low, and although there are some fairly advanced collieries no more than 50 per cent of all Chinese coal is extracted, loaded, and conveyed mechanically, whereas these operations are virtually 100 per cent mechanized in the two other coal superpowers. Even more serious is the shortage of coal preparation capacity; the latest reliable account found its total at 83.62 Mt in 1970[29] and if it would have since grown even by sustained 10 per cent per year—certainly a too optimistic assumption—the 1978 total could not be greater than about 180 Mt, that is no more than one-third of the country's total raw coal production. And the share of the most efficient and most progressive method of extraction—large-scale mining—is even lower, perhaps no more than 10 per cent.[30]

These problems are certainly well recognized, and the Chinese have tried to move toward their solution by re-establishing

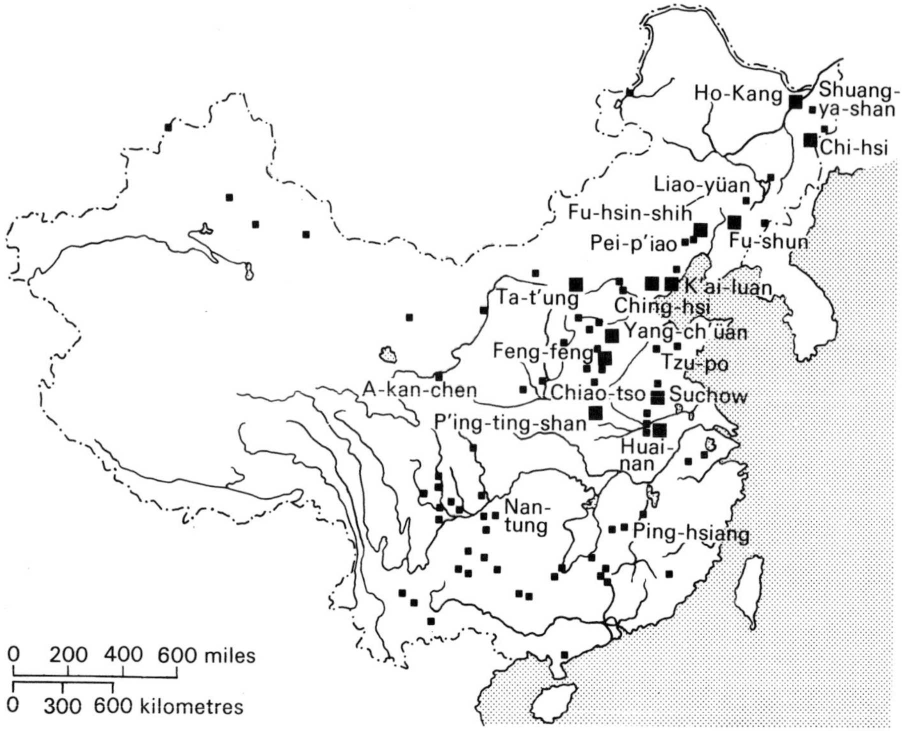

Fig. 10.3. China's major coalfields. Large squares show collieries with more than 10 Mt of annual raw coal production in the mid-1970s.

a separate Ministry of Coal Industry in January 1975 and by embarking on a 10-year plan of comprehensive modernization in October of the same year. The major tasks announced were the general mechanization (80–85 per cent of all operations) of principal large mines, concentration of the future developments in the existing major coalfields and in new large mines currently under construction as well as the continuing expension of small mines.

Nevertheless, it will be a difficult and costly effort to modernize the industry and to maintain its historical output exponential growth of 5.4 per cent annually in the decade ahead as the need for heavy investment in this relatively neglected—yet still absolutely essential—field will have to be weighed against, and adjusted to, the no less pressing requirements of other branches of modern energetics.

Hydrocarbon industries

Very high growth rates of China's hydrocarbon extraction, first crude oil exports to Japan and other East Asian countries, expansion of oilfields and refineries, new major gas discoveries and the promising offshore potential have brought widespread international attention to China's oil and gas industry[31]—as well as numerous predictions of the country's emergence as a Saudi Arabia of the Far East. Admittedly the country's annual crude-oil production increments have been quite substantial—though not without many precedents around the world—during the first half of this decade, but critical analyses had to conclude that China's future export potential is limited, and that the fast growth rates are unsustainable.[32] Recent developments have confirmed these conclusions and there is little doubt that the Chinese hydrocarbon production will require large investments and far reaching technological modernization just to keep up the pace with the growing demand.

This is owing to a multitude of deficiencies which have accompanied the Chinese oil and gas development. The technology has been very much Soviet-oriented and the Chinese problems are similar to the Soviet ones, only more widespread: shortage of sophisticated geophysical equipment (modern seismic devices, computerized field units) limits the capability of locating deep structures; inefficiencies in field operations are caused by shortages of high quality drilling and casing pipes, continuing reliance on old turbo-drills, poor drill bits and mud pumps, lack of gas treating facilities, and until recently, the prevalent use of line-drive waterflooding.[33] This all spells low ultimate recovery rates and slow pace of development in any but rich and shallow fields. The Chinese offshore drilling and production technology is especially rudimentary: their drilling fleet for 1976–7 consisted of only two shallow-water barges, two shallow-water jackup rigs, one older jackup and its near copy, and two catamaran drillships.

In spite of several major additions since 1975 the pipeline network is still quite thin, totalling about 7500 km. Similarly, major improvements have also been achieved in the Chinese oil ports but Lü-ta in Liaoning is still the only installation able to accommodate 100000-tonne tankers and there are only two other terminals—Chan-chiang in Kwangtung and Huang-tao in Shantung—which can handle 70000-tonne vessels. However, the largest domestically built tankers have only 25000 tonnes (a single 50000 tonne tanker was also built) and the Chinese will have to build or import bigger ships to take the advantage of significant economies of scale which they could enjoy by using larger vessels for their north–south coastal shipments of crude oil.[34] With the increasing consumption of oil products in large southern cities, as well as in the countryside, these shipments are bound to increase substantially because the regional disparity in crude oil production is even stronger than in the case of coal extraction. Five giant oilfields in the north-east and the north are producing nearly 90 per cent of the nation's oil (Fig. 10.4), an imbalance which cannot be remedied easily.

Yet another serious deficiency affecting China's oil industry has been the persistent shortage of refining capacity. According to the official claims, crude oil output had grown more than six times between 1965 and 1974, but the refining capacity increased less than four times, and only a slightly smaller disparity between the two volumes was reported during 1977. Even after subtracting the exports and the crude oil burned directly in power plants, the difference between the production and refining estimates suggests that China must be stockpiling large amounts of crude oil.

Unfortunately much less is known about China's increasingly important natural gas industry; it has been predominantly concentrated in Szechwan Basin, but Po Hai fields and the newly opened Ta-ch'ing zone will undoubtedly become more prominent with further large-scale expansion of the nitrogen industry and even more so in the case of eventual exports of liquefied natural gas to Japan.

Future developments in fossil fuel energetics, as well as those in hydrogeneration, will be, of course, critically influenced not only by investment priorities and technological capabilities: magnitudes, quality, and location of energy resources will be the essential variables.

Fossil fuels and renewable energy resources

China has been always credited with abundant coal resources—some of which have been exploited in a modern commercial way since the 1870s—and, at least since the early decades of this century, with sizeable oil shale deposits. Liquid crude oil and natural

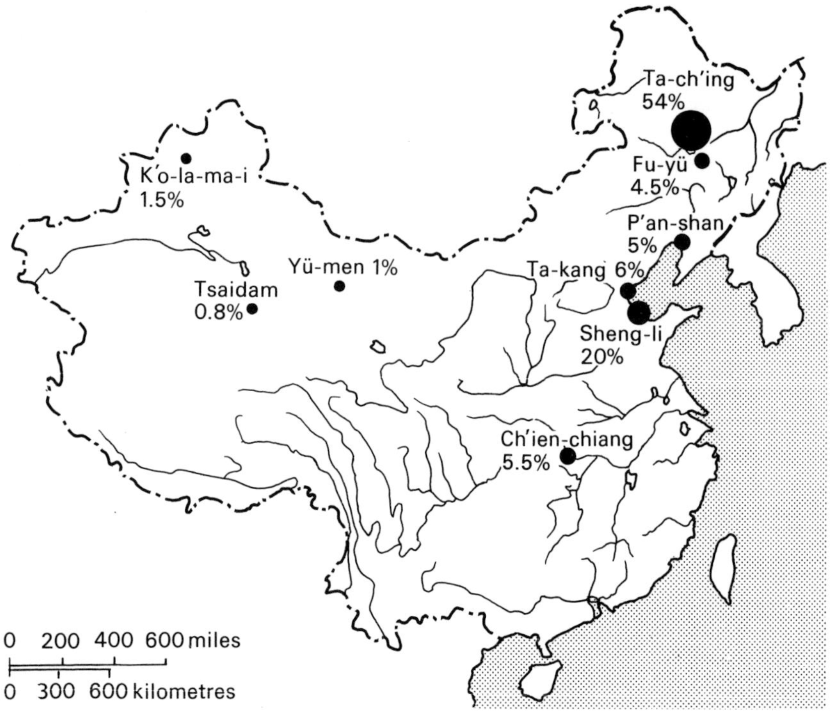

Fig. 10.4. China's major oilfields. Shares of the 1975 crude oil production (according to the CIA, 'Economic indicators' op. cit., pp. 28–9) are shown for nine major fields, which provide 94.7 per cent of the aggregate output of 77.1 Mt.

gas resources were considered rather insignificant for such a large country. Extensive geological and geophysical prospecting carried out after the establishment of the PRC in 1949 has considerably increased the magnitude of all fuel resource categories and affirmed the country's third—and conceivably second—place on the list of global fossil energy endowments. Moreover, large quantities of fissionable materials have also been discovered.[35] Solar energy converted by green plants has been sustaining the Chinese civilization for millennia but among its many important forms only the hydro potential has been systematically appraised, while the direct radiation, wind and thermal sea power—as well as geothermal and tidal energy—have just become a target of interest and preliminary evaluation.

Solid fuels

The first nationwide totals of coal deposits in China (excluding Manchuria), presented at the 12th International Geological Congress in 1913, spanned a very wide range—the resources estimated were at least 38.765 Bt and as much as 996.613 Bt. Reserve figures claimed by the Nationalist Government in the 1930s and 1940s were between 250 to 300 Bt and rose after several years of Communist exploration to 1000 to 1500 Bt in the mid-1950s. Total potential resources up to 1800-m depth were placed during the 'great leap' period (in 1958) at 9000 Bt, undoubtedly a very generous estimate as the proved reserves at the end of 1958 were put by an official publication just in excess of 80 Bt.[36]

No new nationwide figures have been

released since then, and all foreign observers are left to juggle these 20-year-old totals. Soviet experts, who worked extensively in China, accept the highest totals—1500 Bt for reserves and 9000 Bt for resources.[37] The World Energy Conference uses 80 Bt for 'recoverable reserves' and 1000 Bt for 'total resources in place'. Perhaps the best current interpretation of the Chinese coal resource figures is that the recoverable reserves are no less than 100 Bt and the total resources are at least 1500 Bt.[38]

Different resource estimates are in an excellent agreement as far as the fuel categories are concerned. Bituminous coals account for four-fifths of the total, anthracites for slightly less than one-fifth, and lignites for only a few per cent. The quality of coal is mostly very good and seams are of above average thickness and are predominantly horizontal or only slightly inclined. In sum, China's coal resources are outstanding both in their quantity and quality.

Hydrocarbons

During the 1920s the Standard Oil Co. estimated crude oil resources in Shensi, Kansu, Sinkiang, and Szechwan at 188 Mt; in 1935, the Chinese Bureau of Mines put the total for hydrocarbon liquids at 620 Mt (including oil potentially extractable from Fu-shun and Shensi shales). The highest Kuomintang estimate was about 780 Mt, and the post-1949 exploration increased this total to 2.75 Bt in 1953 and to 5.9 Bt in 1959. Two-thirds of this latest official resource figure were in shale oils, and only 200 Mt belonged to the measured reserve category.

Continuing absence of authoritative Chinese oil resource figures is, of course, much more unfortunate than the lack of updated coal resource estimates: coal deposits are much easier to discover and to quantify than are the hydrocarbons, and it is highly unlikely that the solid fuel totals underwent any drastic change; on the other hand, China's largest producing oilfields were discovered only after the latest official estimate was released and, consequently, even the best outside estimates are hardly more than educated guesses.[39]

A review of estimates published in the 1970s (Table 10.5) shows an extremely wide range of values (due above all to the near total lack of any hard knowledge about offshore resources and to a rather liberal treatment of oil shales); non-uniform categorization of resources also precludes direct comparisons.

Certainly the most detailed attempt to estimate China's natural crude oil resources has been the field-by-field account of A. A. Meyerhoff who was given access to Soviet geological appraisals in the late 1960s and who has since, in co-operation with Willums, revised his figures.[40] On the other hand, resource appraisals leaked by the Chinese to some visitors from the United States are patently useless.

Leaving aside the undoubtedly sizeable shale oil resources, whose oil content and recoverability are largely unknown, the best currently available geological evidence compatible with production totals and growth rates would indicate that China's crude oil reserves are certainly no less than 3 Bt and most likely no more than 10 Bt.[41]

There is even more uncertainty about China's natural gas deposits. Based on the Soviet data, Meyerhoff estimated the Szechwanese reserves at 528.6 Bm^3 and Tsaidam reserves at 81.4 Bm^3 as of the beginning of 1969; World Energy Conference 1974 total for proved recoverable reserves was 680 Bm^3 and the latest Oil and Gas Journal estimate is 708 Bm^3. These estimates are not widely apart, but they are undoubtedly extremely conservative: ultimately recoverable volume has been put by Meyerhoff and Willums one order of magnitude higher—8571 Bm^3 with 5714 onshore and 2857 Bm^3 offshore. Conservative figures of less than 1000 Bm^3 would not place China's reserves even among the top 15 in the world ranking, while just taking the onshore total around 5000 Bm^3 would elevate the country to fourth place, behind the USSR, Iran, and the United States.

Table 10.5. Estimates of China's crude oil reserves

Estimator	*Year*	*Total amount (billion tonnes)*	*Reserve category*
Meyerhoff[1]	1970	0.78	Total probable ultimate recovery from known fields
		0.96	Minimum estimate of proved and probable reserves
		1.72	Minimum estimate of potential reserves
		2.68	Total proved and probable and potential reserves
Chen[2]	1971	10.00	Total reserves
Kambara[3]	1973	1.20–1.80	Proved and probable reserves
Koide[4]	1973	3.00–10.00	Reserves
World Energy Conference[5]	1974	1.73	Proved recoverable reserves
		5.00	Estimated recoverable reserves from estimated total reserves
		21.00	Estimated recoverable oil from shales
National Council for United States–China Trade[6]	1974	6.00–10.00	Onshore reserves
		20.00	Potential offshore reserves
Willums[7]	1975	5.5–8.9	Total ultimately recoverable onshore reserves
		4.1–8.51	Total ultimately recoverable offshore reserves
		10.3	Total ultimately recoverable reserves
Williams[8]	1975	1.116	Proved reserves
		5.9	Proved and probable reserves
		7.6	Total proved, probable, and potential reserves
Terman[9]	1976	4.1–4.8	Total onshore reserves
		1.4–2.1	Total offshore reserves
		5.5–6.9	Total reserves
Meyerhoff and Willums[10]	1976	5.398	Produced, proved, probable, and potential onshore reserves
		4.110	Produced, proved, probable, and potential offshore reserves
		9.507	Total reserves
Oil & Gas Journal[11]	1977	2.75	Estimated proved reserves

[1]Meyerhoff, A. A. Developments in mainland China, 1949–1968. *American Association of Petroleum Geologists Bulletin* **54** (8), p. 1573 (August 1970).
[2]Cheng-siang Chen and Kam-nin Au. The petroleum industry of China. *Die Erde* **3–4**, 319 (1972).
[3]Kambara, T. The petroleum industry in China. *China Quarterly* **60**, 711 (Oct.–Dec. 1974).
[4]Koide, Y. China's crude oil production. *Pacific Community* **5** (3), 464 (April 1974).
[5]WEC, op. cit., pp. 136 and 188.
[6]Cited by Auldridge, L. Mainland China striving to boost crude exports. *Oil & Gas Journal* **73** (1) p. 27 (6 Jan. 1975).
[7]Willums, Jan-Olaf. China's offshore oil: application of a framework for evaluation of oil and gas potentials under uncertainty. Cambridge, Mass., unpublished Ph.D. dissertation, MIT, (1975), p. 265.
[8]Williams, B. A., op. cit., p. 235.
[9]Terman, M. J. Sedimentary basins of China and their petroleum potential. In *SEAPEX Proceedings* **111**, p. 127. Singapore SEAPEX (1976).
[10]Meyerhoff and Willums, op. cit., p. 201.
[11]Worldwide oil and gas at a glance. *Oil & Gas Journal* **75** (53) p. 101 (26 Dec. 1977).

Reneweble energy resources

As for any large territory spanning comparable latitude, solar radiation received by China represents a vast potential resource of clean energy—somewhere between 9 to 12×10^{18} kcal annually—whose commercial exploitation faces a multitude of technical and economic problems. The best opportunity for collecting direct radiation is in high-lying, clear and clean mountain plateaux and deserts of Tibet, Tsinghai, Sinkiang, and Inner Mongolia, all sparsely populated and mostly very remote from industrial and agricultural concentrations of the eastern half of the country.[42] Indirect harvesting of solar flow in green plants and hydro-power stations will thus remain by far the most important renewable sources of energy in China for decades to come.

Estimates of net annual productivity of China's vegetation have already been presented and the total for forests should be appreciably enlarged through further afforestation, better choice of species, and better management. Hydro-energy resources were known to be huge for decades but the Nationalist Chinese total of 136 761 800 kW of potential power was expanded quite considerably through a Soviet-aided Communist survey of 1598 rivers with a total length of 226 000 km during the 1950s. The theoretical capacity was estimated to be about 540 GW under conditions of average flows with approximately 300 GW suited for actual industrial exploitation.[43] The latest WEC estimate is 330 GW for the average flow (G_{av}) and 60 GW for the flow available 95 per cent of the time (G_{95}), placing China respectively first and second in the world in these two hydraulic resource categories.[44]

Chinese tidal energy potential appears to be relatively small but the still mostly unexplored geothermal resources are undoubtedly very large. Most of China is influenced by the 40 million-year-old—and continuing—collision between Indian and Eurasian land masses, which gave rise to profoundly disarranged geological conditions, diverse landforms, the severest earthquakes—and abundant geothermal phenomena, especially on the Tibetan plateau. Chinese have three tiny geothermal stations, apparently all of them based on inefficient vaporization of hot water, and have recently put into operation the country's first direct steam geothermal station in Yangpaching steam field in Tibet, which was discovered during the interdisciplinary survey of Tsinghai–Tibet plateau by the Peking University geothermal group.[45] While it is impossible to present any quantitative appraisal of the geothermal endowment, it is safe to conclude that should the Chinese eventually decide to develop these resources they have one of the world's richest potentials.

Regional distribution of resources

Sufficient magnitude of the resources is far from being a guarantee of a smooth development in a country so large, so relatively poor, and so unevenly settled and accessible as China: spatial distribution is of critical importance and while it is impossible to offer a reliable provincial breakdown the available regional estimates for coal, crude oil and hydro-energy (Table 10.6) are a good indicator of fortunes and problems with China's distributions of major energy resources.

North-east and north with nearly 30 per cent of China's population and more than 45 per cent of gross industrial output are fortuitously provided with abundant reserves of both coal (nearly 75 per cent of the total) and crude oil (about 63 per cent). However, as already pointed out, these reserves are supplying the bulk of the country's production and they are being extracted faster than any other fuel deposits throughout China. Consequently, unless they will be substantially enlarged by further exploration, the more remote regions will have to balance their decline, which could come in the case of crude oil as early as the late 1980s—but more likely sometime in the 1990s. Northern

Table 10.6. Regional distribution of China's energy resources

	*Coal**				*Crude oil reserves*†					
	Reserves		*Resources*		*Produced, proved, probable*		*Total ultimate*		*Hydroenergy potential*§	
	Billion tonnes	*Per cent*	*Billion tonnes*	*Per cent*	*Million tonnes*	*Per cent*	*Million tonnes*	*Per cent*	*Gigawatts*	*Per cent*
Total	1500.0	100.0	9000	100.0	1620.1	100.0	5393.0	100.0	535.6	100.0
North-east	40.2	2.7	414	4.6	410.4	25.3	1368.8	25.4	14.8	2.8
North	1051.2	70.1	1368	15.2	615.0	38.0	923.0	17.1	10.5	1.9
North-west	280.7	18.7	4986	55.4	460.7	28.4	2424.2	44.9	49.2	9.2
South-west	49.2	3.3	585	6.5	134.0	8.3	408.0	7.6	392.5	73.3
Central–South	56.3	3.7	747	8.3			274.0	5.0	57.3	10.7
East	22.4	1.5	900	10.0					11.3	2.1

*Bazhenov, Leonenko, and Kharchenko, op. cit., p. 44.
†Calculated from basin totals in Meyerhoff and Willums, op. cit., p. 201.
§Wu, op. cit., p. 167.

coal reserves are so huge that the regional shift will not come because of physical exhaustion but rather because of the increasing cost as well as the need to distribute the production more equally.

In contrast to the richly endowed north and north-east, the east, with one-fifth of the total population and nearly 30 per cent of industrial output, is almost devoid of any significant fuel, as well as hydro, resources. Barring unlikely early discoveries of huge and cheap offshore oil and gas deposits the east will remain a large importer of energy. A large territory of central–south and south-west, housing over two-fifths of China's people and producing 20 per cent of its industrial goods is only slightly better off than the east—with the notable exception of a large hydro-power concentration in extremely inaccessible eastern Tibet and western Szechwan.

It is to the north-west—remote, severely inhospitable, thinly populated (less than 7 per cent of the total), unindustrialized (less than 5 per cent of gross industrial output) and still only tenuously linked to the rest of the country—where the Chinese will have to turn for their future fuel needs, a westward shift of energy centres comparable in its magnitude to the eastward shift of the Soviet energetics.[46] The north-west has no less than half of China's ultimate coal resources and nearly half of her estimated recoverable onshore oil supplies. The only major way to postpone this costly and complicated shift would be to turn offshore first and to plunge into certainly no less expensive and difficult search and production of undersea hydrocarbons. This is not as yet a pressing dilemma—but it will have to be resolved sometime during the next decade; otherwise it would be extremely difficult to keep China's energy consumption on its fast, and much needed, exponential rise.

Energy consumption and future demand

Judged in absolute terms, the record has been quite impressive: China's primary energy consumption, which was barely over 20 Mtce in 1949, grew nearly tenfold in a decade, topped, after years of politically-induced stagnation, 300 Mtce in 1972 and is now exceeding 500 Mtce. In aggregate terms, China has thus become the world's third largest energy consumer, just ahead of Japan—and very far behind the Soviet Union and the United States (Fig. 10.5). Consumption per capita naturally remains rather low: at around 500 kgce annually it is more than double of India's modern energy usage, but less than half of Mexico's figure—and an order of magnitude less than the consumption of developed nations; addition of the still important traditional fuels increases the aggregate value to some 600 Mtce in 1976 and the annual usage per capita to nearly 650 kgce.[47]

Even after leaving out the economic recovery period of the years 1949–52, the long-term (1952–76) exponential growth rate of energy use equalled 9.3 per cent annually, a pace superior to the consumption increases of all other large (more than 50 million) developing nations. Naturally this fast consumption rise fuelled the strong, though erratic, expansion of industrial output and construction—as well as the costly nuclear capability.

However, almost until the beginning of this decade, agricultural production was receiving only minuscule amounts of the growing consumption and even today the energy flows into farming are still much less than desirable. And although the industry has been consuming by far the largest share of the national total it, too, is short of fuels and electricity.

Future energy requirements of the Chinese economy are thus truly immense, especially should the country move vigorously toward the goal outlined by its late Premier: to accomplish the comprehensive modernization of agriculture, industry, natural defence, and science and technology so that China's economy will be advancing in the front ranks of the world by the end of this century.[48] Restructuring of sectoral uses, improved efficiency of industrial consumption and

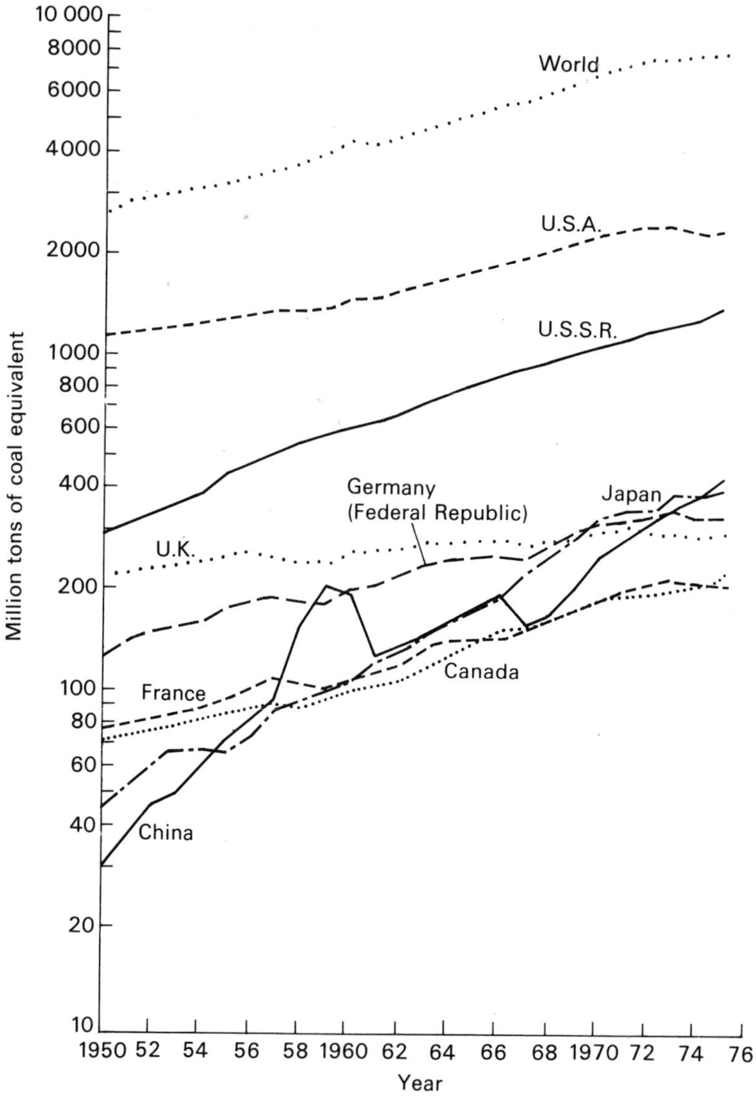

Fig. 10.5. World's leading energy-consuming nations. Primary energy consumption according to the UNO, *World energy supplies* (New York, UNO, annually), except for China. Chinese totals are from V. Smil, *China's energy*, op. cit., p. 141.

increased energy subsidies into agriculture will have to be the major tasks on the difficult road toward that ambitious goal.

Sectoral uses

Direct information about final energy uses in China has been extremely scarce, a problem which might not be difficult to overcome by calculations should the appropriate sectoral output and conversion data be available. Unfortunately such figures are very fragmentary and, consequently, our sectoral consumption data must be built on cumulative assumptions and estimates. While the absolute values, especially for the 1960s

Table 10.7. Sectoral consumption of primary energy in China, 1950–1976*
(All values are in million tonnes of coal equivalent and, in parentheses, in per cent)

	Total	*Electricity generation*	*Industry*	*Transportation*	*Agriculture*	*Residential and commercial*
1950	30.4 (100)	3.6 (12)	3.9 (13)	3.3 (11)	Negligible	19.6 (64)
1952	47.5 (100)	4.4 (9)	12.6 (27)	5.0 (11)	0.1 (<1)	25.4 (53)
1957	96.5 (100)	8.8 (9)	28.9 (30)	9.3 (10)	0.6 (1)	48.9 (51)
1960	198.3 (100)	20.0 (10)	105.3 (53)	15.5 (8)	5.5 (3)	52.0 (26)
1965	178.4 (100)	16.7 (9)	75.2 (43)	14.3 (8)	6.1 (3)	66.1 (37)
1970	251.4 (100)	21.6 (9)	115.4 (46)	19.9 (8)	13.0 (5)	81.5 (32)
1974	377.0 (100)	33.6 (9)	193.5 (51)	26.4 (7)	18.2 (5)	105.3 (28)
1976	445.0 (100)	42.0 (9)	228.4 (51)	31.5 (7)	27.6 (6)	115.5 (26)

*1950–74: V. Smil, *China's energy*, op. cit., p. 150; 1976: my calculations using the same derivation procedures as for 1974 and appropriate inventory and performance figures for 1976 estimated in CIA, *China: Economic Indicators*, op. cit., passim.

and 1970s may be arguable, the relative importance of individual sectors and the general consumption trends can be portrayed satisfactorily (Table 10.7).

The most striking feature of the Chinese sectoral energy use is the large share of the industrial consumption; even with power generation requirements classified separately, industry now draws about half of all China's primary energy, a sharp increase in comparison with the early 1950s.[49] On the other hand, relative importance of residential and commercial uses has declined considerably since the late 1950s and, significantly, both the power generation and transportation shares, in spite of large absolute increases, have also diminished. Agriculture consumed about 46 times more commercial energy in 1976 than it did at the end of the first 5-year plan two decades ago—but in relative terms it is still no more than about 6 per cent.

A more detailed look at the recent consumption pattern—by sector and source (Table 10.8 and Fig. 10.6)—reveals important weaknesses in the Chinese energy use. About one-third of raw coal is consumed for residential heating, one of the least efficient —and relatively most polluting—fuel conversions, while the household use of refined oil products remains negligibly low. Some four-fifths of energy consumed in transportation are solid fuels which are very inefficiently converted into motion by steam locomotives, still the principal power sources of the Chinese railways. Most importantly, a great deal of energy is wasted in virtually all industrial processes.

Table 10.8. China's consumption of primary energy by sector and source in 1974*

	Total	*Industry*	*Agriculture*	*Transportation*	*Household and commerce*
Coal	251.2 (100)	140.9 (56)	2.5 (1)	22.3 (9)	85.5 (34)
Crude oil	75.9 (100)	55.7 (73)	15.1 (20)	4.1 (6)	1.0 (1)
Natural gas	46.6 (100)	28.0 (60)			18.6 (40)
Hydroelectricity	3.3 (100)	2.5 (76)	0.6 (18)		0.2 (6)
Total	377.0 (100)	227.1 (60)	18.2 (5)	26.4 (7)	105.3 (28)

*For derivation of the estimates see V. Smil, *China's energy*, op. cit., pp. 146–9.

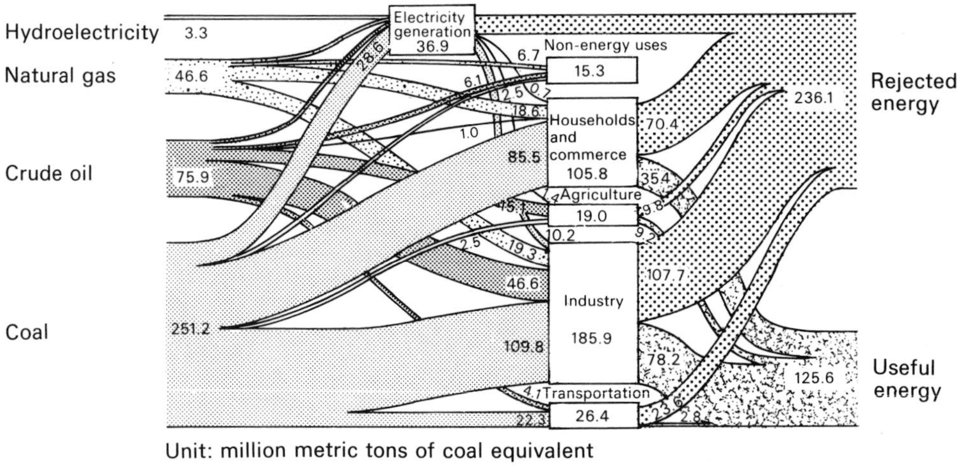

Fig. 10.6. Commercial energy flow pattern for China in 1974. For comparison identically structured energy flow patterns for the United States in the years 1960, 1970, 1980, and 1985 can be found in the Joint Committee on Atomic Energy's *Certain background information for consideration when evaluating the national energy dilemma*, Foldouts A-D. USGPO, Washington DC (1973).

Industrial consumption

Recent research efforts to disaggregate the energy demand into detailed components and to subject individual industrial processes to a systematic energy analysis have abundantly illustrated numerous savings to be made through production adjustments, conservation measures and material or energy substitutions even in the most advanced economies. Although the Chinese have been engaged in almost incessant campaigns to save fuel and electricity—and have also taken some desirable steps toward residual heat utilization—the potential energy savings in the country's industries are immense.

In absolute terms, the Chinese iron and steel industry is certainly the branch with the greatest energy waste. Conversion of poor quality coking coal results in high benefication losses even in the case of large enterprises;[50] coke charging in modern plants was still about 700 kg per tonne of pig-iron in the late 1960s and was estimated at 650 kg in 1974; moreover, in small local plants, which now produce 27 per cent of China's iron and 11 per cent of her steel, coke requirements are as high as 900–1000 kg per tonne of pig-iron.[51] Poor ore, relatively small blast furnaces, still infrequent partial substitution of coke by an injection of fuel oil or natural gas, scarcity of scrap and the heavy dependence on energy-intensive open-hearth furnaces in steelmaking are other principal factors explaining China's inordinately high energy consumption in this essential industrial activity: iron- and steel-making require nearly one-fourth of the national raw coal consumption and this, in turn, accounts for almost 30 per cent of the total industrial energy usage.

International comparisons of energy consumption in steel industry reveal still better China's unenviable situation. In China, raw coal requirements alone translate into approximately 17000 kcal per kg of crude steel in 1974, while in the same year total direct energy inputs (solid fuels, fuel oils, gases, and electricity) to produce 1 kg of crude steel in major Western producers and in Japan ranged between 4400–5500 kcal.

Another important sector where small plants are turning out an exceedingly energy-intensive product is the fertilizer industry, above all the enterprises synthesizing aqueous ammonia and ammonium bicarbonate.[52] Available evidence shows that the production of one kg of nitrogen in these small units—which provided one-half of the domestic output in 1974—requires energy inputs (coal, coke, coke oven gas, electricity) between 23000–31000 kcal;[53] in comparison, large, modern ammonia and urea plants, which the Chinese purchased from the United States, Netherlands, Japan, and France, synthesize 1 kg of nitrogen with no more than 11300–17700 kcal of total feedstock and process energy.[54] Similar, though very likely not so glaring, efficiency differences could be certainly found in other industrial processes, above all in colour metallurgy, cement production, and crude oil refining.

Lowering of specific fuel consumption in thermal power generation has been a constant preoccupation in the Chinese electricity production but the last reliable published average national heat rate—640 g of standard coal per kWh in 1957—was some 20 per cent above the comparable Soviet value and nearly 50 per cent greater than the average US consumption. Although this huge gap has been certainly narrowed during the past two decades, great differences must prevail even in the case of large modern power-plants because the typical sizes of the Chinese turbo-generators—25–125 MW—are still too small to approach the thermal efficiencies of large Western or Soviet units.

In view of these numerous conversion inefficiencies the share of useful energy—estimated to equal one-third of the total consumption in 1974 (Fig. 10.6)—may be actually even lower.[55] In any case the Chinese energetics faces a difficult, though rewarding, task to improve its conversion rates by elimination or modification of appealingly simple but energetically wasteful production processes, widespread conservation, introduction of new technologies and larger units to benefit from considerable economies of scale and by the increased use of the total energy systems. A no less important task for China's industries will be to provide greatly increased energy subsidies for the country's agriculture.

Agricultural modernization

Undoubtedly the most important near-term goal for the Chinese economy is to modernize the country's agriculture and village life by sharply reducing the reliance on renewable animate power and phytomass and to make the countryside much more dependent on fossil fuels and electricity. This is, of course, the aim of the 'basic farm mechanization', a rather loosely defined programme which means that more than 70 per cent of all principal field, forestry, animal husbandry, fishery, and side-line activities should be taken over by machines. The year 1975 was Mao's original deadline for this complex and costly accomplishment; now 1980 is Hua's new target and it is quite clear that it, too, will not be met. Slogans and deadlines aside, this is, naturally, a crucial task and it is revealing to evaluate the quantities of modern energy needed to accomplish—and to sustain—this unprecedented rural transformation.

To begin with, how much energy will be required to eliminate some three-quarters of all animate labour in the Chinese countryside? In mechanized farming, virtually all fieldwork (tilling, sowing, transplanting, cultivating, applying fertilizers and pesticides, and harvesting) and transportation of products and provisions would be performed by tractor-drawn implements (and also some trucks), while irrigation, drainage, crop processing (grain milling, oil pressing, sugar extraction), and fodder preparation require machinery powered either by internal combustion engines or by electric motors.

Although the Chinese are building 75-horsepower tractors (and importing even bigger ones) and increasingly installing high-power water-pumping equipment, most of this machinery has been—and will continue to be—rather small. Nearly 20 per cent of the tractor park in 1976 were garden tractors, with drawbar horsepower of four, and among the wheel tractors the one produced in the greatest volume has been a 54-horsepower (36 horsepower at the drawbar) machine;[56] similarly, most of the more than 1 million tubewells on the North China Plain have a capacity of only 1.5–2 m^3 per second.[57] Average power of farm machinery in Wu-sih County, a showplace of rural mechanization in Kiangsu, typifies the situation in rice-growing areas: mean power of tractors is slightly over 12 horsepower and that of electrical and diesel motors only about 7 horsepower.[58]

Gross efficiency of this small-scale machinery is rather low. Depending on a host of circumstances (rolling resistance, soil and crop conditions, work speed, engine and its state, etc.) the useful work performed by small and medium tractors (drawbar horsepower 4–40) is equal to anywhere between 5–20 per cent of the total fuel consumption; assuming the average 15 per cent efficiency is not certainly too conservative. Power unit energy efficiencies for common motor use in water pumping range, with well-maintained equipment, between 20 per cent for natural gas engines and 27 per cent for diesel engines; 25 per cent may be taken as a somewhat liberal average. Water pumping efficiencies vary greatly with pump type and age and with the rate of pumping: assuming the average efficiency better than 60 per cent is quite unrealistic. Multiplying the two average values (0.25×0.6) results in the overall efficiency of 15 per cent.

Consequently replacing three-quarters of the current 60 trillion kcal of the useful human and animal rural labour with machinery whose gross efficiency is not higher than 15 per cent would call for an annual direct expenditure of at least 300×10^{12} kcal ($60 \times 0.75/0.15$) or about 43 Mtce; inadequate maintenance and inexperienced operation and management might raise this total easily to about 50 Mtce per year. To this must be, of course, added the not inconsiderable energy requirements for producing chemical fertilizers, field, water pumping and processing machinery and many other minor farm inputs.

When the large number of recently built ammonia and urea plants will have become fully operative, they will produce 3.5 Mt of nitrogen annually and the national total should reach 8 Mt of nitrogen in 1980. Taking the average value of 17600 kcal of feedstock and process energy per kg of nitrogen the aggregate fuel and electricity inputs to supply the country with nitrogen fertilizers would be about 140×10^{12} kcal—or 20 Mtce—per year at the beginning of the next decade. Approximately another 14×10^{12} kcal (2 Mtce) would be needed to produce adequate amounts of phosphorus and potassium.[59]

To displace three-quarters of animate labour, inventories of fossil-fuelled or electricity-powered machinery would have to be at least double in comparison with the mid-1970s. Assuming approximately 50 kg of steel per horsepower and no less than 20000–25000 kcal per kg of machinery, annual production of some 20 million horsepower would require 3–3.5 Mtce energy and adding the energy cost of scores of field implements and crop processing machinery, trucks, spare parts, storage sheds and repair shops, as well as the feedstock and process energy requirements for insecticides and herbicides, would easily double this figure.

Indirect energy subsidies in agricultural chemicals and machinery would be thus about 30 Mtce annually and direct liquid fuel and electricity inputs for tractors and water pumping would bring the total energy cost of basic farm mechanization to no less than 80 Mtce per year. Furthermore, cutting the rural dependence on forest fuels, grasses, and crop residues also by about three-quarters from its mid-1970s level would require—even when assuming doubled combustion efficiency—another 50–60 Mtce of solid and liquid fuels.

This approximate analysis makes clear the enormous energy cost of what would be merely basic rural modernization in the world's most populous nation. Further energy subsidies would be, of course, needed to raise the crop yields, extend the irrigated land, increase multicropping, mechanize construction and repairs of water projects, build modern roads, and improve the living conditions of the peasants. Regardless of how fast and with what real success the Chinese move toward the still distant goal of nationwide rural modernization, direct and indirect energy-flows into agriculture will have to take up a much larger share of the country's future energy consumption.

Future energy needs

If China wants to achieve her ambitious developmental goals, her economy will have to maintain expansion rates at least equal to the best periods of its past performance. The annual exponential GNP growth rate for both the first 5-year plan (1953–7) and for the post-Cultural Revolution years of renewed economic expansion (1969–76) was 7.2 per cent; the long-term rate for 1949–76 equalled 6.85 per cent. It would thus seem that the Chinese economy would do very well maintaining 7 per cent growth rate for another decade—and thus doubling its size—and it would not do badly to advance at 6 per cent rate.

As in any other nation, economic growth and energy consumption in China are closely related: GNP-energy linear regression for the years 1949–76 has a correlation coefficient 0.973 and explains 94.77 per cent of the variance.[60] This strong relationship offers a better short-term forecasting tool than the often used GNP-energy elasticity coefficients.[61] Taking 6 and 7 per cent as the desirable lower and upper limits, China's GNP (in 1976 US dollars) would grow to approximately $410–$425 billion in 1980 and to $550–$600 billion in 1985 and primary energy required to support this growth would range roughly from 530 to 560 Mtce in 1980 and between 730–800 Mtce in 1985.

Continuation of the historical production growth rate of about 9 per cent until the mid-1980s would bring the primary energy output to approximately 650 Mtce in 1980 and to 1000 Mtce in 1985 and leave a considerable surplus for export (about 100 Mtce in 1980 and perhaps over 200 Mtce in 1985). However, while not impossible, such a growth rate is not very likely: it is the basic property of any growth process that large, complex systems cannot simply continue to expand at fast pace.

The only two countries which had topped 500 Mtce energy production level and went on to expand it beyond 1000 Mtce—the United States and the Soviet Union—have both experienced much lower growth rates. The Soviet analogy is certainly more appropriate: the country's primary energy output topped 500 Mtce as recently as 1956 and surpassed the 1 billion mark in 1966, growing at about 6.7 per cent annually; the expansion had not been limited by availability of energy resources but solely by investment and technological considerations. It must be also remembered that the Soviets profited from major transfers of advanced foreign technology.

Expansion of the Chinese primary energy production by 7 per cent per year for another decade would have to be then termed a success; it would bring the output to just over 600 Mtce in 1980 and to some 850 Mtce in 1985, meeting the likely domestic requirements and leaving a small, though valuable, export surplus equal, in crude oil terms, to some 40 Mt in 1980 and 60 Mt in 1985.

The actual course of affairs will be, of course, determined by the Chinese choice of developmental strategies.

Developmental strategies

Erratic course of the Chinese economic development during the 27 years of Mao's fluctuating leadership had left hardly a trace of a 'normal' policy record which might be used to extrapolate at least into the near future. And although virtually all events since the autumn of 1976 point to a deepening shift away from Maoist-inspired radicalism to sensible pragmatism, the generational succession has yet to run its full course and the stability of the post-Mao leadership has yet to be tested.

Nevertheless, as 'the true powers of individuals, groups, and political bodies lie in the useful potential energies that flow under their control',[62] vigorous expansion, qualitative improvement, and a more equal distribution of energy flows must be the goals of any but a suicidal leadership. Their pursuit in the Chinese setting will inexorably require the continuation and intensification of many recent trends.

Modernization of coal-mining and transportation, intensive hydrocarbon recovery from the largest producing oil and gas fields and extensive exploratory drilling (including shallower offshore waters), construction of interprovincial pipelines, further substitution of coal by liquid and gaseous fuels, greatly increased energy subsidies into agricultural production and significant improvement of conversion efficiencies must be at the top of any list of priorities if China is to make significant progress in economic modernization and improvements in the standard of living. The scale of this effort is staggering and just a few quantitative indicators and comparisons illustrate the immensity—and impossibility—of an attempt to surpass world's advanced levels before the end of this century.

To maintain a fast pace of primary energy production, the Chinese coal industry is to double its output in the next 10 years:[63] This means an average exponential growth rate of 7 per cent per year and the total output in excess of 1 billion tonnes of raw coal in 1988. However, as both the Soviet Union and the United States have been finding out, the cost, the environmental problems, and the logistics of producing more than half a billion tonnes of coal annually is sharply curtailing any fast growth rates; since topping that mark, the US coal output has been growing by only 2.1 per cent per year and the Soviet production by mere 1.4 per cent.

Crude oil production will have to be expanded considerably—but exponential growth of no more than 10 per cent per year would exhaust the Chinese onshore reserves of around 5 Bt by the mid-1990s. Chinese are, of course, well aware of this fact, as exemplified by Hua's call to discover 10 more Ta-ch'ings; even should the required reserves be in the ground, the Chinese investment to discover and to develop them might be of the same order of magnitude as the Soviet oil industry's expenditures during the past 20 years.[64]

Every step of large-scale fossil fuel development—exploration, production, transportation, and conversion—requires complex and expensive technology (virtually all of it based on high-quality steel) and well-trained labour force backed up by long-range planning and management and by intensive research. So far the Chinese have not excelled in any of these activities. In spite of impressive progress in many areas, China's domestic energy technologies lag considerably behind the world standards and resemble the United States or European status of, depending on particulars, two to four decades ago; Communist Party's ever-changing 'line' has been hardly conducive to serious long-range planning and the disdain of intellectuals and scientists —a practice only recently discarded—has damaged the country's research and development effort immeasurably.

Consequently China's modernization pace will depend to a considerable degree on the willingness and ability to promote rational planning, research, and management, and to import advanced foreign technologies. The option of complete self-reliance has been always a useless myth: even the most advanced industrialized nations are not self-sufficient in certain major branches of increasingly complex energy technologies.

This raises, of course, the problem of

hard-currency payments and the question of how far China's barter of energy for technology might go. Because the country's potential needs for foreign technology are so immense, it seems safe to conclude that unless the country would open herself to long-term joint ventures or choose to accept large loans or amass sizeable trade deficits it is most unlikely that they could be satisfied by regular trade alone.[65] The post-Mao leadership has initiated a relatively massive transfer of the most advanced Japanese and Western technology but it will take years before clear-cut, long-range policies will emerge from the continuing discussions about the extent of the self-reliance and integration with the global economy.

Chinese planners also face difficult decisions regarding the future state of small-scale technologies which have played such a critical part in the rural industrialization. Their low quality output and inordinate energy cost do not make them very suitable in more advanced stages of modernization—but their total, or near total, substitution by centralized large-scale production would not be an appropriate solution in a capital-short country so badly equipped with good roads and railways.

In modernizing the countryside, Chinese should also avoid sinking into an excessive dependence on fossil fuels; there are definitive advantages in keeping and improving certain functions of a society running on solar energy.[66] For example, energy flow analysis shows that draught animals do not put an excessive burden on the country's ecosystem and consequently many of them should be kept even in largely mechanized farming to contribute useful work and valuable protein and organic fertilizer. Similarly, establishment of fuelwood lots in suitable deforested regions complete use of logging residues in forested areas, generation of biogas from animal wastes and crop residues and operation of small hydro stations provide an excellent alternative, or at least a welcome supplement, to non-renewable fuels.

In sum, China's energy development strategy should be multi-faceted and flexible. Taking into account the richness, location, and quality of resources, ancient traditions of solar energetics and enormous regional disparities within the nation, it should strive to modernize the countryside without cutting it completely off its traditional renewable energies and without abandoning appropriate small-scale industries; it should aim for sustainable growth rates of coal and hydrocarbon production by, among others, tapping the still sizeable economies of scale and introducing as many advanced foreign technologies as practicable;[67] and it should attempt to improve conversion efficiencies and encourage proper final uses and widespread conservation.

Given a stable, rational government, these strategies would not only maintain China's energy self-sufficiency for the remainder of this century, but would even allow for modest growth of fuel exports. They would also firmly establish China as the world's third largest economy and might bring a modicum of prosperity to her vast population.

Appendix A: Units

Abbreviations	*Units*
Bm^3	billion cubic metres
Bt	billion tonnes
Btu	British thermal unit
°C	degree Celsius
cm^2	square centimetre
GW	gigawatt
hp	horsepower
J	joule
kcal	kilocalorie
kg	kilogram
kgce	kilogram of coal equivalent
km	kilometre
kW	kilowatt
kWh	kilowatt hour
m^3	cubic metre
Mt	million tonnes
Mtce	million tonnes of coal equivalent
MW	megawatt
W	watt

Appendix B: China's fossil fuel production

	Coal (thousand tonnes)				
	Total	*Large mines*	*Small mines*	*Crude oil (million tonnes)*	*Natural gas (million cubic metres)*
1949	32430	22117	10313	0.121	Negl.
1950	42920	32607	10313	0.200	Negl.
1951	53090	45405	7685	0.305	Negl.
1952	66490	56184	10306	0.436	Negl.
1953	69680	61527	8153	0.622	—
1954	83660	75545	8115	0.789	—
1955	98300	89650	8650	0.966	—
1956	110360	101862	8498	1.163	—
1957	130732	—	—	1.458	600
1958	230000	—	—	2.264	—
1959	300000	—	—	3.700	—
1960	280000	—	—	5.100	—
1961	170000	—	—	5.500	—
1962	185000	—	—	6.100	—
1963	200000	—	—	6.700	—
1964	215000	—	—	9.000	—
1965	232200	197370	34830	11.400	9200
1966	271400	—	—	14.600	—
1967	190000	—	—	13.900	—
1968	235800	—	—	15.200	—
1969	281600	—	—	21.400	—
1970	327400	240600	86800	30.129	20700
1971	353600	—	—	38.700	—
1972	376500	—	—	44.900	—
1973	398100	286640	111460	56.900	—
1974	409000	—	—	68.200	—
1975	478000	330900	147100	77.060	34600
1976	483000	325300	157700	86.760	38020
1977	550000	364400	185600	93.640	47140

Source: CIA, *China: economic indicators*, Washington DC: CIA, (1978), p. 22; CIA, *China: a statistical compendium*, Washington DC: CIA (1979), p. 9.

Notes and references†

1. Most of this information has been summarized and evaluated in my *China's energy: achievements, problems, prospects* (New York,Praeger Publishers, 1976).
2. Socolow, R. H. Energy conservation. In Hollander, J. M., Simmons, M. K., and Wood, D. O., eds., *Annual Review of Energy* **2** (Palto Alto, Annual Reviews, 1977), p. 241.
3. The selected year, mainly because of a relative abundance of available data at the time of researching this complex topic, is 1974, the 25th year of the PRC's existence. Derivations of the flows are presented in detail in an appendix to the original publication.
4. Abbreviations of all units used in the text, and notes to this paper are explained in Appendix A.
5. Global net energy fixation of land plants is nearly 0.3 per cent of annual solar radiation (full spectrum) at the Earth's surface; lower conversion rate for China is due to a very low productivity of the country's vast, dry, and barren interior. Net primary productivity of China's vegetation is thus only about 3.5 per cent of the world total, although the

† For reasons of space the number of references and notes in the original text has been greatly reduced.

country's territory covers nearly 6.5 per cent of the global landmass.

6. Odum, H. T. *Environment, power, and society* (New York, Wiley-Interscience, 1971), pp. 105–9.
7. For comparison, the 1974 food supply for other populous developing nations was calculated by the FAO as follows (all figures in kcal/capita): India 1971; Indonesia 2128; Brazil 2515; Bangladesh 2023; Pakistan 2132; Nigeria 2084; Mexico 2725; Philippines 1963 (FAO, *1976 Production Yearbook* (Rome, FAO, 1977), pp. 243–245).
8. Smil, V. China's food. *Current History* **75** (439) (September 1976), 69–72, 82–84.
9. Richardson, S. D. *Foresty in Communist China* (Baltimore, Johns Hopkins 1966), p. 14, and Westoby, J. Whose Trees? Whose science?, *New Scientist* **74** (1013) (12 August 1976), pp. 341–343.
10. This time-consuming task—essential yet unrewarded by any workpoints—is usually done by children or grandparents to free the parents for communal work.
11. For comparison, in the same year the Indian consumption was 110 million m^3, the Soviet 83.4 million m^3 and the US firewood harvest was only 14.1 million m^3 (FAO, *1975 Yearbook of Forest Products*, Rome, FAO, 1977), pp. 17–18.
12. CIA estimate is 24 million tonnes of coal equivalent, which would be exactly 168×10^{12} kcal (CIA, China: economic indicators (Washington, DC, CIA, 1977), p. 27).
13. In 1974 inventory of powered irrigation equipment reached 36 million horsepower and the tractor park totalled 12.5 million horse-power: CIA, China: Economic Indicators, op. cit., p. 13.
14. Total animal power was calculated from figures in Table 10.2 assuming, once again, that only two-thirds of animals are actually available for work; total human potential was calculated by assuming rural working population of about 390 million people and power of 0.075 hp/person (that is around 5.5 kilogram-metres per second for continuous work).
15. Erisman, A. L. China: Agriculture in the 1970s. In: *China: A reassessment of the economy* (Washington, DC, USGPO, 1975), p. 333.
16. It should be stressed that about half of all plant energy is the animal feed and bedding, about one-quarter is fuel and only about 16 per cent is vegetal food (Fig. 10.1); caloric equivalent of primary commercial energy is based on the 1974 consumption of 377 Mtce.
17. According to the USBC, *1976 Statistical Abstract* (Washington, DC, USGPO, 1976), p. 549, the 1974 national primary energy consumption equalled $72\,933 \times 10^{12}$ Btu or 18.4×10^{15} kcal. Energy equivalent of all US food and feed crops harvested in 1974 totalled about 1.5×10^{15} kcal (data on field crop, fruit and hay harvest were taken from USDA, *Agricultural Statistics 1976* (Washington, DC, USGPO, 1976), pp. 1–296) and that of timber and fuelwood (according to the USBC, op. cit., p. 681) was about 0.95×10^{15} kcal for a total of about 2.45×10^{15} kcal.
18. Schumacher, Ernst F. Economics should begin with people, not goods. *The Futurist* **8**, (6) (December 1974), p. 274.
19. Most of the following material on small coal mines and small hydro stations is taken from my previous summaries of the topic: Smil, V. China opts for small scale energy technologies. *Energy International* **13** (2) (Feburary 1976), pp. 17–38; Smil, V. Intermediate energy technology in China. *World Development* **4** (10–11) (November 1976), pp. 920–937; Smil, V. Intermediate energy technology in China. *The Bulletin of the Atomic Scientists* **33** (2) (February 1977), pp. 25–31.
20. New China News Agency (NCNA) in English, SWB, FE/W910/A/6 (5 January 1977).
21. NCNA in English, SWB, FE/W952/A/13 (26 October 1977).
22. CIA. China: The Coal Industry (Washington, DC, CIA, 1976), pp. 8–9.
23. You Jishou, quoted in *China Reconstructs* **28** (4) (April 1979), p. 10.
24. NCNA in Chinese and provincial broadcasts, SWB, FE/W881/A/7 (9 June 1976); FE/W913/A/8 (26 January 1977); FE/W949/A/11) 5 October 1977).
25. For details on the Chinese biogas generation see Smil, V. China claims lead in biogas energy supply. *Energy International* **14** (6) (June 1977), pp. 25–7 and Smil, V. Energy solution in China. *Environment* **19** (7) (October 1977), pp. 27–31.
26. Anaerobic fermentation destroys 50 per cent of *Escherichia coli* in 3 months and 95 per cent of *Schistosoma japonicum* (blood fluke) eggs are eventually destroyed in the process, a fact of high importance for still large schistosomiasis areas of southern China.
27. The problems with small coal mines have been already mentioned: low quality of fuel, making it unsuitable for modern efficient enterprises, low productivity, and poor safety. Many mines are also only shortlived

and seasonally operated and cannot be relied on supplying steady base requirements. The same is true about many small hydro stations with their very low load factors, erratic service and silting-up reservoirs. Biogas digesters cannot be used in colder regions of the country and even in temperate and warm provinces their efficiency, and hence their gas output, drops sharply during the winter months.

28. For details on K'ai-luan's development, production, and national importance see Smil, V. Earthquake strikes at China's energy centres. *Energy International* **13** (12) (December 1976), pp. 21–2.
29. Ikonnikov, A. B. The capacity of China's coal industry. *Current Scene* **11** (4) (April 1973), p. 8.
30. US surface production was 54.7 per cent in 1975 and, in the same year, the Soviet open mines produced 32.2 per cent of the total: USBC, op. cit., p. 710; TsSu, op. cit, p.242.
31. The most valuable publications have been Williams, B. A. The Chinese petroleum industry: growth and prospects. In: *China: A Reassessment of the Economy*, op. cit., pp. 225–63; Ling, H. C. *The petroleum industry of the People's Republic of China* (Stanford, Hoover Institution, 1975): Chen, Chu-yan. *China's petroleum industry* (New York, Praeger Publishers, 1976) and CIA, China: Oil Production Prospects (Washington, DC, CIA, 1977).
32. See, among others, Smil, V. Communist China's oil exports: a critical evaluation. *Issues and Studies* **11** (3) (March 1975), pp. 71–8; CIA, China: Energy Balance Projections (Washington, DC, CIA, 1975); Hardy, R. W. *Chinese oil* (Washington, DC, The Center for Strategic and International Studies, 1976).
33. Meyerhoff, A. A. and Willums, J.-O. Petroleum geology and industry of the People's Republic of China. CCOP Technical Bulletin **10** (1976), pp. 204–5).
34. The Japanese and European experience has shown that the largest economies of scale are realized when increasing the tanker size between 20 000 and 200 000 deadweight tons; gains are much smaller for larger ships—while the problems with them (manoeverability, accident and pollution chances) are greater.
35. Communist Chinese have never released any figures on the resources of fissionable materials; Western estimates credit the PRC with 20000 to 100000 tonnes of uranium (World Energy Conference (WEC), *Survey of energy resources 1974* (London, WEC, 1974). p. 205). Considering that the reasonably assured US resources at up to $20 per kg of uranium were at least 330000 tonnes in 1974 (WEC, loc. cit.), the estimates for China would seem to be rather low. In any case, China has enough fissionable materials to support not only her nuclear armaments but also to develop an independent nuclear power industry.
36. State Statistical Bureau, *Ten great years* (Peking, Foreign Languages Press, 1960) p. 14.
37. Bazhenov, I. I., Leonenko, I. A., and Kharchenko, A. K. *Ugolnaya promyshlennost Kitaiskoi Narodnoi Respubliki* (Moscow, Gosgortekhizdat, 1950), p. 44.
38. For comparison, the US recoverable coal reserves are about 180 Bt and total resources about 2900 Bt: WEC, op. cit., p. 78.
39. It must be pointed out that estimates of recoverable oil and gas resources are very contentious even in the case of the world's most extensively explored area—the United States. For details on varying totals and interpretations see, among many others, McCulloch, T. M. Oil and Gas in Brobst, D. A. and Pratt, W. P., eds., *United States mineral resources* (Washington, DC, USGPO, 1973), pp. 477–496; and Riva, J. P., Jr., and Franssen, H. T. Energy Supply: Oil and Natural Gas in *Project Interdependence*, op. cit., pp. 130–207.
40. Another detailed study is now being conducted by M. J. Terman of the US Geological Survey. The most significant difference between Meyerhoff's and Terman's interpretation is in their assumptions about tectonic genesis of the offshore basins, particularly those under the East China Sea. Unlike Meyerhoff, Terman believes their oil-bearing strata are analogous to the heterogeneous continental and lacustrique Upper Tertiary facies of the graben of North China, having, possibly, high oil content but a rather low economic recoverability.
41. Values close to the upper limit of this range would make China's crude oil reserves nearly as large as are currently the Soviet ones and just slightly in excess of the Iranian and Kuwaiti totals.
42. Consequently, there have been only isolated small-scale applications of solar heat collectors in Tibet, where the largest glass absorber (280 m^2) is used for water heating in Lhasa's public bath: NCNA in English, SWB, FE/W866/A/10 (25 February 1976).
43. Berezina, Y. I. *Toplivno-Energeticheskaya Baza Kitaiskoi Narodnoi Respubliki* (Moscow, IVL, 1959), p. 58.
44. China's 330 GW for G_{av} represent 13.5 per

cent of the global total; USSR's share is 11.1 per cent, US share 7.2 per cent and Zaire's 6.7; however, Zaire can utilize its waters most of the time, its G^{95} resources are 77.6 GW, followed by China, USSR, and Brazil.

45. Ko Tze-yuan, Tibet's Abundant Geothermal, Resources, Ta Kung Pao (8 April 1976), p. 13; Chang Ming-tao, Tibet's Geysers, *China reconstructs* **26** (11) (November 1977), pp. 44–6.
46. In 1960 Siberian crude oil accounted for mere 1.1 per cent of the national production, natural gas for 0.7 and coal for 28 per cent; in 1980 these shares will be about 50, 35, and 38 per cent and the strong eastward shift will continue afterwards (Smith, A. B. Soviet Dependence on Siberian Resource Development, in *Soviet economy in a new perspective* (Washington, DC, USGPO, 1976), p. 482).
47. Per capita primary energy consumption (all values are in kgce/year/capita) is over 11 000 in the United States, nearly 4000 in Japan and averages around 5000 in both the EEC and Comecon countries. Inclusion of traditional fuels (firewood, crop residues, dung) in Indian energy consumption raises the per capita value quite dramatically: from about 200 to some 490 kgce/year/capita (Revelle, R. Energy Use in Rural India, *Science* **192** (4243) (4 June 1976), p. 969.
48. Chou. En-lai, Report on the Work of the Government. *Peking Review* **18** (4) (24 January 1975), p. 23.
49. However, these industrial consumption estimates are certainly somewhat exaggerated because they were determined as residuals after accounting for all other sectorial uses and include also transportation and storage losses, fuel stocks, non-fuel uses (these are separated in Fig. 10.6) and military needs. For comparison, the 1974 industrial energy consumption in the United States was 23.3 per cent of the total use, in Japan 36.8 per cent and in major Western European nations between 25–30 per cent (OECD, *Energy balances of OECD countries* (Paris, OECD, 1976) passim).
50. Usack and Egan estimate that about 3 tonnes of raw coal are needed to produce a tonne of coke concentrate in large enterprises and that the ratio is as high as 4.5. 1 for small plants: Usack, A. H., Jr. and Egan, J. D. China's iron and steel industry, in *China: A reassessment of the economy*, op. cit., p. 272. For comparison, in the United States coke ovens 1.43 tonnes of coal are needed to produce a tonne of coke: Federal Energy Administration, *Project Independence*, **3** (Washington DC, USGPO, 1974) pp. 6–15.
51. Because metallurgical coke is still the most expensive fuel used by iron and steel industry, its partial replacement by injections of fuel oil or natural gas has recently led to input values of well below 500 kg of coke per tonne of pig iron in many Western European nations and in Japan.
52. Small plants producing mainly these two fertilizers accounted for one-half of 3.2 Mt of nitrogen output in 1974 (CIA, People's Republic of China: chemical fertilizer supplies, 1949–74 (Washington DC, CIA, 1975), p. 14).
53. These are my calculations (using rather conservative assumptions as far as the energy content of fuels is concerned; if the actual raw material and process fuel inputs are of better quality, the energy cost of fertilizers would be even higher!) based on about half a dozen input budgets given in Sigurdson, J. Rural Industrialization in China in *China: A reassessment of the economy*, op. cit., pp. 420–1.
54. The average value for the United States 1973 ammonia output was 11 318 kcal/kg of N (Hayes, E. T. Energy implications of materials processing. *Science* **191** (4228) (20 February 1976), p. 664); European values for ammonia and urea at the beginning of this decade were between 13 400–17 700 kcal/kg of N (Leach, G. and Slesser, M. *Energy requirements of network inputs to food producing processes* (Glasgow, University of Strathclyde, 1973), pp. 21–5).
55. For comparison, the useful energy in the United States amounted to 49.3 per cent in 1960, 50.5 per cent in 1970 and it would—without a significant conservation effort—decrease to about 45 per cent in 1980 and to only 40 per cent in 1985 (Joint Committee on Atomic Energy, op. cit., pp. 4–6).
56. CIA, Production of Machinery and Equipment in the People's Republic of China (Washington DC, CIA, 1975), pp. 13–14.
57. Perkins, D. D. A Conference on Agriculture. *The China Quarterly*, No. 67 (September (1976), p. 606.
58. Chin. Chi-chu, Revolutionization in command of mechanization. *Peking Review* **20** (33) (12 August 1977), p. 38.
59. This assumes attainment of the optimum ratio of approximately 100 units of nitrogen to 50 units of phosphorus and 33 units of potassium, and the average energy costs according to Leach G. and Slesser, M. op. cit., p. 34.

60. Calculated on the basis of the CIA's GNP data (CIA, China: economic indicators, op. cit., p. 3) and my energy consumption estimates (Smil, V. China's Energy, op. cit., p. 141 for 1949–74; the values used for 1975 and 1976 were 415 Mtce and 447 Mtce). The linear equation has the form $Y = -6.0633 \times 10^7 + 1.4499 \times 10^{-2} X$, where Y is the energy consumption in Mtce and X is the GNP in billions of 1976 US dollars.
61. Major problem with elasticity coefficients is that regardless which method of calculation is used, one obtains different results for different periods. For example, using the data described in footnote 60 and the classical formula for period elasticity—$e = ((\Delta E/E)/(\Delta G/G)$—China's energy/GNP elasticities are 3.2 for 1953–76, 1.9 for 1969–76 and 2.6 for 1973–6. Similarly, division of the compound GNP growth rate into the compound growth rate of energy consumption (the annual method) results in elasticity coefficients 1.8 for 1953–76, 1.6 for 1969–76 and 2.4 for 1973–6. These temporal variations do not make energy/GNP elasticities a reliable forecasting tool. On the other hand, energy-GNP linear regressions for individual countries are uniformly and extremely high, providing a reasonable basis for short-term forecasts (Smil, V. and Kuz, T. Energy and the economy—A global and national analysis, *Long Range Planning* **9** (3) (June 1976), pp. 65–74).
62. Odum, H. T., Environment, Power and Society, op. cit., p. 206.
63. This goal was revealed by Hsiao Han, Ministry of Coal Industry, in his article Developing Coal Industry at High Speed, *Peking Review* **21** (8) (24 February 1978), p. 6; another doubling is to be achieved between 1987 and 2000.
64. Conservative estimates of Ta-ch'ing's ultimate production are at least 400–500 Mt (Meyerhoff and Willums, op. cit., p. 179). Discovery of 10 more Ta-ch'ings would thus entail crude oil reserves of no less than 4–5 Bt, the mass about equal to the best current estimates of China's total recoverable onshore deposits (see Table 10.5). Comparison with the Soviet effort is based on the fact that the Soviet crude oil production rose from 98.3 Mt in 1957 (about equal to China's 1978 output) to 519.7 Mt in 1976, the total which would be reached by the Chinese with 10 per cent exponential growth by 1995. It should be pointed out that the Soviets achieved this growth with a considerable transfer of Western, as well as Comecon, technology, with tapping of extraordinary supergiant Samotlor field—and without virtually any expensive offshore drilling.
65. Chinese crude oil exports totalled US$760 million in 1975 and $665 million in 1976; in relative terms these shipments provided only about 10.6 and 9.2 per cent of China's export earnings (CIA, China's Internationl Trade, 1976–7 (Washington DC, CIA, 1977), p. 12), and their value was virtually identical with foodstuff imports in those 2 years.
66. It would be ironic for China to discard all of her precious renewable energetics in time when the world's most industrialized nations are searching for ways to cut their dependence on fossil fuels by increasingly engaging in research and applications of solar energy—as direct radiation, crop and forest fuels, wind and ocean thermal power—for heating and electricity generation.
67. Perhaps the only exception should be nuclear energetics. Although the Chinese believe that nuclear power has 'outstanding merits' and is a safe and clean source of energy (Feng Tse-chun, 'Nuclear Power', K'o-hsueh Shih-yen, No. 12 (December 1976), pp. 29–31), introduction of commercial fission generation in the near future could be hardly justified as necessary or economical.

11

China's electric power industry

WILLIAM CLARKE

There exists a widespread shortage of electric power in the People's Republic of China (PRC) today that is adversely affecting the economy and which must be corrected quickly if the programme to modernize industry, agriculture, science and technology, and national defence is to be successfully implemented. Electric power is a 'vanguard' industry which in a developing country like China must advance at a pace 1.3 or 1.4 times that of industry generally.

The short-term solution to the power shortage is being sought in the directives of Chairman Hua issued in the autumn of 1977 calling for conservation, fuller utilization of existing generating capacity, and its more efficient operation. In the longer run, China will place reliance on the continued development of both hydroelectric and thermal power stations. No nuclear stations are currently operative, but the Chinese will probably soon begin one. Although both large and small power stations will continue to be built, the greater emphasis will be placed on development of China's hydroelectric potential, the largest in the world. Currently the PRC is the fourth largest producer of primary energy in the world after the United States, the Soviet Union, and Saudi Arabia.

In 1977 the PRC's electric power industry generated about 223 billion kilowatt-hours of power or 9.5 per cent that of the United States. This was enough to place China seventh in power output. Installed capacity on 31 December 1977, was estimated to be 40 500 megawatts. The bulk of this capacity is found in the 192 known thermal and hydro-stations of 30 megawatts capacity and over. Of these, 126 units are thermal stations and 66 are hydroelectric, some are currently under construction or are being expanded. Additional stations of this capacity or greater are thought to exist. About 62 per cent of the capacity is thermal, the balance hydroelectric.

To adequately support a 10 per cent rate of industrial growth, the power industry would need to add about 5300 MW to capacity this year, a 13 per cent rate of growth, and about 12 700 MW in 1985 to provide capacities of 45 800 and 108 000 MW respectively. The domestic power equipment manufacturing industry, while quite substantial, does not appear capable of meeting this requirement. Thus, if a 10 per cent industrial growth is to be achieved, Peking will have to import power plants and equipment from abroad possibly expending as much as $300 million annually during the period 1978–85.

It does not appear that between now and 1980 the electric power industry can accelerate growth to the level to support a

From *Chinese Economy Post-Mao*, A Compendium of Papers Submitted to the Joint Economic Committee, Congress of the United States (US Government Printing Office, New York, 1978), pp.403–27.

10 per cent industrial rate of growth, 1978–80. It does seem possible, however, that by 1981 acceleration of developments in the industry could support such industrial growth. To achieve this the Chinese will need to:

(a) invest heavily in the development of the coal industry;
(b) improve rail transport and develop 'mine mouth' thermal plants to reduce coal hauling;
(c) sharply reduce station construction times, especially on large hydro plants;
(d) develop higher capacity transmission systems;
(e) accelerate the development of 600-MW boilers and turbogenerators;
(f) expand the domestic power equipment manufacturing industry; and
(g) engage in a consistent and planned import of complete foreign powerplants and equipment.

The energy base

The People's Republic of China is the fourth largest producer of primary energy in the world after the United States, the Soviet Union, and Saudi Arabia. Output is about one-fifth that of the United States and one-third that of the Soviet Union. It ranks third in the consumption of energy after the United States and the USSR, and ahead of Japan. Reserves of energy are among the most extensive in the world and are still in a relatively early stage of exploitation. The hydroelectric potential is the greatest in the world and coal reserves are third after the United States and the USSR. China has been awakened to the size and potential of its petroleum resources only in the past 15 years. To this day it is doubtful if the People's Republic of China has a full and accurate appraisal of the extent of its petroleum reserves. Information available outside of China on natural gas reserves is sketchy.

The hydroelectric potential of the People's Republic of China has been given recently as 540000 MW located principally in Tibet and in the mountainous south-western provinces.[1] The Yangtze River alone constitutes about 40 per cent of the potential. To the north of the Yangtze in drier regions lies the Yellow River with the most developed hydroelectric facilities, but with only 5 per cent of the run-off of the Yangtze. Currently, only about 1 per cent of China's primary energy supply is derived from hydro resources, placing China 12th in the world in hydroelectric power generation; production is about 14 per cent of the United States, the world leader.

Coal has long been China's traditional source of energy. Proven reserves run about 80 billion tonnes and are located in many parts of the country, but principally north of the Yangtze River. Although development of the industry has been hampered by inadequate investment, coal production was 483 million tonnes in 1976 and was around 550 million tonnes in 1977. Recent investments in foreign mining equipment indicate that some priority is now being given this industry, but it will take years to bring productivity up to world standards. Coal now supplies about two-thirds of the primary energy of the People's Republic of China. Such minor fuels as peat and firewood are excluded from this energy analysis.

With the opening of the Taching, Shengli, and Takang oil fields in the 1960s, China became an oil producer of world rank running 10th in production in 1976; about 80 per cent of a daily production of 1.8 million barrels at the beginning of 1978 came from these three fields. China's onshore reserves of oil are believed to total 40 billion barrels while estimates of offshore reserves are much more speculative, but potentially quite significant. Oil accounts for 21 per cent of the energy supply. About 90 per cent of the natural gas reserves, estimated at 25 trillion cubic feet, are found in Szechwan Province with the gas share of total energy supply being 10 per cent. China ranks fifth in natural gas production, but output is only about 7 per cent of the world leader, again the United States.[2]

Development of the industry (1949–1975)

Early stages

The economy of China was severely damaged by the Sino-Japanese War (1937–45) and by the civil war that ensued after the close of the Second World War and up until 1949 when Communist forces consolidated control over the country. Industrial production was reduced, agriculture was curtailed and the transport system disrupted. After the Japanese surrendered to the Russians in Manchuria in 1945, the Soviets dismantled heavy industrial facilities and shipped the equipment back to the USSR. Surveys later showed that about 50 per cent of the Manchurian industrial capacity was affected in this way. Included in these shipments were about 1000 MW of turbo-generating capacity, including both thermal and hydro units. By 31 December 1949, the total installed electric power generating capacity of the People's Republic of China stood at only 1800 MW, down from the 1944 peak of 3100 MW.[3] Thus, China's electric power generating capability at the end of the revolution was less than the present capactiy of the Grand Coulee hydroelectric station or the Kansas City Power & Light Co.

As the Chinese leadership surveyed the task ahead, they were quite aware of Lenin's dicta that 'communism equals Soviet power (strength) plus electrification' and 'without an electrification plan we cannot carry out real construction'. Later, in a 1958 directive, Chairman Mao put it more simply when he said, 'electric power is the pioneer of the national economy'.[4] The years 1949–51 were devoted primarily to restoring order in the economy and in the power industry preparatory to the planned development under the first 5-year plan.

China's first 5-year plan (1952–7) projected additions of new capacity of 2050 MW or a doubling of the installed capacity at the end of 1952. The actual additions turned out to be about 2900 MW, well above plan. Of this, new units at the Tafengman and Supung hydro-stations in the north-east to replace those removed by the Soviets totalled 600 MW. The feat of more than doubling capacity was accomplished by significant help from the Soviet Union, Czechoslovakia, and East Germany, who supplied turbines and generators and who established power generating equipment production facilities which, even today, remain the backbone of the Chinese equipment supply capability. By the end of 1957, installed capacity reached 4900 MW; 1000 MW of which were in hydroelectric facilities. China's electric power generating capacity for selected years is shown in Table 11.1.

Table 11.1. Electric power generating capacity, 1949–1977* (in thousand megawatts)

Year§	*Capacity*	*Year†*	*Capacity*
1949	1.8	1971	21.1
1952	2.0	1972	23.6
1957	4.9	1973	26.8
1961	10.7	1974	30.0
1965	11.8	1975	34.0
1966	13.8	1976	36.9
1970	19.4	1977	40.5

*Power generated is 3-phase, 50 hertz at main stations; small plants are generally single phase.

†CIA, *Handbook of economic statistics*, September 1977, p. 87, and older volumes. Estimates for 1976 and 1977 by the author are discussed in the section on the current situation.

§31 December of the year cited.

The 'Great Leap Forward'

At the close of the first 5-year plan in December 1957, the People's Republic of China began the great leap forward phase of economic development. In an attempt to move the economy forward at extraordinary rates of growth, power generation during 1958–60 was to increase at 18 per cent per annum. At this time plans called for a large number of new hydroelectric stations, some of 1000 MW, but most were never started and some that were, like Liuchia and Tanchiangkou were not completed until after 1970. Generating capacity in 1958 and 1959 was nearly doubled, however, with the addition of 4500 MW.[5]

Soviet aid continued during the 'Great Leap', but the excesses of the programme soon began to disrupt the economy. As a result by 1960 a severe slump had set in as production dropped. Difficulties were compounded by the decision of the USSR to withdraw all of its assistance, including personnel, and by the end of the summer of 1960 the Russians were gone.

Output of power is estimated to have dropped from 47 to 31 billion kilowatt-hours between 1960 and 1961, a decline of 34 per cent. If accurate, this decline illustrates the severity of the depression following the 'Great Leap Forward'. Six years elapsed before the 1960 level of output was again attained.[6] Additions to generating capacity 1960–5 were only 2600 MW, an average of just over 500 MW annually. Recovery was well under way by the mid-sixties only to receive another setback with the onset of the cultural revolution in 1966. By 1968, however, production rose sharply and growth of power output in the period 1968–70 grew at an average annual rate of 17 per cent.[7]

Resumption of growth

The beginning of the seventies saw attainment of a new level of confidence in Chinese power-development capabilities. The void left by the Soviet departure in 1960 had been overcome or to paraphrase Chairman Mao, the Chinese electric power industry 'had stood up'. The manufacture of basic units such as 100 MW turbogenerators had matured. The first large generators for long-deferred major hydro projects had become operational.

The fourth 5-year plan (1971–5) projected the further development of still larger turbogenerators and of higher voltage transmission lines. New power-generating equipment manufacturing facilities were to be erected in the interior. To accelerate growth during this period, the PRC leadership made a decision to import significant quantities of plant and technology including electric power stations. During the period 1972–5 about $2.8 billion in foreign plants were contracted for.

Contracts with foreign suppliers in the power sector approached $350 million and upon completion will add about 4500 MW to capacity. These foreign purchases are shown in Table 11.2. During the 1971–5 period, the expansion of generating capacity was uneven but averaged about 11 per cent annually.[8]

Organization

The electric power industry of China is controlled from Peking by the Ministry of Electric Power, although daily operations are managed by provincial power manatement bureaux.[9] A significant amount of local control is exercised at the prefecture and county level among the medium- and small-sized plants. The thousands of small hydros that dot the countryside, unlike other small-scale industries in China, are controlled by an electric power and water conservancy bureau probably at the level necessary to effect unified control over water use. This would not be at the commune or brigade level, but at the county level and often probably much higher, including the province. Although operated at the commune or brigade level, the small hydros are required to feed the power they generate into the area's state power grid. The operators of the small stations get paid for the power they supply to the grid, but the commune in turn must pay for the power it consumes.[10]

The electric power industry is no exception to the policy followed in various other sectors of the economy known as 'walking on two legs'. That is, parallel with the erection of relatively modern, large- and medium-sized central thermal stations and hydroelectric

Table 11.2. Electric power generating plant and equipment purchased by China, 1972–1976

Thermal station turbo-generators

USSR—1972: 4 units at 75 MW each; $8.2 million.

USSR—1973: 7 units at 100 MW each; $16.7 million.

USSR—1974: 1 unit at 200 MW; $2.7 million.

USSR—1975: 2 units at 200 MW each; $6.8 million.

USSR—1976: 2 units at 200 MW each; about $7.0 million.

Czechoslovakia—1974: 3 units at 100 MW each.

Italy—1972: 1 unit at 125 MW; supplied by Gruppa Industrie Elettromeccaniche (GIE)—over $8 million.

Italy—1974: 2 units at 320 MW; oil-fired plant under construction at Tientsin, December 1975; value about $79 million.

Japan—1972: 2 units at 125 MW each; supplied by Hitachi; operation scheduled for 1975; value, $30 million.

Japan—1973: 2 units at 250 MW each; supplied by Hitachi; operation at Tangshan originally scheduled for 1975; value, $72 million.

France/Switzerland—1974: 1 unit at 300 MW brown coal-fired plant supplied by CEM/France and Sulzer and Brown Boveri/Switzerland; transaction is 70 per cent French; operation scheduled for mid-1976; value, about $55 million.

France—1972: 2 units at 60 MW each; supplied by Alsthom-Neyrpic and Creusot-Loire; delivery scheduled 1975; value $10 million.

Sweden: 3 units supplied by ASEA; went into operation 1974; value, $4 million.

Gas turbines and generators

United Kingdom—1972: 5 units at 20 MW each; supplied by John Brown Ltd. (G. E. licensee); in use for base and peak load service, value $8.2 million.

United Kingdom—1973: 3 units at 20 MW each; supplied by John Brown Ltd.; at least one unit in use for mechanical drive, not power generation; value $8.2 million.

Belgium/Canada: 3 units at 8.5 MW each; supplied by ACEC/Belgium and Westinghouse/Canada (Model W–101–G); for base load service; delivered 1975; value $5 million.

Japan—1975: 2 units at 25 MW each; supplied by Hitachi (Type G–5); delivered 1976; value $5.2 million.

Canada—1973: 2 rail mobile units at 9 MW each; supplied by Orenda Division of Hawker Siddeley; arrived in PRC in 1975; value $5–6 million.

plants is the construction of simple, small-scale, relatively inefficient facilities. The number of these small stations is very large and by 1975 totalled 60000 with additions being made at the rate of over 5000 annually. At the beginning of 1979, China had a total of 87000 small hydros. By 1980 the installed capacity of these small hydros is expected to double.[11]

The great increase in these facilities since 1965, mostly hydro units whose average capacity is only 50–100 kW came about with the development of rural water conservation projects and the need in rural areas for power for agriculture and for the many, locally operated, small-scale industries. About 80 per cent of these small stations are found in the eight water-rich southern provinces of the PRC; Kwangtung leads with about 20000 hydros.

Technological base

In a general sense, the technological level

represented by the Chinese electric power industry trails that in the industrialized countries by more than 20 years. This lag can be seen in the scale of plant, the size of generating units, in the capacity of transmission lines, and in the near absence of interconnected systems and the creation of power pools.[12] It can also be seen in the design of equipment, in the near absence of gas turbines, in less sophisticated instrumentation, in centralized control of thermal stations, in power dispatch and load management, and in the absence of nuclear power stations. The real question, of course, is not so much the current technological lag, but the willingness and the ability of the Chinese to accelerate technological growth in the years ahead based on proven power industry technologies available from the industrialized countries. (See section on prospects.)

If the Chinese were to report publicly some meaningful operational data about their electric utilities, it would probably reveal additional problems associated with an inadequate technological base. There are, for example, reports by visitors to the PRC of serious voltage drops and frequency fluctuations in the power supply. Such drops in voltages and frequencies probably indicate that the demand for power is greater than the generating capacity in the grid. There is some indication that to try and meet demand the Chinese keep an unusually high percentage of available capacity operating in base load service.

Voltage and frequency variations can be damaging to electrical machinery and the lack of control can pose dangerous problems of stability in the grid and in the transfer of power to connecting systems. Moreover, there would appear to be insufficient reserve capacity to meet peak demand. All of these factors are probably the concern behind a July 1977 commentary from Shanghai which stated, 'Because of excessive consumption, the power network is overloaded, thus affecting power generation. If such a situation is allowed to continue, it will bring serious harm to the power network.' And from Kiangsi Province, 'We must strive—to achieve safety.'[13] Conversely, in Shantung province where major additions to capacity have been made in the past few years, the statement has been made which says that 'the level of safe and economic operation is steadily rising'. This is taken to mean that it has been possible to raise reserve capacity in Shantung.[14]

The technological feat in the power field that the Chinese have praised most has been the development of water-cooled rotors and stators for their 125- to 300-MW turbogenerators (the 125-MW stator is air cooled). Although such a development leads to smaller sized generators, there are difficult engineering problems to be overcome, for example, non-magnetic stainless steel rotor end shields. It is not clear why the Chinese went to this development that has not been found necessary in the West in these relatively small-sized generators. One possible explanation is that Chinese metallurgical and metalworking practices are not sufficiently well developed to handle the large shafts necessary (hydrogen embrittlement in the shafting can cause catastrophic destruction).[15] An insufficient number of the new 300-MW turbogenerators with distilled water-cooled rotors are in operation to prove that all developmental problems have been solved. Nevertheless, the development of water-cooled rotor turbogenerators indicates a noteworthy Chinese engineering and design capability.[16]

The PRC should take pride in the substantial technical growth that has been made since 1949 in bringing generating capacity from 1800 MW up to 40 500 MW on 31 December 1977. The steady technical progress made over this span of years may be seen in the milestones of achievement shown in Table 11.3.

Regional power capacity

At the close of the revolution in 1949, the PRC's power industry was centred in the

Table 11.3. Milestones in Chinese electric power development

1952	First 3-MW electric generator.
1953	First 6-MW hydrogenerator set. First 44 KV/20000-kVA transformer.
1954	First 6 MW steam turbogenerator set. First 154-kV/20000-kVA transformer.
1955	First 40-ton/hr steam boiler. First 10-MW hydrogenerator set. First 120-kV/31500-kVA transformer.
1956	First 12-MW steam turbogenerator set. First 15-MW hydrogenerator set. First 3.5-kV high-tension cable.
1957	First 130-ton/hr steam boiler. First 220-kV/20000-kVA single-phase transformer.
1958	First 110-kV/60000-kVA 3-phase transformer. First 220-kV/40000-kVA single-phase transformer. First 220-kV oil-filled high-tension cable.
1959	First 50-MW steam turbogenerator. First 72.5-MW generator for hydro use.
1960	First 230-ton/hr high-temperature and pressure steam boiler. First 50-MW high-temperature and pressure steam turbine.
1965	First silicon-controlled rectifier. First 500-kV standard condenser. First 6-MW gas turbine. First 220-kV air circuit breaker. First 330-kV rod insulator.
1966	First 125-MW hydrogenerator set. First 100-MW steam turbogenerator with water-cooled rotor and stator. First 100-MW hydrogenerator set. First 1000-kV standard condenser. First 330-kV suspension-type insulator. First 1000-kV standard condenser.
1968	First 150-MW generator for hydro use operational at Tanchiankgou. Initial construction of 300-MW hydroelectric turbogenerator at Harbin. First variable control transformer. First 110-kV underwater cable.
1969	First 125-MW steam turbogenerator with water-cooled rotor and stator. First 225-MW generator for hydro use operational at Liuchia. First 330-kV high-tension cable. First 250-kV transformer.
1970	First 60000-kVA transformer. First 110-kV aluminium cable current sensor. First 154-kV high-tension cable fault detector.
1971	First 60-MW hydrogenerator set for low head. Initial construction of 200-MW steam turbogenerator with water-cooled rotor and stator. First experimental geothermal power generator operational at 86 kW. Initial construction of 300-MW steam turbogenerator with water-cooled rotor and stator. First 750-kVA, 3-phase, water-cooled transformer. First 15000-kVA water-cooled transformer.
1972	First 220-kV/300000-kVA aluminium-wound transformer. First transmission of power at 330 kV over short distances.
1973	First 300-MW hydrogenerator set with water-cooled rotor and stator operational. First 11-MW pumped storage facility.
1974	First power station in China with over 1000 MW capacity into operation. First 330-kV mutual inductance voltage transformer. First sodium hexafluoride high-voltage standard condenser. First 670-ton/hr super high-pressure boiler for 200-MW steam turbines. First use of gas turbine exhaust heat to preheat boiler feedwater.
1975	First computer control of a 100-MW steam turbogenerator. First 10-MW gas turbine for power generation. First 200-MW steam turbogenerator operational at the Chinghsi station, Peking. First 330-kV high-tension transmission line completed, 534 km long.
1976	First 300-MW steam turbogenerator operational at the Wangting station, Wuhsi.
1977	Initial construction of 600-MW generators at Harbin. Initial construction of 600-MW subcritical power boilers at Harbin.

three provinces of the north-east and in the coastal areas. The first 5-year plan policy of locating industry as close to raw material and fuel sources as to centres of consumption promoted the dispersion of industry away from the coast. To support the industrial growth, centres of power also had to be established in the inland provinces which led to the development of a power industry in all of China's provinces. Table 11.4 indicates the approximate portion of generating capacity to be found in each province at the end of 1977.

Since 1970 power systems in some provinces have undergone rapid expansion. Between 1970 and 1977, about 1340 MW of capacity were added in Shantung to support the growth of industry, which brought the province from eleventh to fourth place. Completion of major hydro facilities on the Yellow and Han Rivers has significantly increased capacity in Kansu and Hupeh Provinces. Liaoning remains the province with the greatest capacity with Kansu, Szechwan, and Shantung following in that order.

Table 11.4. Electric power generating capacity by province, 31 December 1977

Province	*Share (per cent)*
Anhwei	4.8
Chekiang	5.1
Fukien	1.8
Heilungchiang	3.1
Honan	3.2
Hopeh	4.0
Hunan	2.4
Hupeh	5.7
Inner Mongolia	1.1
Kansu	8.1
Kiangsi	1.4
Kiangsu	4.1
Kirin	4.3
Kwangsi	1.8
Kwangtung	5.7
Kweichow	2.2
Liaoning	9.5
Ningsia	0.8
Peking	4.1
Shanghai	4.0
Shansi	2.6
Shantung	6.1
Shensi	2.4
Sinkiang	0.6
Szechwan	6.8
Tibet	0.2
Tientsin	1.6
Tsinghai	0.3
Yunnan	2.2

Power generation and demand

Information available does not permit an accurate or detailed picture of the demand for electric power in China for recent years, although it has been clear for some time that demand has not been fully met. Estimates show that industry consumes about 62 per cent of the primary energy generated with approximately 6 per cent used for agriculture, 5 per cent for transport, and 27 per cent commercial and residential use.[17]

Of the 6 per cent consumed by agriculture, a major share is produced by the thousands of small hydroelectric facilities found in the PRC. In addition to pumping for irrigation purposes, electric power is required on China's many communes to support repair facilities, small industrial establishments, and the increasing mechanization of agriculture.

New figures show that China generated 256.6 billion kilowatt-hours during 1978. While this was sufficient to put the PRC in seventh place in the world, the annual consumption per capita at 250 kilowatt-hours is very low and only on a level with other developing countries. Power generated in selected years is shown in Table 11.5.

Very little of the power generated is exported although some transfer has occurred with North Korea; the last reported figures show that in 1956 the PRC exported 154 million kilowatt-hours and in 1958 they imported 400 million kilowatt-hours. The PRC and North Korea also share the output of several hydroelectric facilities on the Yalu River.

China does not publish sufficient

Table 11.5. Generation of electric power in the PRC* (in billion kilowatt hours)

Year	*Generation*
1949	4.3
1952	7.3
1957	19.3
1961	31.0
1965	63.0
1970	107.0
1971	128.0
1972	139.0
1973	150.0
1974	164.0
1975	187.0
1976	203.5
1977	223.4
1978	256.6

* CIA, *China: Major Ecanomic Indicators*, 21 Sept. 1979.

information to permit estimates of the average demand or load on power-plants and systems. Plant factors (ratio of average power load to rated capacity) usually cannot be determined. One measure of efficiency is the annual hours the rated capacity must be operated to produce the kilowatt-hours of power generated. In 1962 when the lack of demand idled industrial capacity following the 'Great Leap Forward', the annual hours of operation dropped below 2800. Hours of operation for thermal and hydro-stations differ markedly. At times of low water or when the demands of irrigation are high, the operation of small hydro facilities can drop below 2000 hours per year. By 1976 and 1977, this hourly figure of merit was estimated at 3500 and 3525 hours, respectively.[18]

Transmission of power

The most important electric power grids in the PRC are located in the north-east (centred on Liaoning and Kirin), north (centred on Peking, Tientsin, and Tangshan) and east (centred in the Shanghai area). Provincial grids are gradually being expanded to cover most important centres of power consumption in Kwangtung, Hupeh, and Shantung. China's longest transmission link runs from Yumen in the north-east through Lanchou to Chengchou in the east. The portion from Lanchou running 333 miles to Paochi is the PRC's only 330 kilovolt line; first power was transmitted in 1972. To further develop China's hydro potential properly, higher voltage transmission will have to be employed, probably on the order of 500 kV. Development is under way. Interchange capabilities will have to be expanded (the key north-east and north grids are linked by a single 110 kV line so the interchange is limited).[19]

Current situation (1976–1978)

The power shortage

In the early autumn of 1977 Chairman Hua Kuo-feng issued a series of state directives giving the development of electric power a position of high priority. In stressing the need to conserve electric power, to utilize capacity more fully, and to generate power more efficiently, Hua was clearly indicating that all was not well within the Chinese power industry.

That China has been short of power for years was evident from official statements, from reports of visitors, from staggered hours of industrial operations and from a nationwide campaign that preached conservation. But now recognition was being given the fact that if the ambitious programme to modernize agriculture, industry, science and technology, and national defence by the year 2000 was not to be jeopardized, the existing situation in the power industry would have to be rectified quickly. The seriousness of this problem was underscored by the November 1977 statement from Peking that 'solving the notable contradiction (shortage) of supply and demand of electric power has become an important task facing the new leap forward in the national economy . . . present contradictions in supply and demand are fairly large and have directly affected the development of industrial and agricultural production'.[20]

Perhaps one of the clearest indications of the immediate concern for power supplies came in December at the Miyun reservoir near Peking, when Chairman Hua said, 'it [the reservoir's water] must first be used to generate electricity and then to irrigate the land'. This appears to reverse the generally held first priority accorded the production of agricultural products. The Chairman had told the Minister of Water Conservancy and Electric Power that 'power output must be increased by fully utilizing hydroelectric power and that when increased power output is achieved throughout the country, the gross value of industrial output will be greatly enhanced without even increasing the amount of industrial equipment'.[21]

Causes

The causes of the current situation are primarily attributable to years of insufficient investment in the electric power industry and in the supporting fuel and rail transport sectors. Investment in mine development, mine mechanization, and coal preparation facilities has lagged for many years. The destruction at the important underground Kailuan mines in Tangshan resulting from the July 1976 earthquake also impaired supplies. While coal output is now around 600 million tonnes annually, the Chinese rail system and the fleet of rolling stock are not up to the task of expeditiously moving coal from mines to power plants. The rapid development of the Chinese petroleum industry and the conversion of some thermal stations to the firing of oil has somewhat eased the coal bottleneck.

In the power industry itself capital construction plans have gone unfulfilled and the number of turbine and generator sets to be placed on-line has fallen short. Maintenance of plant and equipment has been neglected, in part owing to the failure to create the normal reserve generating units commonly found in the developed industrial countries. This has resulted in overuse of units in base load service and an inability to meet loads at time of peak demand. The limited number of transmission lines and the absence of many interprovincial power grid connections have caused problems of load management that has resulted in outages. All of these factors have brought the safety and reliability of the Chinese power system into question.

Short-term solution

To ameliorate the immediate shortcomings of the industry and to provide the basis in 1978 for an acceleration of power growth by 1980, Chairman Hau's directives focus particularly on conservation and full utilization of generating capacity. To balance supply and demand with the needs of the national economy, a specific planned power consumption quota emphasizing conservation will be assigned each and every urban and rural area, enterprise, workshop, and work unit.[22] Based on experiences in the important north-east power grid (Liaoning, Kirin, and Heilungkiang Provinces), a careful, planned programme can result in a 10 per cent reduction in consumption.[23]

Additionally, attempts will be made to utilize more fully existing capacity, although it would appear that in some cases this will come in conflict with the need to take equipment off-line for maintenance and it will interfere with the creation of adequate reserve capacity. As noted earlier, the greater utilization of hydroelectric facilities may also interfere with irrigation and agricultural production. Finally, equipment is to be used more efficiently and coal and oil conserved.

Power capacity and generation

In both 1976 and 1977, the capacity of the Chinese power industry increased substantially. In 1977 over 40 large and medium-sized hydro and thermal power generating units having a considerably greater generating capacity than those built in 1976 were put in operation. Information concerning the commissioning of a number of individual turbo-generator units has been released by Peking. The capacity estimated to have been added in turbo-generators of all sizes was about 2900 and 3600 MW in 1976 and 1977 respectively. Based on an 8.5 per cent growth in 1976 and 9.8 per cent in 1977, generating capacities at the end of 1976 and 1977 are estimated at 36.9 and 40.5 thousand megawatts. US capacity at the end of 1976 was 531.3 thousand megawatts.[24]

How this installed generating capacity was used in 1976 and 1977 to produce power was highly dependent on the rate of industrial growth. Apparently, there was no industrial growth in 1976.[25] Despite this, more power was produced, probably because the industry had not been fully meeting demand in 1975.[26] Shantung, in fact, generated 20 per cent more power in 1976 than in 1975.[27] Power generated in the PRC in 1976 was an estimated 203 billion kilowatt-hours, an increase of 8.8 per cent over 1975. Power generated in the United States in 1976 amounted to just over 2 trillion kilowatt-hours.

The year 1977 witnessed a reported 14 per cent increase in industrial output.[28] Some of this growth, of course, was simply reactivation of capacity idled by the political turmoil of 1976 when plants in various industries were shut down, in some cases for extended periods. During the first 6 months of 1977, power output set a record high; 6 of the 11 largest power systems surpassed all previous records. Although China's plan for power was fulfilled by 12 December 1977, shortages persisted. During the period July–October 1977, Hofei, capital of Anhwei Province, suffered a '30 per cent power shortage' despite being tied into the East grid.[29] For 1977 power generated ran an estimated 136 billion kilowatt-hours or an increase of 9.8 per cent over 1976.[30]

At the end of 1977, thermal electric stations had 62 per cent (25.1 thousand megawatts) of the PRC's total power-generating capacity while hydroelectric plants contained nearly 38 per cent (15.2 thousand megawatts). This represents a further increase in hydro's share compared to most earlier reports. With emphasis now to be placed on the further development of hydraulic resources, this figure can be expected to rise slowly. In the short term, thermal capacity, which can be brought on line more quickly, may rise faster, but the long-term trend is toward placing a greater share of the industry in hydroelectric capacity.

The larger share of power generated, however, continues to be principally from thermal stations. During 1977, an estimated 71 per cent of all power produced came from these facilities, about 159 billion kilowatt-hours. The reason that hydroelectric stations with 38 per cent of the capacity produced only 29 per cent of the power is attributable to the reduced hours of operation stemming from low water and irrigation and other demands on the water resource. This natural feature of hydroelectric operations may be improved on some as the share of hydro capacity in larger dams increases and if the priority use of water in reservoirs is accorded to power generation as suggested by Chairman Hua in December 1977.

Hydroelectric stations

There are 66 known hydroelectric stations in China of 30 MW capacity and greater, of which seven are under construction and have produced no power. These 59 operative stations comprised about two-thirds of the hydroelectric capacity at the end of 1977 while the balance consisted of the 70 000 or so small- and medium-size hydros. Because of the completion of a number of major dams on the Yellow and Han Rivers and because of the large increase in small hydros, the share of capacity held by hydroelectric stations has been rising in recent years.

In 1974 there were some 73 concrete and 438 stone masonry dams, 15 m (49 ft) or higher in China and more than 250 reservoirs with storage in excess of 100 million cubic metres (35.3 billion cu. ft) of water. In addition to power generation, Chinese dams are designed with irrigation, flood control, and enhanced river navigation in mind. Fish breeding and water for municipal use are also factors.

Liuchia and Tanchiangkou are China's two largest hydroelectric plants and are among the newest constructed, being completed in 1974 and 1973, respectively. Liuchia, the largest powerplant in the PRC, is in Kansu on the Yellow River above Lanchou. This Chinese designed and equipped facility has a powerhouse with one 300 MW and four 225 MW units providing a rated capacity of 1225 MW. It supplies power to several 220 kV lines and China's only 330 kV line. Liuchia is nominally capable of delivering about 5.7 billion kilowatt-hours per year, an annual rate of operation of 4643 hours. Started at the time of the 'great leap forward' construction at Liuchia was long deferred and the facility did not deliver its first power until 1969.

Tanchiangkou was also started in the late fifties with the first generator not being put on line until 1968. The sixth and last 150 MW generator was turned over in 1973. This Chinese-designed and equipped facility is located on the Han River about 430 miles above its confluence with the Yangtze at Wuhan in Hupeh. Tanchiangkou's 900 MW capacity, second largest in the PRC, provides a major share of the power needed in Hupeh.

The Sanmen dam on the Yellow River, designed by the Soviets, has been revamped by the Chinese and will not reach its originally intended capacity of 1080 MW. The Yellow River's silt load, heaviest in the world, forced a revision in the dam and the installation of specially-designed smaller turbines of 50 MW each. Several turbines are thought to be operating and a total of either four or five will be installed giving the facility a capacity of 200 or 250 MW.

China has nine hydroelectric stations with capacities of 300 MW and greater; two more are at 290 MW. Two of these are on the Yalu River where the output is believed to be shared 50–50 with North Korea; operations are controlled by the China-Korea Yalu River Hydroelectric Power Co. The hydro stations of 300 MW or more and the major systems of dams, including cascade systems, are shown in Table 11.6.

The drive to assist the modernization of agriculture and to bring electricity to China's rural communes from small hydroelectric plants saw its greatest surge in this decade when the number of small hydros grew from 15000 to about 90000. Typically, these stations average only 50 kilowatts in capacity, and some are as small as several kilowatts. In the mini-turbine range, the Tientsin Electric Gear-Drive Design Institute has designed seven models from 250 watts to 12 kilowatts which can be manufactured on the commune itself. Although inefficient compared to larger units, both in hours of operation and in cost per installed kilowatt of capacity, China's small hydros, have a major impact on the local economy providing flood control, irrigation, and some power without making demands on major production facilities or on the underdeveloped power transmission systems.

Thermal powerplants

There are 126 known fossil-fuelled thermal electric power stations in China with capacities of 30 MW and higher, of which seven are under construction and are not believed to have produced any power in 1977. Currently the Wangting station in Wuhsi at over 700 MW is the largest. There are no nuclear-powered thermal power plants. About 75 per cent of all thermal stations are fired with coal ranging from lignite through bituminous types to anthracite. The rest of the plants are oil-fired, although a few units in Szechwan are gas-fired. A number of units have been converted to coal and oil-firing or oil-firing alone to ease the coal supply bottleneck.

The coal most widely used in raising steam at thermal plants is a sub-bituminous type with heating values running from 3000 to 5000 kilocalories per kilogram. Lignites will

Table 11.6. Major Chinese hydroelectric systems

	Megawatts
Yellow River (moving upstream):	
Sanmen, Honan	150.0*
Tienchiao Shensi	50.0*
Shihtsuishan, Ningsia	(†)
Chingtung, Ningsia	225.0
Papan, Kansu	180.0
Yenkuo, Kansu	300.0
Liuchia, Kansu	1225.0
Lungyen, Tsinghai	(†)
Yalu River (moving upstream):	
Supung Dong Sui, Liaoning	700.0
Hulutao Unbong, Kirin	400.0
Sungari River: Tafengman, Kirin	590.0
Han River and tributaries (moving upstream from the Yangtze River):	
Tanchiangkou, Hupeh	900.0
Huanglungtan, Hupeh	150.0
Shihchuan, Shensi	135.0
Tatu River: Kungtsui, Szechwan	508.0
Yangtze River: Three gorge area, Szechwan/Hupeh	(†)
Fuchun River and tributaries (moving upstream):	
Fuchun, Chekiang	260.0
Chililung, Chekiang	420.0
Hsinan, Chekiang	652.5
Cascade systems:	
Kutien, Fukien (4 stages)	158.0
Maotiao, Kweichow (6 stages)	250.0
Lungchi, Szechwan (4 stages)	108.0
Ili, Yunnan (4 stages)	172.0

*Partial capacity.

†Under construction.

continue to be used as seen in the erection of the Swiss/French-supplied thermal station. Coal consumption per kilowatt-hour of power generated has dropped, but no national averages for this indicator of efficiency are available. Recently, the Chinese have talked about blending in 5 to 10 per cent of very low grades of 1000 to 2000 kilocalorie coal.[31]

A typical oil-fired Chinese thermal station will use Taching, Takang, or Shengli crude. At the Wuching plant in Shanghai, crude from Shengli is fired having a heating value of 10000 kilocalories and a sulphur content of 1 to 1.8 per cent.[32] Taching crude exported to Japan is also often directly used for firing thermal station boilers because its high paraffin content makes processing difficult in Japanese refineries.

For thermal station work, the Chinese appear to have standardized on steam turbogenerators of 25, 50, 75, 100, and 125 kW. These are serially produced. Units of 200 and 300 MW with water-cooled rotors are now being manufactured and are in operation, although their numbers are not great and it is questionable whether they can be considered to be in serial production. Initial production is under way at Harbin and probably Shanghai on 600-MW turbo-generators and the associated boilers. Based on past experience, the first 600-MW unit will probably not be online before 1981–2.

There is no evidence of the use of combined cycle plants (where gas turbine exhaust is used to drive a conventional steam turbine) for peaking or intermediate load service. This is the most efficient system for generating electricity from liquid or gaseous fossil fuels, but is probably not found in China owing to the relatively undeveloped nature of power gas turbine production and technology. There is no evidence of significant Chinese development in gas turbines for peaking or baseload service, although the Chinese do have some foreign units of this type (see Table 11.2).

To increase efficiency, the Chinese are utilizing waste heat from hot flue gases and warm cooling water at power stations to heat other industrial plants. Some 120 facilities in Liaoning are using such residual heat. Although not used much in the United States, combined district heat and electric power stations are extensively utilized in Europe, especially in the Soviet Union.

At a Tientsin powerplant, where much of a gas turbine's exhaust heat was formerly wasted, 80 per cent is now recovered and used to preheat the feedwater for a steam generating unit. Still, there is a little evidence of the more advanced concept of 'energy centres' where steam is delivered to industrial process use after passing through a steam turbine in a central power station or where 'byproduct' electricity is produced from excess industrial process steam using an extraction or back-pressure turbine. In Kiangsu at Changchou, one-tenth of the power produced is generated from waste industrial steam, and at the Harbin cement plant a 4.5-MW station uses waste heat to provide one-third of the power needed.

Other sources of electric power under development in China include geothermal units, solar power, and tidal stations. The Chinese have at least four experimental geothermal power generators in operation: Fengshun County, Kwangtung, 86 kW, started in 1971; Ninghsiang County, Hunan, operation stabilized at 300 kW in 1975: Huailai County near Peking, started in 1974; and Yangpaching, Tibet, where the first 1000-kW unit began producing the high-pressure vapour in 1977. Trial projects in both geothermal and solar electric power production are under way at Tientsin University.

There is no significant amount of electric power developed via solar means or from generators based on gas from methane digesters, although millions of families in China use digester methane for cooking and heating. In certain localities, these developments could become of some importance.

The Chinese have at least one tidal power station, Kanchutan in Kwangtung, although it is only unidirectional and not a true tidal station. Depending on flow, capacity is 200 to 250 kW.

Plans

The Minister of Power speaks

The national economic development plan is to modernize agriculture, industry, science, and technology, and national defence in order to propel China into the front ranks of the industrialized nations of the world by the year 2000. Announced by Premier Chou En-lai in January 1975 and revalidated by the important Taching conference in May 1977, this four modernizations programme will place a heavy burden on the electric power industry—an industry characterized by Chairman Mao as one of the two 'vanguards' (the other is transportation) which must lead in economic development.[33]

That the Chinese are already engaged in preparing this vanguard industry for the difficult task ahead is seen currently in Chairman Hua's directives concerning power development. At no time have actual capacity targets been released, but at the recent National People's Congress, Hua stated that the 10-year plan calls for the building or completion of 30 power stations.[34] As a result of Hua's directives, the convening in December 1977 of a national power conference, and as indicated by the foregoing quotation, a very high priority effort is currently being directed at the acceleration of electric power development in an effort to place the industry in a strong position to support orderly growth of the economy.

Again, without revealing plan targets, the Minister of Water Conservancy and Electric Power, Chien Chen-ying in a significant November 1977 article and later at the national power conference provided some general information on how the PRC plans to develop electric power over the remainder of the twentieth century.[35]

The guiding policy laid down by the party and the state council in 1977 stresses the simultaneous development of both hydroelectric and thermoelectric power in large, medium, and small stations. Emphasis is to be given, however, to the creation of large hydroelectric stations as the future backbone of the Chinese power industry.

The Minister spoke pointedly of the need to complement hydro developments with erection of thermal plants in the vicinity of the hydros to meet regional demand when low water and irrigation reduce hydro operations. Expressing concern over the lengthy time required for the construction of hydros, she urged that construction continue in the winter of 1978 through the dry period in order to accelerate by 1 year the introduction of new hydroelectric facilities. While citing long construction times for hydros, she noted the cheaper cost of the power produced from them and the more rapid recovery of investment. Finally, and apparently as a preview of future plans, Minister Chien referred to Premier Chou's earlier call for the building of hydroelectric projects in the three gorges of the Yangtze River astride the Szechwan-Hupeh border.

The construction of thermal electric stations near coal mines, the so-called mine-mouth type of plant, is to be stressed to ease the burden of hauling coal by rail, one of the current problems causing power shortages. This in turn places the burden of transporting energy on the transmission systems which also may be a problem. The need to utilize low-grade forms of coal such as lignite and even peat is to be promoted. Chien cited the need for more thermal powerplants where waste or excess steam is used for heating purposes in adjacent towns and factories; this is extensively done in the Soviet Union but there are only a few such plants in the PRC. At no time did she mention thermal stations based on nuclear power, but there are indications China will soon move into such facilities although they would only play a minor role in the total picture.

Minister Chien noted the need for increasing the reserve capacity of the industry. In this connection she devoted an entire paragraph to the discussion of safety in the industry as a means of preventing serious damage to the national economy. This is taken to mean plans must recognize the need for a larger reserve capacity to insure stability in the power supply. The need for improved transmission systems coupled with a call for greater automation and mechanization also relates to improved load management and great reliability of supply.

All of the Minister's plan information, although very general, is useful in aiding in the assessment of just what prospects are in store for the Chinese electric power industry.

Prospects

Constraints on growth

In pushing for rapid development of the economy the Chinese are faced with a number of critical problems: improvement of agricultural productivity; the need for better management and more discipline in the industrial work force; higher wages; better scientific and technical education; and increasing exports to earn foreign exchange to support acquisition of foreign plant and technology. The strengthening of rail transport, the coal industry, and the iron and steel industry—all weak links in the economy—must be accomplished. Coupled with these problems is a need for political stability and relative freedom from natural disasters.[36]

Understanding plans for industrial growth in a developing country such as China is important because of the close relationship to the demand for electric power. If the electric power industry cannot be developed at a faster pace than industry generally, then industrial growth is likely to be inhibited. As Vice Premier Li Hsien-nien put it in December 1977, 'unless the problem of the power supply is solved the national economy cannot possibly grow at a high speed'.[37]

In the 23-year period 1952–75, industrial growth in China averaged an estimated 11 per cent annually, although in 1976 it was close to zero and in 1977 about 14 per cent.[38] In the period 1978 to 1985 and even beyond to the year 2000, industrial growth could average anywhere from 6 to 14 per cent annually, depending on the success Peking has in coping with the problems enumerated above. Sustained industrial growth at a higher rate seems unlikely and if it falls even as low as 6 per cent, the announced programme of modernization could only be considered a partial success.

Growth in generation capacity

A study of 12 rapidly industrializing countries in the 1960s showed that to support industrial growth adequately, electric power needs to be advanced about 1.4 times as rapidly. To date, the Chinese experience has been similar with this ratio at 1.6 during the period 1952–75, but dropping to 1.3 times during 1971–5. Using a 1.3 relationship, Table 11.7 shows what installed generating capacities would be required for selected years in order to support average industrial growth rates of 8, 10, and 12 per cent annually over the period to the year 2000.

At a 10 per cent rate of industrial growth—13 per cent for the power industry—Table 11.7 shows that at the end of this year

Table 11.7. Required electric power generating capacity to support industrial growth rates of 8 per cent, 10 per cent, and 12 per cent, selected years
(in thousand megawatts)

	Generating capacity (per cent)		
*Year**	*8*	*10*	*12*
1978	44.7	45.8	46.8
1979	49.4	51.7	54.1
1980	54.5	58.4	62.6
1981	60.2	66.0	72.3
1982	66.4	74.6	83.6
1983	73.3	84.3	96.7
1984	81.0	95.3	112.0
1985	89.4	108.0	129.0
1986	98.7	122.0	149.0
1987	109.0	137.0	173.0
1990	147.0	198.0	267.0
2000	394.0	673.0	1140.0

*31 December of year cited.

capacity should be 45 800 megawatts, an increase of 5300 MW over 1977. Construction projects currently under way where turbo-generators appear likely to come on-line in 1978 would contribute about 2500 MW. Other projects, chiefly hydroelectric, where information is sketchy, would contribute additional capacity as would the introduction of many more of the small hydros. The only 300 MW thermal turbo-generators that have been announced as entering production are those at the Wangting station, yet indications are that the Chinese have produced more than this so several more may be operative elsewhere. Still, the total estimated new 1978 capacity from a review of construction projects would not appear to reach the required increment of 5300 MW needed to sustain 10 per cent industrial growth.

Power equipment industry

A review of the Chinese power equipment manufacturing industry reveals a considerable productive capacity. In fact, for many years this industry has appeared to produce more turbo-generator capacity than can be accounted for by annual increments to capacity as reflected by the electric power capacity series or by a power station by station analysis.

The power equipment plants, for example, are estimated to have produced 21 300 MW of capacity, 1971–5. During this time, imports of turbo-generators ran at least 1900 MW for a total of 23 000 MW. China does export a few small turbo-generators—the largest, a 100 MW unit, went to North Korea. But during the period 1971–6—slipped a year to allow time for equipment installation after manufacture—the electric power capacity series (see Table 11.1) shows an increase of only 15 800 MW or less than 70 per cent of the equipment capacity apparently available for installation. Retirement of obsolete facilities would account for only a small part of this. Information is lacking on whether some equipment produced was just not usable. A basic unexplained difference appears to remain.

From the analysis contained in this study and from the pronouncements of the Chinese leaders concerned with the economy, it appears questionable whether the equipment industry has the capability to supply the capacity needed in 1978 to maintain a 13 per cent rate of growth in electric power capacity. It should be noted that long lead time items like turbines and generators had to be laid down in 1976 and 1977, if they are to be shipped to construction sites, installed, and be ready to produce power in 1978, moreover, 1976 was not a good year for industrial production. Additional capacity may be derived from imports, but no turbo-generators were noted in Sino-Soviet trade for 1977, nor were any imports, other than those already mentioned, seen in China's imports from the industrialized West.

Equipment imports

Shortfalls, therefore, have to be made up by imports. During 1977 one would have expected to hear about negotiations in Peking concerning the purchase of large-scale thermal plants, but such was not known to have been the case, possibly indicative of greater difficulty in retrenching the economy in 1977 and planning for 1978 and beyond than had been thought. While it is assumed negotiations are now under way in Peking, it should be noted that for major projects such as large thermal stations, a contract in 1978 means online power no earlier than 1981–2. Hence, it is hard to see how any new purchases of foreign plants will materially assist in the required increments of electric power capacity until 1981 at the earliest.

1985

Industrial growth of 10 per cent would require a power capacity in 1985 of 108 000 MW or nearly 2.7 times 1977's generating capacity. The increment to capacity in 1985 of 12 700 MW is perhaps even more imposing.[39] This would appear to require a major expansion of power generating equipment manufacturing plant. And it would also require a sustained programme of significant imports of foreign plant and equipment, possibly as much as 2500–3000 MW annually calling for minimal annual outlay of at least $300 million.

At a 10 per cent industrial growth rate, Table 11.7 projects a need in the year 2000 for a generating capacity of 673 000 MW. This is less than 50 per cent of one estimate of US generating capacity for the same year and reduces the Chinese goal of overtaking the United States economically to an exhortatory call for action.[40]

Assessment

To achieve the four modernizations, the Chinese under the leadership of Chairman Hua and Vice Premier Teng Hsiao-ping plan to achieve at least an annual 10 per cent increase in industrial growth by 1980 and sustain it through 1985 and possibly beyond. Given the 8.5 per cent and 9.8 per cent increases in power-generating capacity in 1976 and 1977 and the lead time required to install new capacity, it would appear difficult to accelerate developments to the required 13 per cent level prior to 1980. This is one reason why Chairman Hua's directives of late 1977 place such heavy emphasis on conservation and allocation of electric power.

Key features of the effort to increase capacity and power production will have to include:

(a) Heavy investment in the development of the coal industry to forestall more thermal plants from being converted from coal to oil firing. This will help maximize the availability of oil for export earnings.
(b) Improvement in rail transport to eliminate bottlenecks in coal deliveries and the development of coal-fired, mine-mouth type thermal plants to ease the burden on the rail system. Increased use must be made of locally available low grade coals to reduce the long haul of higher grade coals.
(c) Commencement of major hydroelectric developments in the 1000 MW and greater capacity. This means development of new dams in the main gorges of the Yangtze above Ichang. The first Yangtze River hydroelectric station is under construction now.
(d) Reduction in construction time for both hydro and thermal station projects. The 15–16 years spent on Liuchia and Tanchiangkou should be reduced to perhaps 8 years.
(e) Development of 500 kV transmission lines to serve centres of consumption far from remote hydro sites. Greater interconnection of grids to provide security for the power supply is essential.
(f) Large thermal stations and units. Work currently under way on 600 MW boilers and turbo-generators will have to be accelerated.
(g) The import of complete one- and two-unit thermal stations in the 600 and 1200 MW class.
(h) Expansion of the power equipment manufacturing capability.

With their relatively abundant hydraulic resources and reserves of oil and coal, the PRC need not be driven into a rapid nuclear power programme. Nevertheless, it seems likely that the Chinese will soon construct or contract for one or more nuclear stations if only to keep up with technological developments. It would also make sense for the Chinese to enter into a technical assistance agreement for the manufacture of gas turbines of 25 MW and higher for both peak shaving and base load service. And while China's self-reliant stance might prevent such a contract, the Chinese would probably benefit greatly from obtaining consultative advice from abroad on numerous aspects of power industry operations.

What is not so evident in the above quantitative analysis of what China may require by 1985 are the changing technological characteristics of the capacity to be added. A major portion of the new capacity will be larger and more complex. Technological problems will require solution as higher operating temperatures and pressures are encountered, as improved process control and environmental equipment are required, and as the plant and equipment size scale-up continues to affect new design in all areas of power generation, transmission, and distribution. These qualitative aspects of the incremental capacity required add another dimension to the problems facing the Chinese electric power industry. Nevertheless, if all or most of the problems facing the electric power industry are solved, the industry probably could support an industrial growth rate of 10 per cent for a sustained period commencing about 1981.

Bibliography

Ashton, John, *Development of electric energy resources in Communist China*, Joint Economic Committee Report, *An economic profile of mainland China*, pp. 297–316. US Government Printing Office (1967).

Carin, Robert, *Power industry in Communist China*. Union Research Institute, Hong Kong (1969).
CIA, *China: energy balance projections* (1975).
Clarke, William, China's electric power industry. *The China Business Review*, pp. 22–37, September–October (1977).
Hydraulic engineering and water resources in the PRC, Report of the US Water Resources Delegation, August–September (1974).
JETRO, *China's electric power production.* Tokyo, January (1975).
Perkins, D., de Angelis, A., Denberger, R., Halford, S., Khan, A., Livingston, O., Parish, W., Rawski, T., Simmons, L., Stitchcombe, A., Timmer, P., and Van Slyke, L., *Rural small scale industry in the PRC*, pp. 107–9. University of California Press (1977).
Report of the Canadian Electric Power Mission to the People's Republic of China, 29 August–18 September (1973).
Smil, Vaclav, *China's energy achievements, problems, prospects*. Praeger (1976).
Wu Yuan-li, *Economic development and the use of energy resources in Communist China.* Praeger (1963).

Notes and references

1. Hydro reserves that are technically feasible to develop are thought to be about half of this. Relevant figures for the United States are 390000 and 179000 MW.
2. For details on China's primary energy base, see Vaclav Smil elsewhere in this volume. Also see US Congress Committee on Energy and National Resources, Project Interdependence, US and World Energy Outlook Through 1990, 1978. For other selected readings on the power industry of China, see the bibliography.
3. Ashton, John, Development of Electric Energy Resources in Communist China, JEC, 1967, p. 306.
4. FBIS, 10 November 1977, E13.
5. Ibid.
6. CIA, *China: economic indicators*, October 1977, p. 1 and older volumes.
7. Ibid.
8. It should be noted that \$350 million is an insufficient amount to buy 4500 megawatts of capacity as complete thermal power stations. The units sold to the People's Republic of China by the USSR and Czechoslovakia are turbo-generator sets only. The four complete thermal stations sold to China range in cost from \$120 to \$183 per kilowatt of capacity added. To add 4500 MW of capacity as complete plants would entail an outlay of \$550 million or more.
9. At the beginning of 1978 the Minister was Madame Chien Cheng-ying.
10. *Rural small scale industry in the People's Republic of China*, p. 107, University of California Press (1977).
11. FBIS, 31 January 1978, E20.
12. Largest thermal station: United States, 3199 MW; and PRC-713 MW. Largest hydroelectric station: United States, 2195 MW; and PRC, 1225 MW. Largest turbo-generator: United States, 1300 MW and PRC, 300 MW. Largest transmission voltages; United States, 750 kilovolts (kV); and PRC, 330 kV.
13. FBIS, 29 July 1977, G2. FBIS, 30 September 1977, G4.
14. Chung-kuo Hsin-wen, Hong Kong, 21 January 1976.
15. For example, *People's Daily* on 30 October 1977, said, 'the quantity of large forged pieces (rotors) for power stations was unable to meet the demand for protracted periods of time. Do we lack the ability to turn out such pieces? No. Are we ignorant of the advanced techniques in the production of large forged pieces? No. The major reason is low quality in production'.
16. A large-scale model of the 300 MW unit at the Shanghai Industrial Exhibition shows this 3000 rpm model GFS-300-2 to consist of a 9-stage high-pressure turbine, an 11-stage medium pressure turbine, and two double-expansion low-pressure turbines, each with two 6-stage turbines.
17. *Project Interdependence*, in the work cited in Ref. 2.
18. See Appendix 2 for more detail on hours of operation.
19. For additional detail on China's transmission lines see Appendix 1.
20. FBIS, 2 December 1977, E1.
21. Ibid.
22. FBIS, 21 October 1977, L3.
23. FBIS, 14 November 1977, E8.
24. For additional detail on estimating generating capacity in 1976 and 1977, see Appendix 2.
25. Indicators, op. cit.
26. FBIS, 12 January 1977, E20.
27. FBIS, 15 July 1977, E17.
28. FBIS, 27 December 1977, E8 (11 mos. growth was 13.7 per cent).
29. Ibid. Also Peking NCNA Domestic Service, 24 November 1977.
30. FBIS, 27 December 1967, E9 (For additional detail on estimates of power, produced in 1976 and 1977, see Appendix 2).
31. FBIS, 15 December 1977, E13.

32. For more detail on a typical Chinese thermal powerplant, see Appendix 5 of the original (unabridged) paper.
33. FBIS, 12 September 1977, E23.
34. FBIS, 7 March 1978, D17.
35. *Red Flag*, November 1977 and FBIS, 10 November 1977, E13-19.
36. For more detail on Chinese economic and industrial growth see Field, Chen, and others in the JEC volume (*Chinese Economy Post-Mao*).
37. FBIS, 19 December 1977, E2.
38. *Indicators*, op. cit. n. 7 and FBIS, 27 December 1977, E8.
39. This is greater than the 11 000 MW of capacity the Soviet Union plans to add in 1978.
40. Federal Power Commission projects 817 000 MW for the United States for 31 December 1986. The period 1987–2000 for the United States was taken at a growth rate of 4.5 per cent annually.

Appendix 1: power transmission

Transmission lines in China are found at 66, 110, 154, and 220 kV, and at the one 330 kV circuit. Lines are generally carried on steel or reinforced concrete towers or poles. For example, the 173-mile-long, 220 kV Maoming-Chiangmen line, completed in 1975, is carried on 177 steel and 597 concrete pylons; the tallest steel pylon is 184 ft, the shortest is 79 ft. Distribution lines are 6, 11, and 35 kV carried primarily on concrete poles in woodshy China. Domestic consumption is at 380 and 220 volt, 50 hertz.

Experimental work is being carried out in China on 500 kV transmission systems. The Shenyang transformer works is doing practice repairs on a 500 kV test line. There is no direct evidence of test work on high voltage direct current (HVDC) transmission, but it is known that the Chinese have a strong interest in this area. A move to HVDC may be necessary if the PRC is to efficiently move large blocks of power from major hydro facilities on the upper reaches of the Yangtze and Yellow Rivers to distant industrial centres.

The Chinese have done considerable work in live-wire maintenance of transmission lines, including the transformation of lines to higher voltages without interruption. The Fushin-Chinchou line in Liaoning had its capacity doubled in 1973 without interruption in the power supply.

A notable Chinese achievement is the 220 kV Yangtze River transmission line crossing at Nanking. The south channel crossing is on towers 635 ft high spanning 6340 ft, the longest span and tallest transmission towers in China. The towers are constructed of steel tubing with pre-stressed cross arms. Transmission cable is composed of 19 high-strength steel wires and 38 aluminium-covered steel wires. Construction of the crossing, which connects the Nanking thermal station north of the river with the city to the south, was begun in May 1974 and completed in September 1976.

Appendix 2: power capacity and generation (1976–1977)

In 1976 the Chinese published information about turbo-generator units totalling about 2000 MW of capacity, including the following units that were installed; 300 MW-Wangting; 200 MW-Hsintien, Chaoyang, and two at Huantai; 125 MW-Huainan, Hsintushan, and Laiwu; 100 MW-Wulashan and Hsinhua; 75 MW-Ansha, Pikou, and Kungtsui; and several others that are less certain. This does not include the contribution to capacity made by new units at thermal and hydro plants in the 1 to 29 MW range nor does it include the capacity from approximately 5000 small hydros added (at an average of 50 kW per hydro, this would yield an additional 250 MW of capacity). There is also probably some unknown residual that was not announced.

It is not clear what damage the political turmoil did to the construction effort in the power industry in 1976. Certainly the July earthquake impacted heavily on the construction of the new 750 MW Japanese-supplied power plant in Tangshan and possibly on the 640 MW Italian-supplied thermal station at Tientsin. No information is available on whether the French and Swiss-supplied, 300 MW coal-fired station became operable in 1976 as originally scheduled. The assumption is that none of these foreign-supplied plants contributed to capacity in 1976. But given the four 200 MW units imported from the Soviet Union in 1975 and 1976 and the possible addition of another Chinese-built 300 MW unit, it seems reasonable to postulate that around 2900 MW of turbo-generating capacity were added in 1976. This represents a growth in capacity of about 8.5 per cent.

For 1977, about 1950 MW of additional capacity was announced, including the following units: 300 MW-Wangting; 200 MW-Hsintien and Chaoyang; 125 MW-Taoho (2), Huaipei, and Huainan; 100 MW-Matou (3) and Chingshan; 75 MW-Pikou and Kungtsui; 50 MW-Panshan, Tienchiao, and Yungan; 30 MW-Mashek; and several others that are less certain. The same situation as in 1976 applies to the medium sized plant additions, the Soviet generators, possibly an unannounced 300 MW unit, and to the estimated 5000 small hydros added.

In mid-year pledges, the Peking Electricity Administration undertook to add 800 MW of generating capacity in 1977 and the Shensi and Shantung power authorities to add 500 MW of capacity. At the end of the year it was announced that 465 MW of a planned 765 MW became operative in the Peking-Tientsin-Tangshan triangle, including two units at the Taoho station in Tangshan. Of the 500 MW, 250 represents new units, not otherwise announced.

It is also known that a total of 40 large and medium size units became operational in 1977 leading to Peking's New Year's Day statement that a 'considerably greater generating capacity than those built in 1976 were put into operation'. No allowance is made for the Italian or French/Swiss-supplied thermal stations whose construction has likely been delayed. This suggests the addition of 3600 MW and a growth in generating capacity in 1977 of about 9.8 per cent over 1976.

The power generated by the installed capacity in 1976 and 1977 is derived from estimates of the number of hours the mid-year capacity is operated annually. Ordinarily in the face of a power shortage, this figure would be expected to rise, however, if an above average share of capacity is already in base load service, as appears to be the case in the PRC, then this places a limit on how much more the capacity could be operated safely. The amount of planned maintenance and unexpected outages is another factor for which little information exists. In the face of no industrial growth, the rate might remain rather static. Political turmoil as occurred in 1976 might cause interruptions in power service although there is no information this actually took place as it did in other industries. Interruptions in the supply of coal, which did take place, could cause fossil-fuelled thermal stations to curtail operations, however. Drought and irrigation requirements can impact rather heavily on hydroelectric operations and in China, with around 38 per cent of all capacity in hydro units, this is a significant factor often causing reduced hours of operation. Natural disasters as at Tangshan also cause interruptions.

In 1977 there was a sharp rise in industrial output requiring more power and there was some improvement in worker morale and plant discipline contributing to more efficient operation. Little is known, however, of the industrial operations of heavy power consumers such as aluminium and nuclear weapons manufacture. The power shortage persisted and the question remains whether the generating capacity already heavily engaged in base load service could be much more extensively operated. Given these circumstances and in comparisons with operations in other developing and developed countries, it is believed that 3500 hours of operation annually in 1976 and 3525 hours in 1977 are reasonable (the extra 25 hours added to reflect increased efficiency). The 3500 hour figure is a composite rate based on 2000 hours for small hydros, 3000 hours for large hydros and 4000 hours for thermal stations. These yield power outputs of 124 billion kilowatt-hours in 1976 and 136 billion kilowatt-hours in 1977.

The reader should be impressed by the tenuous nature of these estimates.

* * *

Editor's note

In the absence of any official statistics all power capacity and generation estimates for China in the 1970s could be only tenuous, a fact noted in W. Clarke's closing sentence. In summer 1979 the State Statistical Bureau in Beijing released China's first official statistics in nearly two decades and these have shown much higher power generation figures than previously estimated, Consequently, I have updated appropriately all production statistics in W. Clarke's paper—but I have left unchanged his generation capacity estimates because no new statistics have been released in this regard, except a statement that the end of 1978 installed total was about 50000 MW. This would indicate that the CIA series (Table 11.1) is most likely no more than 10 per cent lower than the new Chinese figures. Naturally, the new generation total of 256.6 billion kilowatt-hours and installed capacity of around 50000 MW in 1978 imply a much higher load factor than estimated by Clarke in Appendix 2: about 5100 hours rather than 3500 hours.

V. S.

IV India

TOP: A gobar gas plant. Cow dung is fermented in a digester, producing methane gas that rises through tubes into kitchen of village home. The remaining sludge is much better fertilizer than the original dung.

BOTTOM: Tarapur Nuclear Power Station near Bombay. Tarapur is India's first nuclear power plant; its two 200 MW(e) reactors were put into operation in November 1969.

US Agency for International Development Photo.

India, the world's second most populous nation, has an immense need to increase its energy supply. Usage per capita of fossil fuels and hydroelectricity amounts merely to less than 200 kilograms of coal equivalent annually—and, moreover, this average hides the distressing fact that at least 60, and perhaps as much as 80, per cent of the country's nearly 650 million people do not have the purchasing power to buy modern, commercial energy and must survive on traditional fuels. Energy consumption per capita of these poorest 60 per cent of the population is possibly as much as nine times less than that of the richest tenth belonging to India's urban elite.

As Reddy and Prasad scathingly remark, this population 'below and just above the poverty line has been in the grip of a very grave energy crisis for a long, long time, even though there have been no conferences to highlight this age-old crisis' (Reddy and Prasad, 1977).

Only dramatic increases in energy use would lift these hundreds of millions above crushing poverty (annual per capita GNP much below \$US100), widespread malnutrition (India's *national* average is only around 1950 kcal of food per day per capita), premature death (infant mortality is much above 100 per 1000 live births and the mean life expectancy at birth is no more than 50 years), and illiteracy (at present only one-third of the population is literate).

Unfortunately India is not rich in the easily convertible, high-quality energy resources which could speedily effect such a transformation. As P. D. Henderson makes clear in his thorough inventory ('Energy resources, consumption, and supply in India'), the country has extensive coal reserves but most of them are in non-coking, high-ash fuels; identified hydrocarbon deposits are very small and, although the current offshore drilling (centred on Bombay High Field in the Gulf of Cambay which was discovered in 1974) will boost the domestic supply, it is not expected to free the country from costly oil imports (today some two-thirds of India's oil supply is imported). The nationwide total for hydro power is rather large, but predictably most of the potential is in remote locations: the isolated and politically unstable north-east has alone nearly one-third of the country's theoretical water-power capacity, much of which is moreover in the Brahmaputra Valley in Arunachal Pradesh claimed by the People's Republic of China. Reserves of fissionable materials are huge, but as they are mostly in thorium, rather than in uranium, they cannot be utilized without a major technological breakthrough.

Consequently, traditional energy sources—firewood, crop by-products and cow dung—are retaining their importance: Henderson's figures show that these fuels supplied about one-half of India's total energy consumption at the beginning of the 1970s and the *Report of the fuel policy committee* (Ministry of Energy, 1974) estimates that they will still account for nearly one-quarter of the nationwide energy usage at the beginning of the 1990s.

Most of these traditional fuels are, naturally, used in India's more than half a million villages and Roger Revelle ('Energy use in rural India') has attempted to trace their flows, as well as to account for the sizeable animal and human energy inputs into farming and village industries. Although he finds that rural energy use is surprisingly high, he stresses the need for further increases in fuel supply and for its more efficient utilization.

One of the appropriate ways to achieve these goals is greatly to expand the generation of biogas. No other country has a larger number of cattle than India—some 260 million head in 1975—and using their manure for widespread methane generation rather than as primitive, inefficiently burned and unhygienic dried fuel cakes would be a major step towards rural modernization. Chaman Kashkari ('Biogas plants in India') offers the basic technical description of typical Indian biogas digesters and provides essential cost estimates for a small (3 m^3) plant. Wallace E. Tyner and John Adams ('Rural electrification in India: biogas versus large-scale power') offer a more detailed look at the economy of small-scale biogas-fuelled power generation in comparison with the centralized power production, and although they conclude that, based on financial considerations alone, current centralized power facilities are more advantageous than the biogas based systems they also point out that 'a biogas programme may be desirable solely as a means of producing both cooking fuel and fertilizer from cow dung with no associated power generation'.

Undoubtedly the expansion of biogas generation will be a major ingredient in future efforts to solve India's energy needs: that is, as argued eloquently by Reddy and Prasad, to pursue above all a strategy of discriminatory and biased increase of energy supply to the country's villages, which are the home of four-fifths of the subcontinent's people.

Energy in India: selected readings

Central Water and Power Commission (1970). *Power atlas of India*. Central Water and Power Commission, New Delhi.
Chaudhuri, M. R. (1970). *Power resources in India*. Oxford and IBH Publishing Company, New Delhi.
Chitale, V. P. and Roy, M. (1975). *Energy crisis in India*. Economic and Scientific Research Foundation, New Delhi.
Dagli, V. (ed.) (1971). *Natural resources in the Indian economy*. Vora and Company Publishers Private Ltd., Bombay.
Dasgupta, B. (1971). *Oil industry in India: some economic aspects*. Frank Cass, London.
Henderson, P. D. (1975). *India: the energy sector*. Oxford University Press, Oxford.
Kashkari, C. (1975). *Energy: resources, demand and conservation with special reference to India*. Tata McGraw Hill, New Delhi.
Kumaramangalam, S. M. (1973). *Coal industry in India: nationalisation and task ahead*. Oxford University Press, New Delhi.
Mehta, B. (1974). *India and the world oil crisis*. Sterling Publishers, New Delhi.
Ministry of Energy (1975). *Report of the fuel policy committee*. Manager of Publications, New Delhi.
National Council of Applied Economic Research (1965). *Domestic fuels in rural India*. National Council of Applied Economic Research, New Delhi.
Pachauri, R. K. (1977). *Energy and economic development in India*. Praeger Publishers, New York.
Parikh, K. S. (1976). *Second India studies: energy*. Macmillan Company of India, New Delhi.
Reddy, A. K. N. and Prasad, K. K. (1977). Technological Alternatives and the Indian Energy Crisis. *Economic and Political Weekly*, Special Number, August 1977, pp. 1465–1502.
Sankar, T. L. (1977). Alternative Development Strategy with a Low Energy Profile for a Low GNP/Capita Energy-Poor Country: The

Case of India. In *The energy syndrome* (ed. L. N. Lindberg). D. C. Heath and Company, Lexington, Mass.

Sathianathan, M. A. (1975). *Biogas: achievements and challenges*. Association of Voluntary Agencies for Rural Development, New Delhi.

Tyner, W. E. (1977). *Energy resources and economic development in India*. (Martinus Nijhoff Press, Leiden.

12

Energy resources, consumption, and supply in India

P. D. HENDERSON

The energy resources of India

In the present state of scientific and technical knowledge, it is convenient to list the main energy resources of India under five headings. Four of these can be grouped under the general description of 'commercial energy'. These are: coal; oil and natural gas; hydroelectric power; and nuclear fuels, both actual and potential. The fifth category comprises the various kinds of resources in India which provide 'non-commercial' energy, so called because much of it is not ordinarily bought or sold, at any rate in recorded transactions. In this last category, much the most important item is forest resources, which provide the basis for a considerable volume of firewood and charcoal consumption. The other main forms of non-commercial fuel in India are vegetable wastes, which chiefly consist of crop residues, and dried cow dung.

Coal

India has large and extensive reserves of coal. Published estimates of their extent have varied appreciably, and in any case much exploratory work has still to be done before a confident assessment can be made. The figures given in Table 12.1 are taken from estimates recently published by the Geological Survey of India.

It can be seen from the table that total estimated reserves of all types of coal are now put at some 81 billion tonnes, of which just over one-quarter comes into the category of proved reserves. Out of the proved reserves of some 21 billion tonnes, about 42 per cent consists of coking and 58 per cent of non-coking coal. The share of non-coking coal in other reserves, both indicated and inferred, exceeds 80 per cent, so that for all forms of reserves coking coal accounts for about one-quarter and non-coking coal for three-quarters.

As remarked in the notes to the table, these figures in general refer only to coal seams lying at a depth not exceeding 2000 ft, and in seams exceeding 1.2 m in thickness, though in the case of a few coalfields, including much the two largest of Raniganj and Jharia, the depth goes up to 4000 ft and reserves also include seams of between 1.2 m and 45 cm in thickness. In so far as it became worthwhile to mine coal at greater depths than these, further reserves would be identified. In this respect the table gives a somewhat conservative picture.

On the other hand, the figures refer to all forms of coal, including coal with such a high content of ash and moisture that so far it has not been generally worked. Thus, for example in the case of proved reserves of non-coking coals, it appears that out of the total of 12 billion tonnes only about

From *India, The Energy Sector* by P. D. Henderson (Oxford University Press for the World Bank, New Delhi, 1975), pp. 6–35. Reprinted by permission of the World Bank and Oxford University Press, India Branch.

Table 12.1. Estimated coal reserves in India (million tonnes)

	Proved reserves	*Other reserves* *Indicated*	*Inferred*	*Total reserves*
Prime coking coal	3650	1540	460	5650
Medium coking coal	3850	4310	1270	9430
Semi- and weakly-coking coal	1520	2600	910	5030
Total coking coal	9020	8450	2650	20120
Non-coking coal	12340	22310	26180	60830
Total coal reserves	21360	30760	28830	80950

Source: Geological Survey of India, *G.S.I. News*, April 1972. The figures are based on data supplied by the G.S.I. itself and by the former National Coal Development Corporation.

Notes: (1) The figures which have been rounded off here to the nearest 10 million tonnes, refer in general only to coal in seams exceeding 1.2 m in thickness and to a depth not exceeding 2000 ft (610 m). However, in the case of a few coalfields including the two largest, the figures cover seams exceeding 45 cm in thickness and to a depth of 4000 ft. (2) *Proved reserves* are those within 200 m of workings, outcrop or borehole. *Indicated reserves* are those within points of observation no more than 1000 m apart, or 2000 m for beds of known continuity. *Inferred reserves* are those based upon broad knowledge of the measures even though there is no quantitative evidence within 1000 or 2000 m.

three quarters can be assigned to grades with an ash content of less than 40 per cent, which has normally been the maximum acceptable figure. Applying this factor to total reserves of non-coking coal, proved and other, would reduce the figure of 60 billion tonnes shown in Table 13.1 to 45 billion.

Another factor to be taken into account is that not all reserves *in situ*, even of acceptable quality, can actually be worked. Moreover, only a certain proportion of workable reserves, which in Britain for example is normally put at 50 per cent, can actually be turned into saleable coal. This ratio largely depends on geological conditions and the methods of coal-getting that are used. For non-coking coal in India, it appears that in underground mines the ratio under present conditions may vary between 35 per cent and 60 per cent, with an average figure of perhaps 45 per cent. For open-cast mines, a figure of 80 to 90 per cent would be typical. Taking both together, an average of about 55 per cent for non-coking coal might be appropriate. If for illustrative purposes this ratio is applied to the figure of 45 billion tonnes derived in the preceding paragraph as a possible rough estimate of reserves of non-coking coal of acceptable quality *in situ*, a figure of about 24 billion tonnes is derived for reserves of recoverable and saleable non-coking coal.

At the present level of output of non-coking coal, a reserve of this size would be adequate for between 350 and 400 years. If however allowance is made for possible future increases in output, the prospect is less reassuring. If for example it is assumed: (a) that the Fifth Plan production target for non-coking coal of over 100 million tonnes in 1978/79 is attained; and (b) that output increases thereafter at a constant rate of 5 per cent per annum until it reaches a figure of 500 million tonnes a year (about the year 2011), after which it remains constant, this level of reserves would suffice only for a further 65 to 70 years from now. This may well be an unduly pessimistic figure, since an annual level of coal production in India as high as 500 million tonnes is at present hard to envisage, while in recent years the rate of increase in production has been well under 5 per cent per year. On the other hand, output did in fact rise at an average rate of about 5 per cent per annum over the past 20 years as a whole, in a period when the rate of economic growth was lower than planned and coal was losing ground to oil. It is hoped in future to increase the rate of growth of the economy as a whole, while the recent sharp increases in oil prices have greatly improved the competitive position of coal and strengthened the case for greater reliance on indigenous fuels. In view of this, to project the past increase in coal output into the future for a period of just over 30 years from 1978/9, and to assume no further growth in output thereafter, may be taken as a possible illustrative hypothesis.

On present evidence, the reserve position with respect to coking coal appears rather less favourable. A critical factor here is the availability of prime coking coal, with which the other coking coals must be blended for metallurgical use. It can be seen from Table 12.1 that the total reserves of prime coking coal are put at about 5600 million tonnes. Of this, the amount that can actually be charged to coke ovens may only be of the order of 1600 million tonnes, because of losses arising not only in mining but from the washing process that is necessary in view of the high ash content. It has been estimated that this amount, together with the other coking coals that would be blended with it, might be adequate to meet demand for a further period of between 40 to 50 years if the steel industry's consumption continues to rise at the rate that is currently projected. This figure however is probably on the low side, not only because it takes no account of possible changes in the technology of steelmaking but also because the very limited area of the coking coal fields is likely at some stage to set a physical upper limit to annual rates of output—with the possible result that eventual future demands might have to be restricted to this limit or met from outside India.

The arithmetic of the previous two paragraphs takes no account of the strong possibility already mentioned that existing estimates of coal reserves in India may well be revised upwards in the course of time. Moreover, the estimated duration of given reserves would be increased in so far as improvements in mining techniques made it possible to raise the proportion of reserves *in situ* which could be recovered and used. Increasing scarcity and higher relative prices of coal would make it more profitable to develop and exploit such improvements.

In addition to coal, deposits of lignite exist at the Neyveli field in Tamil Nadu. Total reserves are estimated at nearly 2000 million tonnes. Current production of lignite is at the rate of about 3 million tonnes a year, and a target of 6 million tonnes has been set for the end of the Fifth Plan period. At this level of output the reserves would last for over 300 years.

Because of the conditions under which they are formed, the Indian coal deposits have two related characteristics which create problems both in working and in marketing. The first of these is that seams tend to be very thick, sometimes exceeding 45 m. The second characteristic, which has already been noted, is the high ash content. In earlier years, when some 80 per cent of the industry's output came from the higher quality and lower ash coal of the Jharia and Raniganj fields on the border of West Bengal and Bihar, an average ash content of 14 per cent could be maintained. But over time the ash content of coal from these fields has risen, while the proportionate share of output from other fields with generally lower quality coal has increased. Inevitably the average ash content has gone up, and it now exceeds 20 per cent.

The coal deposits of India are distributed very unevenly as between different regions of the country. There are no coalfields in the north-west regions, none in the west except for the small fields in the eastern part of Maharashtra, and none in the south except for the Singareni fields in Andhra Pradesh, which are also small, and the lignite deposits of Neyveli in Tamil Nadu. Hence long and costly haulages are necessary if coal is to be supplied to these regions, particularly if it has to be brought from the main producing areas of West Bengal and Bihar.

Even within the areas in which coal is mined, there is a strong element of concentration of both output and reserves in particular coalfields and geographical areas.

The total number of coalfields at present is 82, excluding the few small fields in Assam. Within this total, the four largest fields—namely Raniganj in West Bengal, Jharia and North Karanpura in Bihar, and Singrauli in the northern part of Madhya Pradesh—together account for some five-eighths of the total reserves. Raniganj and Jharia alone produced about 58 per cent of the industry's total output in 1969/70, the latest year for which published information on this subject is available at the time of writing.

As the distribution of output and reserves by area, a dominating position is still held by the two states of West Bengal and Bihar, where the industry originally developed. Of the total reserves of coking coal, approximately 86 per cent are in Bihar and virtually all the remainder in West Bengal. Thus all but a very small fraction of coking coal output comes from the Bengal–Bihar area.

With respect to non-coking coal, and for both types of coal taken together, the approximate percentage shares of Bengal–Bihar and the other (or 'outlying') fields are shown in Table 13.2. The first four columns of the table relate to output and the last two to reserves.

Over the past 20 years or more, a deliberate attempt has been made to increase the production of non-coking coal in the outlying fields, both absolutely and relatively, so as to minimize the difficulties and costs of transporting coal long distances from Bengal–Bihar. As can be seen from Table 12.2, a good deal of progress has been made in this direction, while under the Fifth Plan programme a further increase is projected in the share of output from the outlying fields. From the last two columns, however, it appears that over a longer period there are limits to the extent to which this process

Table 13.2. Respective shares in coal production and reserves of Bengal–Bihar and outlying fields (percentages)

	Production				*Reserves*	
	1954	*1960–1*	*1972–3*	*1978–9*†	*Proved*	*Total*
Non-coking coals						
Bengal–Bihar	70	71	60	50	46	58
Outlying fields*	30	29	40	50	54	42
Coking and non-coking coals						
Bengal–Bihar	81	80	68	61½	68	68
Outlying fields*	19	20	32	38½	32	32

*This term is used in India to refer to all coalfields outside the two states of West Bengal and Bihar. These are very largely to be found in four states, namely, Andhra Pradesh, Madhya Pradesh, Maharashtra, and Orissa.

†Planned.

Sources: For *reserves*, the figures given in Table 13.1 are used, in conjunction with other information from official sources. For *production*, the figures for 1954 are derived from Ministry of Steel and Mines, Coal Controller, *Monthly review of coal production and distribution*, May 1971; those for 1960–1 are from the *Report of the energy survey committee;* those for 1972–3 from Coal Controller, *Provisional coal statistics*, November 1973; and those for 1978–9 from data supplied by the Planning Commission.

Note: As remarked in the text, the share of Bengal–Bihar in coking coal, both production and reserves, is virtually 100 per cent.

can be continued. For all forms of coal the estimated share of Bengal–Bihar in both proved and total reserves is 68 per cent, while even for non-coking coals alone the share in total reserves is not far short of 60 per cent. Thus for as far ahead as can be seen at present, India will continue to depend for well over half of total coal supplies on production from West Bengal and Bihar.

Oil and natural gas

By comparison with coal, proved reserves of *oil* in India are at present exceedingly small. However, a great deal of survey and exploration work remains to be done, so that large areas in which productive deposits of oil or natural gas might possibly be found have yet to be investigated thoroughly. Hence the potential for further discoveries may be considerable, though it is still at present very uncertain.

The total sedimentary area of India, onshore and offshore, comprises 27 basins. On land, these cover an area of about 1.41 million square kilometres, some 43 per cent of the country. Offshore, a further 0.38 million square kilometres of possible oil-bearing rock have been identified up to the 200 metres isobath line, of which about two-thirds lie within the 100 metres isobath.

To judge from past experience in the world as a whole, perhaps only about 3 per cent of the total sedimentary area is likely to prove productive. Within the 27 basins that have been identified in India, the prospects vary considerably. The basins are at present grouped into four main categories of promise. Those with high prospects comprise Cambay and a large part of Assam–Arakan—the basins in which all the existing productive wells are to be found. The area which falls into this category comes to about 300000 square kilometres, or some 18 per cent of the total sedimentary area, onshore and offshore, up to the 200 metre isobath line. A second category with medium prospects comprises a further 15 per cent of the total sedimentary area. Here the basic geological conditions appear similar to those of Cambay and Assam, but so far neither oil nor gas has been found in quantities which would make commercial development worthwhile.

The remaining two-thirds of the sedimentary area consists of basins where the prospects are assessed only as fair (which make up some 40 per cent of the total area) or poor (about 27 per cent). It is thus probable that in many of the basins little or no oil or gas will be found.

Up to now, geological and geophysical studies have been conducted in 14 of the 27 basins, while exploratory drilling has taken place in nine. The presence of hydrocarbons has been proved in seven of these nine, but as noted above only two of these, the onshore portion of the Cambay basin and Assam, have been shown to contain oil and gas in exploitable quantities. Of the total number of wells so far drilled, about 90 per cent have been in these two areas, and they account for an even higher proportion of the total meterage drilled.

The result of the exploratory and drilling activities of the past 15 years is that an estimated 185 million tonnes of proved and indicated crude petroleum reserves have been discovered, all in the two areas of Gujarat and Assam. The fact that oil-bearing reservoirs are still being discovered in these producing areas suggests that further useful deposits of oil remain to be found.

The chances of finding oil in remunerative quantities offshore appear to be good. It has often been the case that offshore areas of coastal basins have provided greater yields per well than onshore; and the offshore portion of the Cambay basin, where the first exploratory drilling now in progress has already found oil at shallow depths, holds considerable promise. An encouraging feature is that the oil has been found in limestone reservoirs, as in the Middle-East fields, and in rocks that are of younger age than those in which oil discoveries have been made in the other producing areas of the Indian subcontinent.

Even before these recent discoveries, it

Table 12.3. Crude petroleum: proved and indicated reserves* and domestic production, 1966–73 (million tonnes)

	*Reserves**	*Production*	*Ratio of reserves to production (duration period)*
1966	153.0	4.65	32.9
1967	154.8	5.67	27.3
1968	141.0	5.85	24.1
1969	132.3	6.72	19.7
1970	127.8	6.81	18.8
1971	113.8†	7.19	15.8
1972	125.2†	7.37	17.0
1973	n.a.§	7.20	n.a.

*Strictly speaking, the figures for reserves shown here refer to what are known in India (where the classification system used in the USSR is followed) as categories A, B, and C1. Category A covers oil in areas fully outlined by wells, while category B includes oil that has been proved by the presence of wells with favourable reservoir data. Categories A and B together are probably equivalent to what in the US are termed proved reserves. Category C1 comprises accumulations where the porosity and permeability of formations are known and in which at least one well has been drilled. This category corresponds to what are known in American practice as indicated reserves.

†Figures for 1971 and 1972 reserves are provisional.

§n.a. = not available.

Sources: Government of India, Ministry of Petroleum & Chemicals, *Indian petroleum & chemicals statistics*, 1972; data for reserves at the end of 1971 and 1972, and for production in 1973, supplied by the Ministry.

had been conjectured that recoverable reserves in the Bombay High area of the Cambay basin might amount to some 125 million tonnes. An earlier broad appraisal of total reserves in India, made by the Soviet geologist Kalinin on the basis of geological analogy alone, concluded that there should be, all told, some 3 billion tonnes of oil on land within India and a further 1 billion tonnes offshore. Thus the potential for new discoveries could be very great.

At the same time, the position is not altogether an encouraging one. Judgements made on the basis of broad geological evidence alone are subject to a wide margin of error. Until a great many more exploratory drillings have been done, the amount of oil resources that may exist will remain a matter of speculation. Recent onshore developments, moreover, have been disappointing. The main producing wells, actual or prospective, were all discovered in the 1950s or early 1960s; there has been no addition to their number in the past 10 years. Most of the recent discoveries are marginal, and represent small accumulations of oil. Since the mid-1960s, the additions to proved and indicated reserves have been small, and as shown in Table 12.3 the current level of proved and indicated reserves in 1972 was appreciably below the figure for 1967, which is the highest so far attained. As domestic production of crude is now above the levels reached in 1967 and 1968, the ratio of production to reserves is correspondingly lower. Any long-run sustained increase in the level of domestic crude production has now become critically dependent on the discovery and development of substantial new producing oilfields.

Production of crude oil in India is at present concentrated in a small number of fields. It is estimated that in 1973 well over 90 per cent of output came from the six main producing fields. Within this group, two in particular are predominant. These are Ankleshwar in Gujarat, which is operated by the public sector Oil and Natural Gas

Commission, and Nahorkatiya in Assam, which is operated by Oil India Limited, a joint sector enterprise in which 50 per cent shares each are held by the Government of India and Burma Oil Company.

The costs of finding, producing, and distributing oil depend on a variety of factors, including the difficulties of the terrain, the depth and accessibility of oil deposits, and the productivity of producing wells. In most of these respects the Gujarat fields are more favourably placed than those of Assam. The fields in Assam are relatively inaccessible and distant from markets, and petroleum occurs in a large number of separate pools at depths which vary from 3000 to 4000 metres. The average depth of wells in the onshore Cambay basin is just under 1700 m (550 ft), while the corresponding figure for Assam is over 3300 m (10800 ft). Annual production per well, or well productivity, is not very different between the two regions, but is generally higher in Gujarat. For India as a whole, productivity averages about 270 barrels per day. This is low compared with big Middle Eastern fields, but not much below the current level in Venezuela.

The quality of Indian crudes is good. In the Gujarat fields, the crude produced is very light (36–48° API) with a sulphur content of less then 0.1 per cent. A problem arises, however, in production and refining, because of the rather high wax content, which averages between 11 and 13 per cent. This results in a high pour point, and in winter the oil must be heated to flow. Assam crudes tend to be heavier (averaging about 34° API), with an average sulphur content of 0.3 per cent and a lower pour point.

The cost of producing crude oil is higher in Assam than in the onshore Cambay fields. For all domestic production, the average direct producing costs at present may be in the region of $1.50 to $1.65 per barrel.[1] This is very high in comparison with the really big Middle-Eastern fields, but not in relation to the costs incurred in a number of other producing countries. The comparable figure for Mexico, for example, is about $2.20 per barrel. In future, costs are liable to rise, even apart from general increases in input prices, because new onshore supplies are likely to have to come from reservoirs which will be deeper and costlier to develop. However, the main factor determining production costs will be the size of any new fields that are discovered, which cannot be accurately predicted. In any case, at present and anticipated levels of world crude oil prices Indian production even at appreciably higher unit production cost will certainly be competitive with imported crude.

Natural gas is found in India both alone and in association with crude oil; but most of the output comes from associated sources, and the only non-associated gas field is that at Cambay in Gujarat. The gas–oil production ratio tends to be low in India, but as shown in Table 12.4 the output has increased rapidly in recent years. From the final column of the table, it can be seen that over 40 per cent of output is still not utilized, but is flared.

Because of their generally very close association in India, the prospects for future discoveries of natural gas, and for later consequent increases in output, are as hopeful but also as highly uncertain as those for crude oil.

Hydroelectric power

The basis for assessment of the hydroelectric power reserves of India is a comprehensive initial survey which was undertaken during the period 1953–60 by the Central Water and Power Commission. The method used in this survey was to examine each basin in detail, and to estimate the firm power potential that it was felt could be provided at a cost which would be low enough to be competitive with other sources of power. The calculations were made on the basis of prevailing techniques of hydro construction and utilization, and of the constraints believed to be imposed by topographical and hydrological conditions and by other demands on available water resources.

The firm power potential defined in this

Table 12.4. Natural gas: reserves, production, and utilization, 1965–73

	Reserves (billion cubic metres)	*Production*	*Utilization*	*Flared gas*	*Ratio of utilization to production (per cent)*
		(million cubic metres)			
1965		737	346	391	47
1966	63.15	803	373	431	46
1967	67.25	1221	465	756	38
1968	63.34	1317	604	712	46
1969	65.60	1384	730	654	53
1970	62.48	1424	676	748	47
1971	62.29*	1509	761	748	50
1972	62.51*	1565	927	628	59
1973*	n.a.	1674	913	761	55

*Reserves figures for 1971 and 1972 are provisional, as are all figures for 1973.
Sources: Ministry of Petroleum and Chemicals, *Indian petroleum & chemicals statistics*, 1972; data on reserves for 1971 and 1972, and on production in 1973, supplied by the Ministry.

way was estimated by drawing up a complete inventory of actual or putative hydro stations, with specified design parameters in each case. The total of assessed hydro resources was then arrived at by summing the individual figures for each of these stations.

This aggregate total, which is still normally quoted as the accepted estimate of India's hydro potential, is just over 41 million KW at a load factor of 60 per cent. In Table 12.5, the percentage shares of this total figure are shown according to (1) regions and states, (2) the main river systems, and (3) the types of hydro project which comprised the CWPC inventory.

From the first two columns of the table it can be seen that there is a broad correspondence between regions and river systems. The very large potential resources of the north-eastern region, just over 30 per cent of the total, come from the rivers of the Brahmaputra basin and neighbouring drainage areas. The northern region's resources, which form just over one-quarter of the total, correspond almost exactly to the potential of the Ganga and Indus basins. The river systems of central and southern India, which provide over 40 per cent of the potential, are the sources of hydro power for the southern, eastern, and western regions.

To some extent the availability of hydro power redresses the differences which arise from the very uneven regional distribution of coal reserves. The main coal-producing states of Bihar and West Bengal are not well favoured with respect to hydro resources. On the other hand a number of states in the south and north-west, which have no coal reserves and are remote from the coal-producing areas, are well endowed with, or have relatively simple access to, hydroelectric potential. These include Haryana, Himachal Pradesh, Jammu and Kashmir, Karnataka, Kerala and Punjab.

The estimated total potential of 41 million KW at 60 per cent load factor is equivalent to an annual output of 216 TWh. This figure can be compared with the present level of hydro generation, which at 27 TWh is only one-eighth of it. The corresponding planned level of output for the final year of the Fifth Plan period is about 46 TWh, which is rather more than 20 per cent of the total. Hence, even on the basis of an assessed potential of 41 million KW, the scope for further development of hydro resources is considerable.

In fact there are grounds for regarding this estimate of hydro potential as conservative. Even at the time when it was arrived at it was in the nature of a prudent minimum figure rather than the most probable one.

The main reasons for this were the following:

(a) The estimates of the firm power potential were made on the basis of the minimum average flows that could be expected to be available with a probability of 90 per cent, taking into account the regulation afforded by the storage envisaged. Hence no account was taken of the energy that

Table 12.5. Estimated shares of hydro potential by states and regions, river systems, and types of project (percentages)

States and regions		*River systems*		*Types of project*	
Southern region		1. Southern India			
Andhra Pradesh	6.0	(a) West flowing rivers	10.4	(a) Run-of-river	25.0
Karnataka	8.2	(b) East flowing rivers	21.0	(b) Storage projects	75.0
Kerala	3.7	Total	31.4	Total	100.0
Tamil Nadu	1.7				
Total	19.7				
Western region					
Gujarat	1.6				
Madhya Pradesh	11.2	2. Rivers of central India	10.4		
Maharashtra	4.6				
Total	17.4				
Eastern region					
Bihar	1.5				
Orissa	5.0				
West Bengal	0.1				
Total	6.5				
Northern region					
Himachal Pradesh	4.5				
Jammu and Kashmir	8.7	3. Ganga Basin	11.4	(a) High head	33.1
Punjab and Haryana	3.3			(b) Medium head	58.0
Rajasthan	0.4	4. Indus Basin	16.0	(c) Low head	8.9
Uttar Pradesh	9.1			Total	100.0
Total	26.1				
North-eastern region					
Assam*	28.2	5. Brahmaputra Basin and neighbouring drainage areas	30.3		
Manipur	2.1				
Total	30.3				
Total	100.0		100.0		

*Including Meghalaya, Nagaland, and Mizoram.

Source: Government of India, *Report of the energy survey of India committee*, New Delhi.
Notes: (1) The Ganga basin is formed on the north by the rivers draining the Himalayan range, and on the south by the rivers that drain the northern part of the Central Plateau. For both the Ganga and Brahmaputra basins, the CWPC inventory of possible projects included some which would be situated outside India, but the total for assessed firm power potential of 41 million kW at 60 per cent load factor took account of projects only within India. Similarly the figure for the Indus basin covered only that portion of the basin which lies within India. (2) High-head projects are defined as those in which the head exceeds 1000 feet, while in medium-head projects the height is from 100 to 1000 feet and in low-head projects from 25 to 100 feet.

could be produced on a secondary basis corresponding to inflows higher than dependable flows, nor of the energy that could be supplied on a seasonal basis.

(b) The estimates referred only to sites within India, and no allowance was made in the estimated total for the possibility that hydro power from Nepal might become available for use in India.

(c) It was known that in the light of further survey work the estimates of the hydro potential of the Himalayan rivers might be revised upwards.

(d) No account was taken of the possible effects of improvements in the technology of hydro design, construction, and operation.

Since the original CWPC survey was completed, a number of developments have established that a higher estimate of total hydro potential is now warranted. These are summarized in the 1971 *Report of Power Economy Committee*.[2] This suggests that the firm power potential of the Indus basin might now be put at some 12 or possibly 14 million KW, instead of between 6 or 7 million as shown in the survey. Hence even on the former somewhat conservative basis of assessment a figure of close to 50 million KW would now seem to be indicated.

As to new factors not taken into account in the above estimates, two developments which have occurred since the original CWPC survey was made have improved the outlook for hydro resources. One is that the estimated potential of the Karnali Valley in Nepal has been raised considerably. The possibilities of some form of joint development of this resource, with substantial sales of hydro power to India, now appear more promising. A second factor is that recent improvements in the technology of pumped storage schemes have considerably raised the potential for seasonal supplies of hydro power in the river systems of the Deccan.

A further point is that in its assessment of firm hydro potential, the CWPC has followed the practice of estimating demands for irrigation and for industrial, commercial, and domestic water supplies, and deducting the losses arising from these from the potential available for hydro generation. These categories of demand are treated as 'priority uses', so that hydro power becomes the residual claimant. It is possible that a more flexible optimizing approach to water resource developments, in which all forms of demand were permitted to vary in relation to one another so that a greater number of possibilities could be explored, might suggest a larger role for hydro power in the development of river systems. If so, this again would be a reason for regarding current estimates of potential as being on the low side.

On the other hand, it has to be remembered that for a substantial part of the hydro potential that has been identified, the date at which it might be put to use is uncertain and probably remote. This applies particularly to the resources of the north-eastern region. Even if the cost of providing hydro power at a particular location would be low, it does not follow that generating facilities should be established there. The case for this will depend on how far potential consumers would be prepared to pay a price which would cover the estimated costs to society of the power that would be generated. For as far ahead as can be foreseen at present, it seems unlikely that power consumption in the north-eastern region will warrant the exploitation of any but a small part of the identified hydro potential there: its remoteness, the difficulties of communication, and the lack of raw materials which require ample supplies of electric power for processing, are likely to hold down the pace of development. Hence the value of these hydro-power resources may largely depend on further progress in the technology of extra-high voltage transmission lines which would reduce the losses from conveying power over long distances, and on the development within India of a more fully articulated power grid of which these lines would be a constituent part. These developments can be foreseen, but their time has yet to come.

Looking ahead towards the end of the century, a very rough assessment of the possible contribution of hydro-power can be made on the basis of some projections made by the Power Economy Committee 3 years ago. They suggested that over the coming two or three decades it might be worthwhile to install about 80 to 100 million KW of hydro capacity. If we take the lower of these two figures as being applicable, and assume an average plant load factor of 40 per cent which takes account of the use of hydro-power for meeting peak loads, an output of some 280 TWh is indicated at a time perhaps 20 to 25 years from now. It will be seen that this figure considerably exceeds the estimate of 216 TWh mentioned above, which corresponds to the assessment of firm hydro-power potential of 41 million KW at a 60 per cent system load factor.

This possible output of 280 TWh from hydro plant has to be compared with a corresponding figure for total electricity generated. This is necessarily a matter of conjecture. For illustrative purposes, we may take the target level for the final year of the Fifth Plan period, which is 128 TWh, and assume thereafter a constant annual growth rate of 8 per cent. This would yield a figure of some 475 TWh by the middle of the last decade of the century.

Hence the existing known potential of hydroelectric power can be judged to make possible a substantial contribution to a total power output some four times as high as that which it is hoped to achieve in the Fifth Plan, and some seven times as high as at present. Since hydro resources are renewable, this would be a continuing contribution, and it seems likely that estimates of potential will continue to be revised upwards. These however will depend on further advances in knowledge and techniques, and on the cost and availability of alternative sources of energy.

Nuclear fuels

Resources of nuclear fuels in India consist of uranium, and potentially of thorium also. The first of these is already in use for the generation of electric power in India, and the current nuclear power programme provides for further construction of power-stations with CANDU-type heavy water reactors using domestically produced natural uranium as fuel.

The main concentration of uranium ores at present, and the only source in which uranium is being actively mined within India, is in the Singhbhum district of Bihar. In addition to the two mines that are now being worked or developed, other exploitable deposits may exist in Bihar. Besides this principal area, deposits near Udaipur in Rajasthan may prove worth developing, though the uranium concentration is expected to be considerably lower. Prospecting and exploration work for uranium is being carried out in a number of different regions in India, under the direction of the Department of Atomic Energy in collaboration with other government agencies.

The existing proved minable ore reserves in the Bihar mines have been estimated at some 3.5 million tonnes. The grade of ore is believed to average some 0.060 to 0.065—that is, just under two-thirds of 1 per cent—of U_3O_8, which is a lower level than that generally found in the existing mines of other producing countries. With this concentration, the existing proved reserves of ore would yield some 22000 tonnes of U_3O_8. In addition, a figure somewhat larger than this has been suggested as the present estimate of inferred as distinct from proved reserves.

On the basis of these reserves of uranium, and with the technology that is currently in use, uranium supplies would suffice for a rather restricted period, the length of which would depend on the rate at which the installed nuclear power capacity was built up. This period would be extended by improvements in fuel technology in the present reactors, and by the discovery and proving of further reserves of uranium. Each of these, however, appears to offer only limited scope.

The main possibility for increasing the available resources of nuclear fuel, in India as elsewhere, arises from the development of fast breeder reactors. These would be able to make use of the plutonium that is now being produced by the present generation of nuclear reactors, but which is not used in them, and by producing more plutonium than they would themselves burn, they would enormously increase the total resources of nuclear fuel that could be developed from a given amount of uranium.

Moreover, the development of fast breeder reactors would open up the prospect of using thorium, of which India has very large reserves, in order to supplement uranium as a basic fuel.[3] The thorium would be converted in the breeder reactors into the fissile material U-233 which itself can be used directly as a nuclear fuel. If and when this process becomes established, so that breeder reactors based on thorium can be introduced, the capacity to generate electricity from domestic sources of fuel would be extended virtually without limit. Known reserves of thorium, which are found chiefly in the monazite sands of Kerala and in the Ranchi plateau on the border of West Bengal and Bihar, are currently put at 450000 tonnes. It is estimated that the energy potentially available from this amount is about 18Q, or more than 5 million TWh. This compares with a current level of electricity generation of about 70 TWh, and a possible level by the end of the century of perhaps 500 TWh.

This tremendous increase in fuel resources depends, however, on the successful development both of fast breeder reactor on a commercial scale and of the thorium-based process for adding to nuclear fuel supplies. Both the development time and the costs of realizing these objectives are extremely uncertain. Some very difficult technical problems remain to be solved.

Although a great deal of money and effort is now being put into the development of fast breeder reactors in several countries, the eventual payoff from all this activity is still in doubt. It is true that breeder reactors would bring about a substantial reduction in the fuel costs of nuclear power-stations, but this advantage may well be outweighed, at any rate for a considerable time to come, by higher capital costs. Much will depend on further progress in the technology involved, and also on trends in the price of uranium, which will largely determine what happens to the fuel costs of existing types of nuclear power-station. Uranium prices in turn will be affected by the rate of expansion of nuclear power generation in the world as a whole, and by the extent of new discoveries of uranium ores. All these factors are subject to a great deal of uncertainty.

Because of these uncertainties, it is not yet possible to say with confidence when fast breeder reactors will reach the stage of being able to generate useful amounts of power at an acceptably low cost. This is true even for countries where development work has gone much further than in India, and where the scale of expenditure greatly exceeds what is planned or could be contemplated in the Indian programme of development. The present official expectation in India is that full-scale fast breeder reactors developed within India will be producing power by the second half of the 1980s. This may well prove to be too optimistic a projection.

Superimposed on the problems that may arise with fast breeder reactors in general are those of developing the use of thorium. Effective ways of producing from natural ore deposits the metallic thorium required, and of developing on a commercial scale reactors in which it will be converted to U-233, have yet to be devised and proved. For these to be developed independently within India may take a considerable time. Moreover, even assuming that it were possible and acceptable for the Indian programme to make use of foreign as well as indigenous technology in order to speed up the process of development, the scope for this may be limited because the possible gains from turning to thorium may be rated less highly in other countries, with the result that relatively little would be spent on proving them. Thus the full potential of India's thorium reserves, and the time by which it will be possible to begin exploiting them seriously, still remain to be established.

Forest resources

Forests and woodlands are an important element in the inventory of fuel resources in India, since they are the source of firewood and charcoal which are the main items of domestic fuel consumption. Although the total amount of firewood consumed is not known precisely, it is currently put at some 130 million tonnes. This exceeds by some 50 per cent the present level of output of the coal industry.

Not a great deal seems to be known about the sources of firewood, the implications of current or higher levels of consumption for the inventory of forest resources, or the extent to which well-conceived programmes of forestry development would permit the maintenance or increase of firewood supplies in the long run.

The total forest area of India is put at some 75 million hectares, which is about 23 per cent of the total area of the country. Of the forest area itself, some 60 per cent is classified as exploitable (which means that the forests are actually in use), and a further 20 per cent as potentially exploitable. Virtually the whole of the forest area comes under the ownership of the States, and all recorded production of timber is from State forests. In round terms, the most recent available production figures (for the year 1969–70) are 22 million cubic metres for total timber production, of which 13 million cubic metres consisted of fuelwood. In terms of tonnage this latter figure comes to only 9 million. It follows that out of the 130 million tonnes referred to above, which is believed to be a reasonable current estimate of total fuelwood consumption, only about 7 per cent is accounted for from recorded production. As to the remainder, it can only be said in general terms that it must come from three sources: (1) forest areas not owned by the States; (2) unrecorded production from State forests; and (3) woodlands, such as those belonging to villages and at roadsides, which do not fall within the definition of forest areas. Since so little of the present forest area is in the hands of agencies other than the States, the first of these sources must be relatively unimportant.

The effects of fuelwood consumption on this scale, and the resultant extent of felling, are generally believed to be serious; but even the broadest quantitative indicators of the possible amount of damage and depletion are lacking. At the same time, no estimates or assessments exist of the future levels of firewood consumption which might be consistent with sound management for forest and woodland resources. However, the need for greater attention to this problem, and for action designed to increase the supply of fuelwood by planned investment, has been recognized in a number of recent reports including that of the Fuel Policy Committee, and in the Draft Fifth Plan itself.

Vegetable wastes and cow dung

On the present most widely accepted estimate of consumption of non-commercial fuels, and allowing for differences in thermal value, firewood accounts for almost two-thirds of the total, vegetable wastes for about 20 per cent, and cow dung for about 15 per cent.

Since vegetable wastes are mainly derived from crop residues, the available quantities largely depend on the amounts harvested of the crops concerned, and the total is therefore likely to rise over time in line with aggregate crop production. It is not thought that any problem of resource use arises in connection with this source of domestic fuel.

The burning of dried cow dung is a more controversial practice, because of the alternative use of dung as a fertilizer. The present cattle population of India, including buffaloes, is probably of the order of 250 million, which would perhaps yield 1550 million tonnes of wet dung in a year. Since it takes about 5 tonnes of wet dung to produce 1 tonne of dried dung for fuel purposes, and since current consumption of dried cow dung as fuel is put at some 70 million tonnes, it appears that on these estimates between one-fifth and one-quarter of the total supply is burned as fuel.

It is sometimes argued that any use of cow dung for this purpose is extremely unfortunate, since its value as fertilizer greatly exceeds its value as a fuel. The strength of this argument depends on what it is reasonable to assume about (a) the cost of alternative fuels, and (b) the effectiveness with which dung is actually likely to be used as a fertilizer. What does seem to be clearly established is that much more effective use could be made of this resource both as a fuel *and* as a fertilizer, by methods which are both proved and reasonably simple to introduce.

The growth and pattern of energy consumption and supply

In order to measure aggregate changes in energy production or consumption, it is necessary to express the various constituent forms of energy in terms of some common unit of measurement. None of the methods used is clearly superior to the others, and indeed it is arguable that no measure derived purely from the physical or technical characteristics of fuels is very satisfactory.

In India the Energy Survey Committee in its Report of 1965[4] initiated the practice of measuring the amounts of different fuels in terms of a common unit specified as *million tonnes of coal replacement*. Since then this measure has been generally chosen for the analysis of energy trends within India, and in particular it has been adopted by the Fuel Policy Committee. It is therefore used in the discussion which follows.

Total energy, commercial and non-commercial

A striking feature of energy consumption in India is the very important position still held by the traditional or non-commercial sources of supply.

One such source which has not yet been referred to, and for which only very rough estimation is possible, is the animal power which still constitutes a substantial share of the energy input into agriculture. Although this is increasingly being replaced by mechanical power, it remains extremely large in absolute terms. A recent estimate[5] is that the energy derived from animal power came to about 110 million tonnes of coal replacement in 1965/6. This amount was estimated to be over one-third of all energy consumption at that time, expressed in terms of coal replacement, and to exceed the amounts derived both from commercial sources of energy and from other non-commercial sources, each of which was put at under one-third of the total.

So far as fuels are concerned, the main forms of non-commercial energy, as already noted above, are firewood and charcoal, dried cow dung, and vegetable wastes. It is these sources alone which are referred to below as non-commercial energy, with animal power excluded.

The amounts of these non-commercial fuels consumed can also be estimated only roughly. A set of figures has been derived here, but the results have little more than illustrative value. Estimates of consumption per head of non-commercial fuels in 1962/3 were made by the Energy Survey Committee from evidence which had then recently become available. In the absence of more recent evidence, these values are assumed here to have held good both before and after this period, so that *consumption per head* is taken to be constant over a long period of years. Different values of consumption per head apply for urban and rural areas, so that total *consumption* for a given year is derived by multiplying each of these by the estimated urban and rural population for that year.

Table 12.6. Estimated energy consumption, commercial and non-commercial, 1953/4 to 1970/1

	1953/4	*1960/1*	*1965/6*	*1968/9*	*1970/1*
Amounts consumed (m.t.c.r.)*					
Commercial energy	60	101	147	177	197
Non-commercial energy	127	147	164	175	183
Total	187	248	311	352	380
Percentage shares					
Commercial energy	32	41	47	50	52
Non-commercial energy	68	59	53	50	48

*Million tonnes of coal replacement.
Sources: For commercial energy, data were supplied by the Planning Commission.

The set of estimates of aggregate consumption of non-commercial fuels is shown here in the third line of Table 12.6. This table compares in aggregate terms and for selected years the absolute amounts and relative shares of commercial and non-commercial fuels, which together comprise total estimated consumption of energy as defined here.

It can be seen from Table 12.6 that over the whole period covered by the figures—that is, from 1953/4 to 1970/1—the estimated consumption of commercial energy measured in coal replacement terms more than tripled, while total consumption of commercial and non-commercial fuels taken together approximately doubled. As a result of its faster rate of growth, the share of commercial energy in the total rose considerably over this period, from under one-third in 1953/4 to over one-half in 1970/1. On the assumption that per capita consumption of non-commercial fuels remains constant, this share will have risen further since 1970/1, and will continue to increase with time.

Again using the coefficients given in the report of the Energy Survey Committee, for each of the three main non-commercial fuels rather than for the total, it is possible to show the estimated composition of the total consumption of non-commercial fuels. This is given for 1970/1 in Table 12.7, which also gives the estimated amounts consumed of the three fuels in original units as well as in million tonnes coal replacement.

From Table 12.7 it can be seen that some two-thirds of the estimated consumption of non-commercial fuels, measured in coal replacement values, consists of firewood. Cow dung accounts for about 30 per cent

Table 12.7. Estimated consumption in India of non-commercial fuels, 1970/1

	Amounts consumed		
	Original units (million tonnes)	*Million tonnes coal replacement*	*Relative share of consumption in m.t.c.r. (per cent)*
Firewood and charcoal	126	120	66
Dried cow dung	68	27	15
Vegetable wastes	39	37	20
Total	233	183	100

of consumption by weight, but in terms of coal replacement its estimated share is only 15 per cent. The remaining 20 per cent of non-commercial fuels consists of vegetable wastes. The consumption per head of non-commercial fuels is probably rather higher in rural than in urban areas: while the urban population is estimated to have been almost 20 per cent of the total population in 1970/1, its share of non-commercial fuel consumption is put at over 17 per cent. Household consumption of commercial fuels—kerosene, soft coke, and electricity—is appreciably higher in urban than in rural areas.

Commercial energy

Within the total consumption of commercial energy, the shares of the different principal fuels can be shown in two alternative ways: by sources of primary energy, or by sources of final consumption of energy. The difference lies mainly in the treatment of electricity.

There are four chief primary sources of commercial energy in India: coal, petroleum, hydroelectricity, and (from 1970 onwards) nuclear power. On this classification, electricity generated from coal or petroleum is regarded as a secondary fuel, and therefore excluded from the list. If however commercial energy consumption is broken down according to final sources, then the three main components become coal, petroleum, and electricity. Under this classification, only the amounts of coal and petroleum products that are directly used for energy consumption are shown and not the amounts that are converted into electricity before being used as energy, while all electricity is included whatever the source of energy that is used in generating it.

It would be preferable to show the growth of commercial energy consumption according to both these classifications, by primary sources and by final sources. Unfortunately, however, there are no figures for consumption by primary fuels which are fully consistent with the most recent estimates of coal, petroleum, and electricity consumption; and these estimates themselves at present go only up to 1970/1. Hence in the tables which follow in this section, commercial energy consumption is analysed over the period from 1953/4 to 1970/1 only in terms of consumption of coal, petroleum, and electricity and not according to primary sources.

Total consumption of commercial energy, as shown in the first line of Table 12.6, and also the amounts consumed within this total of coal, petroleum and electricity, are shown in Table 12.8. The upper half of the table shows absolute amounts consumed in million tonnes of coal replacement, while the lower half shows the relative shares of each of the three fuels.

Over the whole period covered by the figures in Table 12.8—from 1953/4 to 1970/1—consumption of all three fuels rose considerably. Direct use of coal, measured in coal replacement units, has almost doubled since 1953/4, though almost the whole of this increase took place in the earlier part of the period up to 1965/6, when the average annual rate of increase was about 6 per cent. Since 1965/6 coal consumption has changed very little (though this does not take account of sales of coal to thermal power stations, which continued to rise), and for the period as a whole the average rate of increase is 3.5 per cent per annum.

The amount of petroleum directly used for energy purposes has more than quadrupled between 1953/4 and 1970/1, with an average annual rate of increase of 8.6 per cent. Energy consumed in the form of electricity rose approximately sixfold over the whole period, with an average growth rate of about 11.5 per cent.

As a result of these disparate rates of increase, the share of coal fell from just under a half to just over one-quarter; that of petroleum has slowly increased from 40 per cent to almost one-half; and the share of electricity has more than doubled, from 13 per cent to 25 per cent.

Table 12.9 compares consumption of commercial energy in 1960/1 and 1970/1,

Table 12.8. Commercial energy consumption by main fuels, 1953/4 to 1970/1

	1953/4	*1960/1*	*1965/6*	*1968/9*	*1970/1*
1. *Absolute amounts* (m.t.c.r.)					
Coal (direct use)*	28.7	40.4	51.8	53.0	51.4
Petroleum† (direct use)*	23.8	43.9	64.6	82.3	97.2
Electricity	7.6	16.9	30.6	41.5	48.6
Total	60.1	101.2	147.0	176.8	197.2
2. *Relative shares* (percentages)					
Coal	48	40	35	30	26
Petroleum	40	43	44	47	49
Electricity	13	17	21	23	25
Total	100	100	100	100	100

*'Direct use' excludes coal and oil that is used for conversion into electricity.

†Figures for petroleum exclude consumption of non-energy products, such as naphtha for use as feedstock, lubes and greases, and bitumen.

Source: Data supplied by the Planning Commission.

distinguishing the main categories of consumers. In the first four rows of the table, consumption of each fuel is shown by each of four producing sectors into which the economy is divided and which among them account for the whole of output (or gross domestic product). The fifth line gives the total for these four producing sectors. In addition, commercial energy is consumed by the domestic or household sector, and this is shown in the sixth row of the table. Total commercial energy consumption, shown in the final row of the table, is the sum of energy consumed by the four producing sectors and by households. In the last four columns of the table the changes in consumption between 1960/1 and 1970/1 are also shown.

Looking at the figures for 1960/1, marked differences appear in the amount and pattern of fuel consumption by sector. Mining and manufacturing and transport were the two dominant consumers, with almost 75 per cent of the total energy consumption. In each case about half the energy consumed in that year came from direct use of coal, but with respect to the other half transport was almost entirely dependent on oil, while for mining and manufacturing electricity was more important than oil. With respect to oil, household consumption was almost double that of mining and manufacturing, while in the case of electricity the mining and manufacturing sector accounted for over two-thirds of the total.

This pattern was broadly maintained in 1970/1, but with certain modifications. With respect to coal, the mining and manufacturing sector has become more dominant as a consumer; the whole of the net increase in coal production over the 10-year period is accounted for by this sector. The transport sector became more dependent on oil, as a result both of the more rapid expansion of road transport than of rail and also of the change on the railways from steam to diesel locomotives. Big increases took place in proportionate though not absolute terms in consumption by agriculture and 'other sectors'. In agriculture both oil and (still more) electricity consumption rose, largely because of the spread of pump sets for irrigation. In the other sectors the increase was concentrated on oil.

Looking at the increases between 1960/1

Table 12.9. Commercial energy consumption by sector, 1960/1 and 1970/1 (m.t.c.r.)

	Total consumption								*Change in consumption 1960/1 to 1970/1*			
	1960/1				*1970/1*							
	Coal	*Oil*	*Electricity*	*Total*	*Coal*	*Oil*	*Electricity*	*Total*	*Coal*	*Oil*	*Electricity*	*Total*
1. *Producing sectors*												
Agriculture*	—	2.7	0.8	3.5	—	4.5	4.5	9.0	—	1.8	3.7	5.5
Mining and manufacturing	20.9	7.2	11.6	39.7	31.9	10.9	34.4	77.2	11.0	3.7	22.8	37.5
Transport and communication*	16.0	17.4	0.8	34.2	15.1	47.2	1.4	63.7	−0.9	29.8	0.6	29.5
Others†	0.7	—	2.2	2.9	0.3	7.0	4.5	11.8	−0.4	7.0	2.3	8.9
Total	37.6	27.3	15.4	80.3	47.3	69.6	44.8	161.7	9.7	42.3	29.4	81.4
2. *Household consumption*	2.8	16.5	1.5	20.8	4.1	27.6	3.8	35.5	1.3	11.1	2.3	14.7
3. *Total consumption*	40.4	43.9	16.9	101.2	51.4	97.2	48.6	197.2	11.0	53.3	31.7	96.0

*Consumption of oil in agriculture in the form of tractor engine fuel is here included in consumption of the transport and communications sector. It is a relatively small amount.

†These comprise the following service activities: (1) trade and hotels and restaurants; (2) banking and insurance; (3) real estate and ownership of dwellings and business services; (4) public administration and defence; and (5) other services.

Source: Data supplied by the Planning Commission.

Table 12.10. Growth rates of total commercial energy consumption, GDP, and industrial production, 1960/1 to 1970/1 (average annual compound rates of growth, in percentages)

	1960/1 to 1965/6	*1965/6 to 1970/1*	*1960/1 to 1970/1*
1. Commercial energy consumption (m.t.c.r.)	7.8	6.1	6.9
2. Gross domestic product at 1960/1 prices	2.9	3.2	3.0
3. Industrial production*	9.0	3.3	6.1

*Increases are for calendar year periods 1960–5, 1965–70, and 1960–70.

Sources: Energy consumption figures are derived from Table 12.8. Data on gross domestic product are from *Estimates of national product, saving and capital formation, 1960/1–1971/2*, published by the Government of India, Central Statistical Organization, November 1973. The industrial production series is taken from *Basic Statistics relating to the Indian economy*, published by the Government of India, Planning Commission, 1972.

and 1970/1, it can be seen that despite the very rapid growth in agriculture and the 'other' sectors, over two-thirds of the total increase was in mining and manufacturing and in transport. Well over half the increase in oil consumption took place in the transport sector, but only about 7 per cent in mining and manufacturing.

The rate of increase in total energy consumption for different periods can be compared with the growth of income and production in India. In Table 12.10 the comparative growth rates are given for the period from 1960/1 to 1970/1, and for two sub-periods within it, of energy consumption, gross domestic product at constant prices, and industrial production.

It can be seen that total commercial energy consumption increased during the decade at a considerably faster rate than national product. For the decade as a whole, the growth of energy consumption was close to that of industrial production, but this close relationship did not hold good in the two 5-year sub-periods considered separately.

The relationship between changes in national product and changes in energy consumption over this 10-year period can be analysed in rather more detail by means of the data given in Table 12.9, where the four main producing sectors are separately distinguished. For this purpose household energy consumption, which was about 20 per cent of consumption in 1960/1 and 18 per cent in 1970/1, is excluded from the total, and only the use of energy in producing sectors is considered.

Table 12.11 sets out for the 2 years 1960/1 and 1970/1, for each of the four sectors and for the economy as a whole, the contributions to gross domestic product (i.e., gross value added) at 1960/1 prices and the total consumption of all forms of commercial energy in million tonnes of coal replacement. By dividing for each sector in each year its output by its consumption of commercial energy, we derive a measure of the intensity of energy use. For each sector and for the whole economy, these *energy coefficients*, which show the amount of commercial energy consumed (in million tonnes of coal replacement) for each billion rupees of value added, are set out in the third and final column under each of the 2 years.

For the economy as a whole, the intensity of use of commercial energy increased appreciably between 1960/1 and 1970/1: the overall energy coefficient rose from 0.57 units of energy per billion rupees of value added to 0.80 units, an increase of 40 per cent. Within the four sectors, energy intensity in agriculture doubled, though the figure in 1970/1 remained extremely low, while for the 'other sectors' category it more than doubled. Energy intensity also increased in mining and manufacturing and in transport, but by much

Table 12.11. Main producing sectors: contributions to GDP, commercial energy consumption, and energy-intensity, 1960/1 and 1970/1.

	1960/1			*1970/1*		
Main producing sectors	*Contribution to GDP (Rs bn)**	*Commercial energy consumption (m.t.c.r.)*	*Energy used per unit of output (m.t.c.r. per Rs bn)**	*Contribution to GDP Rs. bn)**	*Commercial energy consumption (m.t.c.r.)*	*Energy used per unit of output (m.t.c.r. per Rs bn)**
1. Agriculture	70.1	3.5	0.05	86.3	9.0	0.10
2. Mining and manufacturing	28.7	39.7	1.38	49.4	77.2	1.56
3. Transport and communication	6.8	34.2	5.03	11.6	63.7	5.49
4. Others	35.4	2.9	0.08	55.2	11.8	0.21
Total	141.0	80.3	0.57	202.5	161.7	0.80

*In 1960/1 prices.

Source: Energy consumption figures are taken from Table 12.9, and contributions to GDP from the official estimates of national product referred to under Table 12.10.

less in proportionate terms than in the sectors which are less heavy users of commercial energy.

The changes in energy consumption over the period, for each of the four sectors and for the economy as a whole, can be separated into three constituent elements. First, there are the increases that resulted from rising output by itself, taking no account of the changes in energy coefficients. Second, there are the effects of the changes in energy coefficients in themselves, taking no account of changes in output. The third element consists of the increases that arose from the changes in the energy coefficients with respect to the increase in output, and therefore takes account of both output changes and changes in energy coefficients.[6]

These three elements of the changes in energy consumption are shown in Table 12.12. Reading along the rows of the table, it can be seen that in the case of the main energy consuming sectors, namely mining and manufacturing and transport, much the greater part of the increase in their energy consumption resulted from the increase in their output alone. For agriculture and for other sectors, the increases were mainly accounted for by an increase in energy intensity. Summing up for all four sectors, in the fifth row of the table, the output effect is dominant because of the very large weight of industry and transport in total consumption of commercial energy. Out of the total increase over the decade of 81.4 million tonnes in coal replacement values, about two-thirds (55.4 million tonnes) came from increases in sector output, just over one-fifth (16.7 million tonnes) from greater energy intensity within each sector, and just over 10 per cent (9.4 million tonnes) from the greater energy intensity in relation to the increase in output.

In the final row of the table the same separation is made for the economy as a whole. It is clear that while the total increase of 81.4 million tons is the same, as it must be by definition, the relative importance of the three elements is noticeably different. The effect of increases in output is smaller, and that of the increase in energy intensity is greater. This is explained by the fact that the proportionate increase in the output of the energy intensive sectors, industry and

Table 12.12. Analysis of changes in commercial energy consumption by sector, 1960/1 to 1970/1 (million tonnes of coal replacement)

	Increases arising from			
	Changes in output alone†	*Changes in energy coefficients alone*†	*Changes in energy coefficients applied to increases in output*§	*Total changes*
1. Agriculture	0.8	3.8	0.9	5.5
2. Mining and manufacturing	28.7	5.1	3.7	37.4
3. Transport and communication	24.3	3.1	2.2	29.5
4. Others	1.6	4.7	2.6	8.9
5. Total of individual sectors‡	55.4	16.7	9.4	81.4
6. Total of all producing sectors taken together‡	35.1	32.3	14.1	81.4

*In terms of the notation of note 6 this column shows the values of $k_1 \Delta X$.
†In terms of the notation of note 6 this column shows the values of $\Delta k X$.
§In terms of the notation of note 6 this column shows the values of $\Delta k \Delta X$.
‡It will be seen that for the first three columns of the tables, the sum of the increases for the individual sectors is not equal to the total for the economy as a whole, which they comprise. The reason for this divergence is set out in the text.
Source: As for Table 12.11.

transport, was more than that of agriculture and other services. The result of such a change in the composition of national product is to raise the average energy coefficient for the economy as a whole even if the separate coefficients for each particular sector remain unchanged. By comparing the figures in the last two rows of Table 12.12, it is possible to assess how far the increase in energy intensity for the economy as a whole can be explained by changes in the relative output of different sectors, and how far it results from more intensive use of commercial energy within each of these sectors. For instance, if all producing sectors had grown over this period at the same rate as the economy as a whole, with no change in intensity of use of energy (i.e., with the 1960/1 energy coefficients remaining unchanged), then the total increase in commercial energy consumption would have been 35.1 million tonnes of coal replacement, as shown in the first column of the final row of the table. Since however the energy-intensive sectors gew faster than the others, the actual increase in consumption arising from output changes, even with the 1960/1 intensity of energy use, was 55.6 million tonnes.

To analyse the pattern of energy consumption in terms of four sectors only is not very satisfactory. Within each of these, the behaviour of constituent sub-sectors, and particularly those which are energy-intensive, needs to be looked at more closely. Such an analysis cannot be made on the basis of the data at present available; but it is indispensable to a thorough and systematic account of the relationship between energy use and economic change in India.

Notes and references

1. At current levels of crude production, the total costs of the Oil and Natural Gas Commission operations considerably exceed this figure, since they include the cost of carrying shut-in wells, research and design

facilities, and the overhead of the central staff. In order for ONGC to meet all outlays from revenues derived from the sale of crude from its fields, a price of perhaps \$4 per barrel would probably be necessary. As outlays continue to increase, and unless and until a higher level of production is attained by ONGC, this figure can be expected to rise. Neither this figure nor those quoted above for direct production costs take account of recent and prospective increases in costs arising from general inflationary trends, and from associated rises in input prices.

2. Government of India, Ministry of Irrigation and Power, *Report of Power Economy Committee*, Chapter 2. New Delhi, March (1971).
3. The use of thorium as a fuel is not limited to breeder reactors; on present plans it will be used in a number of nuclear power plants of the HTGR (high temperature gas-cooled reactor) type in Germany and the US. It will not, however, be used in conventional (as distinct from breeder) reactors of the types that are now in service or planned for future construction in India.
4. Government of India, *Report of the Energy Survey of India Committee*. New Delhi, (1965). Although inevitably dated in many respects, this study remains an extremely useful source.
5. Given in Natural resources in the Indian economy, by Narottam Shah, which forms Chapter 1 of *Natural resources in the Indian economy* (ed. Vadilal Dagli). Vora and Co., Bombay (1971).
6. Algebraically, this distinction may be expressed as follows. Let output for any sector in the two periods being compared be X_1 and X_2 respectively, and commercial energy consumption E_1 and E_2. The energy coefficients k are then given by

$$k_1 = E_1/X_1;\ k_2 = E_2/X_2.$$

Let ΔX be the change in output $(X_2 - X_1)$, ΔE be the change in energy consumption $(E_2 - E_1)$, and Δk be the change in the energy coefficient $(k_2 - k_1)$. Then we can express the increase in energy consumption ΔE as follows.

$$\begin{aligned} \Delta E &= E_2 - E_1 \\ E_1 &= k_1X_1 \\ E_2 &= k_2X_2 = (k_1 + \Delta k)(X_1 + \Delta X) \\ &= k_1X_1 + k_1\Delta X + \Delta kX_1 + \\ &\quad + \Delta k\Delta X. \end{aligned}$$

Subtracting E_1 from both sides in this last equation, we get:

$$\Delta E = k_1\Delta X + \Delta kX_1 + \Delta k\Delta X.$$

The three terms on the right-hand side show the increase in energy consumption ΔE separated into: first, the effect of the increase in output ΔX, with no account taken of the change in the energy coefficient; second, the effect of the change in the energy coefficient, Δk, applied to the original output X; and finally, the increase arising from the change in the energy coefficient Δk applied to the increase in output ΔX.

13

Energy use in rural India

ROGER REVELLE

The economic chasm that divides the world also separates two vastly different levels and kinds of energy use. More than five-sixths of all the energy obtained from fossil fuels and hydroelectric and nuclear power is used by the billion inhabitants of the rich countries and less than one-sixth by the 3 billion people of the poor countries.[1,2] The reverse is true of the traditional sources of energy—human and animal labour, firewood, crop residues, and animal wastes—that were predominant throughout history everywhere until the last two centuries. The total quantities of energy from these sources used in the poor countries today are probably about equal to their consumption of fossil fuels, and greatly exceed the uses in the rich countries.

International statistics on energy use are usually based only on consumption of 'commercial' energy and hence seriously underestimate total energy consumption in poor countries. In India, for example, energy use per capita is generally given the UN coal equivalent[3] of 150 to 190 kg[1,2] whereas, as we shall see, total energy use from all sources is close to 490 kg. In the rural areas of poor countries, energy provided by the people themselves is five to ten times that obtained from commercial sources. Nevertheless, usable energy is in very short supply, and the needs both for a large increase in supply and for conservation through more efficient utilization are greet.

From an energy standpoint, rural India can be thought of as a partially closed ecosystem in which energy derived by people and animals from the photosynthetic products of plants is used to grow and prepare human food, which in turn provides an essential energy input to grow more food, and so on in an endless cycle. The ecosystem is being disrupted by rapid population growth.

Estimation of human energy

Several different methods have been employed to compute the human and animal energy used in work.

Pimentel, Hurd, Bellotti, Forster, Oka, Sholes, and Whitman[4] take the total food energy input of a full-time farm-worker (working 40 hours per week) as a measure of the energy utilized in farm labour. For example, they show that 9 hours of labour per acre are used in US corn production, and they calculate the energy input as 9/40 multiplied by the energy in 1 week's food consumption (assumed to be 21 770 kcal), or 4900 kcal per acre.

Makhijani and Poole[5] use the energy in the food intake of all persons in a farming village as the gross energy input for human labour. They give a hypothetical example of

First published in *Science*, Vol. 192 (4 June 1976) pp. 969–75.

a village of 1000 people consuming on the average 2000 kcal per day per capita in food, with a gross energy input of 7.3×10^8 kcal per year or 0.73×10^6 kcal per person. The annual work output per capita from persons more than 15 years of age, taken as half the total population of the village, is assumed to be 0.045×10^6 kcal, giving an 'energetic efficiency' of 3 per cent for all human beings in the village.

Passmore and Durnin[6] and White, Bradley, and White[7] estimate the metabolic energy used in different work activities from measurements of oxygen consumed or carbon dioxide exhaled. East African women, obtaining water for household use by walking to a well or water hole and carrying the water home in jars on their heads, expend on the average 240 kcal each day and take 46 minutes for the task.[7] In unmechanized agriculture in Hungary, Russia, Italy, Germany, and Gambia, 19 groups of men, with a mean weight of about 65 kg, expended on the average 6.0 kcal per minute in a variety of agricultural tasks. Fourteen groups of women in Russia, Italy, Gambia, and Nigeria, with a mean weight of about 55 kg, expended on the average about 4.7 kcal per minute.[6]

The average daily or weekly energy expenditures in most working activities are less than the measured values for particular tasks. A British miner, working a 44-hour week, was observed to expend an average of 269 kcal per hour during working hours, or 4.5 kcal per minute, even though the average energy expenditure for different mining tasks is 6.7 kcal per minute.[6] Approximately one-third of his working time was spent in rest. Even so, the weekly energy expenditure of this miner during working hours was nearly 45 per cent of his total food energy intake for the week.

The different methods of estimating energy expenditure are compared in Table 13.1 in terms of an average Indian rural worker (50 per cent of the rural population), who is assumed to work 1800 hours per year. Obviously the method of Passmore and Durnin[6] and White *et al.*[7] gives the lowest values for yearly energy in work by human beings, particularly for a rural population, such as India's, in which there is considerable underemployment. This method is used in Table 13.2 to estimate energy expenditures for human labour in rural India.

Table 13.1. Comparison of methods of measuring human energy expenditures in agriculture

	Energy per worker (kcal/hour)	
Method	*Gross input (expenditure)*	*Useful output*
Pimentel *et al.*[4]	580*	
Makhijani and Poole[5]	870*	25
Passmore and Durnin[6]	250†	

*The energy in weekly food intake is 20 200 kcal per adult male and 15 050 kcal per person for the entire population (see Table 13.3).

†The average energy expenditure during work is assumed to be 70 per cent of the energy used in specific agricultural tasks.

From Table 13.2 we see that somewhat more than half of the estimated 500 billion hours per year of human labour are spent directly in agriculture. Cooking, obtaining water, collecting fuel, and other domestic activities take up nearly 200 billion hours, or 39.5 per cent of the total hours worked, and all other occupations take up slightly more than 9 per cent. Human energy expended in agricultural work is estimated to be 55 per cent of the annual total of 1.08×10^{14} kcal (120 billion kWh) expended in all labour.

Approximately a third of the food energy consumed by the rural population[8] is used in work (Table 13.3). If our figures are correct, women and girls work harder than men and boys, in terms of the proportion of food energy expended in labour. Women 15 or more years old use 44 per cent of their energy intake in labour while males in this age group use 38 per cent. It would appear that adult women work about as hard as the British coalminer described above.[6]

Table 13.2. Energy expended in human labour in rural India. The energy per hour expended in work (columns 6 and 7) is estimated from data given for various tasks by Passmore and Durnin[6], multiplied by 0.7 to account for the fact that humans in India have smaller body sizes than the workers described by Passmore and Durnin and for observed differences between energy expended per hour while working and energy required for specific work tasks.

	Number of workers (10^6)		*Estimated hours worked per year*		*Energy per hour (kcal)*		*Total energy expended in work* (10^{12} *kcal/year*)		
Occupation	*Male*	*Female*	*Male*	*Female*	*Male*	*Female*	*Male*	*Female*	*Total*
Cultivators*	74.9	4.0	1800†	1000†	250	200	33.7	0.8	34.5
Agricultural labourers*	26.4	21.0	1000‡	1000‡	250	200	6.6	4.2	10.8
Unpaid family workers in cultivations§	40.9	5.0	1550‖	1000‖	200	200	12.7	1.0	13.7
Total directly in agriculture	142.2	30.0					53.0	6.0	59.0
Domestic activities¶		109.4		1800#		200		39.4	39.4
All other occupations**									
Livestock and poultry	1.5		2000		250		0.8		0.8
Fishing	0.5		1500		300		0.2		0.2
Forest products	0.3		2000		300		0.2		0.2
Mining and quarrying	0.4		2000		300		0.2		0.2
Transport and storage	1.3		1500		200		0.4		0.4
Construction	1.5	1.0	1000	1000	250	250	0.4	0.3	0.7
Trade and commerce	3.0		2000		150		0.9		0.9
Other services	7.2	3.0	1500	1000	150	200	1.6	0.6	2.2
Carpentry, wood, and straw manufacture	1.8		2000		200		0.7		0.7
Leather industry	0.9		2000		200		0.4		0.4
Metalwork and blacksmithing	1.0		2000		250		0.5		0.5
Pottery and brickmaking	0.7		2000		250		0.4		0.4
Food preparation and milling	0.7	0.8	1500	1500	200	200	0.2	0.2	0.4
Textiles	1.6	1.0	2000	2000	200	150	0.6	0.3	0.9
Miscellaneous	0.5	0.2	2000	2000	200	150	0.2	0.1	0.3
Total, all other occupations	22.9	6.0					7.7	1.5	9.2
Grand total	165.1	145.4					60.7	46.9	107.6

*According to the 1971 census of India[36] the total rural population was 439 million (228 million males and 211 million females), of whom 151 million were in the (employed or self employed) labour force—120 million males and 31 million females. Within this labour force there were 76.8 million cultivators (farmers owning or renting farmland), 45.3 million landless agricultural labourers, and 28.9 million workers in other occupations. In addition, 2.1 million cultivators and an equal number of agricultural labourers lived in urban areas. About 95 per cent of the cultivator households were headed by males and 5 per cent by females. Most adult females in the families of agricultural labourers work whenever they can find employment, and hence I have assumed that the number of female agricultural labourers was about 80 per cent of the number of males.

†It is assumed that male and female cultivators work 180 10-hour days and 125 8-hour days, respectively, per year.

‡Landless agricultural labourers suffer from severe underemployment. They are employed mainly during peak periods of labour demand in crop production, such as seedbed preparation, rice transplantation, and harvesting. I have assumed that both males and females are able to find about 100 days of employment per year.

§According to the 1961 census of India[37] the average household engaged in cultivation, with or without other occupations, had 2.36 family workers, including the head of the household. I have assumed that a large proportion of these were unpaid family agricultural workers, including all males 10 to 14 years of age and 15 million males 15 years or older in cultivator households. Males 10 to 14 years of age in other households are also counted as unpaid family agricultural workers, together with 5 million females.

‖Nearly a third of unpaid male family workers are assumed to be 10- to 14-year-old children of landless labourers helping their parents; hence the number of hours worked by the average unpaid family worker is less than that for cultivators.

¶All females 10 years of age or older not in the labour force or in the category of unpaid family workers are assumed to be engaged in domestic activities.

#Domestic activities must take place every day in the year and may require about 5 hours a day per domestic worker. For example, East African women take 46 minutes each day in fetching water and expend on the average 240 kcal[7] and these numbers probably apply in India. Collecting wood, straw, and dung for fuel may take several times as much time and energy, perhaps 2 hours a day and 600 kcal. I estimate that procuring and preparing food, cooking, washing, carrying cooked food to farm workers, and other household tasks take at least an additional 2 hours a day per worker.

**The proportions of workers in occupations other than farming are estimated from the proportions in major occupational categories in the state of Haryana in 1971 and in industry in all of rural India in 1961[36,37]

Table 13.3. Food energy intake and estimated expenditure in work for males and females of different age groups living in rural India, 1971. The values in column 4 are from Table 13.2

Age group (years)	*Number of people (10^6)*	*Energy per capita (10^6 kcal/year)*		*Energy intake expended in work (per cent)*
		Food intake[8]	*Expended in work*	
0 to 9	133.3	0.55		
10 to 14				
Males	25.9	0.91	0.32	35
Females	23.3	0.85	0.36	42
15 and older				
Males	135.0	1.03	0.39	38
Females	122.1	0.73	0.32	44
Total	439.6			
Averages		0.78	0.24	31

The estimate of the total number of hours worked in agriculture computed from Table 13.2 is in fair agreement with observations in a World Bank study of cereal production in Bangladesh.[9] The number of man-days of labour ranged from 125 per hectare in wheat production to 150 per hectare in broadcast aus and aman (monsoon) rice, 175 days in transplanted aus and mixed aus and aman, and 218 days in boro (winter) rice. Since about 80 per cent of the 163 million gross sown hectares in India is planted to food grains (cereals and pulses), of which about 30 per cent is in rice, 15 per cent in wheat, and 35 per cent in other cereals and in pulses,[10] it can be assumed that the World Bank figures apply fairly well to Indian agriculture. Taking a rough average of 150 man-days per hectare, and assuming an average working day of 10 hours, a total of 245 billion hours of labour would be spent directly in agriculture. The total from Table 13.2 is 255 billion.

Animal energy

It is less easy to determine the proper way to account for energy expended in bullock work, and the underlying data are less adequate. If a bullock can be thought of as a kind of working machine, then the energy in its 'manufacture' might be included in the accounting—that is, the net energy input (feed energy minus energy in dung) of the entire cattle population, less the energy in milk and other products. Alternatively, the energy consumed annually in feed by the bullock itself, minus the energy in its dung, divided by the number of hours worked, could be taken as its gross energy expenditure per working hour. I have used a third method, which gives smaller values, assuming that a fully employed bullock, like a human manual worker, utilizes about 43 per cent of the energy it consumes in work.

The first method is essentially that used by Odend'hal[11] for the cattle population of a village in West Bengal.[12] Subtracting the energy in dung and milk produced by this population of 3770 animals from the energy in feed consumed, and dividing by 1079, the number of working bullocks, gives an annual energy input per bullock of 14.5×10^6 kcal, or dividing by 1200 hours of work per year, 12.1×10^3 kcal per hour of work. This number should be reduced because not all the male calves produced in the herd are retained by the villagers, and the gross energy expenditure in the herd's milk production (probably between five and ten times the energy in the milk) has not been considered. The energy in milk was 1.83×10^8 kcal per year, and if the gross energy expenditure in milk production was 1.83×10^9 kcal per year, the gross energy input per bullock hour worked was less than 10.9×10^3 kcal.

With Odend'hal's data, the second method gives 5.3×10^3 kcal per hour, and the third 2.3×10^3 kcal per hour, compared with an output of useful work of 0.43×10^3 kcal per hour,[11,12] corresponding for the third method to an 'energetic efficiency' of about 19 per cent. The 1971 population of bullocks in India was 70.4 million,[13] and I have assumed that 83 per cent of the work done by bullocks was carried out in rural areas.[14] Thus, if the average bullock worked 1200 hours per year, the total energy expenditure in bullock work in 1971 was 1.61×10^{14} kcal, or 179 billion kWh.

Part of the bullock work in rural areas was used in ploughing, cultivating, and harvesting farm fields, part in lifting water for irrigation, and the remainder for transportation. In Bangladesh the observed number of bullock days per hectare ranged from 30 for wheat to 49 for transplanted aman rice and 74 for boro rice.[9] Taking an average of 40 days per hectare and 8 hours per day, the bullock working time on India's 163 million gross cultivated hectares is 52 billion hours, or 75 per cent of the total work time in rural areas. Bullock power was also used to lift 4 to 6 million hectare metres of irrigation water in approximately 4 million 'Persian wheels' and other unmotorized wells.[10] A pair of bullocks is able to lift 1 hectare metre in 600 hours.[15] The bullock time in lifting water was between 4.8 and 7.2 billion hours, 7 to 10 per cent of the total working time in rural areas, and the proportion of the work of rural bullocks used directly in agriculture was 82 to 85 per cent, corresponding to about 1.35×10^{14} kcal per year.[16,17]

Locally produced fuels

India is one of the few countries where a systematic attempt has been made to determine the extent of use of 'non-commercial' fuels. Sample surveys in villages and towns were conducted by the Energy Survey of India Committee in the early 1960s. The committee reported that about 120 million tonnes of wood, 50 million tonnes of dried dung, and 30 million tonnes of 'vegetable waste' were burned each year, largely in the villages but also in urban areas.[18] Later authors have given somewhat higher estimates.

For example, Henderson[14] estimates that 126 million tonnes of firewood was consumed in 1970–1, of which 83 per cent (0.24 tonne per person) was burned in rural areas, and Datta[19] gives a total of 142 million tonnes for both rural and urban areas. With an energy content for firewood of 4.4×10^6 kcal per tonne,[20] Henderson's estimate corresponds to a total of 4.60×10^{14} (515 billion kWh) of energy supplied annually by burning firewood in rural areas. This is the energy contained in 61.3 million UN equivalent tonnes of coal (139 kg per capita).

In northern India and Nepal, where the winters are cold, consumption of firewood per capital may be much higher than these figures indicate. Makhijani and Poole[5] estimate that 1 to 1.5 tonnes of firewood per person per year is used even in such warm regions as Nigeria and Tanzania.

Many workers have attempted to estimate the quantity of dung produced by livestock in India and the proportion used as fuel. Briscoe[21] and Odend'hal[11] summarize recent estimates, which range from 1.4 to 3.5 kg of dry dung per head per day, of which 22 to 75 per cent is estimated by different authors to be used as fuel. The combined estimates correspond to a range of 120 to 310 million tonnes per year of dry dung produced by the Indian cattle population of 247 million in 1970–1,[13] and 48 to 97 million tonnes for the quantity used as fuel. I shall accept Henderson's estimate[14] of 68 million tonnes used as fuel, of which 83 per cent was burned in rural areas. Taking the energy content of dried cow dung as 3.3×10^6 kcal per tonne[22] gives a total of 1.86×10^{14} kcal (207 billion kWh) for 56 million tonnes of dried dung burned in rural areas, corresponding to 24.8 million UN equivalent tonnes of coal, or 56 kg per capita.

Briscoe[21] concludes from data given by several other workers that crop residues from wheat and rice in the Indian subcontinent amount to about 1570 kg per hectare annually. Makhijani and Poole[5] give the ratios of straw and chaff to grain from indigenous rice varieties, wheat, and sorghum (called *bajra* in India) as 2.9. 1.75, and 0.85, respectively. The total Indian food grain production in 1971–2 was about 105 million tonnes,[23] of which approximately 42 per cent was rice, 23 per cent wheat, and 35 per cent other cereals and pulses. Using Makhijani and Poole's ratios, we conclude that the total quantity of straw and chaff residues from food grain production was around 200 million tonnes, grown on 130 million gross sown hectares, or 1540 kg per hectare, close to Briscoe's figures. Most of these residues were eaten by livestock (providing somewhat less than half of their food energy) but probably about a fifth (39 million tonnes) was used as fuel,[14] of which 83 per cent was consumed in rural areas. Datta[19] gives a smaller estimate of 34.2 million tonnes for 1968–9 and the National Sample Survey in 1963–4[24] indicated a still lower household use. Accepting the figure of 39 million tonnes and assuming that the energy content of straw and other crop residues is the same as that of dried cow dung (3.3×10^6 kcal per tonne), the total energy obtained in rural areas is 1.07×10^{14} kcal (120 billion kWh), corresponding to 14.3 million UN equivalent tonnes of coal, or 32 kg per capita.

In terms of UN coal equivalents, the energy derived from burning wood, cow dung, and crop residues adds up to 227 kg per capita per year, or a total for rural India of 100 million tonnes, with an energy content of 7.53×10^{14} kcal. In Table 13.4, I have allocated 90 per cent of this energy to cooking and space heating and 10 per cent to other uses, including pottery and and brickmaking, metalworking, and blacksmithing, and sugar making.

'Commercial' energy sources

In recent years Indian farmers have used around 2 million tonnes of nitrogen in chemical fertilizers annually.[23] About 1.55 tonnes of naphtha and other light petroleum fractions is used as a feedstock and as a source of energy in manufacturing a ton of nitrogen in fertilizer in India (about the same weight of natural gas is used in most imported fertilizers), with an energy content of 11.4×10^6 kcal per tonne.[17] Hence the weight of fossil fuels used in manufacturing 2 million tonnes of nitrogen in fertilizer is 3.1 million tonnes, with an energy content of 0.35×10^{14} kcal, corresponding to 4.7 million UN equivalent tonnes of coal or 11 kg per capita per year.

About 16.1 million tonnes of petroleum products were used as fuel in India in 1970–1.[14] Farm usage, mainly as diesel fuel to pump water for irrigation and to a small extent for tractors, was 4.6 per cent of this amount or 0.74 million tonnes, and household usage, mainly paraffin for lighting, was 28.3 per cent or 4.56 million tonnes. Assuming that per capita household usage was the same in the country as in the city, rural households used 80 per cent of 4.56 million tonnes, or 3.65 million tonnes, and total rural use on farms and in households was 4.39 million tonnes of petroleum products, with an energy content of 0.50×10^{14} kcal (56 billion kWh), corresponding to 15 UN equivalent kilograms of coal per capita. In addition, a considerable quantity of petroleum products was used as fuel for trucks and other vehicles, in part for transportation of farm products and fertilizers and other agricultural inputs between rural and urban areas, but I have not tried to account for this.

Henderson[14] estimates that 4.1 tonnes of soft coke made from coal was used in households in 1970–1. Consumption per capita was probably at least twice as high in cities as in rural areas. Average per capita coke consumption in rural areas was then 6.2 kg per year. If the energy content of this coke was the same as that of Indian coal

(5.2×10^6 kcal per tonne) the total energy in coke used in rural areas was 0.14×10^{14} kcal, or a UN coal equivalent per capita of 4 kg per year.

In 1970–1, 9.2 per cent of 48.6 billion kWh of electricity consumed in India was used in agriculture, mainly for irrigation, or 4.5 billion kWh (0.04×10^{14} kcal). In addition, 3.8 billion kWh was used in households. Villages containing 36 per cent of the rural population (160 million people) were electrified. Except for irrigation, per capita consumption of electricity is lower in rural than in urban areas, but since the urban population was only 110 million people we may assume that half of the household use occurred in rural villages, or 1.9 billion kWh (0.02×10^{14} kcal). With this assumption, the average consumption per capita of electricity for all purposes in rural areas was 0.04 kWh per day.[14]

Hydroelectric power accounted for 45 per cent of electricity generated in India in 1970–1 and thermal power (including nuclear) accounted for 55 per cent.[14] Applying this ratio to electricity consumption in rural areas, we obtain 2.9 and 3.5 billion kWh for the total hydroelectric and thermal energy consumed. Indian thermal generating plants have an average efficiency of 22 per cent for conversion of heat energy to electricity.[14] Subtracting transmission losses and electricity used in power generation, the net electricity consumption is 83 per cent of electricity generated. Hence 1 tonne of Indian coal with an energy content of 5.2×10^6 kcal is burned to generate 1000 kWh of electricity consumed.[22] If coal were used exclusively, the coal required for 3.5 billion kWh electrical would be 3.5 million tonnes (actually a considerable fraction of total electricity is generated from heavy fuel oil). The UN coal equivalent at 18 per cent consumptive efficiency is 1500 kWh per tonne of coal. Hence the UN coal equivalent per capita of thermal electricity consumed in rural areas was 5 kg. Taking the consumptive efficiency of hydroelectric power as 70 per cent, the UN coal equivalent for hydroelectric energy is 2 kg per capita.

In terms of UN coal equivalents, the commercial energy use per capita in rural India in 1971 was 37 kg and the total for the rural population was 16.3 million tonnes, with an energy content of 1.20×10^{14} kcal. In Table 13.4, I estimate that 12 per cent of this commercial energy was used for cooking and space heating (soft coke), 40 per cent for lighting (mainly kerosene and a small quantity of electricity), and 48 per cent for agriculture (petroleum products used in manufacturing nitrogen fertilizer, and electricity and diesel fuel).

Fuel efficiency in cooking

The total energy from local and commercial fuels used in cooking and space heating was 6.9×10^{14} kcal, or 1.57×10^6 kcal per capita per year, approximately twice the energy in food eaten. If space heating can be neglected, the energy use in cooking per calorie of food energy consumed was higher than the estimated US energy use per food calorie for cooking and home refrigeration combined.[25]

Two experiments with rice cooking showed that the energy required to bring the cooking water to boiling and to boil away the requisite quantity of water is about 600 kcal/kg, or 17.5 per cent of the food energy content of rice. Assuming that other food grains behave in a similar fashion, and that 75 per cent of the energy from fuels used in cooking and space heating went into cooking food grains, the efficiency of fuel use was less than 9 per cent. This may be compared with an energy efficiency of 30 to 60 per cent in cooking on a modern gas stove (without pilot lights) in the United States.[5]

The large-scale burning of firewood as a source of energy for cooking and space heating has serious implications. Until recent years, forests had completely disappeared from most of China, because the trees had been cut down for fuel. It is likely that a similar process is now occurring in much of India. The total forested area is about 75 million hectares, of which 80 per cent is

Table 13.4. Energy uses in rural India (except for human labour, quantities and uses of energy from different sources are given in the text)

	Energy used (kcal)					
Source of energy	*Agriculture*	*Domestic activities*	*Lighting*	*Pottery, brickmaking, metalwork*	*Transportation and other uses*	*Total*
Human labour*	0.59×10^{14}	0.39×10^{14}		0.01×10^{14}	0.09×10^{14}	1.08×10^{14}
Bullock work	1.35×10^{14}				0.26×10^{14}	1.61×10^{14}
Firewood and charcoal						4.60×10^{14}
Cattle dung		6.78×10^{14} (firewood and charcoal, cattle dung, crop residues)		0.75×10^{11} (firewood and charcoal, cattle dung, crop residues)		1.86×10^{14}
Crop residues						1.07×10^{14}
Total from local sources	1.94×10^{14}	7.17×10^{14}		0.76×10^{14}	0.35×10^{14}	10.22×10^{14}
Petroleum and natural gas						
Fertilizer	0.35×10^{14}					0.35×10^{14}
Fuel	0.08×10^{14}		0.42×10^{14}			0.50×10^{14}
Soft coke		0.14×10^{14}				0.14×10^{14}
Electricity						
Hydro†	0.03×10^{14}		0.01×10^{14}			0.04×10^{14}
Thermal‡	0.12×10^{14}		0.05×10^{14}			0.17×10^{14}
Total from commercial sources	0.58×10^{14}	0.14×10^{14}	0.48×10^{14}			1.20×10^{14}
Total, local and commercial	2.52×10^{14}	7.31×10^{14}	0.48×10^{14}	0.76×10^{14}	0.35×10^{14}	11.42×10^{14}
Daily per capita	1.57×10^{3}	4.55×10^{3}	0.30×10^{3}	0.47×10^{3}	0.22×10^{3}	7.11×10^{3}

*See Table 13.2.

†Potential energy in water used to generate hydroelectric power.

‡Energy in coal used to generate thermoelectric power.

actually or potentially usable. According to Prasad, Prasad, and Reddy.[26] forest areas contain 50 tonnes of wood per hectare. Thus the present reserves, if all were used for firewood, are $7.5 \times 10^7 \times 0.8 \times 50 = 3 \times 10^9$ tonnes, or enough to last for 24 years at present annual rates of consumption, without taking into account new growth. Two other serious problems are the very uneven distribution of the forests, with 50 per cent of the forested area in four states (Madhya Pradesh, Orissa, Andhra Pradesh, and Maharashtra) that have less than 20 per cent of the population, and deforestation of mountainous regions. These are the watersheds for the great rivers that flow through the plains. With the growth of human populations, the forests are being cut down faster than they can grow, partly to make room for new farmlands, and partly for use as fuel. As a consequence, the upland areas are subjected to destructive erosion, while the resulting sediments cause rapid filling of reservoirs and destructive floods in the downstream areas.[10] Small, run-of-the-river hydroelectric generators[27] might provide a substitute source of energy for the mountain and hill peoples and thereby help to conserve the forests.

Intensive reforestation programmes will be necessary if India's forests are not to disappear. Actually, reforestation could considerably increase present energy supplies. Parikh[22] estimates potential annual production in forest plantations at 12.5 tonnes per hectare. Thus, the potential annual production under intensive reforestation could be 7.2×10^8 tonnes, about six times the present annual consumption of firewood.

In the short term, improved stoves and other means for increasing the efficiency of fuels used for cooking and for heating water would appear to be the most promising energy conservation measures.

Comparison of the United States and rural India

In Table 13.4, the quantities and uses of energy from different sources are summarized. Energy utilized per person in 1971 was 7.1×10^3 kcal per day, 3.3 times the energy in food consumed (estimated as 2.15×10^3 kcal per day).[8] In terms of UN coal equivalents, the annual energy expenditure corresponds to 0.346 tonne per capita, compared with 11.15 tonnes per capita in the United States in 1970.[1] More than 89 per cent of this energy was provided by the villagers themselves and less than 11 per cent was from commercial sources, whereas nearly all the energy accounted for in the United States is from fossil fuels and hydroelectric power.

The total quantity of energy utilized in rural India in 1971 was 11.4×10^{14} kcal per year, probably somewhat more than the total used on farms and in farming households in the United States (estimated as roughly 10.65×10^{14} kcal).[28] But the use per capita by the US farm population of 9.5 million was 50 times greater than that of India's 440 million rural people.

Steinhart and Steinhart[25] estimate that the energy used in all components of the US 'food system', including 5.26×10^{14} kcal on farms, 11.66×10^{14} kcal in the food processing and marketing industries, and 4.8×10^{14} kcal in home refrigeration and cooking, is about nine times the energy in food eaten. Assuming that 80 per cent of the food produced and energy consumed in Indian agriculture is chargeable to rural areas the corresponding figure for agriculture and cooking in rural India is slightly less than 2.7 kcal per 1 kcal of food eaten, depending on the (probably small) amount of fuel used for space heating. But the energy utilized in the US food system is less than 13 per cent of total US energy use,[25] whereas 82 per cent of total energy use in rural India is directly related to food.

Dividing Steinhart and Steinhart's estimate of 5.26×10^{14} kcal used on farms in the United States by the 1971 cropped area of 122 million hectares, we obtain an energy use per hectare of 4.31×10^6 kcal, nearly three times our computed value from Table

13.4 of 1.55×10^6 kcal per hectare on India's gross cropped area of 163 million hectares. Estimates by Pimentel *et al.*[29] of energy expenditure in production of food grains (cereals and soya beans) and animal products (meat, eggs, poultry, and milk products) in the United States give a total of 9.2×10^{14} kcal for the 108 million cropped hectares used for these purposes, or 8.52×10^6 kcal per hectare, about twice the value derived from the data of Steinhart and Steinhart. Approximately 55 per cent of this energy (5.06×10^{14} kcal) was used on cultivated fields and 45 per cent (4.14×10^{14} kcal) in the care and management of animals.

It is difficult to compare the energy expenditures per unit of human food in India and the United States because of the very different diets of the two peoples. Comparison is easier if we consider only food grains, which make up 81 per cent of the Indian diet but only 21 per cent of the US diet.[30] The data given by Pimental *et al.*[29] indicate that 4.3×10^{14} kcal is used in US agriculture to produce 271 million tonnes of corn, wheat, sorghum, other cereals, and soya beans, or 1.59×10^6 kcal per tonne. This is 45 per cent of the food energy in the crops. Assuming that 80 per cent of energy expenditure in Indian agriculture goes to food-grain production, which totalled 105 million tonnes in 1971–2,[23] the energy expenditure per tonne was 1.92×10^6 kcal, 55 per cent of the food energy. Most of this was in the form of human and animal work. In so far as energy costs are reflected in food grain prices, such work is apparently more costly than mechanical work based on fossil fuels, even under Indian conditions.

Throughout the decade 1960–70, when grain prices were relatively stable, wholesale prices of wheat, sorghum, and corn in the United States averaged \$54, \$45, and \$45 per tonne respectively,[31] while during the same period in India average wholesale wheat and sorghum prices were \$107 and \$73 per tonne.[32] World prices of these cereals were about the same as US prices. Only rice, which made up about 1 per cent of US food grain production but more than 40 per cent of Indian production, was somewhat higher priced in the United States, averaging \$162 per tonne compared to \$142 per tonne in India. The average wholesale price of a tonne of soya beans in the United States was \$92. Pulses in India averaged \$128 per tonne at wholesale.

The average Indian spent the equivalent of \$48.60 each year on food and beverages, of which about \$40 went for a total of 2060 kcal per day in food grains, sugar, fruit, vegetables, and vegetable oil.[33] The farmers' share was 80 to 90 per cent of these expenditures, or about \$17 per thousand kilocalories per day.[32] In 1970 the American farmers' share of per capita food expenditure in the United States was about \$200.[4] The equivalent of humanly edible plant energy in the American diet is 10900 kcal per day—2000 kcal in plant food eaten directly and 8900 kcal in food grains fed to animals.[29, 30] Thus American farmers received a little more than \$18 per thousand plant calories per day for the average American's diet, very close to the Indian figure. This is in spite of the fact that a large part of American costs were chargeable to the care and management of livestock and poultry.

More energy is needed in India

In order to reduce the costs and energy expenditure per tonne of food produced, let alone provide enough food for the population of 1000 million expected by the year 2000, a considerable increase in energy use will be essential, primarily for three purposes: irrigation, chemical fertilizers, and additional draught power for cultivating the fields. The climate and water supply permit growing two crops per year on most of India's arable land, but this will be possible only if facilities for surface and groundwater irrigation are greatly expanded and if abundant nitrogen fertilizers can be made available, so that the fields do not have to be left fallow to accumulate nitrogen. Estimates by the Indian Irrigation Commission indicate that with full irrigation development, about 46 million net hectare metres should be pumped annually from wells,[10] requiring at least 1×10^{14} kcal of fuel energy, four times the bullock, diesel, and electric energy now used. Applications of nitrogen fertilizer should be raised to around 100 kg per hectare per crop, or 20 million tonnes for 100 million double-cropped hectares, with an energy requirement of 3.5×10^{14} kcal.[17]

More draught power is needed than can be obtained from bullocks, because rapid seedbed preparation is necessary to grow two crops per year. Makhijani and Poole[5] estimate that an additional 5×10^{5} kcal per hectare per crop is required for construction and operation of small tractors, or 1×10^{14} kcal, supposing that 100 million acres are double-cropped. Cultivation of two crops per year would greatly increase farm employment probably by at least 50 per cent, corresponding to an added human energy input of 0.3×10^{14} kcal per year.[34] The total additional energy requirement is 5.2×10^{14} kcal, more than twice the energy now used in Indian agriculture. With these added energy inputs it would be possible, in principle, to approximate the average US yield of 3.28 tonnes per hectare per crop for food grains,[1] instead of the present 0.8 tonne.

Assuming a yield of 2 tonnes per hectare per crop and double-cropping on 100 million hectares, food grain production could be raised to between 300 and 400 million tonnes, depending on the farmland devoted to other crops. This is between three and four times present production and would have a value at 1976 world prices of $35 billion or more. The input of energy from all sources per tonne of food grains would be on the order of 1.8×10^{6} kcal, significantly less than at present. If the average yields per hectare attained in US food grain production were achieved, the energy input would be about 1.1×10^{6} kcal per tonne of food grains.

Where would the energy come from?

With present technology the additional energy required for draught power, pumping water, and manufacturing chemical fertilizers would have to be provided largely by fossil fuels and hydroelectric power. If the requirement were met by using petroleum products, 43 million tonnes would be needed, more than twice the quantity used at present in all of India, costing at today's world prices $3.2 billion. Alternatively, 95 million tonnes of Indian coal could be used. These figures might be significantly reduced by development of the Indian and Nepalese hydroelectric power potential, which is probably from 50000 to 100000 megawatts.[35]

Even if all the additional energy came from petroleum products, and all this petroleum were imported, the cost could be met by exporting about a tenth of the increased food grain production. But the crop residues remaining from 300 million tonnes of food grains would be at least 400 million tonnes, with an energy content of 13×10^{14} kcal, about $2\frac{2}{3}$ times the required additional energy. If this energy provided by photosynthesis could be harnessed, for example in nitrogen-conserving fermentation plants of the type suggested by Makhijani and Poole,[5] the Indian rural ecosystem could continue to be fairly self-sufficient. A major long-range research and development effort along these lines would be of inestimable value.

Summary

An old saying has it, 'slavery will persist until the loom weaves itself'. All ancient civilizations, no matter how enlightened or creative, rested on slavery and on grinding human labour, because human and animal muscle power were the principal forms of energy available for mechanical work. The discovery of ways to use less expensive sources of energy than human muscles made it possible for men to be free. The men and women of rural India are tied to poverty and misery because they use too little energy and use it inefficiently, and nearly all they use is secured by their own physical efforts. A transformation of rural India society could be brought about by increasing the quantity and improving the technology of energy use.

References and notes

1. US Department of Commerce, Bureau of the Census. *Statistical abstract of the United States*. Washington DC, ed. 93 (1972).
2. Fisher, J. L. and Potter, N. In *Rapid population growth: consequences and policy implications*, pp. 222–4. National Academy of Sciences. Johns Hopkins Press, Baltimore (1971).
3. In UN statistical publications 1 equivalent tonne of coal corresponds to 7.5×10^6 kcal of usable energy. In India 103 million UN equivalent tonnes of coal from commercial sources was used in 1970[1]. I estimate that 16 million tonnes was used in rural areas, leaving 87 million tonnes for urban use. Non-commercial energy use in rural and urban areas corresponds respectively to 136 and 28 million UN equivalent tonnes of coal, and total energy use is 267 million tonnes for a population of 550 million people, or 486 kg per capita.
4. Pimentel, D., Hurd, L. E., Bellotti, A. C., Forster, M. J., Oka, I. N., Sholes, O. D., Whitman, R. J. In *Energy: use conservation and supply*. (ed. P. H. Ebelson), pp. 41–7. AAAS, Washington DC (1974).
5. Makhijani, A. and Poole, A. *Energy and agriculture in the Third World*, pp. xv and 168. Ballinger, Cambridge, Mass. (1975).
6. Passmore, R. and Durnin, J. V. G. A. *Physiol. Rev.* **35**, 801 (1955).
7. White, G. F., Bradley, D. J., White, A. U. *Drawers of Water*, pp. 93–107. University of Chicago Press, Chicago. (1972).
8. President's Science Advisory Committee, Panel on World Food Supply, *The world food problem*, Vol. 2, Chap. 1. The White House, Washington DC (1967).
9. International Bank for Reconstruction and Development, *Bangladesh Land and Water Resources Sector Study*. Washington DC (1972).
10. Ministry of Irrigation and Power, Government of India, *Report of the Irrigation Commission, 1972*, Vol. 1, pp. 41–56 and 201–246. New Delhi (1972).
11. Odend'hal, S. *Hum. Ecol.* **1**, 3 (1972).
12. Harris, M. *Curr. Anthropol.* **7**, 51 (1966).
13. Bhatia, R. K. and Mehta, M. *Tubewell irrigation in India: an economic analysis of some technical alternatives*. Working paper, Harvard Center for Population Studies, Cambridge, Mass. (1975).
14. Henderson, P. D. *India: the energy sector*. International Bank for Reconstruction and Development, Washington, DC (1975).
15. Meta Systems, Inc., *Working draft report: analysis of 'Revelle' polders development scheme and design for a long range lake Chad Basin study*, pp. 52–110. Cambridge, Mass. (1974).
16. The Ministry of Food, Agriculture, Community Development, and Cooperation Government of India (*Farm Management in India* (New Delhi, 1966)), quoted in (17), estimates 642 bullock-hours and 615 man-hours per hectare for wheat production in Uttar Pradesh. Using my estimates of energy input per hour, the total expenditure of bullock and human energy per hectare was 1.63×10^6 kcal, or 57 per cent of the food energy in the wheat crop. Pimentel (17), using his method of computing human and bullock energy expenditures, gives 2.85×10^6 kcal per hectare, about equal to the energy in the wheat. Table 13.4 indicates that for a gross cropped area of 163 million hectares, average human and bullock energy expenditure in Indian agriculture is 1.18×10^6 kcal per hectare, 28 per cent smaller than the Ministry's figure.
17. Pimentel, D. *Energy use in world food production*, Tables 6 and 15. Report 74-1, Department of Entomology and Section of Ecology and Systematics, Cornel University, Ithaca, NY (1974).
18. Government of India. *Report of the Energy Survey of India Committee*. New Delhi (1965).
19. Datta, R. L. In *Solar energy in developing countries: perspectives and prospects*, pp. 40–6. National Academy of Sciences, Washington DC (1972).
20. Reed, T. B. and Lerner, R. M. In *Energy: use conservation and supply* (ed. P. H. Abelson), pp. 131–6. AAAS, Washington DC (1974).
21. Briscoe, J., thesis, Harvard University (1976).
22. Parikh, K. S. *India in 2001—Fuels or Second India and Energy*. Discussion Paper No. 105, Indian Statistical Institute, New Delhi (1974).
23. Gavan, J. D. and Dixon, J. A. *Science* **188**, 541 (1975).
24. Indian Statistical Institute, Government of India, *National Sample Survey, 18th Round, February 1963–January 1964*. New Delhi (1964).
25. Steinhart, J. S. and Steinhart, C. E. *Science* **184**, 307 (1974).

26. Prasad, C. R., Prasad, K. K., Reddy, A. K. N. *Econ. Polit. Wkly.* **9**, 1347 (1974).
27. Steadman, P. *Energy environment and building*. Cambridge University Press (1975).
28. Since the average income of farm families from all sources is 71 per cent of the median income of all families in the United States (1), we assume that the farm energy use per capita outside farming operations is 71 per cent of the US average of 80.8×10^6 kcal per capita, or a total of 5.40×10^{14} kcal for 9.5 million persons living on farms. Adding the estimate by Steinhart and Steinhart (25) of 5.26×10^{14} kcal for farming operations gives a total of 10.66×10^{14} kcal used annually on US farms.
29. Pimentel, D., Dritschilo, W., Krummel, J., Kutzman, J. *Science* **190**, 754 (1975).
30. Revelle, R. In *The human population*, pp. 163–70. Freeman, San Francisco (1975).
31. US Department of Commerce, Bureau of the Census, *Statistical Abstract of the United States*. Washington DC, eds. 81 to 92 (1960 to 1971).
32. Moore, J. R., John, S. S., Khustro, A. M. *Indian food grain marketing*, pp. 41–76. Prentice-Hall of India, New Delhi. (1973) I have converted prices given in rupees into dollars using an exchange rate of \$1 = 4.76 rupees up to 1966 and \$1 = 7.50 rupees in 1966 and thereafter.
33. Rao, V. M. *Second India studies: food*, pp. 12–14. Macmillan, New Delhi (1975).
34. Krishna, R. *Indian J. Agric. Econ.* **28**, 20 (1973).
35. International Bank for Reconstruction and Development, *Nepal, Irrigation and Water Resources Development*. Washington DC (1974), pp. 7–11.
36. Office of the Registrar General, Government of India, *Census of India, 1971*. New Delhi (1972–1975), in various parts.
37. Office of the Registrar General, Government of India, *Census of India, 1961*. New Delhi (1962–1965), in various parts.

38. I thank my colleagues in the resources development group of the Harvard Center for Population Studies for many helpful discussions, in particular R. Bhatia, J. Briscoe, J. Gavan, P. Rogers, and R. D. Tabors. This article is based in part on a paper presented at a conference sponsored by the US Agency for International Development at the Georgia Institute of Technology in 1974.

14

Biogas plants in India

CHAMAN KASHKARI

The shortage of fertilizers has created a difficult situation for farmers. Developing countries like India, Pakistan, and Nepal cannot buy chemical fertilizers in the international market at the levels they could in the past, because fertilizer prices have skyrocketed owing to escalation in the price of oil. Moreover, it is the opinion of agricultural experts that fertilizer in itself is not adequate for cultivation; the soil must be supplied with organic manure along with fertilizers. Organic manure in the form of cow dung has been traditionally used by farmers in India. Farmers are also facing a severe shortage of fuel. Firewood is not as abundant as it was once, since no serious effort has been made to replant trees. The cut in oil imports has affected the quantity of paraffin available for cooking and lighting in the villages. The only source of inexpensive fuel left is cow dung, which, when made into dried dung cakes, is an excellent fuel. For millions of people living in the rural areas of India, dried cow dung is the only fuel available for cooking.

What is the farmer to do? Should he burn cow dung and satisfy his fuel needs, or should he use it as manure? Fortunately there is a solution which will meet both requirements. Cow dung can be used as manure after its fuel energy has been extracted, in a biogas generator commonly known as a 'gobar gas plant' on the Indian subcontinent. 'Gobar' in the Indian language means cow dung.

The plant operates on the principle that when dung and other organic materials are fermented in the absence of air, combustible methane gas is produced. This method of using cow dung to produce methane gas has been known in India for over 30 years. The extraction of methane gas does not affect the manure characteristics of dung in any way. In fact, after dung is passed through the gas plant, the manure is not only rich in nutrients but is also innocuous and odourless. It is also free from flies and other sources of infection. The gas produced by the plant burns with a blue flame and without a trace of smell at an efficiency at least five times that of burning cow-dung cakes. Thus both improved fuel and organic manure can be obtained from cow dung by using the inexpensive 'gobar' gas plant.

The history of biogas[1]

The first person to observe that decaying vegetation produced a combustible gas was Alessandro Volta. In 1776 he wrote to a friend that 'combustible air' was being produced continuously in lakes and ponds in the vicinity of Como in northern Italy. Volta had noticed that when he disturbed the bottom sediment of the lake, bubbles of gas would rise to the surface. He noticed that when the sediment contained more plant

From *Energy Resources, Demand and Conservation with Special Reference to India*, by Chaman Kashkari (Tata McGraw Hill Co., New Delhi, 1975), pp. 86–94. Reprinted by permission of the author.

material, more bubbles came up. In 1806 William Henry showed that Volta's gas was identical with methane gas. Humphrey Davy in the early 1800s noticed that methane was present in farmyard manure piles. In 1868 Bechamp demonstrated that methane was formed from carbon compounds by action of micro-organisms. Tappeiner in 1882–4 showed conclusively that methane was of microbiological origin. The first plant for production of methane from wastes was set up in a leper asylum in India in 1900. Another plant was set up in Indonesia in 1914 which used straw-board wastes as the source of gas.

The interest in biogas reached a peak at the beginning of the Second World War. In 1940 French scientists working in North Africa developed the technology of production of biogas from agricultural wastes and it was reported that about 1000 biogas plants were in operation in France and French North Africa by 1950. Owing to the Allied blockade, Germany was forced to develop new energy resources during the war. Reportedly, 90000 vehicles were converted to operate on methane gas in order to save petroleum fuel. The tractors on farms also operated on this gas. Following the war many countries, notably Great Britain, Italy, Russia, Kenya, Uganda, and South Africa, showed interest in biogas technology but the enthusiasm waned because there were cheap petroleum resources. However, the interest in this technology continued in India since it fitted the Gandhian philosophy of self-sufficiency at the village level.

The principle of biogas formation[2]

The decay of dead plants and organic materials is carried out by bacteria. *Aerobic* bacteria produce the decomposition in the presence of air, but *anaerobic* bacteria can effect the decomposition process in the absence of air. When decomposition takes place in the presence of air, the gases escape and the residue left is manure. Since one is interested in collecting the gas, it is necessary to use a chemical reaction involving anaerobic bacteria. During an anaerobic process, three gases are evolved—methane, carbon dioxide, and hydrogen. Therefore, when organic wastes are put in containers insulated from the outside air, conditions are ripe for anaerobic process. However, as long as there is oxygen inside the container, no gas will be produced.

Since the slurry also contains the aerobic bacteria, the oxygen contained in the slurry is consumed in the aerobic reaction. Once the oxygen is used up, the anaerobic reaction commences. Thus, there is a time-lag between feeding the wastes into the digester and the production of gas.

Prerequisites for setting up a gas plant

The Khadi and Village Industries Commission of India (KVIC) has standardized the design of biogas plants in India. Even for the smallest plant, a continuous supply of 45 kg of fresh dung per day is necessary. This facilitates installation of a 1.7-m^3 (60 ft^3) gas plant. The daily droppings from a medium-sized cow, buffalo, or bullock is about 10 kg. Therefore, a farmer should have at least five head of cattle to install a biogas plant. He should have adequate space in his farmyard for the biogas installation and space for the output slurry pits which are connected to the plant by means of a channel. A sufficient quantity of water must be available since the dung must be mixed with water before feeding into the gas plant. There is no objection to the location of the gas plant near residential quarters since there is no danger of explosion nor are there any problems of foul odour or fly-breeding. The plant must not be installed within 15 m of a well supplying drinking water to avoid the possibility of the slurry percolating into the well.

Plant construction

The plant comprises a digester for fermentation of cow dung, vegetables, and

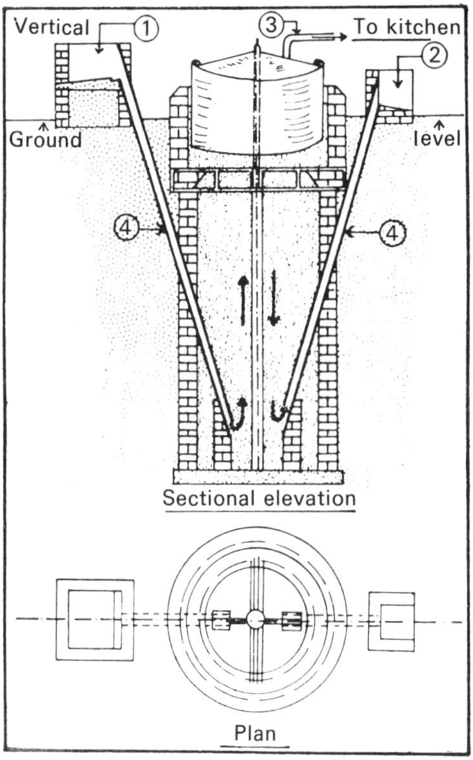

Fig. 14.1 Drawing of a biogas plant: (1) input slurry; (2) output slurry; (3) gas pipe; and (4) input and output pipes.

other organic matter. A gas-holder rests on the digester to collect and direct the gas produced into the kitchen at correct pressure. For daily operation, one collects the cattle dung and other organic materials, drops them into a mixing tank, adds water, mixes properly to form a slurry, and feeds it into the inlet pipe. While the fresh slurry is fed into the digester, an equal amount of ripe slurry is discharged through the outlet pipe. The output slurry is stored in a compost pit where it is covered with farm wastes and finally used as a manure. The construction of the gas plant is illustrated in Fig. 14.1. It has two parts, (1) the digester (2) the gas-holder.

The digester

This is essentially a circular shallow well dug in the ground with sides and bottom made of masonry. The depth of the well varies from 3.5 to 6 m and the diameter from 1.2 to 6 m depending on the size of the plant. A partitioning wall in the middle divides the well into semicircular compartments. As shown in the diagram, two cement pipes, which have their openings at ground level, reach the bottom of the well on either side of the partitioning wall. One is the inlet pipe and the other is the outlet pipe. Fresh cattle dung and water are mixed in the ratio 4:5, forming a slurry which is fed into the inlet pipe, filling up the left compartment. Once it is filled, the slurry flows over the top of the partitioning wall into the right compartment. Gradually the right compartment also is filled, causing some of the slurry to flow out through the outlet pipe since the outlet opening is at a lower level than the inlet opening. The partitioning wall remains submerged in the slurry. As fresh slurry is added, an equal amount of old slurry flows out through the outlet pipe.

The gas-holder

The gas-holder is a mild steel drum which fits like a cap on the mouth of the well and rests on a ledge constructed inside the well. The gas produced in the digester rises through the slurry and is collected in the gas-holder. The pressure of the gas makes the gas-holder rise and float on the slurry. The accumulated gas flows through the gas pipe into the kitchen, or it can be used for gas lamps. A central pipe guides the up-and-down movement of the drum. The pressure of the gas is regulated by means of weights placed on top of the drum. The pressure normally ranges from 7.5 to 14 cm of water column, which is adequate for kitchen appliances and gas lamps.

Gas plant products

The two main products of a gas plant are (1) fuel gas and (2) manure.

Fuel gas

Since the composition of the gas, approximately 55 per cent methane and 45 per cent carbon dioxide, is different from that of coal gas, the appliances must be of special design. After long research, the KVIC has developed appliances suitable for this gas. These appliances have the same efficiency as standard appliances using coal gas. If coal gas appliances are used with biogas, the efficiency is very low (35 per cent instead of 60 per cent). Even diesel oil engines can be run on biogas but the quantity of gas must be sufficient. An engine developing 1 hp will need 425 litres of gas per hour. An engine developing 5 hp, running an electric generator or a water pump, would need 18 m^3 of gas for 8 hours. That would require at least 45 to 50 animals. In order to run an internal combustion engine of diesel or petrol–paraffin type on biogas a special attachment has been designed by the Indian scientists.

Manure

The outlet slurry from the plant is rich in nitrogen and humus. It can be applied to the farmland directly by mixing with irrigation water. In this condition it mixes with the soil very well and the nitrogen content of the slurry is over 2 per cent.

If the slurry cannot be used immediately, it is used for rapid fermentation of compost. A series of pits are dug near the gas plant. The outlet slurry flows into a channel which connects the pits. Vegetable refuse like corn cobs, leaves, and similar waste material is dumped into the pits in a layer, on top of which the outlet slurry is allowed to spread. The slurry is covered with vegetable waste; the process is repeated until the pits are full. The nutrient material in the slurry and the bacteria accelerate the process of composting. The manure output from the biogas plant can also form a good organic base for enriched manure by mixing the manure with chemical fertilizers like ammonium sulphate, superphosphate, etc.

The economics of biogas plant

By using a biogas plant both fuel and manure can be obtained, whereas by converting it into dung cakes or manure only one of the two can be obtained. It has been seen that both of these benefits are obtained to an increasing degree by use of the gas plant. As an example, in the generation of gas about 25 per cent of the dung is consumed, but the useful heat of the gas is about 20 per cent more than the useful heat obtained by burning the entire amount of dung. This is due to very high efficiency of gas (about 60 per cent) as compared to poor efficiency (about 11 per cent) of dung cakes. Similarly, the amount of manure obtained through the gas plant is about 40 per cent more than pit manure. This is perhaps because the decomposition in a gas digester is selective while the manure pit is more rigorous.[3] The minimum number of animals required for different sizes of plants and costs are shown in Table 14.1.

Table 14.1. Capacities of gas plants

Size of plant (cu. ft.)	*Estimated cost (rupees)*	*Minimum no. of animals required*
60	1575	5
100	2075	8
150	2475	12
200	2850	18
300	3675	24
350	4050	30
500	5650	40
700	7450	56
900	8300	72
1250	12300	100
1500	13850	120
2000	17200	160
3000	25200	240
5000	37600	400

Note: The prices are based on estimates made in 1973 in India.

The actual economics of a 3 m^3 (100 ft^3) gas plant would be as shown in Table 14.2. No labour cost is shown because in all cases communal labour is involved.

Table 14.2

		Cost (rupees)
A. *Investment*		
Cost of installation of the gas plant:		
Gas holder and frame		701.00
Piping and stoves		260.00
Civil construction		1114.00
Total		2075.00
B. *Annual expenditure*		
The interest on investment 11 per cent		228.25
Depreciation on gas holder and frame 10 per cent		70.10
Depreciation on piping and stoves 5 per cent		13.00
Depreciation on structures 3 per cent		33.42
Cost of painting every year		50.00
Total		394.77
Say		395.00
C. *Annual income*		
Gas, 3 m^3 per day		
Rs 10 per 29 m^3 (1000 ft^3)		377.58
Manure (pure gobar manure 7 tonnes but composted with refuse)		
16 tonnes Rs 30 per tonne		480.00
Total		857.58
Say		858.00
If entire dung is converted to farmyard manure:		
11 carts @ Rs 15/– per cart		165.00
If entire dung is burnt in form of cakes:		
62.5 quintals @ Rs 5.40 per quintal		337.50
Say		338.00
Surplus if used as manure	858.00	
	−165.00	693.00
Surplus if used as fuel	858.00	
	−338.00	520.00
Cost of depreciation, interest, and maintenance is only		395.00

Note: The above estimate is based on 1973 prices.

Thus it will be seen that construction of a gas plant is actually profitable; also there are the incidental advantages of hygienic operation, absence of smoke and soot, convenience in burning, and richness of manure.

Miscellaneous useful data

Availability of dung (green) per animal. No firm figures can be given since it depends on the size of the animal, the animal feed, and whether the animal is stable-bound or freely grazing. The following figures are broad averages for a stable-bound adult animal of medium size:

Buffalo	14 kg per day
Bullock or cow	10 kg per day
Calves	4 kg per day

Gas production

On an average 1.3 ft^3 of gas can be produced from each kg of wet dung.

Gas plant size

The size of the gas plant is determined by the number of animals available. As shown in Table 14.1, the smallest gas plant is 1.7 m^3 (60 ft^3) size requiring about five animals.

Gas consumption

Cooking	12 ft^3 per day per person
Lighting	4–5 ft^3 per lamp of 100 candle power per hour
Motive power	15 ft^3 per hp per hour

Number of plants in India

The KVIC has been working on the biogas scheme for nearly a decade. Initially the Commission had to reckon with the resistance of farmers to any innovation. With the fuel and fertilizer problems growing alarmingly, the significance of the biogas plant is being understood by cultivators. By August 1973 the Commission had set up a total of about 6250 plants in various states with Gujarat and Maharashtra topping the list with 2816 and 1405 plants respectively. Since 1974 tens of thousands of new plants have been installed in the country. The volume of gas produced by the plants was 10.13 million m^3 in March 1973, valued at Rs. 2.66 million. The corresponding quantity of organic manure produced was 74051 tonnes, valued at Rs. 2.27 million. In the beginning, the programme was mainly concentrated in Gujarat. Now it has spread over the entire country, gathering momentum, particularly in Uttar Pradesh, Haryana, Andhra Pradesh, and Maharashtra. Other organizations which are active in the field are the Indian Agricultural Research Institute (IARI), Gandhi Smarak Nidhi, etc. The IARI had initially worked on the gobar gas plants in the 1930s and had produced a design in 1939.

The present estimates indicate an annual availability of about 324 million tonnes of dung. In 1966 the total dung production was 184 million tonnes and only 0.04 million tonnes were used for biogas plants. There is, therefore, scope to increase the use of cattle dung for generation of gas by at least a factor of 5000 if not more; otherwise this previous source of fuel and manure will be consumed at a very low efficiency.

Central generation of biogas

Thousands of gas plants which have been installed on the Indian subcontinent are mainly of the small single-family type. This means that the farmer must be experienced in operation and maintenance of the plant. This causes problems. While the maintenance of the plants is relatively simple, there have been many instances of poor maintenance resulting in the plants becoming inoperative. This has caused dissatisfaction with the plants, with the result that the farmers go back to other sources of fuel for cooking requirements. The farmer must also spend a considerable amount of time in preparing the slurry and feeding it into the plant, which he would like to avoid if possible.

If the gas could be produced at a central plant in quantities sufficient for an entire village, that would be an ideal situation, since most of the present problems would not arise. This would involve installation of compressors, for which electricity must be available. Thus it is not possible in those villages which have not been electrified. But where electricity is available, every effort must be made to produce the gas at a central plant. Owing to economy of scale, it is better to have a larger plant to cover the requirements of, say, a dozen homes even in those areas where no electric power is available. Maintenance personnel could then be hired to take care of the plant, resulting in reliability of service. Since the gas production goes down in cold weather, larger plants can be provided with temperature control, which is difficult with small single-family units. It should also be possible to utilize solar energy to increase the temperature of the slurry in the digester, resulting in increased gas production.

Research and development

The KVIC has a research centre at Korakendra, near Bombay where research and development work on various aspects of biogas generation is undertaken. The scientists at the centre have developed burners and lamps which run efficiently on biogas. They have installed an experimental 3 kW electrical generating set driven by a dual fuel 5 hp engine operating on 15 per cent diesel oil and 85 per cent biogas. The centre has designed a water heater operating on biogas which has been installed at a laundry in Thana, near Bombay. The heater heats 200 litres of water to 200 °F every 20 minutes. Biogas for burning in the water heater comes from a 2000 ft^3 per day plant installed in the laundry compound.

While the progress in biogas technology in India is impressive, considerable research and development work needs to be done as outlined below:

(1) to work out better and cheaper plant designs using, whenever possible, local or easily available materials;
(2) to better understand fermentation chemistry and conditions which influence greater generation of methane, like temperature, pH, enzymatic and microbial action, suitability of catalysts, etc.;
(3) to evolve cheaper designs and materials for gas-holders and to improve the efficiency of burners; and
(4) to evolve more effective techniques of maintenance.

It has been observed that the gas production goes down in winter because the temperature is below the optimum for microbial activity. Some research should be aimed at:

(i) isolation of a microbial strain that will remain active under low temperature; also, evolving strains which will produce methane instead of the mixture of 55 per cent methane and 45 per cent carbon dioxide, as at present;
(ii) to try inexpensive additives which will stimulate production of more gas; and
(iii) to devise a simple and inexpensive solar heating system which will automatically provide hot water for preparing inlet slurry so as to maintain a higher temperature in the digester.

References

1. Sathianathan, M. A. *BIO-GAS achievements and challenges*, p. 14. Association of Voluntary Agencies for Rural Development, A/1, Kailash Colony, New Delhi, India.
2. Ibid., p. 26.
3. *Gobar Gas—why and how*. Khadi and Village Industries Commission, Irla Road, Vile Parle (West) Bombay 400056 (1974).

15

Rural electrification in India: biogas versus large-scale power

WALLACE E. TYNER AND JOHN ADAMS

One possible means of providing electricity to India's 550000 villages is the use of animal, human, and perhaps some forms of vegetable waste to make methane, a fuel that can be employed in small generators located in or near the communities to be served. This method is often called the gobar gas process in India because 'gobar'—cattle dung—is the main ingredient. The principal alternative, and the one that has been pushed in recent drives for rural electrification, is large-scale power works using coal, hydroelectric potential, atomic energy, or now possibly oil or gas. The large-scale system mandates an extensive power grid, but the local system does not. The Indian government is considering a commitment to a sizeable small-scale power programme, perhaps assisted by multilateral foreign aid. The economic basis of this decision and its ramifications for rural society have not, however, been systematically assessed.

In this paper we will undertake a cost analysis of the two major rural power options: central power facilities and biogas units. We will contrast our findings with the estimates of the major previous studies of biogas electrification. In our judgment, their cost estimates have been substantially biased towards local units. Our conclusion is that, on average, centralized power production and distribution have an appreciable cost advantage over local units. Where villages are remote from transmission lines, however, small-scale units may provide cost savings. There are thus numerous locations in rural India where gobar gas facilities may serve at least as a transitional source of power. We will comment upon the administrative problems associated with providing and servicing these decentralized generators and mention some of the implications of implanting this new technology in the Indian village setting.

That biological materials can be used to generate combustible gases has been known for some time. In northern Italy in 1776, Alessandra Volta recognized the correspondence between the volume of combustible gas generated by lake sediments and the amount of plant material in the sediment. During the Second World War a number of vehicles in Germany were converted to methane operation. Research in India began at the Indian Agricultural Research Institute in 1939. Although a number of experimental plants were developed, it was not until the early 1960s that a practical design was available for field use.

The principal energy ingredient in biogas is methane (CH_4) or natural gas. Biogas is formed in one of two ways. (1) When organic material is left exposed to the air, the gaseous by-products of decay escape into the atmosphere, and the residue is compost. This

First published in *Asian Survey*, Vol. 17, No. 8 (August 1977), pp. 724–34.

decay process is termed 'aerobic' because it is enabled by bacteria that work in the presence of oxygen. (2) The process of forming useful biogas is known as anaerobic digestion since it occurs in the absence of oxygen. During the first phase, sludge materials are broken down into smaller molecules. Organic compounds are oxidized to acids or alcohols, the oxygen in the material fed to the digester is used up, and large amounts of carbon dioxide are formed. In the second phase, bacteria convert the acids and alcohols into methane and carbon dioxide. Generally, 60 per cent to 70 per cent of the gas formed is methane. A delicately balanced environment is required. Changes in acidity, temperature, input mix, and other factors affect the pace and yield of the reactions. For example, the amount of gas generated is a function of temperature. About twice the amount of gas per tonne of manure is produced at 75 °C (167 °F) as at 25 °C (77 °F). Methane generation stops completely below 10 °C (50 °F). Temperatures in North India in the winter frequently fall below this threshold and under such conditions some biogas may have to be used to provide heat for the plant, thereby reducing its net yield.

Cost of centralized power generation

In order to calculate an estimated cost of electricity per kilowatt hour, it is necessary first to estimate the initial capital costs. Capital costs of either biogas or central power facilities include three components; the cost of the power plant, transmission costs, and the cost of village electrification. The ultimate calculation of capital costs per kilowatt hour depends not only upon these cost estimates but upon utilization factors—that is, the degree to which installed capacity is utilized. Unreasonable assumptions regarding any of the capital cost components or the utilization factors will substantially bias the final cost per kilowatt hour estimate.

A number of studies have attempted to compute the costs of installing and operating gobar gas units. Among these, only a few have compared rural electrification using biogas with centralized generation alternatives.[1] Makhijani and Poole estimated the total capital cost for coal-fired generating plants in India at $500 per kilowatt. This cost estimate included $250 per kilowatt for the generating station, $50 per kilowatt for transmission, and $200 per kilowatt for rural electrification. Capital cost for thermal generating plants in 1970 was about $200 per kilowatt.[2] The generating station and transmission costs reported by Makhijani and Poole for 1974 appear somewhat high but reasonable, allowing for inflation. At a 12 per cent discount rate, the annual amortization per kilowatt is $60.[3]

Mikhijani and Poole's rural distribution cost estimate assumes that the average transmission distance from the main line to each village is 8 kilometres. Joint distribution to several villages would reduce these costs. It is clear, too, that costs for a given village will be lower the nearer it is situated to major power lines and that with the growth of India's national power system more and more villages will be closer to such lines. Without knowing the exact distribution costs for a particular village, it is impossible to determine whether central or biogas costs per kilowatt hour would be lower. Estimates that use average distribution costs can thus only provide a basis for a general comparison of the two systems.

To convert the annual capital charge of $60 per kilowatt to a cost per kilowatt hour, utilization factors must be employed. For centralized power generation, a proper approach is to separate rural distribution costs from generation and transmission costs and apply an appropriate utilization factor to each portion. The average generating plant utilization factor for India as a whole has been in the range of 48 per cent to 55 per cent, which is comparable to the average plant utilization factor for the United States.[4] The plant utilization factor should be applied to the generation and transmission portion of total capital cost ($300 or $36 per year at a

12 per cent discount rate). The appropriate factor for rural distribution cost ($200 or $24 per year at a 12 per cent discount rate) is derived from the rate of power consumption per kilowatt of connected load in rural areas. From 1966 to 1971, agricultural sector consumption in India ranged from 657 to 842 kilowatt hours per kilowatt of connected load representing distribution network utilization of 8 per cent to 10 per cent.[5] Total rural sector consumption rates would be somewhat higher.

In their analysis, Makhijani and Poole used the same utilization factors for both generation and transmission and rural distribution. They used two different factors: 1150 and 800 kilowatt hours per kilowatt per year which represent 13 per cent and 10 per cent utilization factors respectively.[6] These factors are appropriate for the rural distribution component but not for the generation and transmission components of total capital cost. Makhijani and Poole evidently believe that a power plant would serve only rural areas, and that no urban or industrial consumption would be serviced from the plant.

Table 15.1 displays a range of unit costs of centralized power supply; it includes our estimates as well as those of Makhijani and Poole and others. Items 1 and 2 are actual unit cost calculations by Henderson (2.2 cents per kilowatt hour) and Venkataraman (1.5 cents). The two Makhijani and Poole estimates for their assumed 10 per cent and 13 per cent capacity utilization factors are 8.5 cents and 6.2 cents per kilowatt hour, respectively. Item 5 is our estimate. We assume a plant utilization factor of 45 per cent which yields a capital amortization cost for generation and transmission of 0.9 cent per kilowatt hour. We assume rural consumption of 1100 kilowatt hours per kilowatt of connected load (12.6 per cent utilization) which yields a capital amortization cost for rural distribution of 2.2 cents per kilowatt hour. Hence, our total value for amortized capital cost is 3.1 cents per kilowatt hour (using a 12 per cent discount rate). If Henderson's operating cost per kilowatt hour of 1.3 cents is raised to 1.5 cents to allow for inflation, the total unit cost of centralized fossil fuel power generation for rural areas becomes 4.6 cents per kilowatt hour. Because this cost estimate was calculated using conservative utilization factors, it should be considered the upper limit for centralized power costs for villages an 'average' distance from power lines. This cost estimate will be compared with the

Table 15.1. Unit cost of centralized electricity supply in India

	Capital cost-amortization (cents per kWh)	*Operating cost (cents per kWh)*	*Total unit cost (cents per kWh)*
1. Actual 1971–2 costs	0.9	1.3	2.2
2. Actual 1967–8 costs	0.8	0.7	1.5
3. Capacity utilization = 10 per cent (800 kWh/kW/year)	7.5	1.0	8.5
4. Capacity utilization = 13 per cent (1150 kWh/kW/year)	5.2	1.0	6.2
5. Plant capacity utilization = 45 per cent and Rural distribution utilization = 13 per cent (3942 and 1100 kWh/kW/year)	3.1	1.5	4.6

Sources: (1) P. D. Henderson, *India: The Energy Sector* (Washington DC: World Bank, 1975), p. 87; (2) Venkataraman, *Power Development*, pp. 84–8; (3) and (4) Makhijani and Poole, *Energy and Agriculture*, pp. 97–8; (5) authors' calculations.

Table 15.2. Assumptions used for biogas power generation

	Units	Authors' values	Prasad, Prasad and Reddy	Makhijani and Poole
1. Dry dung/cow/day	kg	3.0	3.18	2.96
2. No. of cattle in village		300	250	300
3. Dry dung/village/day	kg	900	795	888
4. Collection efficiency	per cent	75	75	70
5. Usable dry dung/village/day	kg	675	596	622
6. Biogas yield/kg dry dung	ft^3	11	6.6	13.5*
7. Energy content/cu. ft of biogas†	Btu	620	620	620
8. Conversion factor	kWh/Btu	3413	3413	3413
9. Power generating efficiency	per cent	25	83§	25
10. Maximum power generation/day	kWh	337	593	381

*Biogas yield for the Makhijani and Poole study was calculated by multiplying the energy content of dry dung (14000 Btu/kg) by the assumed conversion efficiency 60 per cent, and dividing the result by 620 Btu/ft^3 This yield is equivalent to 6 ft^3/lb of dry dung which is the expected biogas yield at 27 °C (80 °F). Clearly, a net yield of this magnitude is not currently attainable during winter months in North India.

†Sathianathan, *Biogas*, p. 62.

§Prasad, Prasad, and Reddy make the direct conversion from cubic feet of biogas to kWh using a factor of 0.15 kWh/ ft^3 biogas. Assuming 620 Btu/ft^3 of biogas, this conversion amounts to a generation efficiency of 83 per cent.

biogas generation cost estimates discussed below.

Biogas-based power generation

The physical parameters controlling the generation of electricity using a decentralized biogas system are summarized in Table 15.2. Column one contains our estimates; columns two and three show comparable data from other sources. In an average village there are in the neighbourhood of 250 to 300 cattle. Assuming that each animal will provide about 3 kilograms of dry dung each day and that three-quarters of that amount is collected for use, the total amount available will be 675 kilograms. Our estimate is thus higher than those of Prasad *et al.*[1] (596 kilograms) and of Makhijani and Poole[1] (622 kilograms). Multiplication of usable dry dung by the biogas yield per kilogram (11 ft^3) and by the Btu content of a cubic foot of gas yields the total Btu content. When this total is divided by the energy conversion factor and multiplied by the efficiency of the power generator, a maximum power generation estimate is derived. This is 337 kilowatt hours per day, and is lower than those calculated by Prasad *et al.* and Makhijani-Poole. We believe, however, that this is an optimistic value and an upper limit with current technology.

The differences among the three results are due to the use of different yield and conversion estimates. Makhijani and Poole assumed a 60 per cent conversion efficiency, which is near the highest observed in experimental plants.[7] Prasad *et al.* assumed a conversion efficiency of only 30 per cent and this is slightly below the year-round average for India. We think that 50 per cent net energy conversion may be generally attainable after additional applied research and development and have used this figure, which is comparable to 11 ft^3 of biogas per kilogram of dry dung. The next key assumption concerns power generation efficiency, that is, the efficiency of the internal combustion engine and generator in converting biogas energy into electric power. Makhijani and Poole assume a generation efficiency of 25 per cent, which is probably near the upper limit.[8] Although petrol engines usually run at less than 25 per cent efficiency, we selected a generation efficiency of 25 per cent as the best possible case. Based on these assumptions, the maximum power that could be generated per day is 337 kilowatt hours.

The costs of generating power may be estimated on two different bases: (I) assuming a portion of the biogas is used for cooking to replace dung that was previously used for this purpose; and (2) assuming a substitute (perhaps solar energy or water hyacinths) could be found for cooking so that all biogas could be used to generate electricity. The adjusted initial capital and annual costs of these two alternatives are given in Table 15.3. Following Makhijani and Poole, 46 per cent of the biogas generated is assumed to be adequate to serve the cooking needs of two hundred families in the village. This fraction may be low in light of the technical difficulties in maintaining a high level of production. Nonetheless, we will proceed with the analysis of capital costs based on this assumption. For the applications with and without biogas used for cooking, it is asserted that the costs of the biogasification plant, the gas plant auxiliaries, land, and gas storage and compression would be identical. This procedure is valid for the first three items but is open to question for gas storage and compression. Storage facilities adequate for 50 per cent of the annual production of gas were assumed in both cases. This assumption is reasonable for the case without cooking fuel, but appears to be too high for the case with cooking fuel because daily utilization of gas for cooking would even out the consumption pattern through time relative to the case without cooking fuel. Hence, we reduced the storage and compression cost for the case with cooking fuel.

Table 15.3 displays the revised capital and annual costs for the two cases assuming generator capacities of 66 kilowatts and 123 kilowatts. Makhijani and Poole used generator sizes of 75 kilowatts and 140 kilowatts for the cases with and without cooking, respectively. Because we arrived at a lower maximum daily generation figure, we reduced the generation capacities and recalculated the cost figures. Makhijani and Poole assumed no economies of scale for the higher capacity generators, an hypothesis we retain.

Gross annual cost for a biogas plant is calculated by amortizing at a 12 per cent discount rate the total initial plant investment and adding four additional costs: collection costs, labour and maintenance, market town services, and distribution costs of fuel. A 25-year life is assumed for the biogas plant and other equipment, which may be somewhat long given the corrosive nature of some of the materials used in biogas generation.

After estimating gross annual operating costs, it is necessary to subtract credits for cooking fuel sales and a credit for fertilizer sales to obtain a figure for net annual operating costs. Annual electricity generation was figured on the basis of 1000 kilowatt hours per kilowatt installed, the figure used by Makhijani and Poole,[1] which represents a capacity figure of 11.4 per cent.[9] Since all of the electricity generated from the biogas plant would be used in a limited rural area, this capacity utilization represents an upper limit. Using the above assumptions and cost input data, the cost per kilowatt hour of electricity with biogas used for cooking would be 6.7 cents and with no cooking provided from the biogas, 5.1 cents. Since assumptions favourable to biogas generation were used when no firm data were available, these costs represent lower limits of the costs for biogas-based generation.

Comparison of cost estimates

Clearly both of the biogas cost estimates are significantly greater than the 4.6 cents per kilowatt hour cost for the centralized power generation system. It should be emphasized that 4.6 cents/kWh represents the upper limit for the 'average' village and that 5.1 cents/kWh represents the lower limit for power generation using the biogas system.

Table 15.3. Costs of a decentralized biogas generation and electrification plant

Cost items	*Gas used for cooking*	*Alternative cooking fuel*
Capital costs	($)	($)
Biogasification plant	8000	8000
Gas plant auxiliaries	1000	1000
Land cost	1000	1000
Gas storage and compression	1000	1500
Cooking fuel distribution cylinders and gas stoves	8000	—
Cost of water hyacinth or other cooking system	—	10000
Electric generator with reciprocating gas engine and switchgear @ $160/kW installed	10600	19700
Construction supervision and training	1000	1000
Subtotal	30600	42200
Interest on capital during 6 months' construction @ 12 per cent	1800	2500
Total	32400	44700
Cost per kW	491	363
Annual costs		
Capital cost amortization	4100	5700
Residue collection at $2/tonne fresh manure	2600	2600
Local labour and maintenance	1300	1300
Market town services	500	500
Labour for distributing cooking fuel	300	600
Gross annual costs	8800	10700
Credit for cooking fuel sales	2000	2000
Credit for fertilizer	2400	2400
Total credits	4400	4400
Net annual operating cost	4400	6300
Annual electricity generation at 1000 kWh/kW	66000 kWh	123000 kWh
Cost per kWh	6.7 cents	5.1 cents

Source: These cost estimates are adapted from cost values contained in Makhijani and Poole, *Energy and agriculture*, pp. 112–6.
Note: All costs are rounded to the nearest $100.

Actual differences may be considerably greater. Based on economic considerations alone, the conclusion of this analysis is that *electricity generation using centralized power facilities is on average more cost advantageous than adopting decentralized systems based on biogas generation.*[10]

In some situations, however, power generation from gobar gas may be a reasonable alternative. In isolated regions, the transmission costs would be higher than those estimated. Small villages, or even caste or lineage neighbourhoods, might use biogas as an interim alternative to a central source. Even if only 20 per cent of India's villages fall into these categories, over 100000 units would be installed.

It should be noted that our conclusion applies only to the use of biogas as a means of decentralized electric power generation. We have not considered the merits of gobar gas as a cleaner, more healthful cooking fuel, nor have we examined the potential of the residue being a superior fertilizer, considerations which would enhance its appeal. A biogas programme may be desirable solely as a means of producing both cooking fuel and fertilizer from cow dung with no associated power generation.[11]

Potential problems with a biogas power generation programme

Before biogas is adopted in those circumstances where it is deemed desirable, there are a number of political and administrative problems that need to be resolved at the national level. In addition, if past experience with agricultural assistance, community development, and co-operative credit institutions at the village level is any guide, the villagers of India are likely to find their lives deeply affected by the programme; and, in turn, they are likely to bend biogas installations to their own purposes and thereby upend the calculations of policy makers who ignore the human factor.

The general administrative problems likely to be encountered are those typical of any new programme. These include co-ordination of finance, production, distribution, and political activities together with assuring adequate numbers and competence of staff to carry forward the assigned tasks. Any massive diffusion of technology depends upon the dissemination of information, guidance of production and distribution by co-operation between technicians and the service population, and adequate provision for maintenance. A successful biogas programme must be based on a technically sound plant which can function under a wide range of operating conditions. Much research needs to be done on plant design for improved efficiency, improved winter operating performance, use of solar energy to heat the biogas plant, proper utilization of the sludge output to conserve nutrients, and biogas plant operations in water-short regions. Initial breakdowns in administration, maintenance, or technical components may sour villagers on the programme, and they and their neighbours may become progressively unresponsive.

There is also the danger that new biogas units will be emplaced in villages which are close to existing roads, towns, and power lines. This pattern may tend to result from ease of access for construction, maintenance, and monitoring. Yet these are the sites where biogas power generation offers little or no cost advantage. Officials will have to take special steps to ensure that decentralized rural electrification reaches into the more remote areas where it will do the most good and does not end up as merely another facility provided to the already developed regions.

Major obstacles to the successful dissemination and utilization of biogas plants in Indian villages are found at the village level. Currently, cow dung is used directly for fuel and compost in many Indian villages, and there is an existing social-cum-economic structure that provides for the collection, drying, and distribution of the dung fuel. The institutional structure is so arranged that, generally, fuel is available for the cooking needs of villagers in all castes or economic classes, and without regard to the distribution of cattle ownership.

If a biogas plant is established, then cow dung would not be used directly as a fuel but would be 'transformed' into another type of fuel and fertilizer. One could anticipate that many of the types of tensions associated with commercialization of the village economic system and with the adoption of new farm technologies would recur. As in these previous cases, the new development provides novel opportunities for gain for some in the village and threatens to deprive others of existing income rights. In turn, these economic changes will interact with caste and status relationships and with the village political system. At present, dung is a non-marketed commodity subject to rules and rights that govern its sharing. As with crops, labour, land, and water, dung will become a marketed and priced item subject to distribution through the market system. It is reasonable to suppose that the village cattle owners, who are likely in the main to be the wealthier peasant farmers, will attempt to assert latent property rights to their beasts' dung. Their power and status are likely to enable them to get their way. The losers will be the poorer families whose women and children collect dung for use as a cooking fuel. They will have to seek alternative sources of fuel. Some may even lose small incomes from the sale of dried dung.

On the distribution side, some equitable and enforceable method must be devised for governing the flow of gas, electricity, and fertilizer. Even if initial efforts to ensure even-handed community control and to design an equitable pattern are successful (which is not likely), it would be surprising if the big men of the village were not able to abort these, place themselves astride power and gas lines, and appropriate more than their share of energy and fertilizer.

One may with some confidence predict a worsening of the internal distribution of resources and incomes inside the village. A prerequisite to taking the biogas system into village India must be the design of a set of locally intelligible property rights and payments that do not do excessive violence to existing economic relationships—it is too much to expect a change for the better. At a minimum, some serious thought must be given to determining what effects the new technology will have on village institutions and how the villagers will respond.

Notes and references

1. See Makhijani, Arjun and Poole, Alan. *Energy and agriculture in the Third World.* Ballinger Publishing Co., Cambridge (1975); Prasad, C. R., Krishna Prasad, K., and Reddy, A. K. N. Biogas plants: prospects, problems, and tasks. *Economic and Political Weekly*, Special Number pp. 1347–64; (August 1974), Sathianathan, M. A., *Biogas: achievements and challenges.* Association of Voluntary Agencies for Rural Development, New Delhi, 1975); a more general survey is found in Revelle, Roger, Energy use in rural India. *Science* **192**, 969–75 (1976).
2. Government of India. *Report of the Fuel Policy Committee*, p. 84. Government of India Press, New Delhi (1975).
3. Makhijani and Poole used a 15 per cent discount rate, but to achieve consistency with their analysis of a typical decentralized unit it is necessary to use a 12 per cent rate.
4. *Statistical yearbook of the electrical utility industry for 1974*, pp. 6–15. Edison Electric Institute, New York (1975); G.O.I., *Report of the Fuel Policy Committee*, p. 80.
5. G.O.I., *Report of the Fuel Policy Committee*, p. 87.
6. Makhijani and Poole, *Energy and Agriculture*, p. 97.
7. Ibid., p. 149; also see Sathianathan, *Biogas*, pp. 31–4; Prasad *et al.*, Biogas plants, pp. 134–9.
8. Sathianathan, *Biogas*, pp. 68–9.
9. This capacity fraction is somewhat lower than that used for the centralized system because greater capacity is required in the decentralized system for the same load due to the heavy demand of motor starting requirements (Makhijani and Poole, *Energy and agriculture*, p. 116).
10. Venkataraman reports that the average cost of electrifying a village in India is about $9000, much less than the cost of a biogas electrification unit (p. 94). Venkataraman, K. *Power development in India, the financial aspects.* Wiley Eastern Pvt. Ltd., New Delhi (1972).
11. See Tyner, Wallace E. *Energy resources and economic development in India*, Chapter VI. Martinus-Nijhoff Press, Leiden, the Netherlands (1977).

V Brazil

The construction site of the Estreite hydro-electric power project on the Rio Grande in Brazil which is being constructed by Furnas with the aid o World Bank.

World Bank photo by J. R. Nenate.

Cattle-drawn cart in Brazil. Potential for agricultural and industrial growth large, and the Government has emphasized the need for transport to open up new lands and to move agricultural products from the interic to coastal consumption areas and po for export.

Before the Second World War, Brazil was thought of mainly as a producer of coffee and sugar. But during the past two and a half decades, Latin America's largest nation has striven rapidly to convert its vast agricultural and mineral resources into a base for its development as a major industrial power. Modern industries, patterned after those of the advanced industrial countries and ranging from steel mills to car-assembly plants, have been vigorously promoted through policies of import substitution and development of an infrastructure of large ports, highways, and electric power grids.

Rapid and impressive though this industrialization has been, it has been severely hampered in recent years by Brazil's heavy reliance on imported fossil fuels. Coal deposits, concentrated in southern Brazil, are very modest in quantity and generally poor in quality. The Brazilian iron and steel industry has therefore had to rely principally on charcoal or on imported coke. The situation has been even more severe for liquid petroleum fuels. Despite an extensive drilling programme since 1939, proven Brazilian petroleum reserves amount to only about 106 million tonnes, and provide barely 20 per cent of domestic petroleum demand. The bulk of Brazil's petroleum, now amounting to some $3 billion a year in foreign exchange, must be imported.

Brazil is blessed, however, with the world's sixth largest hydro-power potential and with the planet's largest resources of biomass. The Itaipu hydro project alone (on the Parana River, shared with Paraguay) will, when completed in the 1980s, produce more than six times the electric power of the Aswan High Dam in Egypt. And the Amazon rain forest, still covering some 36 per cent of the country's territory, is the single most extensive tract of tropical forest land remaining in the world. Not surprisingly, therefore, Brazil has begun seriously to explore the means fully to exploit these vast renewable resources. At the same time, the country continues to search for offshore hydrocarbons and has also set to acquire a sizeable nuclear generation capacity.

J. Goldemberg, Director of São Paulo University's Institute of Physics, reviews in his paper ('Brazil: energy options and current outlook') the availability and distribution of fossil fuels and renewable resources, describes the nature of the current Brazilian energy problems and discusses some possible solutions including biomass, hydro-power, and nuclear energy.

E. J. Jeffs, editor of *Energy International,* concentrates much of his paper ('Energy profile of Brazil') on the conditions, performance, and organization of the country's expanding power generation and points out the great dilemma facing Brazilian energy planners: what next after the rich hydro resources in the south are developed? The work on the largest southern hydro station—Itaipu on Parana with 18 Francis sets and the total installed capacity of 12600 MW—is already well under way and J. Mazzone ('Itaipu: the world's largest power station) provides a detailed description of the project's dams, power house, and generating units.

Besides abundant hydro-power Brazil can exploit many other renewable energies: direct solar radiation, ocean thermal gradients, hydrocarbon-producing plants, and, most importantly, some of its highly productive crops which might be transformed through bioconversion of fuels and feedstock. J. M. Miccolis ('Alternative energy technologies in Brazil') reviews all of these options and argues for a systematic, co-ordinated, and comprehensive approach for their development.

Partial substitution of petrol by ethyl alcohol produced from sugar-cane and manioc has attracted perhaps the greatest attention abroad, both for its enormous potential and for the large scale on which Brazilian planners eventually intend to implement the technology. Allen L. Hammond ('Alcohol: a Brazilian answer to the energy crisis') surveys the advantages as well as the many outstanding problems of the programme, which, if successful, would go a long way toward improving Brazil's balance of payments, promoting industrial growth, and reducing urban pollution and rural unemployment.

Brazil's continuing desire to industrialize, coupled with its particular resource situation, may prove of special significance to many other nations. Because the country is generally lacking in the conventional coal and oil deposits that fuelled the industrialization of the major powers of the northern hemisphere, it is being compelled to harness effectively those resources which it does possess. Many of these resources—biomass, hydro-power, direct solar energy—are shared in abundance by other tropical nations. Brazil also shares with other developing countries the characteristics of having a large and growing rural population and an even larger and faster growing urban population, with success thus far in extending the benefits of urbanization and industrial production only among a relatively affluent minority. If, in its drive for industrial power, Brazil is able to develop its indigenous energy resources in a manner that incorporates an increasing proportion of its population, the country will have also pioneered some technologies and energy-use systems of great importance to other developing countries. And certain of these technical developments might be of considerable interest to industrialized countries as well.

Energy in Brazil: selected readings

Brazilian National Committee of the World Energy Conference (biannually). *Estatistica Brasileira de Energia*. Brazilian National Committee of the WEC, Rio de Janeiro.

Ciência E Cultura (September 1976). Special energy issue **28**, No. 9.

Goldemberg, J. (ed.) (1976). *Energia no Brasil*. Academia de Ciências do Estado de São Paulo, São Paulo.

Licio, A. M. A. (1976). *Etanol: combustível e matéria prima*. Semana de Tecnologia Industrial, Ministério da Indústria e Comercio, Rio de Janeiro.

Ministério de Minas e Energia (1977). *Balanco Energético Nacional*. Ministério de Minas e Energia, Brasilia.

Muthoo, M. K. (1978). Forest energy and the Brazilian socio-economy with special reference to fuelwood. Paper presented at the 8th World Forestry Congress, Jakarta, 17 October 1978.

Wilberg, J. A. and Brito, A. S. (1974). *Energy resources and their utilization in Brazil*. 9th World Energy Conference, Detroit.

16

Brazil: energy options and current outlook

J. GOLDEMBERG

Brazil has an area of 8 511 965 square kilometres and a population of approximately 110 million people.[1,2] The country was kept dormant as a Portuguese colony for more than 300 years and, after gaining political independence in the last century, remained as a producer and exporter of agricultural products, mainly coffee and sugar, until the Second World War.

After the Second World War, Brazil entered a phase of accelerated industrialization, which resulted in the growth of very large cities in the southern (and more temperate) part of the country, and consequently in an exodus of rural populations to urban centres. The fraction of the population living in cities increased from 36 per cent in 1950 to 45 per cent in 1960 and 56 per cent in 1970.

The energy consumption per capita of the average Brazilian therefore increased enormously in a brief span of time; in addition, the profile of consumption changed very significantly. Fig. 16.1 indicates that by 1976 Brazil had reached a level of consumption comparable to some of the less developed European countries (approximately 10 megawatt-hours per year per capita).[3]

Energy consumption as a function of income per capita has increased in recent years in a manner similar to that in developed countries. Thus the country has entered a phase of modernization in which the energy-intensive consumption patterns of the great industrial countries have been adopted, without any critical assessment, through the transplantation of modern, foreign industries. As shown in Fig. 16.2, the relation between per capita energy consumption (E) and per capita income (I) is practically linear, a characteristic of highly developed countries.[4,5]

The ratio of total energy used to income per capita has also remained almost constant in the last 10 years at the level of 60×10^3 British thermal units (Btu) per dollar. This is approximately two-thirds of the value in the United States[6] and indicates that the efficiency of energy use has been slowly improving (Fig. 16.3); however, less energy is needed in Brazil to produce one dollar of income than in the United States, indicating a smaller use of energy-dissipating devices such as air-conditioners and freezers.

The profile of consumption[3] changed in a somewhat predictable fashion in the era of cheap and abundant petroleum (Fig. 16.4). The relative importance of biomass in the balance of the energy consumed decreased dramatically from 1940 to 1975, with a corresponding growth of petroleum consumption.

Coal has had an insignificant role in energy consumption in Brazil, but hydroelectric power has increased its share to 20 per cent of the total energy consumption in recent

First published in *Science*, Vol. 200 (14 April 1978), pp. 158–64.

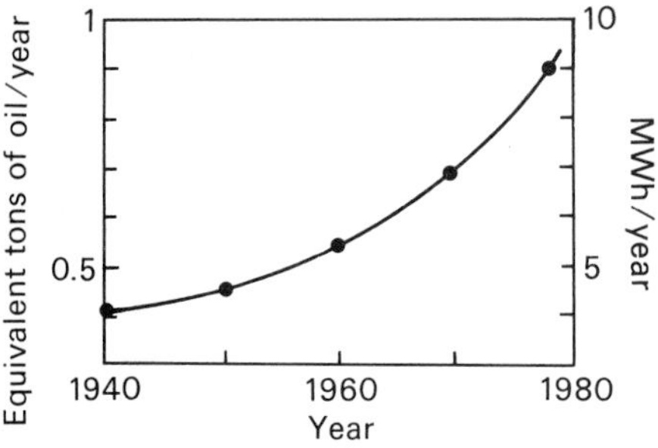

Fig. 16.1. Brazil's energy consumption per capita in the period 1940 to 1977.

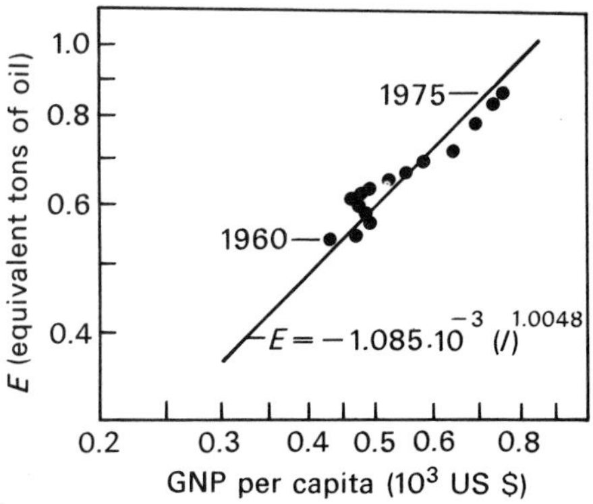

Fig. 16.2. Energy consumption (E) versus income (I). The data indicate p close to unity.[4]

years. The balance is taken by petroleum; its contribution has grown from 9.2 per cent in 1941 to 28.0 per cent in 1952 and to 44.8 per cent in 1972 (Fig. 16.5). Natural gas consumption has been negligible.

The energy profiles of Brazil and the United States are compared in Table 16.1. Petroleum represents approximately 44.8 per cent of the total energy consumed in Brazil and only 20 per cent of it is produced internally. The remaining 80 per cent (700000 barrels per day) is imported at a cost of more than $3 billion per year. To compensate for this deficit in the balance of trade, the country has to export large quantities of raw minerals, agricultural products, and semi-industrialized goods.

The future prospects for energy consumption are presented in Fig. 16.6, which shows the official projections for consumption of different sources up to 1985: The contribution of biomass remains approximately constant, whereas hydroelectric production increases significantly but not enough to avoid a strong increase in the use of liquid combustibles (predominantly petroleum, although other sources such as alcohol and shale oil are also considered). Energy consumption is expected to grow at a rate of approximately 10 per cent a year; the population growth rate per year is 2.9 per cent which, by itself, represents a great stress on the Brazilian economy.

In this article I review the known resources in Brazil and their possible utilization. As I will show, the prospects for a greatly increased petroleum production in Brazil are limited. Alternatives must therefore be found if an extremely serious situation is to be avoided in the next 10 to 15 years.

Table 16.1. Energy resources in Brazil and the United States in 1972

Source	*Brazil (per cent)*	*United States (per cent)*
Coal	3.6	17
Petroleum	44.8	46
Gas	0.3	32
Hydroelectric power	20.8	4
Biomass*	30.5	1
Total	100.0	100

*Including wood and suger-cane bagasse.

Energy resources in Brazil

The data given below are taken from the compilation made by the Brazilian National Committee of the World Energy Conference. The data refer in all instances to 1972.

Crude oil

Sedimentary basins onshore extend over an area of 3168000 km^2, plus about 800000 km^2 offshore on the continental shelf. The first basins to be explored were those in the

Table 16.2. Petroleum reserves (1972) in 10^6 tonnes

Locality	*Reserves* *Total*	*Reserves* *Recoverable*	*Past cumulative production*
Bahia	515.7	83.2	81.0
Alagoas	6.2	0.4	0.3
Sergipe	212.7	20.4	7.4
Offshore	14.9	2.6	
Total	749.5	106.5	88.7

north-eastern region (state of Bahia) near the Todosos-Santos Bay, and all locally produced oil has come from this region. Since 1939 more than 3900 wells have been drilled all over the country; 1985 of the wells produced oil, and 108 natural gas. The overall results have been disappointing, however; the recoverable oil reserves are only about 106×10^6 tonnes, and the annual production of 8.2×10^6 tonnes covers only one-fifth of the country's needs, the balance being imported (Table 16.2).

The remaining possibility for increased oil production in Brazil seems to be the offshore exploration that led to the discovery in 1976 of new fields off the shore of Rio de Janeiro. These reserves increased the figures shown in Table 16.2 by about 15 per cent, and there are hopes for doubling the Brazilian production of oil by 1982.

Natural gas reserves

Natural gas reserves (Table 16.3) are usually associated with crude oil deposits. Although the production of natural gas was 1.2 km³ in 1972, only 18 per cent was used for energy and industrial uses; the balance was either reinjected into the wells—to increase pressure or for storage—or flared locally. The principal reason for flaring is that the main producing centres are located in Bahia, which is not an industrial state. The recent establishment of a petrochemical industry near the crude oil and gas fields will encourage further use of gas.

Table 16. 3. Gas reserves (1972) in 10^6 cubic metres

Locality	*Reserves* *Total*	*Reserves* *Recoverable*	*Past cumulative production*
Bahia	49.3	28.9	12.5
Sergipe	4.1	1.6	0.1
Alagoas	0.9	0.6	
Offshore	5.9	4.7	
Total	60.2	35.8	12.6

Shale oil

Depending mainly on economic factors, the oil recovered from shales could complement conventional crude oil. The known shale oil reserves in the southern region of Brazil are given in Table 16.4. Most shale deposits contain 4 to 8 per cent oil. The recoverable oil, considering only the formations in the southern region, is estimated at about 500×10^9 barrels, almost five times more than the known crude oil deposits.

Studies are under way for the commercial exploitation of shale deposits in Paraná.

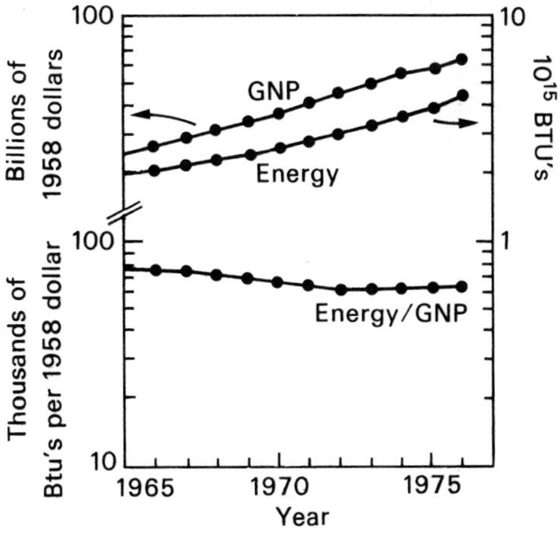

Fig. 16.3. Energy and gross national product (GNP) in the period 1965 to 1975. The ratio of energy to gross national product is approximately constant over the period and somewhat smaller than the equivalent value for the United States.

Table 16.4. Shale oil reserves (1973)

Locality	*Deposit area* (km^2)	*Oil content (kilograms of oil per 1000 kg of shale)*	*Total recoverable oil* (10^6 *tonnes*)
São Paulo	200	40 to 130	288
Parana (Iratí)	82	70	95
Rio Grande do Sul	350	20 to 80	114
Total	632		497

Operation of the oil-producing facilities is expected to begin in 1978 with a daily production of about 10000 tonnes of oil, 900 tonnes of sulphur, 400 tonnes of liquefied petroleum gas, and 1.7 million cubic metres of light heating gas. Environmental problems associated with these plans have yet to be solved. For the oil to be recovered, large quantities of rock have to be removed (200000 to 400000 tonnes) daily, and material remaining after extraction is highly acidic and presents a disposal problem.

Coal

Coal deposits are scarce in Brazil and all those that have been discovered are in the southern region (Table 16.5). The total known reserves are 3256×10^6 tonnes of which 2014×10^6 tonnes are of the sub-bituminous type, 1240×10^6 tonnes bituminous, and only about 2×10^6 tonnes anthracite. Coal of a metallurgical grade suitable for coking can only be obtained after complex processing. Prewashed coal has an ash content of up to about 30 per cent. The sub-bituminous coals of the states of Rio Grande do Sul and Parana are also of poor quality and produce only steam coal for local use. Fluidized bed combustion of poor-quality coal might be used to advantage in Brazil.

Table 16.5. Coal reserves (1972). The total recoverable quantity is 688×10^6 tonnes

Locality	*Total reserves* (10^6 *tonnes*)	*Annual production* (10^3 *tonnes*)
São Paulo	1	
Parana	35	346
Santa Catarina	1200	4536
Rio Grande do Sul	2020	978
Total	3256	5860

Uranium and thorium

Only very recently did prospecting for the so-called fissile fuels begin in Brazil. Coastal monazite-sand deposits containing both thorium and uranium are known to exist, but the cost of exploiting them commercially has not been evaluated.

The only known uranium deposits (Table 16.6) are in the south-eastern region, in the State of Minas Gerais (Pocos de Caldas). They occur in an intrusive pipe of alkaline rocks covering an area of about 900 km^2. The economic thorium reserves (Table 16.7) come from monazitic beach sand deposits. The monazite occurs in association with zircon and rutile, and the deposits are located along the eastern and

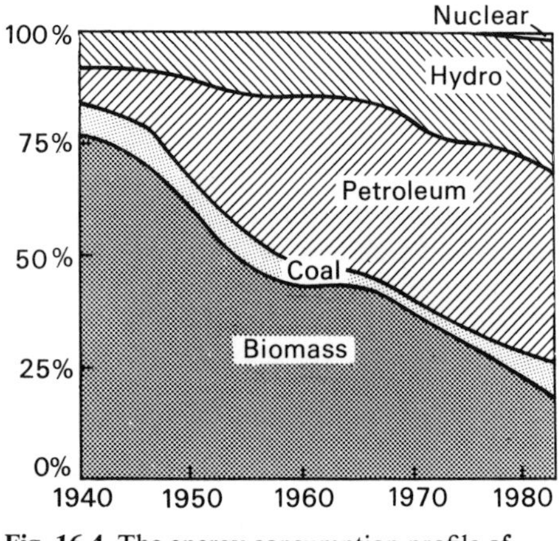

Fig. 16.4. The energy consumption profile of Brazil indicating the rapid decline of biomass consumption.

Table 16.6. Uranium reserves (1972). Costs are in US dollars. New findings, raising these numbers to perhaps 10000 to 20000 tonnes, have recently been reported

Locality or deposit	*Range of maximum recovery cost ($/kg)*	*Quantity recoverable (tonnes)*	*Average grade of ore (per cent of U^3O^8)*	*Estimated additional resources (tonnes)*
Minas Gerais	Up to 33.0	3195	0.15 to 0.19	4250
Monazite sands	Up to 22.0	49	0.18	37
Total		3244		4287

north-eastern Atlantic Coast. A total of only 408 tonnes of thorium was produced in 1972.

Other possible sources of fissile fuels, not yet sufficiently known in terms of economic exploitation, occur in the State of Minas Gerais. These include thorite and thorogummite, in connection with highly decomposed alkalic rocks. In the Araxá niobium deposits, thorium appears associated with monazite. Still other sources could be fluvial monazite-sand deposits and monazite-bearing pegmatites in the states of Minas Gerais, Goiás, and Rio Grande do Norte.

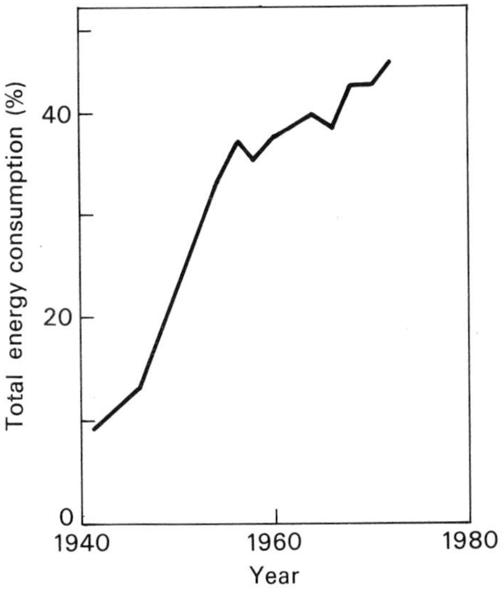

Fig. 16.5. The rapid rise of petroleum consumption in the period 1940 to 1977.

Hydroelectric energy

The geomorphology of Brazil is such that water resources are spread over the whole country, with a certain predominance in the northern region where the world's biggest basin—the Amazon—is located.

Table 16.8 shows the main characteristics of the local hydroelectric potentials. Figures are presented by geographic region. Of the overall installable hydropower capacity of 118980 megawatts, approximately 17000 MW are being used and this number should increase to 35000 MW by 1985 with the completion of the huge Itaipu central dam, with a capacity in excess of 10000 MW, on

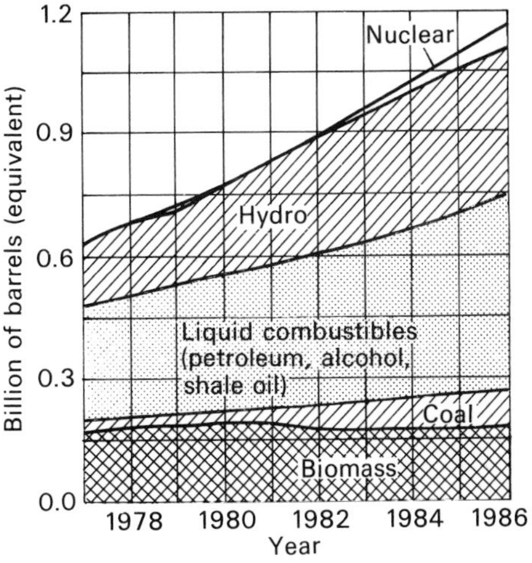

Fig. 16.6. Projections of energy consumption of different sources in the period 1977 to 1986. All sources converted to oil equivalent.

Table 16.7. Thorium reserves (1972). Costs are in US dollars

Locality or deposit	*Range of maximum recovery cost ($/kg)*	*Quantity recoverable (tonnes)*	*Average grade of ore (per cent)*	*Estimated additional resources (tonnes)*
Minas Gerais	Not available	65000	0.09 to 1.0	1200000
Monazite sands	Up to 20	1350	5.9	1000
Total		66350		1201000

Table 16.8 Hydroelectric potential in Brazil

Region	*Installable capacity (MW)*	*Potential annual generation* (GWh)*	*Power generated in 1975 (GWh)*	*Fraction utilized (per cent)*
North	46200	202400	1020	0.5
North-east	13349	58500	8800	15
South-east	39577	183700	51570	27
Central-west	1164	5100	1730	34
South	18690	67200	8390	12.5
Total	118980	516900	71510	14

*Available 95 per cent of the time.

the Paraná River, and a few other dams. At present, only 14 per cent of the total hydroelectric power of the country is being used, although in the most populous south-eastern region this fraction is 27 per cent (Table 16.8). There remains a potential of almost 50000 MW mainly in the tributaries of the Amazon River in the northern region (Tocantins, Araguaia, Xingu, Tapajós, Cotinga, and Trombetas).

A serious transportation problem may develop because these sources are located at least 2000 km from the great population centres (Rio de Janeiro and São Paulo) in the south-eastern part of the country that has a total population of 40 million people.

Biomass

Wood accounts for approximately 30 per cent of Brazil's present energy needs; this represents approximately 170 million cubic metres, most of it used as fuel. These numbers probably represent a lower limit.

The utilization of wood for charcoal is important in the steel industry and it is estimated that 40 per cent of the needs of this industrial sector are supplied from this source (approximately 2 million tonnes yearly).

As indicated in Table 16.9, forests originally covered 55 per cent of the Brazilian territory. The Atlantic and Brazilian pine (*Araucária braziliensis*) forests have now been almost completely decimated, but the Amazon forest remains almost intact.[7]

Total reserves

The proved recoverable energy reserves of the country for 1972 are summarized in Table 16.10.

The nature of the problems

In the southern part of Brazil the patterns of energy consumption are not very different from those of the great industrial nations.

Table 16.9. Brazilian vegetation. All numbers represent percentages of total territory

Forest	*Primitive*	*Present*
Amazon	40	36
Atlantic	10	1
*Araucaria**	5	0.5
Total	55	37.5

*Brazilian pine.

Table 16.10. Brazil's energy resources

Resource	*Proved reserves* (× 10^6 *tonnes*)	*Total energy content* (10^{15} *joules*)	*Percent-age of total*
Non-renewable			
Crude oil	106.53	4687	11.1
Natural gas*	35.8	1468	3.5
Shale oil	497.0	21 868	52.0
Mineral coal	688.0	13 760	32.7
Uranium†	0.0032	309	0.7
Total		49 092	100.0
Renewable			
Hydroelectric power (present)		649	
Biomass (present)		954	
Hydroelectric power‡ (potential)		3023	

*Proved reserves are in cubic kilometres.
†Figures are for pressurized water reactor without plutonium recycling.
‡Annual generation based on potential of 119 GW and on historical average hydrological conditions, converted at substitution basis (1 kWh = 12.75 × 10^6 joules).

This part of Brazil suffers from crowded cities, roads clogged with automobiles, and air pollution, and there is a general deterioration of the quality of life in the urban centres.

The number of automobiles in Brazil has grown from a few thousand 30 years ago to about 5 million in 1975. For the transportation of goods and services, road transportation has been emphasized, often because of the availability of subsidies for road construction, with the result that the energy spent in road transportation is approximately 83 per cent of the total transport energy.[8]

In addition to the petrol consumed in cars there is an industrial energy-intensive sector that uses large quantities of petroleum derivatives and electricity. The transportation of electricity to these urban centres from distant locations in the Amazon basin poses a serious technological problem, and for this reason the construction of nuclear reactors was considered as a solution to the energy problem. The Brazilian government has now begun an ambitious programme of installing several nuclear reactors, mainly in the south-eastern part of the country. This programme could alleviate the energy shortage in the urban and industrial south-east, but would have little effect on the automobile and the automotive industry, which is the leading industrial sector in Brazil.

Since most of the petroleum consumed in Brazil is imported, the price of petrol is now among the highest in the world: $US1.80 per gallon (approximately three times the current price in the United States).

Because of strong pressure to reduce consumption of petrol (and other oil products), the government has made a determined effort to promote the use of ethyl alcohol (ethanol) as a partial (or total) substitute for petrol in automobiles.

Even if the programmes to produce nuclear energy and to substitute alcohol for petrol succeed, the problem remains that the development patterns which 'modernized' the southern part of Brazil—in the sense of introducing the latest gadgets and products of industrialized countries—have benefited only approximately 20 per cent of the population, who are concentrated in large cities. Thus a situation has arisen in which there are, in effect, two countries in one: a reasonably well-developed section that includes 20 per cent of the population, and an underdeveloped section that includes the remaining 80 per cent of the population living either in the north-east under conditions of poverty or in slums in the big cities.

Although the total population growth rate in Brazil is 2.9 per cent per year, the growth rate for the rural population is 2.3 per cent whereas that for the urban population is 6.13 per cent per year. Thus, in addition to meeting the requirements of the high general rate of growth, energy production must meet the requirements of the even higher rate of urban population growth. Up to now, the high rates of growth of energy production (approximately 10 per cent per year for all sources; 12.5 per cent per year for hydroelectric power) (Fig. 16.6) have been able to keep pace with population growth, but how long this rapid growth rate can be sustained is a fundamental question because, in developed countries, such growth rates in general are not higher than 5 per cent per year.

The possible utilization of wind energy, thermal gradient of oceans, tidal power, and other new sources of energy has been discussed in Brazil, but the work being conducted on these techniques can be generally regarded as following the 'state of the art'.

Possible solutions

There are several possible solutions to Brazil's energy problems. Here I will discuss biomass and the alcohol programme, hydroelectric power, solar energy, nuclear energy, and conservation measures.

Biomass and the alcohol programme

The average intensity of solar radiation over most of Brazil is approximately twice the intensity in the United States, and this, together with other conditions, such as humidity, permits rapid growth of most types of vegetation.

Wood is not being extensively utilized in Brazil for the production of ethanol and methanol. Recently, however, with the alcohol programme becoming an important government priority, much research is being conducted on the possibility of growing various plant crops for alcohol production.

Technically the idea of using alcohol as a petrol substitute is feasible: present internal combustion engines can use or be converted to run on ethanol, and the huge amounts needed could be produced, mainly from sugar-cane, in Brazil.[9] Alcohol can be mixed with petrol without any changes in present day internal combustion engines in any amount up to 20 per cent. Although ethyl alcohol has a calorific content that is 39 per cent lower per litre than petrol, there are other compensating factors: ethanol has a higher density than petrol, and the power of a motor running on alcohol is 18 per cent higher than a motor running on petrol. The overall result is that only 1.4 per cent more alcohol is consumed than petrol. Motors running on 100 per cent alcohol can be produced with minor modifications of the present ones.[10]

Typical goals of the Brazilian alcohol programme are given in Table 16.11.[11] The amounts of land that would be needed for some of these scenarios are very large.[12] Of Brazil's total area of 850×10^6 hectares,

Table 16.11. Goals of the alcohol programme in Brazil. The scenarios are as follows: (1) 20 per cent alcohol added to petrol plus 10^9 litres for industry; (2) 100 per cent alcohol plus 10^9 litres for industry; (3) 100 per cent alcohol plus 50 per cent of the diesel oil consumption; (4) 100 per cent alcohol plus 100 per cent diesel oil consumption

Scenario	*Production (litres/year $\times 10^9$)*	*Cultivated area needed in 1000 ha of sugar-cane**
1	4	1000
2	16	4400
3	22	6000
4	33	9000

*The average agricultural productivity was taken as 60 tons per hectare and industrial output as 70 litres per ton. One hectare is equivalent to 10000 m² or 2.47 acres.

approximately 70 × 10^6 ha are fertile lands. If one assumes that by the year 2000 the total amount of fertile land will increase to 14 per cent (120 × 10^6 ha), approximately 20 per cent of that land would be necessary to produce all the alcohol needed by then (almost twice the amount for scenario 4 in Table 16.11). This would correspond to 3 per cent of the Brazilian territory being covered by sugar-cane—a difficult goal to achieve and probably an undesirable one.

The overall efficiency of alcohol production from different crops is indicated in Table 16.12.[13] In the case of sugar-cane, the energy gain is 2.40 with a total production of 3564 tonnes per hectare. This corresponds to an efficiency of solar energy utilization of a few tenths of a per cent (0.3 to 0.4 per cent). It is assumed that the bagasse is used as a combustible in the alcohol distillation plants. There is, however, a surplus of bagasse that could be used to generate electricity as a by-product in a 'cogeneration' process.

Hydroelectric power

The average annual growth of Brazilian hydroelectric consumption in the last 15 years has been 12.5 per cent. By 1985 all the reserves of the south-eastern part of the country will have been used up and it will be necessary for the southern region to consume electricity generated in the Amazon tributaries.

Long-distance lines will therefore be needed, and possibly the use of direct-current high voltage transmission to minimize losses that are inevitable with the usual methods of transmission. The construction of a 4.5 million-kilowatt hydroelectric power plant located on the Tucurui River in the Amazon Basin is being considered; the electricity produced would be consumed locally in the production of aluminium from bauxite instead of being transported long distances. Ideas of this type have been studied in some detail by Strout[14] and probably deserve further consideration.

Some smaller hydroelectric power plants remain to be built in the State of São Paulo such as Porto Primavera and Ilha Grande on the Paraná River. Water resources might also be used more economically; for example, reversible stations could be constructed on the Serra do Mar where water could be pumped uphill during off-peak hours.[15] Another 10000 MW could be made available through this method.

A new idea receiving much discussion involves the use of 'bulb type' generators that can work efficiently in small waterfalls (2 to 20 metres) or in fast-moving streams.[16] Costs of these turbines compete favourably with the conventional ones, and they produce from 10 kW to 10 MW of electricity. Such 'mini' hydroelectric generating stations are adequate for decentralized electricity dispensing with expensive transmission lines. They are economically competitive and have been used for at least 15 years in France, Germany, Japan, England, and a few other countries, but have been used in only a few locations in the United States.

Solar energy

The most significant projects for the use of solar energy in Brazil are those for drying

Table 16.12. Annual energy balance in alcohol production

Crop	*Agricultural yield (tonnes/ha)*	*Alcohol production (litres/ha)*	*Energy (Mcal/ha)* Required	*Energy (Mcal/ha)* Produced	*Energy (Mcal/ha)* Gain
Sugar-cane	54	3564	14952	36297	2.40
Cassava	14.5	2523	12751	18783	1.45
Sorghum	32.5	3775	16554	31689	1.92

agricultural products and for heating water for industrial or hospital use. In one such project, 1000 m^2 of flat plate collectors are being installed in the roof of the University Hospital at São Paulo (400 beds). The water heated by the collectors will be used to provide steam and for other purposes. The total energy consumption of this hospital is approximately 1800 tonnes of fuel oil per year, and it is expected that 15 to 20 per cent of this fuel oil will be saved by solar energy utilization. The same method will be used in some textile and food industries; it has been estimated that the total energy consumption in the industrial sector in Brazil could be reduced by 5 per cent by this method.[17]

The project for grain drying is being developed at the University of Campinas where it has been shown that 10 tonnes of sorghum per day can be successfully dried under economically competitive conditions.

Nuclear energy

The strong pressure to guarantee the supply and prosperity of the large cities in the São Paulo–Rio de Janeiro area has encouraged the inclusion of nuclear reactors in plans to provide alternative energy sources in Brazil, although paradoxically there are enormous hydroelectric reserves in other parts of the country. After a long period of hesitation, a 624-MW nuclear reactor was purchased in 1969 from Westinghouse for construction in Angra dos Reis, Rio de Janeiro. This pressurized water reactor (PWR), which is due to start operation in 1979, is fuelled with enriched uranium, and it was almost totally constructed by US technicians. No transfer of technology was contemplated and participation of Brazilian industry was restricted to the civil works and some low technology equipment. The decision to purchase this reactor was strongly criticized by many scientists and by industry spokesmen because it increased Brazil's dependence on foreign imports. Sensitive to that criticism, the government in 1974 embarked on an ambitious nuclear programme in co-operation with West Germany whereby Brazil would achieve complete autonomy in the nuclear field over a period of 15 years.

Eight PWR's (1300 MW each) were scheduled to be installed in Brazil with an increasing index of nationalization that should come close to 100 per cent in 1990. A semi-industrial uranium enrichment plant (250 tonnes per year) was to be built in Brazil based on the jet-nozzle method. In addition, a plutonium-reprocessing plant was to be built by German enterprises. In all cases companies were to be formed in which the Brazilian government would be dominant but there would be German associates (and in some cases private Brazilian capital).

Although there was some initial enthusiasm for such a comprehensive nuclear programme, the difficulties soon became apparent. First, the feasibility of uranium enrichment (which is essential if any real autonomy is sought) was viewed with strong scepticism by many scientists because the Becker jet-nozzle method to be used was not considered a proved method; for many years to come, therefore, enriched uranium would have had to be purchased from other suppliers. The achievement of 'nuclear independence' was therefore in the far distant future.

Secondly, the transfer of technology was not successful from the very start; disagreements on the role to be played by Brazilian local industry and German industries surfaced and it became apparent that the programme would benefit the German nuclear industry in Germany and not in Brazil.

Thirdly, the role of Brazilian scientists and technological institutes was neither properly defined nor given much attention; this strengthened the suspicions that no real transfer of technology was to occur.

Finally, the planned installation of a plutonium-processing plant raised strong objections in the United States because such a plant would constitute an added danger to nuclear proliferation.

These problems caused the programme to

be delayed, and the urgency of nuclear energy in Brazil is now being reassessed. Most Brazilian scientists and industrialists would probably prefer a more modest programme in which they could play a dominant role and acquire the necessary technology. The construction of a prototype nuclear reactor—preferably working on the thorium cycle—would probably be the most appropriate choice from the point of view of Brazilians familiar with nuclear problems.

Conservation measures

Although a number of energy-saving methods have been suggested, the only practical actions taken by the government have been in the direction of reducing petrol consumption in private automobiles and in trucks. To this effect the following measures were adopted about a year ago: (i) limitation of the maximum speed on roads to 50 miles per hour; (ii) gradual banning of cars from the centres of large cities to discourage people from driving their own cars to work or to go shopping; (iii) improvement of the bus system with the introduction of 'executive' buses and exclusive bus-lanes; (iv) closing of petrol stations in the evenings and weekends; (v) gradual price increases for petrol; (vi) the addition of up to 20 per cent ethyl alcohol to the petrol used by cars in some cities.

A precise evaluation of these measures has not been made, but a modest decrease (7 per cent) in petrol consumption occurred in 1977 which is encouraging if one considers that the number of cars increased by about 10 per cent. Some of the more drastic suggestions made were not adopted, such as allowing the use of cars only on alternate days according to the last digit in their licence plates (odd digit, odd days; even digit, even days), or rationing petrol according to quotas. The suggestion to limit the power of cars produced by manufacturers (which is a better petrol-saving measure than velocity limitation) was also refused. Many industries and bus and truck companies, however, are shifting away from petrol to diesel oil, which is cheaper by a factor of 2.

Cars are generally smaller in Brazil than in the United States, but they are not very efficient; this upsets the gain due to the smaller weight. Although detailed data are not available for comparison, the average consumption seems to be 20 to 30 per cent higher for cars of corresponding sizes in the United States; this may be related to the lower quality of the petrol used in Brazil and to less efficient motors. Important improvements could be made on these two counts as in other countries.

It is interesting to point out, however, that price increases alone were not very successful in Brazil in discouraging people to drive cars. This indicates that the class of people owning cars has enough money—and a strong adherence to the established habit of driving—to afford price increases; or, perhaps, they give up other goods so that they can continue to drive their cars. People with lower incomes are discriminated against by high prices; the number of prospective car owners is reduced, and this creates a situation that ultimately will affect the economic health of the automobile industry.

Conclusions

It is evident that Brazil has plenty of renewable energy resources but very modest reserves of fossil fields. The present energy problems of the country are the consequence of industrialization having been based largely on imported fossil fuels in an era of cheap and abundant petroleum.

In order to utilize Brazil's renewable energy sources—mainly hydroelectric power and biomass—the people will have to make considerable social adjustments. These adjustments will probably include the relocation of some of the producing centres so that they are closer to the hydroelectric plants, and a general decentralization of the urban centres. This does not mean a 'return to the fields' or to a more primitive type of civilization, but a redistribution of the amenities of modern life in a way more compatible with nature. The pollution in the air and water of the city of São Paulo has already reached such proportions that there is strong political support for decentralization.

To reduce energy consumption, restrictions on the use of automobiles will probably have to be imposed, and there will have to be a stronger emphasis on mass transportation. The use of rail and hydro transportation will have to be encouraged. Solar energy will probably be used directly in water heating, mainly for industrial purposes, and solar dryers may well be used in agriculture. Innovation is very fast in this area and the direct use of solar energy could become important in the future.

Biomass, for the production of alcohol as well as charcoal, will have an enormous role in the future. The historical association of the use of wood with underdevelopment will have to be counteracted by pilot projects and demonstrations of the utility of biomass. The reorientation of the steel industry towards the use of charcoal instead of mineral coal has been done to some extent and should be encouraged, together with a co-ordinated programme of reforestation.

Nuclear energy will have only a secondary role in energy production in Brazil; efforts to promote a widespread use of this form of fossil energy cannot be justified. High-grade uranium resources are small in Brazil, and serious risks would be asscciated with a new dependence on imports of nuclear fuel.

Although oil shale is abundant, the extraction of the oil poses serious technical and environmental problems, and this resource should probably be used only in the chemical and pharmaceutical industries. Recovery *in situ* might eventually prove to be an attractive technology.

In the overall picture, Brazil seems to be capable of finding within its own frontiers most of the energy needed to sustain its population.

New patterns of energy consumption will have to be adopted in Brazil. The construction of completely enclosed buildings—requiring constant air conditioning—in Brasilia and other cities in the temperate regions of the country indicated a total disregard for efficient energy use. The Portuguese colonizers some 200 years ago constructed simple but functional buildings and with some effort it should be possible for Brazilians today to design a new type of 'tropical civilization' that is appropriate to the environment.

References and notes

1. Except when specifically noted, data in this article are taken from *Anuário Estatístico do Brasil 1975*. Instituto Brasileiro de Geografia e Estatistica, Rio de Janeiro (1975); *Balanco energético nacional*. Ministério de Minas e Energia, Brasilia (1977); and from (2).
2. *Estatistica Brasileira de Energia*, Biannual Bulletin of the Brazilian National Committee of the World Energy Conference No. 19, Rio de Janeiro (1974).
3. Wilberg, J. A. *Energia Elet.* **35**, 25 (1973).
4. Wilson, C. L. *Energy—global prospects 1985–2000, report on the Workshop on Alternative Energy Strategies*. McGraw-Hill, New York (1977); Goldemberg, J. unpublished data.
5. The exponent p, in the relation $E = k(I)^p$, which is called 'income elasticity of energy demand', can easily be shown to be the ratio of the rate of growth of energy consumption ($\Delta E/E$) to the rate of per capita income ($\Delta I/I$). For developed countries this ratio is approximately one or even smaller; it is much larger than one for underdeveloped countries.
6. Ross, M. H. and Williams, R. H. *Energy and economic growth*. Report prepared for the Joint Economic Committee of the US Congress. Government Printing Office, Washington DC (1977).
7. Beirutti, P. A. *Ciênc. Cult.* (*São Paulo*) **29** (No. 3), 274 (1977).
8. Colombi Neto, J. thesis, Universidade de São Paulo (1975).
9. Goldemberg, J., paper presented at the Fourth Annual College of Biological Sciences Colloquium, Columbus, Ohio (1977).
10. Stumpf, U. E., paper presented at XI Reunião Anual da Sociedade Brasileira de Física, São Paulo (1977).
11. Licio, A. M. A. *Etanol: combustível e matéria prima*, Semana de Tecnologia Industrial, Ministério da Indústria e Comercio, Rio de Janeiro (1976).

12. Gomes da Silva, J., paper presented at XI Reunião Anual da Sociedade Brasileira de Física, São Paulo (1977).
13. Gomes da Silva, J., Serra, G. E., Moreira, J. R., Goncalves, J. C., Goldemberg, J. *Science* (in press).
14. Strout, A. The future of nuclear power in developing countries (unpublished paper). MIT Energy Laboratory (1976).
15. Garcez, L. N., in *Energia no Brasil* (ed. J. Goldemberg), p. 73. Academia de Ciências do Estado de São Paulo (1976).
16. Luca, C., Koelle, E., Junqueira, J. L. A., in ibid., p. 83.
17. Martin, J. V. and Goldemberg, G., unpublished data.
18. Roa, G. and Villa, L. G., personal communication.
19. I thank R. H. Williams of the Center for Environmental Studies for a complete revision of the manuscript and for useful discussions.

17

Energy profile of Brazil

ERIC J. JEFFS

Brazil is the largest, most populous, and potentially the wealthiest country in Latin America. It has an abundance of water power and some of the richest and most extensive deposits in the world of such important industrial raw materials as iron ore, bauxite, and manganese. But if, in the present economic climate, foreign observers are apt to temper their enthusiasm with caution, the mood of ministers is one of quiet confidence that everything will come right in the end. Above all, Brazil wants to be in a position to deliver the goods when the world wants them.

Energy is a key element in the country's development; energy for industry, mining and mineral processing, transport, and the affluent society of the industrial south-east. Brazil's great strength is in water power and here lies a dilemma: most of the remaining hydroelectric potential is in the wrong place, far from the major load centres. There is coal in the south, of relatively poor quality and worked on a scale far short of that of hydroelectric energy supply. The search for oil off the coast has not fulfilled the promise of early discoveries; and the extent of uranium reserves as a whole has yet to be determined.

Within Brazilian territory are two of the world's great river systems—the Amazon and the Parana—the one an accumulation of the flows of several mighty jungle rivers, each a substantial energy source in its own right, and the other, flowing south-west from the coastal ranges and the southern highlands, destined to become a power staircase, like its tributaries, serving the burgeoning industrial load centres of São Paulo and Rio de Janeiro.

But what will happen when the Parana has been fully developed? This is the question preoccupying Brazilian energy planners. The Amazon tributaries are the obvious alternatives if water-power development continues, but the most promising sites are so far away that economic transmission of their energy can be bought only with a new technical development for which the rest of the world has yet to show any need, or else massive, energy-intensive industrial developments must be made in the mineral-rich, sparsely populated, jungle-clad Amazon Basin.

Such developments, to be of an economically viable size, are beyond the scope of Brazil to finance herself. Yet they need to be done to earn foreign currency to service international loans and sustain industrial development at home. There is a triangular relationship with which Brazil has to come to terms. New mining developments must earn income which can help finance the energy projects which are a necessary adjunct to the development of the mines and processing plants.

First published in *Energy International*, Vol. 13, No. 9 (September 1976), pp. 21–3. Reprinted by permission of *Energy International*.

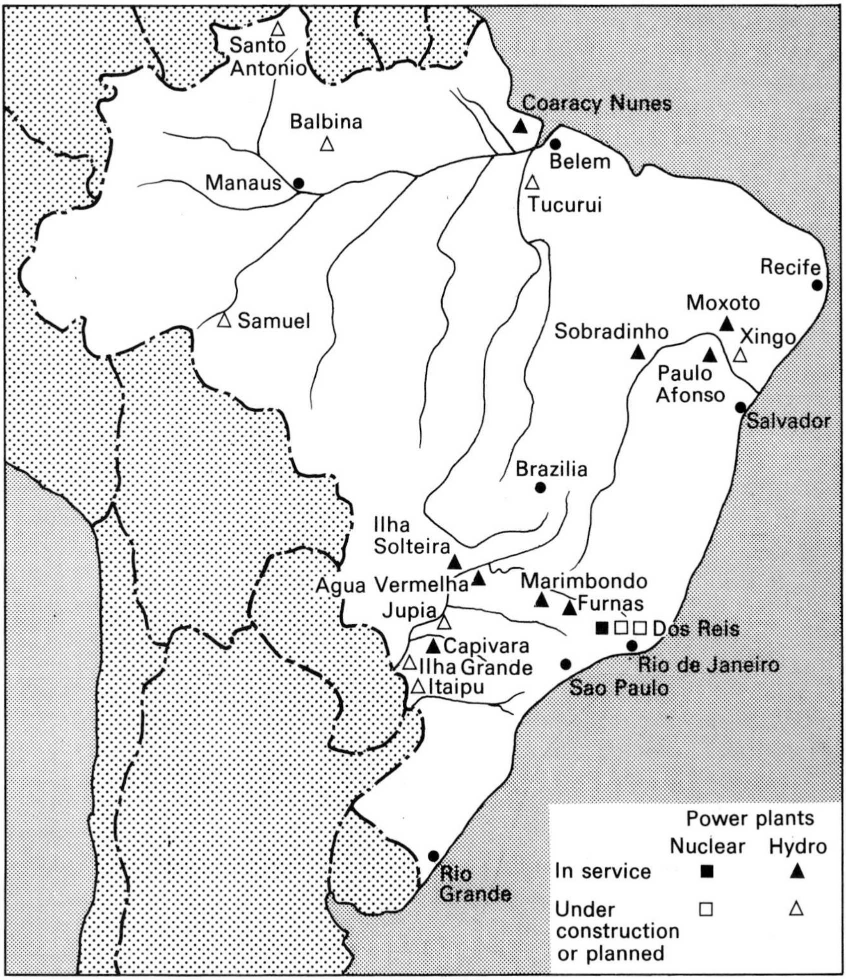

Fig. 17.1. The extent to which the major river systems of Brazil have already been, and will continue to be, exploited for energy supply is shown on this map on which, for the sake of clarity, only the major power projects are marked.

Significant to this process is the capacity of Brazilian industry to manufacture what would otherwise be imported. This is most noticeable in consumer goods where most of the familiar European names appear in the shops and three cars out of four on the streets of São Paulo are Volkswagens, all locally manufactured. Brazil also manufactures water turbines, transformers, motors and other electrical products, a wide range of industrial equipment, and even a commuter aircraft—the twin-turbo prop Bandeirante, which flies many of the low-density regional routes from the major cities, stands favourable comparison with similar products from Canadian and US aircraft factories.

Energy demand

According to Federal Energy Minister, Shigeaki Ueki, primary energy demand in

Brazil is doubling every 10 years. In 1965 it was 49 million oil-equivalent (to-e). By 1975 it had risen to 95 million to-e and the forecast for 1985 is 190 million to-e. But in parallel with this growth, federal policy is to reduce the share of the primary energy market covered by oil and gas while building up the contributions of hydro and nuclear energy.

In 1975, oil accounted for 46 per cent of primary energy demand over the whole country (substantially more in the north-east). Nationally, the aim is to cut back this share to 41 per cent by 1980 and 37 per cent by 1985. One contributory factor will be the development of electrified mass transit systems in the major cities and the electrification of new and existing railway lines.

Development of major hydroelectric schemes in the south-east will boost the contribution of hydro-power in the years ahead. In 1965 it accounted for only 15 per cent of total energy demand and had only climbed to a 22 per cent share 10 years later. The forecast is for 27 per cent of the market by 1980 and 32 per cent by 1985. In the longer term, much depends on the proportion of national primary energy demand taken by mining and mineral processing, and dependent infrastructure activities in the Amazon Basin.

The last decade has seen a dramatic fall in the consumption of the natural renewable organic fuels, such as wood, charcoal, and bagasse. Their share of the market has fallen from 46 per cent in 1965 to 22 per cent in 1975. It is expected that the decline will continue and stabilize with these fuels holding a 15 per cent share of the 1985 energy market.

The fact that these are renewable fuels has been seized upon by researchers elsewhere seeking new energy sources and has not been overlooked by the Brazilians. With a tropical climate over most of the country, the possibility of growing crops specifically for fuel is intriguing, be it for making charcoal or liquid fuels. Charcoal has certain attractions for the steel industry—a better quality alloy at 30 to 40 per cent lower cost with a 100 per cent natural carbon source. But such a strategy—a steel industry using charcoal—depends on efficient forestry practice with a short growth cycle plant.

A more promising line of approach is the use of alcohol from sugar-cane residues as a petrol stretcher. It is also used as feedstock in the chemical industry. Present production is about 700000 m^3/year, for all uses, but it is planned to bring a new plant in service with a capacity between 2.5 and 3 million m^3/year. Mixed with petrol, alcohol offers an improvement in octane rating, though more important in the future is the extension of petrol supplies and hence the reduced rate of oil consumption for transportation that would result from such practices applied on a larger scale.

Nuclear energy is late appearing on the scene. The country's first nuclear power plant—a 600 MW(e) Westinghouse PWR at Angra dos Reis—was delayed in the early stages of construction and will not be in service until the latter half of 1978. On an adjacent site, trial borings were in progress earlier this year, preparatory to construction of the first four units initially ordered from Kraftwerk Union last year. So far only two of the 1300 MW(e) plants have been allocated to the Angra dos Reis site, 200 km south of Rio. Other sites have yet to be determined, but it is thought possible that one will be in the south of the country in Rio Grande do Sul or Santa Catharina Provinces and another may go to the north-east.

Massive though the nuclear deal was with the Germans—four 1300 MW(e) power plants, four options, and technical assistance and hardware to develop a complete fuel cycle capability from mining through enrichment and fuel fabrication to reprocessing, in exchange for a guarantee of uranium supplies for German nuclear power stations—it must be seen in the context of electricity supply overall. The nuclear plan is long-term, a total of 11000 MW(e) of plant, the last of which will come into service some time after the 12600 MW, 18-unit Itaipu hydro plant is complete in the late eighties. Indeed, by 1990, nuclear generating capacity will account for about 15 per cent of electricity supply, with the remainder, some 70000 MW overwhelmingly hydroelectric.

Hydro, in fact, is destined to be the dominant component of electricity supply for many years to come, and base-load hydro at that. Much of future development, particularly in the northern rivers feeding the Amazon, will initially be linked with mineral developments, but even at remote distances when the costs of construction are inevitably higher and transmission costs add a disproportionately large component to the delivered price of a unit of electricity to the consumer, it is a competitive alternative to other and newer energy supply systems that could be built in the south of the country where the energy loads are greatest. There are doubts, for instance, on the wisdom of pursuing oil distillation from shales, of which there are deposits in the country. A 50000 bbl/day (net) plant would require an investment of $1.5 billion: the same money could build a hydro plant that would represent a saving of 150000 bbl/day of oil.

Hydro-energy represented 92 per cent of total electricity supply in 1975. Nuclear power was adopted as a back-up to provide a much needed thermal component. In present circumstances it is significantly cheaper than other fossil-fuelled base load capacity. Hydro is still the cheapest, at 10 to 13 mill/kWh, with nuclear at 17 to 20 mill and fossil-fuelled plant at 30 to 35 mill/kWh.

Regional utilities

There are approximately 500 public and private utilities in Brazil, of which there are 15 which are considered the most important in terms of their size, technical capabilities, and financial resources. At the head of this structure is Eletrobras, the state-owned management company.

Eletrobras was founded in 1962 to co-ordinate the operations of the major utilities and to draw up plans for development of electricity supply in the regions. This it does through a series of monthly report meetings with the major utilities and through the submission of regional plans to the Government each year. There are four regional operating subsidiaries responsible for bulk power generation and transmission within their spheres of influence.

Largest of these subsidiaries is Furnas, which covers the main industrial and population centres of the south-east. Its area of operations covers principally São Paulo and Minas Gerais States, and includes the Parana River and its major tributaries—Rio Grande, Tiete, and Paranaiba. It operates six hydroelectric plants and one oil-fired plant, the 450 MW Santa Cruz plant south-west of Rio. Two other hydro plants are under construction—Marimbondo and Itumbiara, and the nuclear plant at Angra dos Reis. Total generating capacity is at present about 4500 MW.

CHESF (Centrais Hidroelectricas São Francisco) serves the north-eastern states, which include the cities of Salvador and Recife. It is a poorer region of the country, dependent on agriculture and prone to, alternatively, drought and flooding. The major generating resource is the Sao Francisco River which rises in the vicinity of Brasilia and flows north and eastwards to the sea, about 200 km south of Recife. On this river is situated the Paulo Afonso–Moxoto complex, which is the largest generating resource on their system.

The southernmost states, south of São Paulo state are served by Eletrosul. This region of the country contains less hydro power potential than the others and is the centre of the coal industry. However, the coal is of poor quality and is unlikely to be developed for electricity generation on any large scale.

Lastly, there is Eletronorte, created in 1974 to further the development of electricity supply in the north and study the power potential of rivers feeding into the Amazon. Unlike the other Eletrobras subsidiaries it is permitted to sell energy direct to the consumer and assist in the social and economic development of the region. The utility serves a very thinly populated region of isolated networks, and much of its future growth will be tied in the development of mining and mineral processing and transportation links out of virgin jungle.

After Eletrobras and its subsidiaries, the next most important are the State utilities and the major private companies serving the major centres of population. The most important of these are CESP, serving São Paulo, CEMIG, in Minas Gerais, and LIGHT, a private Canadian financed distribution utility serving the metropolitan areas of Rio and São Paulo, which account for almost 50 per cent of all electricity sales.

Electricity consumption is concentrated in the south-east. In 1975 it amounted to 68 603 GWh, of which 75 per cent was in the central (Furnas) region and 11 per cent in the north-east, 12 per cent in the south and 2 per cent in the north. Eletrobras forecast that by 1980, the central region will be taking 70 per cent of an estimated 122 700 GWh, with the north-east taking 14 per cent, the south 13 per cent, and the north 3 per cent. Almost all of this additional energy will be derived from hydro plants now under construction.

18

Itaipu: the world's largest power station

JERRY MAZZONE

The Itaipu power project on the Parana River, on which work has now started, when completed, will produce 12600 MW and will have cost between \$5 and \$6 billion. According to Rubens Vianna de Andrade, construction superintendent of Itaipu Binacional, the joint company set up by the governments of Brazil and Paraguay to oversee the construction of the power station, it does not involve any new technological problems that have not already been solved in similar Brazilian projects. The only real problem is the sheer magnitude of the enterprise, which demands enormous financial, technological, and organizational resources.

The first decisions on this giant hydroelectric project were taken by the two countries in 1966 when an agreement was signed under which a survey was to be made of the hydroelectric potential of the Parana between the Sete Quedas Falls and the mouth of the Iguacu River. It was also agreed that the power produced by an eventual plant would be equally shared by both countries with each having first rights to the purchase of power from the other. In this case, Brazil, which will use the bulk of the power generated to supply its industrialized south-east, will pay Paraguay for her share in dollars.

The first studies to find an ideal location for the dam and to estimate the river's energy potential were made by a consortium of International Engineering Co (IECO) of San Francisco and Electroconsult SpA of Milan, Italy.

Ten locations were studied as possible dam sites in the Sete Quedas–Iguacu stretch of the river and 50 different system combinations of dams, channels, and power houses were considered. In the consultants' final report to the two governments, two proposals were submitted: a single dam at the point of the river called Itaipu to exploit the entire power potential in one giant power plant; or two dams, one at Itaipu and the other at Santa Maria 150 km up-river with a power house at each dam. A single dam at Itaipu was chosen by the joint Paraguay–Brazil commission.

Finally in 1974 Itaipu Binacional was created to oversee the project. In that same year this organization chose the IECO–Electroconsult consortium to draw up overall plans for the project as well as those for the diversion channel and the left-bank rock dam. Brazilian and Paraguayan consultants and engineering firms were chosen to plan the main dam and penstocks, the power house, the earth dams and navigations works, and the spillway.

The 4000 km-long Parana River, with a basin covering an area of 3 million km^2, is one of the world's largest waterways. It begins with the confluence of the Parnaiba and Rio Grande in South Central Brazil,

First published in *Energy International*, Vol. 13, No. 9 (September 1976), pp. 23–5. Reprinted by permission of *Energy International*.

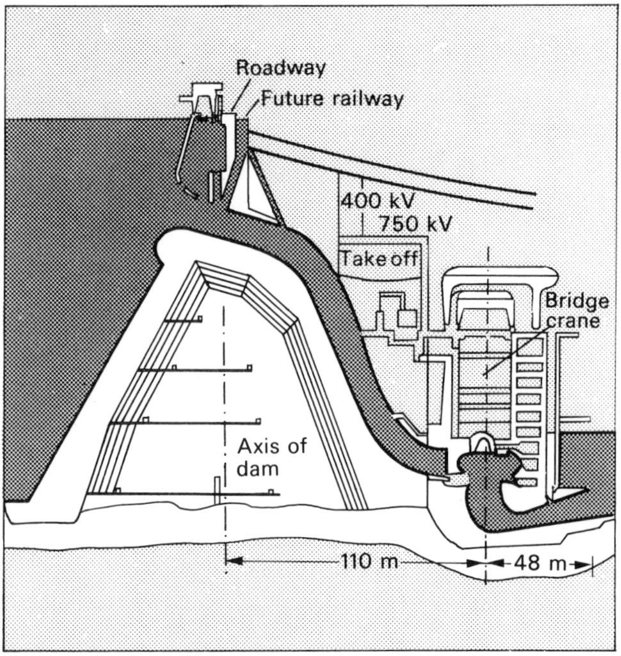

Fig. 18.1. Section through power house and hollow gravity section forming central region of the total dam structure.

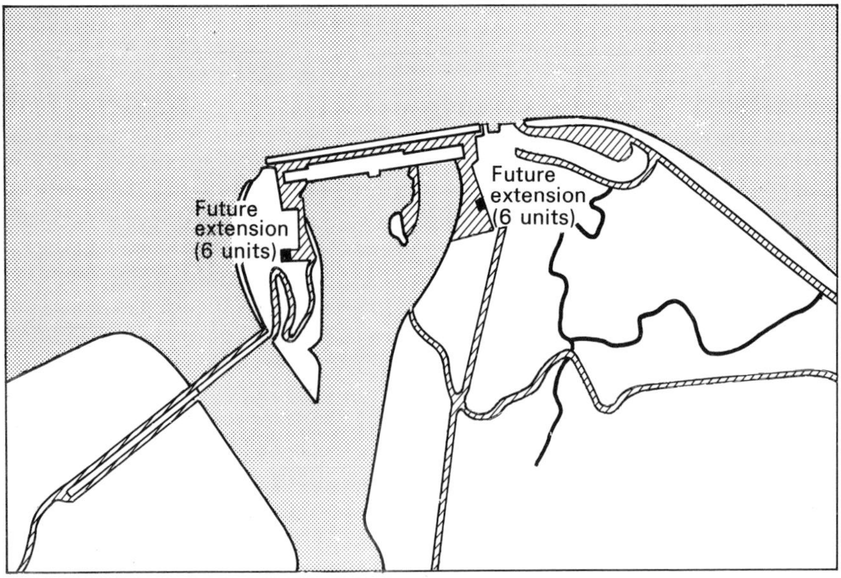

Fig. 18.2 The overall plan of Itaipu with 14 units of the plant installed in the river bed and 4 in the diversion channel. The wing dam creates an area in which a further extension could be built in the dry in later years.

runs south-east over the Sete Quedas Falls between Paraguay and Brazil to the point where it receives the Iguacu River. From there it runs between Paraguay and Argentina, turns west, and, after receiving the Paraguay River, its main tributary, continues south through Argentina until it is joined by the Uruguay at Buenos Aires to form the River Plate Estuary in the South Atlantic. The Itaipu project is located between Sete Quedas Falls and the Iguacu River, this 190 km stretch of the river flows through a deep valley carved in basalt. In the first 60 km to Porto Mendes the river drops 100 m and in the remaining 130 km to the Iguacu, by 20 m.

At Itaipu the Parana is 400 m wide and from 25 to 45 m deep. The power project itself consists basically of a main concrete dam across the river with the power house in the base of this dam. On the right bank of the river there will be a lateral concrete dam, a spillway with gates and canals for flooding as well as an earth dyke. On the left bank the main dam is complemented by a rock dam and a compacted earth dyke. Damming the river will create a reservoir 170 km long covering a total of 1460 km^2 and with storage of 29 billion m^3 of water.

A diversion channel was built so that the main concrete dam and the power house can be built in a dry bed; it has a flow of 30000 m^3/s. The average flow of the river from 1931 to 1970 was 8460 m^3/s. A structure will be built in the diversion channel for control and for eventually closing it when the reservoir is filled. Later, this structure can be used for the penstocks of four of the generating units. Two cofferdams each 70 m high, built in the main channel will enclose a dry area where the foundation of the main dam and the power house will be built. When the project is completed the upstream cofferdam will remain in place while the one downstream will be partly removed.

Two basic alternatives were proposed for the main dam: a gravity dam which would require 915 million m^3 of concrete, or a hollow gravity type with 7.6 million m^3 of concrete. The second option was chosen, but, although more economical, it is more difficult to execute. However, it appears that the civil contractors are well prepared for this type of operation. The main concrete dam will be 1500 m long and its crest 224 m above datum. The foundations will rest on solid basalt 48 m above datum. Lower breccia layers will be sealed and drain curtains will be installed, together with restoration of decomposed layers by concreting.

On the right bank, the principal dam will link up with the spillway by means of another curved, concrete dam 775 m long and 224 m above datum and 40 to 55 m high. Here, 460000 m^3 of concrete will be used. This lateral curved dam is designed to guide the flow of water during discharges towards the spillway which will be connected with the bank by an earth dam 840 m long, 30 m high with 300000 m^3 of compacted fill. A lateral earth dyke 4.5 km west of the main dam, near the Paraguayan town of Hernandarias, will close off a depression where drainage would occur when the reservoir is full. On the left bank there will be a rock dam 2200 m long and 70 m high. In continuation from this rock dam there will be a compacted earth dam 2000 m long, 30 m high. The two dams will total in length 4200 m and will be 225 m above datum, 1 m above the crest level of the main dam.

Located on the right bank to take advantage of more favourable morphological conditions, the spillway will include an entrance channel and concrete floodway with 13 steel radial gates 20 $\times$ 20 m at the 200 m level and three more radial gates 13 $\times$ 13 m at the 207 m level. The concrete-covered floodway that will carry the discharge back to the river downstream from the main dam will be divided into five separate channels to facilitate flood control as well as maintenance of the system. The project is planned for a maximum flood of 50000 m^3/s and 58000 m^3/s for reservoir levels of 200 m (maximum normal) and 222 m (maximum exceptional) respectively. Studies are being made to cut down depletion. For discharge of floating trash there will be a small channel with a 9 $\times$ 4 m gate.

The power house is planned for 18 Francis-type turbine-generator sets at intervals of 37 m. Fourteen of these generators will be located in the river channel and the other four in the diversion channel. The total length of the power house is 945 m including three assembly areas and a central control room 91 m high and 70 m wide. The generating units will be installed in pairs which will be hydraulically independent, each pair isolated from the others in case of flooding. Each pair will also have its own pumping equipment.

The nominal potential of each unit is 635 MW with a guaranteed minimum—during minimum lows—of 520 MW and a maximum of 700 MW. This means that the total nominal potential of Itaipu will be 11 430 MW with a minimum of 9 360 MW and a maximum of 12 600 MW. The turbines will be rated for a minimum flow of 625 m^3/s and a maximum of 750 m^3/s with a head range from 90 to 124 m. The transformer platform will be located at the 139 m level between the power house and the dam and the transformers will be connected to the generators by 23 kV lines. It has been planned to have 18 groups of three single transformers of 250 MVA with nine groups of 23/400 kV and nine groups of 23/800 kV with transmission lines to substations on both banks.

The power house will have auxiliary equipment and services such as a heavy overhead crane of 1900 tonnes and two others of 250 tonnes each for assembly and maintenance purposes. Three assembly areas have been planned, each with its own 50-tonne overhead bridge crane.

Itaipu will produce other benefits such as flood control and navigation systems which will permit the use of the Parana River for transportation. Locks will be installed at the dam and in the area of Sete Quedas Falls there will also be a canal and locks.

19

Alternative energy technologies in Brazil

J. M. MICCOLIS

It is imperative that Brazil should consider alternative energy production and conservation techniques in order to cope with one of the most demanding crises of its modern history: the so-called 'energy crisis'. To mention just one of the most serious consequences of the current situation, Brazil imports about 650000 barrels of petroleum per day, which accounts for more than 78 per cent of total consumption, at an annual cost of more than $3 billion. Oil amounts to 50 per cent of the total energy utilized in Brazil. Over the past few years several steps have been taken in the direction of reducing Brazilian dependence on external sources of energy. Alternative energy production technologies have been examined. Some of them are very promising medium-term solutions, and are mostly in the research and development stage. Others offer attractive short-term possibilities and are currently in the initial stages of implementation.

Energy conservation measures that have been undertaken in the past 3 years have not been very successful. Despite sharp rises in fuel prices, internal consumption is rising consistently at a rapid rate. More recently, however, the Brazilian government has enacted much tougher conservation measures that are expected to change substantially the energy consumption pattern in the country. This paper is an attempt to report the major alternative energy activities under way in Brazil.

Solar energy

Brazil occupies a vast region in which solar energy is conveniently available. The country encompasses an area of more than 8.5 million square kilometres, almost entirely located between the Equator and the Tropic of Capricorn. Solar energy is now considered capable of playing an important supporting role on a medium- and long-term basis in the country's energy matrix, since the economic comparisons that always made it unwise to convert solar energy into other forms of energy are no longer valid. Although several scattered efforts to develop solar energy applications in Brazil occurred before 1973, by the end of that year the first comprehensive government attention was devoted to solar energy with the creation of a task force, within the government's planning structure, to examine all possible alternative energy technologies that could be applicable to the Brazilian situation. Solar energy was chosen as one of the potentially successful candidates. A national solar energy research and development plan was prepared

The full version of this paper was first published in Norman L. Brown (ed.) *Renewable Energy Resources and Rural Applications in the Developing World*, AAAS Selected Symposium No. 6 (Westview Press, Boulder, Colorado, 1978). This volume is based on papers presented at the 143rd Annual Meeting of the American Association for the Advancement of Science, Denver, Colorado, 23 February 1977. Reprinted by permission of the author and the AAAS.

by the task force, and following approval by the proper authorities resources were allocated and the plan's implementation started by the end of 1974.

The underlying philosophy of the research and development plan for solar energy in Brazil took into account several different factors: socio-economic and natural resources particular to the country, which differ from region to region; the immediately available and easily improvable capability of local research institutions; and what appeared to be the state-of-the-art of solar energy conversion techniques at that time.

The plan's budget for the period 1974–5 was $2.5 million, in 1974 prices, and focused mainly on solar energy conversion processes that could be classified as 'low-technology' applications. Some basic research was also funded. The main projects within the plan included the development of collectors, dryers, distillation and refrigeration units, bioconversion, solar architecture, and solarimetry.

Ocean thermal gradients

Harvesting the solar energy collected and stored in tropical waters (Ocean Thermal Energy Conversion: OTEC) has received considerable attention in the US in the past few years. A heat engine can operate by means of using warm surface-water as a heat source, and the much colder deep ocean water as a heat sink. The idea is not technically new and it seems feasible with current technology. Some regions along the Brazilian coast present optimum natural conditions for the development of this process. In the Cabo Frio region of the Brazilian coast, east of Rio de Janeiro along the Tropic of Capricorn, the deep sea water, cold and nutrient-rich, comes to the surface. An attempt will be made to generate power using this water, related to an aquaculture research project which is also using this water for ice-making, and as a basic feed for its marine cultures.

Wind power

Although windmills have been traditionally used in some regions of Brazil, regional wind patterns are not well known. A small-scale research project aimed at developing a vertical axis Savonius* wind conversion system is under way.

Solar energy perspectives

If solar energy is going to play any role in the Brazilian energy picture, then the north-east would have to be considered as the most suitable region for successful solar energy applications. Occupying a considerable portion of the Brazilian territory, the north-east includes all of the country's semi-arid region, where droughts are common, heavy rains occur within a very short period of time, and the average daily temperatures are very high. Furthermore, even measured by Brazilian standards, the north-east is an underdeveloped region. The average annual income per capita is well below the national level, birth and mortality rates are rather high, the economy is basically rural and based upon an outdated ownership and land-use model. The national solar energy research and development plan took into consideration all these factors. That is why several projects were recommended and funded: solar stills for areas where an adequate source of fresh water is not available, and where it is not relevant to make economic comparisons with technologies that cannot even be applied; crop dryers designed so that a variety of crops, maturing at different times, can be dried in sequence by use of the same equipment; solar refrigeration intended primarily for food preservation and for the storage of seasonal and perishable crops; water pumping with small solar engines for irrigation purposes; and others.

The programme has thus far failed to accomplish the development of most of the prototypes intended for an eventual

*S. J. Savonius, a Finish engineer, invented this windmill in the 1920s.

industrial production and commercialization in Brazil. This failure cannot be attributed merely to the fact that only 2 years have passed since the initial projects were funded and that, naturally, some projects have been more successful than others. It was also in part due to a lack of co-ordination among several government agencies which could have taken a much more active role in the process. For example, the federal housing agency in charge of financing thousands of low-income units throughout Brazil could have made economically feasible the large-scale production of solar water-heaters to replace the widely used, inefficient, and electricity-hungry electric resistance water heaters. Simply by changing current building regulations and by incorporating into construction costs and financing the added costs for the solar heater, an insured market would have existed, thus creating an incentive for industrial production of solar heaters. The government could also have provided incentives for the replacement of conventional fuels with solar energy to provide the low-temperature process heat used in several industries.

Bioconversion is another very promising solar energy conversion technology. Because of recent developments in Brazil and to the considerable attention that it has recently received, bioconversion possibilities in Brazil will be discussed as a separate topic in this paper.

Bioconversion

Green plants are able to utilize sunlight to produce stored chemical energy, usually but not necessarily in the form of carbohydrates. Currently, with the stored production of ancient photosynthesis—fossil fuels—running out, it appears that harnessing the renewable energy stored in green plants is not only highly desirable but increasingly feasible. The stored chemical energy can be recovered by different processes, at the end of which solid, liquid, and gaseous fuels, as well as chemical feedstocks and other products, can be obtained.

Brazil is in a very privileged position to make use of this natural energy collection process, not only because Brazil occupies a huge area where the incident average solar energy is abundant, but also due to particular local conditions such as a satisfactory combination of appropriate soils, water resources, and rainfall needed for growing green plants. Furthermore, the labour-intensive characteristics of the related agricultural processes, coupled with the availability of relatively inexpensive and arable land, could very well match the socio-economic requirements of a developing nation like Brazil. It should also be noted that owing to the extensive forest resources that are available in Brazil, it is quite probable that a number of other possibilities might exist in addition to the ones that are mentioned here. However, the possibilities described below do represent current knowledge and give a fairly accurate view of projects under consideration or presently being carried out.

Fuels and chemical feedstocks from sugar-cane

Since early in the sixteenth century, sugar-cane has been one of the major Brazilian agricultural products. In 1972 Brazil became the world's largest producer of cane-sugar (6 million tonnes per year), with about one-third of domestic production going for export. High prices in world markets during 1973–4 stimulated further increases in production to a level of 7.2 million tonnes per year.

Ethyl alcohol. Among the many by-products of the sugar-cane industry, ethyl alcohol or ethanol has been traditionally obtained in Brazil by fermentation of surplus molasses from sugar manufacture and used as an adjunct in petrol. The percentages of alcohol in petrol have varied over the years (2 to 15 per cent alcohol content); ethanol has served as a regulatory device to maintain a reasonable and profitable level of sugar-cane production in the country. Whenever there was a surplus of sugar, the production of alcohol was increased and greater amounts added to petrol.

Over the past few years ethyl alcohol production in Brazil has oscillated between 570 and 700 million litres per year (150 to 185 million gallons), of which about half was anhydrous (for mixing with petrol).

Measures recently taken by the federal government have insured the sugar-cane growers that whenever it is possible to obtain ethanol or sugar from a sugar-cane crop, both commodities would be worth the same; that is, the price is set so that the 90 kg of sugar or the 30 l of ethanol obtainable from 1 tonne of sugar-cane yield the same monetary return.

Those measures are clearly designed to stimulate ethanol production in the country, and are tied to an ambitious plan to have 75 per cent of the total liquid fuels consumed in Brazil replaced by ethyl alcohol. According to one scenario being considered, domestic petroleum production will increase from the 1975 level of 200000 barrels per day to 500000 b.p.d. in 1980, and to 1 million b.p.d. in 1990, remaining at that level to the year 2000. In the first phase (to 1980) ethyl alcohol would be blended with petrol at a 1:10 ratio, wlich does not require any major adjustments to automobile engines. In the following decade, engines would be gradually adapted to use pure alcohol so that by 1990, 50 per cent of all liquid fuels could be replaced by ethanol. By the year 2000, ethyl alcohol would account for 75 per cent of the country's consumption of liquid fuels.

In order to achieve the goals set forth by the plan, about 400 new distillaries would have to be operational by 1980, 1150 by 1990, and 3500 by 2000. This assumes distillaries of an average capacity (12500 litres/day) and harvesting periods of 160 days. It should be noted, however, that of the approximately 200 sugar mills that are responsible for the current sugar production in Brazil, more than 50 per cent are operating at only marginal profits.

Ethyl alcohol has further useful properties. Blended with petrol, it increases the octane rating of the fuel, thus reducing the need for cyclic hydrocarbons. Also, as an anti-knock additive, ethanol makes the use of lead unnecessary. As a pure fuel, ethanol does have a lower energy content per unit weight than does petrol; however, the energy content per unit weight is not the determining factor for the power generated by an internal combustion engine. Factors like the heat of combustion, thermal efficiency, etc., are important. When these factors are taken into account for petrol and for pure ethanol, it is clear that ethanol generates about 18 per cent more power. That is one of the reasons, by the way, that several racing engines use ethanol as a fuel. Ethanol consumption, though, is about 50 per cent higher than petrol consumption in a conventional, unadjusted automobile engine. However, for higher compression rates, about 10:1, and with some pre-heating of the air–ethanol mixture in the carburettor, ethanol consumption has been experimentally demonstrated to be about 15 to 20 per cent higher than that of petrol. It should also be noted that an ethanol-fuelled engine drastically reduces the emission of pollutants such as nitrogen oxides, carbon moxoide, and cyclic hydrocarbons.

Brazil is considering not only sugar-cane as the source for ethanol. Cassava, or manioc, a root-crop that grows everywhere in the country, has been the focus of considerable government attention, and will be discussed later.

Just recently the Brazilian government approved about $US500 million for implementation in 1977 of a National Alcohol Programme that includes both sugar-cane and manioc as raw materials for ethanol production.

Other fuels. Besides ethanol, a number of other fuels could be obtained from the sugar-cane biomass. By means of thermal conversion processes, the fibre could either be used as a boiler feed (combustion), which is currently done in Brazil and which makes the sugar-cane industry practically self-sufficient in energy, or converted to synthesis gas by means of processes such as Bailie, Kellog, Koppers–Totzek, Syngas, Purox, etc. Synthesis gas in a mixture of carbon monoxide and nitrogen with smaller proportions of water, carbon dioxide, ethane, and propane. It can be directly used as a low Btu gas, or processed into a pipeline gas (methanation), and/or methanol and a motor fuel by processes such as Fischer–Tropsch, Mobil. Also, by microbiological conversion techniques, similar to those used for the fermentation of molasses or cane juice into ethanol, substitute natural gas (SNG) could be obtained by fermenting the bagasse.

Chemical feedstocks. A number of chemical feedstocks are obtainable from sugar crop biomass. Through fermentation the sugar-cane juice, or the surplus molasses, can be transformed into acetone, isopropanol, butanol, butadiene, ethylene, acetaldehyde, acetic acid, xanthane, and several other polymers. Some of those products would require an initial fermentation and additional chemical synthesis, steps for which the technology is already available. Furthermore, recent advances in the field of microbial biosynthesis that make possible the production of a specific organic chemical by microbial fermentation could indeed shorten the additional chemical synthesis steps that are currently necessary, dramatically changing the economics for the production of those products.

Other products by fermentation. Sucrose is an excellent raw material for fermentation. Together with starch and starch-derived sugars it served well as a feedstock for the microbial production of several chemicals. During the post-Second World War petroleum-glut period, many of these fermentation processes were discontinued in lieu of lower-cost petroleum-based chemical syntheses. However, some products, such as citric acid, penicillin, and other antibiotics not readily derived from petroleum, continued to use fermentation as their commercial source. Since raw materials account for at least 60 per cent of the total cost of the average fermentation end-product the low cost of petroleum led to the demise in 1945–73 of many fermentation processes.

It must also be mentioned that for the most part the current reconsideration of fermentation does not yet take into account the new capabilities of present-day microbiology. Rapid, automated, and systematic, genetic-strain-improvement skills can now replace improvement efforts that were formerly the province of chance. Achievements in the antibiotic field stand as evidence of such claims.

While an in-depth study is needed to determine for local Brazilian conditions the best of the many specific product opportunities, numerous candidates may be suggested for consideration: amino acids, such as L-lysine, L-methionine, L-tryptophan; vitamins like vitamin C (ascorbic acid), vitamin B12 (cyanocobalamin), vitamin B_2 (riboflavin); food chemicals such as acetic acid, citric acid, nucleotides, and microbial polysaccharides; antibiotics like penicillins G and V, tylosin, gentamicin, and the cephalosporins.

Ethyl alcohol from manioc (cassava)

Manioc is a large, somewhat bushy herb which grows everywhere in Brazil. The roots, which have the appearance of sweet potatoes, yield a starchy product. Although 2.1 million hectares were planted in 1973, no commercial-scale operations have been established. All the manioc is grown in small farming units, manually planted and harvested.

The starch content of manioc, about 25 per cent, is far greater than the 13 per cent sucrose content in sugar-cane. The result is that a tonne of manioc yields considerably more ethyl alcohol than does a tonne of sugar-cane. However, one hectare of sugar-cane crop yields about 50 tonnes of cane, and 1 hectare of manioc yields only about 15 tonnes.

Manioc crops for energy purposes present problems related to mechanization, and to the fermentation process itself. Since starch cannot be directly fermented, it requires enzymatic action, and there is a lack of industrial experience with its processing. Furthermore, an overall energy balance would probably reflect the fact that the manioc industry cannot benefit from burning the residues of its industrial processing, as the sugar-cane industry does by burning bagasse.

Anyway, manioc crops are very much within the government plans for ethyl alcohol production. A pioneer manioc distillary is being built, a fairly large manioc research programme is under way, and official estimates assume an increasingly large contribution of manioc to alcohol production, even surpassing that of sugar-cane in less than a decade.

Socio-economic considerations of ethanol production

Brazil has abundant land and can continue expanding its cultivated cropland at present rates for most of this century. Thus, a major agricultural issue consists of finding ways to make the land resource contribute more toward raising national and per capita incomes. Brazil is currently dependent on foreign petroleum, for which the country has to pay about 10 million dollars per day, and it needs to change both the pattern of the farm labour force, which constitutes a disproportionately large component of the low-income group, and to modify somewhat land-ownership distribution. Therefore, it is not only very welcome, but necessary, to expand acreage for energy crops, and thus cash crops.

Estimates indicate that more than 200000 people are directly employed by the sugar-cane industry in Brazil, including factory, sugar-cane farm, cane and sugar transportation, and other service workers. Most of these people reside in the areas in which they work. Given the government goals for ethyl alcohol production, and the increasingly larger contribution of manioc, by 1980 about 700000 new hectares will be planted, with the corresponding settlement of 65000 farm worker families; by 1990 about 9 million new hectares will be added to production and 730000 families will be settled; and by 2000 there will be 18 million new hectares and 1.4 million families.

Considering that the growth rate of another cash crop, soya beans, has been an amazing 34.8 per cent per year over the period 1967–72 (about 5 million hectares), the goals set forth by the plan do not seem unattainable. Much to the contrary, they represent a unique opportunity for tackling the problem of poverty in the agricultural sector, for embarking on a land redistribution programme, and for implementing a large-scale credit programme for the acquisition of agricultural machinery, fertilizers, and other modern agricultural inputs. Such development offers the possibility of solving most of the current problems caused by petroleum imports which are now facing the Brazilian economy.

The economics of ethanol production in Brazil are such that at the moment its market price is highly competitive with that of petrol. However, there are many different and attractive technologies and products which are alternatives to obtaining ethanol from sugar-cane, and which should be considered together with ethanol production for the establishment of a more complete and efficient industrial complex. A comprehensive feasibility study is very much needed. Raw material considerations, disposition of by-products, marketing of all products, costs of different processes, availability of appropriate technologies and overall energy balances are but a few of the topics that should be investigated.

Additional bio-conversion alternatives

Charcoal. Charcoal produced by carbonization of wood is widely used in Brazil as a raw material for the production of pig-iron and steel. Currently more than 2.5 million tonnes of pig-iron and more than 1 million tonnes of steel are produced in this manner in the state of Minas Gerais alone.

Owing to the limited availability of Brazilian coal and its characteristics (it is mainly high-ash, high-sulphur-content, low-grade coal), charcoal production will have to be increased by more than twofold in the next 5 years. However, production methods still being used are quite outdated. By switching to the more modern technique of wood distillation, considerable amounts of various by-products could be obtained. For example, from the production of 1 million tonnes of pig-iron using charcoal, it is technically feasible to recuperate 146000 tonnes of fuel gas, 18000 tonnes of acetic acid, 12000 tonnes of methanol, and 70000 tonnes of tar, which add up to an additional value of about 200000 dollars.

A fairly comprehensive feasibility study encompassing different aspects of charcoal production has been conducted for the state of Minas Gerais. Commercial charcoal production utilizing more appropriate technology will follow. Furthermore, considering the very extensive forest areas that are currently being cleared for agricultural production (more than 2 million hectares in the northern state of Para alone), wood pyrolysis could be of significant value in the overall Brazilian energy matrix.

Hydrocarbon-producing plants. Hydrocarbon (rubber) producing plants that naturally grow in the Amazon basin are being considered as a potential source for the direct photosynthetic production of hydrocarbons. It has been suggested that proper manipulation of rubber tree (*Hevea*) production could control the molecular weight of its principal hydrocarbon product, polyisoprene, which has a chemical composition similar to that of petroleum, thus obtaining a renewable 'fuel' tree. This is still only a research idea. However, other *Euphorbia* species (of which there are more than 3000 different species in Brazil), like the *Euphorbia tirucalli*, are also potential candidates for this kind of chemical manipulation and are being investigated.

Waste recycling. Organic wastes might prove to be of considerable significance on the local level for supplying energy whenever large waste concentrations occur within a relatively small area. A project that includes the future construction of a pilot plant for pyrolyzing the municipal solid wastes of the city of Rio de Janeiro (5 million inhabitants) is currently in the stage of feasibility studies. Pyrolysis consists of heating organic material at high temperatures for a prolonged period of time in the absence of oxygen. Different combinations of gas, oil, and residues can be obtained, depending on the organic waste composition, and on the temperature, pressure, and duration of the process.

The anaerobic fermentation of sewage is another way of disposing of organic wastes. The methane produced by bacteria (typically 60 per cent methane and 40 per cent carbon dioxide) can provide the energy needs of the sewage treatment plant itself, or be used as a pipeline gas. The residues, unfermented sludge, can be used as a fertilizer. The process is simple; presently it is being used in several locations in the world, and could contribute to the overall economic feasibility of treating sewage in Brazil. Small-scale sewage digesters are now being built for future larger scale developments.

Water hyacinth/fresh water algae. Water hyacinth, or *Eichhornia crassipes*, is widespread in tropical and sub-tropical regions. Submitted to anaerobic digestion it yields methane and carbon dioxide.
Fresh water algae like *Chlorella* can grow in a sewage oxidation pond, and are readily subject to bacterial attack. Algae are also a good protein source, and can be grown very efficiently, with productivity greater than that of agriculture, although at somewhat higher costs. Experiments with water hyacinth and fresh water algae anaerobic digestion are being conducted in Brazil to

determine both their possible use as a fuel and as a protein source, and the possibility of growing them in sewage oxidation ponds.

The hydrogen economy

Although not exactly an energy-production technology, the 'hydrogen economy' was chosen to be included with other production technologies since its appropriate uses can result in a very interesting, almost unique, possibility for Brazil. Owing to the huge water-power resources available in Brazil and the large distances between the major electric energy consumer centres, hydrogen was initially regarded as a possible 'energy vector' that could conveniently solve the energy transportation and storage problems associated with those conditions which are almost peculiar to Brazil.

However, studies conducted in 1974 by the above mentioned task force on alternative energy technologies concluded that other useful hydrogen characteristics should be regarded on a priority basis for a short-term research and development programme, and that they would be more readily applicable to satisfying the national needs.

The National Hydrogen Research and Development Programme was completed in the beginning of 1975. It incorporated two different but inter-related lines of projects: research projects, and technical–economic feasibility studies. The former was intended to foster research both in some frontier areas and in some established areas in which the development of Brazilian know-how was thought to be necessary. The latter was designed to answer questions concerning the applicability of already available technologies and processes to short-term industrial developments.

Petroleum and fertilizer imports are causing an extremely acute balance-of-payments problem for Brazil. As a natural consequence, a major portion of the hydrogen programme effort has been dedicated to studying the feasibility of producing ammonia from pure electrolytic hydrogen. The results of several studies conducted by FINEP indicate that ammonia production near a hydroelectric power plant is competitive with the naphtha-reforming process currently used in Brazil, provided that electricity could be supplied at a cost of about 12 mills per kilowatt-hour (at 1975 prices), and provided that the plant would produce at least 600 tonnes per day of ammonia. Even for an ammonia plant located up to 400 km from the power station, and thus from the hydrogen-producing plant, the studies found that for an installation producing in excess of 1000 tonnes per day, the ammonia so obtained would still be economically competitive with that from other processes. Those conditions (12 mills/kWh electricity, proximity to a power plant, and ammonia production of more than 600 tonnes/day) are very much feasible today in Brazil.

Plans are now under way for building an industrial-scale ammonia plant which, if successful, would constitute a major contribution of the hydrogen programme to the country's energy and economy picture, and would also serve as a catalyst for the several other research activities being funded by the programme.

Fossil fuel alternative technologies

Coal gasification

Coal gasification processes are under consideration in Brazil. Different technologically established processes (Winkler Lurgi, Koppers-Totsek, Otto) were examined as alternatives for ammonia production, and for the direct reduction of iron ore in steel production. However, owing to the high-ash content of Brazilian coal (55 per cent) it is not at this point clear whether any one of those applications will find its way from the feasibility-study stage to the pilot and demonstration plant scale.

Shale oil

Petrobras, the state-owned Brazilian oil

company, has developed the technology for shale oil production. A pilot plant (1000 barrels per day) has been operating for the past several years in southern Brazil. Plans were recently announced for building the first commercial-scale shale-processing plant. The plant is expected to yield 51 000 barrels of shale oil, and 1.8 million cubic metres (63.5 million cubic feet) of pipeline gas per day. For that production, approximately 112 thousand tonnes of shale will be necessary. About 94000 tonnes of residue will result. An advanced research project is under way for determining other possible applications for Brazilian shale, as well as for the residues of shale oil distillation (polymers, fertilizers, medicines, construction materials, etc.).

Energy conservation measures

Forced by the increase in petroleum products consumption, despite stepwise price increases during the past 3 years, the Brazilian government recently (January 1977) enacted very tough fuel conservation regulations. Those regulations consist basically of a petrol surtax of about 63 cents per gallon (the surtax is to be returned to the consumer after 2 years, without any value corrections to compensate for inflation and no interest paid. Petrol prices, as a result of the surtax, will be about $US2.20 per gallon); a similar measure for fuel oil (the surtax will be $US21 per ton of fuel oil; prohibition of automobile circulation in city-centre areas in major Brazilian cities; closing of petrol stations all over the country on Sundays and holidays; the establishment of different working schedules for industry, commerce, and government agencies, including staggered hours; raising by 50 per cent the toll fares on state and federal highways during weekends; incentives for the use of alternative energy sources; for the use of electricity as opposed to energy from fossil fuels, and incentives for the expansion of public transportation systems; reduction by 10 per cent of fuel bills of government agencies; limitation of power output of government automobile engines to 89 hp; enforcing the national maximum speed limit (50 m.p.h.); fining owners of badly tuned diesel engines; surtaxing petrol or diesel oil-fired electricity generators; restricting imports of aeroplanes by the government, and raising diesel-oil prices.

Since those measures were taken quite recently, there is no way to evaluate how effective they really are. Furthermore, it is not very clear at this stage what the meaning is of some of them which were phrased more as recommendations than as regulations. However, it is fair to assume that their reach and potential use open up a wide spectrum of possibilities for stimulating the development of alternative energy technologies in Brazil.

Incentives for the use of alternative energy sources include not only the gradual replacement of petrol and other liquid fuels by ethyl alcohol, but also the 'more efficient use' of other natural resources. Notwithstanding the possibilities that have been mentioned, at this point it is not possible to determine definitively which of them will be developed on a priority basis.

Some implications for conservation can be suggested. Public transportation systems (buses) are responsible for 75 per cent of the total number of passengers in the 10 largest metropolitan areas in Brazil. Increasing this number, say, to 85 or 90 per cent, could save an estimated 430 to 640 thousand gallons of fuel per year. Also, increasing the person-per-automobile average number (now 1.35 in the largest metroplitan areas) to 2.0 could save an estimated 10 per cent of the total annual petrol consumption in the country. The government hopes to achieve these goals not only by restricting the use of automobiles in city centres, but also by a number of complementary measures such as creating special traffic lanes for buses, and car pools, charging special toll fares for cars carrying only one motorist, stimulating the production of electrically-powered trolleys and of small, low-petrol consumption automobiles, increasing parking rates around city centres, and a number of other measures. Also, the federal investment in railways and construction and in electrically powered railways equipment will be substantially increased and the highway construction programme will be kept at a minimal acceptable level.

Conclusions

The possibilities for developing alternative energy technologies in Brazil are many and varied. Some of them are peculiar to the country; others are applicable elsewhere. Some are fairly well developed and need only be adapted or improved, to take advantage of local conditions. Others, although very promising, are still a few years away from being used on a commercial scale.

Nevertheless, for a country like Brazil, as for many other countries, there is no simple solution for meeting its energy needs. Different possibilities, though, are not mutually exclusive. They should contribute to the overall solution by solving some specific, local problems. It seems clear that the country's energy policy cannot restrict itself to short-term planning in this field. Research and development efforts have to be considered as an integral part of the policies being formulated—which, in all fairness, cannot be said to have happened in the past.

The variety of methods, technologies, processes, and end-products that appear to be feasible in the Brazilian case, require a very well co-ordinated and executed comprehensive approach toward the problem. A systems treatment is a must. In the first few iterations, a definite answer is not going to be found; however, a trial-and-error process should be conducive to a much better solution than the random approach which results from focusing attention on isolated alternatives.

20

Alcohol: a Brazilian answer to the energy crisis

ALLEN L. HAMMOND

While the United States languishes in protracted debate over synthetic fuels and other means of alleviating dependence on imported oil, Brazil has moved decisively in the direction of growing its own fuel. The Brazilian government has launched a bold programme to replace much of that country's imported oil with ethyl alcohol produced from sugar-cane and other crops. If successful, the alcohol programme has the potential to establish Brazil not only as the world leader in renewable energy sources but also as the first developing country without large oil resources to find a path to energy independence—a path uniquely its own.

José Goldemberg, director of the physics institute at the University of São Paulo and co-ordinator of an academic energy policy group has claimed that an energy strategy based on biomass 'is a natural for Brazil'. 'We have lots of land, lots of water, and an ideal climate for growth'. Indeed, figures released at a week-long symposium* on the national alcohol programme held in Rio de Janeiro in December indicate that less than 2 per cent of the land-area of Brazil could produce enough fuel to replace all imported petroleum. Brazil imports more than 80 per cent of its oil, about 700 000 barrels a day, and finding the $3 billion annually to pay for this oil has seriously interfered with the country's economic growth in recent years. A measure of the importance attached to reducing this dependence on imports is the amount of money—more than $400 million—that the Brazilian government has committed to the alcohol programme since it began in November 1975.

Alcohol programme

The programme has the personal backing of Brazil's President, General Ernesto Geisel, and is one of the few to have emerged unscathed from the recent round of government budget cutting. Already proposed are more than 70 new distilleries and additional sugar-cane plantings totalling about 500 000 hectacres, although only 15 projects have actually received funding. As a result of the delay, an unofficial but widely mentioned target of the programme, producing enough alcohol to replace 20 per cent of Brazil's petrol by 1980, now seems unlikely to be achieved on time. Nonetheless, the programme appears to be rapidly gathering momentum, and few Brazilian observers now doubt that it is destined to play a major role in their country's future.

A number of factors account for the rapid

*Ethanol: Combustível e Matéria-Prima, sponsored by the Ministry of Industry and Commerce, Rio de Janeiro, 1 to 4 December 1976.

First published in *Science*, Vol. 195 (11 February 1977), pp. 564–6.

emergence of alcohol as a high-priority ingredient in Brazil's energy planning—not least that country's extensive prior experience with alcohol–petrol blends as motor fuels—but three stand out as having been of paramount importance. One was the demonstration that ethyl alcohol (ethanol) is superior to petrol as a motor fuel, delivering litre for litre as much power with much less pollution in a properly tuned engine. A second was the realization that the manufacture of alcohol need not depend solely on sugar-cane, which requires relatively good soils, but could ultimately utilize the far larger potential of manioc (cassava), a root crop that grows in all parts of the country and for which Brazil is already the world's largest producer. A third and politically decisive factor was the role played by Geisel in establishing a national programme to exploit what is now widely described as Brazil's 'fuel of the future'.

The rapid establishment of an ambitious alcohol plan is apparently due in large part to Geisel's previous experience in the energy field and a chance visit to a little-known research laboratory in 1975. Before becoming President he headed Brazil's national oil company, Petrobras, and he is described as uncommonly knowledgeable about energy matters for a national leader. In the course of a visit to Brazil's space agency in San José dos Campos, he stopped at a newly founded laboratory investigating alcohol as a motor fuel and was fascinated by the experimental results. He is said to have prolonged what was to have been a brief ceremonial visit into a lengthy session, and to have quickly grasped the possibilities. A few months later the alcohol programme was established, elevating what had been a modest research effort largely within the Commerce Ministry to a national programme headed by an interministerial council directly responsible to the President.

Using alcohol as a fuel for automobiles actually has a long history in Brazil, dating back to the 1920s. At that time the effort consisted of a few experimental vehicles, including one driven from Rio to São Paulo and back on pure ethanol. By the 1930s it was legal in Brazil to blend alcohol with petrol, but really large-scale use did not begin until after the Second World War. Then, in an attempt to make the sugar industry more competitive, Petrobras agreed to purchase the growing quantities of alcohol produced as a by-product of sugar-refining and blend it as a minor constituent in essentially all petrol sold in Brazil. Depending on the region of the country, the alcohol content of Brazilian petrol has ranged between 2 and 8 per cent in recent years—a level for which no adjustments to automobile engines are required.

Following the sharp rise in international oil prices that began Brazil's current economic troubles, however, the Commerce Ministry in 1974 began a research effort to explore the possibility of blending much higher percentages of alcohol in petrol and of burning pure alcohol. A principal figure in the ethanol utilization effort has been Urbano Ernesto Stumpf, an aeronautical engineer who had devoted years to exploring the properties of alcohol as a fuel and whose expertise had now catapulted him into sudden prominence. Stumpf and his colleagues were rapidly able to show both theoretically and experimentally that ethyl alcohol, despite its low caloric heat-content compared with petrol, is a competitive fuel when burned in a properly designed engine. One reason for this is that an alcohol engine ideally operates at a higher compression ratio than a petrol engine—a ratio of about 10 rather than the value of 7 appropriate for Brazil's low-octane petrol. Stumpf's data indicate that, with appropriate engines, pure alcohol delivers 18 per cent more power per litre than petrol and is consumed at a rate between 15 and 20 per cent higher. The two factors effectively cancel, leaving neither fuel with a clear advantage from an energy standpoint. Moreover, because an alcohol engine can be tuned to run much leaner than a petrol burning motor, the fuel is more completely combusted, giving alcohol a slight practical edge in the kilometres-per-litre figures and dramatically lowering the amount of pollutants emitted—by as much as 50 per cent for carbon monoxide and oxides of nitrogen. Since alcohol does not contain hydrocarbons and does not need tetraethyl lead additives to boost its octane, emissions of these substances are eliminated altogether.

Stumpf has also shown that alcohol is a far more flexible fuel than petrol, since it can be used (although less efficiently) in motors designed for petrol and can be blended with petrol in proportions as high as 20 per cent with no adjustment to ordinary automobile engines. Alcohol can also be burned in a 50–50 mixture with diesel fuel in truck and bus engines through use of an ingenious double carburettion system and seems to be an ideal turbine fuel for use in electric generating plants. To illustrate these virtues, the Commerce Ministry equipped three automobiles to run on hydrated alcohol (95 per cent alcohol and 5 per cent water) and toured them all over Brazil, accumulating more than 100000 kilometres of use in 1976.

The publicity stunt and the research data behind it have attracted considerable attention in Brazil and eliminated or at least muted the initial scepticism of automobile manufacturers. Last November, for example, the supervisor of motor engineering for Chrysler–Brazil announced that the company was demonstrating a high-compression engine suitable for pure alcohol; he also said that existing Chrysler motors could operate with up to 20 per cent alcohol without retuning and, with the alcohol blend, 'could run in California without controls and pass pollution specs'. Petrobras is reported to have been conducting large-scale tests of a 20 per cent alcohol–petrol blend by the simple means of increasing the admixture in the petrol delivered to particular localities. The city of São Paulo where air pollution is a serious problem, is planning to test a 300-car fleet operating on pure alcohol this year.

Large-scale production

Producing enough alcohol to make a major contribution to Brazil's energy supply is a more difficult problem. Some 800 million litres of alcohol are now produced annually from sugar-cane, and the technology and economics of the distilling process are well established. Cane production can clearly be expanded and all but two of the proposed new distilleries are to be based on cane. If they are funded, they will nearly triple the current output of alcohol. But cane can be grown in only a few parts of the country and much of the ideal land is already under cultivation, so that a 50-fold increase in alcohol production—which would be required to essentially eliminate oil imports—could probably not be based on cane. Cane, moreover, is a seasonal crop with a harvesting period of at best 160 days and, once cut, must be quickly processed before the sugar-content degrades; the distilleries would thus stand idle more than half the year.

Hopes within the government for really large-scale production of alcohol seem accordingly to rest on manioc. With an estimated 2 million hectares already under cultivation, largely for food, manioc is already a major crop in Brazil. The root of the plant contains between 20 and 40 per cent starch, depending on the variety, and it is from this material that alcohol is made. Starch cannot be fermented directly, however. Although several methods exist for breaking it down into sugar, ranging from brute-force hydrolysis to the use of enzymes to catalyse the process, their commercial feasibility for manioc was unproved. Then early in 1975 a research group at the National Institute of Technology in Rio obtained promising laboratory results with a particular enzymatic method, and they have since successfully tried the process in commercial-scale equipment. Commercial production of the appropriate enzymes is now beginning, and Petrobras is building the pioneer manioc distillery, which is scheduled to begin operations late this year.

Large-scale production of alcohol from manioc remains in the future, however. Manioc is now grown almost exclusively in back-yard plots and the agricultural infrastructure for commercial cultivation will have to be built from scratch. Government officials argue that this is an advantage, since modern techniques for both cultivation and distillation can be introduced from the start. (Many existing cane distilleries employ outmoded techniques, and the sugar industry has shown no great interest in upgrading its plant or operating procedures.) Nonetheless, scepticism abounds among Brazilian observers not directly connected with the alcohol programme. Cane distilleries are often self-sufficient in energy, generating heat and electricity by burning bagasse, the fibrous residue of the cane. Manioc residues have too high a water content to burn, however, and so an additional energy source will be needed to operate the distilleries. More crucial to the ultimate feasibility of obtaining alcohol from manioc is the question of the net energy output from this crop when fertilizers and other energy-intensive inputs of large-scale cultivation and production are included in the balance. No detailed assessment of this balance has yet been published and, although government officials assert that making alcohol from manioc is feasible, the subject is hotly debated by Brazilian energy scientists. In any case, the Ministry of Agriculture has established a research institute devoted to manioc and alcohol programme officials talk about a 'new agricultural frontier'.

Officials of the national programme estimate that about 4 billion litres of alcohol per year will be required to substitute for 20 per cent of petrol consumption by the early 1980s. This level of production would require either 1.3 million hectares of cane or between 1 and 2 million hectares of manioc. (Typical yields of manioc as it is now grown in Brazil are 10 to 15 tonnes per hectare, but agricultural planners hope to achieve 30 tonnes per hectare with modern methods.) The prospect of opening a million hectares of a new crop or even 10 times that amount does not seem insuperable to the planners, however, despite the lack of an agricultural infrastructure for manioc. At the Rio symposium, a representative of the Agriculture Ministry, Antonio Licio, pointed out that the area planted with soya beans in Brazil has grown from nearly nothing to 6 million hectares in the span of 8 years. He estimates the arable, readily accessible land in Brazil to be in excess of 40 million hectares.

The key to the economics of the national alcohol programme in Brazil is cheap agricultural labour, and it is not in short supply. Brazil has millions of unemployed, especially in the impoverished north-eastern part of the country, and a high birth rate. As a result of this and the high petrol taxes imposed by the government, alcohol is already competitive with petroleum products; it sells for about $1 per gallon, a price fixed by the government, compared to $1.50 per gallon for petrol. Despite their inefficiencies, existing distilleries operate profitably under these conditions. To stimulate production even further under the alcohol programme, new distilleries can be financed with government loans at low interest rates, and Petrobras guarantees that it will buy all alcohol delivered to it. These conditions are so generous that they have been described as 'a licence to print money', and it is no wonder that companies are standing in line to take advantage.

The financing scheme, moreover, is designed to be self-perpetuating. In December, the government announced the establishment of a revolving fund for financing of these projects. The fund is to be continually replenished from the profit that Petrobras realizes from buying alcohol at the wholesale price and selling it, blended with petrol, at the petrol price.

The alcohol programme seems likely to have an unusually broad impact on Brazil. In addition to providing what is potentially a major and inexhaustible source of energy and reducing the disastrous economic effects of importing foreign oil, it may have equally profound effects in other areas such as the following.

Pollution. Even a partial switch from petrol to alcohol could substantially reduce the air pollution that in large Brazilian cities is already a substantial health hazard.

Employment. Government officials expect the alcohol programme to create between 0.25 and 1 million new jobs, primarily agricultural, in coming years. They also hope the availability of jobs in rural areas will help to slow the migration to the cities that is overwhelming Brazil's major urban areas.

Industrial growth. The proliferation of distilleries is expected to stimulate the capital goods industries by adding a major new internal market. Government officials also hope to develop a complete chemical industry based on alcohol rather than oil. Production of vinyl chloride, for example, is said to be an immediate possibility. In the long run, Brazil may be able to export the resulting technology and know-how.

National self-confidence. The psychological impact of successfully developing a Brazilian solution instead of copying an imported model would be enormous. Indeed, so widespread is the attitude in Brazil that 'imported is better' that some opposition to the alcohol programme appears to have been based on the fact that it was an indigenous idea. In addition, Brazil would stand to gain substantial international prestige from securing its energy independence, not to mention a market for its alcohol expertise in other land-rich tropical countries. Finally, many scientists believe that the success of the alcohol programme would establish the value of research to Brazilian industry, heretofore a sceptical and unenthusiastic customer.

Despite its enormous potential, it is too early to judge the alcohol programme a certain success. It requires, for example, a degree of co-operation among several different ministries that is unusual in Brazil. Moreover, as one Brazilian official observed, 'we Brazilians are mad for plans but their execution is another matter'. Delays in approving financing for new distilleries have given rise to additional concerns. Despite the programme's high priority, for example, the first funds were released only in early October 1976, nearly a year after the programme was launched, and the rate of approvals continues to be slow. Most Brazilian observers believe that these delays reflect opposition to the alcohol programme by entrenched and powerful economic interests; at the Rio symposium two senators commented independently on what they described as 'strange forces' holding up the programme. Most frequently mentioned in private speculation is the sugar industry, which is controlled by a few families that, in this view, are resisting the entry of potential competitors into the business. It was evident at the meeting that sugar producers are not entirely happy with the alcohol programme. Some university scientists believe that Petrobras, a power unto itself in Brazil, was also less than enthusiastic initially.

José Bautista Vidal, Secretary for Industrial Technology of the Commerce Ministry and the government official most closely identified with the alcohol programme, denies that there has been any concerted opposition. In an interview he admitted, however, that getting the programme off the ground involved 'a process of consensus' within the government and that he spent much of 2 years convincing people.

If there is a struggle going on, the alcohol forces clearly seem to have won at least one battle. The Rio alcohol symposium was held at Petrobras headquarters, a fact that Bautista Vidal says is 'very significant' because it shows, he told the meeting, that 'in Brazil, oil and alcohol are not enemies'. General Araken de Oliveira, president of Petrobras, told the meeting that his company 'is more interested in the development and welfare of the country than in its own profits'.

Clearly the alcohol programme has some

way to go before it can significantly contribute to Brazil's energy supplies. But the Brazilian alcohol venture is just beginning, its potential is enormous, and it may yet become a model for an energy-hungry, and increasingly oil-poor world.

VI Africa

One of four Kaplan type turbines bei assembled for driving an 80 MW generator at the site of the Niger Dar at Kainji.

World Bank photo by Yutaka Nagata.

View of the spillway, as seen from the tailrace, at the Kainji Hydro-electric development project built with the aid of World Bank funds on the Niger River about 260 miles north of Lagos and about 65 miles upstream from the town of Jebba in Nigeria.

World Bank photo by Yutaka Nagata.

In terms of average consumption per capita of modern energy, Africa is the poorest continent. Half of the nearly 50 African nations and territories for which the commercial energy statistics are available have consumption rates below 100 kg of coal equivalent per capita annually. In many nations, in fact, fossil fuel and electricity use is limited to only a small fraction of better-off urban population, resulting in the world's lowest annual consumption averages: Rwanda and Burundi use around 10 kg of coal equivalent per person, Upper Volta and Chad about 15, Mali 25, Niger and Ethiopia 30, Somalia 40, and Uganda 50. Only South Africa and hydrocarbon-rich Libya have substantial domestic usage.

By far the most populous nation in Africa is Nigeria, with about 80 million people, and its economic development has been fortuitously helped, after two decades of unproductive search, by the discoveries of crude oil in 1956. Extraction was quickly restored and expanded after the civil war of the late 1960s and Nigeria is currently OPEC's sixth largest producer. It can offer crude oil of outstanding quality: very light (gravity 38° API) and with a low sulphur content, yielding high percentage of petrol. Consequently the Nigerian crude is in demand both in the USA and in Western Europe and, with increased OPEC prices, its exports provide the bulk of the country's badly needed foreign earnings.

Martin Quinlan ('Nigeria's oil industry') describes in some detail the recent hydrocarbon production, government oil policy, development of the state petroleum company, downstream ventures, company relationships, and future production and export prospects for Nigerian light crude and natural gas.

Although a major crude-oil exporter, Nigeria has so far done relatively little to expand the domestic consumption of modern energy: the nationwide average per capita is just around 70 kg of oil equivalent annually and the power generation amounts to mere 50 kWh per year per capita. One of the best ways how Nigeria could spend the oil revenues is to develop its considerable renewable energy resources. G. V. Eckenfelder ('Hydro power plans in Nigeria') reviews the power potential of the Niger Basin and describes the large Kainji hydro stations, started in 1963, and other major projects planned for Africa's third largest river and for some of its tributaries.

E. Eskilsson ('Energy resources and demands in Zambia and in Africa south of the Equator') reviews fossil fuel deposits, hydropower potential, and crude oil import needs in Zambia and in 15 other African nations. Although southern Africa is a relatively oil-poor part of the continent, it has rich hydro resources of which so far less than 3 per cent have been developed. Eskilsson sees their gradual harnessing, culminating in the creation of interstate long-distance direct-current high voltage interconnections, as the best strategy to provide energy not only for the region's important mineral industries but also for developing its considerable food production potential.

Zaire (formerly the Belgian Congo) is perhaps the most fortunate among black nations south of the Equator. Significant deposits of crude oil have already been discovered and prospects of further hydrocarbon strikes, especially offshore, appear excellent. Above all, the country has the world's fourth largest hydro potential (about 660 billion kWh/year at average rate of flow, almost as much as the USA and about half of China's total) in the mighty flow of Zaire (Congo) River and its tributaries.

With the construction of first phases of giant Inga Dam near Kinshasa the harnessing of Zaire's power has barely started. Inga can eventually reach nearly 30000 MW of installed capacity and it has already been tied via a record-length high-voltage link with mineral-rich Shaba province 1700 km to the south-east. K. L. Adelman ('Energy in Zaire') outlines the details of this favourable situation and stresses Zaire's energy strength as the key factor in making it a future great continental power.

In contrast, Tanzania's energy situation is unenviable. The country produces only negligible amounts of coal and hydroelectricity and has to rely on imported oil to support a meagre modern energy consumption of below 100 kg of coal equivalent per capita. It is precisely in such circumstances where small-scale solar technologies might offer the best solution to the rural energy modernization.

The US National Academy of Sciences and the Government of Tanzania held a joint workshop in 1977 to determine the cost of five solar technologies—small hydrogeneration, windmill power, biogas, photovoltaic cells, and flat-plate solar collectors—and to compare it with costs of diesel-generated electricity and with the transmission from the national grid. N. L. Brown and J. W. Howe ('Solar energy for Tanzania') present detailed results of the workshop's estimates and see them as encouraging enough to initiate serious testing of the technologies in Tanzanian villages.

The future development of most African countries will continue to be one of the least successful chapters of the world's economic progress. The continent's energy reserves are relatively poor: less than 3 per cent of the global coal, and about 14 and 11 per cent of crude oil and natural gas, the latter two being overwhelmingly concentrated in Arab Africa. Barring major new hydrocarbon discoveries or a massive and speedy harvesting of solar energy, most of the black African states thus face an energy-poor future, a situation made worse by low export earnings, chronic indebtedness, and widespread political instability.

Energy in Africa: selected readings

Amann, H. (1976). *The role of the energy sector in agriculture-oriented economic development: the Tanzanian case study*. Economic Research Bureau, University College, Dar es Salaam.

Brace Research Institute (1976). *A study of the feasibility of establishing a rural energy center for demonstration purposes in Senegal*. McGill University, Montreal.

Brokensha, D. and Riley, B. *Forest, foraging, fences, and fuel in a marginal area of Kenya*. US Agency for International Development, Washington DC.

Digernes, T. H. *Wood for fuel: the energy situation in Bara, Sudan*. Department of Geography, University of Bergen.

Ernst, E. (1977). *Fuel consumption among rural families in Upper Volta, West Africa*. Peace Corps, Ougadougou.

Eskilsson, E. (1978). African Rivers Hold Promise of Major Energy Supply. *Energy International* **15**, n. 7 (July 1978), 19–21.

Ezzati, A., Mubayi, V., Lee, J., Palmedo, P., and Allentuck, J. (1978). *A preliminary assessment of the Egyptian energy outlook*. Brookhaven National Laboratory, Upton, NY.

Floor, W. M. (1977). *The energy sector of the Sahelian countries*. The Netherlands Ministry of Foreign Affairs, Amsterdam.

Fraenkel, P. L. (1975). *Food from windmills*. Intermediate Technology Publications, London.

Holz, P. (1977). South Africa's Largest Hydro Scheme Nears Completion. *Energy International* **14** (7) (July 1977), 37–40.

Howe, J. W. *et al.* (1977). *Energy for the villages of Africa*. Overseas Development Council, Washington DC.

International Atomic Energy Agency (1976). *Prospects for utilization of nuclear power in Africa*. Economic Commission for Africa, Accra.

Kabagambe, D. M. (1976). *Aspects of resource conservation and utilisation: the role of charcoal industry in the Kenya economy*. Institute for Development Studies, Nairobi.

von Lazar, A. and Duersten, A. L. (1976). Oil and Development Planning: Implications for Nigeria. *Energy Policy* **4** (4) (December 1976), 330–42.

McDowell, J. (ed.) (1976). *Village technology in Eastern Africa*. UNICEF Eastern African Regional Office, Nairobi.

United Nations Environment Program (1976). *Environmental impacts of energy production and utilization on the African continent*. Economic Commission for Africa, Accra.

United Nations Industrial Development Organization (1976). *Development of petroleum refineries in Africa: present status and future prospects*. Economic Commission for Africa, Accra.

Walton, J. D., Jr., Roy, A. H. and Bomar, S. H., Jr. (1977). *A state of the art survey of solar-powered irrigation pumps, solar cookers, and wood-burning stoves for use in sub-Sahara Africa*. Georgia Institute of Technology, Atlanta.

21

Nigeria's oil industry

MARTIN QUINLAN

Through its oil revenues, Nigeria has rapidly become sub-Saharan Africa's most rapidly developing country. Its wealth, in terms of natural resources, income per capita, and state spending, vastly exceeds that of neighbouring states, and has led in recent years to an increasingly influential role in African politics. But Nigeria's own development problems are very real: it is still a young nation, and its wealth has brought difficulties as well as opportunities. How the former are resolved, and the latter exploited, will influence the development of its neighbours in West and Central Africa.

Nigeria, which is approximately the size of Spain and Portugal, supports a population of some 80 million—by far the largest in Africa. The economy is heavily dependent on oil, to the extent of about 95 per cent in terms of export earnings, 80 per cent in terms of government revenues, and well over one-third in terms of gross domestic product. Agriculture (together with forestry and fishing providing a contribution to GDP which is less than half that of oil) has been allowed to decline in importance in recent years, although groundnut production is still the highest amongst African countries and cocoa production second-highest. But export earnings from crops are insignificant compared to those from oil. With a relatively low level of industrialization—Nigeria is very much a nation of traders, not manufacturers—and minimal education (only 4 per cent of the age-group receiving secondary education in 1970), the domestic problems facing the government are immense.

Although a relatively recent oil producer, Nigeria's crude is of high quality—it is light in gravity and nearly free of sulphur—and is therefore well suited to refineries in the USA and Western Europe, where output profiles are normally adjusted to meet the dominant demand for petrol. Nigeria's oil also has the advantage of its geographical location: it is a number of days' steaming for a supertanker nearer to the main markets than oil produced in countries of the Gulf. Owing to its quality and 'freight advantage', Nigeria's oil was in high demand in the 1960s and early 1970s, resulting in very rapid development of the country's oil regions. At one time Nigeria was the sixth-largest producer in the Organization of Petroleum Exporting Countries (which it joined in 1971), and is the largest producer in Africa.

Early development

Oil was first discovered in Nigeria in 1956, following two decades of fruitless exploration by Shell and BP, operating as the Shell–BP Petroleum Development Company of Nigeria. Exports began on completion of the pipeline to Port Harcourt (the first field, at Oloibiri in the Niger River delta, was some 45 miles to the west), and by 1960 Shell–BP was producing some 17 500 barrels/day. Completion of the tanker terminal and related facilities at Bonny in 1961 allowed production to rise to over 46 000 b/d, although Mobil and other explorers were still unsuccessful.

But with large-scale exploration in the 1960s, reserves, production, and exports increased at a startling pace. In 1965 the trans-Niger pipeline was completed, allowing oil from fields in the mid-west to flow to Bonny terminal, and in the same year Gulf Oil began lifting oil from the company's first find—which was also Nigeria's first offshore oilfield. These developments allowed production to rise to some 275 000 b/d in 1965 and to nearly 420 000 b/d in 1966 prior to the Biafran war. In spite of the almost total breakdown of administration, transport, and communications resulting from the war, and the impeded flow of machinery to production sites, oil output recovered rapidly from the very low levels of 1968 to reach 1.08 million b/d in 1970, 2.06 million b/d in 1973, and 2.25 million b/d in the following year.

In 1975 the government imposed production ceilings on the major producing companies, in response to reduced world demand (itself a reflection of the sharp oil price increases made by OPEC over the previous 2 years and the resulting recessions in western economies). Output was accordingly held down in that year to 1.79 million b/d, but a modest increase to 2.08 million b/d was allowed in 1976 and 2.10 million b/d was recorded in 1977.

The marketing problem

The following year (1978) gave the first indication, from the viewpoint of most Nigerians, that their oil boom was not without limit. Production, on a monthly average basis, had begun to decline in June 1977—at a time when it would normally have peaked, in view of the high summer demand for petrol in the USA—and had fallen month by month until it reached 1.57 million b/d in February 1978. This was the lowest rate recorded since the period of recovery from the Biafran war. The message was brought home by Colonel M. Buhari, the last Federal Commissioner for Petroleum prior to the October 1979 return to civilian rule, who appeared on television to warn Nigerians that the three main African oil producers (Nigeria, Libya, and Algeria) faced a cut in their combined production of some 600 000 b/d.

The reason, according to Colonel Buhari, was the increasing production of oil from 'new' sources outside OPEC—in particular from the North Sea, Alaska, and Mexico. Production from the UK and Norwegian North Sea had by early-1978 built up substantially and was being sold at a price competitive with that for Nigerian crude; additionally, it was nearer to the important European refining centres and thus had a freight advantage. The same advantages applied to oil from Alaska and the Mexican offshore production, which were backing out sales of Nigerian crude on the US east coast market.

Colonel Buhari's solution was to suggest that the three African producers should agree to limit their production by the same proportion. The 600 000 b/d cut required represented a fall of 11.5 per cent from the three countries' combined output, which averaged 5.20 million b/d for the second half of the previous year; in Nigeria's case this would result in production falling to about 1.80 million b/d. If production cuts could not be agreed, he warned, Nigeria's output would remain at about 1.50 million b/d.

Although the three countries did meet to discuss their common problem, the results of the meeting were more apparent in terms of oil prices, rather than as an immediate rescheduling of production. At about that time (mid-1978), Nigeria's pricing policy became much more attuned to the market, with the state sales price being cut in April for the second time that year; and there were additional discounts offered to contract buyers and to producing companies which lifted their full output quota. The result was that production improved steadily, and then rose sharply in the latter months of the year in response to the shut-down of exports of Iranian crude and the resulting world shortage. Output averaged 1.91 million b/d in 1978 and rose to 2.40 million b/d in first-half 1979.

State participation

At present, nine companies or partnerships produce oil in Nigeria. The largest, accounting for over 50 per cent of the country's output from just under half of the licensed area, is Shell (which operated jointly with BP until BP's nationalization in August 1979). Producing from 79 onshore fields in the Niger delta region, Shell also manages a large network of crude oil pipelines and operates two big export terminals at Bonny and Forcados. Gulf, Mobil, and Agip-Phillips produce from 16, 12, and 13 fields respectively, Gulf accounting for about 15 per cent of total output and the others a little less. (Gulf with fields in the west of the delta, exports via the Escravos terminal, while Mobil's fields in the eastern part of the delta supply Qua Iboe terminal. Agip-Phillips export at Brass River terminal.) Of the smaller producers, Elf and Texaco account for just over 5 per cent of total output between them, with Ashland, Pan Ocean, and the Tenneco–Mobil–Sunray group contributing the remainder.

All of these companies operate in partnership with the Nigerian National Petroleum Corporation. This is the state-owned oil company, formed in 1977 through the merger of its predecessor (known as the Nigerian National Oil Corporation) with the Ministry of Petroleum Resources. NNPC thus meets two important needs: as a state-owned company, active in its own right as well as in partnerships with the international oil companies, it is playing a part and reaping the rewards from Nigeria's oil; while as an arm of the government, its acts in a regulatory capacity to ensure that the oil is being exploited in the nation's best interests.

The NNPC also holds the state's 60 per cent shares in producing companies. State participation in Nigeria's oil industry began in 1971, the year the country joined OPEC and the first year of operations of the NNOC. An agreement with Elf's subsidiary Safrap gave it a 35 per cent interest in concessions including the Obagi producing field in return for permission to bring the field back on stream—it had been shut down during the civil war. This first hurdle crossed, NNOC went on to take a 33 per cent share in Agip-Phillips' licence areas, while new offshore licences claimed for the state a 51 per cent share. The breakthrough came in the middle of 1975, when the largest producer, Shell–BP, agreed to a 35 per cent state share in its operations, backdated to April of that year.

Such participation shares were considered high—and undoubtedly were, in view of the 25 per cent agreements usual in Middle East countries at the time—but General Gowon's government went on to seek a 40 to 45 per cent stake in the remaining three producers. Gulf, Mobil, and Texaco–Chevron (as it then was) entered into protracted negotiations over the package of terms, but were overtaken by events: in early 1974 the government demanded, and was granted, a 55 per cent share in each of Nigeria's producing companies. This was raised to 60 per cent in July 1979.

With title to over half of Nigeria's oil output the state company can in theory sell about 1.4 million b/d at peak production. It experienced at first some difficulty in building up its direct international sales, however. Companies were asked to take some 'buy-back' crude, and on occasions part of NNPC's 60 per cent entitlement was left in the ground. (This latter practice does not affect the companies' liftings, which are calculated at 45 per cent of the 'allowables' production rates for each field, fixed by the NNPC in consultation with the companies with the objective of achieving the best production consistent with maximum overall recovery from the reservoir.)

Although NNPC has held a share in the operations of the producing companies since April 1974—and over the subsequent 4 years gained a full equity share through the completion of the government's compensation arrangements—it has been content to confine its intervention to general policy matters, leaving the day-to-day running of the producing companies to its US and European partners. But this is a matter of expediency rather than policy; the state company has found it consistently difficult to attract qualified personnel in the numbers required, despite terms of employment which are said to compare well with those offered by private companies. It has also been hampered by the somewhat limited degree of independent action allowed it by the government.

New relationship

However, after several years of steadily gaining expertise and the nucleus of its staff, the state company appears now to be in a position to play a more positive role in the development of Nigeria's oil. This is evidenced by the issue of exploration permits for new areas on terms other than the previous 60 per cent participation basis. The NNPC proposes to issue exploration and production licences for blocks within its reserved territory—which amounts to the whole of the country and the offshore with the exception of existing concessions in the Niger delta, plus relinquished concessions—on terms related to the likely prospects in each block. In each case, NNPC will take a more active involvement in development of these areas, a policy which amounts to a new relationship between the state company and the international oil companies.

Under the new terms, development contracts (which retain for the NNPC ownership of the oil) will be offered for areas where oil has been found but not as yet exploited, while production-sharing contracts and work-obligation contracts which could lead to a production share will be offered for areas where the prospects are more uncertain. NNPC will therefore make a contribution in terms of manpower and finance towards the development of these areas, and will be entitled in return to a greater share of the proceeds than it receives under 60 per cent participation terms.

Greatest interest will be shown in blocks likely to be offered in the Niger delta area's near-offshore—an offshore area of great potential which is already being exploited by the major companies under existing terms. It was here that the NNPC carried out its first drilling programme on its own account, which concluded in the spring of 1977 with four of the six wells drilled testing oil from multilayered reservoirs. (Reservoir thickness with the fifth well was considered insufficient, while the sixth was dry.) Twelve wells are scheduled under the second drilling programme, the first of which has been completed as a discovery.

Drilling work is also expected to begin, under the new terms, in Nigeria's other main petroleum prospects (besides the Niger delta)—the Anambra basin (just to the north of the delta), in the Chad basin (in the north of the country to the south of Lake Chad) and in the Sokoto basin in the north-west. A considerable amount of seismic work has been carried out in these areas but, owing to their distance from the coast, companies have not been enthusiastic about their potential. Finds would need to be very sizeable to justify the cost of a pipeline, and in any case geologists feel that the Niger delta still has good potential for producing worthwhile oil finds.

The Niger delta, in fact, has been one of the most productive areas in the world in terms of the relationship between wildcat wells drilled and oil finds. But it is a feature of the delta that oil is found in relatively small deposits, instead of in large Middle-East-type reservoirs, which can only flow at economic rates for a short time. A continual programme of exploration must therefore be maintained, if proved reserves are not to be progressively run down. This is a costly operation, in the swampy conditions of the delta. The difficulties are exemplified by the project to build a 24-inch pipeline running just 103 kilometres from oilfields to the Brass River terminal, a few years ago. The pipeline involved no less than 56 river crossings, 14 of which had spans of over 400 feet, with much of the rest of the route crossing mangrove swamps and jungle.

In view of the difficult conditions and the need for continual exploration, production costs in Nigeria are appreciably higher than elsewhere; the government allows a nominal US$1 per barrel for the cost of production in its tax calculations—it can frequently be higher—compared with Middle-East levels of 10 cents or less. But there has, nevertheless, been concern that company profitability was falling below the level needed to finance the development work necessary on existing fields and the wildcat drilling called for in the search for new fields.

The government's response came—in mid-1977—in the form of a package of financial measures intended to boost exploration without necessarily increasing profitability. This was achieved by 'expensing' (i.e. allowing as an expense against tax) of all exploratory drilling and the first two appraisal wells in each field; previously, all successful wells had been regarded as capital assets for tax purposes. The rate of petroleum profits tax was reduced from 85 per cent to 65.75 per cent—the lowest rate applying in any OPEC country—until the pre-production costs of new fields had been recovered. Additionally, offshore work was encouraged by a reduction in the rate of royalty from 20 per cent to 18.5 per cent and 16.6 per cent, depending on water-depth, and there were concessions over amortization and investment tax credits.

These incentives were generally well received by the oil companies, and most announced increases in their exploration budgets as a response. However, the slump in production levels previously discussed, which began to be noticeable soon after the exploration incentives were announced, did not provide the right background for increased exploration, and there was concern that a considerable amount of work had to be carried out to 'replace' the reserves used in earlier years.

This was voiced by Colonel Buhari, architect of the exploration incentives, who claimed that they were giving 'negative returns'. According to Colonel Buhari, oil companies can now recover their exploration investment in 5 years—'a situation which cannot be bettered anywhere else'—and had also benefited through the government's not being able to market its full share of production; in return, he called for a boost to exploration, even though production might not increase accordingly for some years. But the exploration scene is far from stagnant. Shell–BP announced plans for a 40 per cent increase in exploration drilling and seismic work over the 1977 total as a result of the financial incentives, while Gulf said it would employ six rigs for a number of years, believing that it has the potential to double production from its existing concessions.

Rate of exploitation

Nigeria's production potential is a matter for some speculation. Maximum output was given officially up to the end of 1978 as 2.25 million b/d, without allowance for wells temporarily out of production for work-overs or other maintenance work—a figure which was somewhat below the 2.33 million b/d recorded in October 1974. But in first-half 1979, in response to the Iranian revolution and resulting dislocations in world oil markets, Nigeria's fields produced at the rate of 2.4 million b/d. The production cuts which followed in the second half, although presented as a conservation measure, are viewed as of political origin; oil revenues had increased dramatically to the point at which the government feared the economy could not usefully absorb them. Given the right conditions, the 3 million b/d target envisaged under the Third National Development Plan (for 1976–80) could still be reached within a few years, it is considered.

But, in 1978, it was not in Nigeria's long-term interest to boost its oil production in a period of over-capacity. The military government showed, according to some observers, commendable restraint in resisting the temptation to significantly lower the price of their oil, and thus to increase output by making it more competitive with Libya's Brega light crude. But as a result Nigerian oil was undoubtedly overpriced in the period up to mid-1978; if it had not been for the unusual circumstances of the US market, where refineries were operating at near-capacity to meet the demand for light products, production would have dipped much earlier than it actually did.

On the other hand, there was at that time a clear argument for an increase in oil revenues. Owing to production limitations and price discounting these were nearly 10 per cent lower in 1978 than in the previous year, and the fall in the value of the US dollar (in which oil accounts are settled) togther with internal and external inflation had reduced the country's spending power by perhaps one-third.

This situation was sharply reversed in the following year (1979) when, as a direct result of the world oil shortage following the Iranian revolution, Nigeria was able to produce at a record 2.4 million b/d throughout the first half. Prices also increased sharply—by over 75 per cent from January to November—for the same reasons, and the very large surge in oil revenues led the government to limit production in order to keep revenues to manageable proportions.

The 'oil revenue now or later' question hinges, of course, on the probable life of Nigeria's oil reserves. The most authoritative unofficial figure—there are no official ones—for proved reserves is about 20000 million barrels, which indicates a life of under 30 years at a production level of 2.25 million b/d. This is not a particularly long time in which to develop alternative sources of comparable wealth. But this figure makes no allowance for improved recovery techniques, and of course makes no allowance for the possibility of new discoveries in the delta and its offshore, the deep offshore (still to be explored) and elsewhere on land. It is safe to assume that the oil will last very much longer than the 30 years indicated.

The government's concern over the size of Nigeria's proved reserves may have been prompted by estimates of the growth to be expected in internal demand for oil products. Excluding LPG, greases, and other solid products such as bitumen, consumption is currently running at over 100000 b/d, and is said to be increasing at an annual 25 per cent. Projected 10 to 15 per cent growth rates over the years to 1988 will raise internal consumption to some 350000 b/d and 500000 b/d respectively.

In addition to reducing significantly Nigeria's oil export availability, growth of this order will necessitate a new programme of refinery construction in the early 1980s. Capacity is expected to increase to 260000 b/d in 1980 with the completion of the 100000 b/d plant at Kaduna, on which good progress has been made. There are now two operational refineries—the original Shell (20 per cent) and NNPC (80 per cent—following the nationalization of BP's 20 per cent share) plant at Port Harcourt, currently running at its full 60000 b/d capacity and due to be expanded, and the 100000 b/d installation at Warri, commissioned in September 1978.

The latter, wholly owned by NNPC but operated with Italian assistance, is designed to process crude from Shell–BP's Ughelli blending station (some 25 kilometres away) and from Gulf's Escravos terminal (62 km distant). A full range of products is available, with facilities capable of producing a high proportion of light products for the local market. However, the absence of further downstream ventures (e.g. petrochemicals plants—although units are now under construction) means that high-value streams such as aromatics from the refineries are, of necessity, being used in petrol. This is wasteful, and results in the anomaly of 97 octane fuel being supplied for the local market —which, in view of the preponderance of Japanese cars in the country, could be met with fuel of a much lower grade. Warri's production is to be distributed throughout the country via a 3000 km network of pipelines and 19 storage depots, promising 'an end to gasoline shortages', according to the NNPC.

Using the gas

In common with many other OPEC countries Nigeria has only recently realized the potential of its second-largest energy resource—natural gas. For many years the gas, known as associated gas and produced together with the oil, was regarded as a by-product of little value; small quantities were used for electricity generation and other purposes at oilfields, but the rest was flared off. This is still the situation in Nigeria, with only a few per cent of the 18000 million cubic metres produced annually being utilized. But the technology for liquefying the gas and transporting it in refrigerated tank ships to consumers in Europe and the USA has developed rapidly; it is costly energy compared with crude oil, but in the view of many forecasters natural gas is the fuel which is best placed to meet the predicted 'energy gap' of the mid and late 1980s.

Nigeria's plans for exploiting its gas now centre on the construction of one large liquefaction plant at Bonny, to have an eventual capacity of 1600 million cubic feet/day (equivalent to some 16500 million cubic metres/year). This is to be built by a consortium of oil companies, with the state's NNPC taking a 60 per cent share; the cost is estimated at between $4500 million and $4900 million, with completion planned (very optimistically) for the early 1980s.

The plant will be fed with gas from the number of gas-only fields found in the delta in the course of oil exploration, in addition to associated gas. There should be no lack of supplies—one geologist commented recently that the delta is considered more of a gas province than an oil province. Nevertheless, a large pipeline network to gather the gas at Bonny will be necessary, and in view of the difficult terrain the cost of this is likely to be very great. Recognizing the difficulties, the government has said that it expects to be involved in this stage of the project to the extent of at least 85 per cent. The government will also take a 50 per cent holding in shipping facilities.

But Nigeria's reserves of gas are believed to be very substantial, and it would clearly be undesirable to continue wastefully flaring a premium, clean, and sought-after energy resource. Gas reserves have been estimated variously at 1250000 million cubic metres (a Shell figure), 1422000 million cubic metres (an end of 1974 US Federal Power Commission figure), and between 1650000 and 2100000 million cubic metres (according to Nigerian scientists), indicating a life of 75 years at the liquefaction plant's full capacity. Reserves could therefore be as great, on an energy-equivalent basis, as two-thirds of the country oil reserves.

Bibliography

Readers are directed to oil industry journals, particularly *Petroleum Economist* (5 Pemberton Row, Fleet Street, London EC4), for further material on Nigeria's oil industry.

The following may also be of interest:
Evamy, B. D. *et al.*, Hydrocarbon habitat of tertiary Niger delta. *The American Association of Petroleum Geologists Bulletin* Vol. 62, No. 1, pp. 1–39 (January 1978). (Geological aspects of the delta.) Scorcelletti, P. Giorgio. Petroleum developments in central and southern Africa in 1977, *The American Association of Petroleum Geologists Bulletin* Vol. 62, No. 10, pp. 1844–97 (October 1978). (Drilling and exploration summary for 1977.) Panter-Brick, K. (ed.), *Soldiers and oil: the political transformation of Nigeria*. Frank Cass & Co. Ltd., London (1978). (Contains some material on oil policy.)

22

Hydro power plans in Nigeria

G. V. ECKENFELDER

The Niger, 4300 km from source to mouth and draining 1.9 million km^2 ranks third among the rivers of Africa, after the Zaire and Nile, in the extent of its region of influence. The main stem of the river traverses four countries—Guinea, Mali, Niger, and Nigeria, flows along the boundary between Benin and Niger, and its tributaries reach into Ivory Coast, Upper Volta, Benin, Chad, and Cameroun. Much of its course is in the Guinea, Sahel and savannah regions of West Africa where it forms the only significant source of water. Its influence and that of its tributaries are thus felt in nine countries. It has been called the River of Sorrow and of Hope—sorrow because in times of drought those who depend upon it sometimes starve, but when the rains come and the floods flow over the bottom lands, there is plenty and people rejoice.

The Niger rises in the highlands of Guinea, less than 300 km from the Atlantic Ocean. It thence flows north-east 600 km to the great inland delta of Mali where it is dispersed in a maze of channels, lakes, and swamps, and where a substantial amount of its flow disappears in evaporation and into the aquifer. This region is, economically, one of the most valuable of the Upper Basin because, in normal years, it supports an important agricultural society, and its channels and backwaters teem with fish. Below the delta region the channel is once more well defined, and the river continues its course across arid plains and through the cities of Timbuktu, Gao, and Niamey, entering Nigeria below Goya, at a point where the three countries, Niger, Benin, and Nigeria come together. The Niger then courses through open and lightly wooded and semi-arid savannah country to Lokoja, where it is joined by the Benue, its major tributary. Below Lokoja the climate changes to humid equatorial, with increasingly heavy forest. The river enters its coastal delta below Onitsha, where swamp and rain forest prevail and where it divides into a myriad of channels. Here, the great wealth of Nigerian oil is found.

Hydrologically, the river in Nigeria is characterized by two distinct floods. The Black Flood, named because the resulting water is relatively free of sediment, thus appearing dark, is derived from the summer rains of the Guinea highlands. Because of the delaying effect of the delta region of Mali, combined with the flat gradient and slow velocity, the Black Flood does not appear in central Nigeria until the following December.

The second flood, the White Flood, so called because the silt it carries gives the water a light colour, comes from the rain which falls on the basin in northern and central Nigeria during August and September.

First published in *Energy International*, Vol. 14, No. 7 (July 1977), pp. 20–2. Reprinted by permission of the author and *Energy International*.

The existence of two flood seasons is reflected in the typical natural flow hydrograph of the Niger at Kainji. The historic minimum monthly flow is 30 m^3/s, and the maximum is 4072 m^3/s. The regulated outflow during the period 1954–75 was 865 m^3/s. Average flow at Kainji during this period was 1474 m^3/s.

The gradient of the Niger is very flat and there are few places where the height of the banks exceed 40 m. The potential hydro sites on the main stem are therefore limited to low head developments. The only existing development in Nigeria, Kainji, has a maximum net head of 40.4 m. On the other hand, the gentle gradient and generally broad valley provides the opportunity for a number of large storage reservoirs. At Kainji, the live storage is 11.5 billion m^3.

Upper Basin development

While this article is concerned mainly with the hydroelectric potential of the Niger Basin, it is worth noting the situation upstream. In Guinea, at Dabola on the Tinkisso tributary of the Niger, there is a 1.5 MW plant. In Mali there are two plants on the Niger itself, Sotuba just downstream of Bamako with an installation of 4.85 MW, and Sansanding Dam, 50 km below Segou. This development provides regulation for irrigation, navigation, and also constitutes a fish pond. The dam is equipped with navigation locks. A number of potential sites have been identified, as shown in Table 22.1.

Power production is the main objective of the schemes in Guinea and Upper Volta, but in Mali and Niger the sites under consideration would be developed as multi-purpose projects involving power, irrigation and navigation with some flood-control benefits. In Mali there are large areas adjacent to the sites which are suitable for irrigation, and the same applies, but to a lesser extent, in Niger. In this respect the Niger is a vital resource to these countries where food production is a tenuous and uncertain activity. Storage reservoirs, permitting two or three irrigated crops per year and with some carry-over capacity to alleviate the extreme low-flow cycles, would mean the difference between dire scarcity and adequate food supply with some surplus. Following the disastrous drought of the early 1970s a number of programmes were initiated with the long-term objective of a more stable agricultural industry. These programmes are under the auspices of the River Niger Commission, which represents the nine countries drained by the river.

Kainji is the most important river-use development built thus far. It is owned by the National Electric Power Authority (NEPA) and is the largest generating plant in Nigeria. Located some 1000 km above the mouth and 580 km from Lagos, its power plant contains four 80 MW units, and two 105 MW units just installed. Two 128 MW units have been in operation since mid-1978, thereby raising the total capacity to 836 MW. After these additions are complete there will still be space for four

Table 22.1. Potential dam sites on the Niger and major tributaries

Country	*Site*	*River*	*Capacity (10^9 m^3)*	*Output (MW)*
Guinea	Fomi	Niadan	5.0	85
Guinea	Kamarato	Baoule		1.7
Mali	Selingue	Sankarani	2.0	11.2
Mali	Tossaye	Niger	2.0	Unknown
Mali	Labezanga	Niger	Unknown	Unknown
Niger	Kandadji	Niger	15.0	200
Niger	Le W	Niger	Unknown	Unknown
Benin		Mekrou	Unknown	Unknown

more units. The extension is being carried out under the direction of Montreal Engineering Co. Ltd.

The Kainji project as a whole consists of a 65.5 m-high concrete gravity dam, which contains the intake gates and penstocks for existing and future units, and adjacent to the intake a spillway composed of four sector gates 15.3 m square. Adjacent to the left abutment of the concrete dam is a navigation lock 198 m long and 12.2 m wide with a lift of 24.7 m. Downstream of the lock is a short length of canal followed by a second lock.

Flanking the gravity dam on the right is a section of earth dam. A second earth dam about 2 km to the left of the main structures closes a saddle in the reservoir rim. The reservoir has an area at full supply of 1200 km^3 and extends 136 km upstream.

The power from Kainji is transmitted to the NEPA grid over two 330 kV transmission lines. A third line, partly energized at 330 kV and partly at 132 kV, carries power to the north of Nigeria and to Niamey, the capital of Niger. This 560 km line is extremely important to Niger as it provides energy at a lower cost than can be generated in that country by other means. The construction of the line was in part a tangible result of the mutual international co-operation which is the policy of the River Niger Commission.

The five existing units at Kainji can pass 1560 m^3/s at full head. The three units under construction will increase the plant discharge to 2630 m^3/s. The design maximum spillway capacity is 7900 m^3/s at full supply level. Construction of Kainji started in 1963 and the initial four units were commissioned in 1968. A new town, New Bussa, was built to house the construction workers, and later housed many of the people who had lived in the villages flooded by the reservoir. New Bussa also is the home of the Kainji operating staff.

Kainji is a well conceived, well constructed and well maintained development and will serve Nigeria for many, many years. In these times of growing cost of fuels it is indeed a priceless asset.

Navigation potential

In its natural state the Niger possessed little possibility of becoming a useful waterway for any craft larger than the picturesque and graceful canoes which have plied its water since time immemorial. Only during periods of high water were the rapids, reefs, and sandbanks submerged, and even then the swift current was a hazard. When Kainji was built, some 130 km of previously difficult navigation channel was submerged and replaced by a deep and slow-moving lake. It was foreseen that in the future other dams on the river would each in turn remove other obstructions. Furthermore, with its regulated discharge, Kainji would provide adequate flow even during the dry season to float vessels of one or more metres draught. Accordingly, when Kainji was designed, locks were included as a first step in a waterway which ultimately would carry commercial vessels the whole length of Nigeria and into land-locked Niger and Mali. This has actually become a reality, and tows of barges have penetrated from the Niger Delta into Niger during high-water seasons. As further dams are built the objective of year-round navigation will be achieved. The locks at Kainji can accommodate tows of two barges and one tug with an overall length of 150 m and a draught of 2.7 m at normal low water level. A tow of this size can carry 1000 tonnes of freight. The dimensions of the Kainji locks will become the minimum standard for the locks in future dams downstream.

One hundred kilometres below Kainji, just above the town of Jebba, is the site for a project with a potential head of approximately 30 m. The possibilities of this site were recognized many years ago and preliminary studies were made in the 1950s prior to the selection of Kainji with its large reservoir. Once Kainji was built its regulated discharge added greatly to the potential value of Jebba, and it was only a matter of time before serious studies would be carried out. In early 1975 NEPA engaged Montreal

Engineering Company to undertake detailed investigations and a feasibility study of the site, which has now been completed. The firm are now proceeding with detailed engineering and design. Construction is scheduled to start in 1978, with completion in 1982.

In addition to the regulated flow from Kainji, Jebba will utilize the discharge from 41 000 km^2 of intervening drainage area. Records dating from 1954 indicate a minimum incremental flow of near zero during the driest period and a maximum monthly flow of 1820 m^3/s. The average, for the period 1954 to 1975, is calculated to be 132 m^3/s. On the basis of these flows added to the discharges from Kainji, an installation of 500 to 600 MW is warranted.

Whereas at Kainji, massive igneous and metamorphic rock exists at shallow depth along the entire length of the dam, the situation at Jebba is less attractive. At some distance below Kainji the Niger enters a deep submerged gorge, evidently carved at a time of low sea-levels or possibly during a period of continental uplift. At Jebba this sand-filled slot meanders from side to side of the river, and has a depth of about 75 m and a width of some 150 m. The banks, as well as a number of islands in the reach under consideration, are mainly composed of hard, jointed gneissic quartz-rich rock. These geological characteristics govern the type and arrangement of structures. The spillway, intake, powerhouse, and navigation locks must be situated on the shore where the rock is exposed or at shallow depth. The river section, with its great depth of unconsolidated sediments, requires a fill-type dam with a suitable measure of seepage control. This could consist of a concrete diaphragm wall placed in a slurry-filled excavation, a slurry trench, or an upstream blanket. The studies thus far lean towards a blanket. A number of alternative layouts, on three possible axes have been examined, in the field and in the course of the office studies, and the optimum arrangement is emerging from an examination of safety, cost, schedule, and convenience.

Jebba is well situated with respect to NEPA's transmission system, there being already in existence near Jebba a 330 kV sub-station fed by Kainji. Access to the site is favourable, with both railway and paved highway from Lagos crossing the river within 3 km. There is also the possibility of transport to the site by shallow-draught river craft from the mouth of the river.

The Niger, below Jebba and in its tributaries, offers a substantial potential for additional development. The sites at Lokoja, under investigation, and Onitsha have an estimated capacity of 1950 and 750 MW respectively: dams here will further improve conditions for navigation. On the Kaduna, the Shiroro site now under development will produce 600 MW, and Makurdi on the Benue, now under investigation, 660 MW. The Cross River, which rises in Cameroun and flows into the sea at the eastern extremity of the Niger Delta, has a number of sites, the most interesting of which is Ikom, where a preliminary feasibility study is being carried out. It has an estimated potential of 400 MW. The foregoing six sites, including Jebba, are considered to be the most promising, and have a total estimated capacity of 4650 MW at 50 per cent capacity factor. Other sites in the Niger and Cross Basins have been subject to reconnaissance or preliminary surveys. The 10 best of these have an estimated total capacity of about 2700 MW at 50 per cent capacity factor.

It is not possible, within the scope of this article, to discuss the sequence and timing of the expansion of NEPA's generating facilities. It suffices to say that the six projects—Jebba, Shiroro, Lokoja, Onitsha, Makurdi, and Ikom—are being seriously considered for development over the next decade or so and Jebba and Shiroro are being investigated in depth.

We have seen that Nigeria is relatively well endowed with hydro sites. This, combined with substantial reserves of oil and gas, places Nigeria in a fortunate situation with regard to electrical power.

23

Energy resources and demands in Zambia and in Africa south of the Equator

ENAR ESKILSSON

Energy situation in Zambia

Zambia is fortunate in being blessed with enormous amounts of sunshine and with plenty of water in its many rivers which offer suitable sites for hydro-power development. Apart from this, Zambia has appreciable coal reserves, but no other fossil fuels and so far no useful geothermal resources, and, though further investigations may be worthwhile, petroleum products have to be imported.

The main river systems of Zambia are the Zambesi and the Luapula. The former rises where the borders of Angola, Zaire, and Zambia meet. In its lower reaches it forms the boundary between Zambia and Rhodesia. It has two main tributaries—the Kafue and the Luangwa, both confined to Zambia, except that the latter forms the boundary between Zambia and Mozambique for a short distance before its confluence with Zambesi which finally through Mozambique, discharges itself into the Indian Ocean. Luapula flows northwards along the border between Zaire and Zambia into Lake Mweru and then to Zaire river.

The three major existing hydro developments in Zambia are Victoria Falls on Zambesi river 108 MW, Kafue Gorge on Kafue river 900 MW, and Kariba North on Zambesi river 600 MW, giving altogether 10 500 GWh firm energy.

Further hydro development on Kafue river would produce 3000 GWh. On the border with Rhodesia new sites for hydro development on Zambesi river as joint ventures with Rhodesia will ultimately yield around 20 000 GWh, of which 10 000 GWh for Zambia. An extension of Kariba North may add 600 GWh to the available energy.

A development on Luapula river with a number of stations could produce 5000 GWh which has to be shared with Zaire, thus for Zambia 2500 GWh. Minor schemes in different rivers will add altogether around 400 GWh to the available energy.

The future hydro-power development in Zambia which now can be foreseen corresponds to a total amount firm energy of 16 500 GWh. Together with the existing supply of 10 500 GWh Zambia's total hydro-power resources thus amount to 27 000 GWh which is almost five times the present total electricity consumption in the country.

The main transmission system in Zambia is arranged for 330 kV. This interconnected system covers both Zambia and Rhodesia and is over a 220 kV transmission line connected with the transmission system in the Shaba Province of southern Zaire with the industrial area around Lubumbashi. An international exchange of electric power with Zaire has been in existence since 1956

First published in the *Transactions of the Tenth World Energy Conference*, Istanbul, Turkey, September 1977. Paper 1.4–5. Reprinted by permission of World Energy Conference.

and with Rhodesia since 1959.

The mining of coal in Zambia was introduced in 1964 and has gradually increased to around 900 million kg per year. Coal is used very little for electricity generation and only occasionally in the old thermal power stations belonging to the mining companies in the copper-belt area. The main quantities, however, are used for the mines. The rest is delivered to the railways and to different industries. The recoverable reserves of coal in Zambia are around 50000 million kg and the total resources around 150000 million kg. The calorific value is about 25000 kJ per kg.

Another type of energy is charcoal, which might be of some importance in the future since there are rich woods in the country. Charcoal can be used not only for cooking, heating, etc., but also for distillation processes for production of certain acids and oils, and above all methanol for vehicles.

The total requirement of petroleum products in 1974 was 900 million kg. The main part is imported through a pipeline from Dar-es-Salaam 1700 km to Ndola. The original pipeline was commissioned in 1968. A refinery was built in Ndola commencing operation in 1973 and designed for 1100 million kg per year. The present pipeline is 200 mm with a loopline 300 mm over a distance of 770 km. The work is under way of completing the second pipeline. The system will thus be duplicated and used both for crude oil for the refinery and for light petroleum products.

There are limited possibilities for converting the energy from the sun into usable electricity or other forms of energy. Electricity can be obtained by solar cells but only in small quantities and at a high price. On the other hand solar energy can be used for water heating, for industrial drying, for solar cookers, etc.

Zambia has already several houses prepared with special equipment for taking advantage of the solar energy for different purposes especially for heating. A hospital is under construction where all requirements of heated water will be obtained from solar energy collected from the roofs of the buildings. But more research has to be carried out and more experimental houses to be built.

It should not be forgotten that nature allows us to use the sun's energy in indirect ways, for example by evaporating moisture from the ground to deposit it as rain elsewhere. This keeps our rivers flowing and makes it possible to use them to produce hydroelectric power.

The most important utilization of solar energy is, however, for producing agricultural commodities. The growth of plants has to be considered a rational use of solar energy so abundant in Zambia like other countries in tropical regions. Zambia has suitable soil, huge areas of undeveloped land, many rivers for irrigation, plenty of manpower, and an excellent climate created by the sun.

Main energy resources and significant power plants in the other countries

The electricity output in Angola has expanded rapidly with utilization of the considerable hydroelectric potentials. The largest plant is Cambambe in Cuanza river opened in 1962, but the major development will be the Cunono Dam scheme undertaken jointly with Namibia. The total resources of hydroelectric power are estimated at some 50 times the present requirement of electricity.

With regard to reserves of oil and natural gas, Angola (Cabinda not included) is second among the 16 countries in southern Africa. Oil production started in 1956 and a refinery was built at Luanda in 1957. Except for crude oil there are big oil reserves in bituminous sand. The estimated recoverable oil in these deposits is in fact larger than the reserves of crude oil and natural gas. Angola has also some resources of uranium for nuclear power.

In Botswana electricity is generated in diesel-electric plants or in a steam-power plant. The available national energy resources in the country are moderate amounts of hydro-power not yet utilized and small amounts of coal partly utilized in steam power-plants.

In Burundi electricity is partly imported from Zaire but Burundi has considerable hydro-power resources and there are plans to develop several sites. One scheme under review is to exploit Kagera river.

In Kenya there are no known deposits of fossil fuels on adequate scale for economic exploitation. Kenya, however, has except for Zaire and Tanzania the highest hydro-power potential in southern Africa with the biggest resources in Tana river. Here are ultimate plans to install 205 MW at Citaru. Transmission systems are built for 132 kV. Oil is imported and a refinery in Mombasa has a capacity of 4000 million kg a year. An indigenous source of energy which is being developed is geothermal steam. From an investigated area in Rift Valley Province can be expected a power potential between 170 and 1400 MW for 25 years.

Lesotho has moderate amounts of hydro-power under development. The biggest plan is Oxbow hydroelectric scheme in co-operation with South Africa.

Malawi has small amounts of coal and some amounts of thorium for nuclear power but the important energy source is hydro-power. The regulation of Lake Malawi gives a minimum reliable discharge of 170 m^2/s in Shire river. This river has over a distance of 84 km a concentrated series of rapids totalling 390 m with suitable sites for hydro development, in the first place Nkula and Tedzani. Together with hydro potentials in other rivers there are possibilities to obtain 5300 GWh firm hydro-power of which less than 50 per cent is expected to be utilized before the year 2000.

There are appreciable reserves of coal and natural gas in Mozambique but the most important energy source is hydroelectric power both in Zambesi river and in other rivers. The big project is Cabora Bassa, recently completed in its first stage for 2000 MW with a high voltage direct current, transmission link to Apollo outside Pretoria in South Africa, a distance of 1400 km. The line voltage is ± 533 kV and the ultimate capacity 1750 MW. A second stage of Cabora Bassa is envisaged for 1600 MW.

Namibia has significant hydro-power resources as well as coal. The biggest station is for 90 MW and coal-fired. A sizeable hydro development is under way at Ruacana in the Cunene river on the border to Angola with an ultimate capacity of 240 MW.

In Rhodesia the considerable coal resources have long played an important role for the supply of energy, and Rhodesia is in this respect third among the 16 countries in southern Africa. The utilization of hydro-power has been increasing over the last 15 years and electricity is now mainly generated in hydro-power plants. The biggest plant is Kariba South for 660 MW in Zambesi river. This river has on the border with Zambia several suitable sites for hydro development. The main transmission system has a voltage of 330 kV. All petroleum products have to be imported. For this purpose there is a pipeline from Beira in Mozambique to Salisbury in Rhodesia.

Rwanda's electric system is connected with Zaire for exchange of power however on a small scale. The country has probably hydro-power resources. In addition there are prospects for exploitation of natural gas from Lake Kivu.

The main coal resources in the 16 countries in southern Africa are located in South Africa. The recoverable reserves amount to more than 10×10^{12} kg and the total resources in place amount to between 45 and 75×10^{12} kg corresponding to about 1000 times the annual production. South Africa has smaller amounts of natural gas and oil shale resources of which most are developed.

Electricity is imported from Cabora Bassa in Mozambique over a high voltage direct current transmission system. The distribution of electricity includes parts of Lesotho, Mozambique and Swaziland. South Africa has transmission systems for 400, 275 220, and 132 kV. The total generation in South Africa amounted in 1974 to 67000 million kWh and the corresponding installed capacity in all power stations was 13400 MW.

South Africa has thorium resources and extremely rich uranium resources of lower cost and is in this respect the second country in the world. There are 298 million kg of uranium with a maximum cost of $36 per kg. A nuclear power station is being planned near Cape Town to be commissioned late 1982.

Petroleum products are imported, most of the crude oil being refined in Durban. Of the total needs of refined oil of around 11 000 million kg in 1974, more than 10 per cent is produced from coal within the country.

Swaziland has appreciable hydraulic resources which are partly developed and quite large coal resources, and in this respect ranks second among the 16 countries in southern Africa. A 132 kV interconnection exists with South Africa. Plans have been discussed to erect a large thermal station, thus creating a more viable project and to export the main part of the energy.

In Tanzania there are appreciable resources of coal but above all there are great hydro resources. Tanzania in this respect being the second country after Zaire in southern Africa. The biggest hydro plant is Kidatu in Great Ruaha river with a capacity of 200 MW. From the site goes a 220-kV transmission line to Dar-es-Salaam.

Uganda possesses no fossil fuels but has an abundance of hydro power resources, most of them unharnessed. The river Nile has a drop of over 500 m between Lake Victoria and Lake Albert corresponding to a generating capacity of 3000 MW. However, the major energy source has been Owen Falls for 150 MW at the outlet of Lake Victoria. A part of the capacity has been delivered to Kenya over a 132-kV transmission line.

Zaire's hydroelectrical potential is from one source estimated at 100000 MW but other sources have indicated 180000 MW. This sum corresponds to one-third of Africa's hydroelectric resources and amounts to around 700000 GWh. The biggest project for power generation is the Inga complex in Zaire river with one of the highest hydroelectric potentials in the world but with an ultimate capacity of some 40000 MW. The first stage has a capacity of 351 MW and the second near completion 1272 MW. This second stage is combined with a high voltage direct-current transmission link to Shaba Province near the border to Zambia. The voltage is $\pm$500 kV, the distance 1700 km, and the ultimate capacity 1120 MW. The huge hydro-power resources in Zaire could, as far as energy is concerned, be sufficient to meet the total electricity requirements in all the 16 countries in southern Africa up to the year 2000.

Zaire has not only great hydro-power resources but also appreciable amounts of coal, oil, natural gas, oil shale resources, and uranium.

With regard to petroleum products the total requirements in 1974 amounted to 800 million kg. These products were mainly imported as crude oil and refined in a refinery for 750 million kg per year located at Matadi near the western coast of Zaire. Different products have been imported from neighbouring countries but also exported, especially fuel oil.

Summary of electricity requirements

The result of the study regarding electricity requirements in the different countries is shown in Table 23.1. A forecast has been made for every country giving the estimates for 1984. It should be added that it has been difficult to obtain information from a few countries. It has therefore in a few cases been necessary to make rough estimates or guesses.

To make the picture of the countries more significant, figures are given both for the size of the country and the number of inhabitants. The most densely populated rural areas in Africa are Burundi and Rwanda with 132 and 162 inhabitants respectively per square kilometre. This can be compared with

Table 23.1. Estimated population and electricity requirement

Country	*Area thousand km²*	*Population million end 1974*	*Electricity requirement (GWh)*	
			1974	*1984*
Angola	1246	6	1000	3000
Botswana	712	0.6	300	500
Burundi	28	3.8	300	700
Kenya	644	12.8	1100	2400
Lesotho	30	1.2	30	100
Malawi	118	5	210	550
Mozambique	783	10	700	2000
Namibia	835	0.8	400	1200
Rhodesia	389	6.1	5700	14000
Rwanda	26	4.2	300	700
South Africa	1223	24	67000	130000
Swaziland	17	0.5	150	350
Tanzania	936	14.5	570	1500
Uganda	236	11	700	1000
Zaire	2344	24.5	4000	15000
Zambia	752	4.7	5700	11000
Total	10319	129.8	88160	184000

Botswana and Namibia with less than 1 inhabitant per square kilometre or with Angola and Zambia with 5 or 6 inhabitants respectively per square kilometre.

The total electricity requirement increases from 88160 GWh in 1974 to 184000 GWh in 1984 or from 679 to 1418 kWh per capita counted as an average value and related to the population in 1974. If the yearly population increase is 2 per cent the consumption per capita in 1984 will be 1163 kWh. Assuming an average load factor of 70 per cent and a necessary stand-by with margin for the different systems of 20 per cent the result is a total required capacity of 18000 MW in 1974 and 37500 MW in 1984.

World energy conference survey of energy resources 1974

The survey has information about most of the 16 countries but the material is in some cases rather old and dated between 1960 and 1973. It gives the amounts for installed and installable capacity based on average annual flow conditions and is expressed in GWh (millions kWh) shown in Table 23.2.

The result is around 1 million GWh which is about half of the estimated hydroelectric resources in Africa which are estimated at around 2 million GWh.

The survey gives the amounts for recoverable solid fuel reserves in thousand million kg, as shown in Table 23.3. The

Table 23.2

Angola	48320
Botswana	8952
Kenya	53760
Lesotho	2600
Malawi*	400
Mozambique	45160
Namibia	3600
Rhodesia	20000
South Africa	8546
Swaziland	10080
Tanzania	83200
Uganda	72000
Zaire	660000
Zambia†	15336
Total in GWh	1031954

*The actual resources are 5300 GWh.
†The actual resources are 27000 GWh.

Table 23.3

Botswana	506
Mozambique	80
Rhodesia	1390
South Africa	10584
Swaziland	1820
Tanzania	180
Zaire	720
Zambia	51
Total	15331 thousand million kg

corresponding amount for total resources in place is 58 162 thousand million kg.

The survey gives the following amounts for recoverable reserves of crude oil expressed in thousand million kg.

Angola	49.4
Zaire	68.2
Total	117.6 thousand million kg

The survey gives the amount for recoverable reserves of natural gas expressed in cubic kilometres shown in Table 23.4.

Table 23.4

Angola (excluding Cabinda)	39.6
Mozambique	72.4
South Africa	11.3
Zaire	29
Total	152.3 cubic kilometres

The survey gives the following amounts for recoverable reserves of oil from shale and bituminous sand expressed in thousand million kg.

Angola	200
South Africa	20.2
Zaire	1550
Total	1770.2 thousand million kg

Table 23.5 indicates for every country the electricity consumption in 1974, the potential of hydroelectric resources per year and the corresponding potential factor or relationship between the two values. The table also indicates the potential values from non-renewable resources converted to electricity which means 1 kWh = 10.5×10^6 J instead of 3.6×10^6 J referring to the energy content. Finally the table shows the corresponding years of supply if all non-renewable resources should be used for generating electricity at the present consumption level.

To summarize:

Hydroelectric energy per year 1032000 GWh or 3.7×10^{18} J
Solid fuels 15331 thousand million kg equal to 374.5×10^{18} J
Crude oil 117.6 thousand million kg equal to 5.1×10^{18} J
Natural gas 152.3 cubic kilometres equal to 5.8×10^{18} J
Oil from oil shale and bituminous sand 1770.2 thousand million kg equal to 76.6×10^{18}
Total fossil fuels 462×10^{18} J

The following conclusions can be stated. The most important energy resources are no doubt the hydroelectric resources overwhelming and inexhaustible. The total generation of electricity in 1974 in all 16 countries corresponds to only 8.4 per cent of the total hydroelectric resources. In spite of this fact the main part or more than two-thirds of the electricity consumption is generated in thermal power plants mainly in South Africa. Less than 3 per cent of the hydroelectric resources are exploited.

The energy content in fossil fuels is enormous and the resources are well spread over the region. The big problem seems to be the conversion to suitable forms of energy either in processing coal into oil or in exploiting oil shale formations.

Transmission

Alternating current transmission lines have been used for transmitting electric power since about 85 years ago. With increasing demand of power came the request for

Table 23.5. Electricity consumed and electric energy available in GWh

Country	*Consumption in 1974*	*Potential of hydroelectric resources per year*	*Corresponding potential factor*	*Potential from non-renewable resources*	*Corresponding years of supply*
Angola	1000	48430	48	1170000	1170
Botswana	300	8952	30	533000	1780
Burundi	300				
Kenya	1100	53760	49		
Lesotho	30	2600	87		
Malawi	210	5300	25		
Mozambique	700	45160	65	378000	540
Namibia	400	3600	9		
Rhodesia	5700	20000	4	3880000	681
Rwanda	300				
South Africa	67000	8546	0.125	23860000	357
Swaziland	150	10080	67	5080000	33900
Tanzania	570	83200	146	481000	844
Uganda	700	72000	103		
Zaire	4000	660000	165	8490000	2120
Zambia	5700	27000	5	126000	22
Total	88160	1048518	12	43998000	500

gradually increased voltages. Early in 1952 the first 400 kV system was commissioned. Since then several power systems have been introduced with 500 kV and lately with still higher voltages 735 and 765 kV. Systems exist for up to 5000 MW over distances of up to 800 km. Studies and designs are on the way for creation of ultra-high voltages (UHV) above 1000 kV. Plans are thus made for 7000 MW over distances of about 1500 km. Equipment for 1100 kV has been tested. It is no doubt feasible to use levels of at least 1500 kV. The determining factors for the economic choice of system voltage is the power to be transmitted and the distance. The first high voltage direct current transmission line carrying 20 MW at 125 kV was built already in the 1800s but the real development utilizing converters came much later. The first commercial high voltage direct current (HVDC) scheme with converters was commissioned in 1954 for 20 MW at 100 kV. Gradually new schemes for higher voltages and longer distances as well as greater capacity were created. The largest, the longest, and the highest voltage scheme is designed for 1920 MW at ± 533 kV between Cabora Bassa and Apollo in South Africa and in operation since 1976. The still longer Inga Falls transmission system was commissioned in 1978. During the next decade there is every reason to believe that HVDC transmission systems are going to be developed for still higher capacities and longer distances. Direct current transmissions have usually been used when the task has been to transmit a large load over a long distance without taps on the way. This does not mean that a tap cannot be arranged, but it is costly. If it is a question about an interconnector between several stations or systems alternating current is usually the economic solution. Here again for big systems stability and security requirements might cause problems.

The biggest international transmission system has its centre in Zambia and Rhodesia and consists of around 3000 km 330 kV lines. The system has through a 220 kV line, which is built for 330 kV, connection with Victoria Falls power stations in Zambia and through another 220 kV line connection with the Lubumbashi industrial system in the Shaba Province of Zaire. This link over a distance of 200 km has proved to be of great importance for both Zaire and Zambia. Large amounts of energy have been transported over the border from time to time in different directions aiming at improving the power balance and strengthening the reliability.

The connection might be of still greater importance after the completion of the HVDC link between Inga Falls and Lubumbashi, but only after a strengthening of the link, for instance with a 330 kV line, giving possibilities for a firm transfer of up to 600 MW.

With Cabora Bassa, only 350 km from the nearest point of the existing 330 kV transmission system in Zambia and Rhodesia, there seem to be ample opportunities and great advantages with a connecting 330 kV line. Such a line could be useful both for general exchange of electric power and for facilitating further development on both sides. The cost for a single line would be around 30 million dollars. The corresponding unit cost for a transfer of 600 MW at a load factor of 70 per cent is around 0.08 cent per kWh.

Owing to the fact that Zambia would be located in the centre of the envisaged interconnected system it seems natural that the national control centre under erection in Lusaka could play an important role in the administrative and operative achievements necessary for an efficient utilization of available resources.

Co-operation regarding electricity distribution started a long time ago between Kenya and Uganda and has been seriously discussed between Kenya and Tanzania. These three countries (the East African Community) are rather densely populated and have similar requirements of electricity. They have advantages of short distances in erecting interconnections. Suitable voltages 132 and 220 kV are already established and a further development for mutual benefit seems natural.

With regard to electricity connections it is in the first place a question about extensions of existing lines and at a later stage a possible introduction of a higher voltage. Owing to the fact that several big hydro developments are under construction or being planned the justified interconnections have to be carefully studied.

A co-operative movement has been introduced regarding petroleum products and this arrangement has certainly contributed to the development in the energy field. It concerns import with shipping and agreements with oil-producing countries and oil companies. It also concerns refineries, storage facilities, and distribution.

In South Africa there is a large transmission system with, in 1974, around 5000 km of 400-kV lines and 14 000 km of lines for 275, 220, and 132 kV. Connections are established with Lesotho, Swaziland, and southern Mozambique. This system is being used for distribution of 75 per cent of all electricity generated in the 16 countries in southern Africa. In 10 years this percentage might be reduced to 70 but here is still a dominating centre from many points of view.

The long-range planning to meet the overall energy requirements in southern Africa must be to utilize the enormous inexhaustible hydro-power resources in the northern countries, especially in Zaire, to meet the growing demand of energy in the southern countries. Two important initiatives have been taken in this respect with HVDC lines, one in the West from Inga Falls to Lubumbashi 1700 km, and one in the East from Cabora Bassa to Apollo 1400 km.

It seems realistic to consider such connections in a future with higher capacities and over longer distances. The distance from Inga Falls to Johannesburg is about 3000 km. A double bipolar line for 6000 MW would probably, with present prices, cost around $1600 million. The corresponding unit costs for a transfer of 6000 MW at a load factor of 70 per cent will be around 0.45 of a cent per kWh.

If and when available hydro-power resources for reasonable costs in the East African Community cannot keep pace with the requirements one could envisage another big transmission connection from the Inga Falls to reinforce the supply in Uganda, Kenya, and Tanzania. Such a connection ought to have a distance of around 3000 km to the centre of the region.

The conclusion is that utilization of direct current has provided ample opportunities for transfer of high amounts of electric energy over vast distances at reasonable cost.

Petroleum products and pipelines

Crude oil has been found in Angola and Zaire, in both countries in rather large quantities. Natural gas has been found in Angola, Mozambique, Rwanda, South Africa, and Zaire. The total amount is about the same as for crude oil. The total amounts of recoverable reserves of crude oil and natural gas are small as compared with coal, and also in comparison with oil from oil shale and bituminous sand which have been found in Angola, South Africa, and Zaire with especially large quantities in Zaire.

The total consumption of petroleum products may be estimated at around 18 000 million kg (in the whole of Africa around 50 000 million kg). Known refineries are established at Luanda in Angola, Mombassa in Kenya, Salisbury in Rhodesia, Durban, and other places in South Africa, Matadi in Zaire, and Ndola in Zambia. The total refinery capacity might be somewhat larger than the consumption (in the whole of Africa 62 000 million kg). The recoverable reserves of crude oil for all 16 countries in southern Africa are only around eight times the present annual consumption.

Known pipelines are the following:

Dar-es-Salaam in Kenya to Ndola in Zambia 200 + 300 mm 1700 km;
Beira in Mozambique to Salisbury in Rhodesia 500 km;
Durban to Rand in South Africa, 300 mm, 700 km.

A comparison between costs for transporting energy in the form of electricity and the corresponding costs for transport of oil in pipelines does ordinarily result in lower costs for electricity over transmission lines. For very large quantities, however, the result can be the opposite. An example is given below.

The costs vary within a wide range, depending upon the site conditions. 6000 MW electricity can be transported 1000 km over a double bipolar high voltage direct current line costing 555 million dollars. The transported energy in a year at 100 per cent load factor is 52 560 million kWh or 189×10^{15} J. The unit cost is thus 0.106 of a cent per kWh or 0.029 of a cent per MJ.

A corresponding transport of 4360 million kg oil per year containing the same amount of energy can be done with a pipeline with a diameter of 360 mm costing around $150 per m or in total $150 million. This gives a unit cost of 0.008 of a cent per MJ.

If the oil is going to be used for generating electricity the transported amount has to be 12 600 million kg. Thecorresponding cost for a 610-mm pipeline is $255 per m or totally $255 million. The unit cost in this case will be around 0.05 of a cent per kWh or 50 per cent of the transmission line costs.

It can be finally concluded that there seems to be no justification for such large transfers of energy in the form of oil in southern Africa but certainly with regard to electricity. To transport gas is more expensive than to transport oil. A pipeline with a certain diameter can transport four to five times as many calories of oil than calories of gas.

Conclusions and recommendations

Southern Africa is a region with enormous natural possibilities and potentials of value for mankind. It has firstly in many countries, a good climate and suitable soil for agriculture, and in addition vast areas of undeveloped land which could be cultivated. Increased initiatives could create huge crops of different kinds and a variety of fruits, plants, etc., not only to meet the existing demands, but also to arrange export to other needy peoples and for building up a positive trade balance.

Secondly, we have to deal with the mineral wealth of tropical Africa. Southern Africa has rich resources of ferrous metals such as iron ore, cobalt, chrome ore, manganese ore, columbite, and tantalite. Better known are base metals, for instance copper, tin, lead, and zinc. Of the light metals there are magnesium and of precious metals there are gold and silver. Of the other minerals there are diamonds, asbestos, and fertilizers and also radioactive minerals. Finally, there are the mineral fuels.

Thirdly, southern Africa has rich resources of energy not only in mineral fuels but above all in hydroelectric resources. The energy situation is most favourable not only for the existing demands but also for an expected development both with regard to the agricultural products and the mineral products both so manifold and promising.

With regard to petroleum products, existing reserves could be better utilized in some parts of the region but in the long run and for overall conditions the resources are moderate. Greater efforts should therefore be devoted to produce oil from coal and from the large woods. A promising solution is processing methanol for vehicles from wood.

The main energy resource is after all the inexhaustible hydroelectric energy, so abundant in many parts of the region. A natural development is in general to start with local resources and local systems and as soon as larger networks have been created of production and consumption, to proceed with transmission systems and finally to take the third step in creating interconnected systems. All the time expansion has to be justified and controlled by economic factors. At the same time it is important to apply and make use of the latest technical achievements especially to spread and extend the beneficial use of electricity from the hydro sites to the centres in need. The purpose of distributing electricity is to meet the demand where there is a capability and a will to pay the cost.

24

Energy in Zaire

KENNETH L. ADELMAN

One month after the 1973 Middle-East War and start of the ensuing energy crisis, President Mobutu Sese Seko asked Zairians, 'Where would we be today if we had not finished the first stage of Inga?' Inga of course refers to the gigantic hydroelectrical power complex in Bas-Zaire (formerly Lower Congo). Important as it is, Inga is only one element in Zaire's total energy picture. The recent discovery of offshore oil reserves and the operation of a petroleum refinery in Moanda, together with Inga, give Zaire one of the brightest energy prospects in all of Africa.

Petroleum supply and distribution

Zaire is a relatively large energy consumer in Africa because of its huge size and developed mining industry. The country's total petroleum consumption has grown as its industrial output increases. In 1970, 761.217 billion litres of petroleum were consumed in Zaire; in 1971, 820.42 billion; in 1972, 879.725 billion; and 918 billion litres for 1973. Of these totals, a bit over 40 per cent was used for diesel-type fuel; 15 per cent for premium petrol; 12 per cent for regular petrol; 12 per cent for paraffin; 11 per cent for jet fuel; 8 per cent for fuel oil; and 2 per cent for regular aviation fuel.

To meet these fuel needs, Zaire long relied upon the large oil companies, primarily Fina, with over half the business, and Shell, Mobil, and Texaco. All parties were pleased with the arrangement until 1974. Then, during the first stages of the oil crisis, the companies sought to raise their domestic prices to offset rising costs. The Zairian government, wary of aggravating the already high rate of inflation, refused to allow the increase and, about the same time, ordered the companies to standardize their prices for petroleum products throughout the country. This in effect made them absorb some of the high transportation costs in Zaire. The companies became increasingly distressed as their profit margin dwindled, but they continued to meet the country's needs in all but jet fuel, which was in short supply on the world market. They still hoped for future government concessions and were reluctant to complain too loudly for fear of jeopardizing their long-range investment prospects. Many had been doing business in the country for over half a century and wanted to continue for another 50 years.

They were in for a surpise when, instead of making concessions, the government simply nationalized the entire industry. On 19 December 1973, the day President Mobutu returned from three Arab countries, the Minister of Energy announced that as of 10 January 1974, a government corporation called PetroZaire would be the sole supplier and distributor of petroleum products

First published in *Africa Today*, Vol. 22, No. 4 (October–December, 1976), pp. 49–55). Reprinted by permission of the author and *Africa Today*.

throughout the country. He assured the oil companies that just compensation would be forthcoming, which somewhat eased the jolt.

There are a host of possible reasons for Zaire's nationalization of the petroleum industry. First and perhaps foremost, the industry was the largest foreign concern after the President's dramatic 30 November 1973 speech which effectively Zairianized the economy by ordering the takeover of all medium and small businesses and agricultural activities. The decision to create PetroZaire, announced just 3 weeks later, was merely a further step in the nationalization process already under way. Secondly, Zaire was obviously disturbed by the oil companies' continual requests for prices increases and by their difficulty in supplying jet fuel, a precious commodity for President Mobutu who considers the Air Zaire fleet, especially the Jumbo jets, his biggest prestige item.

In addition, Zairian officials may well have believed that the oil companies were making a fortune in the country, a profit they would like to have, and that they would get a better deal from doing business directly with the Arabs. This seems to have been a key factor. President Mobutu had been courting the Arabs before this time, breaking diplomatic relations with Israel shortly before the outset of the latest war despite years of friendly relations between the two countries and extensive military training programmes in Israel for Zairian officers. The President further cultivated 'our brothers, the Arabs' with a highly publicized trip to Algeria, Libya, and Egypt just before nationalization (November 1973) and to Saudi Arabia, Kuwait, and Iran just afterwards (December 1973 and January 1974). Despite the diplomatic offensive, the Zairian efforts have in the main proved futile since the Arabs have refused to give Zaire any special arrangements, whether in terms of long-term supply contracts or reduced prices. In fact, Zaire now pays $2 or $3 per barrel more to the Arabs than to the large oil companies for petroleum products.

Finally, there are the inevitable rumours that the government nationalized the oil industry for some more mysterious reason. One hears that the government was furious at Fina, a Belgian company, for allegedly diverting tankers from Zaire to Belgium during the crisis in Europe. Also, rumour has it that the Arabs were contemplating large investments in the copper industry of Zaire, foreign capital that the President would eagerly welcome. These and other stories persist even though there are no hard facts to substantiate them.

Regardless of the government's motives, the oil companies soon found themselves nationalized. Some minor exceptions were allowed, such as the oil refinery in which Zaire already owns 50 per cent with an Italian firm, Ente Nazionale Idrocarburi (ENI) owning the rest. Part of the distribution network in the East was left in private hands for another year. Still, for all intents and purposes, PetroZaire became the oil industry in Zaire, even though for months it existed only as a name, and not as an organization, while the oil companies continued to supply and transport petroleum throughout Zaire.

For over 6 months following the nationalization announcement, PetroZaire actually consisted of only two persons, the Director and his deputy, who were busy preparing plans to consolidate the four major companies into one Zairian structure. In December 1973, there were approximately 150 expatriates working for the companies, most of whom continued to work as before until April or May 1974. At that time, Fina released much of its staff—now about 33, down from 85—and Shell removed all of its expatriate employees. Out of the original 150 executives and managers, there are now some 40 or 45 expatriates working either for the oil companies under PetroZaire or for PetroZaire directly.

Hence the transition from a private to public petroleum industry in Zaire was a smooth one with the major companies co-operating. Of course they helped PetroZaire get established in part to assure receipt of compensation for all the equipment and facilities taken over in the country. While the government has fully agreed to just compensation—which the companies estimate at upwards of $160 million—little has actually been done. Zaire has not even begun negotiating amounts as the officials consider the matter still under 'careful study'. Even after 1 year, the oil companies remain optimistic about getting their money, though perhaps not as much as requested. They believe that Zaire must pay, or ruin its international financial rating. It simply cannot keep encouraging large foreign investment after refusing to compensate a large industry which was nationalized.

The oil companies have helped PetroZaire not only to encourage full compensation but also to protect their future business arrangements in the country. All four of the major companies are involved in exploration activities in Zaire, efforts which have not been affected by nationalization. In addition, some continue to work on contract for Petro-Zaire. For example, Mobil Oil still operates the elaborate machinery for making lubricants, and supplies aviation fuel, some crude oil, and special products used for the paint and textile industries. Hence the companies have had their own reasons for helping PetroZaire through the transition period, which formally ended on 1 January 1975 when final consolidation of the industry in Zaire took place. The four accounting, sales, distribution, public relations, and administrative offices of the oil companies are now centralized and effectively integrated in PetroZaire.

The new, consolidated PetroZaire should not have any major supply problems during its first year of full operations. Present plans call for Zaire to receive half its crude oil from Libya and the other half from Iran or possibly Algeria and the major oil companies. In the past, Zaire imported 669193 tonnes of crude oil, valued at $12.7 million in 1970; 672033 tonnes valued at $14 million in 1971; 717018 tonnes valued at $16.2 million in 1972; and 179095 tonnes valued at $4.1 million for the first 3 months of 1973.

While the Arabs have agreed to supply this crude oil, and some refined products as well, they do so at fairly high prices since Zaire is a relatively small consumer. Also the Arabs have refused to sign any long-term contracts with Zaire to guarantee continual supply over the years. It seems that they regard Zaire more as a burden than a brother. Because of such treatment, over which Zaire has not publicly protested as yet, the government found itself in the embarrassing position of doubling domestic petroleum prices on 1 May 1974, just a few months after the oil companies requested slight price increases. At present, domestic prices are extremely high, though they are uniform throughout the country. Premium petrol sells for $1.55 per gallon, regular petrol for $1.44 per gallon, paraffin for 76 cents and diesel-type fuel for 93 cents per gallon.

Many of these products are produced in Zaire at the refining plant outside Moanda on the Atlantic Ocean. SOZIR, as it is called, plans to increase its production from an annual output of 750000 tonnes in 1972–3 to over 1.7 million tonnes of refined products per year. Actually the refinery was specifically designed to process the type of crude oil supplied by the large companies. Consequently, it works less efficiently refining the Libyan crude, which is of a slightly lower quality. There has been some thought given to changing the equipment or expanding the plant to better accommodate Libyan oil, but nothing has been done. No action is likely until Zaire's offshore oil is analysed and production begins.

Zaire gets most of its imported refined oil from Algeria. The supply to eastern Zaire comes by ship to Lobito, Angola, and along the Benguela Railroad into Zaire, and from Kenya and Tanzania. Zambia also supplies the Shaba (ex-Katanga) Region, sending mostly diesel fuel for the heavy mining equipment, motor oil, and jet fuel for the Lubumbashi airport.

PetroZaire's outlook for the immediate future appears fairly good. One main problem area is the supply of 15000 tonnes of aviation fuel needed in the country. This product is in short supply throughout the world, in part because of increased use of the premium part of the barrel in the United States and Europe to meet the pollution standards in new environmental laws. Also, PetroZaire may be concerned about assuring supply of half its crude oil requirement, the half coming from Iran and the oil companies in the past. While the contract for Libyan crude oil is in effect for 1975, the remainder needs to be negotiated.

Oil exploration and production

PetroZaire's outlook for the long-range future appears excellent, owing primarily to the production of offshore oil. In 1969 Zaire gave concessions for exploratory drilling to a consortium composed as follows: 50 per cent Gulf Oil Zaire (subsidiary of Gulf Oil); 32.28 per cent Japan Petroleum Zaire (subsidiary of Teikoku Oil); and 17.72 per cent Littoral Zairois (subsidiary of Cometra Oil). The group spent approximately $25 million on exploration and is now spending an additional $30 or $35 million to begin production, scheduled to start by the summer of 1976. The current plans are to begin producing 25000 barrels per day, which is slightly more than total Zairian consumption, and to increase production upwards during the months following. There has been no public announcement on the total amount of oil located on the small 25-mile coastline nor the type of crude oil there, although it seems to be the low-sulphur type crude. In that case Zaire may possibly export its total production of this valuable type oil and continue to import its own fuel requirements. These decisions have not yet been made and all arrangements have to be worked out between Gulf, the Japanese firm, and Zaire once production begins.

Whatever is decided, however, Zaire stands to gain, whether in the form of crude oil to meet domestic needs or great increase of foreign reserves to more than cover its own petroleum costs.

In addition to this offshore find, Zaire is hopeful that oil can be found on-shore along the coastline. At present, a consortium of Fina (50 per cent), Shell (25 per cent), and Mobil (25 per cent) is conducting exploratory drilling. No results have been announced as yet. Even if there is only a small reserve found, it may still be exploited since the drilling equipment is in such close proximity. In the interior of Zaire, Texaco (50 per cent) and Shell (50 per cent) have rights for exploratory drilling in the central basin, between Mbandaka and Kisangani, but no findings are reported as yet.

On top of this, Zaire is extremely interested in the future of Cabinda, the small territory lodged between the People's Republic of the Congo and Zaire, politically considered a part of Angola, and economically valuable with offshore oil. The Angolan liberation movements have proclaimed that Cabinda is and must remain an integral part of Angola, even though the two territories share no common border. Others are eager for Cabinda to be totally independent. President Mobutu seems to be supporting both sides at once. He fully backs the FNLA movement which seeks to unite Cabinda and Angola while allowing the Cabinda liberation movement to raise arms and money in Kinshasa. Certainly the Zairian government is eager to share in Cabinda's treasures, which now add up to more than 150000 barrels per day or over six times initial production offshore Zaire.

Hydroelectric power

Zaire's future supply of hydroelectrical energy looks as good if not even better than petroleum. Zaire's total consumption is high: 3437283 MWh in hydro power and 103079 MWh in thermal power in 1971; and 3436920 MWh in hydro and 117090 MWh thermal in 1972. Over 70 per cent of this consumption goes for the mineral and metallic industries located in the Shaba region. Zaire can easily meet the huge demand because of the Inga Dam project.

The idea of capturing the tremendous power of the Zaire (Congo) River—second in the world after the Amazon with a discharge of over 11 million gallons per second—was first conceived in 1885. The site for the dam, at Inga near the mouth of the river, was chosen because the water drops some 330 feet in less than 9 miles. In 1929 a special committee gave serious study to the construction of the power station on the site. The plans moved ahead slowly and by 1960 a special proposal was handed to the World Bank for financing. Nothing became of this portfolio since the country was thrown into turmoil with civil wars and rebellions. In 1967, after President Mobutu had seized power and the country settled down, an Italian team again took up the plans and pushed the project.

The plans finally adopted call for a successive construction of the power plant. This is possible at Inga since the dam is being built not across the Zaire River but on dry land with the river to be diverted later to run through its generators. As a result the project becomes financially and technically feasible since construction continues on one section after another section is already completed and supplying energy. Upon completion of the final stage, Inga IV or 'Grand Inga', the price of the energy per unit will be the cheapest of any hydroelectrical plant in the world and far cheaper than nuclear power.

The first stage, Inga I, was dedicated on 24 November 1973. Its present output of 360000 kW is only a fraction of that expected from Grand Inga. The construction cost totalled $110 million, of which the government of Zaire paid two-thirds and obtained loans, mostly from the Italians, for the remainder. The cost (more than $280) per kilowatt, ran high, but the energy was needed for Kinshasa and the industrial development of Bas-Zaire with its cement factories and planned iron and steel factory at Maluka designed to produce 250000 tonnes of steel.

Inga II is scheduled for completion sometime in 1976. Its output will be three times that of the first stage, 1.3 million kW, at a total estimated cost of $150 million or under $150 per kilowatt. Construction of Inga II is being directed by Italinga, the same firm involved in building Inga I, and includes participation by American (General Electric, Westinghouse), French, Italian, British, and German firms.

Certainly the unique aspect of Inga II is that it will supply energy to the copper mines of the east. This is made possible by the 1700-km long Inga-Shaba line, a high tension power line going through more than 400 km of dense forest land. This line will be the longest in the world, surpassing the 1500 km Cabora-Bassa–Pretoria line, and its construction constitutes the largest single contract in history, $250 million. A consortium of American firms, including Morrison Knudsen, International Engineering Co., and Fischback and Moore International, landed the contract for building the line and two conversion stations, one at Inga and one in Kolwesi (250 km north-west of Lubumbashi). Construction is well under way and the first steel tower was dedicated in December 1974. The final tower and conversion stations should be in place by September 1974. After the initial tests and adjustments, full working operations to provide Shaba with Inga's power are scheduled for 1 January 1977.

This task is a staggering engineering feat of the first magnitude. To install the 9400 towers, some 3350 persons will be employed, including 375 Americans and 325 Brazilians who have done construction work in the Amazon jungle. The plans call for the importation of 170000 tonnes of materials including 150 trucks and a fleet of gigantic tractors to tear down trees. Where the tractors cannot clear a path, dynamite will be used. Besides the technical difficulties of working on a project 1700 km long through near-impossible terrain the team faces problems of importation, transportation, bureaucratic delays, and of course the usual mishaps of working in a developing country. For example, the initial survey team dropped small aluminium poles by helicopter along possible construction routes, only to find that when they flew back, all the carefully placed markers were gone. Apparently, they were hot items in the local markets, selling for a few cents apiece.

Following the construction of Inga II and and Inga–Shaba line comes Inga III, presently in the planning stages. Its output could reach 1.8 million kW with the cost per installed kilowatt around $210. At the completion of Inga IV and Grand Inga—still in the discussion stage—there is the potential for more than 30 million kW with the final cost per kilowatt around $70. This would make Inga far and away the most powerful hydroelectrical plant in Africa, more than ten times the capacity of the Aswan Dam (2.1 million kW) and five times that of Cabora Bassa, Mozambique (6.32 million kW).

Naturally this tremendous energy potential has important political repercussions, both domestically and internationally, for Zaire. The Inga–Shaba power line binds the country together, perhaps irrevocably. The Shaba Region with all its copper production and the one region with a strong sense of solidarity and a history of secessionist sentiments, will be almost totally dependent on the Kinshasa area for its power. Apparently this factor was decisive in the construction of Inga and especially of the Inga–Shaba line. Government leaders well realized that the power for the copper industry could be supplied from Zambia and from local water sources, probably at considerably less cost than the Inga project.

Conclusion

Internationally, the country's exportation of both petroleum and hydroelectrical power will place Zaire as a key energy provider for central and much of southern Africa. There are already plans afoot to export energy to Zambia, Tanzania, Rwanda, Burundi, Mozambique, Rhodesia, and the small African republics to the north of Zaire. This places Zaire in a strong position, along with Nigeria, as a leading political and economic force of Africa, and may prove invaluable in helping President Mobutu realize his dream of great continental power and world prestige.

25

Solar energy for Tanzania

NORMAN E. BROWN AND JAMES W. HOWE

Most of the people in the developing countries of Asia, Africa, and Latin America live in rural areas. Progress in these areas depends on finding substitutes for human muscle energy, which is now relied on for many village tasks.

The prohibitive costs of large central generators and massive transmission and distribution systems, as well as the slow pace of the spread of rural electrification programmes, discourage hopes that rural energy needs can be met with a national electric grid. Hence, we have inquired into the potential of small-scale technologies that use renewable energy sources coming from the sun. Current solar energy comes from four major systems: (i) photosynthesis, which is the basis of all life, both plant and animal; (ii) the water cycle, which is driven by the sun; (iii) wind, caused by the atmospheric pressure differences due to changing amounts of solar energy falling on different places; and (iv) direct sunshine. Proven small-scale technologies exist for using each of these solar energy systems.

In photosynthesis, biogas plants use anaerobic bacteria to turn animal, human, and crop wastes into methane gas and, at the same time, leave a residual slurry that is useful for fertilizer. It has been reported that there were 1.2 million biogas plants installed in China in the first 6 months of 1976 alone, and that 4.7 million are now in operation.[1] The technology appears to be proving itself and is improving all the time. Methane can be used for cooking, crop drying, power generation, and various other purposes.

To make use of the water cycle, a number of very small hydroelectric generators are now being manufactured for as little as $800. Miniature units producing only a few hundred watts or a few kilowatts can operate either with a small dam or simply by the flow of a small stream. In China, it is reported, there are 60000 such units averaging about 40 kilowatts in capacity that successfully supply most of the electricity used by three-quarters of China's rural communes.[1] In the nineteenth and early twentieth centuries, most of New England's commercial power came from small hydro facilities.

Windmills had long since proved themselves in Holland and the plains of the United States before they were driven out of existence by rural electrification—originally based on coal and later on cheap oil.

At least two small-scale technologies are available to make use of the direct rays of the sun. One is a flat-plate collector for space- and water-heating, but which could also serve for activities such as crop and fish drying, distilling water, and refrigerating.

First published in *Science*, Vol. 199 (10 February 1978), pp. 651–7. Copyright 1978 by the American Association for the Advancement of Science. Reprinted by permission of the authors and *Science*. A revised version of this paper appears in P. H. Abelson and A. L. Hammond (eds.) *Energy II: Needs, Conservation and Supply* (AAAS, 1978).

Table 25.1. Solar energy applicability matrix. Animals are included as a solar technology (based on photosynthesis). For many villages the use of animals would represent a modernizing step. It includes the use of dung for burning or fertilizing.

	Energy use													
								Heating						
Solar technology	*Water pump-ing*	*Light-ing*	*Cool-ing*	*Com-muni-cations*	*Water desalt-ing*	*Spin-ning*	*Saw-ing*	*Cook-ing*	*Space*	*Domes-tic water*	*Grind-ing*	*Dry-ing*	*Trans-port*	*Ferti-lizer*
Solar cells (flat plate)	+	+	+	++	−	+	−	−	−	−	+	−	−	−
Flat-plate collectors	+	−	+	−	++	−	−	+	++	++	−	++	−	−
Concentrating collectors	+	+	+	−	+	+	+	+	−	−	−	−	−	−
Solar, stirling	+	+	+	+	−	+	+	−	−	−	+	−	−	−
Solar, rankine	+	+	+	−	−	+	+	−	−	−	+	−	−	−
Wind (mechanical)	++	−	−	−	−	+	+	−	−	−	++	−	−	−
Wind generator	++	++	++	++	−	+	+	−	−	−	++	−	−	−
Water (mechanical)	++	−	−	−	−	++	++	−	−	−	++	−	−	−
Hydroelectric	++	++	++	++	−	++	++	−	−	−	++	−	−	−
Bioconversion	−	+	−	−	−	−	−	++	++	++	−	++	−	+
Biogas	+	++	+	−	−	−	−	++	−	+	−	+	+	++
Draught animals	++	−	−	−	−	−	−	+	−	+	++	−	++	++

Symbols: ++, applicable; +, potentially applicable; −, not applicable.
Source: Adapted from a presentation by J. R. Williams at the Tanzanian workshop.

The other technology for collecting the direct rays of the sun to generate electricity is a solar cell or photovoltaic array such as that used to power spacecraft.

Such promising technologies could be useful for a variety of tasks in rural areas. This potential is described in Table 25.1, where 14 technologies are applied to 15 common village tasks with the result that there are 34 applications that seem useful and 39 applications that seem marginally useful.

But what of costs? Are these not all technologies that require years more of research or the establishment of mass markets to become cost competitive with conventional energy sources? So few good data have been kept on the costs and performance of such technologies in actual village situations that we cannot answer this question completely. However, some preliminary calculations suggest that at least five technologies now 'on the shelf' are, or soon will be, cost effective when compared with either diesel electric generation or the existing electric grid in the case of Tanzanian villages. These calculations were made in Tanzania during a 10-day workshop jointly sponsored by the US National Academy of Sciences and the Tanzanian National Scientific Research Council. For a week, this workshop group[2] poured over calculations of the costs of performing certain village tasks (i) with diesel motors, (ii) with electricity from the Tanzanian electric grid, and (iii) with five small-scale renewable technologies. The results surprised even the experts. Each of these five technologies appeared to be now, or soon would be, competitive with diesel. A number of them compete well with the electric grid for certain village tasks. These results are valid despite the assumption that capital to build the facility costs 10 per cent and must be repaid during the life of the equipment. In actual fact, a great deal of capital is often available to developing countries on far more generous terms. This is more advantageous to solar energy over the life of the project than to diesel power, because capital costs of the former are high relative to operating costs while the reverse tends to be more true of diesel power. Thus, for example, it may be possible to borrow nearly 100 per cent of the total life of project costs for a photovoltaic installation (since such costs consist nearly entirely of initial capital), whereas for the initial capital for diesel one could borrow only about one-eighth of the life of project costs. Hence cheap capital favours solar over diesel energy.

Of course the panellists recognized that a final determination of whether a given technology should be applied to a given village situation depends not only on the financial costs, but also on availability of resources, social obstacles, social benefits, institutional barriers, long-range power requirements, and long-range development goals. In the short time available to them, they focused on estimating financial costs of the technologies considered most likely to be applicable with the understanding that this was but a first step in the decision-making process.[3]

Basis for cost comparison

A hypothetical village of 300 families was chosen as a basis for estimating the magnitude of financial investment needed. It was assumed, for these initial installations, that the needs of each family could be met, on the average, by the use of 1 kilowatt-hour per day (300 kWh total) to be applied to lighting, operation of a village television receiver, radio communications, pumping water, or grinding grain. At this rate of energy consumption, Tanzanians receiving central-station generated electricity from TANESCO (Tanzania Electric Supply Company) would pay, on the average, about 0.93 shilling (*s*) per kilowatt-hour[4] (the US equivalent is $0.113/kWh). It was assumed further that the 300 kWh/day could be supplied either on a 5-hour basis, that is, at the rate of 60 kW, or for 20 hours, that is, at a rate of 15 kW.

Technologies of energy supply

Five technologies were chosen as illustrative examples, on the basis of their immediate or short-term availability (or both).[5]

Photovoltaic power generators. The analysis of the cost of supplying electrical power by a solar-cell array was based on a cost estimate of $20 (US) per watt-peak ($W_p$). Although, in a recent large-scale purchase by the US government, the cost was $15/$W_p$, a cost of $20/$W_p$ was used in these estimates on the assumption that the more favourable price would not be available for an initial small-scale purchase.

Cost calculations are summarized in Table 25.2.[6] The size of the array needed to supply 300 kWh daily was based on World Meteorological Organization insolation data for Tanzania.[7] These figures indicate that an array with a peak power capacity of 1 kW will produce, on the average, 5.3 kWh daily. Thus, for 300 kWh/day, a generous estimate of 60 kW_p was used. An interest rate of 10 per cent per annum, the prevailing rate in Tanzania, was used to calculate financing costs. The estimated cost of energy provided by photovoltaics, 11*s*/kWh, is approximately 12 times the average current cost of electricity in Dar-es-Salaam, as noted above.

In view of the predicted drop in the cost of photovoltaic devices—the Department of Energy looks to a cost of $0.50/$W_p$ by 1985, or earlier—it is interesting to see how sensitive the electricity cost is to the array cost. For an array cost of 4.1*s*/W_p ($0.50/$W_p$) the total system cost for this example would be 528 000*s* with the same battery costs assumed. The annual cost would then be 94 000*s*, and the cost of electricity 0.83*s*/kWh, or 10 per cent less than the current cost of electricity from the grid. The 'break-even' array cost, that is, the cost of photovoltaics that would enable electricity to be generated at the average current selling price in Dar-es-Salaam, would be 5.28*s*/W_p or $0.64/$W_p$. Thus, the use of photovoltaic devices to generate electricity for the villages of Tanzania is likely to be economically competitive within 10 years.[8] Moreover, for any village that wants small amounts of electricity now but is

Table 25.2. Cost of supplying electricity by means of photovoltaic generators. Financing costs were based on amortization of the loan in equal yearly instalments

Base data	
Lifetime of silicon solar cells	20 years
Lifetime of batteries	6 years
Efficiency of batteries	85 per cent
Cost of silicon solar cells	160*s*/W_p
Cost of batteries	800*s*/kWh
Equipment costs	
Solar-cell array, 60 kW_p at 160*s*/W_p	9 600 000*s*
Battery storage	
(300 kWh at 85 per cent efficiency)	
353 kWh at 800*s*/kWh	280 000*s*
Total equipment costs (approximate)	10 000 000*s*
Financing costs	
Solar-cell array	1 100 000*s*/year
9 600 000*s* at 10 per cent for 20 years	
Batteries	
280 000*s* at 10 per cent for 6 years	64 000*s*/year
Total cost of financing (approximate)	1 200 000*s*/year
Cost of electricity	
Total energy generated	110 000 kWh/year
Unit cost	11*s*/kWh

not within reach of the grid (discussed later) photovoltaic devices may already be cost-effective compared with conventional alternatives.

Small-scale hydro-power. In the mountainous regions of Tanzania there are many small streams and rivers with a flow of water sufficient in quantity and reliability to be considered as a source of small-scale hydroelectricity. This technology is a mature one, with devices of a variety of sizes available 'off the shelf' not only in the United States, but in many other countries.[9] With known cost figures as a basis, four cases were considered, as shown in Table 25.3. These four cases provide for two basic situations—one in which the needs of the village (300 kWh/day) would be supplied directly by the generator during the hours of use (that is, 60 kW), and one in which a smaller generating capacity (that is, 15 kW) would be used with storage batteries to supply the required 300 kWh/day over a period of 20 hours.

The cost calculations for these four ways of supplying hydroelectric power are summarized in Tables 25.4 to 25.6. For the purposes of this exercise, it was assumed that dams and penstocks, if needed, could be constructed with local labour and materials (timber and earth) at no significant capital costs.[10] The water requirement estimates were based on data supplied by manufacturers of turbine or generator (or both) systems of the scale discussed. In all cases, where battery storage was required, it was assumed that the cost of the batteries would be amortized over the 6-year life expected for that sub-system, in order to allow for its replacement as needed, independent of the lifetime or amortization rates (or both) for the other equipment. As with the dams and penstocks, no cost figures were included for protective housing for batteries or power-conditioning equipment, on the assumption that locally available materials would suffice. (For all of these cases, some maintenance would be advisable. At an estimated cost of 1000*s*/month, this would add 0.10*s*/kWh to each of the cost figures.) Any of these assumptions might not be valid in specific circumstances; nevertheless the estimates show that small-scale hydroelectric installations are cost competitive with present large-scale systems—to say nothing of the serious environmental and social consequences of large-scale hydroelectric projects—and are worth serious consideration in rural areas.

As a result, the panellists felt that it would be useful to extrapolate these estimates to the case where a large region of, say, 500 villages would be supplied with perhaps as many as 500 small hydroelectric generating units—assuming, of course, that sufficient rainfall and water-flow rates were available. As an example, the total capital requirement for case 1 would be 330 million shillings. If a loan from the International Development Association (IDA) (the 'soft-loan window' of the World Bank) were available, the economics of small-scale hydroelectricity applied on a large scale are very attractive.

Table 25.3. Types of hydroelectric power equipment considered

Case	*Power* Type generated	Type used	Conditioning required	Storage required	Generating capacity (kW)
1	d-c	a-c	Yes	No	60
2	a-c	a-c	No	No	60
3	d-c	a-c	Yes	Yes	15
4	a-c	d-c	No	Yes	15

Table 25.4. Water requirements for supplying hydroelectricity by small-scale systems

Power (kW)	*Head (m)*	*Flow (m^3/min)*
	48	12
60	24	25
	12	50
	6	100
	24	6
15	12	12
	6	24

Table 25.5. Base data for cost of supplying hydroelectricity by means of small-scale systems

Item	*Lifetime (years)*	*Unit cost (s)*
Generator/turbine	30	4000/kW
Power conditioning	30	6/W
Batteries		
(85 per cent efficiency)	6	800/kWh

For such a loan, no payment is required for the first 10 years; the loan is repayable, in equal annual instalments over the next 40 years, at an annual interest rate of 0.75 per cent. For this example, this would mean a financing cost of 9.6 million shillings per year from years 11 through 50. If the energy generated were sold to the villagers at the cost figures calculated in Table 25.6, the annual income would be 53 million shillings if the loan were a conventional 10-year loan, and 35 million shillings if it were a conventional 30-year loan. This would provide the government with between 25 and 40 million shillings for other projects. On the other hand, if energy were sold at a rate just sufficient to meet the 40-year cost of the IDA loan, the rate would be 0.17*s*/kWh, a figure less than one-fifth the current price of electricity in Dar-es-Salaam, and a cost well supportable by the villages electrified in this scheme. (This is approximately 1*s* per week.)

The four hydroelectric cases considered were based on a use by the villagers of 200 watts of electricity for 5 hours per day. For cases 3 and 4, this is the total capacity of the system. For cases 1 and 2, however, the system would be capable of supplying energy at the same rate (60 kW) day and night for 24 hours. If this capacity were used

Table 25.6. Cost of small-scale hydroelectric systems (in shillings). The cost of dams and penstocks was not included

Item	*Case 1*	*Case 2*	*Case 3*	*Case 4*
Cost of equipment				
Generator/turbine	240000	240000	60000	60000
Power conditioning	360000	0	90000	0
Installation	60000	24000	15000	6000
Subtotal*	660000	265000	165000	66000
Battery storage	0	0	280000	280000
Installation	0	0	28000	28000
Subtotal	0	0	308000	308000
Total (approximate)	660000	270000	470000	370000
*Financing costs at 10 per cent annual interest rate**				
Annual cost in shillings†				
30-year loan	70000	29000	89000	78000
10-year loan	107000	44000	99000	82000
Cost of electricity (*s*/kWh)‡				
30-year loan	0.64	0.26	0.81	0.71
10-year loan	0.97	0.40	0.90	0.75

*Based on amortization of the loan in equal yearly instalments.
†In both cases, it was assumed that the cost of the battery storage would be amortized over 6 years.
‡Based on 110000 kWh/year.

Table 25.7. Cost of supplying cooking fuel, lighting, mechanical power, and electricity by biogas.

Base data	
Cattle dung	10 kg/day per cow
Biogas production (at 0.06 m^3 per kg of dung)	0.6 m^3/day per cow
Energy content of biogas as 60 per cent methane*	6.4 kWh/m^3
System lifetime	20 years
Conversion efficiencies	
Internal-combustion engine‖	25 per cent
Electrical generator	90 per cent
Plant cost	
Single-family plant (3 m^3)	6000*s*
Financing costs†	
Single-family plant, 6000*s* at 10 per cent for 20 years	705*s*/year
Engine/generator to provide 1 kWh/day, 5400*s*‡ at 10 per cent (5 hour/day)	5940*s*/year
Engine to provide 1 kWh/day, mechanical energy, 3200*s*‡ at 10 per cent (4 hour/day)	3520*s*/year
Energy costs§	
Cooking and lighting directly by gas (20 kWh/day)	0.10*s*/kWh
Cooking and generation of electricity at 1 kWh/day	18.2*s*/kWh
Cooking and generation of mechanical power at 1 kWh/day	11.6*s*/kWh

*Approximately 4 kWh of biogas energy is available daily from each cow.

†Based on amortization of loan in equal yearly instalments.

‡Retail costs, Dar-es-Salaam, August 1977.

§Cost of energy production only—does not include cost of appliances or cost of collecting dung.

‖Assuming peak loading.

for more than 5 hours daily, the cost per kilowatt-hour could be reduced by as much as a factor of 4 or 5. That is, with load factors greater than 0.2 (5 hours' use per day), the cost of electricity production by small-scale hydropower systems of the type considered would approach 0.1 to 0.2*s*/kWh.

Biogas generation. The generation of methane from human, animal, and agricultural wastes is a process that is finding more and more use in developing countries, as people grow more aware of the potential of these 'waste' materials as a source of both energy and fertilizer.[11] Indeed, several biogas plants are operating in Tanzania, and a body of experience in their construction and operation is being accumulated.[12] Thus, it was natural for the workshop participants to consider the use of biogas not only for village lighting and cooking, but for the generation of electricity or mechanical power. For this exercise, the use of cattle dung was assumed, with average production rates and methane concentrations. Furthermore, lighting both by a gas-mantle lantern and with generated electricity was considered. The calculations are outlined in Table 25.7.

Analysis of the data shows that gas requirements for cooking three times a day are approximately 1.4 m^3/day per family, which could be supplied by dung from three to four cows. In contrast, to supply the electric lighting needs of a family (1 kWh/day) by using the biogas to operate an engine-generator set would require heat energy of 5 kWh/day, which could almost be supplied by one cow. This method of lighting, therefore, is almost four times as efficient, in energy use, as a gas-mantle lantern, albeit requiring a much greater capital investment. Finally, this same amount of gas—the gas supplied by one cow—would provide mechanical power alone at 1 kWh/day.

Another potential use for biogas, as a replacement for wood and charcoal, is in firing clay pottery used for water and cooking

Table 25.8. Cost of supplying electricity by means of windmill generators.

Base data	
Useful life of windmill generator	15 years
Lifetime of batteries	6 years
Efficiency of batteries	85 per cent
Equipment costs	
Windmill generator (10 kW)	170 000*s*
Wiring, controls	42 000*s*
Installation	42 000*s*
Battery storage—(100 kWh at 85 per cent efficiency) 118 kWh at 800*s*/kWh	94 000*s*
Total equipment costs (approximate)	350 000*s*
*Financing costs**	
Windmill generator, wiring, installation, 254 000*s* at 10 per cent for 15 years	33 000*s*/year
Batteries, 94 000*s* at 10 per cent for 6 years	22 000*s*/year
Total cost of financing (approximate)	55 000*s*/year
Cost of electricity	
Total energy generated	36 000 kWh
Unit cost	1.5*s*/kWh

*Based on amortization of loan in equal yearly instalments.

vessels. For small-scale production, estimates based on gas-fired firebrick kilns indicate that about 8 m^3 of methane, over a period of about 5 hours, would be required to fire earthenware at 1000 °C in a kiln having a volume of about 0.2 m^3 (6 cubic feet). This is the equivalent of about 13 m^3 of biogas, which could be supplied by a 4-day accumulation from the dung of five cows. Larger production capacities—for instance, for a village industry—could be available by scaling-up the above estimate accordingly, and would represent another potential use for community digesters.

To summarize then: (i) heat energy, even from a single-family biogas plant, can be supplied at well below (less than one-ninth) the equivalent energy cost of electricity, and (ii) Ujamaa villages lend themselves readily to communal systems. Because of the economies of scale in biogas plant construction such communal systems (for example, schools, community latrines, community cattle-dung digesters in Masai villages) should be seriously considered.

Windmill generators. The use of windmill generators to supply a village's proposed electrical energy needs was considered in this exercise. However, even though the financial costs can be reasonably well estimated, measurements of wind-velocity and duration must be made to determine the suitability of any proposed site before any plans for a windmill project are contemplated.

The estimates that were made (Table 25.8) assume minimum wind speeds of about 12 miles per hour (5 m/s) for an average of about 10 hours daily throughout the year. With windmill generators of a size reasonably available (10 kW), this would provide an average of 100 kWh daily, with electricity costs of less than 2*s*/kWh. This means, also, that to provide the proposed 300 kWh daily to a village of 300 families, three such installations would be required. If the task to be performed is pumping water, serviceable wind pumpers can be made with substantial savings by using local materials and skills. Thus, for example, in the Omo River Valley in Ethiopia, simple sail wind pumpers were built with Ethiopian materials following a design long used in Crete. The costs of mills that pumped 800 imperial gallons of water per hour, an elevation of 9 feet in winds of

Table 25.9. Cost of solar refrigeration of fish

Base data	
Lifetime of equipment	5 years
Weight of fish (M) chilled daily	500 kg
Specific heat of fish (C_p) (estimate)	1 cal/g °C
Storage time (t)	24 hours
Ambient temperature	25 °C
Cold storage temperature	5 °C
Surface area (A) of insulated box	6 m²
Thermal conductivity (K) of walls*	10^{-4} cal/s·cm·°C
Wall thickness (d)	10 cm
Hours of sunshine (average)	6
Heat requirements	
Cooling (Q_c)	
$Q_c = M \cdot C_p \cdot \Delta T = 10000$ kcal/day	
Losses (Q_L)	
$Q_L = K \cdot A \Delta T \cdot t/d = 1000$ kcal/day	
Total heat requirement	22000 kcal/day
Equipment costs	
Chiller ($\frac{2}{3}$ tons = 2000 kcal/hr)	(estimated) 20000
Collector (10 m²)	(estimated) 17200
Total equipment cost (coefficient of performance = 0.5)	(approximated) 37000
Financing cost†	
19000*s* at 10 per cent for 5 years	9800*s*/year
Cooling cost	
Energy required for cooling (22000 kcal/day)	9200 kWh/year
Unit cost	1.06*s*/kWh

*Based on the use of a material, such as sisal, with a thermal conductivity similar to that of sawdust.
†Based on amortization of loan in equal yearly instalments.

13 miles per hour, was only \$375 for each sail mill.[13]

Solar refrigeration. Having visited a village where fishing was one of the major activities, the workshop panellists considered the possibility of using solar cooling to enable the villagers to preserve their fishing catch long enough to market the excess over their local needs. The cost of cooling and preserving a catch of 500 kg—typical for a day's fishing at the village visited—was calculated, on the basis of the use of local materials and labour for the container and its insulation, and commercially available collector. Estimates were based on the assumption that ammonia-based cooling systems could be used since the units will be located out of doors, and that they could be constructed in Tanzania. The container was assumed to be 2.5 m × 1 m × 1 m, the cost of the chiller unit was estimated from known costs of available machines, and current US costs of collectors were used. The results, based on the assumptions stated, are shown in Table 25.9. They indicate that solar refrigeration would cost only slightly more than the current cost of electricity alone, assuming a 5-year equipment life.

Conventional technologies

The preceding analyses, as was noted earlier, compared the cost of generating electricity to the current selling price from the grid. To provide a useful context for this comparison, the costs of supplying electricity by extension of the present grid, and by local diesel generators, were examined.

Distribution grid to a village. This situation is based on either eventual extension of

Table 25.10 Cost of supplying electricity from existing grid

Base data	
Grid voltage	33 kV
Distance from grid to village (assumed)	20 km
Distribution voltage to substation	11 kV
Local distribution voltage	400 V
Number of substations assumed*	45
Average hook-up distance for 45 substations and 300 families in 16-km² village	0.2 km
Fixed costs	
High voltage step-down transformer	
33 kV to 11 kV, 500 kW at 10000000*s*/500 kW	1000000*s*
11-kV transmission line 20 km at 500*s*/km	10000*s*
Substation transformers	
11 kV to 400 V, 50 kW at 10,000*s*/50 kW	450000*s*
Local distribution lines (400 V); 300 families at 0.2 km per family and 12*s*/m	720000*s*
Fixed costs	2180000*s*
Financing† costs	
2180000*s* at 10 per cent for 20 years	256000*s*/year
Cost of electricity‡	
Total annual capacity 500 kW × 8760 hour/year	4380000 kWh
Unit cost of capacity (load factor = 1)	0.06 *s*/kWh
Unit cost at 10 per cent load factor	0.58*s*/kWh

*Because local distribution is so expensive, in this example it is cost effective to underutilize the substations by using many of them to reduce local hook-up distance.

†Based on amortization of loan in equal yearly instalments.

‡This calculation represents the unit cost of transporting electricity from the 33 kV transmission line to the consumer. It does not take into account maintenance costs for the system nor the cost of electricity delivered to the point where the 11 kV line starts.

transmission lines to cover the country to the extent of coming within 20 km of every village, or constructing distribution systems to villages within 20 km of present transmission lines. In view of the overwhelming cost of the first alternative, serious thought was given only to the second. On this basis, it was assumed that a village of 300 families would occupy about 16 km² at a distance of some 20 km from a 33-kV transmission line. A summary of the analysis is given to Table 25.10. Transmission line costs (33 to 11 kV with a transformer of 500 kW) and substation (11 kV to 400 V at 5 kW) costs and connection costs came to an estimated total of about 2.18 million shillings. Financing costs, based on a 20-year life for the system, and a 10 per cent annual rate of interest, would be about 256000*s* per year. If this system were fully utilized (that is, load factor of 1.0) the unit cost would be 0.06*s*/kWh. Usually a grid system is poorly matched to village needs, however. In the case considered, for example, a village of 300 families has a 500 kW supply continuously available, much more than it can reasonably use on a continuous basis. A more reasonable load factor to assume would be 0.1, which would make the transmission costs 0.58*s*/kWh. With the average generating cost in the existing grid 0.30*s*/kWh, the cost for delivered electricity by this scheme would be 0.88*s*/kWh—a figure comparable to current consumer prices in Dar-es-Salaam. This modest cost, it must be remembered, would be available only to those fortunate few villages within 20 km of the existing grid assuming, of course, that TANESCO would be willing to sell electricity to the distribution point for its cost of generation.

Table 25.11. Cost of supplying electricity by small-scale diesel generators

Base data	
Operation	5 hour/day
Useful life (about 10 years)	20000 hours
Fuel consumption	0.35 litre/kWh
Overhaul	every 5000 hours
Fixed costs	
Retail cost, 6-kW diesel generator	29000*s*
Overhaul costs	15000*s*
Installation	2900*s*
Annual costs	
Equipment and installation, 32000*s* at 10 per cent for 10 years*	5200*s*/year
Overhaul, 15000*s* at 10 per cent for 3 years*	6000*s*/year
Maintenance, operator	7000*s*/year
Total annual costs (less fuel) (approximate)	18000*s*/year
Cost of electricity	
Total energy generated annually	11000 kWh
Unit cost, less fuel	1.6*s*/kWh
Fuel cost, at 2*s*/litre	0.7*s*/kWh
Total unit cost	2.3*s*/*k*Wh

*Based on amortization of loan in equal yearly instalments.

A more realistic estimate would take into account the cost of transmission to the distribution point, but this information was not available to the panel.

Small-scale diesel generation. In view of the ubiquity of diesel electric generators, it is instructive to examine the cost of generating electricity by this technology. Table 25.11 summarizes the cost figures based on current retail prices in Dar-es-Salaam. At a cost of 2.3*s*/kWh for diesel-generated electricity, it is apparent that, with the exception of photovoltaics at present prices and biogas-generated electricity, the alternative technologies considered in our discussion would be preferable on a unit-cost basis. Even photovoltaic devices will be preferable in a few yeers.

One of the problems with such solar energy technologies that depend on wind or sunshine or even flowing streams is that these are intermittent sources of energy, so that in the United States they require a back-up system based, for example, on gas, oil, or electricity. The cost of the solar-based system plus the back-up system may be prohibitive. However for many village tasks in the developing countries, the back-up system may be the traditional energy system. If the wind fails to pump water, the villagers simply revert to carrying it on their heads. If the sun fails to shine to refrigerate fish, they are smoked over a wood fire, and so on. Moreover, a number of tasks can be performed whenever primary energy is available—for example, grain can be ground or water pumped and then stored for later use.

Thus far we have established that there are good technologies, that there is preliminary evidence that some of them may be cost effective and that, in many cases, there is a ready back-up system that entails no capital costs. But there is still very little experience with installing such technology in rural villages of the Third World under circumstances where good cost and performance data have been kept. In fact, many of the experiments in placing technology in villages have ended in failure. A number of windmills and a few methane digesters have been tried in African villages, for example, with far from encouraging results. Outside technicians came into the villages with a preselected technology to perform a preselected village task, and without very much interaction with villagers they erected and operated the energy producing hardware. A few weeks or months later, the visiting technicians left and shortly afterwards the technology fell into disuse. But this pattern is not unique to small-scale renewable energy hardware. Whether it be farm machinery, or transport or construction equipment, to provide such capital goods to a village without first training a cadre of people able to operate, maintain, and repair it, and without ensuring that there is local institutional infrastructure to support it, has universally proved to be futile. The latter might be a government institution such as a school, or a co-operative society, or a private entrepreneur. Without trained people and a responsible institution the chances are that energy technology will not be properly or long used. To give such technology a fair chance for success, it is necessary to enlist the enthusiastic co-operation of appropriate villagers. This means villagers must be involved in selecting the village task to be energized, in selecting the technology, and in determining what village institutions should be responsible for its maintenance and use.

The subject of finding renewable energy sources for Third World rural areas is not just a matter of humanitarian concern for those people. It may directly affect the availability of world energy supplies. Third World rural areas are not significant commercial energy users at present. However, influential leaders in the international community have set a target of eliminating the worst aspects of absolute poverty by the end of the century. The Overseas Development Council has examined the energy consumption of the 25 developing countries that have largely achieved this target to gauge what might happen to energy demand if all developing countries were to do so. Three preliminary important conclusions appear warranted. First, those nations (such as Brazil and Mexico) that have emphasized growth alone are relatively much higher energy users per capita than those countries (such as Taiwan) that have pushed growth with equitable distribution of incomes, or those (such as Sri Lanka) that have focused exclusively on equitable income distribution and have not made such headway on growth. Second, even if all Third World countries follow the relatively energy-efficient growth with equity strategy, the goals of eliminating the worst aspects of absolute poverty cannot be met without imposing a claim on world oil resources larger than world oil production will permit. Third, therefore these development goals can only be met if non-petroleum sources of energy are made available to these rural areas. Under these circumstances, exploring the use of small-scale renewable sources of energy appears to be an attractive path.

References and notes

1. Smil, V. *Bull. At. Sci.* **23** (No. 2), 25 (1977).
2. The US team, in addition to the authors of this article, included Dr J. R. Williams, associate dean for research, College of Engineering at the Georgia Institute of Technology; Dr T. Lawand, director of field operations of the Brace Research Institute, McGill University, Montreal, Canada; Dr B. Williams, director of the Energy Systems Research Laboratory of RCA; and Dr P. Reining, Office of International Science of the AAAS. The Tanzanian participants included representatives from the sponsoring council, the Prime Minister's office, relevant ministries and interested organizations, and the University of Dar-es-Salaam.
3. Calculations such as those in the following pages will be included in a forthcoming NAS publication on the proceedings of the workshop. Although these calculations are based on the work done at the NAS workshop, the particular numbers in this article are those of the authors and have not been checked yet with other members of the workshop.
4. The rate is 0.93 shilling per kilowatt hour. Actually the rate is graduated according to the amount used. The exchange rate is approximately $US1 = 8.2 shillings.
5. The estimates made by the panel for the renewable resource technologies aimed at

producing electricity as well as for diesel did not include the cost of power distribution in the village. Such costs are treated in the discussion of extending grid to the villages.

6. In view of the uncertainties in the cost estimates, all numbers are given only to two significant figures.
7. World Meteorological Organization, average of data for June 1966.
8. In this analysis, and those to follow, the cost of generating electricity is compared with the current price to the consumer. The principal justification for this approach is the assumption that the communal nature of the Ujamaa villages lends itself to eventual communal ownership of the generating system—hence the important datum for the villagers is the energy cost.
9. National Academy of Sciences, *Energy for rural development*. National Academy of Science, Washington DC (1976). See 'Hydropower' in Part 2, *Indirect uses of solar energy*, for a discussion of the growing use of small-scale hydroelectricity in the People's Republic of China.
10. Tanzanian participants thought that this was reasonable since village labour and materials would be volunteered and hence would not need to be included in the funds budgeted for the project. In a similar situation, techniques in which local labour and materials were used to construct dams and penstocks for installations capable of producing power in tens of kilowatts have been developed in Colombia at the Centro de Desarrollo Integrado 'Las Gaviotas'.
11. See *Methane generation from human, animal, and agricultural wastes*. National Academy of Sciences. Washington DC (1977).
12. Mhina, P. S. 'A brief description of manufacture and utilization of gobar gas in Tanzania', presented at a Seminar on Appropritae Technology in Small-Scale Industries, 15 to 17 December 1976. Dar-es-Salaam Technical College (Small Industries Development Organization (SIDO), Box 2476, Dar-es-Salaam): Mzee, A. *Pilot project on utilization of gobar gas in small I.C. engines*. Ministry of Water, Energy and Minerals, PO Box 9153, Dar-es-Salaam, Tanzania (1977).
13. Fraenkel, P. *Food from windmills*. Intermediate Technology, Ltd., London (1975).

VII Various energy profiles

Electrification in a town in Nicaragua.
World Bank photo by Paul Conklin.

The surge towers of the power station rise above the Seyhan Dam on the Seyhan River in Turkey. This multi-purpose dam controls water supplies to the Adana Plain and was built with the aid of World Bank funds.
World Bank photo by Mary M. Hill.

Reviews and analyses of energy status and prospects have recently become available for virtually all of the major developing countries and their exhaustive coverage in one volume is clearly impossible. The purpose of this section is thus to complete the book with a handful of detailed profiles selected to inform about the energetics of three populous Asian nations—Indonesia, Bangladesh, and Turkey, and about Central America, an increasingly important developing region whose combined population will shortly surpass 100 million people.

The chapter's selections start with an informed energy profile of Indonesia, today the developing world's third most populous country—about 140 million people and growing at an annual rate of 2 per cent—and it is fortunate in having sizeable resources of hydrocarbons, not yet fully appraised but significant coal deposits, fairly large hydro-power potential, and very rich supply of fuelwood from its tropical rain forests. However, as A. Arismunandar ('Conventional energy resources in Indonesia') points out, the sense of resource abundance is, unfortunately, illusory.

The nation has massive demand for modern energies and the domestic crude oil consumption has been growing at such a fast rate that hardly anything of Indonesia's total crude oil output as early as in the mid-1980s would be left for exports. To maintain the country's principal source of export revenue Indonesia will have to embark on a new energy development policy, aiming above all at comprehensive exploitation of solid fuels, geothermal steam, and a variety of renewable resources.

While Indonesia's planners argue about the best strategy to harness the country's relatively abundant energy resources, Bangladesh does not seem to have many choices. One of the world's poorest nations (GNP per capita about $US100 annually) with extremely high population density (in excess of 500 people per km^2) and frequent and devastating environmental hazards, Bangladesh produces and consumes only negligible quantities of modern energy and has not, so far, discovered any major fuel deposits.

M. Azizur Rahman and A. M. Z. Huq open their paper ('Energy resources in Bangladesh—problems and prospects') with brief information about the country's environment and economics, describe total energy and electricity production and consumption by sources and sectors and then survey all of the nation's resources of fossil fuels and hydro-power and point out some problems associated with their exploitation. They conclude by stressing the urgent need for effective population-control measures.

The energy outlook for Turkey is certainly more comfortable: sizeable lignite deposits exploitable by surface mining and the economical potential for 70 billion kWh of hydroelectricity annually are the country's most readily available resources and they will be increasingly relied on to satisfy as much of swiftly growing demand as possible. However, as M. Cetelincelik, President of the Turkish Nuclear Forum, makes clear ('Energy resources in Turkey,') domestic fuel and hydro-energy production will have to be supplemented by rising oil imports, a situation which would favour a move toward nuclear generation starting in the mid-1980s.

Energy situation of Mexico is, in many ways, similar to that of Indonesia. Population of Latin America's second largest nation is also growing very fast (the annual rate in excess of 3 per cent is among the highest in the world), the country has rich hydrocarbon resources whose development is under national control, as well as significant quantities of coal, hydro-power, and geothermal steam. Moreover, domestic demand for Mexico's rich crude oil resources is growing so fast that the country must also reduce its dependence on petroleum by initiating, as soon as possible, a major shift toward coal and renewable energies.

Unlike Indonesia, whose energy consumption per capita is only 150 kg of coal equivalent annually, Mexico—with about 1400 kg—is already much more advanced. According to J. Eibenschutz, A. Escofet, and G. Bazan ('Energy in Mexico') the nation's aggregate energy consumption by the end of the century is to expand five to seven times in comparison with 1975, and this would at least double the current consumption per capita or it could, with a slower population growth, lift it to over 4000 kg of coal equivalent annually, that is to a developed country level.

Other nations in Central America—Costa Rica, El Salvador, Guatemala, Honduras, Nicaragua, and Panama—are not as fuel-rich as Mexico but, as A. M. Strout of MIT argues in his review ('Energy and economic growth in Central America'), they have adjusted with relatively little difficulty to increased prices of necessary oil imports and they have considerable potential for enlarging hydrogeneration and for exploiting geothermal energy. Accelerated development of these resources might even enable a considerable expansion of energy-intensive industries which would reduce, above all, the imports of fertilizers and cement.

Dealing with both Bangladesh and Mexico, this section spans the extremes of energy situation in the developing world that is composed of emerging oil superpowers (leaving the already rich OPEC nations aside) and of impoverished nations with deteriorating economies. It also indicates well the future outcomes: potential for achieving the basic goals of development in some nations and almost inevitable worsening of the current state for others.

Energy in Asia: selected readings

The Asia Society (1977). *Report of a Seminar on Development of Small Scale Hydroelectric Power and Fertilization Production in Nepal.* The Asia Society, New York.

Bhudraja, P. S. Mekong development prospects revive. *Energy International* **14**, (10) (October 1977), 30–2.

Bogazici University (1977). *An energy modelling system for Turkey: summary report.* Tenth World Energy Conference, Istanbul.

Bourcier, P. (1977). *Growth and prospects of the Korean economy.* World Bank, Washington DC.

de Carmoy, G. (1974). Energy and development policies in Iran: a Western view. *Energy Policy* **2**, (4) (December 1974), 293–306.

Department of Energy, Republic of the Philippines (1978). *Ten year energy development program.* Department of Energy, Manila.

Energy Research and Development Group (1976). *Nepal: the energy sector.* Tribhuvan University, Kathmandu.

Htun, Maung Nay *et al.* (1976). *Some applications of solar energy in Thailand.* Asian Institute of Technology, Bangkok.

Islam, N. and de Lucia, R. J. (1977). *Energy sector planning in a developing country. Some general needs and a specific approach in*

Bangladesh. Tenth World Energy Conference, Istanbul.

Jeffs, E. J. (1977). Energy profile of Iran. *Energy International* **14**, (9) (September 1977), 33–41.

Khan, M. A. (1974). *Pakistan's energy requirements, energy resources and nuclear power programme*. Ninth World Energy Conference, Detroit.

C. Lotti & Associates, Meta Systems, Montreal Engineering Company and Snamprogetti. (1976). *Bangladesh energy study*. United Nations Development Program.

Pathmanathan, M. (1978). *Nuclear technology transfer and international safeguards: a case study of Malaysia*. Universiti Malaya, Kuala Lumpur.

Sherman, M. S. (1978). *Household use of energy in Pakistan*. US Agency for International Aid, Islamabad.

Tyers, R. (1976). *Energy in rural Bangladesh*. Harvard Center for Population Studies, Harvard University, Cambridge. Mass.

United Nations Economic and Social Commission for Asia and the Pacific (ESCAP) (1974). *Proceedings of the intergovernmental meeting on the impact of the current energy crisis on the economy of the ESCAP region*. United Nations, New York.

Unit, J. G. (1972). *The importance of rural electrification in Pakistan*. US Agency for International Development, Washington DC.

Energy in Latin America: selected readings

Commission Economica para America Latina (CEPAL) (1975). *America Latina y Los Problemas Actuales de Energia*. Fondo de Cultura Economica, Mexico.

Fitzsimmons, A. K. and McIntosh, T. L. Energy planning in Guatemala, response to crisis. *Energy policy* **6**, n. 1 (March 1978), 14–20.

Instituto Mexicano de Petróleo (1975). *Energéticos: Demanda Sectorial. Análisis y Perspectivas*. Instituto Mexicano de Petróleo, Mexico.

Interciencia (1978). Reports and recommendations of workshops. Symposium on Energy and Development in the Americas, March 12–17, 1978. *Interciencia* **3**, (3) (1978), 182–90.

McGranahan, R. and Taylor, M. (1977). *Urban energy use patterns in developing countries. A preliminary study of Mexico City*. Institute for Energy Research, State University of New York at Stony Brook.

Secretaria del Patrimonia Nacional (1976). *Propuesta de Lineamientos de Politica Energetica*. Commission de Energeticos, Mexico.

World Bank (1975). *Cost and benefits of rural electrification—a case study in El Salvador*. World Bank, Washington, DC.

26

Conventional energy sources in Indonesia

A. ARISMUNANDAR

From whatever data is available at present, it would be reasonable to assume that Indonesia is endowed with a relative abundance of energy resources, conventional or otherwise. The former includes non-renewable or exhaustible resources (i.e., petroleum, natural gas, and coal) and renewable resources (i.e., hydro-energy). The unconventional category in the Indonesian case includes solar energy, geothermal energy, wind energy, and tidal energy.

In assessing the availability of the above resources, this paper examines the past and present demands, projects the future demand, and evaluates the available reserves to meet the demand. With regard to the demand primarily the conventional and the commercially available forms of energy will be discussed. Non-commercial energy (notably firewood) will be discussed only in passing, in view of the scarcity of data, although its share in the Indonesian energy market is very large.

With regard to the past and present demands, this chapter examines the Indonesian energy situation and problems associated with it. In projecting into the future this paper assumes a set of mean commercial energy demands and based thereon calculates the cumulative commercial energy demand during the next 26 years.

The availability of conventional, non-renewable commercial energy sources is thence computed by subtracting production to date and future production from the known reserves. Future production is the sum of cumulative demand and export. Thus, positive availability can be calculated for any future date. Renewable energy sources (i.e. hydro-energy) are not included in the calculation in view of their inherent positive availability wherever they are found to be technically and economically feasible.

In anticipation of negative availability in the future since non-renewable energy sources are finite, this paper recommends a set of measures to be taken with regard to exploration of resources, pattern of energy supply, and energy utilization.

Projections on future energy demand

The energy crisis of October 1973 has provoked considerable concern and a sudden interest in energy problems throughout the world, Indonesia included. This concern and interest grew in part as a result of the anticipation of a probable impact of the crisis on the world economy, i.e. the danger of collapse of the world economy caused by the stream of petro-dollars which could not be invested, thus threatening to destroy the balance of the international monetary system, and the rapid increase of a negative balance of payments in many industrialized and developing countries. The former did not

First published in the *Transactions of the Tenth World Energy Conference*, Istanbul, Turkey, September 1977. Paper 1.4–1. Reprinted by permission of World Energy Conference.

materialize, because the oil-producing countries showed a much greater import capacity than had been foreseen, and they invested to a high degree in capital goods and infrastructure. The rapid increase of a negative balance of payments was lessened because many countries have managed to save energy to a considerable degree, thus reducing overall oil demand by at least 10 per cent.

Furthermore, it is significant to note that most member states of the Organization of Petroleum Exporting Countries (OPEC) have employed the increased oil revenues to build their national economies. This is also true with Indonesia. The share of the oil sector in the government's revenues has increased from 39 per cent in fiscal year 1972/3 to 60.4 per cent in 1975/6.[1,2]

The impact of the energy crisis and its associated price rises which resulted in the swelling of oil revenues (to more than six times in 3 years) stimulated considerable interest in Indonesia on policy matters pertaining to future energy development patterns and the role of oil as the nation's principal revenue earner in such patterns. Seminars and symposiums were held to discuss such matters and to recommend measures to cope with the rapidly increasing demand for energy. These include:

(a) the National Energy Seminar, held in July 1974;
(b) the Symposium on Energy, Resources, and the Environment, held in February 1975, and
(c) the Second Seminar on Electric Power, held in October 1975.

Besides, study groups were organized by governmental departments and universities. The reports submitted by these groups and the papers presented at the meetings made some attempts at estimating the energy demand in the years to come.

The National Energy Seminar (NES) which was held in Jakarta from 24 to 27 July 1974, was sponsored by two ministries and three government agencies, and was attended by 152 participants representing the government (policy makers), energy producers, energy consumers, the scientific community, and the general public. The conference was the first of its kind ever held in Indonesia, and its objective was to discuss various aspects of energy and to submit recommendations to the government to be used as a basis in defining a national policy on energy.

The Seminar recommended policy measures consisting of two parts,[3] firstly, an energy development pattern to meet the projected demand in the year 2000, and, secondly, suggestions pertaining to policies to sustain such a pattern. The Seminar advised that the energy sector should be developed in such a way as to fulfill its principal function as the prime mover in the long-range national economic development. The energy demand per capita projected by the Seminar for the year 2000 was 2.3×10^{10} J, of which 85 per cent, or 2.0×10^{10} J, was commercial energy.[4] The latter figure was adopted from an earlier, pre-oil crisis Seminar which based its projection on a 7 per cent growth-rate of gross domestic product (GDP) during the period 1970–2000, an expected population growth-rate of 2.3 per cent per annum and an energy–GDP elasticity of 2 in the beginning (1973–6), and gradually decreasing to 1 towards the end (1993–2000) of the projection period.[5] Based on a population of 231 million, the total energy demand in the year 2000 would be 5.3×10^{18} J, of which 4.5×10^{18} J would be commercial energy. The Seminar (NES) suggested that, since the growth rate of GDP could be higher than 7 per cent per annum,[6] the energy demand could be higher than the projected figures.

The demand projections made by the NES was evaluated in a report submitted by the Netherlands Economic Institute (NEI) to the Minister of Mines of Indonesia.[7] This report suggested that the initial value of the growth elasticity of energy consumption was rather high and the terminal value rather low. The combined effect of the two would balance out and the level of commercial energy consumption in the year 2000 would thus be the same as that of NES. Thus, according to NEI, the projected multiplication of the level of commercial energy consumption in the year 2000 by a factor of 18 compared with that of the year 1970 would be a fair estimate.[8] The level in the year 2000 could even be 30 per cent higher than the NES projection, because NEI used a 30 per cent higher figure for the base (1970) year. This would lead to a consumption per capita of 2.5×10^{10} J of commercial energy in the year 2000.

The Symposium on Energy, Resources, and the Environment (SERE) which was held in Jakarta from 25 to 28 February 1975, was organized by the Minister of State for Research in co-operation with the Mitre Corporation (USA). The objective of SERE was to obtain an overall conclusion and synthesis of all previous conferences on energy, natural resources and the environment in Indonesia and abroad, to be used as a basis in defining a national policy for development and conservation in the years ahead.

At this Symposium one paper offered some comments on the demand projection made by NES.[9] Using a higher percentage for population growth-rate than that used by NES, higher figures were obtained for commercial energy and non-commercial energy demands. Furthermore the share of non-commercial energy was initially (1970) higher than the figure used in the NES. However the share in the year 2000 was projected to be lower (4.8 per cent) than the NES figure (15 per cent).

The Second Seminar on Electric Power (SEP) which was held in Bandung from 30 October to 1 November 1976, was organized by the Bandung Institute of Technology and sponsored by the Minister of Public Works and Electric Power and the State Electricity Corporation (PLN). Although primarily concerned with the development of the electric power sector towards the year 2000, the Seminar also dealt with energy problems. One paper proposed somewhat revised figures for the energy demand in the year 2000, namely:[10]

Total energy:	5.5×10^{18} J.
Commercial energy (only):	4.8×10^{18} J.
Total energy per capita:	2.3×10^{10} J.

The figures for total energy and commercial energy suggested here are 12.2 per cent and 16.1 per cent higher than those produced by NES. The commercial energy demand for 1980 and 1990 as projected in the paper were 0.7×10^{18} J and 1.9×10^{18} J, respectively. The projected share of commercial with respect to total energy for 1980 and 1990 were 45.9 per cent and 65.0 per cent, respectively. This increasing share was assumed in the paper consistent with the world-wide trend of people's desire to live in greater and greater comfort and less and less inconvenience.

During 1975–6 two independent studies were made by two separate groups in Indonesia. The first was made by an energy study group for the National Economic and Social Affairs Institute (LEKNAS) within the framework of a broader study on the long-term growth perspectives of the Indonesian economy. The second was made by a team formed by the Director General of Oil and Natural Gas (MIGAS) to study the energy demand and supply in Indonesia, with special reference to oil.

The LEKNAS report projected energy demands of 140 million barrels of oil in 1980, 260 million in 1985, and more than 420 million in 1990.[11] Expressed in SI units,[4] they are, respectively, 0.8×10^{18} J, 1.4×10^{18} J, and 2.3×10^{18} J in 1980, 1985, and 1990.

The MIGAS study obtained three demand projections for the year 2000:[12]

(a) a low estimate of 139.3 million tonnes of coal equivalent (t.c.e.), based on the econometric method;
(b) a high estimate of 266.5 million t.c.e., based on the analytic method.
(c) a probable figure of 202.9 million t.c.e., which is the average of the low and the high estimate.

Table 26.1. Summary of all energy demand projections 1975–2000

	1975		*1980*		*1985*		*1990*		*1995*		*2000*	
Ref.	(*a*)	(*b*)	(*a*)	(*b*)	(*a*)	(*b*)	(*a*)	(*b*)	(*a*)	(*b*)	(*a*)	(*b*)
3											5.3	2.3
9	0.9	0.7	1.2	0.8	—	—	—	—	—	—	5.1	2.1
10	—	—	1.6	1.1	—	—	2.9	1.5	—	—	5.5	2.3

(*a*) Total demand (10^{18} J).
(*b*) Per capita demand (10^{10} J).

Table 26.2. Summary of all commercial energy demand projections 1975–2000

	1975		*1980*		*1985*		*1990*		*1995*		*2000*	
Ref.	(*a*)	(*b*)	(*a*)	(*b*)	(*a*)	(*b*)	(*a*)	(*b*)	(*a*)	(*b*)	(*a*)	(*b*)
3											4.5	2.0
7												2.5
9	0.4	0.3	0.8	0.5	1.4	0.8	2.2	1.2	3.4	1.5	4.8	2.0
10	—	—	0.7	0.5	—	—	1.9	1.0	—	—	4.8	2.0
11	0.4	—	0.8	—	1.4	—	2.3	—	—	—	—	—
12	0.4		0.7		1.0		1.5		2.3		3.5	1.4
L												
P	0.4		0.8		1.3		2.1		3.2		5.1	2.1
H	0.4		1.0		1.6		2.6		4.1		6.7	2.7

(*a*) Total demand (10^{18} J).
(*b*) Per capita demand (10^{10} J).
L = Low; P = Probable; H = High.

Expressed in SI units,[4] the demand estimates for the year 2000 are, respectively 3.5×10^{18} J, 6.7×10^{18} J, and 5.1×10^{18} J. Using the same population estimates as in earlier studies one obtains energy demands per capita of, respectively, 1.4×10^{10} J, 2.7×10^{10} J, and 2.1×10^{10} J.

The results of known energy demand projections made during the past 2 years expressed in SI units are summarized in Table 26.1 for total energy and Table 26.2 for commercial energy. For total energy the demand projections for the year 2000 vary from 5.1×10^{18} J, to 5.5×10^{18} J, a variation of only 10 per cent. The difference between total energy and commercial energy is due to non-commercial energy, primarily firewood and charcoal. The latter's share in the total energy demand is large: an earlier paper estimated it to be 65 per cent in 1970, later estimates were 70.9 per cent in 1970[9] and 64.1 per cent in 1973.[10] This share will definitely decrease because, as one paper[9] suggests, 'more and more commercial energy will be required to support the rapidly growing industrial developments in the years to come, and because more and more non-commercial energy will be replaced by commercial energy due to the effects of modernization and the increasing desire for convenience and cleanliness'. The share of non-commercial energy in the year 2000 was estimated to vary between 4.8 and 12 per cent.

As can be seen from Table 26.2 if the high and low estimates of the MIGAS study are taken out, the results of the different studies agree quite well. The mean commercial

Table 26.3. Mean values of known commercial energy demand projections 1975–2000

		Commercial energy demand			*Rate of growth per annum (per cent)*		
Year	*Population* (10^6)	*Mean* (10^{18} J)	*Per capita* 10^{10} J	*Max. deviation (per cent)*	*GDP*	*Comm. energy*	*Energy–GDP elasticity coefficient*
1975	132.1*	0.4	0.3	0	—	—	—
1980	148.3*	0.8	0.5	7.8	8.10*	12.6	1.6
1985	167.0*	1.4	0.8	3.3	8.87*	12.1	1.4
1990	189.3†	2.1	1.1	11.1	7.0†	9.0	1.3
1995	214.5‡	3.3	1.5	2.0	7.0†	9.2	1.3
2000	243.1*	4.8	2.0	6.2	7.0†	7.4	1.1

*Note 6.
†Note 13.
‡Computed from Note 13.

energy demand in the year 2000 is 4.8×10^{18} J with a maximum deviation of 6.2 per cent. The mean for the year 1975 is 0.4×10^{18} J with a maximum deviation of 0 per cent.

Proceeding in a similar manner one obtains the mean commercial energy demand and the maximum deviation for the year 1980, 1990, and 1995, as shown in Table 26.3. This table also shows the rates of growth of energy demand and the elasticity coefficients within each 5-year period. The table indicates consistency of the Indonesian situation with the world-wide trend of decreasing growth rate of energy demand with increasing economic development and that the energy–GDP elasticity coefficients will tend over time to approach unity.[15]

Furthermore it can be seen from Table 26.3 that the demand growth rates for Indonesia are three to four times higher than the world average of 3.3 per cent per annum[16] through to 1990. This also seems to be consistent with the above-mentioned trend and with the low demand per capita in Indonesia compared with that the world's average. The projected demand per capita in Indonesia in 1980 of 0.5×10^{10} J is even lower than that of average of the Third World in 1971 of 1×10^{10} J.[17] The situation in Indonesia would not improve much in the year 2000 because the projected demand per capita for that year of 2.0×10^{10} J is only one-third of the Third World's average of 6.2×10^{10} J.[17] Even with China and Arab countries excluded, the demand per capita in Indonesia in the year 2000 would still be lower than that of the average of the rest of the Third World[17] of 3.7×10^{10} J. From this point of view, the projected commercial energy demands suggested in this paper would seem to be on the pessimistic side and be considered realistic.

Using the mean commercial energy demands and their respective annual growth rates, as shown in Table 26.3, the cumulative commercial energy demands from 1975 to 2000 can be computed. This is shown in Table 26.4. The total commercial energy demand for the 26-year period would be 52.6×10^{18} J. This is equivalent to any one of the following quantities of energy source:[4]

(a) 9599 million barrels of petroleum;
(b) 2104 million tonnes of bituminous coal; and
(c) 53 trillion cubic feet of natural gas.

Availability of conventional energy resources to meet the demand

In order to be able to assess availability of energy resources to meet the demand, data on resources should be known and the

Table 26.4. Cumulative commercial energy demand 1975–2000

	Mean commercial energy demand (10^{18} joules)	
Period	*Total*	*Cumulative*
1975–9	2.8	2.8
1980–4	4.9	7.7
1985–9	8.2	15.9
1990–4	12.8	28.7
1995–9	19.2	47.9
2000	4.7	52.6

demand should be estimated as accurately as technically feasible. At present, no consistent data on the conventional energy resources of Indonesia is known.[18] The official figure for petroleum reserves,[18,19] for example, is 57.5×10^{18} J whereas one foreign source[20] estimated it to be 98.6×10^{18} J. These low and high estimates are respectively 1.5 and 2.5 per cent of the world measured crude oil reserves[16] of 3955.3×10^{18} J. An often-quoted figure of 2 per cent would yield 79.1×10^{18} J, which is the nearest to the 82.2×10^{18} J figure mentioned by the Indonesian Minister of Mines[11] than any one of the previous estimates.[21]

There are widely differing estimates of the natural gas reserves of Indonesia. One official estimate made in 1973 was 30×10^{18} J, whereas one foreign source estimated it to be 3×10^{18} J, only one-tenth of the former.[22] These estimates are, respectively, 1.5 and 0.15 per cent of the measured world reserves of natural gas of 1935×10^{18} J.[16] Judging from existing commitments for the supply of liquefield natural gas (LNG) to other countries, the higher estimate would seem to be more reasonable.

The coal resources of Indonesia seem to be quite large. Officials of both the Indonesian Ministry of Mines and the Shell Mining Company (Dutch) estimated the coal resources of South Sumatera[23] alone to be of the order of tens of billion of tonnes.[11] However, the coal reserves of Indonesia are presently estimated[16] to be 46.0×10^{18} J). These reserves amount to 0.3 per cent of the world measured reserves of solid fuels[16] of 15250.2×10^{18} J.

Data on the uranium resources of Indonesia is not available as yet. However, survey and systematic prospecting which have been carried out since 1969 in co-operation with the French Atomic Energy Commission (CEA) have indicated existence of uranium deposits in West Kalimantan.[11]

Based on presently available data as outlined above the total conventional non-renewable energy resources of Indonesia range between 106.5×10^{18} and 174.6×10^{18} J, or between 0.5 and 0.8 per cent of the world reserves; see Table 26.5. The list does not include the potential energy resources of Indonesia, non-renewable or otherwise. The latter include hydro-energy (0.5×10^{18} joules per annum),[25] geothermal energy, and firewood (0.8×10^{18} J per annum).[9]

To give some indication[26] on the past and present demand,[12] it is useful to note that the total consumption of primary energy

Table 26.5. Conventional, non-renewable energy reserves of Indonesia in comparison with Asia and the world (10^{18} J)

	Fossil fuels			*Uranium*	*Total*	
Area	*Solid fuels*	*Crude oil*	*Natural gas*		*(10^{18} J)*	*World (per cent)*
Indonesia	46.0	57.5–98.6	3.0–30.0	—	106–5–174.6	0.5–0.8
Asia (less USSR)	2753.6	2332.6	456.8	3.2	5546.1	25.0–25.3
World	15250.2	3955.3	1935.0	765.0–1070.9	22210.9	100

(oil, natural gas, coal, and hydro-energy) in Indonesia during the period 1960–74 was roughly 3.2×10^{18} J. Thus it is obvious that available, conventional non-renewable energy resources (see above paragraph) far exceed the past and present demands. It is true that Indonesia still imports some of her needs. Oil imports in 1976, according to the Minister of Mines,[27] is expected to reach 4.9 million m^3. However, this is purely due to technical and economic reasons, i.e. the capabilities of Indonesian refineries to meet domestic requirements and the substitution of higher-priced, low-sulphur domestic oil with less-expensive, high-sulphur imported oil.

The large excess of resources with respect to demand is definitely no reason for complacency, because if the trend of demand during the past few years continues, the future must be envisaged with extreme caution. Firstly, the rate of growth of commercial energy consumption has increased annually from 6.6 per cent during the period 1960–70 to 14.9 per cent during 1970–4.[12] Secondly, whereas the share of oil has continually and steadily increased from 86 per cent in 1960 to 90.8 per cent in 1974, the share of coal has declined from 12.4 per cent to less than 1 per cent during the same period. Production of coal has decreased from a record of 2000680 tonnes in 1940 to 156153 tonnes in 1974.[11] Thirdly, a large portion of energy consumed has been for non-productive purposes. Commercial energy consumption in the household sector, notably paraffin, has been substantial, varying between 31.9 per cent and 39.2 per cent during the period 1968–74.[12]

To this figure should be added the consumption of electricity for household purposes, which is 29 per cent during fiscal year 1975/6.[28] Non-productive uses of commercial energy tend to increase for two reasons, namely, the growth rate of population and the increasing share of population demanding more comfort, convenience, and some degree of modernization.

In order to find out whether or not any one source of non-renewable energy will be available at any given time in the future, the following simplified equations can be used:

$$\text{Availability} = \text{reserves} - (\text{production to date}) - (\text{production henceforth}) \qquad (1)$$

$$\text{Production} = \text{Demand} + \text{Export} \qquad (2)$$

Since production to date is 32.5×10^{18} joules,[29] if the 1975-level of export of 2.0×10^{18} joules[30] is assumed to be maintained and if the total commercial energy demand until 1984 is to be met by oil (see Table 26.4), then availability of oil in 1985 will be -2.7×10^{18} joules. This means that, if the lower figure of the crude oil reserve of Table 26.5 is used, oil will no longer be available for export and to fulfil a portion of the domestic demand by as early as 1984, 5 years hence.

The latter statement would not necessarily prove to be correct for the following reasons:

(a) oil reserves might be as high as the higher figure indicated in Table 26.5, in which case the availability might be extended for another 10 years.

(b) oil is not the only energy source available; coal and natural gas could be used, although their share would be small and it would be difficult to replace the role of oil significantly within less than 20 years.

(c) the amount of reserves would tend to increase with time because, through new discoveries and extractive technology, undiscovered and below-economic resources are continually moved into the reserve category.[18] In this case, again, availability would be extended further; and

(d) if none of (a), (b), and (c) materializes the other unknown (uranium) and the renewable energy sources (hydro and geothermal) could still be counted upon.

If the other non-renewable energy sources (coal and natural gas) could be used and if they could be made available at any time during the period under consideration, then there might be sufficient energy sources available to meet the demand until the year 2000. However the shift in pattern from a 90.8 per cent oil supply in 1974 to, for example, an 82.1 per cent oil supply in 1985,[11] might be difficult to realize. To meet the balance of the demand efforts must be made by all governmental agencies concerned to produce in 1985: 0.2×10^{18} J of natural gas and 0.1×10^{18} J of coal.[11]

Measures to enhance the availability of energy resources to meet the demand

Thus, it became obvious that the most logical method to enhance availability is to change 'resources' into 'reserves', or to move 'resources' into the 'reserve' category. Therefore, exploration of new oil and other resources should be accelerated and in certain areas intensified. The discovery of new reserves, and how much, plays a decisive role in determining future policies on domestic uses and export of energy. One report suggests that if newly discovered reserves of crude oil until the year 2000 amounts to only one-half of the present reserves then:[7]

(a) in the case of constant export (at 2×10^{18} J per annum) the ratio of reserves to production becomes 10 in 1985 and reserves will be exhausted in 1977; and
(b) in the case of constant production (at 2.8×10^{18} J per annum since 1974)[4] the reserve-production ratio becomes 10 in 1989.[31]

The discovery of new oil reserves is most important because, as indicated earlier, it would seem that the role played by oil could not be readily replaced by coal or natural gas. To this effect exploration technology should be improved,[16] especially in the face of adverse sea-state conditions in offshore regions of Indonesia. To add more coal reserves to cope with the worldwide (Indonesia included) rejuvenation of interest in coal, intensive exploration should be carried out to find new deposits or to define recoverable reserves in known deposits. There is also a need to discover uranium reserves in the shortest possible time in order that nuclear energy may contribute its share in meeting the future energy demand since 1985.

Furthermore, since the amount of reserves is finite, efforts should also be made to improve the recovery of deposits to enhance the availability of known energy sources. In the case of crude oil these efforts would be justified because escalating prices would improve the economic prospects for advanced (e.g. 'third generation')[16] recovery methods. In the case of coal all available methods to improve the recovery of deposits should be applied both in open-pit and underground mining in order that coal may in the future reduce the burden presently carried by oil as soon as technically feasible.

Availability of energy sources can also be enhanced by technological improvements in the use of low grade resources. If energy sources become scarce and if the era of cheap energy belongs to the past, then extraction of energy from sources previously regarded as too low grade[32] can be considered attractive. Low-grade coal, i.e. of low calorific value can and should be used to meet domestic energy demands. Specialized techniques[16] for dealing with low-rank coals should be applied if necessary. Some improved conventional processes which have been applied to brown coal and lignite in many countries should also be tried in Indonesia.

Once the reserves are known and once the demand can be reasonably projected, then the availability of all energy sources can be determined. Thus the share that each energy source should contribute to meet the total demand can be rationally decided. For reasons already stated, the first decision to be made is to gradually reduce Indonesia's dependence on oil. The share of oil in the

Indonesian commercial energy market should be lowered, consistently and conscientiously, from 90.8 per cent in 1974 to as low a figure as technically and economically feasible. The LEKNAS study suggested 82.1 per cent in 1985,[11] an average drop of 0.8 per cent per annum. Another report recommended 75.1 per cent in the year 2000,[33] an average drop of 0.6 per cent per annum.

This decision to reduce dependence on oil requires a strong political will by the people and concerted actions by all governmental agencies concerned. To fill in the gap created by the reduction of oil supply, the share of coal should be increased, especially to produce electric energy. The LEKNAS report suggested that the share of coal could be 6.8 per cent in 1985,[11] an average rise of 0.4 per cent per annum. Percentagewise, this might be considered low. However, in view of the physical constraints and the state of the coal-mining sector at present, the projected share of coal supply might be slightly on the optimistic side. A pessimistic view is presented in another report where the share of coal in the energy market is projected to be 5.7 per cent in the year 2000,[33] a slow average rise of 0.2 per cent per annum.

Complementary to coal, nuclear energy should be introduced as soon as technically and economically feasible. According to a study by the International Atomic Energy Agency (IAEA) the first nuclear power plant of 600-MW size should be operational by as early as 1983.[34] Judging from what has been accomplished hitherto it would be difficult to have one plant on-line by 1985. However, the study has proved that sooner or later Indonesia has to 'go nuclear' for economic and technical reasons. Even with a low forecast of peak demand of 23238 MW for Java alone in 1997, the study suggested[34] that the share of nuclear power capacity could be 17400 MW.

Other rational measures to enhance availability include the utilization of all resources effectively and efficiently and the utilization of energy largely for productive purposes. The former would be difficult to achieve at this early stage when the sense of abundance of resources with respect to demand still prevails. However, as implied earlier, this sense of abundance is in fact merely an illusion, because oil reserves are limited and the large reserves of coal have not contributed much (and would not in the immediate future) in the share of the energy market in Indonesia. The effective and efficient use of all non-renewable resources is therefore imperative because, however large these resources might be, their life could be measured only in terms of decades than centuries. The effective and efficient use of resources should also be considered in the light of a broader and better-known energy conservation programme, which is necessary, among others, because of the environmental effects of unrestrained demand (because people's wants are infinite) and because energy is a fundamental ingredient in any economic system.[35]

More and more energy should be used for productive purposes, rather than consumptive, because only productive uses of energy can sustain and maintain acceleration of economic growth so vital for the development of the nation. To meet the demand of an increasing number of the population at large which consumes energy largely for non-productive (i.e. household) purposes, the quantity of energy supplied for these purposes should be increased. However, the share of non-productive uses of energy should be gradually but consistently reduced from 33.7 per cent of oil consumption in 1974 (plus 29 per cent of electric energy consumption in 1975/6) to a level which would be considered technically and economically feasible, while maintaining socio-political stability within the nation. All previous estimates should be re-examined with regard to the latter constraint. One such estimate[33] was 10.5 per cent of oil consumption in the form of paraffin for household uses in the year 2000. Whether or not this is possible should be evaluated in the light of the above policy, and also in view of:

(a) the increasing number of population desiring convenient forms of energy;
(b) the necessity of substituting inconvenient and ecologically disturbing forms of energy (such as firewood in critical land areas) with others (such as biogas from waste); and
(c) the possibility of assigning priorities to renewable resources (such as hydro-power and geothermal energy) in carrying the balance of the energy demand.

Conclusions

From what has been elaborated above, the following conclusions can be drawn:
1. The projected energy demands reported in the various papers and studies seem to be in close agreement. The mean commercial energy demands in Indonesia were computed from the above projections; the value for the year 2000 was found to be 4.8×10^{18} J and the per capita demand 2.0×10^{10} J. The latter figure is a meagre one-third of the projected per capita demand in the Third World in the year 2000.
2. The mean commercial energy demands in Indonesia in the future indicate: firstly, consistency with the world-wide trend of decreasing growth rate of energy demand with increasing economic development; and secondly, that the energy–GDP elasticity coefficients will tend over time to approach unity (from 1.6 during 1975–80, gradually decreasing to 1.1 during 1995–2000).
3. From what is presently thought to be known the conventional, non-renewable, energy reserves of Indonesia are relatively large, namely between 106.5 and 174.6×10^{10} J, especially if these are compared with the past and present demands.
4. However, if the reserves are compared with a cumulative commercial energy demand of 52.6×10^{18} J during the next 26 years plus the need for export, they may be considered small. If the 1975-level of export is maintained and if the total commercial energy demand in the future is to be met entirely by oil, then the availability of this energy source might become negative by as early as 1984 The sense of absolute abundance of energy resources would thus be illusory because oil reserves are limited and the large reserves of coal have not contributed much in the share of the energy market.

In view of the above, measures would have to be taken to enhance the availability of energy resources to meet the demand in the future, as follows:

(a) exploration programmes should be carried out intensively and extensively and accelerated wherever possible to determine present reserves and to move more 'resources' into the 'reserve' category;
(b) efforts should be made to reduce dependence on oil, gradually but consistently;
(c) coal and nuclear energy should be used to meet the demand for electric energy;
(d) renewable energy resources (notably hydro and geothermal) should be used wherever feasible;
(e) all energy sources should be used effectively and efficiently and in the light of a broader conservation programme; and
(f) the share of the productive uses of energy should be increased, relative to the non-productive ones, as high as technically and economically feasible, while maintaining socio-political stability within the nation.

Notes and references

1. *Pidato Kenegaraan Presiden Republik Indonesia Jendral Suharto di Depan Sidang Dewan Perwakilan Rakyat 16 Agustus 1975*, pp. 70–8. Departemen Penerangan R.I., Jakarta (1975).
2. RAPBN Th. '76/77 3,5 Trilyun Rupiah. *Sinar Harapan* (newspaper). Jakarta, 7 January (1976).
3. See *Hasil-Hasil Seminar Energi Nasional 1974*. Komite Nasional Indonesia, World Energy Conference, Jakarta (1974).
4. SI units are used throughout this paper; for conversion factors see Position Paper for Division 1: Development of conventional

energy resources by C. H. Smith and R. B. Tombs, Tenth World Energy Conference, Istanbul, 19–24 September 1977; here, 10^{18} joules (J) of energy is assumed to be equivalent to 182.5 million barrels of petroleum, or 40 million tonnes of bituminous coal, or 1 trillion cubic feet of natural gas.

5. *Permasalahan Minyak dan Gas Bumi Indonesia menjelang Tahun 2000*. Hasil Seminar SUSPI-MIGAS Angkatan I, Jakarta, October (1973). The Seminar was held upon request by the President-Director of PERTAMINA (the state oil and gas company), and attended by senior officials of the nation's oil and gas industry.
6. This was confirmed in a recent report: figures of 8.10 and 8.87 per cent were estimated for 1975–80 and 1980–5, respectively; see *Perspektip Perekonomian Nasional Indonesia Tahun 1985*, Lembaga Penyelidikan Ekonomi dan Masyarakat, Fakultas Ekonomi Universitas Indonesia, Jakarta, April (1976).
7. The development of the energy sector in Indonesia 1970–2000, with special reference to crude oil (unpublished report).
8. The 1970 level of commercial energy consumption was 51 million barrels of oil equivalent (see Ref. 5), or 0.3×10^{18} J. This is roughly 1/18 of the level in the year 2000.
9. Arismunandar, A. Indonesian energy demand in the year 2000 views and comments. Symposium on Energy, Resources and the Environment, Jakarta, 25–28 February 1975.
10. Sudarsono, Budi and Arismunandar, A. Peranan tenaga nuklir dalam memenuhi kebutuhan tenaga listrik tahun 2000. Seminar Ke dua Teknik Tenaga Listrik, Bandung, 30 October–1 November 1976.
11. Sudarsono, Budi, Surjadi, A. J., Iljas, Jasif. *Laporan proyek penelitian energi Indonesia dalam Jangka panjang*, Lembaga Ekonomi dan Kemasyarakatan Nasional-LIPI, Jakarta (1976).
12. Team Kerja Tetap Peneliti Perkiraan Kebutuhan Energi dan Bahan Bakar Minya. *Perkiraan konsumsi energi di Indonesia 1975–2000*, Direktorat Jendral Minyak dan Gas Bumi, Jakarta, June (1976). (Draft report.)
13. Djojohadikusumo, Sumitro. Indonesia towards the year 2000. Symposium on energy, resources and the environment, Jakarta 25–28 February (1975).
14. Kadir, Abdul. Pola Pengembangan energi di Indonesia serta peranan tenaga listrik dalam pola tersebut, Seminar Energi Nasional, Jakarta, 24–7 July (1974).
15. Darmstadter, J. with Teitelbaum, P. D. and Polach, J. G. *Energy in the world economy*, pp. 32–44, 65–74. The Johns Hopkins Press (1971).
16. See Smith and Toombs (note 4).
17. Pierre Daures, Jean-Romain Frisch, *Perspectives energetiques pour le Tiers Monde*, Groupe Prospective de l'Energie de la Maison des Sciences de l'Homme, Paris January (1975).
18. Definition of 'resources' and 'reserves' is according to V. E. McKelvey.
19. Throughout this paper all energy figures are rounded off to the first decimal point (of 10^{18} J); original data is 10.5 billion barrels, see *Statistik Perminyakan Indonesia 1974*. Divisi Development & Information Centre PERTAMINA, Jakarta (1975).
20. Original data is 18 billion barrels, see Ingersoll, J. M. *Energy and the Third World*. Hudson Institute Research Memorandum 4 (HI–2094–P), New York, September (1974); see also Ref. 11.
21. The Minister's figure was 15 billion barrels.
22. In original units, they are, respectively, 30 trillion cubic feet (see Ref. 5) and 85 billion m^3 (see Ref. 20).
23. Indonesia is an archipelago in South-East Asia consisting of more than 10000 islands with a total land area of 1.9 million km^2. The five major islands are Java, Sumatera, Kalimantan, Sulawesi, and Irian Jaya. Petroleum can be found in Java, Sumatera, Kalimantan, and Irian Jaya, and their offshore areas. Coal can be found in South and West Sumatera and East Kalimantan. Indications of uranium resources have been found in West Kalimantan, West Sumatera and in the southern part Sumatera.[11] Hydro energy resources can be found in almost all major islands. Geothermal energy can be located along the volcanic belt from Sumatera, Java, the Moluccas, and on to Sulawesi.
24. This figure has been estimated by the author from data submitted by the Indonesian National Committee of the World Energy Conference (WEC) for the forthcoming issue of *Survey of energy resources* to be published by WEC Central Office, as follows: bituminous, sub-bituminous and brown coal 341 million tonnes, and lignite 1872 million tonnes.
25. 155 billion kWh; see Notodihardjo, Mardjono. Hydro power resources of Indonesia. Thirteenth Pacific Science Congress, Vancouver, Canada, 18–29 August (1975).
26. If the demand can only be partially met, as is the case in Indonesia, then consumption constitutes merely a fraction of the demand.
27. Sadli, Menteri Pertambangan M. Impor

BBM tahun ini 4891—Juta kilo liter. *Berita Yudha* (newspaper), Jakarta, 16 September (1976).

28. *Statistik Pengusahaan 1 April 1975–31 Maret 1976*, Perusahaan Umu Listrik Negara, Jakarta (1976).
29. 5928935000 barrels (see Ref. 11).
30. 363069249 barrels; see Adin, A. Peranan Minyak dalam Pembangunan Ekonomi Indonesia, *Prisma* (magazine), Jakarta, No. 4, May 1976, Tahun V.
31. This latter option of constant production is consistent—at least temporarily—with the recent decision by the Organization of Petroleum Exporting Countries (OPEC) to maintain daily production at 30 million barrels; see Mulai Tanggal 1 January 1977 Harga Minyak RI $US12.70/barrel. *Sinar Harapan* (newspaper), Jakarta, 20 December (1976).
32. According to Smith & Toombs (see Ref. 16), the 'grade' of a deposit is determined by:
    (a) internal factors, i.e. impurity content, water content, dispersion of the resource, etc.;
    (b) external factors, i.e. environmental penalties, transport distances, infrastructure cost, etc.
33. Wijarso. Beberapa Aspek Pengelolaan Energi di Indonesia menuju Tahun 2000. *Prisma* (magazine), Jakarta, No. 2, pp. 69–74, April (1975).
34. Nuclear power planning study for Indonesia (Java Island). Unedited Draft Report, International Atomic Energy Agency, Vienna October (1975). Remarks on the low forecast are contained in an IAEA letter No. SC/502–1 dated 7 October (1975).
35. Hannon, Bruce. Energy conservation and the consumer. *Science* **189** (4197), p. 95, 11 July (1975).

27

Energy resources in Bangladesh—problems and prospects

M. AZIZUR RAHMAN AND A. M. Z. HUQ

Bangladesh is a country which was born as late as December 16 of 1971, with a population of nearly 75 million confined within an area of 141 122 km^2. The fact that the independence of Bangladesh was achieved after an initial period of about 9 months of seriously disturbed conditions arising out of a resistance movement accompanied by guerilla warfare, and finally a full-scale war for about a fortnight, is one of the main causes, along with some others, responsible for the large-scale disruptions of economic and social life of this country, and the consequent low level of economic activity in the recent post-liberation period.

The land and environment

In this context, therefore, before taking up a detailed consideration of the question of energy as related to the present and future conditions of Bangladesh, it might be worthwhile to start with a few basic facts relating to this country of rather small area but a large population, giving an average population density of 531 persons per km^2, a figure amongst the highest in the world.

To give a very broad picture about the 'environment' of Bangladesh one may mention the following facts. Nearly 80 per cent of the working people of this country are dependent on agricultural activities for their livelihood. Out of a total of 94 204 km^2 of cultivable land, 89 719 km^2 are actually under cultivation. Forests occupy 22 000 km^2, or nearly 16 per cent of the total area; area under water of a few big rivers and a large number of branches and tributaries is approximately 7800 km^2. The southern part of the country consists largely of the vast deltaic regions of the rivers Ganges and Brahmaputra. The topography of the country is mainly monotonous plains, except the hilly regions of Chittagong Hill Tracts in the extreme south-east, bordering on Burma, and the extreme north bordering on the lower reaches of the Himalayas. During the monsoons floods are therefore a very frequent occurrence is such plain land, and an area actually much more than cited above goes under water and remains so for considerable lengths of time. Add to this the fact that heavy and long monsoons characterize the climate of this region, producing rainfalls ranging from 1.12 m in the north and western regions to about 5 m in the north-east, a region close to the deep forests of Assam, in certain places of which Indian State the world's heaviest rainfalls are recorded. The short winters extending roughly from November to the end of February are very mild, and a large variety of winter crops can be produced provided a reliable water supply for irrigation can be arranged.

First published in the *Transactions of the Ninth World Energy Conference*, Detroit, 1974, Paper 1.2–7, Vol. II, pp. 203–21. Reprinted by permission of the authors and World Energy Conference.

Economics and energy in Bangladesh

As there is a distinct correlation between the energy consumption in a country and its overall economic condition, a few figures showing the state of energy production and use, as well as the level and nature of economic activities of the country would be useful as a basis for consideration of problems and prospects in this matter.

The GDP for the year 1969–70, the last 'normal' year before the large-scale economic disruption caused by the liberation war, was 50030 million Taka (based on 1972–3 prices), giving a per capita GDP of 656 Taka (7.75 Taka = 1 US dollar), of which 57.6 per cent came from agriculture, livestock, forestry, and fishery. The contribution of manufacturing, trade, transport, and other services amounted to 33.7 per cent.

The effect of the war devastation is reflected in the figure of 42940 million Taka to which the GDP of the country fell in the year 1972–3. The percentage contributions from the main components mentioned above remained nearly the same. The predominantly agricultural character of the economy is clearly evident from the GDP figures.

Existing electrical power generation capacity is 545 MW, giving an installed capacity per capita of 7.5 watts.* The total electrical energy generated in 1970 was 1123 GWh giving an electrical energy consumption per capita of 16 kWh. It is also of interest to note here that the peak electrical demand was only 222 MW in 1970, and that the peak demand fell to as low a figure as about 100 MW during the disturbed months of 1971, and that owing to various types of damage caused to industrial establishments as well as to power system equipment as a result of the war it was possible to achieve a peak demand of only 189 MW by December 1972.

Considering the figures cited in the preceding sections, it would be quite appropriate to state that an 'energy crisis' definitely exists in the country but the nature of this crisis is almost exactly of an opposite nature to that existing recently in some of the highly industrialized countries.[1] The high standard of living which has been achieved, and which is being sought to be raised still higher by more intensive as well as extensive application of advanced technology in industrialized countries, has both called for and encouraged the consumption of energy at a very fast rate, and the risk of exhaustion of the known resources of energy in those countries in the very near future has assumed threatening dimensions by now. The particular character of the crisis has made it imperative to investigate and develop various types of unconventional methods of energy conversion to supplement the already highly developed technologies of conventional energy conversion.

In the developing nations, on the other hand, very little energy is being used, so that the impact of energy utilization on achieving a higher standard of living is almost negligible. Although in such countries there does exist considerable amounts of the conventional energy resources, the financial capability and technical and managerial adequacy essential for the exploitation and distribution of even the available known resources are sadly lacking at the moment. More precisely the problems (which in the last analysis mainly boil down to economic in nature) in the field of energy exploitation in developing countries, even with conventional and well known established technology, are such that they stand in the way of adoption of measures which could solve the same problems.

Energy structure

The data in this section will be presented so as to show the total energy consumption and electrical energy consumption of the country. The sources from which the total energy used only in the form of electricity are

*By the end of 1977 the installed capacity rose to about 750 megawatts.

Table 27.1. Electrical energy sources

Source	*Quantity used*	*Energy generated (GWh)*	*Coal equivalent (10^6 kg)*	*Percentage of total*
Coal	8524 (tonne)	13.44	8.7	1.20
Natural gas	233×10^6 (m^3)	482.2	311.0	42.70
Petroleum products	96790 (tonne)	234.5	151.0	20.70
Hydroelectricity		394.0	254.0	35.40
Total		1123.94	724.7	100.00

obtained will also be given. While electrical energy consumption in a country is an indication of its economic condition, the total energy use gives a more comprehensive and 'living' picture of the character and 'quality of life' of that same country. Besides this, it has been realized only recently that the sources from which the energy is produced, and the ways in which it is converted and consumed, may have a significant influence on the environment and ecology of the region.[3] It will be evident from the data presented, that while in the highly industrialized countries the aspects of environmental pollution due to energy use have received great attention in recent times, the problem in the developing nations is more related to ecological imbalances originating from deforestation, soil erosion, and related phenomena.

Natural gas and water are the two purely indigenous resources which contribute towards the production of electrical energy in Bangladesh. The other major resource—oil—is at present entirely imported. The one existing refinery is almost fully dependent on imports. Only a small portion of available coal, which has also to be imported wholly at present, is used for the production of electrical energy; most of the imported coal goes to supply certain industrial requirements, such as the firing of brick kilns, re-rolling mills, foundry shops, etc. Consumption of coal for railways and waterways transportation is negligible at present. Table 27.1 shows the contributions made by different kinds of resources[2] towards the generation of electrical energy in 1970.

The conversion rates used for the preparation of Table 27.1 are shown in the Appendix to this chapter. It will be noted that there is no nuclear power generation in Bangladesh at present, and that natural gas, which is indigenous, contributes the largest portion towards electric power generation in this country.

Table 27.2 showing the consumption of electrical energy in 1970, has been compiled from data based on the sale of electrical energy under the Bangladesh Power Development Board,[2] which is the only public electric utility organization of the country. The amount of energy produced and consumed by a few private industrial organizations is insignificant.

Table 27.2. Use of electrical energy

Load type	*Energy used (GWh)*	*Percentage of total*
Residential	153.670	18.1
Industrial	584.752	68.9
Commercial	93.844	11.1
Agricultural (pumps)	16.709	1.9
Total	848.975	100.0

It will be noted that there is a significant difference (nearly 25 per cent) between the total amount of electrical energy generated and the total amount of energy sold. Part of this is of course due to the unavoidable losses in transmission and distribution, which is not expected to be more than 10 to 12 per cent. The rest of the loss must therefore be due to some or all of the following causes: (a) excessive leakage due

Table 27.3. Total energy consumption and sources

Source	*Quantity used*	*Energy produced (10^{12} kcal)*	*Coal equivalent (10^6 kg)*	*Percentage of total*
Coal	286238 (tonne)	1.940	292.0	3.14
Petroleum products	1260344 (tonne)	13.150	1975.0	21.21
Natural gas	254×10^6 (m^3)	2.262	340.0	3.65
Hydroelectricity		1.695	254.0	2.73
Firewood, farm and animal waste, etc.		43.00	6450.0	69.27
Total		62.047	9311.0	100.0

to inadequate insulation, (b) intentional pilferage through illegal connection or meter tampering, (c) faulty metering, (d) error in recording and billing. The losses due to avoidable causes seem to be excessive at present. It is also to be noted that a negligible amount of electrical energy is being used in agriculture.

In addition to the generation of electrical power, the available resources—indigenous and imported—are used to produce energy required for various daily activities, such as transportation, cooking at home, and some industries which use fossil fuels directly. One fact of great importance at present is that all motorized traffic of the country, and nearly all railway locomotives are being powered by imported oil. Table 27.3 gives a breakdown according to source of total energy used in Bangladesh in 1970.

The most significant fact that emerges from Table 27.3 is that by far the largest amount of energy in Bangladesh still comes from sources which are neither fossil fuel nor hydro-power. A very approximate figure for the amount of energy consumed mainly for the purpose of cooking in the homes of Bangladesh has been arrived at as follows. Assuming a population of about 75 million, and each family consisting of 7.5 persons (large families being common in the developing countries), it may be estimated that nearly 10 million families cook their daily meals by burning a type of 'resource' most easily available to them. It is known that only a handful of families at present use either gas or paraffin oil or electrical energy to cook their meals; the amount of gas, oil, or electrical energy used as domestic sources of power have been duly considered in preparing Tables 27.3 and 27.4. With above considerations, it has been considered reasonable to assume, keeping in view the standard of living of the majority of the population, that each family would need to run a 1000 watt electrical cooker for 3 hours each day to cook the usual type of meal. This gives 3 kWh per day per family;

Table 27.4. Total energy consumption and sectors

Sector	*Energy used (10^{12} kcal)*	*Coal equivalent (10^6 kg)*	*Percentage of total*
Industrial	5.287	793.0	8.3
Transport	7.885	1178.0	12.74
Commercial	0.535	80.5	0.847
Agriculture	0.1374	19.5	0.233
Residential	48.2026	7240.0	77.88
Total	62.047	9311.0	100.00

for 10×10^6 families a round figure of 10000 GWh for a year has been arrived at. For obtaining the heat energy required, and the coal equivalent, same conversion rates as for Table 27.1 have been used. It may be stated that although the basis of calculations is very rough, the consumption per capita of coal equivalent (90 kg) seems to be a figure close to actual, as has been ascertained from families which have the experiences of using coal. The implications of the fact of a very large fraction of total energy consumed in this country being derived from sources such as firewood, farm and animal waste, etc., in its relation with the environmental conditions of Bangladesh will be discussed later.

The uses to which the total generated energy was put in 1970 is shown in Table 27.4. A study of this table is helpful in forming an idea regarding the state of economic life of the country; in fact some idea regarding the social pattern can also be formed.

The residential energy consumption in Table 27.4 includes, in addition to electric light and fan in some urban areas, the major demand for cooking. Residential use also includes the significant amount of kerosene oil for lighting village and urban homes.

Energy resources of Bangladesh

The foregoing survey of the energy usage pattern of Bangladesh clearly points out the following characteristics of the energy situation in this country, in addition to providing some vital information in this matter:

(a) A very small fraction (7.8 per cent) of the total energy requirement of the country is at present being provided in the form of electricity (Tables 27.1 and 27.4).

(b) Only a very small percentage (8.3 per cent) of the total energy consumed in the country is being used for industrial purposes. Moreover, the amounts consumed for commercial and agricultural purposes are negligible (Table 27.4.)

(c) An alarming proportion of total energy consumed in the country is being derived from fuels which require destruction of the vegetation, not quickly restored either naturally or in a planned way. The use of animal waste (especially, cow dung) represents diversion of natural fertilizer away from the soil. For overpopulated developing countries, of which Bangladesh is a typical example, this aspect is of grave consequence.

In order to be able to arrive at some strategies which could be helpful in altering some of the undesired characteristics highlighted above regarding the energy situation in Bangladesh, it is necessary to look at the complete energy potential of the country.

Hydro-power

The Karnafuli river in Chittagong Hill Tracts is at present providing 80 MW of power and a further 50 MW will be obtained for peaking purposes, so that the addition of energy would be nearly 100 GWh from the peaking generators. The Sangu river in the same region could be harnessed to yield nearly 90 MW. The big river Brahmaputra, in its course through the northern regions of the country, is capable of supplying about 400 MW firm capacity and 1000 MW peak power, when a barrage is constructed.

In addition to the above, there are a number of areas that have not been well investigated, so far. The Garo Hills regions in the north of Mymensingh district, bordering on the Assam forests of India, is likely to have some potential. The Hydroelectric Survey of India, in its detailed report in 1922, drew attention to the northern districts of present Bangladesh, and specially to Mohananda river at Tetulia, and Dharla river at Kurigram, and to Jamuneswari river, which had large maximum discharges in March–April. Harnessing of the river Tista which enters the district of Rangpur after crossing Sikkim and parts of India could be a major source of hydro-power. Development work on a barrage scheme, which could be the basis of a multipurpose project, providing some electric power, in addition to flood control and irrigation facilities was taken up some years ago, and was subsequently abandoned for unspecified reasons. It appears from the Hydroelectric Survey of India report, mentioned above, that if the Tista, along with its tributaries, could be harnessed on a regional co-operative scheme, a considerable source of power amounting to no less than 500 MW could be available for these undeveloped regions of the countries concerned. In a similar way, regional development schemes across international borders, both in the Chittagong Hill Tracts area as well as in the Garo Hills area are likely to prove as substantial sources of hydroelectric power.

Coal

As mentioned earlier, at present the entire requirement of coal is imported. However, intensive prospecting has established that there are considerable deposits of fairly good quality coal in the northern part of the western zone at Bangladesh, at Jamalganj and Jaipurhat in the districts of Rajshahi and Bogra.

Table 27.5 gives some data on the known coal resources in Bangladesh.[5] The better quality coal of Jamalganj having heat value of 6700 kcal/kg, is considered to be exploitable to the extent of 777 206 million kg.

It is estimated that if mining operations to exploit the better quality Jamalganj coal were started immediately, about 0.2 million tonnes would be available per year by 1985, and 2.0 million tonnes per year by 1990.[4] The deposits being at considerable depths below mainly alluvial soil, special and costly mining techniques, including freezing, will be called for, affecting the cost of coal to a large extent. The problem of procuring and the cost of huge quantities of sand, required for filling at the mining sites at Jamalganj, will also be an additional factor influencing the cost of indigenous coal.

Natural gas

As noted earlier, apart from hydroelectric sources, natural gas is the main indigenous source of electric power in Bangladesh. Up until now eight gas fields, all in the eastern parts of the country, have been discovered, out of which four gas fields are at present being exploited. It is estimated that, considering the three as yet untapped fields, the total reserves[5] may be nearly 570×10^9 m^3. The gas is of very high quality, containing 95.2 to 99.05 per cent methane.

No gas has been found in the north and western regions of the country yet, but there are indications that there may be some

Table 27.5. Coal resources in Bangladesh

Region	*Known reserves (10^6 kg)*	*Type of coal*	*Carbon content (per cent)*	*Heat value*	*Maximum depth (m)*	*Minimum thickness of seams (cm)*	*Recent annual production*
Jamalganj	1 438 448	Bitumen	47	M	1172	152	Nil
Lamakata	3048	Lignite	31.7	M	310.8	91	Nil
Kola	30 481	Peat	24.6	L	2.07	8	Nil
Baghia	127 008	Peat	24.6	L	3.73	8	Nil

M is from 19000 to 282000 Btu/kg and L is less than 19000 Btu/kg.

reserves in the western part. Exploratory drilling for new reserves may be undertaken soon. It may be mentioned here that gas is also being used (nearly 35 per cent in 1970) for the manufacture of fertilizers. Table 27.6 shows natural gas resources, total consumption figures and other pertinent data.

Oil

Exploration activities over past several years have not yet been successful in locating oil in this country. As a result all oil, consumed for the purposes of power generation, transportation, running irrigation pumps, domestic lighting in the rural areas (and some cooking, mainly confined at present in urban areas), is imported. Consumption figures are given in Tables 27.1 and 27.3.

Although no oil reserves have yet been located in Bangladesh, it is believed by geologists[6] that prospects of finding oil in the country are not insignificant. The reasons for such belief are the following: (i) the geological history and structure of Bangladesh, particularly the eastern and southern regions are similar to those of Assam and Burma where considerable oil reserves exist, (ii) natural gas reserves have been found to be well distributed over almost the entire eastern region, and there are many instances where gas and oil have been found to exist together, and (iii) the geological history of Bay of Bengal and the Gulf of Mexico are similar; and the sea-bed in the offshore regions of the Bay of Bengal is considered suitable for intensive exploratory efforts, particularly because part of the Sunderban forests on the Indian coasts of the Bay of Bengal have shown evidences of oil reserve.

Uranium

At present there are no proven uranium resources in the country. The sands of the long beach at Cox's Bazar in the south-east part of the country have traces of thorium, and further exploration is under contemplation.

Problems and prospects

From the information given above, the nature of the problems that exist in the matter of exploitations of energy resources of Bangladesh and their effective use so as to influence the economic situation in the country, will be fairly evident. Very briefly stated, the basic characteristics of the problems are the following:

1. While significant amount of certain types of energy resources are known to exist in the country, very little have so far been exploited; in some cases the exploitations will be very expensive and would require a long time to become effective. At the same time, there is need for much more intensive exploration activities. Owing to lack of

Table 27.6. Natural gas resources in Bangladesh

Region	*Gas in place* (10^{12} ft^3)	*Recoverable gas* (10^{12} ft^3)	*Past cumulative production* (10^{12} ft^3)	*Recent annual production* (10^{12} ft^3)	*Heat value* *Btu*/ft^3
Haripur	0.455	0.280	0.04	0.004	1052
Chatak	0.032	0.020	0.0015	0.00015	1007
Rashidpur	1.720	1.060	0	0	1014
Kailastila	0.732	0.600	0	0	1050
Titas	3.654	2.250	0.022	0.015	1036
Habiganj	2.074	1.280	0.003	0.002	1020
Bakhrabad	4.504	2.780	0	0	1061
Simutang	0.049	0.030	0	0	n.a.

adequate manpower with the required technical skill, the country will have to depend for a long time on both foreign technical know-how, as well as finance. The present low level of economic activities of the country, especially as a result of the liberation war of 1971, is bound to handicap the programmes that should be taken up to improve the situation in the matter of energy consumption.

2. The overwhelmingly large proportion of energy (77.88 per cent) still being used for domestic purposes, i.e. mainly for cooking family meals, is still being obtained from farm and animal wastes, and vegetation of the country. As this situation is likely to adversely affect the environmental condition of the country, especially with a very large population density, it is imperative that either electrical energy or natural gas be made available to houses in the rural areas as early as possible. The question of widespread transmission and distribution of energy all over the country—either through electrical lines or through gas pipelines, assume vital importance in this context. The question of availability and installation of domestic energy consumption devices, such as lights, fans, electric or gas cookers, as well as the necessary accessories such as meters, switches, conductors, etc., in the rural homes, where economic conditions are already much less than satisfactory, also becomes of great significance. As the industrial base is very weak the manufacture and supply of the required energy consumption devices within the very near future cannot also be considered as feasible. The allocation of adequate foreign exchange for the above types of device is a matter which require difficult decision-making *vis-à-vis* present economic circumstances. Large-scale rural electrification for irrigation and other agricultural uses, is also a question that involves considerations mentioned above.

3. It is a well known fact that unless a major portion of the total energy consumption in a country is, or can be, used for productive industries, the economy cannot be self sustaining, or even satisfactory. In the absence of such a situation—and the absence is a fact for Bangladesh—the effect of energy generation and distribution on determining the economic condition of a community is reduced to nothing, if not negative; and energy generation and consumption activities remain at the level of luxury. The question of industrialization of the country—or in other words the major application of different forms of energy to produce goods and services—is therefore of crucial importance in the discussion of the energy situation of any country, and more so for the developing countries. However, building up an effective industrial base which would have a significant influence on the economic life of the people, presupposes considerable investment in equipment and raw material, a major portion of which would have to be procured from outside the country at the present time. This situation would again involve both foreign finance and know-how, and a careful determination of priorities in the context of food production for a rapidly rising population, and other long-standing regional problems such as annual floods, cyclones, or other natural calamities. As an indication of the nature of the problem, it may be as well to consider the fact the installed generation capacity is nearly 550 MW, but the maximum demand of electric power has not so far risen above 225 MW, and is rising at a disquietingly slow rate. It is hoped that by the end of the first 5-year plan, in 1978, the installed generation capacity would be nearly 1000 MW, while the peak demand may attain a value not higher than about 600 MW.

An alternative strategy for attaining a much more intensive application of energy to the more predominantly productive sector of the existing economy of the country, that is to irrigation and to agriculture-based industries, has also to be evaluated carefully. An extensive programme for rural electrification would necessarily involve a rapid and large-scale expansion of electric power transmission and distribution facilities, in addition to plans for making available appropriate consumption devices and accessories to a vast agricultural population. The financial or other implications of this approach will be of dimensions no less than for the approach to the well-known consumer-oriented industrialization pattern of the technologically advanced countries. In view of the general nature of the problems of energy management, briefly stated here, it is necessary that the specific problems relating to the different sources of energy at present being used in Bangladesh or may be exploited in the future, be considered in some detail. Formulation of a suitable and most effective energy policy will depend on realistic appreciation of the relative nature of the various difficulties pertaining to the different types of energy source.

Problems regarding coal

Although it has been established that approximately 700 million tonnes of coal could be available as a source of energy in the future, the occurrence of the deposits, at considerable depth, as stated earlier, makes the exploitation both technically problematic as well as financially expensive. Assuming that these problems can be satisfactorily solved, various other problems exist in the matter of utilization of this resource for supplying energy.

One of the difficult problems would be the transportation of large quantities of coal to various parts of the country by railway or by vehicle on roadways, or by inland-water transport. This would require a swift and extensive improvement of the land and water communication systems of the country. Besides, if the transportation systems are to be run by oil, as at present, then the complete dependence on the imported oil for the distribution of coal has also seriously to be considered.

The next alternative of running large coal-fired generating stations in the mining areas seems to be a technically less complex solution, but this would again presuppose extensive transmission and distribution facilities. However, since the north and western regions of Bangladesh do not, till now, have any other sources of energy, and since both installed electrical generation capacity and maximum load demand in the north and western regions are much lower than in the eastern region, increase of generation capacity in the north and western regions seems a more reasonable choice. It is also a significant fact that all existing generation in the relatively power-starved areas of north and west is done by imported oil, and will continue to be so for perhaps the first two or three 5-year plan periods. Besides, it may be remembered that, owing to the existence of the very large and difficult river Brahmaputra, there exists no energy transmission or exchange facilities, either electrical or gas, between the eastern and north and western regions, and the eastern and western grids are being run entirely independently. This is one of the most significant gaps that have to be filled by the country's future energy management policy.

Another alternative for the utilizations of Jamalganj coal is the possibility of gasification of coal *in situ*, a technique which is being seriously considered recently in certain industrially advanced countries.[3] This could help in overcoming the stupendous difficulties involved in mining operation at depths such as those obtaining at Jamalganj.

Even apart from the need for coal for electrical-power generation, there is considerable demand for this fuel for certain industrial loads in both regions, which needs to be fulfilled soon. Also it is imperative that the present excessive dependence for domestic energy of the country upon farm and animal wastes—but more alarmingly on the vegetation and flora of the country—be relieved as soon as possible so as to reduce the adverse effects of the destructive processes upon the environment. Availability of a fossil fuel, such as coal, to replace firewood, shrubs, and farm wastes, would help to stop large-scale deforestation and soil erosion. A major cause for annual flooding of many rivers in the country may be due to excessive silting, which originates from unchecked soil erosion due to deforestation and devegetation, arising from energy needs of the country.

Problems regarding oil

The country depends for its mechanized transportation entirely on imported oil. Also almost all electrical generation in the north and western regions is at present dependent on oil. It cannot be predicted with certainty if present and future exploration activities will be successful in proving oil. Even at present the transportation and distribution of oil to all the generating stations in the north and west, are extremely difficult and uncertain owing to the meagre communication, cargo handling, and port facilities; and power cuts are a rule rather than exception, in these regions, due to irregular fuel supplies.

Keeping in view therefore the local as well as world situation, dependence on oil as a source of energy, except inevitably for motorized transportation, should be reduced as much as possible.

There is also another aspect in connection with oil as a source of energy in Bangladesh; and this is the vital relationship of oil with the acute food problems of this overpopulated country. While during the monsoons, flooding has become a recurring menace to large areas of the country, inevitably causing destruction of considerable parts of the rice crop almost every year, in some parts of the country, especially the north, acute scarcity of water during the dry seasons prevents extensive winter cultivation, so that food production ultimately suffers from both causes. Effective flood-control measures are therefore essential for more food production, among others reasons; extensive measures to increase winter cultivation also assumes importance for the same reason. The Government of Bangladesh have been giving great stress on rapid increase in food production and the Agricultural Development Corporation of Bangladesh have taken up extensive programmes of artificial irrigation by pumps run by disel engines. Inevitably therefore the food problem of Bangladesh has become directly linked with an energy resource, such as oil. The fact that at present very little electrical energy is being consumed in the agricultural sector (see Table 27.2), makes the question of oil as an energy resource in Bangladesh of much greater consequence than for any other resources at the present time. The recent world-wide uncertainties in oil supply and the consequent oil price hikes have therefore assumed threatening dimensions not only in respect of the general energy problems of Bangladesh, but also with a direct bearing on its food supply situation. It has therefore become urgent and imperative for this country to find alternative sources of energy to operate its irrigation programmes so as to ensure a reliable food supply position in the future years. In the face of a rapidly rising population (growth rate 2.5 per cent) the interrelation of population with total energy resources of the country assumes an acute urgency in the context of such a vital issue of food production. As pointed out earlier, immediate and extensive measures for rural electrification with intensive application to agriculture so as to make the irrigation programmes as much independent of direct oil supply as possible seem to be the need of the moment. In addition to necessitating wide rural electrification schemes a rapid exploitation of all the other energy sources—coal, natural gas and hydro—again acquire added importance and urgency.

Problems regarding natural gas

In the eastern region of Bangladesh, it has already been possible to replace coal and oil as fuels for power generation to a large extent, and it is being hoped the use of gas will become more extensive within a short time. It will be seen from Tables 27.1 and 27.3, that although in 1970 natural gas was responsible for fuelling 42.7 per cent of the electrical energy generation, its contribution to the total energy consumption is only 3.65 per cent, i.e. almost negligible. It is therefore needless to state that the already proven gas reserves will have a very vital role to perform in the future energy structure of the country. However, it must be remembered that at present gas is also being used as a raw material for the manufacture of fertilizer, and it is expected that, in conformity with the overall planning of the country, geared primarily at present to achieving a 'Green Revolution', the future need for gas as a raw material may surpass its consumption as fuel for power generation. At an accelerated and 'desired' rate of consumption of gas, for power, fertilizer, and other petrochemical and industrial needs it is estimated that the total consumption by AD 2000 will be more than the proven reserves. It is thus clear that policy regarding exploitation and use of gas in Bangladesh has to be arrived at after most careful consideration.

Use of natural gas for power generation for industrial and domestic purposes needs extensive transmission and distribution facilities through pipelines as in the case of electric power. Whether for a country like Bangladesh with its characteristic economic, geographical, and environmental conditions, energy should be made available to the consumers, large and small, in the form of gas, or as electricity generated from power stations, situated near the sources of gas, is a problem which needs careful analysis. Whichever alternative is chosen, construction of extensive transmission and distribution facilities, both in urban and rural areas would be involved.

Prospect of hydro-power

As mentioned earlier, apart from natural gas, hydro-power is the only indigenous source of energy of the country at the present time. In view of energy needs of the country, early investigation works must be undertaken; but due consideration must be given to the effects of river training, flood control, and diversion activities, in view of the already existing problems of the country, such as land under cultivation *via-à-vis* food production, flooding, natural irrigation by existing tributaries and canals, etc. It is also not unlikely that some of the possible sites may be in border areas with some neighbouring countries.

In such cases regional planning will be essential, needing co-operation, both technical and financial, with those countries. It so happens that the involved bordering countries are essentially developing in their economies; therefore schemes for regional planning may be greatly welcome by all concerned.

Prospects of nuclear power

Whether Bangladesh should decide in favour of building nuclear power stations, especially in view of the lack of fossil fuels other than gas in the country, is a question that has been under scrutiny for several years. The problem has been evaluated by several national and international agencies in the context of the numerous 'variables' existing in the country at the present time. One of the chief considerations has been the need for power, and the lack of resources, in the northern and western regions. It has been mentioned earlier that all the generating stations in that region are fuelled by imported oil at present, and the prices of oil delivered at the site of the stations have been one of the main deciding factors in finding an answer. The present international problems connected with the supply and purchase of oil are likely to influence the decision in favour of a nuclear power station in the near future, at a site called Rooppur on the bank of the river Padma. The size of the power station will have to be determined in consideration of load demand and growth rates of the north and western regions, as well as of the entire country, coupled with the probability of construction of an east–west interconnector tie-line across the Brahmaputra river in the very near future.

A very important aspect of a nuclear power station, especially in its relation to the environmental conditions as existing in Bangladesh, should be carefully examined before embarking on a nuclear power programme. Conditions being such as they are in Bangladesh, river water still happens to be the drinking water for a vast section of the rural population, and radiation pollution of the discharge water from a nuclear power station should be minutely investigated. As fish happens to be part of the staple diet of the people, the possible effects of discharges from a nuclear establishment on the fish population of all waterways downstream of Rooppur is a problem that would also require serious study.

Energy and environment in Bangladesh

For the generation of nearly 70 per cent of the total energy requirement, the country is depending on the destruction of its immediate environment or on the burning of farm and animal waste which could have been employed more fruitfully in other ways. The situation is further aggravated by the fact that a fast-growing population is already requisitioning larger and larger areas of cultivable land and green belts as well as forests, for human settlement. If this dependence is allowed to persist in the future, serious ecological imbalances are certain to appear. No data are as yet available showing the exact correlation of the extent of deforestation and consequent soil erosion, etc., and the changes in the climatic pattern and other seasonal phenomena inside the country. Detailed investigation of this aspect of energy consumption may produce significant data; however a general impression already exists that the pattern has been changing perceptibly in the past few years, especially in the power-starved and comparatively dry northern regions. In order to avert very serious ecological imbalances, and very frequent natural disasters such as floods and cyclones, a sane energy policy for the country should ensure that either hydro-power or fossil fuels are exploited or nuclear power programmes adopted, or both, as soon as possible to replace that portion of the total energy which is directly dependent on the immediate environment. It seems that this aspect of the energy structure is almost the central problem of the particular type of energy crisis that this country is facing.

Conclusions and the future

Most of the various problems stated above are either technically very complex or quite expensive, and dependent on the availability of adequate funds, with large foreign currency components. Provision of technical know-how as well as finances from appropriate international agencies or other organizations with knowledge and experience would therefore be especially useful in the following aspects of energy development and use in this country:

(i) exploration and exploitation of energy resources such as coal, oil, and hydro-power;
(ii) extensive transmission and distribution networks for more extensive use of both gas and electrical energy, especially in the rural areas for domestic as well as agricultural consumptions; and
(iii) ensuring an adequate supply of energy consumption devices, including accessories, for control, measurement, safety, etc., within the next few years, so that the population can switch over to the new methods of energy consumption.

It may also be conjectured that in order to meet the challenge to supply the large energy requirement for domestic use, especially in the rural areas, the country will find it necessary to take effective measures for the use of solar energy in the comparatively drier and sunnier northern regions. In the southern regions where daily tidal waves from the Bay of Bengal occur regularly, adequate research in the problem of utilization of tidal energy may turn out to be fruitful, perhaps on a scale suitable for the supply of rural domestic energy requirements. In addition to these resources there is the water hyacinth, a quick-growing water-plant, which occurs so profusely all over Bangladesh that it has been considered a menace to the waterways system, as well as a health hazard, breeding mosquitos and other insects. It appears now[7] that this abundant plant has a great potential for being used as a solar-energy converter through the process of photosynthesis. This conversion may turn out to be economic in the context of Bangladesh, as the climatic conditions are almost ideally suitable for profuse natural growth of this plant, and in fact this weed in dried form is already in use to some extent in the rural areas. In a similar way the special treatment of animal wastes, such as the considerable amounts of cow dung in the rural areas, to produce significant amounts of gaseous fuel without losing its fertilizing property, seems to have a somewhat attractive prospect.

As a concluding remark, especially in the context of the specific nature of the problems existing in Bangladesh, it may be stated that unless the rate of growth of the population of Bangladesh can be very effectively checked in the immediate future almost all of her existing problems will continue to assume more and more threatening proportions, the energy problem or 'crisis' being one of the problems very vitally and inextricably linked up with the others.

Appendix

Assumed conversion rates and other data:

$$12000 \text{ Btu/lb} = 26450 \text{ Btu/kg} \quad \text{for coal}$$

$$1000 \text{ Btu/ft}^3 = 35400 \text{ Btu/m}^3 \quad \text{for natural gas}$$

$$\text{Average } 18500 \text{ Btu/lb} = 40800 \text{ Btu/kg} \quad \text{for petroleum products}$$

Thermal conversions from kcal to kWh have been made at an overall system heat rate of 4300 kcal/kWh = 17065 Btu/kWh. This heat rate has also been assumed to be applicable for firewood, farm and animal waste, etc. Energy generated from hydroelectric source has also been converted at the same heat rate.

References

1. Friedlander, G. D. Energy crisis and challenge. *IEEE Spectrum*, pp. 18–27, May (1973).
2. *Electric power statistics*. Bangladesh Power Development Board, February–March (1970).
3. Dalal, V. Environment, energy and the need for new technology. *Energy conversion* **13**, 85–94 (1973).
4. *Market survey for nuclear power in developing countries—Bangladesh*. International Atomic Energy Agency, Vienna, September (1973).
5. Bangladesh National Committee, World Energy Conference, Data Table for the 9th WEC.
6. Latif, A. Presidential address. *Proceedings of the 2nd Convention, Geological Conference, Dacca, September 16–17* (1973).
7. Schneider, T. R. Efficiency of photo synthesis as a solar energy converter. *Energy Conversion* **13**, 77–85 (1973).

28

Energy resources in Turkey

MUAMMER CETELINCELIK

Rapid changes in the structure of the Turkish economy from the agricultural to the industrial have resulted in a rapid increase in electrical energy requirements. Electricity demand in the country of Turkey is expected to rise from the 15.5 TWh in 1975 to 146 TWh by the late 1990s, while installed capacity is expected to reach 9000 MW in 1982. Now counted among those countries whose resources are almost adequate to cover their needs, Turkey will become a large energy importer by the year 2000. In almost all the alternatives nuclear power plants inevitably start to be installed in the mid-1980s, and nuclear capacity could reach 20000 MW by the end of the century in the case of high oil prices.

Turkey is a link between Asia and Europe from geographical point of view. The country is roughly rectangular in shape, measuring about 1600 km from east to west, and 650 km from south to north. The total area is 780000 km^2 of which 23600 km^2 constitute the Thrace peninsula in Europe. Last year the total population was about 42 million, of which about 65 per cent was rural. However, the rapid economic growth and industrialization over the last decade has been accompanied by urbanization. The growth rate in population has remained at about 2.5 per cent in recent years, and it is assumed that this figure will remain unchanged for about 10 years more, thereafter declining gradually to 2 per cent towards the year 2000. The rapid economic growth over more than a decade has been accompanied by substantial structural changes of the economy. The Turkish Five-Year Development Plan for 1973–8 aimed at an economic growth rate of 7.9 per cent. Past and projected national income growth rate for the period of 1977–82 is 6.7 per cent; per capita national income growth 4.2 per cent.

The gradual change in the structure of the Turkish economy away from agriculture toward increased industrialization will be accompanied by an increase in total energy requirements. Future energy demand will increase with the growth of population and the increase of energy consumption per capita. The total energy consumption of Turkey is given in Table 28.1. In developing countries and also in Turkey non-commercial energy sources, such as firewood, animal dung, and farm waste products, are also occupying an important place beside the commercial energy sources. The portions of the consumption met by commercial and non-commercial sources are indicated separately.

In the year 2000, the commercial energy consumption per capita of Turkey is expected to reach 2843 kcal, the same as for France in 1963. On the other hand, the commercial energy consumption per capita of Turkey in

First published in *Energy International*, Vol. 14, No. 9 (September 1977), pp. 27–30, 41. Reprinted by permission of *Energy International*.

Table 28.1. Past and projected total energy consumption in Turkey (10^3 million tonnes coal equivalent)

Year	*Commercial*	*Non-commercial*	*Total*	*Rate of commercial to total energy (per cent)*
1950	4226	5797	10023	42.2
1955	6261	6857	13118	47.7
1960	7971	7910	15881	50.2
1965	12551	8994	21545	58.3
1970	18443	9700	28143	65.5
1971	21320	9800	31120	68.5
1972	22275	10397	32672	69.7
1977	41500	10600	52100	79.7
1982	64750	10550	75300	86.0
1987	95620	9280	104900	91.2
1992	133100	6900	140000	95.1
2000	199000	5100	204100	97.5

the same year will be at or near the world average.

Projected energy consumptions up to 2000 have been found by using trend and international comparison methods and the results are checked by the econometric methods. In estimating the shares of non-commercial energy consumption in total, it is assumed that, in coming years, consumption of animal dung as fuel, will decrease in proportion to the increase in the ratio between city and village populations. Consumption of firewood and farm waste products will decrease to match the available firewood production level of Turkish forests. Electricity consumption trends and average annual growth rates are shown in Table 28.2.

The electrical energy consumption forecasts of Turkey up to the year 2000 have also been made by making use of the methods employed for the commercial energy consumption estimates. The annual growths in the electrical energy consumption are continuous and higher than the growth of commercial energy consumption.

National energy resources

Turkey has one deposit of carboniferous coal in the district of Zonguldak. The coal basin has an average thickness of 1.5 m partly in flat formation, and partly in steep formations with many faults. The tectonic structure and vein correlation of coal beds occurring in Zonguldak basin have not yet been completely studied. The extent of the deposit and the structure of the basin will become better known after the completion of these studies.

The total deposits of Armutcuk, Gelik, Uzulmez, and Kozlu, which are in the Zonguldak basin and now in production, are:

Exploitable	32726000 tonnes
Proven	109129000 tonnes
Probable	394604000 tonnes
Possible	393720000 tonnes
Total	930197000 tonnes

The average calorific value of the coal is 6300 kcal/kg. The saleable part of the mine production is 60 to 65 per cent. Coal is mined by the long-wall method with the lowest working depth 425 m below sea level. The basin is under the administration of (TKI) Turkish Coal Mining Enterprise which is a state department.

Saleable coal production in Turkey kept pace with demand up to 1973 when it reached 4.64 million tonnes. This year, production could reach 5.85 million tonnes towards meeting a total demand of 7.88 million tonnes. By the year 2000, a projected demand of 24.2 million tonnes will compare

Table 28.2. Past and projected total and electricity consumption per capita in Turkey

	Consumption		*Per capita consumption*	
Year	*GWh*	*Growth (per cent)*	*kWh per capita*	*Growth (per cent)*
1950	790		38	
1955	1580	14.9	66	11.7
1960	2815	12.3	101	8.9
1965	4953	13.2	157	9.2
1970	8623	11.6	241	8.9
1971	9701	12.5	265	9.9
1972	11242	15.8	289	12.8
1977	20700	12.8	492	10.4
1982	36800	12.2	776	9.5
1987	62900	11.3	1185	8.8
1992	100000	9.2	1675	7.2
2000	180000	7.6	2580	5.5

with a projected output of only 7.6 million tonnes.

The total lignite reserves in Turkey, owned by state and private enterprise are given below, in millions of tonnes.

Proven	2.74
Probable and Possible	2.4
Total	5.14

The lower heat content of the Turkish lignite deposits varies from 1300–5500 kcal per kg. The most important deposit appears to be in the basin of Afsin-Elbistan (*Energy International*, May 1976, p. 24) which are now starting to be exploited. The reserves are estimated to be about 3160 million tonnes; however, only 50 per cent will be exploitable by open pit. The other lignite deposits in Turkey are dispersed and of less importance, and distributed over 43 basins.

Lignite is our economic fuel for the thermal power plants and factories which are close to the mines. The transportation requirements mean that in some regions lignite costs three to four times higher than in the mine area.

Total lignite production in Turkey was 9.12 million tonnes last year, of which 6.2 million tonnes came from state owned mines and 2.92 million came from privately owned mines. Production has effectively doubled in the last 10 years, since in 1965, private production was 2 million tonnes and state production was 2.51 million tonnes, a total of 4.51 million tonnes.

The existence of oil in Turkey has been

Table 28.3. Turkish oil reserves

Firm	*Total known reserves (in barrels)*	*Economically recoverable reserves (in barrels)*	*(in million tonnes)*
Turkish Petroleum Co.	1990	220	36.1
N V Turkse Shell	400	40	6.6
Mobil Expl. Mad. Inc.	220	25	4.1
Ersan Petroleum Industry Co.	200	20	3.2
Total	2840	305	50

known for a long time. The suitable zones for oil exploitation in Turkey can be classified as follows:

Very convenient	12 100 000 ha
Convenient	16 500 000 ha
Less convenient	38 900 000 ha
Total	67 000 000 ha

The known reserve fields corresponding to licensed areas by domestic and foreign corporations are given in Table 28.3.

In general, the oil deposits are located in the south-eastern part of the country. Economically recoverable reserves of crude oil in Turkey will be exhausted around the year of 1985.

Mineral hydrocarbon exploration has been conducted by (MTA) the Mineral Research and Exploration Institute of Turkey in Ankara which, in the 1940s, discovered the *Raman* and *Garzan* oilfields in the south-east which are now of prime importance. After the Petroleum Law was passed in 1954, exploration was also carried out by (TPAO) Turkish Petroleum Company and private companies on the basis of petroleum exploration licences and leases.

Four refineries are operating in Turkey, with a total capacity of 14 million tonnes. Crude oil consumption in Turkey is currently 19.26 million tonnes /year, against production of 3.66 million tonnes. Production is expected to peak at 3.83 million tonnes/ year in 1982 when consumption is predicted at 30.65 million tonnes, rising to 100 million tonnes/year by the end of the century.

At the present there are no known commercial fields of natural gas in Turkey. Natural gas has been found in association with oil, but the experiments did not show satisfactory results. However, oil and gas explorations are being continued by the private corporations and the Mineral Research and Exploration Institute of Turkey. It is possible that new gas fields may be discovered in future. Natural gas deposits in the Middle Eastern countries constitute an important portion of the world supply. Natural gas imports from Iraq are under negotiation.

The existence of bituminous shales in Turkey has been known for a long time. In the old surveys the emphasis was on the possibilities of the liquid fuel production, but the areas searched did not give favourable results and no further studies were made. The total of probable bituminous sand reserves is estimated to be 3350 million tonnes according to the survey. In general, discovered sands contain 1 to 1.5 per cent bitumen. Their average heat value is 1000 to 2000 kcal/kg. The possible use of the large bituminous shale reserves in Turkey should be investigated as soon as possible in order to determine how best to meet the energy requirements in future.

Turkey ranks high in hydraulic energy potential among European countries. Average precipitation is 670 mm and varies markedly from one region to another. It is believed that many projects can be developed within economical cost limits, although some of them have not yet been carried through to the feasibility stage. Therefore it is safe to believe, that the figure of 70 billion kWh is the economical hydroelectric potential of Turkey.

In spite of the high total hydroelectric potential, development in Turkey has been very slow. The great distance between the principal watersheds and the load centres, substantially high initial costs, and a low electricity consumption level in the country are the main reasons for this delayed development. In Table 28.4, the actual and estimated ratio of hydraulic potential utilization for several years are shown. It is estimated that the utilization of hydraulic potential will rapidly increase in the coming years and will be 61 per cent in the year 2000.

Nuclear potential

Geological and mineralogical investigations in the area of Salihli-Koprubasi have been completed and indicate the existence of uranium reserves estimated to be in the

Table 28.4. Hydroelectric potential and exploitation

Year	*Electricity generation* *Total* *GWh/year*	*Hydro* *GWh/year*	*Ratio hydro to total (per cent)*	*Ratio hydro to total hydro potential (per cent)*
1950	790	40	3.8	0.06
1955	1580	89	5.6	0.13
1960	2815	1001	35.6	1.4
1965	4953	2167	43.9	3.2
1970	8623	3033	35.2	4.3
1971	9701	2587	26.7	3.7
1972	11242	3209	28.5	4.6
1977	20700	8300	40.1	11.9
1982	36800	15800	42.9	22.5
1987	62900	23700	43.4	34.0
1992	100000	40000	40.0	57.0
2000	180000	50000	27.7	72.0

vicinity of 2500 tonnes of U_3O_8 equivalent. However, additional surveys must be carried out to confirm this initial evaluation. About three-quarters of these reserves have an average U_3O_8 content of 4.5 per cent, the remainder has a lower average grade in the region of 2 per cent U_3O_8. Among the other areas investigated, Gure, Sebinkarahisar, and Ayvalik have shown dispersed locations or uranium ores which added together would reach 800 tonnes of U_3O_8 equivalent.

Prospecting for thorium in Turkey has received less attention than for uranium in the neighbourhood of Eskisehir-Sivrihisar-Beylikahir, the first investigations have indicated thorium reserves of approximately 4500 tonnes of ThO_2 equivalent with an average content of 0.18 per cent. To the north-west of Malatya thorium reserves have also been discovered in the neighbourhood of Hekimhan.

Systematic geological and geophysical prospecting for radioactive mineral deposits was started in Turkey by (MTA) the Mineral Research and Exploration Institute in 1957. Many detailed investigations have been carried out in several regions of Turkey. The latest find was made below an existing mine which already accounts for five-eighths of Turkey's annual output of 4000 tonnes of uranium. An ore-processing pilot plant with a capacity of 2 tonnes of ore per day (350 kg U_2O_8 per year) is under operation in Koprubasi.

Turkey's interest in nuclear energy goes back to the mid-1950s. The (TAEK) Turkish Atomic Energy Commission was established in 1956 following the signing in July 1955 of a bilateral agreement between Turkey and USA on the application of atomic energy for peaceful purposes. Construction of their first research reactor (swimming pool type) started in August 1959 and the first critical experiment was carried out in 1961. It was then gradually brought up to its design power of 1 MW. This research reactor was set up at Kucukcekmece Nuclear Research and Training Centre. This 1 MW reactor is going to be extended to 5 MW by Belgonucleaire this year.

Studies of a nuclear power generation programme siting and economic evolution of nuclear power plants are being carried out by TAEK and TEK the National Power Utility. TAEK submitted a nuclear energy programme in connection with the preparation of the new 5-year Development Plan for Turkey. The first nuclear power station, a 600 MW MW(e) PWR is to be built at Akkuyu, near Silifke, in south-western Anatolia, and is scheduled to start generating in the winter of 1984. The optimal development programme envisages nuclear capacity additions of 600 MW(e) year from

1984 to 1986, and 800 MW/year in each of the next 2 years. This will increase to 1600 MW in 1989.

Geothermal energy may be an important energy source for Turkey in the future. Important geothermal fields at Denizli-Kizildere, Izmir-Seferihisar, Aydin-Germencik, Afyon-Gezek, Manisa-Balikesir Kizilcahamam, Kozakli, Dikili, are being investigated.

At the first of these a pilot plant is under construction by TEK with a capacity of 15 MW. Projections of total geothermal power production suggest 136 MW(e) of plant could be in service by 1992.

In planning adequate supply from various sources to meet estimated energy consumption of Turkey up to year 2000, the following principles have been considered:

(1) to give priority to the indigenous sources,
(2) to make provisions for the efficient use of all kinds of fuel;
(3) to give priority to hydro sources, with the proviso that multi-purpose projects are built first;
(4) to reduce the consumption of wood as a fuel to a level that can be supplied from our forests without destroying them and replace the part of wood consumption in excess of this amount by the most suitable commercial fuels;
(5) to utilize animal dung more efficiently as fertilizer instead of fuel;
(6) to reduce the amount of imported energy as far as possible by directing those consumers who can be supplied with indigenous sources in order to meet their energy demands domestically; and
(7) to introduce nuclear power systems as soon as possible to meet the country's electricity requirements.

Table 28.5 shows supply of total energy consumption on the basis of the aforementioned principles in terms of coal equivalent.

Turkey has become today a country where energy is much used. The gradually changing structure of the Turkish economy from agricultural to increased industrialization will be accompanied by increasing energy requirements. There is an extensive energy potential to meet the increasing needs of the nation. Water power, coal, lignite, petroleum, and uranium produced in Turkey are raw materials of economic value which can meet the country's demands for energy now. The share of domestically produced resources averages 70 per cent of the requirements and is mainly coal, lignite, and petroleum. Production of coal is expected to increase 5.85 million tonnes and lignite production will be increased to 10.0 million tonnes by

Table 28.5. Estimates of total energy consumption in Turkey (10^3 tonnes coal equivalent)

Year	*1972*	*1977*	*1982*	*1987*	*1992*	*2000*
Coal	4180	7100	8600	13300	17200	21800
Lignite	4200	8320	14340	20000	22200	30000
Crude oil	13495	25040	39835	58150	86100	130300
Hydro	400	1040	1975	2960	5100	6300
Nuclear	—	—	—	1210	2500	10600
Total commercial	22275	41500	64750	95620	133100	199000
Wood	5780	6000	5150	4280	3400	2800
Dung	4617	4600	5400	5000	3500	2300
Total non-commercial	10397	10600	10550	9280	6900	5100
General total	32672	52100	75300	104900	140000	204100

Table 28.6. Primary energy sources for electricity generation (GWh)

Year	*1972*	*1977*	*1982*	*1987*	*1992*	*2000*
Coal	1432	1400	1000	1000	1000	1000
Lignite	1489	4500	13500	22000	30000	35000
Oil and others	5112	6500	6500	6500	9000	9000
Hydro	3209	8300	8300	23700	40000	50000
Nuclear	—	—	—	9700	20000	85000
Total	11242	20300	36800	62900	109000	180000

1980. Turkey has identified hydroelectric resources amounting to about 50000 GWh/year in addition to the nearly 25000 GWh/year that is planned to be in operation by 1986. The overall energy consumption is expected to increase at an average yearly rate of 7.5 per cent during this decade. The market for electricity generating units in Turkey to be commissioned between 1980 and 1989 would be nearly 7000 MW(e) based on a low load forecast, and 11000 MW(e) based on a height forecast. Because of abundance of economically exploitable hydroelectric power, the market for new thermal plants was expected to be in the approximate range of 2900 MW(e) to 4800 MW(e)

An evaluation of the conventional fuels available in Turkey indicates that lignite was the fuel which was most likely to be competitive with nuclear power, and since such deposits of bituminous shale as exist in different regions of Turkey are difficult to mine, their production would be more expensive.

The forecast of the energy demand shows that Turkey should probably introduce nuclear power plants with a total capacity of 6000 MW(e) up to 2000. Generating costs of nuclear power stations are in the same range as the producing costs of the oil-fired thermal power plants when the appropriate taxes on fuel are included. But the generating costs of the nuclear power station would be lower than for a thermal power plant burning imported fuel-oil, especially when account is taken of nuclear fuel from the Turkish uranium reserves.

In this respect, with added electric power in Turkey, it will be quite possible to provide the electro-metallurgical and electro-chemical industries, as well as all the villages in the nation with electric power at a very low cost.

29

Energy in Mexico

J. EIBENSCHUTZ, A. ESCOFET, AND G. BAZÁN

Energy sector development

The responsibility of supplying the country's energy needs has been assigned to two decentralized government agencies: Petróleos Mexicanos and Comisión Federal de Electricidad, whose co-ordination is carried out by the Secretaría de Patrimonio y Fomento Industrial.

The oil industry was nationalized in 1938, through the acquisition of the then existing private and foreign enterprises. As a result Petróleos Mexicanos (Pemex), one of the largest oil enterprises of the world, was formed. It is organized as a wholly integrated industry, covering all aspects from exploration to distribution of products, and at the same time having an increasingly important role in petro-chemistry.

During 1976 Pemex processed 142000 m^3 per day of crude and produced 60 million m^3 of gas per day. Of its total production, 15000 m^3 per day of crude were exported.

Comisión Federal de Electricidad is the only electric utility of the country. It was established in 1937 to promote the electrification of those areas in the country that were not economically attractive for the private utilities, having at the same time the aim of eventually integrating a national electrical network. In 1960 the private electric utilities were purchased by the government and integrated into CFE. In 1976 the total installed capacity was of 9830 MW, of which 4045 MW are hydroelectric. The total number of consumers was of about 7 million, of which 25000 were industrial. The total generation in that year was 44 TWh.

The Instituto Nacional de Energía Nuclear, established in 1972, originated from the Comisión Nacional de Energía Nuclear that had been created in 1956. Until now, the main activities in the energy field of this institution have been exploration of uranium and research and development work in reactors and fuel fabrication.

Mexico does not have an integrated coal industry. This resource is mined and utilized basically by the steel industry, public and private, through a system of concessions administered by the Secretaría de Patrimonio y Fomento Industrial.

In February of 1973 the Comisión Nacional de Energéticos was established as a co-ordinating body of the energy sector. Its main objective is to define the long-range policy guidelines for energy, based on the availability of primary energy resources, within the frame of the overall economy as defined by the government.

The Commission is also a forum for analysing the problems that are common to the enterprises in charge of satisfying the energy needs of the country. Its structure includes a small Secretariat that complements and co-ordinates the resources supplied by the energy industry for the planning activities.

First published in the *Transactions of the Tenth World Energy Conference*, Istanbul, Turkey, September 1977. Paper 1.4–7. Reprinted by permission of World Energy Conference.

The development of the energy sector has taken place under the following basic policy guidelines:

(1) self-sufficiency;
(2) nationalization of the energy supply service;
(3) extension of energy supply to the rural areas; and
(4) supply without restrictions and at the lowest possible cost of the energy demand.

Energy outline

The energy sector is worth approximately 6 per cent of the gross national product. The average growth rate of energy consumption has been approximately 8.2 per cent per year.

Energy consumption is roughly distributed in the following way: 28.6 per cent by the transport sector; 28.1 per cent by the industrial sector; 10.7 per cent by the residential and commercial sector; 2.5 per cent has corresponded to the non-energy applications of energy resources and conversion, and transmission losses and self-consumption of the energy sector itself amount to roughly 30 per cent.

The overall energy demand for 1975 was 23.86×10^{17} joules and for 1976 was 25.36×10^{17} joules, 88 per cent being supplied by oil and gas, hydroelectricity* 7 per cent and coal 5 per cent. This distribution of the energy supply has been maintained roughly over the last 20 years, with a slight increase in favour of oil and gas due to the relatively decreasing participation of hydroelectric energy, (Fig. 29.1).

The high dependency on hydrocarbons is a logical consequence of oil and gas availability. Between 1901 and 1975, the accumulated production has been of 1288 million m^3 of oil equivalent, with up to date reserves of 1749 million m^3.

Future energy demand

For the year 2000, energy demand has been estimated with a basis on constructed scenarios considering different variables as defined by the WAES (Workshop on

*Considered at 3074 kcal/kWh.

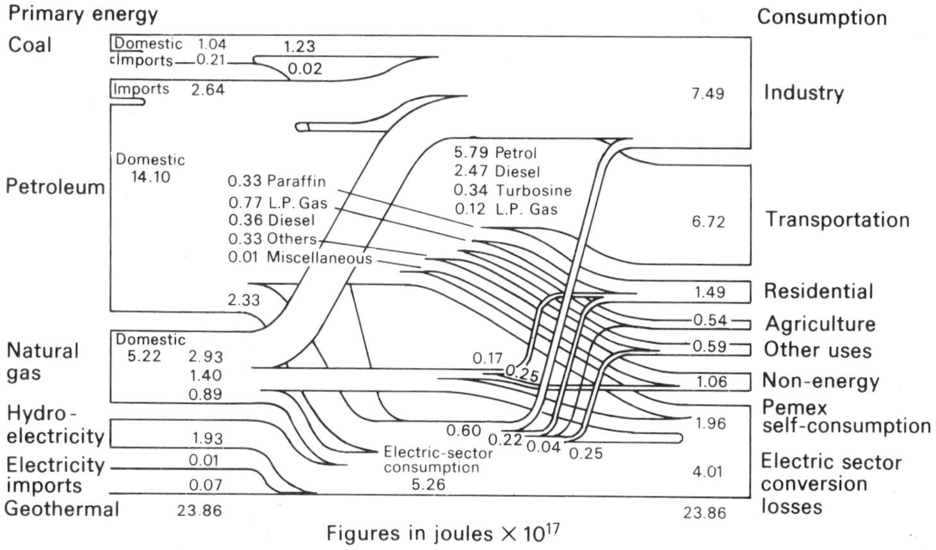

Fig. 29.1. Energy balance 1975.

Alternative Energy Strategies) and which presented two numerical values for economic growth (high and low), two oil prices (high and middle) and government policy designed as vigorous and restrained, and the main substitution fuels were coal and nuclear power.

According to these scenarios, for the year 2000, and considering energy conservation in the industrial and transport sectors, the energy needs were estimated to range between 125 and 162 $\times 10^{17}$ joules; five to seven times the consumption in 1975.

The scenarios that were used are also based on certain national objectives. Mexico is a country with 60 million people, a very unequal distribution of wealth and a high rate of development. Therefore we must sustain a relatively high rate of energy growth to supply the needs of the 125 or 140 million people that Mexico expects to have by year 2000.

Energy resources

Mexico is undoubtedly a country rich in energy. It has oil, gas, coal, uranium, hydroelectric energy, geothermal energy, and lots of sun.

The high dependency on hydrocarbons for the satisfaction of the energy requirements is a logical consequence of the availability of oil and gas. In January 1977 the usable oil and gas reserves were of 1749 million m^3 of crude oil equivalent. The total accumulated consumption of oil and gas is of the order of 1288 million m^3 of crude oil equivalent.

Several estimates have been made of the oil and gas potential of the country. Some of these put Mexico among the richest countries of the world, only slightly behind some Middle Eastern countries. Other estimates are less optimistic. The reality, so far, is that we are in the process of trying to assess the potential of the country in order to better define the energy strategies.

The characteristics of the new production fields in the south-eastern part of the country, which began during the oil crisis, give good grounds for optimism in connection with our oil and gas resources. In spite of the substantial effort that has to be carried out and that will have to be sustained and increased in the future years, it is highly probable that Mexico will be able to continue to satisfy its energy requirements with domestic oil and gas, leaving a margin for exports.

In the case of coal, some experts consider that reserves are at least of the same order of magnitude as those of oil and gas. It is therefore expected that coal will have an increasing participation in the Mexican energy market, both as energy source and as an input to the steel industry. The proven reserves in the State of Coahuila to December of 1975 were of the order of 1685 million tonnes. Based upon a recent study, the Consejo de Recursos Minerales is undertaking a serious exploration programme that will permit a better definition of the coal potential of the country, which has been estimated to lie between 6 and 10 $\times 10^9$ tonnes (in 1975 the probable reserves were estimated at 462 million tonnes and the inferred ones at 5992 million tonnes).

The hydroelectric potential of the country has been evaluated at 83 TWh per year, of which about 60 TWh per year should be possible to develop; the present hydroelectric production lies in the range of 15 TWh/year. According to the characteristics of the sites, it is estimated that the total installed capacity should lie in the range of 25 GW.

In the case of uranium, less than 1 per cent of the area of the country has been explored. The positive reserves in December of 1975 were of about 6000 tonnes of U_3O_8 plus roughly 2000 tonnes of inferred reserves. However, according to the estimates of some experts, based on the work carried out by the Instituto Nacional de Energía Nuclear, the uranium potential of the country could be very important.

Geothermal energy has been known to exist in Mexico for a long time. About 20 years ago a small, 300 MW unit was installed in the State of Hidalgo relatively close to Mexico City. In the Mexicali Valley, close to the north-western tip of the country, the Cerro Prieto geothermal station has been operating with two 37.5 MW units and two more units are under construction. The potential of this field has been estimated to be capable of feeding 400 MW during 30 years. Aside from this, the tectonic characteristics of the country suggest a considerable geothermal potential. The country has several thermal manifestations mainly along the volcanic belt which crosses the country from east to west in its central part.

Solar energy is abundant, particularly in the desert areas that lie north of parallel 23. This implies that for the coming century, when solar energy utilization becomes a reality, Mexico should be in a very interesting position to establish its solar farms in several enormous extensions that have no alternative use for the time being.

Supply-and-demand balance

A comparison between expected demand and our estimate of supply shows that it is possible to satisfy the energy needs of our economy, dominated by hydrocarbons, with our own resources until the end of this century. However, the expected quantity of energy consumption is of such magnitude that a major effort directed towards incorporating new energy sources will be needed as soon as possible.

Given the abundant quantities of coal in comparison to the current rate of production, it is expected that this source will play an important role in the diversification of our energy supply.

The practical hydroelectric resources should be totally developed by the year 2000, but their contribution will only be 20 per cent of the estimated requirements of electric energy for that year.

The development of geothermal and solar energy, which represent interesting perspectives in our country, is not likely to be very significant before the end of this century.

Policy considerations

Taking into consideration the results of the integration of supply and demand, the following energy-policy guidelines were added to those exposed: (a) promote the diversification of our primary sources of energy in order to diminish the dependency in oil and gas; (b) promote the co-ordination of planning in the energy sector as a whole; (c) promote a more efficient utilization of energy; (d) develop the local manufacture of capital goods associated with the energy sector; (e) promote research and development activities in the energy field.

30

Energy and economic growth in Central America

ALAN M. STROUT*

In the single year of 1974, the Central American balance-of-payments deficit on current account increased by four times, from $US12 per capita to $US49 per capita.[1] yet the six countries of the region have managed to adjust to higher prices for petroleum and other imports with little apparent difficulty. Buoyed by heavy capital inflows and agricultural export earnings, the six economies grew at about 5.5 per cent per year between 1970 and 1974, only slightly below the 1960 to 1970 annual trend of 5.9 per cent.[2] The effects of the world-wide recession caught up with the region in 1975, but the balance-of-payments situation remained strong, and prospects of future export growth appear good.

The nature and pace of future economic growth may, however, be strongly affected by decisions made over the next few years about the exploitation and use of energy. Energy is still a relatively minor element of production costs but can be expected to increase as the Central American countries become more industrialized. The present high cost of imported energy (representing the bulk of the region's consumption) can be safely ignored only as long as agricultural export prices remain high or the current large inflow of compensating foreign capital continues. As yet there appears to be little awareness within the region of the role of fuel and power in economic growth, nor do governments show much sense of urgency in reassessing their energy supply-and-demand situation in a comprehensive and long-term manner. At the same time it is likely that Central America still has considerable freedom of choice with regard to the character of future economic growth.

The current energy and economic situation

Costa Rica, El Salvador, Guatemala, Honduras, Nicaragua, and Panama (excluding the Canal Zone) had a combined population of 15.7 millions in 1970. The six countries occupy an area about the size of France (with a population of 59.4 millions) or Thailand (with 34.2 million inhabitants). At $US416 per person, per capita income in 1970 placed the region among the better-off of the developing areas. The region's population is still largely agricultural (60 per cent of the total), but use of fertilizer is relatively modest (44 kg/ha of arable land plus land planted to permanent crops). The amount of arable and permanently cropped agricultural land per person in agriculture was 0.59 ha in 1970, only slightly more than

*This review is largely based on observations made and data collected during a visit to El Salvador and Nicaragua at the invitation of the Instituto Centroamericano de Empresas and the Harvard Institute for International Development in March 1976.

First published in *Annual Review of Energy*, Vol. 2 (1977), pp. 291–305.

in Thailand (0.49 ha/person) or the Philippines (0.40 ha/person). Only 3 per cent of the arable land was irrigated. See Table 30.1 for a description of physical and economic characteristics.

Each country in the region has a cement plant and at least one refinery. In general, however, light industry predominates. There is no basic metal production in the region and only a small pulp and paper industry. For some time there has been chemical manufacturing in El Salvador and Panama, and more recently Nicaragua began production of hydrochloric acid, caustic soda, and plastics. Some fertilizer production occurs in Costa Rica and El Salvador, but the industry supplied only 10 per cent of the region's requirements in 1970. Judged in terms of the 'normal' pattern of energy-intensive materials production (see the following section), Central America in 1970 produced only a little over one-fourth of what might have been expected from countries with similar population and per capita income (see Table 30.1). However, output from this group of energy-intensive commodities (largely cement, fertilizer, and paper) has been increasing rapidly in recent years.

Energy production in Central America is characterized by a relatively large use of hydroelectricity (52 per cent of the total electricity generated between 1969 and 1971). Almost all of the remaining 'commercial' energy is obtained from imported petroleum. Consumption of non-commercial fuel (wood, charcoal, and bagasse) is relatively high and may have amounted to 64 per cent of commercial energy consumption in 1970. Table 30.2 describes selected characteristics of energy use in Central America.[3]

In terms of international norms (see below) based on population, per capita gross national product, and production of energy-intensive materials, the region consumes slightly more total energy (including wood and charcoal but excluding bagasse) than might be expected. Most of the differences are found in Honduras and Nicaragua. (See Fig. 30.1.) The differences may occur because peculiarities of industrial structure—for example, the vegetable oils and organic chemicals industry in Nicaragua—were not taken sufficiently into account when the expected energy consumption in these two countries was calculated. In sharp contrast, electricity consumption is considerably greater than what might be expected in similarly situated countries. The differences exceed 150 per cent (see Table 30.2) in Costa Rica, Nicaragua, Panama, and El Salvador. They probably reflect governmental interest in electrification as a modernizing influence and also the availability of funds from abroad for both thermal and hydroelectric plants.

'Normal' patterns of production and consumption

In assessing the Central American energy situation, it is helpful to refer to 'normal' patterns of energy consumption and production of energy-intensive materials. Typical patterns for several kinds of energy use are available from cross-country statistical regressions, based on 1969–71 data from 31 of the world's largest and most urbanized countries. Principal explanatory variables were per capita income and population size. Although 17 of the 31 countries can be classified as less developed, including five Latin American countries, there were no countries in the original sample with populations as small as those found in Central America.

References to statistically derived normal relationships are included for purposes of rough comparison only. Nevertheless, their use is felt to be an improvement over the expression of consumption or production in simple per capita terms. This is because the process of normalization helps adjust for intercountry differences not only in population but also in per capita income and to some extent in industrial structure. Furthermore, in spite of the fact that the Central American countries fall outside the range of the original statistical sample, the

Table 30.1. Selected physical and economic characteristics of Central America, 1970*

	Costa Rica	*El Salvador*	*Guatemala*	*Honduras*	*Nicaragua*	*Panama Republic*	*Total (or average)*
Population (millions)†	1.7	3.4	4.9	2.5	1.8	1.4	15.7
In agriculture‡	0.8	2.0	3.2	1.8	1.1	0.6	9.5
Per capita GNP (1970 US$)§	571	315	380	284	478	757	(416)
Land area (thousand ha)‡							
Total	5070	2139	10889	11209	13000	7565	49872
Forested	2518	250	5400	3019	6450	5800	23437
Arable and permanent crops	989	651	1498	823	873	542	5376
Irrigated	46	24	40	24	25	20	179
(Arable land/agricultural population)	(1.23)	(0.33)	(0.47)	(0.46)	(0.77)	(0.86)	(0.57)
Fertilizer use (tonne $\times 10^3$ nutrients)‡	60.8	67.7	42.4	22.8	27.7	14.9	236.3
(kg/ha arable land)	(61)	(104)	(28)	(28)	(32)	(27)	(44)
Energy-intensive materials production							
(tonne $\times 10^3$ coal equivalent)‖	73	61	84	48	36	63	365
'Normal'¶	238	189	364	118	191	303	1341
(actual/normal)	(0.31)	(0.32)	(0.23)	(0.41)	(0.19)	(0.21)	(0.27)

*Data for the Panama Canal Zone are not included.

†See Ref. 4.

‡See Refs. 5 and 6. In some cases interpolations of FAO land area figures were made to arrive at an approximation for 1970. The figures for fertilizer represent averages for 1969–71.

§See Ref. 2.

‖Selected sample of materials whose production has been weighted by using direct-plus-indirect energy coefficients found for the United States in 1967. Materials included (and the energy weights in tonnes of coal equivalent per tonne of production) are crude steel (1.87), refined copper (4.47), primary aluminium (8.97), primary lead (1.10), smelter tin (1.42), slab zinc (3.04), hydraulic cement (0.32), fertilizer in nutrient (NPK) content (0.77). pulp from wood and other fibres (0.99), and paper and paperboard excluding energy content of pulp (0.44). [See Ref. 7, Annex Tables I and II]. In Central America these materials consist mostly of hydraulic cement and small amounts of fertilizer and paper. Chemicals and plastics have not been included in the measure shown but were significant in El Salvador, Nicaragua, and Panama, and should be included in a more comprehensive measure for the region.

¶'Normal' computed from equation 30.1 in text.

Table 30.2. Selected characteristics of energy use in Central America, 1970*

	Costa Rica	*El Salvador*	*Guatemala*	*Honduras*	*Nicaragua*	*Panama Republic*	*Total (or average)*
Consumption							
Commercial†	950	797	1176	626	798	1049	5396
Fuelwood + charcoal‡	311	555	932	497	316	182	2793
Subtotal	1261	1352	2108	1123	1114	1231	8189
(ratio to 'normal')§	(1.07)	(1.04)	(0.98)	(1.25)	(1.15)	(1.01)	(1.06)
Bagasse‡	117	129	156	75	144	61	682
Fuelwood + bagasse (as percentage of commercial)	(45)	(86)	(93)	(91)	(58)	(23)	(64)
Total (including bagasse)	1378	1481	2264	1198	1258	1292	8871
Electricity (million kWh)‖	1026	677	777	318	612	886	4296
(ratio to 'normal')§	(2.19)	(1.62)	(1.19)	(1.05)	(2.07)	(1.91)	(1.65)
Production							
Hydroelectricity†	350	183	106	81	104	7	831
(as percentage of total commercial energy consumption)	(37)	(23)	(9)	(13)	(13)	(1)	(15)

*In thousand tonnes of coal equivalent, except where noted. Data for the Panama Canal Zone are not included.
†See (8, Table 2). Hydroelectricity has been included at the thermal-plant-equivalent heat rate of 384 tonnes coal per million kWh instead of at the direct calorific equivalent of 125 tonnes coal per million kWh.
‡See (14, Cuadro A-1). A factor of 1.3 tonnes coal per tonnes petroleum was used to convert the 'petroleum equivalents' in the CEPAL table to 'coal equivalent'.
§See text, equations 30.2 and 30.4.
‖See Ref. 8, Table 21.

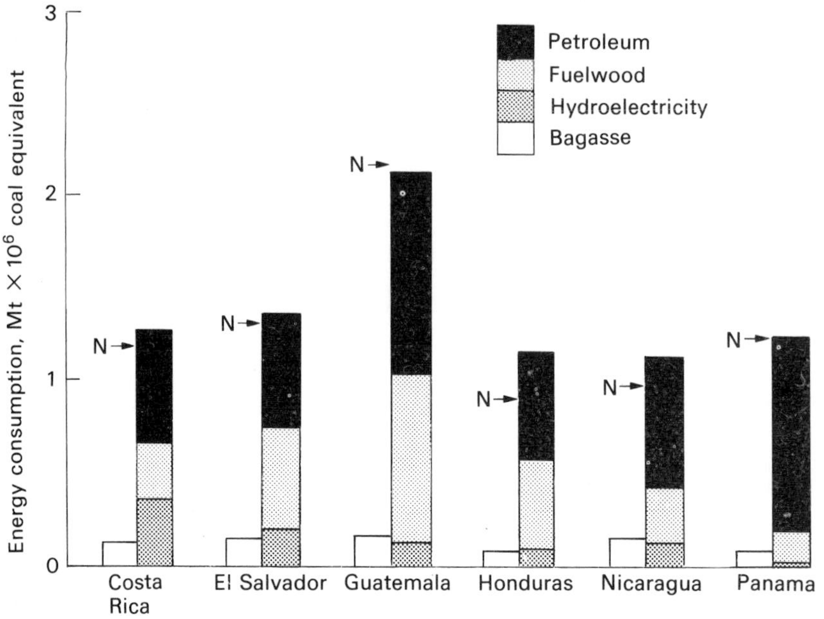

Fig. 30.1. Energy consumption in six Central American countries, 1969–71 averages. (Source: Table 31.2). Arrows show 'normal' (N) consumption of total energy based on equation 31.3 in text.

countries as noted above appear to fit the normal pattern moderately well with respect to total energy consumption. (See Table 30.2 and Fig. 30.1. The correspondence is much less close, as already mentioned, for electricity consumption and the production of energy-intensive materials.) When regional, as opposed to country, totals are used to estimate normal consumption of commercial energy only, actual consumption in the past appears to have been consistently less than predicted by the equivalent of roughly 600000 tonnes of coal per year. Because this difference has been almost constant over time, it increases our confidence in using the same normal relationships, less the 600000-tonne difference, for future projections (as in Fig. 30.4).

The statistical relationships used for the various calculations follow. $\overline{R}^2$ refers to the coefficient of multiple determination corrected for degrees of freedom; *t*-ratios are given in parentheses below the appropriate coefficient; and definitions of symbols follow the last equation.

Energy-intensive materials

$$\ln(\mathrm{MTL/POP}) = \underset{(5.37)}{-4.918} + \underset{(11.21)}{1.552}\ln(\mathrm{GNP/POP}), \qquad \overline{R}^2 = 0.839. \tag{30.1}$$

Commercial energy consumption

$$\begin{aligned}\ln(\mathrm{COMENERGY/POP}) &= \underset{(3.18)}{-1.550} + \underset{(2.60)}{2.160}\ln(\mathrm{GNP/POP}) \\ &\quad \underset{(1.70)}{-0.101}[\ln(\mathrm{GNP/POP})]^2 \\ &\quad \underset{(2.90)}{-1.92}\ln \mathrm{POP} + \underset{(2.97)}{0.141}(\ln \mathrm{POP})^2 \\ &\quad \underset{(2.40)}{+0.269}\ln(\mathrm{MTL/POP}) \\ &\quad \underset{(2.40)}{-0.692}\ln \mathrm{COSCR}, \qquad \overline{R}^2 = 0.956.\end{aligned} \tag{30.2}$$

Total energy consumption

$$\ln(\text{TOTENERGY/POP}) = \underset{(10.64)}{1.572} + \underset{(5.91)}{0.764} \ln(\text{GNP/POP}) + \underset{(2.07)}{0.163} \ln(\text{MTL/POP}) - \underset{(2.30)}{0.702} \ln \text{COSCR}, \qquad \bar{R}^2 = 0.919. \tag{30.3}$$

Total electricity consumption

$$\ln(\text{ELEC/POP}) = \underset{(18.18)}{0.052} + \underset{(5.64)}{0.555} \ln(\text{GNP/POP}) + \underset{(9.09)}{0.544} \ln(\text{MTL/POP}), \qquad \bar{R}^2 = 0.974. \tag{30.4}$$

Symbols and definitions

COMENERGY = commercial energy consumption, in kg of coal equivalent, including hydro and geothermal energy at a thermal generating heat rate of 384 kg of coal per kWh (the average US heat rate used for the original regressions); TOTENERGY = coal equivalent of total energy consumed (including fuelwood and charcoal plus COMENERGY as defined above), in kilograms; ELEC = electricity consumed, in kWh; MTL = production of selected energy-intensive materials, in kg of coal-equivalent energy needed for their direct and indirect production (see Table 30.1, footnote II, for further details); POP = mid-year population, number of persons; GNP = gross national product, 1970 US dollars; and COSCR = index of coal scarcity, which equals 2.0 for all of Central America since coal production in each country was zero (index will equal 1.0 when coal production matches coal consumption and it will fall below 1 when a coal export surplus exists).

Effects of the oil crisis

In this section I examine briefly the effects of the recent oil crisis on energy demand. The cost of crude and partially refined oil delivered to the refineries in Central America apparently rose almost fivefold between 1970 and 1974.[9] Refined petroleum products followed suit; for example, regular petrol in early 1976 cost between $US0.63 and $US0.94 per gallon in the region. Electricity rates also increased but to a lesser degree because of the large use of hydro-power.

The higher energy prices have undoubtedly hurt some categories of users, but government subsidies (bus transportation and rural electricity) have helped some of the poorer consumers, and energy costs continue to be a relatively small fraction of total operating expenses for most users. One US dollar for a gallon of premium petrol may not appear unduly high to a car owner who has paid $8000 for a small new car. If all fuel and power were valued at the former imported oil price of $19.25 per tonne (equal to $2.75 per barrel and to $14.81/tonne coal equivalent), 1970 total commercial energy costs for the region would amount to only 1.2 per cent of regional GNP. By 1975, at a petroleum price of $91.77/tonne[10] the percentage had increased dramatically to the equivalent of 7 per cent of GNP.

From partial data obtained in El Salvador and Nicaragua, it appears that there has been little or no decline in the use of petroleum products. Higher electricity prices caused a slowdown of electricity use in El Salvador for a year, but the upward historical trend may have since been resumed. The 1975 economic slump in the region as well as the earthquakes in Nicaragua (end of 1972) and Guatemala (1976) and Hurricane Fifi in Honduras (1975) may make it difficult to untangle the effects of price on consumption in the past few years. In any case short-run changes may be less pronounced than longer-run effects, which will involve changes in capital equipment and industrial structure.

Institutional factors may also affect future demand as a result of governmental policies designed to encourage or restrict the use of certain types of energy. Governmental policies, in turn, may be influenced by the availability of foreign assistance funds (for example, for exploitation of local resources) and by the ability of the countries to pay for rising energy imports through increases in export earnings.

Both of these factors appear to be moderately favourable in the short run. In an assessment report prepared for the Regional Office for Central America and Panama, US Agency for International Development, it was estimated that crude petroleum imports amounted to 7 per cent of export earnings (for the region excluding Panama) in 1973.[11] Petroleum prices had already increased by 60 per cent above the 1970 level. By 1975 the further increase in petroleum prices added $229 million to the cost of imports (up by 300 per cent, including the normal increases in physical quantities consumed). This was more than matched by a $649-million increase in export earnings, and the cost of oil imports was held to a still tolerable 15 per cent of total export earnings. Non-petroleum imports increased by an even larger absolute amount, largely reflecting price increases, and very large current-account deficits were encountered in both 1974 and 1975. An equally large deficit probably occurred in 1976. These deficits, in turn, were more than matched by compensatory borrowing and by increased foreign capital flows on official account.[12] The foreign exchange reserves of the region actually increased in 1974 and rose again between 1975 and 1976.[8]

These figures help explain why the governments of Central America may feel no great sense of urgency in redirecting their economies to consume less energy. Steps are under way, however, to accelerate the exploitation of hydroelectric sites, and petroleum exploration is being encouraged, although the only marginally commercial discovery so far has been in Guatemala. Considerable publicity is being given in both El Salvador and Nicaragua about the potential of geothermal power. El Salvador has a 30-MW power plant on stream using geothermal steam, but costs ran $15 million more than expected—equal to an almost prohibitively high $500 per kilowatt, at least for the initial unit—because of difficulties in disposing of excess hot water. Active geothermal drilling is proceeding, with some success, in Nicaragua, but a geothermal power plant is still in the future. Geothermal reserves in both countries are believed to be large, and prospects for geothermal energy are considered favourable in all other countries except possibly Guatemala.[10]

Creation of an isthmus-wide electric power grid, a proposal that gained some momentum in the early days of the current energy crisis, appears to have been hampered by differing rate structures among countries and in at least one instance by political difficulties between neighbours (Honduras and El Salvador). However, a link between Nicaragua and Honduras was nearly completed in early 1976, and a tie between Nicaragua and Costa Rica was under final study.

There has been some movement by governments to look at each country's energy sector as a whole and to consider probable developments over the next 20 years or more. SIECA[15] (the agency charged with encouraging Central American integration) and the Mexican office of CEPAL[16] have provided leadership in looking at region-wide problems and in collecting initial data on consumption and production. Some electricity modelling is also reportedly being undertaken. SIECA and ECLA are regarded as overly ideological, however, by some members of the private business community and by more nationalistic government officials.

Each Central American country is supposed to establish a National Energy Commission, and all six commissions will constitute, or be affiliated with, a Central American Energy Commission. The regional

Commission had held only one meeting as of March 1976 and, at least in Nicaragua and El Salvador, there appeared to be little activity as yet on the part of the national commissions. In these two countries and probably in the others as well, day-to-day energy affairs are largely in the hands of relatively few electric public utilities and oil refineries. Although some attention is being paid to rural electrification, especially in Costa Rica and Panama where 56 and 46 per cent of the inhabitants, respectively, had electricity in 1970,[17] little appears to be known in any country about the magnitude, use, and ecological effects of the (probably) extensive fuelwood consumption. Attempts at sector-wide analysis and longer-range energy planning for each country are hampered by inadequate statistics, a shortage of energy specialists, and an imperfect understanding of the several roles played by energy in the process of economic growth.

Energy and the prospects for economic development

In addition to the basic geological–engineering problems of locating and evaluating new sources of hydro and geothermal electricity, petroleum, and possibly coal, several economic problems involving energy will become more important in the future. Several of these are essentially short-run matters of product pricing, subsidies, taxation, and, to some extent, the degree of public versus private control. Others are longer-run and may involve major decisions with respect to capital investment, future industrial structure, and foreign trade policy.

The shorter-run problems illustrate the need for considerably more extensive and accurate information on current energy supply and demand, cost structure, marketing margins, and the role of energy in contributing to greater equality of real income. The longer-run problems are on a larger scale and are closely related to larger questions concerning the character and direction of economic growth. Important influences on local decisions will include economic and political developments elsewhere in the world, especially with respect to future shifts in the international division of industrial specialization and technological developments related to energy production and consumption. Important to the decision-making process will be a deeper understanding of energy as a factor (and cost) of production under already existing technology and industrial structure.

As an illustration of two major alternatives facing Central America, development strategies may be considered which emphasize the growth of agriculture and light industry versus those which place greater weight on the development of heavy, more energy-intensive industries.

The case for more intensive development of agriculture rests on the rather large potential that may exist for increasing both arable and irrigated land and for increasing yields through greater use of fertilizer and other modern inputs. Unpublished estimates of the Food and Agriculture Organization suggest that arable land might be increased from the present 5.4 million ha (including land planted to permanent crops) to perhaps 10 million ha. Irrigated land could be increased, according to the same source, from about 0.2 million to 1.0 million ha.[18] These increases in agricultural land plus a quintupling of fertilizer use and associated inputs might enable the value of agricultural crops to increase fourfold over a 15- to 25-year period.[19]

If we assume that economic growth attributed to light industry and agriculture enabled per capita GNP to increase at the rate of about 2.5 per cent per year between 1973 and 1990 and that the population growth rate declined slightly over the period, we might expect use of imported petroleum to grow quite gradually at rates of 2 to 4 per cent per year.[20] (See Fig. 30.2 and Fig. 30.4, Alternative A.) These rates would presumably be considerably lower than the growth of export earnings, and imported

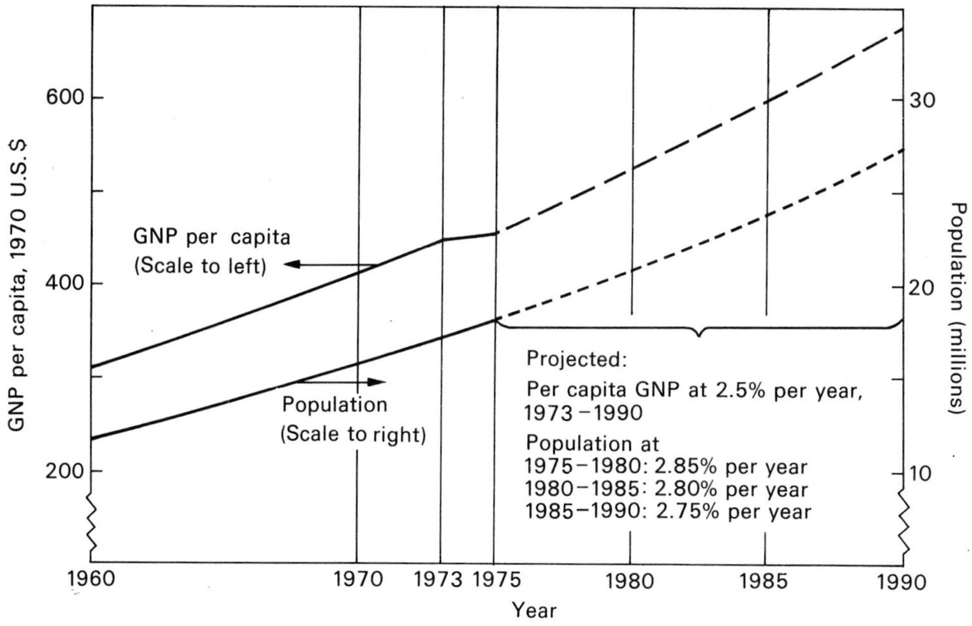

Fig. 30.2. Historical and projected income and population growth in Central America, 1960–90.

petroleum costs should become a progressively smaller burden on the balance of payments.

In contrast, consider the same relatively modest growth in overall GNP, but this time accompanied by a continuation of the historical trend in the production of more energy-intensive materials. (See Fig. 30.3, Projection B.) As noted earlier, in 1970 Central America produced only 27 per cent of what might be considered 'normal' production (based on cross-country comparisons) of a sample of these materials. Production had been increasing relatively rapidly, at 11 per cent annually between 1960 and 1970 and 19 per cent annually between 1970 and 1973, the last year for which complete production data are available. If accelerated growth of these energy-intensive materials were to continue at perhaps 16 per cent per year between 1973 and 1980 and 13 per cent thereafter, the region would achieve a normal level of production in the late 1980s (given the assumptions of GNP and population growth already made).

Under these historical trend conditions (Alternative B of Figs. 30.3 and 30.4), total commercial energy use might grow by 9 per cent per year between 1975 and 1980 and then taper off to perhaps 6 per cent annually by 1990. By the same January 1973 CEPAL projections of hydro and geothermal power as used for the earlier set of assumptions, the growth rate of imported petroleum could be expected to be approximately 6 to 7 per cent per year until 1985 or so and then to decline slightly as new hydroelectric generating plants come into production.

If export earnings under both of these sets of assumptions were to grow at 6 per cent per year, imported petroleum under the 'no further structural change' situation might have only a negligible impact on new foreign exchange earnings between 1975 and 1980 and only a modest effect thereafter. Use of additional foreign exchange earnings to pay for petroleum imports could be significantly more burdensome under the 'continuation

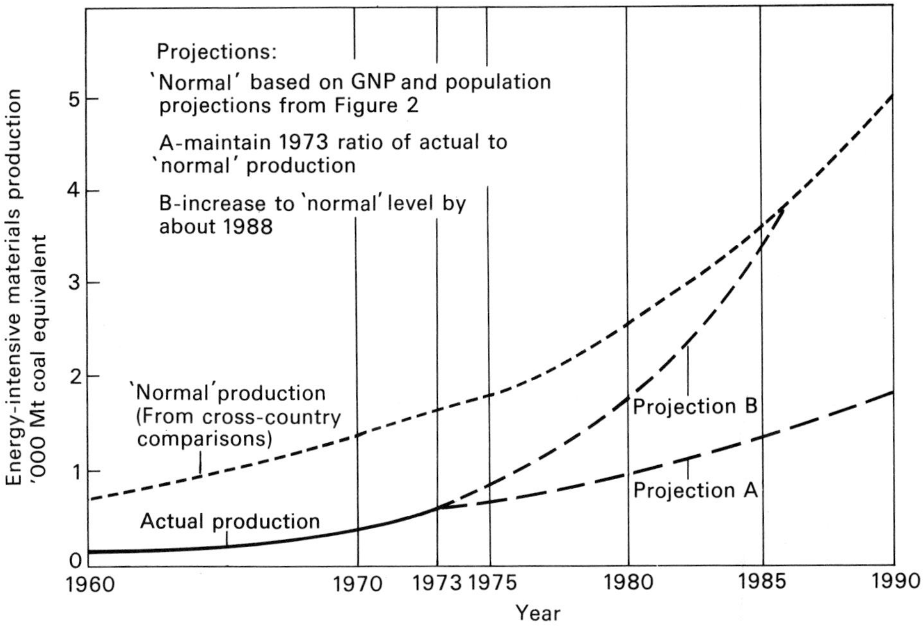

Fig. 30.3. Historical and projected production of energy-intensive materials in Central America, 1960–90. Projection B assumes continuation of historical trends; projection A assumes no further growth in production relative to growth in 'normal' commercial energy consumption.

of historical trends' assumptions. These incremental petroleum imports might equal 13 per cent of new export earnings between 1975 and 1980 and 15 per cent during the next 5 years.

Three important points emerge from these somewhat speculative projections. The first is that because of the relatively low state of development of both agricultural resources and energy-intensive manufacturing, Central America has some very real options still open concerning future industrial structure. The second is that even under the assumption of a considerable increase in energy-intensive manufacturing, much of the increased energy burden could apparently be carried by domestic hydro resources (see Fig. 30.4). These would not only help reduce the balance-of-payments impact of increased energy use, but would probably result in relatively low cost electricity. The 1973 CEPAL projections, which do not include an allowance for geothermal electricity generation, suggest that hydro-power could furnish three-fourths of all electricity in 1985 at an average utilization rate of about 5100 hours of production per year. Installed hydro capacity in 1985, according to the CEPAL study, would range from 9.0 per cent of capacity in Guatemala to 54.5 per cent in El Salvador. The average for all six countries would be about 15 per cent.[21]

The third important point is that accelerated development of hydro and geothermal electricity, with the possible addition of process heat from geothermal waters, could form the basis for a considerable expansion of energy-intensive industries, even above the 'normal' levels envisioned in the second projection. A moderately large group of industries in the United States consumed, directly or indirectly, 200000 or more Btu's per dollar of industrial output in 1967.[23] The energy cost for many of these industries was probably as low as \$0.20 to \$0.60 per million Btu, suggesting

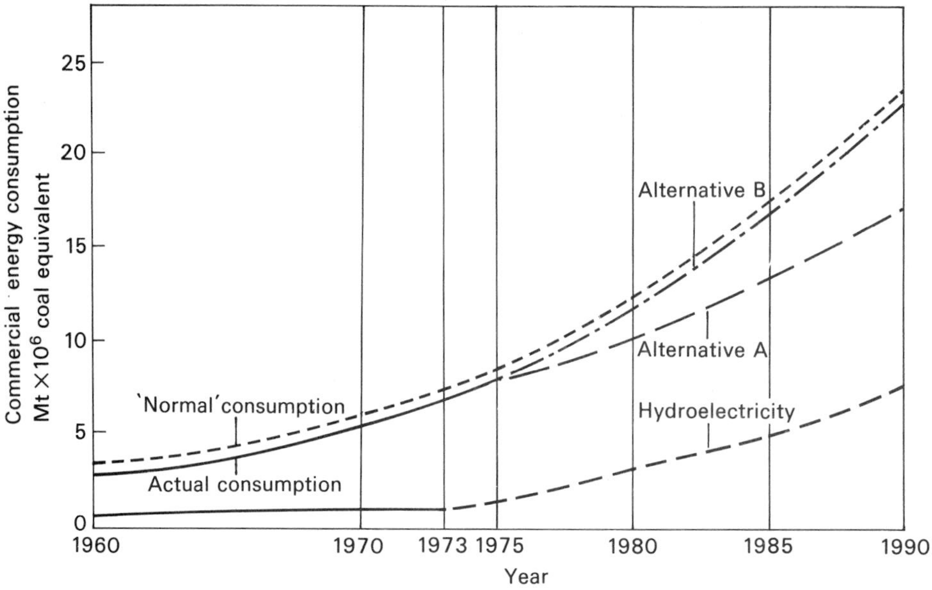

Fig. 30.4. Historical and projected consumption of commercial energy in Central America, 1960–90. Alternatives A and B are based on the projections of energy-intensive materials shown in Fig. 31.3.

that the fuel cost embedded in the final product may have been on the order of 4 to 12 per cent or greater. Today's international cost of energy, derived from a price of $12 per barrel of crude oil, is about $2 per million Btu (although US prices still range, on the average, from $0.30 to $0.90, depending on the type of fuel). Thus fuel costs now and in the future will have become a considerably larger component of more-energy-intensive industries. In the long run, for some of these industries, important advantages may exist in being located near relatively inexpensive sources of hydro and geothermal power.

Summary and conclusions

The Central American countries have adjusted to the recent oil crisis with relatively little difficulty. Foreign borrowing has covered the fourfold increase in the balance-of-payments deficit, and plans are under way to expand hydroelectric capacity substantially. There is little evidence yet that energy consumption trends are slowing down or that governments are interested in dampening the energy growth rate.

Recent energy consumption in the region has conformed closely to international norms. Central America produces relatively low amounts of energy-intensive materials such as cement, heavy chemicals, pulp and paper, and primary metals. If this situation remained unchanged, it is likely that the future growth of imported petroleum would be slower than the growth rate of export earnings. On the other hand, production of energy-intensive materials increased rapidly between 1970 and 1974. Because of the known hydroelectric potential and possibilities for geothermal exploitation in Central America, one option might be to give additional incentives to those industries using low-cost electricity and large amounts of process heat. Under these latter conditions, future petroleum imports might become more burdensome.

To arrive at sensible decisions regarding both short-run questions of supply, pricing, subsidy, and taxation and long-run options involving regional comparative advantage, extensive additional study and effort will be required. As already pointed out by SIECA and CEPAL, some of this effort involves mundane but demanding collection of statistics and other data. At the other extreme, basic studies will be needed to determine how energy enters into the cost of manufacturing (under both current and alternative technologies), how complexes of several industries and related service activities may evolve in ways to minimize energy use and other production costs, and what are the locational advantages and disadvantages of such industrial complexes in Central America. The shortage of Central American economists, engineers, and businessmen having specialized knowledge of energy as a factor of production can be alleviated by local training, workshops, and seminars. Finally, information about available options, costs, and benefits must be assembled in comprehensible language and made widely available to help improve formation of public policy on energy and related development issues.

SIECA and CEPAL, already active in energy and economic development, are the logical leaders for this expanded effort. Individual governments will feel generally more comfortable, however, if their own planners and technicians can become sufficiently knowledgeable in energy-related issues to participate closely in all discussions involving national energy policies. Academic institutions and possibly foreign research groups should be used both to conduct detailed in-country case studies of energy economics and to maintain links with research groups abroad who are examining the future effects of energy costs on industrial structure and geographic locations.

Notes and references

1. Joel, C. *Economic assessment of the CACM Region as of mid 1976*, p. 7. Regional Office for Central America and Panama, US Department of State, Agency for International Development, Guatemala City (1976).
2. World Bank, *Trends in Developing Countries.* World Bank, Washington DC (1973).
3. The high estimate of fuelwood for El Salvador (70 per cent of commercial energy consumption) was disputed as too high (personal communication from Mr Miguel Sandoval, Comisión Ejecutiva Hidroeléctrica del Río Lempa). The total figure for commercial consumption and fuelwood is, however, very close to 'normal' consumption for a country of El Salvador's size and income.
4. United Nations. 1975. Estimates of mid-year population. *Mon. Bull. Stat.* 29(1): 1–5.
5. Food and Agricultural Organization. 1973. *Production Yearbook, 1972.* Rome: FAO.
6. Food and Agricultural Organization. 1974. *Production Yearbook, 1973.* Rome: FAO.
7. Strout, A. M. 1976. Energy and the less developed countries: needs for additional research. In *Changing Resource Problems of the Fourth World*, ed. R. G. Ridker, pp. 124–58. RFF Working Paper PD-1. Washington DC: Resources for the Future, Inc.
8. United Nations, Department of Economic and Social Affairs. *World energy supplies, 1950–1974.* Stat. Pap. Ser. J, No. 19. New York: UN (1976).
9. This statement is based on a petroleum price of $2.75/barrel in 1970 and $13.11/barrel paid by Nicaragua for the mixture of Venezuelan crude and partially refined lighter products—about 25 per cent of the total—that is used as the input to the Nicaraguan refinery. See Ref. 22, Cuadro VIII.11.
10. See Ref. 22, Cuadro VIII.11. Assumes 7 barrels petroleum/MT.
11. Joel, C., op. cit., Table 4.
12. Joel, C., op. cit., Tables 5–7.
13. Joel, C., op. cit., Table 8.
14. United Nations Economic and Social Council, Comisión Económica para America Latina (Comité de Cooperación Económica del Istmo Centroamericana, Subcomité Centroamericano de Electrificación y Resourcos Hidráulicos). *Istmo Centroamericano: Evaluación Regional del Sector Energía* (*Versión preliminar*). Informe preparado por el Señor Eduardo Montano, Asesor de la Oficina de Cooperación Técnica de las Naciones Unites, adscrito á la subsede de la CEPAL en Mexico, doc. No. E/CN. 12/CCE/SC.5/93. TAO/LAT/127, pp. 30–2 (1973).

15. Secretaria Permanente de Tratado General de Integracián Económica Centroamericana.
16. Comisión Económica para America Latina—ECLA in English.
17. United Nations Economic and Social Council, op. cit., p. 70.
18. Personal communication based on unpublished estimates of the Land and Water Development Division, FAO, prepared in early 1974.
19. Based on cross-country relationships for 1969–71. The fivefold increases in fertilizer intensity (from about 44 kg to 200 kg of NPK (nitrogen–phosphorus–potassium) per hectare) and other inputs are well within the bounds of what is presently observed among countries with a more intensively developed agriculture.
20. This estimate assumes that the production of energy-intensive manufactured products continues to increase in proportion to the growth of total GNP (that is, with a 'normal' income elasticity of about 1.55), but that industrial structure remains approximately the same as that of 1973 in relative terms. Petroleum is assumed to account for all energy use after allowing for the growth of hydroelectric power. The latter growth rates are taken from CEPAL projections made at a time (January 1973) when petroleum prices had increased by 40 per cent and were expected to increase by only another 40 per cent by the year 1985.
21. United Nations Economic and Social Council, op. cit., Cuadros A-9 and A-14.
22. Banco Central de Nicaragua, Departamento de Estudios Económicos, *Indicatores Economicos* **2** (1) (1976).
23. Herendeen, R. A. and Bullard, C. W. III. *Energy costs of goods and services*. CAC Doc. No. 140. Urbana-Champaign, Ill: Center for Advanced Computation, University of Illinois (1974).

Appendices

There are five appendices to this volume. Appendix A shows conversion factors for common energy and power units and Appendix B lists typical ranges of energy equivalents of principal fossil and biomass fuels. Average values of these ranges may be used for approximate conversions, whereas any accurate calculations require the knowledge of specific data. Appendix C is a listing of the most important collections of international statistics concerning energy resources, projects, production and consumption, as well as a variety of data regarding economic, social, health, and cultural aspects of development. Most of these databooks contain extensive bibliographies of original national statistics which can be consulted for particulars.

General reviews, detailed analyses, theoretical discussion, suggestions of practical solutions, and a variety of plans, projections, and forecasts about all aspects of energetics and development are published regularly or occasionally in scores of periodicals and Appendix D lists about 50 major English-language titles.

Detailed statistical profiles of individual countries can be compiled from the sources in Appendix C but a convenient concise global review is presented in Appendix E.

Appendix A: Conversion factors for common energy and power units

Energy

To / *From* (Multiply by)	*Joule*	*Kilocalorie*	*Kilowatt hour*	*British thermal unit*
Joule	1	2.389×10^{-4}	2.389×10^{-7}	9.486×10^{-4}
Kilocalorie	4186	1	1.1628×10^{-3}	3.9685
Kilowatt hour	3.6×10^{6}	860.5	1	3412.8
British thermal unit	1055	0.252	2.928×10^{-4}	1

Power

To / *From* (Multiply by)	*Watt*	*Horsepower*	*Kilocalories/minute*	*British thermal units/minute*
Watt	1	1.36×10^{-3}	1.433×10^{-2}	5.688×10^{-2}
Horsepower	745.7	1	10.68	42.44
Kilocalories/minute	69.783	9.351×10^{-2}	1	3.9865
British thermal units/minute	17.58	2.356×10^{-2}	0.252	1

Appendix B: Energy equivalents of principal fuels

Fuels	*Energy equivalents* *J*	*kcal*	*Btu*
Bituminous coals (tonne)	$24 - 33 \times 10^9$	$5.8 - 7.8 \times 10^6$	$23 - 30.9 \times 10^6$
Brown coals and lignites (tonne)	$8.8 - 19.6 \times 10^9$	$2.1 - 4.7 \times 10^6$	$8.3 - 18.7 \times 10^6$
Peats for fuel (tonne)	$6.2 - 14.6 \times 10^9$	$1.5 - 3.5 \times 10^6$	$5.6 - 13.9 \times 10^6$
Crude oils (tonne)	$41.9 - 43.9 \times 10^9$	$10 - 10.5 \times 10^6$	$39.7 - 41.7 \times 10^6$
Gasolines (litre)	$34 - 35.3 \times 10^6$	$8.13 - 8.43 \times 10^3$	$32.3 - 33.4 \times 10^3$
Distillate fuel oils (litre)	$38.9 - 39.3 \times 10^6$	$9.3 - 9.4 \times 10^3$	$36.9 - 37.3 \times 10^3$
Residual fuel oils (litre)	$41.9 - 43.9 \times 10^6$	$10 - 10.5 \times 10^3$	$39.7 - 41.7 \times 10^3$
Liquefied petroleum gases (litre)	$25.1 - 27.2 \times 10^6$	$6 - 6.5 \times 10^3$	$23.8 - 25.8 \times 10^3$
Natural gases (m^3)	$37.6 - 39.7 \times 10^6$	$9 - 9.5 \times 10^3$	$35.7 - 37.7 \times 10^3$
Fuelwoods (tonne)	$14.4 - 16.6 \times 10^9$	$3.5 - 4.0 \times 10^6$	$13.9 - 15.9 \times 10^6$
Crop residues (tonne)	$12.1 - 15.5 \times 10^9$	$2.9 - 3.7 \times 10^6$	$11.5 - 14.7 \times 10^6$
Dry dung (tonne)	$11.7 - 13.8 \times 10^9$	$2.8 - 3.3 \times 10^6$	$11.1 - 13.1 \times 10^6$

Appendix C: Statistical sources

Food and Agriculture Organization. *Production Yearbook*. FAO, Rome.

International Commission on Large Dams. *World Register of Dams*. ICOLD, Paris.

International Labour Office. *Yearbook of Labour Statistics*. ILO, Geneva.

Nuclear Engineering International. *Annual Directory of Data on the World's Power Reactors*. NEI, London.

The Petroleum Publishing Company. *International Petroleum Encyclopedia*. TPPC, Tulsa.

United Nations Educational, Scientific and Cultural Organization. *Statistical Yearbook*. UNESCO, Paris.

United Nations Organization. *Demographic Yearbook*. UNO, New York.

United Nations Organization. *Statistical Yearbook*. UNO, New York.

United Nations Organization. *World Energy Supplies*. UNO, New York.

United Nations Organization. *Yearbook of International Trade Statistics*. UNO, New York.

United Nations Organization. *Yearbook of National Accounts Statistics*. UNO, New York.

World Bank. *Annual Report*. World Bank, Washington DC.

World Bank. *World Bank Atlas*. World Bank, Washington DC.

World Energy Conference. *Survey of Energy Resources*. WEC, London.

World Health Organization. *World Health Statistics Annual*. WHO, Geneva.

Appendix D: Periodical publications

Alternative Sources of Energy
Ambio
American Scientist
Annual Review of Energy
Applied Energy
Applied Solar Energy
Appropriate Technology
BioScience
Bulletin of the Atomic Scientists
Chemical Engineering
Chemical Technology
Current History
Economic Development and Cultural Change
Electrical World
Energy
Energy Conversion
Energy International
Energy Policy
Environment
Environmental Science and Technology
Finance and Development
Futures
Geothermal Energy
Human Ecology
Indian Journal of Power and River Valley Development
Journal of Developing Areas
Journal of Development Studies
Journal of Energy and Development
Journal of Forestry
Mechanical Engineering
Natural Resources Forum
Nature
Nuclear Energy International
Petroleum Economist
Pipes and Pipelines International
Power Engineering
Renewable Energy Bulletin
Science
Scientific American
Solar Energy
Technology Review
The Developing Economies
The Economist
The Futurist
The Oil and Gas Journal
Water Power and Dam Construction
World Coal
World Crops
World Development
World Oil

Appendix E: Economic and social indicators of development, by income groups and by region

Source: Martin M. McLaughlin and Staff of the Overseas Development Council, *The United States and World Development: Agenda 1979*, pp. 156–68. Praeger Publishers for the Overseas Development Council, New York (1978).).

	Population, mid-1978 (*ml*)	*Per capita GNP 1976*[1] (*$*)	*Physical quality of life index (PQLI)*[2]	*Per capita GNP growth rate, 1970–5* (*per cent*)	*Birth rate per 1000*[3]	*Death rate per 1000*[3]
Low-income (45) (p/c GNP < $300)	**1331.2**	**166**	**40**	**0.5**	**39**	**16**
Africa (28)	**241.8**	**191**	**31**	**0.8**	**45**	**19**
*+Benin	3.4	130	27	−1.1	49	22
*+Burundi	4.0	120	25	−1.1	48	22
+Cameroun, Unit. Rep.	8.0	290	27	0.5	41	21
+Cape Verde	0.3	260[6,8]	45	−4.0[8]	28	9
*+Central African Rep.	1.9	230	18	−0.7	43	21
*+Chad	4.3	120	18	−2.0	44	23
Comoros	0.3	180	43	−1.0	45	20
+Egypt	39.6	280	44	1.3	38	12
*+Ethiopia	30.2	100	22	0.4	49	25
*+Gambia	0.6	180	21	7.3	43	23
*+Guinea	4.8	150	20	1.3	46	21
+Guinea-Bissau	0.6	140[8]	14	7.1[8,13]	41	24
+Kenya	14.8	240	39	2.4	48	15
*+Lesotho	1.3	170[8]	48	7.3[8]	40	18
+Madagascar	8.0	200	41	−2.2	47	22
*Malawi	5.4	140	30	7.0	50	26
*+Mali	6.3	100	14	−0.1	50	25
+Mozambique	9.9	170[8]	27	−2.6[8]	42	19
*+Niger	5.0	160	14	−2.8	52	24
*+Rwanda	4.5	110	27	0.2	51	22
+Sierra Leone	3.3	200	28	−0.5	44	19
*+Somalia	3.4	110[8]	19	−0.2[8]	48	21
*+Sudan	17.1	290[8]	34	3.8[8]	48	16
*+Tanzania, Unit. Rep.	16.5	180[15]	30	2.9[15]	47	22
Togo	2.4	260	24	2.0	50	22
*+Uganda	12.7	240	40	−4.5	45	15
*+Upper Volta	6.5	110	16	1.1	48	25
Zaire	26.7	140	32	1.5	45	18

+Considered by the United Nations to be one of the 45 countries 'most seriously affected' (MSA) by recent adverse economic conditions.
*Considered by the United Nations to be one of the 28 least developed countries (LLDC).
○Considered to be a developed country because of its per capita GNP at $2000 or more *and* PQLI rating of 90 or above.
□Member of the Organization of Petroleum Exporting Countries (OPEC).

Life expectancy at birth[4]	*Infant mortality per 1000 live births*[4]	*Literacy*[5]	*Per capita public education expend's, 1974*	*Per capita military expend's, 1974*	*Total exports f.o.b. 1976*	*Total imports c.i.f. 1976*	*International reserves Dec. 1977*
(*years*)		(*per cent*)	($)	($)	($ *ml*)	($ *ml*)	($ *ml*)
48	**135**	**34**	**4**	**6**	**23881**	**27912**	**13124**
45	**146**	**20**	**8**	**10**	**6965**	**10854**	**2446**
41	149	20	6	2	46[6]	150[6]	21
42	150	14	2	2	55	58	94
41	137	19	11	5	511	609	50[7]
50	105	37	n.a.	n.a.	13[6,9]	41[6,9]	n.a.
41	190	7	9	4	47[6,10]	69[6,10]	23[7]
38	160	6	2	5	52[6,7]	115[6,7]	21[7]
46	160	58	n.a.	n.a.	5[11,12]	15[11,12]	n.a.
53	108	26	15	43	1522	3808	435
42	162	6	2	2	278	353	225
40	165	10	6	0	35	74	24
41	175	9	7	5	130[6,9]	80[6,9]	n.a.
39	208	5	n.a.	0	12[6,12]	38[6,12]	n.a.
50	119	20–25	10	3	656[14]	941[14]	524
46	114	59	7	0	15[6,9]	80[6,9]	n.a.
44	102	39	8	3	292[6]	363[6]	69
43	142	22	3	1	148	205	88
38	188	5	2	2	97	150	6
44	140	11	4	0[6]	202[6]	417[6]	n.a.
39	200	5	2	1	85[6]	99[6]	101
41	133	16	3	2	81	103	86
44	136	10	7	2	112	153	33
41	177	5	2	7	89[6]	162[6]	94
49	141	15	11	6	554	980	23
44	167	28	5	5	459[14]	566[14]	282
41	163	16	5	5	126[6]	174[6]	46
50	160	35	8	6	360[14]	80[14]	n.a.
38	182	5–10	2	1	53	144	56
44	160	31	11	8	930	827	145

Low-income countries (continued)

	Population, mid-1978 (*ml*)	*Per capita GNP 1976*[1] ($)	*Physical quality of life index (PQLI)*[2]	*Per capita GNP growth rate, 1970–5* (*per cent*)	*Birth rate per 1000*[3]	*Death rate per 1000*[3]
Asia (15)	**1084.4**	**160**	**41**	**0.6**	**37**	**15**
*+Afghanistan	17.8	160	17	2.1	48	22
*+Bangladesh	85.0	110	32	−2.3	47	20
*Bhutan	1.3	70[8]	n.a.	−0.1[8]	43	19
+Burma	32.2	120	50	0.9	38	15
+India	634.7	150	41	0.5	34	14
□Indonesia	140.2	240	48	3.5	38	14
+Kampuchea (Cambodia)	8.2	70[8,16,17]	38	−6.2[8,17,18]	47	18
*+Lao People's Dem. Rep.	3.6	90[8]	26	−15.9[8,13]	44	21
*Maldives	0.1	110[6,8]	n.a.	0.0[8]	50	23
*+Nepal	13.4	120	27	0.7	44	20
+Pakistan	76.8	170	36	0.8	44	14
+Sri Lanka	14.2	200	82	1.1	26	9
Vietnam, Soc. Rep.	49.2	160[6,8,17]	52	−0.8[8,17,18]	41	19
*+Yemen, Arab Rep.	5.8	250[8]	27	5.8[8,13]	49	19
*+Yemen, People's Rep.	1.9	280[8]	32	−5.8[8,20]	49	19
Latin America (1)	**4.8**	**200**	**40**	**1.5**	**39**	**17**
*+Haiti	4.8	200	40	1.5	39	17
Oceania (1)	**0.2**	**250**	**n.a.**	**−4.3**	**36**	**13**
Solomon Is.[21]	0.2	250[6,8]	n.a.	−.43[8]	36	13
Lower middle-income (38) (p/c GNP $300–$699)	**1227.9**	**429**	**67**	**4.9**	**27**	**10**
Africa (17)	**137.0**	**444**	**31**	**3.6**	**48**	**19**
Angola	6.4	330[8]	16	3.2[8]	47	23
*Botswana	0.7	410[8]	51	8.4[8]	47	21
Congo, People's Rep.	1.5	520	27	4.3	45	19
Equatorial Guinea	0.3	330[8]	28	−1.6[8]	36	18
+Ghana	10.9	580	39	−0.3	49	20
+Ivory Coast	7.2	610	29	1.9	45	19
Liberia	1.7	450	26	0.9	50	21
+Mauritania	1.5	340	18	2.6	45	24
Mauritius	0.9	680	72	5.8	26	8
Morocco	18.9	540	40	3.0	45	14

Life expectancy at birth[4] (years)	Infant mortality per 1000 live births[4]	Literacy[5] (per cent)	Per capita public education expend's, 1974 ($)	Per capita military expend's, 1974 ($)	Total exports f.o.b. 1976 ($ ml)	Total imports c.i.f. 1976 ($ ml)	International reserves Dec. 1977 ($ ml)
49	**133**	**37**	**3**	**5**	**16 837**	**16 937**	**10 643**
40	190	8	1	2	223[6]	350[6]	316
46	153	22	2	1	414	776	235
44	n.a.	n.a.	n.a.	n.a.	n.a.	n.a.	n.a.
50	140	60	4	5	158[6]	170[6]	113
49	129	34	3	4	5424	5515	5184
48	137	60	4	5	8547	5673	2493
45	150	42	4	8	30[6,9]	100[6,9]	n.a.
40	175	28	2	6	10[6,9]	80[6,9]	n.a.
n.a.	n.a.	n.a.	n.a.	n.a.	2[11,12]	3[11,12]	n.a.
44	152	13	1	1	103[12]	166[12]	151
51	139	16	2	9	1144	2134	518
68	47	81	7	2	527	548	292
48	115	65	4	19	60[6,9,19]	700[6,9,19]	n.a.
45	155	10	1	5	8	410	1240
45	155	27	8	23	187[6]	312[6]	101
50	**115**	**23**	**1**	**2**	**79**	**121**	**35**
50	115	23	1	2	79[6]	121[6]	35
57	**52**	**n.a.**	**n.a.**	**n.a.**	**n.a.**	**n.a.**	**n.a.**
57[22]	52	n.a.	n.a.	n.a.	n.a.	n.a.	n.a.
62	**76**	**59**	**11**	**28**	**44727**	**50548**	**18009**
44	**150**	**24**	**16**	**12**	**18418**	**16608**	**5454**
38	203	10–15	9	14[6]	850[6,9]	430[6,9]	n.a.
56	97	33	11	0	90[6,9]	140[6,9]	n.a.
44	180	20	26	18	182[10]	177[10]	12[7]
44	165	20	10	15	n.a.	n.n.	n.a.
49	115	25	13	5	760[6]	805[6]	163
44	154	20	46	9	1620	1296	186
45	159	10	7	3	476	399	27
39	187	11	10	6	178	180	53
63	40	61	25	1	265	359	68
53	133	21	18	12	1262	2618	532

Lower-middle-income countries (continued)

	Population, mid-1978 (*ml*)	*Per capita GNP 1976*[1] ($)	*Physical quality of life index (PQLI)*[2]	*Per capita GNP growth rate, 1970–5* (*per cent*)	*Birth rate per 1000*[3]	*Death rate per 1000*[3]
□Nigeria	68.4	380	27	5.3	49	21
Rhodesia[21]	7.0	550	46	2.8	48	13
São Tome & Principé	0.1	490[8]	n.a.	−0.5[8]	40	13
+Senegal	5.4	390	21	−1.1	47	23
Seychelles	0.1	580[6,7]	73	2.6[8]	28	8
Swaziland	0.5	470[8]	33	7.9[8]	49	20
Zambia	5.5	440	38	0.9	50	19
Asia (6)	**1078.5**	**419**	**71**	**5.2**	**23**	**9**
China, People's Rep.	930.0[25]	410[8]	71	5.3[8]	22[25]	8[25]
Jordan	2.9	610	47	1.9	48	13
Korea, People's Rep.[21]	17.1	470[8]	75	0.9[8]	34	9
Korea, Rep.[21]	37.1	670	82	8.2	24	7
Philippines	46.3	410	71	3.7	35	10
Thailand	45.1	380	71	3.6	33	10
Latin America (11)	**56.5**	**586**	**65**	**3.6**	**38**	**10**
Belize[21]	0.1[6,27]	670[6,8]	n.a.	1.5[8]	39[27]	5[27]
Bolivia	4.9	390	39	3.4	47	18
Colombia	25.8	630	72	3.9	33	9
□Ecuador	7.8	640	69	6.1	40	9
+El Salvador	4.4	490	64	1.9	40	8
Grenada	0.1	420	78	−7.3	27	6
+Guatemala	6.6	630	54	2.8	43	12
+Guyana	0.8	540	84	−0.1	27	7
+Honduras	3.0	390	53	0.8	47	13
Paraguay	2.9	640	75	3.3	39	8
St. Lucia[21]	0.1[6,27]	580[6,8]	67	−2.2[8]	41[27]	9[27]
Oceania (3)	**3.3**	**479**	**46**	**2.3**	**41**	**15**
Papua New Guinea	3.0	490	42	2.3	41	16
Tonga[21]	0.1[6,27]	410[6,8]	78	1.8[8]	35[27]	10[27]
*+Western Samoa	0.2	350	84	2.6	37	7
Europe (1)	**2.6**	**540**	**76**	**3.8**	**32**	**8**
Albania	2.6	540[8]	76	3.8[8]	32	8

Life expectancy at birth[4]	*Infant mortality per 1000 live births*[4]	*Literacy*[5]	*Per capita public education expend's, 1974*	*Per capita military expend's, 1974*	*Total exports f.o.b. 1976*	*Total imports c.i.f. 1976*	*International reserves Dec. 1977*
(*years*)		(*per cent*)	($)	($)	($ *ml*)	($ *ml*)	($ *ml*)
41	157	25	13	14	10565	8199	4250
52	122	39	16	11	500[9,16]	500[9,16,23]	n.a.
53	75	n.a.	n.a.	n.a.	10[6,9]	12[6,9]	n.a.
40	159	5–10	10	6	461[6]	576[6]	34
65	35	58	n.a.	n.a.	3[12,16]	27[12,16]	n.a.
44	168	36	19	0	150[6,9]	110[6,9]	59[24]
44	159	47	30	19	1046	780[23]	70[7]
64	**66**	**63**	**10**	**31**	**20079**	**27721**	**8424**
65[25]	65[25]	50–70[25]	10	33	6600[6,9,26]	10400[6,9,26]	n.a.
53	97	32	18	54	209	1022	678
61	70	85	11	44	n.a.[26]	n.a.[26]	n.a.
65	47	88	13	21	7716	8774	4306
58	80	83	8	6	2574	3953	1524
61	89	79	9	9	2980	3572	1916
58	**87**	**68**	**12**	**6**	**5643**	**5743**	**4122**
n.a.	34[28]	87	n.a.	n.a.	45[12,16]	45[12,16]	n.a.
48	157	40	12	8	443[6]	558[6]	237
61	90	81	10	5	1694	1572	1821
60	66	68	15	11	1127	993	671
58	55	57	13	5	721	705	232
63	24	76	n.a.	n.a.	13[12]	26[12]	n.a.
53	75	46	12	5	760	808	690
68	50	87	32	9	269	363	23
55	103	45	10	4	392	453	180
62	65	80	8	7	179	220[23]	268
63[22]	60[28]	52	n.a.	n.a.	n.a.	n.a.	n.a.
49	**99**	**38**	**n.a.**	**n.a.**	**587**	**476**	**9**
48	106	32	n.a.	n.a.	573	430	n.a.
56[22]	16[28]	90–5	n.a.	n.a.	7[12,16]	17[12,16]	n.a.
63	40	98	n.a.	n.a.	7	29	9
68	**87**	**72**	**19**	**54**	**n.a.**	**n.a.**	**n.a.**
68	87	72	19	54	n.a.	n.a.	n.a.

Upper middle-income countries (continued)

	Population, mid-1978 (*ml*)	*Per capita GNP 1976*[1] (\$)	*Physical quality of life index (PQLI)*[2]	*Per capita GNP growth rate, 1970–5* (*per cent*)	*Birth rate per 1000*[3]	*Death rate per 1000*[3]
Upper middle-income (38) (p/c GNP \$700–\$1999)	**505.4**	**1215**	**68**	**5.1**	**35**	**10**
Africa (6)	**53.5**	**1163**	**48**	**3.2**	**42**	**14**
□Algeria	18.4	990	41	4.3	48	14
Djibouti	0.1	1940[6,8]	n.a.	8.6[8]	48	24
Namibia[21]	1.0	980[6,8]	38	3.7[8]	45	16
Réunion[21]	0.5	1920[6,8]	72	3.0[8]	28	7
South Africa	27.5	1340	53	1.7	40	15
Tunisia	6.0	840	46	6.9	36	13
Asia (8)	**90.5**	**1390**	**62**	**8.3**	**39**	**11**
□Iran	35.5	1930	52	13.3	45	14
□Iraq	12.2	1390	45	6.7	48	14
Lebanon	2.9	1070[8,16]	79	3.7[8,18]	40	9
Macao[21]	0.3	780[6,8]	69	18.6[8]	25	7
Malaysia	13.0	860	73	5.3	31	6
Mongolia	1.6	860[8]	78	2.3[8]	35	8
Syrian Arab Rep.	8.1	780	52	1.8	45	14
Taiwan (ROC)[21]	16.9	1070	87	5.7	26	5
Latin America (16)	**264.0**	**1126**	**72**	**4.0**	**35**	**8**
Argentina	26.4	1550	85	2.9	23	9
Barbados	0.3	1550	90	1.3	19	9
Brazil	115.4	1140	66	6.2	36	8
Chile	10.8	1050	79	−2.7	25	7
Costa Rica	2.1	1040	85	3.7	29	5
Cuba	9.7	860[8]	85	1.0[8]	21	5
Dominican Rep.	5.1	780	64	6.6	39	9
Guadeloupe[21]	0.3	1500[6,8]	81	0.1[8]	28	7
Jamaica	2.1	1070	85	4.0	30	7
Mexico	66.9	1090	75	2.3	42	8
Netherlands Antilles[21]	0.3	1680[6]	82	0.5[8]	28	7
Nicaragua	2.4	750	55	2.5	47	13
Panama	1.8	1310	79	2.2	32	7
Peru	17.1	800	65	3.4	40	11
Surinam	0.5	1370[6]	83	2.3	37	7
Uruguay	2.8	1390	86	−0.3	21	10

Life expectancy at birth[4]	*Infant mortality per 1000 live births*[4]	*Literacy*[5]	*Per capita public education expend's, 1974*	*Per capita military expend's, 1974*	*Total exports f.o.b. 1976*	*Total imports c.i.f. 1976*	*International reserves Dec. 1977*
(*years*)		(*per cent*)	($)	($)	($ *ml*)	($ *ml*)	($ *ml*)
62	**85**	**66**	**35**	**48**	**104798**	**109166**	**47485**
53	**129**	**43**	**33**	**31**	**10842**	**14159**	**3103**
53	145	26	50	17	5163	5312	1918
n.a.	n.a.	n.a.	n.a.	n.a.	20[12,16]	117[12,16]	n.a.
49	177	38	n.a.	n.a.	n.a.	n.a.	n.a.
63	44	63	n.a.	n.a.	94	450	n.a.
52	117	57[29]	21	43	4776	6751[23]	828
55	135	32	34	8	789	1529	357
61	**79**	**50**	**36**	**131**	**47956**	**31598**	**25811**
57	104	37	41	176	23480	12894	12266
53	104	26	38	279	8841	3470	6996
64	59	86	45	48	497[11]	1224[11]	1961
58[22]	78	79	n.a.	n.a.	219	186	n.a.
68	41	53	36	33	5707	4245	2866
61	70	95	18	46	n.a.[26]	n.a.[26]	n.a.
57	114	40	18	63	1065	1986	275[24]
70	25	85	31	62	8147[12]	7593[12]	1447
63	**83**	**73**	**32**	**18**	**30591**	**39523**	**13110**
68	59	93	37	23	3916	3033	3331
69	28	98	n.a.	5	104	237	37
61	109	66	33	19	10128	13622	59947
63	56	88	32	42	2083	1684	485
68	38	89	44	0	584	774	193
70	27	78	32	37	3573	4066	n.a.
58	96	68	9	10	716	764[23]	185
65	35	83	n.a.	n.a.	90	318	n.a.
68	20	82	80	8	633	913	49
65	66	74	28	7	3298	6030	1695[8]
62	28	93	n.a.	n.a.	2519	3668	122
53	110	58	16	10	542	532	149
66	47	78	61	8	227	838	n.a.
56	80	72	31	27	1365	2183	311[8]
66	30	84	n.a.	0[6]	277[6]	262[6]	100
69	49	90	45	24	536	599	459

Upper middle-income countries (continued)

	Population, mid-1978 (*ml*)	*Per capita GNP 1976*[1] ($)	*Physical quality of life index (PQLI)*[2]	*Per capita GNP growth rate, 1970–5* (*per cent*)	*Birth rate per 1000*[3]	*Death rate per 1000*[3]
Oceania (2)	**0.7**	**1127**	**79**	**4.8**	**30**	**7**
Fiji	0.6	1150	79	5.5	29	7
Pacific Is. Trust Terr.[21]	0.1[6,27]	990[6,8]	n.a.	0.9[8]	35[27]	5[27]
Europe (6)	**96.7**	**1326**	**73**	**6.3**	**26**	**10**
Cyprus	0.6	1480	85	−2.4	20	10
Malta	0.3	1390[6]	87	9.4	19	10
Portugal	9.7	1690	80	4.5	19	10
Romania	21.9	1450	91	10.2	20	10
Turkey	42.2	990	56	4.9	34	11
Yugoslavia	22.0	1680	84	5.9	18	8
High-income (48) (p/c GNP ≥ $2000)	**1011.8**	**4976**	**93**	**2.9**	**16**	**9**
Africa (2)	**3.3**	**5746**	**40**	**4.5**	**45**	**11**
□Gabon	0.5	2590	21	7.8	29	21
□Libya	2.8	6310	43	3.9	48	9
Asia (11)	**136.0**	**4860**	**91**	**4.0**	**19**	**7**
Bahrain	0.3	2410	61	20.3[8]	43	8
Brunei[21]	0.2[6,27]	6100[6,8]	n.a.	17.9[8]	33[27]	4[17]
Hong Kong[21]	4.5	2110	87	4.2	18	5
Israel	3.7	3920	89	4.0	28	7
○Japan	114.4	4910	96	4.0	16	6
□Kuwait	1.1	15480	75	−3.3	43	5
Oman	0.8	2680	n.a.	−1.0	49	18
□Qatar	0.1	11400	31	−0.4	44	14
□Saudi Arabia	7.8	4480	29	4.1	49	19
Singapore	2.3	2700	86	7.3	19	5
□United Arab Emirates	0.8	13990	34	1.6	44	14
Latin America (5)	**18.1**	**2528**	**82**	**1.4**	**33**	**7**
Bahamas	0.2	3310[8]	84	−5.0[8]	20	5
Martinique[21]	0.3	2350[6,8]	83	4.5[8]	22	7
○Puerto Rico[21]	3.4	2430	90	0.8	24	6
Trinidad & Tobago	1.1	2240	85	2.5	23	6
□Venezuela	13.1	2570	79	1.5	36	7

Life expectancy at birth[4] (*years*)	*Infant mortality per 1000 live births*[4]	*Literacy*[5] (*per cent*)	*Per capita public education expend's, 1974* ($)	*Per capita military expend's, 1974* ($)	*Total exports f.o.b. 1976* ($ *ml*)	*Total imports c.i.f. 1976* ($ *ml*)	*International reserves Dec. 1977* ($ *ml*)
69	**40**	**64**	**n.a.**	**2**	**127**	**263**	**146**
70	41	64	n.a.	2	127	263	146
62[22]	32[28]	n.a.	n.a.	n.a.	n.a.	n.a.	n.a.
64	**71**	**72**	**42**	**59**	**15282**	**23623**	**5315**
71	27	76	48	28	257	430	324[8]
70	14	83	53	5	229	421	735
69	39	71	35	116	1820	4317	1378
70	31	98–99	59	92	6138	6095[23]	n.a.
57	119	51	22	29	1960	4993	774
68	36	84	65	62	4878	7367	2104
71	**20**	**97**	**224**	**255**	**840661**	**859053**	**237555**
51	**137**	**25**	**164**	**143**	**9336**	**4651**	**4900**
41	178	12	49	21	898[10]	701[10]	10[7]
53	130	27	185	165	8438	3950	4890
72	**20**	**91**	**163**	**78**	**143504**	**107975**	**63376**
63	78	40	80	22	1346	1668	510
n.a.	23[28]	64	n.a.	n.a.	1035[6,12]	270[6,12]	n.a.
72	14	77	n.a.	n.a.	8526	8882	n.a.
71	22	84	159	911	2310	4052	1571
74	9	98	163	38	67225	64799	23260
69	44	55	303	150	9842	3321	2989
47[22]	138	n.a.	27	538	1445[6,12]	668[6,12]	253[30]
47[22]	138	10–15	292	471	2192[12]	817[12]	158[31]
45	152	15	175	190	36119	11759	30034
71	12	75	55	113	6585	9070	3776[7]
47[22]	138	21	364	88	6879[6,12]	2669[6,12]	825
66	**42**	**84**	**78**	**38**	**14365**	**11944**	**9765**
66	35	90	n.a.	n.a.	2879	3560	68
65	32	88	n.a.	n.a.	124	385	n.a.
72	21	89	n.a.	n.a.	n.a.	n.a.	n.a.
66	31	92	60	5	2213	1976	1483
65	49	82	80	41	9149	6023[23]	8214

High-income countries (continued)

	Population, mid-1978 (*ml*)	*Per capita GNP 1976*[1] (\$)	*Physical quality of life index (PQLI)*[2]	*Per capita GNP growth rate, 1970–5* (*per cent*)	*Birth rate per 1000*[3]	*Death rate per 1000*[3]
Oceania (5)	**17.8**	**5737**	**94**	**2.2**	**17**	**8**
○Australia	14.3	6100	94	2.4	17	8
French Polynesia[21]	0.1[6,27]	2770[6,8]	81	−7.2[8]	34[27]	7[27]
Guam[21]	0.1[6,37]	5620[6,8]	n.a.	12.5[8]	35[27]	5[27]
New Caledonia[21]	0.1[6,27]	4460[6,8]	76	−6.6[8]	36[27]	10[27]
○New Zealand	3.2	4250	94	1.5	18	8
Europe (23)	**684.6**	**4022**	**93**	**3.1**	**16**	**10**
○Austria	7.5	5330	93	4.0	12	13
○Belgium	9.9	6780	93	3.9	12	12
○Bulgaria	8.8	2310[8]	92	3.9[8]	16	10
○Czechoslovakia	15.2	2840[8]	93	3.0[8]	19	11
○Denmark	5.1	7450	96	1.7	13	11
○Finland	4.8	5620	94	4.1	14	9
○France	53.4	6550	95	3.4	14	10
○Germany, Dem. Rep.	16.7	4220[8]	94	3.7[8]	12	14
○Germany, Fed. Rep.	61.3	7380	94	1.9	10	12
Greece	9.3	2590	89	4.2	16	8
○Hungary	10.7	2280[8]	90	3.2[8]	18	12
○Iceland	0.2	6100	97	3.2	19	6
○Ireland	3.2	2560	93	1.3	22	10
○Italy	56.7	3050	92	1.7	14	10
○Luxembourg	0.4	6460	92	1.5	11	13
○Netherlands	13.9	6200	96	2.2	13	8
○Norway	4.1	7420	97	3.3	13	10
○Poland	35.1	2860[8]	92	5.8[8]	20	9
○Spain	36.8	2920	92	5.1	18	8
○Sweden	8.3	8670	97	2.3	12	11
○Switzerland[21]	6.2	8880	95	0.7	12	9
○USSR	261.0	2760[8]	91	3.1[8]	18	9
○United Kingdom	56.0	4020	94	2.0	12	12
North America (2)	**242.0**	**7853**	**95**	**1.8**	**15**	**9**
○Canada	23.6	7510	95	3.3	16	7
○United States	218.4	7890	95	1.6	15	9

Life expec-tancy at birth[4]	*Infant mortality per 1000 live births*[4]	*Liter-acy*[5]	*Per capita public education expend's, 1974*	*Per capita mili-tary expend's, 1974*	*Total exports f.o.b. 1976*	*Total imports c.i.f. 1976*	*Inter-national reserves Dec. 1977*
(*years*)		(*per cent*)	($)	($)	($ *ml*)	($ *ml*)	($ *ml*)
72	**15**	**98**	**275**	**132**	**16006**	**15068**	**2830**
72	14	98	291	144	12868	11084[23]	2385
60[22]	38[28]	95	n.a.	n.a.	22	295	n.a.
62[22]	20[28]	n.a.	n.a.	n.a.	20[6,9]	160[6,9]	n.a.
59[22]	41[28]	84	n.a.	n.a.	301	276	n.a.
72	16	98	201	77	2795	3254	445
71	**21**	**98**	**179**	**254**	**505999**	**552632**	**132684**
71	18	98	159	45	8507	11523	4244
71	14	97	339	151	32847[32]	35368[32]	5761
71	23	95	75	181	5382	5626[23]	n.a.
70	21	100	123	204	9035	9706[23]	n.a.
74	10	99	322	144	9113	12419	1670
71	10	99	240	65	6342	7393	570
73	13	97	273	189	55817	64404	10194
72	14	99	155	203	11361	13196[23]	n.a.
71	17	99	254	222	102032[33]	87782[33]	39737
72	23	84	40	90	2543	6013	1020
69	30	98	90	126	4934	5529	n.a.
75	8	99	279	0	404	470	100
71	15	98	108	30	3313	4192	2372
72	19	94	126	79	36969	43428	11608
70	18	98	242	51	32847[32]	35368[32]	n.a.
74	11	98	325	172	40167	39574	8064
75	10	99	304	178	7917	11109	2200
71	24	98	93	134	11017	13867[23]	n.a.
72	11	90	40	67	8727	17463	6590
75	9	99	468	224	18440	19334	3668
73	11	98	342	145	14845	14774	13829
69	28	100	166	421	37169	38108[23]	n.a.
72	14	98–9	203	174	46271	55986	21057
73	**15**	**99**	**389**	**378**	**151451**	**166782**	**24000**
73	14	98	486	130	38128	37910[23]	4607
73	15	99	379	405	113323[24]	128872[34]	19393

Developing countries

	Population, mid-1978 (*ml*)	*Per capita GNP 1976*[1] (*$*)	*Physical quality of life index (PQLI)*[2]	*Per capita GNP growth rate, 1970–5* (*per cent*)	*Birth rate per 1000*[3]	*Death rate per 1000*[3]
Developing countries (141 countries)	**3163.7**	**494**	**56**	**3.1**	**33**	**12**
Developed countries (28 countries)	**1052.6**	**5036**	**94**	**2.8**	**16**	9
World (169 countries)	**4216.3**	**1628**	**65**	**3.1**	**29**	**11**

[1]Preliminary.
[2]Each country's Physical Quality of Life Index (PQLI) is based on an average of life expectancy at age one, infant mortality, and literacy rates.
[3]For countries with complete or near-complete registration of births and deaths, data are for 1975 or 1976. For most developing countries, figures are Population Reference Bureau estimates for 1976 based on UN data.
[4]For countries with complete or near-complete registration of births and deaths, data are for 1975 or 1976. For developing countries, the latest available estimates are shown.
[5]Literacy data are the latest estimates available and generally represent the proportion of the adult population (15 years of age or older) able to read and write.
[6]1975 figure.
[7]November 1977 figure.
[8]Tentative estimate.
[9]UNCTAD, *Handbook of International Trade and Development Statistics* (1976).
[10]Excludes trade among the members of the Customs and Economic Union of Central Africa (CEUCA), consisting of the Central African Empire, Congo, Gabon, and the United Republic of Cameroon.
[11]1973 figure.
[12]IMF, *International Financial Statistics*, **30** (5), May (1977).
[13]Figure is for 1972–5, 1973–5, or 1974–5.
[14]Excludes trade of local products among Kenya, Uganda, and Tanzania.
[15]Figure is for mainland Tanzania.
[16]1974 figure.
[17]*World Bank atlas 1976. Population, per capita product, and growth rates*. Washington DC, World Bank Group (1976).
[18]Figure is for 1965–74.
[19]Figure is for the former Republic of Vietnam only.
[20]Figure is for 1969–75.
[21]Country or territory is not a member of the United Nations.
[22]US AID, Bureau for Population and Humanitarian Assistance. *Population Program Assistance: Annual Report, FY 1973*. US Government Printing Office, Washington DC (1973).
[23]f.o.b.

Life expectancy at birth[4] (*years*)	*Infant mortality per 1000 live births*[4]	*Literacy*[5] (*per cent*)	*Per capita public education expend's, 1974* ($)	*Per capita military expend's, 1974* ($)	*Total exports f.o.b. 1976* ($ *ml*)	*Total imports c.i.f. 1976* ($ *ml*)	*International reserves Dec. 1977* ($ *ml*)
56	**102**	**49**	13	**24**	**276272**	**254141**	**134419**
72	**18**	**98**	**229**	**259**	**737795**	**792538**	**181754**
60	**81**	**62**	**67**	**82**	**1014067**	**1046679**	**316173**

[24]March 1977 figure.
[25]Recent reports of provincial population totals announced through Chinese radio and newspapers during the 1975–7 period indicate that the population of the PRC is much higher than previous estimates have shown; current estimates have been revised to take this into account. Recent reports of the PRC's successful efforts in family planning, health care, and education have also led to downward revisions in estimated levels of fertility and mortality and upward revisions in the literacy estimate.
[26]Figure for the People's Republic of China includes the Democratic Republic of Korea, Mongolia, and the former Democratic Republic of Vietnam.
[27]Population Reference Bureau, Inc., *World population growth and response, 1965–1975*: *a decade of Global action*. Washington DC, (April (1976).
[28]United Nations, *Statistical Yearbook, 1976.*
[29]Literacy among the black population is estimated to be 41 per cent; among the white population, 98 per cent.
[30]February 1977 figure.
[31]September 1977 figure.
[32]Figure is for Belgium and Luxembourg.
[33]Excludes trade between the German Federal Republic and the German Democratic Republic.
[34]Excludes trade between the United States and its possessions (Guam, American Samoa, US Virgin Islands, etc.).

Notes: All members of the United Nations are included regardless of population or availability of data. Other geopolitical entities are included provided they have a population of 100000 or more and data are available for at least seven of the fourteen indicators included in the table.

Bold summary lines for each income-group and each region are cumulative totals for population, export, import, and international reserves figures, and averages weighted by mid-1978 populations for all other indicators.

According to the Population Reference Bureau, demographic data should be used as a time series only with great caution. Significant changes from year to year in a country's birth rates, life expectancy, etc., may reflect actual improvements (or deterioration) in the indicators, but may also be attributable to improved data gathering.

Sources: Unless otherwise indicated, population, birth rate, death rate, life expectancy and infant mortality figures are from Population Reference Bureau, Inc., '1978 World population data sheet' (Washington DC). Per capita GNP and per capita GNP growth rate figures are from *World Bank atlas, 1977: Population, per capita product, and growth rates*, World Bank Group, Washington DC (1977). Literacy figures are from UNESCO, *Statistical yearbook*, 1973 and 1976, and from US Agency for International Development, Bureau for Population and Humanitarian Assistance, *Population Program assistance. Annual report, FY 1973.* US Government Printing Office, Washington DC (1973). Per capita public education expenditure figures are from Ruth Leger Sivard, *World military and social expenditures, 1977* (WMSE Publications, Box 1003, Leesburg, Virginia 22075). Per capita military expenditure figures are from US Arms Control and Disarmament Agency, *World military expenditures and arms transfers, 1966–1975*, US Government Printing Office, Washington DC (1977). Export and import figures are from United Nations, *Monthly bulletin of statistics*, **32** (3), March 1978, International reserves figures are from International Monetary Fund, *International financial statistics*, **31** (4), April (1978).